潘序伦先生

# 美国对华贸易史

## （1784—1923）

潘序伦　著

李湖生　译

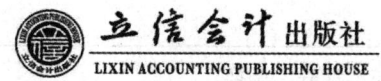

立信会计出版社
LIXIN ACCOUNTING PUBLISHING HOUSE

图书在版编目(CIP)数据

美国对华贸易史(1784—1923)/潘序伦著;李湖生译.
—上海:立信会计出版社,2013.10 (2021.10 重印)
ISBN 978 - 7 - 5429 - 3917 - 3

Ⅰ.①美… Ⅱ.①潘… ②李… Ⅲ.①对外贸易-贸易
史-研究-美国- 1784 - 1923 Ⅳ.①F757.129

中国版本图书馆 CIP 数据核字(2013)第 239322 号

责任编辑 孙 勇
封面设计 周崇文

**美国对华贸易史(1784—1923)**
MEIGUO DUIHUA MAOYISHI (1784 - 1923)

| 出版发行 | 立信会计出版社 | | |
|---|---|---|---|
| 地 址 | 上海市中山西路 2230 号 | 邮政编码 | 200235 |
| 电 话 | (021)64411389 | 传 真 | (021)64411325 |
| 网 址 | www. lixinaph. com | 电子邮箱 | lixinaph2019@126. com |
| 网上书店 | http://lixin. jd. com | | http://lxkjcbs. tmall. com |
| 经 销 | 各地新华书店 | | |

| 印 刷 | 上海天地海设计印刷有限公司 | | |
|---|---|---|---|
| 开 本 | 787 毫米×1092 毫米 1/16 | | |
| 印 张 | 20.25 | 插 页 | 6 |
| 字 数 | 376 千字 | | |
| 版 次 | 2013 年 10 月第 1 版 | | |
| 印 次 | 2021 年 10 月第 2 次 | | |
| 书 号 | ISBN 978 - 7 - 5429 - 3917 - 3/F | | |
| 定 价 | 99.00 元 | | |

如有印订差错,请与本社联系调换

# 足　　迹

（代序）

潘序伦先生(1893—1985)是国内外颇负盛名的会计学家和教育家、我国现代会计事业和会计人才培养的先驱。潘序伦先生从事会计事业达 60 年之久，创办了会计师事务所、会计职业教育和会计书刊编辑出版"三位一体"的立信会计事业，为我国会计事业的发展作出了卓越的贡献，在业界颇受尊崇，被誉为"中国现代会计之父"。研究中国现代会计史，潘序伦的名字要永远铭记。

先生 1893 年出生于江苏宜兴的一个书香门第，6 岁入私塾接受封建时代的启蒙教育。接着在康梁变法维新运动的影响下，他开始接触到新知识，逐渐扩大了视野。1906 年，先生小学毕业，苦于家乡无适当中学可进的现实，背井离乡，到上海进入新式学校——浦东六里桥的浦东中学就学，毕业之际，先生却因故失学，后转入江苏省公办的常州府中学做插班生，就读一年后毕业。1912 年入南京政法大学经济系就学，不久因学校创建条件不合规定，被勒令停办，先生失学返乡。后历经无线电收发报员、造币厂职员等岗位变迁，先生深感选错专业的苦恼，认识到没有一技之长想立足于社会之艰难。经过短暂的迷茫困顿之后，先生决定重走求学之路，经多方引荐，于 1919 年入圣约翰大学就学，凭借勤学苦读的毅力，先生从一名插班生成为正式的大学生，1921年，以全班成绩之冠，获得了圣约翰大学文学学士学位。

在"振兴中华"思想的影响下，先生怀着"工业救国"的理想，于 1921 年远涉重洋，赴美继续深造。进入哈佛大学之后，在选择专业的问题上，先生反复斟酌，煞费心机。如果再继续读文科，难以学到一技之长，选读法科或师范专业，又不是南洋兄弟烟草公司报送所期待的，经过再三考虑，先生选择读商科。在商科专业中，先生首先想到的是选读银行系，因为该专业寻求出路容易，待遇比较好，但是深思熟虑之后，以"人弃我取"的方针，先生毅然决然选择会计专业作为他的终身职业，先生认为会计是一门应用面广泛的学科，各行各业都有需要，且认定我国日后对于会计人才的需要会逐渐增加。哈佛大学工商管理学院会计系科尔(W. M. Cole)教授的教学，使先生获益匪浅，并奠定了先生一生的会计学基础。经过艰苦而又紧张的两年学习生涯，1923 年，先生以出色的成绩获得了哈佛大学工商管理硕士学位。

掌握先进的会计知识和技能，立志报效祖国，是先生留学美国的唯一信念。先生深知经济学科领域知识谱系的不可分割性，作为整个经济学的基础学科，政治经济学对会计等应用类经济学科的发展具有无可替代的支撑作用,为更深刻、全面地了解经济活动的一般规律,更好地开创会计事业、报效社会,先生在取得哈佛大学工商管理硕士学位之后,同年进入哥伦比亚大学攻读政治经济学博士学位。

在攻读博士学位期间,先生与在哈佛大学学习期间一样,谢绝一切娱乐、休闲活动,夜以继日地困守书城。为博览广学,先生先后借阅了英、美、德、奥各学派的经济书籍。由于博士课程上课时间较少,以自习为主,先生干脆把学校图书馆作为自修室,整天在图书馆学习,为了节约时间,他经常随身带着几块面包度日。为了获得博士学位,先生需要提交一篇博士论文并通过答辩。先生选定 The Trade of The United States with China(《美国对华贸易史》)为论文题目,尽管先生始终保持着勤奋读书、刻苦钻研学问的精神,但在初审中,助教对论文提出了不少问题,并要求先生重写某些章节,使得先生"食不甘味,寝不安席",幸而 Seligman 教授复审时,认为其写得不错,并有一定的见解。在答辩中,先生很有条理地对主考教授们所提出的各种问题进行了回答,主考教授们一致决定授予先生政治经济学博士学位。

正是这种曲折多舛的求学经历,锤炼了先生锲而不舍、自强不息的人格特质和执著追求的勇气和魄力,铸就了先生严谨敬业、守信立身、缜密思维、审时思变、实业报国的大师品格。

1924 年,先生怀着"教育救国"、"实业救国"的雄心壮志回国,先后被聘为上海商科大学教务主任兼会计系主任和上海国立暨南大学商学院院长之职。

1927 年,先生在上海设立"潘序伦会计师事务所",并设立簿记训练班,配备专职人员,编译出版立信会计丛书,决心以会计师业务作为终身职业,一心一意为发展我国会计事业奋斗终生。1928 年,先生取孔子《论语》中"民无信不立"之意,将"潘序伦会计师事务所"改名为"立信会计师事务所",将"簿记训练班"改名为"立信会计补习学校",提出"信以立志、信以守身、信以处事、信以待人、毋忘立信、当必有成"的立信准则,在传承东方文化精髓、嫁接西方契约文明内核的基础上,奠定了会计诚信文化的根基;由先生提出的"公正诚信为主,廉洁勤奋为归",旗帜鲜明地标识出会计职业群体的价值追求,成为了中国会计职业群体的"希波克拉底誓言",具有中国特色的现代会计诚信文化自此开启;由先生创办的立信会计学校"管理务其严格",自编教材、切合实用,重视实习、讲究实效,多层次、多形式的办学模式,覆盖面大、适应性强,深受社会青睐,所培养出来的会计人才遍布全国各地,人才辈出,为中国会计的传承和发展奠定了重要的人才基础;由先生创建的会计师事务所、会计职业教育、会计书刊编辑出版"三位一体"的办学模式,开创了现代会计"实业组合链"的先河,成为培育中国现代会计人才的摇篮,是会计实务创新与发展的平台,是先进会计理论与方法的孵化器。作为现代会计"产学研"一体化的拓荒者,这一发展模式至今值得后人深思与借鉴。

先生一生呕心沥血、孜孜以求、著述等身,饮誉海内外。作为会计理论研究的引领者,先生先后出版专著、译著 30 多部,学术论文百余篇,《立信会计丛书》堪称中国现代会计学扛鼎之作,对中国会计学术的发展具有重大启蒙作用;提出的"会计要服务于经济"、"会计师要有独立地位"等会计思想,丰富了我国会计的理论基础,在中国会计融入全球会计的当下,仍然具有很强的现实指导意义。

先生的博士论文《美国对华贸易史》对 1784—1923 年约一个半世纪的美国对华贸易史进行了全面、深入的研究,分阶段论述了中美两国早期贸易的总体状况及其形成原因,详细探讨了两国间主要进、出口商品的贸易发展状况,阐述了美国对华金融投资及美国对华贸易政策的演变历程。论文旁征博引,内容翔实、图表丰富、兼具史料价值,是中美贸易研究领域的开创性文献之一。在论文撰写期间,先生曾将其中若干章节寄回上海,在当时的上海《大陆报》(CHINA PRESS)①英文报纸上发表,见解新颖、文笔畅达,令人刮目,对当时的上海读者产生了很大影响。但目前仅有美国纽约中国商贸局 1924 年出版的英文版本,尚未在国内翻译、出版。

欣逢先生诞辰 120 周年、上海立信会计学院建校 85 周年,出版先生的博士论文,不仅体现了立信同仁对先生的感怀之情,而且为后人追寻先生的足迹,缅怀先生的思想风范,继承先生的学术遗产,提供了宝贵的研究资料。

**唐海燕**

2013 年 6 月于立信松江校园

---

① 经本书译者查阅资料核实,此处所述英文报纸名称应该是:《密勒氏评论报》(The China Weekly Review,原名 Millard's Review of the Far East)。原文系序言作者笔误。

# 译 者 说 明

1. 翻译本着忠实原著的原则,对作者观点不作改动、修正,文字、表格均依原文;带有明显殖民色彩的名称一律改正,如称台湾之所谓"福尔摩沙"等,而满洲(今东北)、奉天(今沈阳)等地名则仍按其旧称,未做处理;大战、世界大战、欧洲战争等,均可从原文知其含意为现在所指"第一次世界大战",遵从原文,不予统一。部分名称以括号方式加以补充,如"(英美)战争"等。

2. 原文所用数据的单位如磅、两、蒲式耳等保持不变,但数量格式弃用西方千分位制,以中国的万、亿为基本单位。

3. 原书中仅为说明正文内容出处的脚注、只为说明数据来源的表格注释一律从略不译,以节约篇幅,研究者可以参见原文。

4. 原文中对正文内容直接解释、说明的脚注予以翻译、并仍作为脚注;译者为说明相关问题而加的注释、对原文明显错误(笔误)部分根据上下文所做的修正与说明,作为脚注与原文注释混排,并以"译注"加以区别。部分表格及其注释稍做调整,以更加简化、直观。

5. 本文之"财年"除特别说明外,其期限均为上一年度 7 月 1 日到本年度 6 月 30 日;而"年份"或"年度"均指公历年(1 月 1 日至 12 月 31 日);表格中各时间段内均为数年均值。

6. 潘序伦先生在其回忆录中称该论文的中文名称为《中美贸易论》,译者根据正文内容及原文题目,将译本定名为《美国对华贸易史(1784—1923)》。

# 美国对华贸易史(1784—1923)

潘序伦　著

纽约·中国贸易局公司
1924 年

# 序一

　　我非常乐意接受邀请，为潘序伦博士的这部优秀著作写几句话。中国文明是最古老、最伟大的文明之一，从文学、艺术和美学的观点考察，中国文明在许多方面都优于我们的西方文明，某种程度上来说正是这种文明让世界明白生命的真正价值究竟为何物。然而，中国目前面临着恢复活力、焕发青春的巨大问题。由于中国在利用自然能源、科学控制自然方面的努力归于失败，中国还停留在欧洲几世纪之前的水平。

　　西方世界产业转移和科学在经济领域的应用带来的革命不仅仅在生活基础方面，还包括达到巅峰的各个方面。现在我们看到一个年轻中国的成长烦恼。如果中国足够明智，它就能够发现缩小东、西方差距的捷径。毕竟西方领先中国的幅度不足百年，也许世界上大部分国家和地区领先中国不超过半个世纪。德国的工业革命发生于50年前，而日本则仅仅发生于一代人之前，在美国，部分地区的工业革命甚至还在进行当中；如果一千年后回头再看现在的情况，也许我们会发现中国只是稍稍落后于世界其他地区，也许已经开始超越其他地区。

　　这一发展自然意味着中国的对外贸易将发生重大变化。潘序伦博士已经对中国外贸的兴起与发展进行了详尽、精确的描述。他最有价值的贡献也许在于对中国出口美国，及从美国进口的每一种重要货物的详细描述。

　　而让人非常感兴趣的则是对美国商业政策的描述，以及近期国际银行财团的失败故事。而其中最有意思的是最后一章，在这一章中，潘先生对中、美两个大国的相互依赖关系进行了分析，并向美国政府和人民发出冷静而科学的呼吁，希望美方尽可能地在中、美双方合作方面作出自己的努力。

哥伦比亚大学 McVickar 政治经济学教授

塞利格曼（Edwin R. A. Seligman，1861—1939）

# 序二

本人非常高兴接受中国南洋兄弟烟草公司的邀请,为该公司的奖学金学生潘序伦先生的学术专著《美国对华贸易史》写一点介绍性文字。

在我看来,这些年来,中、美这两个东、西方最大的共和国之间的各类密切交往越来越多。在这方面,没有其他什么能比撰写有关这两个国家共同利益的论文更有力量了。这一工作由其中一个国家合格的科学代表来完成、并得到了另一个国家最伟大的大学之一的学者和商业人士的热忱合作;这在商业、贸易问题被给予特殊关注的当下尤为重要。

我个人与中国的第一次接触间接地来自于中国政府主动向美国政府请求协助,以建立中国黄金货币本位体系。该请求的起因体系,在中国方面是中国商界和政府与西方世界建立密切贸易关系的需求不断上升;而在美国方面则是基于如下认识:如果建立起这样一个黄金货币本位体系,将能极大地刺激中、美两国间的贸易,也能促进两个国家的政治友好关系。

尽管中国政府当时(1903—1904)并未实现这一目的,但这一努力还是在此后以各种各样的方式留下了印记。在其他国际事务方面,两国之间的关系稳定发展。此后的年份,中、美两国之间的商务活动增长,其特点是两国的共同利益自然加强,表现在物资的互换、特别是美国在华投资快速增长。这一情形不仅在贸易领域发生,也存在于银行业和制造业。

这些以双方商业需求为标志的关系也蕴含着其他动机。美国人民和美国政府在心底里一直认为,美国与远东人民的贸易应该不含领土版图扩张或其他任何政治意图。我们相信,建立在我们开明的利己主义、而非单边利己基础上的政治友好政策是应当长期执行的明智政策。

中、美两国加强交往,无疑将总体上促进一国人民对另一国人民令人钦佩的品质心生尊重;尽管会有偶发的不幸误解,但友好感觉还是会得到提升。

在与中国人民的早期交往中,我注意到了两国人民之间的性格和个人品质的某些相似性,这很自然地增进双方的相互尊重和友好。我所了解的这些特点经常从两国其他人民那里听到,他们的亲身体验和长期观察比我的感受更有说服力。美国人民引以为豪的个人主观能动习惯在中国人的许多方面有同样的体现。甚至在佣人身上也是如此,他们中的大多数人期望被赋予重任、并允许按自己的方法加以实现。尽管中国商人长期以来以精明而闻名,土生的美国人同样追求公平交易。此外,外国人有关中国人民、中国文化的知识越多,他对中国人民的文化也更加尊重,原因在于他们对学习的热爱、勤于实践、怀有崇高理想的品质。人们认识到,尽管我们在技术知识、开展大规模贸易的现代方法和资本运用等方面可以给予中国良多,但我们仍有机会获取重要性不亚于我们的付出的知识和利益。

自从1911年中国辛亥革命,尤其是1914—1918年世界大战之后,出现了许多深深影响两国关系的新情况。中国政府的管治难题使其政治状态一片混乱,以至于我们与中国的交往现在受到了极大的妨碍,被迫去寻找救济的方法。

再者,美国在中国越来越广范围的既得利益,以及我们给中国中央政府、省级政府和私营企业的贷款,我们在中国的银行业和实业投资,可能超出我们教会事业的扩展范围,这些都让我们内心非常担忧我们的利益会受到损失,严重伤及我们的良好关系。中国人的"政治"——这个词在中国、美国使用时都常会有一种贬义——由于个别政治家的过失,严重地干扰着两国贸易的兴盛和两国人民彼此的良好感情。结果,由于物质利益受损,而这些现实问题等待我们的企业和政府来解决,因此,我们的人民有时似乎对中国缺乏同情,不能理解其需求。我们不断感受到实施救济的迫切性。许多人可能缺乏应有的远见或耐心,因此有时倾向于或多或少地直接采纳我们已经习以为常的、以对其他国家实施"掠夺政策"为特点的建议。然而,我自己认为,想法更加周全、更有远见的美国人,应当有这样一种信仰:如果中国人民不再受到外界严重的干扰,给他们一个在没有太多外部压力的情况下解决自身问题的机会,中国人民凭着合理可靠的判断、可敬的天性以及务实的远景,将能够逐步地自我消除本国最大的问题,从而在不太远的将来变得越来越和谐。

中国在国际视野中的重要变化似乎被中国自身与世界之间关系的经济革命所昭示。潘先生的这篇专著里论证了贸易状况正在发生清晰的变化这一事实。相对地讲,中国的奢侈品出口在减少,而支撑世界工业的主要产品如原棉、丝绸、植物油、羊毛——没有提及锑——和皮类等的出口却在增加。当然,中国的原料生产大国地位并不限于上述领域,在煤和铁矿石的供应方面也是如此。显然,中国随着产业链的延伸也在快速地变得更有组织性。棉纺织产业的成长是一个我们在不远的将来就可期望的、值得观察的指标。

对在外国工程、产业界和银行业以及在心理学和政务领域的如此之多的能干的中国人的研究,表明他们正在开始展现强大的影响力。有充足的理由相信,由于这一影响快速壮大,我们一定会在不远的将来发现,中国的一部分国民强烈要求改变自身的命运。过去的数十年间,中国极大地遭受国际强权的控制。如果中国能在经济上更加自主,将能在更大程度上实现政治独立。无可争辩的是,使本国成为一个在世界上有着重要经济地位的国家,是中国许多有才华的思想家的一种愿望和希望,甚至在许多情况下是一种决心；可以相信的是，沿着这条道路，他们能够最大程度地安全、确定地成为掌握自身政治路线和社会路线的命运仲裁者。如果这一工作明智而适度地开展——没有任何针对外国人的敌意，而只是无偏见的思想，为双方利益而进行公平合作——美国将准备持欢迎态度。这样彼此合作、相互尊重的行为，无论如何都不能与潘序伦先生在本书中本着精准的、学术性的和友好合作的精神而进行的中美双边研究相媲美。

纽约大学政府与公共管理研究讲座教授

东方商业和政治学部主任

精琪(Jeremiah W. Jenks,1856—1929)

# 作 者 前 言

在这本专著里,笔者试图尽可能全面地讨论过去 150 年间美国对华贸易之发端、扩张、衰退和复苏等阶段中的经济力量。这一讨论主要立足于中、美两国现有文献中的历史事实和统计数据,而对当前的商业实践则一笔带过。作者试图根据中美贸易的历史发展来解构其未来发展趋势,并提出有助于增加太平洋两岸两个大国间的贸易、增强共同利益的建设性意见。

在本书完成之际,作者诚挚地感谢哥伦比亚大学的 Edwin R. A. Seligman 教授、Wesley C. Mitchell 教授和 Theodore H. Brown 教授;纽约大学东方商业和政治学部副主任 Charles Hodges 教授;中国贸易局经理 Ernest K. Moy 先生;纽约南洋兄弟公司秘书 Alfred S. Lee 先生,以及所有读过全部或部分书稿,并提出许多宝贵批评意见及重要修订建议的人士。

作者委托南洋兄弟公司副总裁、总经理 Tsze E. Pun 先生,完成了所有与本书出版有关的繁杂的事务工作,在此一并致谢。

潘序伦

1924 年 5 月于纽约市哥伦比亚大学

# 目　　录

· 1 ·

# 第一篇

## 美国对华贸易史概述

# 第一章　非正式或非条约性交往期（1784—1844 年）

## 一、概述

　　美中双边贸易已经持续了接近一个半世纪，整个历史可以自然地分为四个时期。我们应当从美国独立开始讨论美中贸易历史，而略去在此之前的非直接商业关系。美中贸易史的第一个时期是非正式或非条约性的交往期，该时期始于 1784 年第一艘美国轮船抵达广州，终于 1844 年美国首任驻华商务专员顾圣①与中国当局签署第一份中美商业条约。这一时期，雄心勃勃的美国水手在中国的外贸中扮演了非常活跃的角色，没有哪个国家的水手能够超越其重要性。这一时期按时间顺序可以细分为如下几个阶段：① 1784—1790 年，贸易起步；② 1791—1814 年，贸易扩张及英美战争；③ 1815—1844 年，从英美 1812 战争结束到鸦片战争爆发及《南京条约》、《望厦条约》签订期间的贸易沉寂期。

　　美中贸易的第二个时期，起始于两国签订《望厦条约》后开始正式交往的 1845 年，终止于 1895 年的中日甲午战争。将 1895 年作为与下一时期的时间分界线，原因在于，在此之前，美中贸易的发展虽然相对较慢，但美国商人在东方市场并没有遭遇日本和欧洲列强非常强烈的竞争。这一时期以美国内战为界自然地分为两个阶段，在前一个阶段，美国商人仍然积极参与东方贸易；但是，美国内战期间其海运业急剧衰退，内战之后国内市场快速发展，因此美国人的智力和资本更倾向于占据其国内市场，所以其东方贸易就有所衰退。

　　美中贸易的第三个时期始于 1895 年，终于 1913 年，这是一个纷乱不安、竞争激烈的时期。这一时期，发生了中日战争、俄日战争、1905 年中国拒买美国货事件、1911 年辛亥革命及中华民国建立等重大事件。所有的这些纷扰因素都对中美两国间的贸易产生了很大影响。日本轻松击败中国从根本上改变了远东的政治局势。西方最强大的殖民帝国，如英国、德国、俄罗斯和法国都迅速抓住这一机会，扩大其在中国的政治、商业影响；已经跻身于工业国家的日本，也倾其全力使中国成为销售其产品的大市场。

---

　　① 译注：顾圣，也称顾盛，原名 Caleb Cushing，1843 年 5 月 8 日到 1844 年 8 月 27 日担任美国驻华特命全权公使兼专员。1844 年 7 月 3 日，与清廷钦差大臣耆英在澳门签订《望厦条约》。

占领和租借中国领土变得非常普遍,各个"势力范围"不怀好意地建立起来了。在这一时期,争夺中国贸易市场的竞争极为剧烈,因此,尽管美国调整了其发展在华贸易的兴趣点,但所获甚少。

美中贸易的第四个时期是一个快速扩张的时期,它自然以欧洲战争的爆发作为开端。战争期间,欧洲无力与中国发展贸易,其对华贸易大部分被美国所接收,结果中美两国之间的贸易得到了极大的增长。这一时期,中国、美国在商业利益方面的关系越发亲密。在前一个时期,中国在双边贸易中较为消极被动,但现在她开始在购买、销售及货运业中扮演积极主动的角色。因此,自 1914 年开始,中美贸易进入了一个新纪元。

## 二、美中贸易的起步

美国对华贸易是过去长时期影响的结果。可以说,新世界被发现之时,美国与中国这个天朝大国的联系就已经存在了,因为哥伦布航海西行的目的就是寻找中国和印度。美国建国之前,中美之间的非直接贸易已经持续很久。广州的茶叶由东印度公司经英国出口;据信,北美人从 1718 年就开始进行本土化栽培西洋参,西洋参在第一艘中国货船的物资中占据了很大部分,很可能是东印度公司通过航运方式向广州运送了一些。美国成为一个独立国家时,这些早期的商贸活动自然为两国直接贸易起了示范作用。

北美殖民地的航运业发展是影响美国对华贸易的另一因素。美国的许多港口,特别是波士顿、塞伦、费城和纽约都因其船东和出色的船舶而闻名。这些雄心勃勃的海员当然发现,他们的出路不仅在大西洋上,更是在太平洋上。还有一个影响因素是,独立革命后,美国失去了与英属西印度群岛间的贸易;独立革命之前,美国当然包含在英国殖民体系之内,但独立后则被排除出来,使得美国人有必要在别处寻找商业投资机会。所以,独立事件关闭了美国人通向西印度群岛的大门,而开启了通往亚洲港口和东印度群岛的门户。

因此,美国独立之后不久即开始广泛开展对华贸易就不令人惊奇了。美国人第一次明确地要与东方古老帝国建立直接贸易的努力发生于 1783 年。当年 12 月,一艘排水量 55 吨的小型单桅帆船"哈里特号"满载西洋参从波士顿驶向中国。"该轮船停泊好望角期间,遇见了一些英属东印度群岛商人,后者提醒这些美国人旅途艰险,并以两倍重量的熙春茶交换其人参。""哈里特号"的船长完成了一次赚钱的买卖,但其在中国升起第一面美国旗帜的荣誉却被另一艘轮船"中国皇后号"所获。

第二年,也就是 1784 年,由纽约商人装备的、开创新纪元的轮船"中国皇后号"首次到达中国,西洋参是其装载的主要货物。"中国皇后号"绕过好望角后,抵达广州,于 8 月 28 日下碇于黄埔港。作为首次航行,这次远航可以说是非常顺利。航务代理人山茂召①在其日记中写道:"中国人对我们非常宽容,他们把我们称为新朋友;我们利用地图向他们介绍我们国家现有人口和日益增长的人口情况时,他们对其产品可能有如此之大的市场这一前景表现出了浓厚的兴趣。"美国人卖掉了西洋参,换回了一船茶叶和各种中国货。"中国皇后号"的返航以 1785 年 5 月 10 日安全到达纽约而结束,带回的一船货物证明美国人再也无需为了茶叶和丝绸而向英国人或荷兰人进贡。这次航行的净利润估计达 30 727 美元,投资回报率约为 25%。

"中国皇后号"成功航行的消息为美国商人已经实施的计划带来了更大的兴趣和产生了进一步的刺激。山茂召向美国国务卿约翰·杰伊②报告了这次旅行的成果,并很快得到了国会的答复,主要内容是"对美国公民与中国首次成功完成直接贸易相当满意"。时隔不久,另一艘船"联盟号"从费城派出,并(从中国)带回一船据说价值 50 万美元的货物。这之后,又进行了多次航行,1786 年山茂召携带国会委任其为美国驻广州总领事的授权,作为"希望号"的船务代理人再次从纽约出发。这是美国在好望角之外的第一个驻外领事馆,也是 1844 年之前美国在中国唯一的一个领事馆。

因此,已经启动的广州贸易自 1790 年开始更加牢牢地建立起来了。仅仅列举一下从事两国贸易的轮船的名字,就足以让人们想象贸易的规模。这其中有,亚洲号和广州号——它们的航行并不很成功,珍妮号、双桅船利奥诺拉号、马萨诸塞州号、男神号、哥伦比亚号、轻骑兵号、大西洋号,双桅船三姐妹号,双桅帆船汉考克号。

为了促进东方直接贸易以及美国航海业的发展,美国国会制定了早期的关税条款。对美国轮船从中国直接进口的茶叶征收较为适中的关税,为 6～20 美分/磅;而美国轮船从欧洲进口茶叶的关税是 8～26 美分/磅;至于外国轮船携带的茶叶,其关税高达 15～45 美分/磅。相应地,由外国轮船进口到美国的其他东方产品,需按货物价值的 12.5% 计征关税,这几乎是美国轮船进口货物税率的 2 倍。很大程度上是得益于这些关税条款,对华贸易成为塞伦、波士顿、纽约、普罗维登斯、费城、巴尔的摩等城市商业活动的重要部分,"为积累巨大财富打下了基础,是许多新英格兰家庭的财富来源"。美国商人"带回大批的茶叶、香料、糖、咖啡、丝绸、本色棉布和其他布匹——所有这些物资的价值与它们的体量成比例,所以在货运业中获取了丰厚利益;在美国国内,无论如何都不可能找到一个可以在新英格兰港重新装船、而在汉堡或北欧销售的市场"。

---

① 译注:山茂召(Samuel Shaw,1754—1794),美国独立战争时期的杰出战将、建国初期著名商人,美国驻中国广州第一、第二任领事。美国建国后第二年,他弃军从商,成为首批来华通商的商人,并写下旅居中国的日记,由乔赛亚·昆西编辑成书,即《山茂召日记》(The Journals of Major Samuel Shaw)。

② 译注:约翰·杰伊(John Jay,1745—1826),1783 年订立美国独立条约的签订人、1793 年独立宣言的起草人;1784 年 5 月 7 日至 1789 年 3 月 3 日任美国外交事务秘书,1790 年 3 月 4 日至 1790 年 3 月 22 日代理国务卿,时任总统乔治·华盛顿。

那时,美国对华贸易局设在广州港,从一开始就被迫去适应称为"公行"的广州贸易体系。"公行"是一个商业组织,由一定数量的、经中国政府授予外国商人事务垄断权的中国商人组成。"行商"成员就"控制"外国人、强制执行贸易规则向中国地方政府负责。中国和外国之间的所有贸易均由该组织操控。

## 三、美中贸易扩张、欧洲战争和 1812 年英美战争的影响(1791—1814 年)

在获得成功的最初兴奋期,美国觉得它与广州的贸易肯定会无限扩张。然而,很明显地,极限马上来到了。美国从中国进口的主要货物是茶叶,但美国的茶叶消费量有限。此外,在广州购买船货难度颇大。几个世纪以来,欧洲人到中国及东方其他地区采购茶叶和丝绸,反过来东方则很少需要西方的产品。双方的贸易差额通过大量航运硬币来平衡,货币流失长期以来都是困扰贸易的因素。美国人从一开始就面临这样的困难。有一段时间,他们寄希望于自己能够供应的产品西洋参;然而,中国市场对西洋参的需求有限,因为它仅被用于某些医疗目的,并不被中国人用于日常消费。美国对华出口西洋参的数量和价值远低于美国人从对方手中购买的丝绸和茶叶。所以,美国有必要输出更多的硬币以弥补其贸易逆差。

1805—1815 年这一时期,美国输出到广州的硬币价值 2 271.9 万美元,占美国出口总额的 70%,而商品出口总额仅为 1 023.9688 万美元,只占美国出口总额的 30%。硬币是美国当时储备最少的商品之一,因其没有重要的银矿或金矿。由于美国人很难用硬币去换回茶叶、丝绸等奢侈品,其与广州的贸易前景似乎相当黯淡。

然而,就在这个时候,两组互不相关的事件部分地消除了双方的障碍,推动了中美贸易快速发展。其一是法国大革命之后的欧洲战争,其影响闻名于世以至于无需在此详加论述。欧洲战争使美国成了全世界及欧洲的公共承运人,它对美国对华贸易的影响,就是为茶叶提供了一个广阔的市场。1800—1812 年间,美国每年进口的茶叶有 1/4～1/2 重新出口;此外,美国轮船直接从中国向欧洲运送了大批的货物。另一组事件就是美国为中国市场的供应开辟了新的物资来源,结果使中国人对美国商人从南太平洋地区得到的、用于交换中国丝绸和茶叶的毛皮、檀香木及其他各种产品产生新的需求。据估计,在这一时期,檀香木贸易在中国市场的重要性甚至超越了西洋参。此类贸易可简单地分为三类:檀香木贸易——从美国内陆地区(大湖地区、密西西比峡谷)到大西洋沿岸港口,然后与普通货物一同航运到广州;与福克兰群岛、南太平洋地区之间的海豹皮贸易;与美国西北海岸沿线地区之间的陆地毛皮、海上毛皮贸易。海豹皮贸易发展得更快,几乎全由一些只有少量船员的美国小轮船独占经营;这种贸易可能是广州贸易中最赚钱的一部分,一直延续到海豹近乎灭绝才终结。然而,这种贸易残忍而不计后果,海豹在一代人的时间内就变得如此之稀少,以至于不再有利可图。

至于毛皮贸易的规模,仅从 Massafuero 岛①捕获并卖到广州的海狗估计就有 350 万只。另一个估计是,在 1805—1834 的 20 年②间,从南太平洋地区卖到广州的海狗数量接近 180 万只,其价值"最保守"也有 350 万美元。同一时间,从美国西北海岸剥来的海獭皮数量达 16 万张,价值不低于 400 万美元。而直接从大西洋港口装船的陆地毛皮的价值,则可能要比它们都低。

檀香木贸易继续由夏威夷土著酋长经营,并导致夏威夷人参访美国,1820 年传教士进入夏威夷,夏威夷最终被美国吞并。尽管现在不能确切知道美国与中国之间的檀香木贸易规模,但可以有把握地说其重要性仅次于毛皮贸易。

广州商船除了在美国西北海岸和南太平洋地区航行以进行毛皮贸易和檀香木贸易外,还有其他一些绕行航线,其中大多是由于欧洲战争才对他们开放的。由于战争,开辟了新的贸易渠道,建立了高效的商船队,中美贸易得到显著的成长。山茂召提到,1789 年在广州仅有 4 艘美国商船,而在 1804—1805、1806—1807、1809—1810 年度分别为 34、42 艘和 37 艘。这三个时期广州的进口额分别是 355.6 万、512.7 万美元和 571.5 万美元。美国贸易总额在 15 年间增长 4 倍多,对华贸易几乎与之同步发展,在美国贸易总额中所占的比例是 4%～5%。

早期在广州进行商业活动的费用非常之高,除了正常的佣金、关税外,还包括"每一环节中用于向河泊(负责监管海关港口的官员)、买办或翻译进行打点的礼物和贿赂"。据说,"哥伦比亚号"首航时装载了 1 050 张海獭皮,销售额 21 400 美元,但扣减各种费用、业务开销和维修费用后,仅余 11 242 美元用于采购返程货物。然而,美国人对中国物资的需求量仍在快速增长,因此两国贸易得以跳跃式发展。

1812 年的英美战争对美中贸易产生了明显的阻断。美国商船担心被英国人俘获,就静静地锚在国内。1812—1815 年的三年间,美中贸易总额几乎不及战前一年(即 1811 年)的 1/2,也不及 1809—1811 年三年的 1/3。

## 四、从英美1812战争结束到美中签订第一份通商条约的和平贸易期(1815—1844 年)

英美 1812 年战争的结束刺激了美国对华贸易。战争导致茶叶、丝绸价格上涨,对贸易恢复的自然增长起到了推波助澜的作用,最初几年美国建立了许多新公司,美国和欧洲市场都充斥着茶叶、本色棉布和丝绸。战后的第一年,就呈现出了决定性的增长态势,第二年则接近战前的最好年份,第三年继续全面超越。但是 1821 年之后,中美贸易回归到正常状况,此后每年的贸易额都非常稳定。表 1-1 为这一时期美中贸易的统计情况。

---

① 译注:南太平洋岛屿名,现名胡安·费尔南德斯(Juan Fernandez),属智利。Massafuero 为西班牙语。
② 译注:原文如此,疑为作者笔误。

表 1-1　1810—1844 年美中贸易统计

单位:万美元

| 财年 | 美国对华出口 | | | 美国从中国进口 | 金银交易 | |
| --- | --- | --- | --- | --- | --- | --- |
| | 国内出口 | 国外出口 | 合计 | | 美国向中国出口 | 美国从中国进口 |
| 1810 | | | 571.5 | 574.5 | 472.3 | |
| 1816 | | | 422.0 | 252.8 | 192.2 | |
| 1817 | | | 570.3 | 561.0 | 454.5 | |
| 1818 | | | 677.7 | 707.7 | 560.1 | |
| 1819 | | | 905.7 | 986.7 | 741.4 | |
| 1820 | | | 817.3 | 818.6 | 629.7 | |
| 1821 | 38.9 | 390.2 | 429.1 | 311.2 | 339.1 | |
| 1822 | 42.9 | 550.6 | 593.5 | 524.3 | 507.5 | 0.1 |
| 1823 | 28.8 | 434.8 | 463.6 | 651.1 | 358.4 | 2.2 |
| 1824 | 33.0 | 497.1 | 530.1 | 561.9 | 446.4 | |
| 1825 | 16.0 | 541.0 | 557.0 | 753.3 | 452.3 | |
| 1826 | 24.2 | 232.4 | 256.7 | 742.2 | 165.2 | |
| 1827 | 29.1 | 357.4 | 386.4 | 361.7 | 252.5 | |
| 1828 | 23.0 | 125.2 | 148.1 | 533.9 | 45.6 | 2.4 |
| 1829 | 26.1 | 109.4 | 135.5 | 468.1 | 60.2 | |
| 1830 | 15.6 | 58.6 | 74.2 | 387.8 | 8.0 | 0.9 |
| 1831 | 24.5 | 104.6 | 129.1 | 308.3 | 36.7 | |
| 1832 | 33.9 | 92.4 | 126.1 | 534.5 | 45.2 | 2.6 |
| 1833 | 53.8 | 89.6 | 143.4 | 754.2 | 29.0 | 0.6 |
| 1834 | 25.6 | 75.5 | 101.0 | 789.2 | 37.9 | |
| 1835 | 33.6 | 153.3 | 186.9 | 598.7 | 139.2 | |
| 1836 | 34.2 | 85.3 | 119.4 | 732.5 | 41.4 | |
| 1837 | 31.9 | 31.2 | 63.1 | 896.5 | 15.5 | |
| 1838 | 65.6 | 86.1 | 151.7 | 476.5 | 72.9 | 0.4 |
| 1839 | 43.0 | 110.3 | 153.4 | 367.9 | 99.3 | |
| 1840 | 46.9 | 54.1 | 101.0 | 664.1 | 47.7 | |

（续表）

| 财年 | 美国对华出口 | | | 美国从中国进口 | 金银交易 | |
|---|---|---|---|---|---|---|
| | 国内出口 | 国外出口 | 合计 | | 美国向中国出口 | 美国从中国进口 |
| 1841 | 71.5 | 48.5 | 120.1 | 309.5 | 42.7 | |
| 1842 | 73.8 | 70.7 | 144.4 | 493.5 | 60.7 | |
| 1843 | 175.5 | 66.4 | 241.9 | 438.6 | 57.2 | |
| 1844 | 111.0 | 64.7 | 175.7 | 493.1 | 56.7 | |

注 1：1910 年为 1812 年美英战争前美中贸易额最大年份。

注 2：本表之"财年"指上年 10 月 1 日至当年 9 月 30 日；自 1844 年起，改为上年 7 月 1 日至当年 6 月 30 日，因此 1843 财年只统计 9 个月数据。

注 3：后文各表中之"财年"，如无说明，均指上年 7 月 1 日至当年 6 月 30 日。

此时，中美贸易出现了变化。随着美国西北海岸海狗的逐渐消失，毛皮贸易已经接近终结；檀香木贸易也已过了全盛期。但是，一些新情况保证了广州贸易的稳定增长。美国商船携带的中国茶叶在欧洲仍然大有市场；同时，与 1790 年相比，美国的人口数量更加庞大，也更为富有，对中国货物的需求也在增长。所以，尽管美中贸易早期繁荣阶段的主要因素已经不复存在，但总体上来说 1814—1844 年的广州贸易还是成功的，尽管其中的大部分业务清淡，没有 1814 年之前二十年的热情和浪漫。

然而，1821 年，发生了一段激烈的插曲——泰拉诺瓦事件。由于外国和中国之间完全缺乏外交关系和外交条约，双方对调解国际问题缺乏共识，两国商贸关系因此暂时中止。泰拉诺瓦是美国"艾米丽号"轮船上的一名意大利水手，中国人指控他在船上杀害了一名中国妇女。中国当局要求予以引渡，但被船长拒绝。因此，广州的所有美国商船都遭到禁运，以迫使美国人屈服。美国人和中国公行商人进行多次协商后，这名水手被交给中国当局接受惩处。美国人最终对中国处理这件事的法律权利表示尊重，广州总督立刻敕令重开美国贸易。除这一插曲之外，这一时期中美关系相当稳定，两国的商人和平、友善地相处。

从综合统计表中，可以看到两国贸易本身的一些明显变化。前五年(1816—1820)间，美国从广州进口 3 326.693 6 万美元，向后者出口 3 393.010 7 万美元(其中包括 2 577.9 万美元的金条和金币)，双方贸易基本平衡。但是，此后十年间(1821—1830)，美国进口总额为 5 295.499 4 美元，出口总额仅为 3 547.758 1 美元，逆差达 1 747.701 3 美元。接下来的又一个十年中，这一差额继续扩大，美国从中国的进口增长至 6 122.322 3 万美元，而对华出口则下降到仅有 1 274.920 3 万美元，逆差高达 4 847.402 万美元。人们可能对这一庞大的贸易逆差感到非常不解。要厘清这一疑问，必须看到这样的事实：美国不仅用中国的信用贷款，而且用英国汇票来支付这些逆差。1826 年之前,美国对华贸易的所有逆差均用金条和金币支付,因此感受不到进、出口之间的差异。1805—1826年期间,美国出口到广州的贵金属价值高达5 870.7891万美元。在被汇票替代之前,贵金属贸易占美国对华出口额的1/2甚至3/4,(最多的)一年接近750万美元[①]。贵金属的消耗是必需的,但(对美国来说)也是沉重的负担;美国商人发现,即使付出高昂代价,进口茶叶也是有利可图的。贵金属中的大部分是来自西班牙属西印度群岛、南美洲、葡萄牙和直布罗陀的西班牙轧边元[②]。然而,1827年左右,英格兰汇票兑付开始代替金币。19世纪快速增长的进口使得两国贸易差额不利于中国,美国人用运送到英格兰的美国货物换回外汇比从西班牙人手中换取银元更加划算。在1827—1833年的七年内,美国人用将近900万美元的英国汇票支付广州贸易的逆差。虽然1833年之后的支付额并不能从现有的两国贸易统计数据中查知,但可以有把握地说这一数字肯定在增大,因为金币的出口数量在快速下降。

1815—1839年这一时期,美国对华进出口贸易的商品构成发生了显著变化。棉开始在美国对华出口中担当重要角色。美国人的确在广州采购本色棉布(中国本国棉布),但是此后数量更大、价格更为便宜的东方粗棉布占领了东方市场。中国对美国原棉的需求很少,因为中国本土及印度的产品更加便宜。其他物资,如水银、铜、铅、大米和少量钢材也被出口到中国。所有这些产品都来自美国本土之外。中国继续从美国进口西洋参,但数量并不大。

中国进口的另一种商品是鸦片。19世纪早期,由美国人运到中国的鸦片总是远少于英国人的出口,其中大部分是土耳其种植的次等品种。然而,要精准地确定美国商人出口到中国的土耳其鸦片的数量是完全不可能的,因为鸦片在1791年之后是违禁商品,走私的数量很大。据一位大鸦片商称,1827—1830年间,美国人每年贩卖的鸦片达1 200～1 400担[③]。美国人从印度贩卖到中国的鸦片数量更难判断,因为美国商船可以自由地将各种货物从英属印度运到广州,其中都会有鸦片。1839年钦差大臣林(则徐)强迫(外商)交出鸦片时,共缴获20 283箱,其中1 540箱属于美国人。

尽管美国人输入中国的鸦片,在中国鸦片总进口或美国的出口贸易中,从来都没有占到很大的份额,但鸦片贸易本身已经给美国人带来了直接收益,因为它降低了硬币进口的必要性。1820年之后,毛皮供应开始减少,而美国的棉花贸易尚处于初期阶段,因此不断增加的鸦片输入成为一个非常重要的交易。

在中国向美国出口的商品中,茶叶通常都占据重要地位。第六章将较为详细地讨论早期的茶叶贸易,这里只需用一组数字简单佐证已经足矣。在美国对华进口总额中,茶叶贸易所占的比例分别是,1822年占36%,1828年占45%,1832年占52%,

---

① 1819年,见表1。
② 译注:又称西班牙碾米美元。曾与法国货币和葡萄牙货币在北美殖民地同时流通。
③ 译注:1担＝100市斤,即50公斤,约合133.33磅。

1837 年占 65％,1840 年占 81％。这些数字表明,1815 年之后,茶叶贸易与其他中国产品的进口相比,呈现稳定上升态势。

丝绸是茶叶之外美国从中国进口的另外一种重要商品。1820 年之后的十五年间,丝绸进口贸易极为重要,其比例有好几次都超过对华进口总额的 1/3。但后来,可能由于时尚的改变,中国丝绸的进口不断减少,到 1841 年,丝绸贸易在美国对华进口贸易总额中的份额已经不足 8％[①]。棉纱布或本色棉布的命运与之有些相似,因为当时美国人已经能够用本国新建的棉工业制造棉制品。美国还进口了其他一些商品,如桂皮、陶瓷器,少量的糖,许多小商品(如屏风、鞭炮、樟脑、大黄和扇子)。

1844 年之前中美交往史上的最后一组事件围绕着第一次中英战争展开,这场战争通常称为鸦片战争,起因是中国政府决定消灭这一使国民意志消沉的鸦片贸易,而英国政府强烈坚持继续这一贸易。此处似乎没有必要描述导致这一臭名昭著的事件发生的错综复杂的英、中关系,因为那样将变成中英政治史而非中美贸易史。只是说美国人在一定程度上参与了鸦片贸易,但没有英国人陷得那么深。因此,美国人对鸦片战争袖手旁观,但其结果对中美贸易未来发展的影响要大于其他任何事情。作为战争的后续,美国与中国于 1844 年缔结了第一份"和平、亲善、通商条约"[②],标志着中美贸易结束了旧的篇章,翻开了新的一页。此后,中美两国就从一个非正式的交往进入了一个外交关系阶段。

1839—1842 年间,由于广州珠江口断断续续发生冲突、扰乱不已,美国对华贸易在短时间内明显下滑。有一段时间,广州港被英国舰队封锁,从海岸向广州城内运货的费用比从美国到中国的费用还要高。然而,美国人在两地运送物资中收益颇丰。随着 1843 年和平的恢复,中美贸易急速回升到正常水平,从表 1—1 可见,只统计 9 个月的 1843 财年,美国对华进口总额为 438.56 万美元,对华出口总额 241.90 万美元,而上一财年(统计 12 个月)的对应数字分别是 493.46 万美元和 144.44 万美元。

① 后见第七章。
② 后见第十四章。

# 第二章 暂时扩张和持续下降期（1845—1894 年）

尽管美中两国间的贸易关系已经持续了半个多世纪，但直到 1844 年（望厦）条约签订，两国才开始了正式的条约性交往。不过，这一正式关系一经建立，美国人在中国的商业活动就立即有了突破性的发展。这一时期的前十五年，美国在中国的对外贸易中占据了非常大的份额，而且看起来，自然应当期待两国贸易迎来迅速且无限的增长。

但是，中美贸易的这一惊人扩张只发生在以中美两国国内局面混乱为特征的这一时期的开始阶段。持续一代人之久的太平天国运动，涉及中国 21 个省份中的 13 个，2 000万人流离失所。据说这是世界上最大的内乱，从来没有一场冲突使如此之多的生命和财产受到损失。这极大地降低了中国人民的购买力，使其国家进步至少延迟了一代人。另一方面，美国也发生了内战，在此期间，美国对外贸易最为倚重的豪华船队陷入衰退，同时为了增加国家收入、保护美国工业而建立了高关税壁垒，使得对华进口的进一步增长严重受阻。由于这些干扰因素的存在，美国减缓东方贸易就变得理所当然、不可避免。

中美贸易发展的放缓对这一时期两国人民之间贸易往来方面的负面影响表现得更明显。这一时期后半段，对两国贸易最有利的因素是距离的缩短。亚洲和美国之间的交流变得快捷、便宜。地球好像突然间缩小到它正常大小的 1/4。继行进速度更快、运送费用更低的快帆船之后，蒸汽动力得到快速发展；美国横贯大陆的铁路线建造起来；远洋蒸汽船首次开通定期客运和货运服务。陆上和海底电报被普遍使用。这些发明，使得美国的制造过程中的省力机器更加完善，蒸汽动力的应用成倍增加。所有这些工业、商业变化对促进美中贸易产生了不可估量的影响。

## 一、短暂扩张期（1845—1860 年）

表 2-1 简要表示了 1845—1860 年这一时期中美贸易的异常扩张。

从表中可以看出，这一阶段中美贸易最显著的特点是进、出口都快速、且无规则地增长。1845 年的贸易总额远远超出上一年，表明中美贸易开始从鸦片战争的烦扰局面中快速恢复；之后的几年里，尽管中国的太平天国运动正处于顶峰状态，中美贸易总额仍然由（期初的）900 万美元稳步增长为 1853 年的 1 450 万美元。1858 年，太平天国运动被平息，中国恢复和平，中美之间的进、出口都受到刺激，贸易总额于 1860 年跃升到 2 250 万美元的高水平。

表 2－1　1845—1860 年美国对华贸易统计

单位:万美元

| 财年 | 美国向中国出口 | | | 美国从中国进口 | 中美金银贸易 | | 中美贸易总额 |
|---|---|---|---|---|---|---|---|
| | 国内出口 | 国外出口 | 出口总额 | | 美国出口 | 美国进口 | |
| 1845 | 207.9 | 19.7 | 227.6 | 728.6 | 15.9 | 2.7 | 956.2 |
| 1846 | 117.8 | 15.4 | 133.2 | 659.4 | 11.3 | | 792.6 |
| 1847 | 170.9 | 12.4 | 183.3 | 558.3 | 3.3 | | 741.6 |
| 1848 | 206.4 | 12.6 | 219.0 | 808.3 | 7.2 | | 1 027.3 |
| 1849 | 146.1 | 12.2 | 158.3 | 551.4 | 1.0 | | 708.7 |
| 1850 | 148.6 | 11.9 | 160.5 | 659.3 | 2.5 | | 819.9 |
| 1851 | 215.6 | 32.9 | 248.5 | 706.5 | 14.7 | | 955.0 |
| 1852 | 248.0 | 18.3 | 266.3 | 1 059.4 | 2.0 | | 1 325.7 |
| 1853 | 321.3 | 52.4 | 373.7 | 1 057.4 | 48.9 | | 1 431.1 |
| 1854 | 129.4 | 10.4 | 139.8 | 1 050.6 | 15.6 | 10.8 | 1 190.4 |
| 1855 | 153.3 | 18.6 | 171.9 | 1 104.9 | 67.5 | | 1 276.8 |
| 1856 | 204.8 | 51.0 | 255.8 | 1 045.4 | 63.4 | 0.1 | 1 301.3 |
| 1857 | 202.0 | 237.5 | 439.5 | 836.0 | 189.8 | | 1 275.5 |
| 1858 | 300.8 | 269.0 | 569.7 | 1 057.1 | 201.6 | | 1 625.8 |
| 1859 | 423.3 | 289.4 | 712.7 | 1 079.1 | 205.0 | | 1 791.9 |
| 1860 | 717.1 | 173.5 | 890.6 | 1 356.7 | 315.6 | | 2 249.3 |

　　综观这一时期,从美国输出到中国的硬币是相对稳定的,但前十年数量较少,每年平均约 10 万美元。其中,1849 年,美国对中国的金条、金币净出口仅为 9 967 美元,几乎可以忽略不计。这足以证明美国巨大的收支差额几乎全部由源于英国鸦片贸易的伦敦汇票支付这样一个事实。但是,1855 年之后,因为美国在加利福尼亚和墨西哥发现金矿、银矿,美国恢复了金币的大量出口。从那时起,硬币特别是银币的输出流动就一直没有中断,并持续到现在。

　　1860 年,在美国最重要的进口来源地中,中国排名第七位,位居英国、法国、西班牙属西印度群岛,英属北美省份、巴西和德国之后。同年,美国对华出口仅占美国出口总额的 1.78%,但中国在美国产品的最佳买主中,排名同样靠前,在美国出口贸易中的地位仅次于英国、法国、英属北美殖民地、德国和西班牙属西印度群岛。

**1. 美国航运业的成长——美国贸易扩张的一个原因**

这一时期美国贸易的扩张有诸多原因,美国航运业的成长排在首位。在前一时期,除 1843 年与 1844 年两个年份外,中美航运贸易量从未超过 1 万吨。但是在这十年中,这一数字超过了 10 万吨,通过对 1840 年问世的美国式快帆船的完善,美国人在一段时期内垄断了茶叶运输——甚至运往英国的茶叶,因为他们比其他竞争对手的运输能力更强,能在更短的时间、更加保鲜的情况下完成茶叶运送。这一时期,船东和水手本身就是商人,因此美国对华进出口贸易得到跳跃式大发展并不令人惊奇。

**2. 美国关税的调低——美国从中国进口增长的原因**

本时期之初,美国从中国及世界其他地区扩大进口的另一个因素,就是美国进口关税的下调。1846 年美国国会通过了一项新的"公开承诺尽可能实施自由贸易原则"的关税法案。茶叶原先是完全的应税货物,现在则免予征收关税,这一松绑措施立刻使得从中国进口的茶叶快速增长。其他物品和产品的关税也下降到 30% 的平均水平,这一措施使得美国从中国进口的生丝和绢丝、香料、羊毛和毛织物、糖等商品大大增加。"1857 年的关税法案更多地消除了美国关税立法的限制性,尽管不能说这一法案完全符合、或坚持自由贸易原则,但与 1860 年之后的关税法律体系相比还是相当温和的。这一状况一直延续到美国内战",部分原因是由于前述美国关税壁垒较为适中,这一时期,美国对华进口从 1845 年的 700 万美元上升到 1852 年的 1 100 万美元,到 1860 年则达到 1 400 万美元。

**3. 中国按照条约建立低关税——美国对华出口增长的原因**

差不多就在美国降低进口关税以促进美国从中国进口的同时,中国也依照《南京条约》《望厦条约》建立了低协定关税制度,这样就消除了中国海关官员的所有非法勒索行为,同时使美国及其他国家商人将其货物运入中国港口的费用大大下降。前一章中,已经列举了广州的外国进口商以前被迫承担的各种沉重费用,如向中国政府、港口官员、买办、翻译缴纳的税收、"佣金"、"礼物"和贿赂。然而,比承担货运费用更糟的可能是不确定性和不够便利。据说,外国轮船的货物被允许上岸之前,中国海关官员通常要花数天甚至数周时间勘定其载货能力,以确定应付款项的数额。贿赂官员以减少官方税收的行为很普遍。如果一艘轮船被征收 1 500 两白银的关税,则其中的 1 300 两作为"勘定费"装入海关官员的私人腰包,只有 200 两白银进入政府国库。在这样一个腐败的关税体系下,美国对华出口无疑不可能大规模增长。

但是,中国与英、美两国分别签订的《南京条约》和《望厦条约》,终结了所有这样的不端习惯,这是中国关税历史的一个转折点。现在,外国商品的进口税都严格地以 5% 为限,这些都列于关税表之中,关税表是这些条约的主要部分,条约文本中明确规定英美进口商人自此以后再也无需支付任何"礼物"或佣金。这些规定使外国商人支付的税收有了实质性的下降,因此成了推动美国对华出口贸易进一步成长的强大动力。正因如此,1845—1847 年间,美国对华出口年均不足 200 万美元,而 1851—1853 期间增长为每年 300 万美元,1858—1860 年则更是达到每年 800 万美元。

**4. "卖猪仔"**

这一时期,中美贸易史上有一件非常重要的事件,即所谓的"卖猪仔"。美国人、英国人、葡萄牙人和西班牙人,都在这一丑陋的"贸易"中占有不小的份额,他们将成千上万无辜的中国劳工置于最悲惨的境地,并将中国移民令人不快的问题归根于中国人自身。20 世纪 50 年代,横跨太平洋的快帆船传回了在旧金山发现金矿、需要廉价劳工的消息。美国及其他一些国家的轮船,开始把中国劳工运送到各自不同的目的地,1854 年"卖猪仔"达到高潮。1855 年,共有 12 只船从广东汕头运出 6 388 名苦力,其中 5 艘美国轮船运送了 3 050 名苦力。香港于 1857 年的劳工贸易统计中显示,在总共 70 艘运送苦力的轮船中,有 22 艘是由美国人雇佣,其中的 9 艘轮船驶向哈瓦那。

"卖猪仔"行为的罪行罄竹难书、影响深远。由于美国对便宜劳工的需求增长,一些刺激招募的虚假方法被使用,大批不知情的中国劳工被骗上轮船,并被暴力扣押,实际上变成了奴隶。他们被塞入拥挤的船舱,其中一些船根本不适合远航,食品和饮水供应不足。所以"在途"死亡率自然是很高的。到达目的地后,苦力通常被转移给或实际上"卖"给承包商,遭受悲惨的待遇,忍受包工制的所有种种恶习,以致他们合同期满时也无法回到中国。因为中国人民不能很好地判别出哪些人是真正的罪行实施者,这些"商人"的法律、道德暴行立刻使中国人民对所有外国人产生了深深的怨恨而在中国南方各港口普遍发生了反对外国人的暴动。这种"贸易"的滥用终于唤醒了一些西方政府的良心行为。1855 年,英国议会通过了所谓"英国乘客法",禁止英国轮船将这样的包身工带到除英国港口之外的地方,并要求接受严格检查。但美国轮船仍在持续参与这种"贸易",直到 1862 年"苦力贸易"被与本着解决美国奴隶问题相同精神的国会法令所禁止。美国驻华大使也在努力制止这种交易的罪行,尽管之前这种交易本身是得到法律支持的。"声誉好的公司已从这一贸易完全退出,但私人公司行为给美国国旗带来了更多的耻辱,加深了中国的反洋情绪"。

就美国和中国的关注点而言,"卖猪仔"的结果是最令人不快的中国移民问题,这个问题使美国人不能公正地对待中国人,并在美国国内引起很多政治冲突。对这一问题进行详细讨论,可能超出这篇论文的范围。然而,它是中美两国贸易中的重要环节,因此笔者至少得在后面的章节对其稍加关注。

**5. 美国对华进、出口贸易的构成**

这一时期,美国从中国进口的商品构成没有太大的改变,而向中国出口的商品则不断变化。如上文所述,在早些年,中国人几乎不需要美国产品,而美国对中国产品的需求则非常大。美国不得不在境外采购物资,以补偿其对中国产品的进口。因此,美国的境外出口通常远大于其国内出口①。但是,19 世纪中期,美国工业革命初见成效,开发出了一些在中国有良好市场的产品。结果,本国产品在美国对华出口中的份额快速增长。1842 年,美国国外出口总额 70.69 万美元,国内出口总额为 73.76 万美元,后者首次超过前者。三年后的 1845 年,美国国内出口总额 207.936 万美元,在美国出口总额中占 92%,而国外出口下降到可以忽略不计的 19.67 万美元,仅占出口总额的 8%。1853 年,美国国内出口总额 321.26 万美元,占比 86%,国外出口则为 52.44 万美元,占比 14%;1860 年,美国的国内出口激增到 717.08 万美元。

在美国对华出口的本国产品中,棉制品具有其他产品不可比拟的重要地位。1860 年,美国向中国出口手绘布、印花布、色染布 59.12 万美元,白色及其他颜色的粗布 26.24 万美元,其他棉制品 304.38 万美元。美国对华棉制品出口总额 389.74 万美元,在 717.09 万美元的美国国内对华出口总额中占 45%。从那时开始,美国棉制品在中国市场的地位平稳增长,直到 20 世纪之初被日本和中国本国的棉布所替代。

该年度(1860 年),美国本国生产的一些大宗商品对华出口情况为:

| 商品种类 | 出口总额(万美元) |
| --- | --- |
| 棉制品 | 389.7362 |
| 肉类、乳制品和其他食品 | 26.9032 |
| 小麦粉(3.7328 万桶) | 30.2304 |
| 煤炭(2.9023 万吨) | 11.7969 |
| 医药产品 | 5.1010 |
| 西洋参(39.5909 万磅) | 29.5766 |
| 钢铁制品 | 8.7731 |
| 制成烟草(66.4289 万磅) | 9.7957 |
| 金(银)条、金(银)币 | 154.5914 |
| 其他物资 | 50.8043 |
| 合计 | 717.3088 |

这一时期的美国国外对华出口实际上全是银币出口,它们从墨西哥及西班牙属西印度群岛转运。1860 年,美国国外出口银币价值 155.6828 万美元,占国外出口总额的 90%。

与前一时期一样,在美国从中国进口的商品中,茶叶仍然保持着优势地位,但其在

---

① 见表 1-1。

美国对华进口贸易总额中的比例,已从 80％降为 60％。不幸的是,茶叶的地位仍在下降。美国从中国进口的商品中,丝绸居茶叶之后,再后是糖、香料和羊毛。1860 年美国从中国进口的商品构成如下所示。

| 商品种类 | 进口总额(万美元) |
| --- | --- |
| 茶叶 | 879.9141 |
| 生丝 | 102.0496 |
| 丝绸和其他制品 | 90.6929 |
| 服装 | 10.8205 |
| 划席 | 27.3709 |
| 精油或挥发压榨油 | 9.9056 |
| 香料(主要是桂皮) | 29.6743 |
| 红糖(1314.3376 万磅) | 62.8668 |
| 羊毛制品 | 20.4352 |
| 其他 | 122.9305 |
| 合计 | 1 356.6604 |

## 二、缓慢发展期(1861—1894 年)

在中美贸易过去一个半世纪的整个发展历程中,没有一个时间段比 19 世纪最后四十年的发展更慢了。19 世纪的前六十年,中美贸易的规模和地位,无论从绝对量还是相对性方面都是增长的,因此有充足的理由期待进、出口都保持快速增长。然而,实际情况却是,中美贸易在一个将近四十年的时间段里没有明显的增长。这一时期,美国与日本之间的贸易从 1860 年的近乎空白(美国进口 13.83 万美元,出口 5.51 万美元)成长为 1894 年的 2 833.07 万美元(美国进口 2 369.60 万美元,出口 463.47 万美元),而同期美国对华贸易仅仅从 1860 年的 2 247.27 万美元微升至 1894 年的 2 299.70 万美元。1860 年,美国对华贸易在美国对外贸易中的份额是 3.15％,而 1880 年则下降到仅为 1.86％,1894 年更是下降至 1.75％。本时段之初,中国是美国进口贸易的第七大商品来源地、美国商品出口的第六大目的地。但十五年[①]之后的 1885 年,中国在美国进、出口贸易中的地位分别下滑到第八位、第十四位。

从另一方面也可以看出这个问题,即对美贸易在中国外贸中的地位也在明显下

---

① 译注:原文如此,疑为作者的笔误。

降,其份额由 1872 年的 8.46％,连续下降为 1877 年的 6.33％、1881 年的 6.5％、1887 年的 6.5％、1889 年的 5.2％、1893 年的 6.4％,而同一时期对日贸易在中国外贸中的份额分别是 3.01％、3.76％、3.4％、4.10％、6.2％和 6.4％。

表 2-2 的前一部分对正在讨论的这一时段内的中美贸易情况做了完全统计。"贸易总额"栏的数字清楚地表明,两国贸易在其后续发展过程中几乎停滞不前。

**表 2-2　1861—1894 年美国与中国内地、香港地区贸易统计**

单位:万美元

| 财年 | 美国—中国内地 | | | 美国—中国香港地区 | | | 美国对华贸易总额 |
|------|--------|--------|--------|--------|--------|--------|--------|
| | 美国进口 | 美国出口 | 贸易总额 | 美国进口 | 美国出口 | 贸易总额 | |
| 1861 | 1 135.2 | 691.7 | 1 826.9 | | | | |
| 1862 | 745.9 | 549.9 | 1 295.8 | | | | |
| 1863 | 1 096.1 | 614.2 | 1 710.3 | | | | |
| 1864 | 1 016.5 | 873.3 | 1 889.8 | | | | |
| 1865 | 513.1 | 710.5 | 1 223.6 | | | | |
| 1866 | 1 013.3 | 1 015.0 | 2 028.3 | | | | |
| 1867 | 1 211.2 | 976.8 | 2 188.0 | | | | |
| 1868 | 1 138.5 | 1 169.1 | 2 307.7 | | | | |
| 1869 | 1 320.9 | 1 237.6 | 2 558.5 | | | | |
| 1870 | 1 462.8 | 904.0 | 2 366.9 | | | | |
| 1871 | 2 006.6 | 206.8 | 2 213.5 | | | | |
| 1872 | 2 675.4 | 293.6 | 2 969.0 | | | | |
| 1873 | 2 635.3 | 339.4 | 2 974.8 | | | | |
| 1874 | 1 815.9 | 254.3 | 2 070.3 | | | | |
| 1875 | 1 348.0 | 145.8 | 1 493.8 | 120.3 | 210.2 | 330.5 | 1 824.3 |
| 1876 | 1 236.1 | 138.3 | 1 374.4 | 49.4 | 324.0 | 373.3 | 1 747.8 |
| 1877 | 1 114.1 | 169.7 | 1 283.8 | 117.1 | 323.0 | 440.1 | 1 723.9 |
| 1878 | 1 589.5 | 359.7 | 1 949.2 | 223.3 | 326.3 | 549.5 | 2 498.8 |
| 1879 | 1 656.6 | 251.7 | 1 908.3 | 165.3 | 329.1 | 494.4 | 2 402.7 |
| 1880 | 2 177.0 | 110.1 | 2 287.1 | 225.1 | 287.7 | 512.8 | 2 719.9 |
| 1881 | 2 231.8 | 544.8 | 2 776.5 | 240.0 | 291.7 | 531.7 | 3 308.2 |

（续表）

| 财年 | 美国—中国内地 | | | 美国—中国香港地区 | | | 美国对华贸易总额 |
|---|---|---|---|---|---|---|---|
| | 美国进口 | 美国出口 | 贸易总额 | 美国进口 | 美国出口 | 贸易总额 | |
| 1882 | 2 021.4 | 589.6 | 2 611.0 | 242.4 | 342.9 | 585.2 | 3 196.2 |
| 1883 | 2 014.1 | 408.0 | 2 422.2 | 191.9 | 377.8 | 569.7 | 2 991.8 |
| 1884 | 1 561.7 | 462.7 | 2 024.3 | 150.5 | 308.2 | 458.6 | 2 483.0 |
| 1885 | 1 629.2 | 639.7 | 2 268.9 | 98.4 | 414.9 | 513.3 | 2 782.2 |
| 1886 | 1 897.3 | 752.1 | 2 649.4 | 107.2 | 405.6 | 512.9 | 3 162.2 |
| 1887 | 1 907.7 | 624.7 | 2 532.3 | 143.6 | 298.4 | 442.1 | 2 974.4 |
| 1888 | 1 669.1 | 458.3 | 2 127.3 | 144.6 | 335.2 | 479.8 | 2 607.1 |
| 1889 | 1 702.8 | 279.1 | 1 982.0 | 148.0 | 368.6 | 516.7 | 2 498.6 |
| 1890 | 1 626.0 | 294.6 | 1 920.7 | 97.0 | 443.9 | 540.8 | 2 461.6 |
| 1891 | 1 932.2 | 271.0 | 2 802.3 | 56.3 | 476.9 | 533.2 | 3 335.5 |
| 1892 | 2 048.8 | 566.3 | 2 615.2 | 76.3 | 489.4 | 565.7 | 3 180.9 |
| 1893 | 2 036.7 | 390.0 | 2 453.7 | 87.8 | 421.7 | 509.5 | 2 963.2 |
| 1894 | 1 713.5 | 586.2 | 2 299.7 | 89.3 | 421.0 | 510.2 | 2 810.0 |

注 1：1874 年前(含)，香港地区的贸易数据计入"中国"，未单列。

注 2：1870 年前(含)，金银贸易也计入其中。

然而，由于香港作为中国与美国，以及所有其他欧洲国家之间中转港的作用，这些数字并不能代表中美贸易的总量[①]。在那些较早的岁月里，美国与英国、荷属东印度公司、印度支那之间的贸易量还很小；美国从香港进口的大部分——如果不是全部的话——一般都发源于华南，出口到香港的商品一定会有同样的比例最终运往中国内地。如果把美国与香港间的所有贸易按美国对华贸易来对待，可以确信不会有什么严重的错误。甚至美国政府报告也是这样做的。在 1874 年之前，美国有关对华贸易的统计数据都包括了"美国—香港地区"的全部贸易。

表 2-2 的第二部分将"美国—香港地区"的贸易单独列出，因为该数据是单独报告的；最后一列是美国与中国内地、香港之间的贸易之和，很明显这有助于全面考察中美贸易。

即使对贸易数据做了这样的修正，美国对华贸易也没有呈现什么实质性的增长，

---

① 关于该观点的进一步的讨论，详见后文第四章之《香港贸易修正》。

只在 2 000 万美元到 3 000 万美元之间徘徊。所以,美国对华贸易在两国外贸中的地位下滑是不争的事实。

### 1. 中美贸易发展缓慢的原因

人们可能会提出疑问,既然存在着运距缩短、工业发展等诸多有利于贸易扩大的因素,为什么中美贸易却并未如它应该有的速度那样发展。这一中肯的问题可以在如下列举的理由中找出答案。

*(1) 美国在华航运业的萎缩*

美国商业船队在美国内战之后显著萎缩,自然地对美国在东方进一步扩张贸易产生了不利影响。在南北时期,美国轮船面临着被敌对双方海军攻击的致命危险。其中的不少船只被卖到了其他国家,剩余的则大多无所事事地停泊在港口,慢慢腐烂。数年之内,内战之前无人出于其右的宏大的美国商业船队突然不再重要、不再活跃。以前由美国轮船承运的往来于中国的大量货物,现在只得依靠其他国家的商人来运输。1860 年,美国国内产品出口 717.08 万美元、进口 1 356.66 万美元,其中,由美国轮船装运的分别为 677.44 万美元和 1 313.53 万美元。但是,到了 1893 年,美国轮船运送的货物仅占对华出口货值的 12.6%,在美国对华进口方面也仅占 13.2%[①]。

*(2) 1862 年后美国重新建立的限制性贸易关税体制*

美国国内战争阻滞了美国对华贸易的自然扩张,不仅是由于庞大的美国船队遭到破坏,而且还由于美国将前一时期的自由商业政策开始转向极端保护体系,从而制约了美国从中国及其他国家的进口贸易。内战爆发后,美国政府立即感到需要额外收入来维持战争,因此通过 1862、1864 年关税法案,对进口税率进行大幅提高。这些法案"无差别地大幅提高关税,导致课税商品的平均税率从 1862 年的 37.2% 上升 1864 年的 47.1%。建立了比美国以往所有法案都要极端的关税保护措施"。这些高关税起初只是作为应付战争的临时性措施,但却在后续的 1872 年、1875 年、1883 年和 1897 年的法案中加以保留、增加并系统化,直到 1909 年也没有任何删减。不只是制成品被课以沉重的进口关税,许多原材料如羊毛、兽皮也是如此。在如此严苛的关税限制下,来自中国的进口在一定程度上被压制就不奇怪了。

*(3) 美国在华商业机构的沉寂(萧条)和倒闭*

也正是一时期,活跃的美国商界先驱从中国市场上消失了。"如果说在美国内战之前,东方的美国商业社群已经达到了发展巅峰和最活跃期,对那些后来进入中国市场的人大概是不公平的。中国市场已经开始萎缩,美国的国内发展已经使得,那些与

---

① 1893 年,美国从中国进口价值 544.36 万两海关银元,对华出口价值 418.3 万两海关银元,其中由美国轮船完成运送的货物价值分别为 141.2 万两海关银元、68.8 万两海关银元(据《中国海关统计》1893 年第一部分)(译注:原文此处-第 33 页注释 2-所列两组数值分别与该页正文及第 22 页之表 3 有冲突,疑有误)。

在亚洲的先驱者有着同样能力、品质的男人在本国的制造业、银行业和运输业同样能够得到充足的报酬"。其结果是,《天津条约》前所有著名的美国商业机构纷纷衰退、收缩或倒闭,且没有新的企业能达到同样水平,这成为 1860—1895 年这一时段的特征。美国在华老牌公司中最知名的两家企业 Russell 公司、Elyphant 公司先后于 1878 年 12 月、1891 年 6 月倒闭,其在中国的声望和商业领导地位被迫让与英、德竞争对手,直至欧洲战争美国人也没有能重新获得这一地位。美国内战之后现身于中国的美国公司,都没有良好的资本支持,有时倾向于采取不能给美国贸易带来任何信誉的投机方式,很少有明显的例外。

(4) 日本在茶叶、丝绸市场的竞争①

这一时期,美国对华贸易增长缓慢的一个更为明显的原因是,中国的茶叶、丝绸在对美贸易中遭到日本产品的激烈竞争。1860 年,(美国)海军准将佩里考察日本,促使这个当时仍然与世隔绝的国家向国际开放市场。在此之前,美国进口的全部茶叶及大部分丝绸都来自中国。只要中国掌控着这两种商品的垄断地位,只要美国这一快速发展的国家对这两种商品的需求不断增长,美国从中国的进口就大大增加;同样,进口的增长反过来会促进对华出口。但是,日本进入美国市场后,立即成为其东方近邻中国最强劲的竞争对手;日本与美国间的丝绸和茶叶贸易在一个比较短的时间里就严重地蚕食了中国丝绸、茶叶的市场,并且几乎使之完全崩溃②。

(5) 银价的跌落

另外还有一个原因,可以解释为什么对美国来说,对华贸易越来越微不足道(美国对华贸易额在美国外贸总额中的比例从 1860 年的 3% 不断下降到 1894 年的不足 2%),那就是银价相对于金价的持续贬低。美国内战之后,对华贸易量尽管增长缓慢,但却相当稳定,不过由于银/金的比价下降,以美元计价的贸易额却在缩水。贸易量的增长甚至不足以弥补贸易额的下降(贬值的影响)。1860 年两国贸易总额为 2 247.260 5万美元,三十年后则仅为 1 920.67 万美元。

表 2-3 表明香港海关银元(中国用于对外贸易的标准银元)兑换美元的汇率在快速下降。1871 年,1 两海关银元可兑换 1.58 美元,仅仅二十四年之后其黄金价值就下降到 0.77 美元,不足原值之一半。这种不利于中国的汇率,自然阻碍了中国人向美国采购的意愿。这就是为什么这一时期美国对华出口总额没有任何增加,反而下滑的主要原因。

在中国人看来,美国对华贸易有不规则的增长,但从美国人角度看并非如此。这一事实可通过表 2-3 中分别以海关银元、美元统计的贸易数据加以观察。

---

① 原文第 35 页标号(c)重复,应系作者笔误,该标号(c)及后续标号(d)(原文 36 页)、(e)(原文 37 页)依次更改为(d)、(e)、(f)。

② 关于日本竞争的更多信息和讨论,见后文《茶叶和丝绸》等章。

表2-3后两栏为美中直接贸易总额。可以看到,如果以海关银计价,则两国贸易总额从1871年的1 080.7万两海关银元跃升为1894年的2 570.6万两海关银元,增长将近120%。但是,如果以金价计值,贸易总额仅仅是从1 706.7万美元上升到1 979.4万美元,增长不足20%。

表2-3　1871—1894年美国对华贸易统计

| 年度 | 汇率 | 美国对华进口 | | 美国对华出口 | | 美国对华直接贸易总额 | |
| :---: | :---: | :---: | :---: | :---: | :---: | :---: | :---: |
| | (美元/银元) | (万两海关银元) | (万美元) | (万两海关银元) | (万美元) | (万两海关银元) | (万美元) |
| 1871 | 1.58 | 1 035.8 | 1 636.6 | 44.9 | 71.0 | 1 080.7 | 1 706.7 |
| 1876 | 1.45 | 725.9 | 1 052.6 | 73.9 | 107.1 | 799.8 | 1 159.7 |
| 1881 | 1.37 | 1 022.2 | 1 686.7 | 330.0 | 450.5 | 1 352.3 | 2 137.2 |
| 1886 | 1.22 | 968.6 | 1 181.6 | 464.7 | 567.0 | 1 433.3 | 1 748.6 |
| 1891 | 1.20 | 903.4 | 1 084.0 | 773.2 | 927.8 | 1 676.5 | 2 018.8 |
| 1894 | 0.77 | 926.4 | 713.3 | 1 644.3 | 1 266.1 | 2 570.6 | 1 979.4 |

(6)中国移民问题引起的美中之间的反感情绪

这一时期中美贸易萎缩、枯竭的原因,除了前面列举的所有因素外,还有另外一个原因要承担最大的责任。商界有一个共识,即买卖双方的亲善(信誉)是扩大贸易的最有效的动因。但在19世纪的后数十年间,由于一个令人非常厌恶的问题——美国不仅排斥1880年条约①中规定的中国劳工,还频繁歧视中国商人和旅行者——中国人对美国的友好态度至少是暂时受到了损伤。随着这一排斥而来的是,几年后,中国人对美国商品展开联合抵制以作为报复。这种情况下,中美贸易怎么可能有什么快速增长呢?

中国移民问题在美国影响如此之大,以至于美国的经济学家、政治家、立法官员、工会人士和作家对此认真关注了近三十年之久。全面描述这一问题超出了本书的范围,但它与美国对华贸易史牵涉颇深,因此必须至少给予简单的描述,以便理解这样一个使中美两国贸易发展至少延迟一代人的重要原因。

中国移民问题源于前一部分已经讨论过的丑恶"卖猪仔"。早些年到达美国——大多在加利福尼亚的华工,是受到欢迎和垂青的。但是,美国矿工被嫉妒心理和种族偏见所挑动,逐渐形成一种反对华工的情绪。由于不同的外表和风俗习惯,华工成为

---

① 译注:1880年11月17日,清廷被迫与美国在北京签订《管制和限制华工赴美条约》,允许美国限制或禁止中国劳工进入美国,为美国歧视害华工提供了法律依据。但同时规定在条约签订之时即1880年已经在美国工作的中国劳工"应允许按其自己的意愿决定其去留"。1888年10月,美国国会修改了相关法律,不加区别地禁止中国劳工,包括那些持有授权其返回美国的有效证明的中国劳工进入美国。

被怀疑和仇恨的对象,以及祸害这些社群的各种罪恶的替罪羊,适时发表反华声明对任何政党或候选人的竞选获胜都是非常必要的。在这样一种公众舆论下,华人的命运必然是非常糟糕的。"他们遭受各种不同方式的抢劫、殴打、谋杀和迫害。外国矿工承受着相当于准合法掠夺的歧视性牌照税。"

为了响应沿岸各州多次要求联邦政府采取措施排斥华人的建议,美国国会于1876年任命了一个关于中国移民问题的特别委员会,对事实真相进行全面调查,随后出具报告。这份报告的基调是完全反华。但是,对证据的认真研究表明,该委员会必然会"完成得出反华结论的任务要求,在其中并没有什么公正可言","证据被蓄意扭曲,以达到预设的结果"。

当时,美国和中国的关系名义上由包括著名的1868年《蒲安臣①条约》②在内的一系列条约③来调整;条约规定,两国在最惠国条款的基础上,明确承认两国人民自愿移民的权利,不过"它不能解释为包括归化特权"。很明显,在现行的条约之下,没有什么联邦立法能使西部各州的政治家感到满意。美、中代表多次会谈之后,于1880年签订了一个新的条约④。该条约最重要的特点是授权美国政府,可以对中国劳工进入或定居美国加以适度调整、限制、中止,但不得禁止;只要美国国家利益需要,无论何时都可以实施这种行动。按照这个条约,各种各样的排华法案在美国国会获得通过。其中的第一个法案于1882年⑤通过,它规定了排除华人劳工的十年期限。1888年通过的第二个法案采取了更为严格的排除措施。1892年法案中,排华期限又延长十年,1902年更是无限期延长。

从1880年条约的最初谈判开始,美国政府确保禁令只针对中国劳工而不及其他阶层,此目的非常明显,对此,中国政府予以认可。"但是排华法案在19世纪末形成时,除了1894年条约列举的学生、商人、旅客和官员四类人群外,以下各类人群均不得进入美国,包括银行家、律师、新闻记者、僧侣和神职人员、内科医师、牙医、保险代理人、经纪人和商业旅行代理人。……事实上,关于这个问题,法案似乎处于一个令人绝望的混乱之中:美国不同的首席检查官对若干规定的含义给予相互冲突的意见,结果使中国移民——无论其是居民商户还是商业旅行代理人,在试图登陆美国的过程中都

---

① 译注:Anson Burlingame(1820年11月14日至1870年2月23日),美国著名的律师、政治家和外交家,美国对华合作政策的代表人物。他是唯一一位既担任过美国驻华公使(1861—1867),又担任中国使节(1867—1870)的美国人。在驻华公使任上,蒲安臣积极执行美国国务卿西华德提出的对华"合作政策";开展"公正的"外交活动,以取代"武力外交"。"在条约口岸既不要求也不占领租界","也永不威胁中华帝国的领土完整。"

② 后见第十四章。

③ 译注:1868年,蒲安臣领衔组成中国代表使团出访美国,代表中国清政府与美国订立《蒲安臣条约》,又称《柏林盖姆条约》、《中美天津条约续增条款》、《中美续增条约》。该条约是近代中国第一个以平等身份签订的条约,在劳工、留学等方面对以后的中美关系产生了重要影响。

④ 译注:即1880年《管制和限制华工赴美条约》。

⑤ 译注:美国于1882年5月6日签署《排华法案》,允许美国暂停入境移民。

要承受巨大的困苦;被允许进入美国后,华工在这个国家从事合法商业活动时,还要不断被美国政府移民代理的住所搜查和不合理干扰所烦扰。"①

移民问题对中美贸易产生的不良后果简单列举如下:

(1) 它伤害了中国人的感情,两国直接贸易以来形成的中国人民对美国人的好感长时间不复存在。其结果不可避免的是反对使用美国货,其极端是形成针对所有美国人的激烈抵制运动。

(2) 对中国银行家、新闻记者、律师、保险代理人、经纪人、商业旅行代理人和其他专业人士进入美国施加不合理的阻碍措施,自然地阻止了这些中国人参与美国的进、出口贸易活动。这一事实,加之由于美国国内发展导致美国商人在对华贸易中收益下降,很大程度上应对中美贸易增长缓慢负责。

**2. 两国贸易的商品构成**

这一时段内,中美贸易的商品构成发生了一个重要的变化,即许多在以后各阶段占据重要地位的新商品开始参与其中。糖、染料、化工产品、草帽、植物油、兽皮、毛皮和羊毛,一个接一个地进入美国对华进口的商品名单之中,美国对华出口的商品名单中则增加了烟草和矿物油。尽管如此,茶叶和丝绸仍然是美国进口的主要商品,绵制品则在美国出口中占据主导地位。这一阶段看上去似乎是一个过渡期。表2-4以五年为一期,显示了两国贸易中主要商品的贸易情况。

表 2 - 4　1870—1890 年美国对华贸易主要商品构成

单位:万美元

| 商品名称 | 1870 年 | 1875 年 | 1880 年 | 1885 年 | 1890 年 |
|---|---|---|---|---|---|
| 美国从中国进口: | | | | | |
| 茶叶 | 979.6 | 874.6 | 999.5 | 803.9 | 685.8 |
| 生丝和绢丝 | 47.7 | 68.2 | 693.7 | 378.7 | 446.6 |
| 麻药、染料和鸦片 | 65.0 | 54.0 | 108.9 | 34.6 | 40.7 |
| 帽子材料 | 21.6 | 44.6 | 82.9 | 98.0 | 89.2 |
| 植物油 | 9.5 | 20.0 | 16.2 | 18.9 | 14.0 |
| 大麻、黄麻 | 37.5 | 40.9 | 52.9 | 3.7 | 0.5 |
| 米、米粉 | 52.0 | 93.1 | 98.0 | 73.0 | 60.3 |
| 香料、糖、水果 | 85.9 | 57.4 | 31.1 | 18.1 | 15.0 |
| 生皮 | | | 7.0 | 38.0 | 13.0 |

① 见第三章"联合抵制"。

(续表)

| 商品名称 | 1870年 | 1875年 | 1880年 | 1885年 | 1890年 |
|---|---|---|---|---|---|
| 美国从中国进口: | | | | | |
| 毛皮 | | | | 22.2 | 29.2 |
| 羊毛 | | | | 10.3 | 81.4 |
| 羊毛服装、棉布 | 7.5 | 8.0 | 7.7 | 15.6 | 8.6 |
| 其他 | 156.6 | 87.2 | 162.0 | 114.2 | 141.7 |
| 美国进口合计 | 1 462.9 | 1 348.0 | 2 177.0 | 1 629.2 | 1 626.0 |
| 美国向中国出口: | | | | | |
| 棉制品 | 62.6 | 55.3 | 33.9 | 344.3 | 123.1 |
| 煤炭 | 62.0 | 5.3 | 1.0 | 0.3 | 0.1 |
| 钢铁制品 | 11.4 | 13.4 | 4.1 | 80.2 | 7.4 |
| 矿物油 | 14.2 | 41.1 | 36.6 | 145.5 | 130.1 |
| 卷烟 | 3.9 | 1.1 | 0.5 | 1.4 | 4.1 |
| 小麦和面粉 | 83.9 | 3.5 | 6.6 | 4.6 | 5.9 |
| 其他 | 66.7 | 26.8 | 27.4 | 74.3 | 24.3 |
| 美国出口合计 | 304.7 | 146.6 | 110.1 | 639.6 | 294.4 |

### 3. 两国间的贸易差额和硬币航运

自1871年起,美国输出到中国内地和香港的金银开始分别记录,因此可以通过表2-5计算出1894年前的贸易差额。有趣的是,这时期与以前一样,美国对华贸易总体上仍然对中国有利,而与香港的贸易则继续不利于香港。假定美-港贸易大多就是美-中贸易的一部分,将同一年份两个相反方向的差额加以冲抵,就可以计算出整个二十四年间的美国对华贸易净差额是3.0亿美元。

表2-5 1871—1894年美国对华贸易差额

单位:万美元

| 年度 | 中国内地对美顺差 | 中国香港对美逆差 | 中国对美总顺差 | 美国向中国硬币净流出 |
|---|---|---|---|---|
| 1871 | 1 799.4 | | 1 799.4 | 357.0 |
| 1872 | 2 381.6 | | 2 381.6 | 599.9 |
| 1873 | 2 529.1 | | 2 529.1 | 715.4 |

（续表）

| 年度 | 中国内地对美顺差 | 中国香港对美逆差 | 中国对美总顺差 | 美国向中国硬币净流出 |
|---|---|---|---|---|
| 1874 | 1 727.6 | | 1 727.6 | 934.1 |
| 1875 | 1 200.9 | 89.9 | 1 111.0 | 659.6 |
| 1876 | 1 096.4 | 244.6 | 811.8 | 792.3 |
| 1877 | 942.3 | 205.9 | 736.4 | 1 542.0 |
| 1878 | 1 228.3 | 103.0 | 1 125.3 | 1 620.5 |
| 1879 | 1 378.0 | 163.7 | 1 214.2 | 729.7 |
| 1880 | 2 066.8 | 62.6 | 2 004.2 | 642.2 |
| 1881 | 1 687.0 | 51.7 | 1 635.3 | 343.7 |
| 1882 | 1 431.8 | 80.4 | 1 351.5 | 441.4 |
| 1883 | 1 606.1 | 185.9 | 1 420.2 | 694.8 |
| 1884 | 1 099.0 | 157.9 | 941.1 | 933.6 |
| 1885 | 989.6 | 316.5 | 623.0 | 1 457.2 |
| 1886 | 1 145.0 | 298.4 | 846.9 | 1 024.5 |
| 1887 | 1 283.0 | 154.8 | 1 128.3 | 1 071.3 |
| 1888 | 1 210.8 | 190.6 | 1 020.2 | 755.2 |
| 1889 | 1 123.7 | 220.6 | 903.1 | 1 403.5 |
| 1890 | 1 331.4 | 346.9 | 984.5 | 1 042.1 |
| 1891 | 1 062.1 | 420.5 | 641.5 | 464.6 |
| 1892 | 1 482.5 | 413.1 | 1 079.4 | 743.0 |
| 1893 | 1 673.1 | 333.9 | 1 339.8 | 853.5 |
| 1894 | 1 127.3 | 331.7 | 795.5 | 911.1 |
| 合计 | 3 403.4 | 4 152.7 | 30 046.7 | 20 732.0 |

注1：1874年之前（含），美国—中国香港贸易未单列，统计于美国—中国贸易之中。

注2：根据表2-5各年度数值，1871—1894年中国内地对美贸易顺差合计应为34 199.4万美元左右，原文此处（43页）明显有误，应系作者笔误。

从美国陆续出口到东方的金银（表2-5最后一栏）无疑部分地支付了这一巨大的贸易差额。1875年起，中国内地、香港地区的数据可以分别统计，可以看出，美国从中国进口或出口到中国的硬币数量波动很大。有些年份如1875、1876年，美国的净进口量通常极低,但 1887 年则达到 50 万美元。然而,如果将香港地区的贸易计算在内,则硬币净出口的数量相当大。表中显示,这段时期共有 2.0732 亿美元的金币和金块运到香港和中国内地,这一数字稍高于同期贸易净差额的 2/3。美国人如何支付剩余的 1/3 不得而知。一个合理的猜测是,与以前一样,美国人用伦敦或(欧洲)大陆国家的汇票支付,因为中、欧间的贸易差额与中美相反,一直是一个不利于中国的庞大数额。

# 第三章 局势纷乱和激烈竞争时期（1895—1913 年）

将 1895 年中日战争结束作为前一时期与本时期的分界线，至少有两个理由。

（1）中日战争导致东方一系列或多或少相互关联的纷扰，对中国与美国及其他国家的贸易产生了很大的影响。中国战败使国人警醒，结果改革派人士于 1898 年对中国政府进行了惊人的改组①。这一行动反而使中国的政治权力重新归于保守势力之手，随即于 1899 年爆发了义和团运动，接着在 1904—1905 年发生了俄-日战争。作为美国国内中国移民这一令人不快问题的最后结果，1905 年在中国发生了声势浩大的针对美国贸易的抵制运动。五年后的辛亥革命完全打破了中国的社会、政治和经济传统。位于太平洋彼岸的美国，通过购买阿拉斯加、吞并夏威夷群岛、强占菲律宾、开挖巴拿马运河，在太平洋上获得了一个个崭新的商业地位。所有这些政局动荡现象都各自影响着美国对华贸易的发展。

（2）中日战争标志着一个时代的开始，中国贸易面临的国际竞争到了最危急的时刻。尽管中国自 1842 年鸦片战争战败之后就被公认为海军力量不足，但直到这次中日战争后才完全暴露于西方世界。日本带头从中国割让了台湾，俄罗斯则租借了中国的南满地区，英国、法国、德国，甚至一度还有意大利，在共同抢夺土地政策下，纷纷冲进中国这个幅员辽阔的帝国。永久租借得到了承认，势力范围立刻在各地被划分。（来到中国的）所有国家——美国是唯一例外——都想让远东地区完全殖民化。

此外，作为这一重要战争的结果，中、日两国于 1895 年签订了《马关条约》②，自此之后，在华外国人的特权快速膨胀。接着，两国又于次年签订了另一份中日通商条约③。这两个条约的重要特点是，中国向外国公民开放内河和运河水域，准许外国人在中国内地购买物资或从事生产、租借仓库而无需另付特种税、在条约港口自由经营各种制造业；同时，准许进口各种机器而只支付规定的进口关税、购买自己在中国制造的产品而只需支付与进口机器应纳税额相同的国内转口税（这一条款在通商条约有修

---

① 译注：即"戊戌变法"，也称"百日维新"。

② 译注：原名《马关新约》，中日两国于 1895 年 4 月 17 日（清光绪二十一年三月二十三日）签订于日本马关（今下关）春帆楼，也称《下关条约》、《春帆按条约》，日本称《媾和条约》。按此条约中国需向日本支付赔款 2.3 亿两白银，这一数字相当于当时日本国家财政四年半的收入。

③ 译注：即中日通商行船条约，1896 年（光绪二十二年）7 月 21 日签订于北京。

订)。中日条约特别指出,这些特权只赋予日本人,但它们立刻适用于所有以"最惠国待遇"原则与中国建立全面条约关系的其他国家的国民。中国这样的全面开放对本国工业和商业是毁灭性的,其立竿见影的结果是各方商界纷纷涌向东方。

事实上,中国的商业竞争变得如此激烈,以至于迄今为止一直被外国人所盼望的中国完全开放,现在却成了他们不满的主要因素。各个西方大国都试图将中国的某几个省份对其他国家关闭,以期通过(在该范围内的)优先权消灭竞争。在这种情况下,原本无意对中国进行任何殖民的美国对华贸易难免会受到妨碍。美国通过国务卿海伊的演说宣布其"中国门户开放政策"[①],从而消除了这一障碍。

还应当注意到,19 世纪后期美国对华贸易萎缩的另外一部分原因是,美国的国内发展吸引了美国所有的资本,占用了美国人民的所有精力。但是 19 世纪结束之际,美国几乎完全完成了国内发展,因此其国内企业释出部分资本和产能,开始重新投入对外贸易的发展。此外,美国庞大的国内产业应当为其产品在本国之外寻找出路;它还需要本国不能充足供应的一些原料。所以,对外贸易又重新回到美国人的视线之内。对美国而言,无论作为买家还是卖家,南美洲都是一个优于远东的市场。不过,美国人也注意到,东方在不久的将来会是世界上最大的市场之一。基于此考虑,美国人将对外贸易的关注点投向了东方。美国人对远东贸易的浓厚兴趣,不仅被中国门户开放政策的声明、还被占领菲律宾及建议开挖巴拿马运河所证明。伴随着贸易利益的增长,中美贸易的总量也在逐步增加。表 3－1 是此时期二十年间的全部贸易统计数据。中美贸易的绝对量无疑在增长,只是增长相当没有规律。1896 年中美贸易总额达到2 900 万美元。接下来的五年里,中美贸易稳定增长,1900 年达到 4 215.6 万美元。但是,此后的 1901 年,贸易总额严重下滑 32%,这可能是由于受到中国北方省份的义和团运动的干扰所致,不过美国在这场反洋起义运动中遭受的损失无法详尽、准确地估计。美国驻烟台领事在其 1901 年报告中估计,美国仅在棉贸易的损失就超过 300 万美元。

但是,这一临时性的混乱很快就过去了,美国对华贸易于 1902 年完全恢复。由于俄日战争,美中贸易于 1905、1906 年达到了全盛,中国东北地区对战争物资和给养的大量需求应该是贸易以惊人速度扩张的原因。

但是,在战时对食品和给养的需求减少之后,美国对华贸易总量重新降至战前水平,维持在 5 000 万美元左右,在 1914 年之前没有明显的增长。

## 一、美中贸易的相对重要性

尽管这一时期美国对华贸易的绝对量有一定增长,但就中国而言,中美贸易的重

---

① 后见第十四章。

表 3-1　1895—1913 年美国对华贸易统计

单位：万美元

| 财年 | 美国—中国内地 | | | 美国—中国租界 | | | 美国—香港地区 | | | 美国对华贸易合计 | | |
|------|------|------|------|------|------|------|------|------|------|------|------|------|
| | 进口 | 出口 | 总额 | 进口 | 出口 | 总额 | 进口 | 出口 | 总额 | 进口 | 出口 | 总额 |
| 1895 | 2 054.6 | 360.4 | 2 415.0 | | | | 77.6 | 425.3 | 502.9 | 2 132.2 | 785.7 | 2 917.9 |
| 1896 | 2 202.3 | 692.2 | 2 894.5 | | | | 141.6 | 469.1 | 611.0 | 2 344.2 | 1 161.3 | 3 505.5 |
| 1897 | 2 040.4 | 1 192.4 | 3 232.8 | | | | 92.4 | 606.0 | 698.4 | 2 132.8 | 1 798.4 | 3 931.2 |
| 1898 | 2 032.6 | 999.3 | 3 031.9 | | | | 74.7 | 626.5 | 701.2 | 2 107.3 | 1 625.8 | 3 733.1 |
| 1899 | 1 861.9 | 1 449.3 | 3 311.2 | | | | 247.9 | 773.3 | 1 021.2 | 2 109.8 | 2 222.6 | 4 332.5 |
| 1900 | 2 689.7 | 1 525.9 | 4 215.6 | 0.5 | 36.7 | 37.2 | 125.6 | 848.6 | 974.2 | 2 815.8 | 2 411.2 | 5 227.0 |
| 1901 | 1 830.4 | 1 040.6 | 2 871.0 | | 37.7 | 37.7 | 141.6 | 801.0 | 942.6 | 1 972.0 | 1 879.3 | 3 851.3 |
| 1902 | 2 105.6 | 2 472.3 | 4 577.9 | 0.8 | 53.9 | 54.7 | 127.8 | 803.0 | 930.8 | 2 234.2 | 3 329.2 | 5 563.4 |
| 1903 | 2 664.9 | 1 889.8 | 4 554.7 | 2.4 | 71.1 | 73.5 | 136.0 | 877.2 | 1 013.2 | 2 803.3 | 2 838.1 | 5 641.4 |
| 1904 | 2 934.5 | 1 286.2 | 4 220.7 | 0.8 | 61.8 | 62.6 | 151.9 | 1 045.9 | 1 197.8 | 3 087.2 | 2 393.9 | 5 481.1 |
| 1905 | 2 788.5 | 5 345.3 | 8 133.8 | 0.2 | 17.2 | 17.4 | 155.2 | 1 077.0 | 1 232.2 | 2 943.9 | 6 439.5 | 9 383.4 |
| 1906 | 2 853.1 | 4 377.4 | 7 230.5 | 3.6 | 25.1 | 28.7 | 182.9 | 704.9 | 887.4 | 3 039.6 | 5 107.0 | 8 146.6 |
| 1907 | 3 343.7 | 2 570.5 | 5 914.1 | 20.0 | 191.3 | 211.3 | 274.1 | 833.2 | 1 107.3 | 3 637.8 | 3 595.0 | 7 232.8 |
| 1908 | 2 602.1 | 2 234.4 | 4 836.5 | 57.9 | 867.7 | 926.5 | 212.9 | 897.5 | 1 110.4 | 2 872.9 | 3 999.6 | 6 882.5 |
| 1909 | 2 879.9 | 1942.0 | 4 821.9 | 64.4 | 52.9 | 117.3 | 176.9 | 726.8 | 903.7 | 3 121.2 | 2 721.7 | 5 842.9 |
| 1910 | 2 999.0 | 1 632.1 | 4 631.1 | 130.8 | 65.0 | 195.8 | 233.2 | 646.7 | 879.9 | 3 363.0 | 2 343.8 | 5 706.8 |
| 1911 | 3 422.8 | 1 928.8 | 5 351.6 | 105.3 | 93.5 | 198.8 | 271.8 | 775.6 | 1 047.4 | 3 799.9 | 2 797.9 | 6 597.3 |
| 1912 | 2 957.4 | 2 436.1 | 5 393.5 | 88.6 | 92.6 | 181.2 | 311.5 | 1 033.4 | 1 344.9 | 3 357.5 | 3 562.1 | 6 919.5 |
| 1913 | 3 901.1 | 2 132.7 | 6 033.8 | 74.5 | 111.3 | 185.8 | 402.0 | 1 043.1 | 1 445.1 | 4 377.6 | 3 287.1 | 7 664.7 |

注：关于香港数据修正，参见第二章、第四章相关脚注。

要性并没有发生变化。表 3-2 是中国对外贸易的国别统计情况。

对美贸易在中国对外贸易中的份额，1896 年是 6.7%，1905 年增加到 15.0%，1913 年重新退至 7.6%。其每年的差值是一条标准的钟形曲线，终点并没有比起点超出很多。包括英属印度在内，英国的份额呈下降趋势，而日本却在持续上升，二十年间翻了一倍。欧洲大陆的份额也在增长，尤其是德国。

反过来看，对华贸易在美国外贸中的地位也呈现出下降趋势。这一时期，美国与远东地区的贸易总体上在增长，特别是与日本、英属东印度群岛之间的贸易，而对华贸易的发展却呈相反态势。

1900 年，美国来自中国的进口在美国进口总额中占有 3.18% 的份额，这一数字在十年之后的 1910 年下降到 1.92%，1913 年稍有恢复，达到 2.15%。1900 年，对华出口在美国出口总额中的份额为 1.10%，十年后下降为 0.94%，1913 年再次下降到 0.87%。同一时期，美国对日贸易在美国外贸总额中的份额却由 1.84% 上升到 4.00%，

表 3 - 2　1896—1913 年各国(地区)在中国外贸中的份额

单位:%

| 年份 | 美国 | 英国 | 英属印度 | 欧洲(不含俄罗斯) | 俄罗斯和西伯利亚 | 德国 | 法国 | 日本 | 香港 |
|------|------|------|----------|------------------|------------------|------|------|------|------|
| 1896 | 6.7 | 16.5 | 7.4 | 8.0 | 5.0 | | | 8.4 | 42.5 |
| 1899 | 9.5 | 11.7 | 7.8 | 10.2 | 2.2 | | | 11.5 | 41.6 |
| 1902 | 10.5 | 12.8 | 6.8 | 10.8 | 8.1 | | | 12.2 | 40.8 |
| 1905 | 15.0 | 14.9 | 5.5 | 9.8 | 4.3 | | | 14.0 | 31.4 |
| 1908 | 9.9 | 12.7 | 5.1 | | 5.4 | 3.1 | 5.8 | 15.3 | 36.1 |
| 1911 | 8.7 | 12.4 | 4.9 | | 4.8 | 4.2 | 5.4 | 17.1 | 29.3 |
| 1913 | 7.6 | 11.4 | 5.5 | | 6.0 | 4.5 | 5.3 | 19.7 | 29.1 |

与英属东印度群岛间的贸易所占份额则由 1.57％上升到 3.28％(见表 3 - 3)。

表 3 - 3　1895—1913 年东方各国(地区)在美国外贸中的份额

单位:%

| 年份 | 美国—中国 | | | 美国—香港 | | | 美国—日本 | | | 美国—英属东印度群岛 | | | 美国—荷属东印度群岛 | | |
|------|------|------|------|------|------|------|------|------|------|------|------|------|------|------|------|
| | 进口 | 出口 | 总额 | 进口 | 出口 | 总额 | 进口 | 出口 | 总额 | 进口 | 出口 | 总额 | 进口 | 出口 | 总额 |
| 1895 | 2.81 | 0.45 | 1.57 | 0.11 | 0.53 | 0.33 | 3.24 | 0.57 | 1.84 | 2.90 | 0.35 | 1.57 | 1.06 | 0.14 | 0.58 |
| 1900 | 3.18 | 1.10 | 1.88 | 0.15 | 0.62 | 0.43 | 3.84 | 2.08 | 2.74 | 5.34 | 0.34 | 2.24 | 3.28 | 0.11 | 1.31 |
| 1905 | 2.51 | 3.52 | 3.08 | 0.14 | 0.71 | 0.47 | 4.64 | 3.40 | 3.92 | 4.80 | 0.50 | 2.32 | 1.65 | 0.11 | 0.76 |
| 1910 | 1.92 | 0.94 | 1.40 | 0.15 | 0.37 | 0.26 | 4.26 | 1.26 | 2.68 | 4.53 | 0.54 | 2.43 | 0.68 | 0.13 | 0.39 |
| 1913 | 2.15 | 0.87 | 1.48 | 0.22 | 0.42 | 0.33 | 5.05 | 2.35 | 4.00 | 6.41 | 0.61 | 3.28 | 0.34 | 0.13 | 0.25 |

　　对华贸易在美国外贸中的地位下降还可以用另一种方式表述:1900 年,中国是美国商品出口的第十大客户,而 1913 年则下滑至第十三位[1];1900 年,中国在美国进口来源地[2]中排名第六位,而 1913 年则跌至了第九位。

　　中美贸易如此明显的下滑自然引起关注,且需要加以解释。但是,如果我们把这一时期前半段时间中美贸易发展的原因,解释为是美国人复兴了远东地区的商业利益,是中国的完全开放不只针对外国商人也针对外国制造业者,是中国东北地区对食品和服装的临时性战争需要,那么该怎样解释其在后一阶段的衰退呢?

---

　　[1] 译注:根据原文第 84 页正文及注释 2 所列 1913 年美国商品出口目的地排名,中国应为第 14 位。原文此处(第 51 页)疑为作者笔误。

　　[2] 译注:原文此处(第 51 页)称"从美国进口",根据本段前文及原文第 83 页正文及注释 1 推断,应为作者笔误。

## 二、1905 年后美国对华出口衰退的原因

1905 年之后,美国对华贸易的萎缩在美国出口方面尤为明显,可以用图形标示贸易额的持续下降。1905 年,美国对华(含香港地区)出口 6 400 万美元,1906 年下跌至 5 100 万美元,1907 年继续下降到 3 600 万美元,1908 年小幅回升至 4 000 万美元[①],1909 年再次滑落至 2 900 万美元,最终于 1910 年降至 2 300 万美元,只比之前五年中峰值[②]的 1/4 稍多一点。1910 年后,美国对华出口逐步回升,但直到 1913 年也没有超过 3300 万美元[③]。

（1）外国在中国的竞争

美国对华出口严重衰退首要、也是最明显的原因是,各国制造业和商人为其不断增长的产量在中国寻找市场而展开了激烈竞争。至于此类竞争的激烈程度,十三年前曾在远东地区从事贸易业务的行业老手 F. 麦考密克先生的如下描述给予我们生动的印象:

"本世纪初之前,外国货物被放在中国沿海码头,供中国人选购……现在,由于竞争,外国商人被迫深入公路或偏僻小路。今天,辛勤地奔波于中国公路之上的,有收集贸易报告的领事官员,还有文职督察以及外商本人,甚至还有贩卖专利药品的外国流动商贩。在满洲,外国商人惊奇地看到了日本零售商人。甚至于,不甚精明的俄罗斯人也在蒙古与中国产生了贸易冲突。对英国和俄罗斯来说,如何在西藏与日本人竞争贸易是一个急需解决的问题;然而在朝鲜边界的长白山脚下,(日本)大阪小刀正在为获得鸭绿江畔伐木人的青睐而与(德国)索林根刀具对决……"

在这一新的竞争态势下,美国商人未能寻觅到合适的切入点。美国收获了 1905 年俄日战争贸易的精华部分,却成为唯一未能分享远东地区战后商业繁荣景象的国家。日本、德国获益最多,英国保持了其原有份额,而美国人则相对落后。

在对华贸易份额已经超越或开始赶超美国产品的国家中,德国和日本在争夺远东贸易的竞争中最为用心。其中,德国更加尽力,其在中国做了大量商业投资,可能超过其他任何大国。德国通过扩充其官方体系持续、有效地整合其在中国的所有商业利益,而德国商人则通过广泛的信用"顺利征服市场"。

其时,日本在华商业同样强大,因为它在贸易补贴、贷款和官方奖励方面得到了最有力的支持。日本煤炭,加上满洲地区的煤炭,不仅成功地与美国煤炭竞争,也与中国煤矿竞争。日本设在大连的面粉厂得到 4％的政府低息贷款,同样能适应各种竞争;

---

① 这一不寻常的上升是由于对南满地区大量出口铁路材料和设备所致。

② 1905 年。

③ 见表 3-1。

这减少了美国面粉的贸易份额,后者的损失无法通过扩大在满洲广泛使用的美国面粉机器贸易来补偿。日本人控制的北海道、鸭绿江木材区的发展也使美国太平洋沿岸的木材出口减少。日本人甚至于 1907 年建造了一些用于南满铁路的机车车辆,与美国产品相比,其做工和材质更好,成本更低。尽管美国是钢铁大国,日本还是挤进了军舰制造领域,中国建造小型炮艇的许多合同都交给了日本人。

这一时期,美国对华贸易中下滑最多的是棉制品和矿物油。棉制品贸易下降是由于中国鼓励棉花生产,也由于印度棉纱比美国原棉更有价格优势而被大量运入中国。其中,后一原因更为重要,因为它与日本棉花工业的兴起及日本人侵入东亚各国商贸有关。所以,日本挟其强大的贸易竞争工具——如俄日战争后对所有重要产业进行国民救助,对商业船队的补助,帝国资金投资工业领域,对盐业、樟脑、烟草和铁路实行国家垄断专营——对美国在华的棉、樟脑、面粉和其他一些工业产生了巨大的冲击。

然而,不只是日本在"消灭"美国的在华贸易。在美国对华贸易下滑最严重的棉、矿物油两个产品领域,印度、俄罗斯、荷属东印度群岛赚取了美国几乎全部的损失;而在钢铁和机器领域,英国、德国、法国和比利时拿走了(原属美国的)贸易份额。

(2)中国的反美抵制活动

在如此激烈竞争的态势下,消费者的亲善关系在决定与何人进行贸易方面自然有很大作用。但就在这个节骨眼上,中国对美国的亲善遭到了破坏,原因在于美国未能公平处理中国移民问题。排华法案条款之严苛,准许中国人进入美国的管理规章之严格,让中国人难以接受,遂于 1905 年决定抵制美国人以作为抗议和报复。

这一抵制运动的直接原因似乎是即将到来的 1894 年中国移民条约的续订谈判。1904 年,中国驻华盛顿公使[①]指责该条约苛待中国商人、学生、旅行者,这种做法在1899 年之后尤其"臭名昭著"。1905 年 5 月,上海的商界领袖和社会名流在上海商务总会召开会议,决定要求全国各地的中国商人停止订购美国货物,以抗议拟订中的新排华条约的苛刻条款。数天之内,抗议运动就得到了中国 25 个条约港口城市的名流、商人和学校教师的支持,世界各地的中国人发来电报表示声援。

在社会激进分子的狂热带动下,运动呈现出普遍反对外国人的煽动情绪。外国人对义和国运动记忆犹新,这种危险的反洋局面比贸易利益(受损)的危险更让他们惊慌。中国政府也担心运动失控,成为革命分子发起另一场暴动的口实。

中国政府依照美国政府的要求,颁布了一道圣旨,警告民众必须遵守条约规定,违者将受严惩,并通过宣扬与美国的长期友好关系,及美国政府已经允诺用友好条款讨论移民条约的说辞来安抚民众;并要求各地总督和省长发布类似的通告,并要为"任何

---

① 译注:即梁诚(1864—1917),原名丕旭,字义哀,号震东,广州市海珠区黄埔村人。先后出使英、美、秘鲁、古巴等国。他曾反复交涉,争回我国"庚子赔款"多出部分用于教育;争回"粤汉铁路"筑路权益。他在美国时多次函知国内,要求对诱骗妇女、华工出洋者"缉拿惩办"。

骚乱"负责,直接逮捕暴力煽动者。但是直到罗斯福总统催促采取行动,对与中国的新约中所诟病的部分加以矫正,这场运动才在表面上平息下来。

然而,这一相当短暂运动的影响却是深远的。尽管美国对华出口在抵制美货当年达到顶峰,还是应当注意到,对美国食品和服装的需求大部分来自满洲的日俄军人。在接下来的几年间,美国对华出口连年下滑,与之相反的是其他国家的对华出口却在增长。这清楚地表明,由于对美国人的敌意,中国人宁愿使用其他国家的产品,而不喜欢美国货。中国人对美国人的这种敌意直到 1908 年美国(向中国)退还庚子赔款①、1912 年美国率先承认中华民国才完全消失。从那时以来,中国认识到美国毕竟还是自己最好的朋友,两国亲善关系的恢复直接表现为从 1910 年开始美国对华出口逐渐增长。

(3)欧洲资本对中国工业发展的控制

美国对华贸易在俄日战争之后处于停滞状态的原因,除了前述两个主要原因外,还有一个原因,即中国工业发展受到欧洲资本的控制。欧洲各国通过向中国提供贷款"垄断"了其贸易,使得美国的对华贸易受到了阻碍。通过借钱获利是给中国放贷的欧洲国家的惯例。就这样,几年来,中国采购钢材和铁路机器、矿山机器、兵工设备、毛织品、丝绸纺织机器、制革机器、铸造机器及钢铁工厂设备的订单都投向了欧洲。这些年,美国只在中国获得了数量毫不起眼的电力供应、工艺印刷材料的订单,而在其他领域则没有收获。欧洲的资本主义国家获益于中国的工业发展及美国的损失。

## 三、美国对华进口的平稳增长

在对这一时期美国对华出口相对下降的原因及其特点加以论述之后,还应当对美国对华进口只是保持稳定而没有达到预期扩张的原因做一些研究。其中的原因不难理解。首先,日本在美国丝绸市场展现了强大的竞争实力,英属东印度群岛仍旧在美国的茶叶市场具有强大竞争力,这影响了美国从中国进口丝绸、茶叶这两种商品——它们迄今仍在美国从中国进口的商品中占据最重要地位;其次,中国丰富的矿产资源、农业资源的开发迟缓,也严重影响了美国对华进口,因为中国很少有商品能在美国有很大的需求。

尽管有这些不利条件,这一时期,美国对华进口还是稳定增长。1895 年,美国对华(含香港)进口总额 2 100 万美元,十年后为 2 900 万美元,1913 年为 4 400 万美元。即使按同期一般价格水准对这一名义增长值做一些调整,美国从中国的进口显然还是

---

① 译注:1906 年,美国伊利诺伊大学校长埃德蒙·詹姆斯建议美国退还庚款资助中国学生赴美留。1908 年 6 月 23 日,美国国会参、众两院根据罗斯福总统年度咨文中的要求,准许将美国庚子赔款数减至 13 655 492.69 美元,将此数与原分给美国赔款 24 440 778.81 美元的差额,计 10 785 286.12 美元退还给中国。

增长的。但是这只不过是一个正常增长,几乎与美国进口总量、中国出口总量保持同步。

## 四、本时期中美贸易的商品构成

### 1. 美国对华出口的主要商品

表 3-4 是本时期美国对华出口的重要商品简表。其中没有几个品种的年出口额超过 10 万美元。

直到本时期结束,棉布在美国的所有出口商品中一直占据最大的份额。1905 年前,棉布通常占美国出口总额的 1/2～2/3。那时,中国是第二大棉纱布市场,仅次于英属印度。1905 年,美国棉制品在中国的销售达到了顶峰,为 2 776.1 万美元,居美国棉制品出口贸易之首位。但是,自这一年开始,美国棉制品出口的绝对值、相对份额都急速下降,如表 3-4 所示。美国棉制品出口贸易的丧失——这一点已在上文简述、并将在后续有关棉制品的章节中进一步全面讨论——主要是由于日本、中国棉纺厂的竞争,对手的优势在于使用价格低廉的中国、印度原材料,生产成本也较低。

美国对华出口的第二种大宗商品是精炼矿物油。尽管中国油品市场的竞争非常激烈,美国仍然在这一时期一直维持其领先地位。美国石油出口贸易的绝对量稳定增长,但其在美国对华出口总额中的相对份额却在 38%(1909 年[①])至 20%(1912 年)间大幅波动[②]。

烟草(制成品、非制成品)在美国对华出口贸易中占据第三的位置。美中烟草贸易的绝对量及相对份额的增长非常明显。1895 年,美国对华烟草出口额不过 10 万美元,不足美国对华出口总额的 3%。很快地,中国人染上了消费美国烟草的习惯,不到二十年的时间,美国对华烟草出口总额就开始超过 200 万美元,接近美国对华出口总额的 10%[③]。

在美国对华出口商品中,排名第四的是钢铁机器及其他产品。1895 年之前,很少有美国机器在中国销售,中国的机器当时大多由英国、德国和比利时提供。原因如前一部分所述,是由于中国的工业发展被欧洲资本所控制。但当美国机器的优点被中国人逐渐了解之后,开展相关的贸易就是必然的选择了。这一时期的最后几年,其他产品如铁板、电线、钉子、工具等也有了广阔的市场。1908 年,满洲地区独自向美国购买价值 305.9873 万美元的 198 节机车、价值 112.1199 万美元的 31 454 吨钢轨、价值

① 译注:原文此处(第 58 页)称"1907 年"。但按表 3-4,1907 年矿物油所占份额仅为 22%,占比为 38% 的年份应为 1909 年。

② 后见第十一章《矿物油》。

③ 后见第十二章《烟草》。

表 3 - 4　1895—1913 美国对华(含租界)出口的商品构成

| 序号 | 名　称 | 1895 年 | | 1898 年 | | 1901 年 | | 1903 年 | | 1905 年 | |
|---|---|---|---|---|---|---|---|---|---|---|---|
| | | (万美元) | (%) | (万美元) | (%) | (万美元) | (%) | (万美元) | (%) | (万美元) | (%) |
| 1 | 面包原料(不含小麦粉) | 0.9 | 0.2 | 2.1 | 0.2 | 14.4 | 1.3 | 3.0 | 0.2 | 29.3 | 0.5 |
| 2 | 面包原料(小麦粉) | 10.4 | 2.9 | 8.9 | 0.9 | 33.4 | 3.1 | 56.4 | 2.9 | 31.8 | 0.6 |
| 3 | 汽车、马车及部件 | | | | | | | | | | |
| 4 | 铜(块、棒、盘等) | | | | | | | | | 994.1 | 18.5 |
| 5 | 棉布 | 170.3 | 47.3 | 519.6 | 52 | 455.3 | 42.5 | 1369.0 | 69.6 | 2776.1 | 51.6 |
| 6 | 棉花,未加工的 | | | 37.1 | 3.7 | | | 12.3 | 0.6 | 17.6 | 0.3 |
| 7 | 水果和坚果 | 1.4 | 0.4 | 3.2 | 0.3 | 8.1 | 0.8 | 5.6 | 0.3 | 6.0 | 0.1 |
| 8 | 钢铁机器 | | | 12.1 | 1.2 | 28.4 | 2.6 | 2.5 | 0.1 | 28.7 | 0.5 |
| 9 | 其他钢铁制品 | 11.8 | 3.3 | 24.4 | 2.4 | 55.4 | 5.1 | 55.8 | 2.8 | 100.0 | 1.9 |
| 10 | 肉、乳制品和其他食物 | 3.5 | 1 | 7.6 | 0.8 | 42.7 | 4 | 16.6 | 0.8 | 101.6 | 1.9 |
| 11 | 皮革制品和鞣制皮 | 0.3 | 0.1 | 0.5 | 0.1 | 2.8 | 0.3 | 2.4 | 0.1 | 13.5 | 0.3 |
| 12 | 精炼矿物油 | 118.1 | 32.8 | 286.5 | 28.7 | 244.5 | 22.7 | 186.6 | 9.5 | 852.7 | 15.9 |
| 13 | 石蜡 | | | | | | | | | | |
| 14 | 烟草,已制成 | 10.5 | 2.9 | 32.8 | 3.3 | 52.2 | 4.9 | 70.1 | 3.6 | 143.9 | 2.7 |
| 15 | 烟草,未制成 | 0.1 | | 1.8 | 0.2 | 2.5 | 0.2 | 1.1 | 0.1 | 46.0 | 0.9 |
| 16 | 木材(木板) | 6.5 | 1.8 | 12.0 | 1.2 | 13.8 | 1.3 | 31.4 | 1.6 | 41.4 | 0.8 |
| 17 | 木制品 | 2.4 | 0.7 | 4.8 | 0.5 | 20.1 | 2.7 | 30.4 | 1.5 | 27.5 | 0.5 |
| 18 | 其他 | 24.2 | 6.7 | 45.0 | 4.6 | 95.7 | 8.9 | 117.8 | 6.0 | 152.3 | 2.8 |
| | 美国对华出口总额 | 360.4 | 100 | 999.3 | 100 | 1 078.3 | 100 | 1 961.0 | 100.0 | 5 362.5 | 100.0 |

（续表）

| 序号 | 名　称 | 1907 年 | | 1909 年 | | 1911 年 | | 1912 年 | | 1913 年 | |
|---|---|---|---|---|---|---|---|---|---|---|---|
| | | （万美元） | （%） | （万美元） | （%） | （万美元） | （%） | （万美元） | （%） | （万美元） | （%） |
| 1 | 面包原料（不含小麦粉） | 143.3 | 5.0 | 3.2 | 0.2 | 4.4 | 0.2 | 5.7 | 0.02 | 5.0 | 0.2 |
| 2 | 面包原料（小麦粉） | 631.2 | 23.0 | 26.6 | 1.3 | 108.9 | 5.4 | 290.0 | 11.4 | 49.3 | 2.2 |
| 3 | 汽车、马车及部件 | 27.9 | 1.0 | 16.6 | 0.8 | 7.1 | 0.3 | 11.6 | 0.5 | 23.3 | 1.0 |
| 4 | 铜（块、棒、盘等） | 27.0 | 1.0 | | | | | 16.4 | 0.6 | 0.1 | |
| 5 | 棉布 | 571.4 | 20.7 | 800.4 | 40.0 | 529.3 | 26.2 | 737.2 | 29.0 | 558.5 | 2.48 |
| 6 | 棉花,未加工的 | 30.1 | 1.1 | 2.2 | 0.1 | | | 259.1 | 10.1 | 46.4 | 2.1 |
| 7 | 水果和坚果 | 9.0 | 0.3 | 4.9 | 0.2 | 4.6 | 0.2 | 6.5 | 0.3 | 7.8 | 0.3 |
| 8 | 钢铁机器 | 14.5 | 0.5 | 30.3 | 1.5 | 48.1 | 2.4 | 58.0 | 2.3 | 78.6 | 3.5 |
| 9 | 其他钢铁制品 | 173.6 | 6.3 | 94.6 | 4.7 | 171.5 | 8.5 | 217.5 | 8.5 | 219.5 | 9.7 |
| 10 | 肉、乳制品和其他食物 | 19.7 | 0.7 | 9.7 | 0.5 | 6.2 | 0.3 | 13.4 | 0.5 | 14.3 | 0.6 |
| 11 | 皮革制品和鞣制皮 | 13.3 | 0.5 | 8.1 | 0.4 | 9.3 | 0.5 | 10.0 | 0.4 | 12.3 | 0.5 |
| 12 | 精炼矿物油 | 615.4 | 22.3 | 755.2 | 38.0 | 730.0 | 36.1 | 518.2 | 20.3 | 669.9 | 29.8 |
| 13 | 石蜡 | 9.7 | 0.3 | 8.5 | 0.4 | 37.7 | 1.9 | 42.4 | 1.7 | 41.9 | 1.9 |
| 14 | 烟草,已制成 | 142.8 | 5.2 | 96.4 | 4.8 | 57.6 | 2.8 | 82.4 | 3.2 | 106.5 | 4.7 |
| 15 | 烟草,未制成 | 35.8 | 1.3 | 27.4 | 1.4 | 76.4 | 3.8 | 93.7 | 3.7 | 106.7 | 4.7 |
| 16 | 木材（木板） | 97.6 | 3.5 | 35.7 | 1.8 | 101.9 | 5.0 | 33.8 | 1.3 | 86.4 | 3.8 |
| 17 | 木制品 | 60.6 | 2.2 | 3.7 | 0.2 | 26.1 | 1.3 | 16.6 | 0.6 | 23.0 | 1.0 |
| 18 | 其他 | 138.8 | 5.0 | 71.4 | 3.6 | 103.2 | 5.1 | 116.2 | 4.6 | 131.7 | 5.8 |
| | 美国对华出口总额 | 2 751.7 | 100.0 | 1 994.9 | 100.0 | 2 022.3 | 100.0 | 2 528.7 | 100.0 | 2 251.2 | 100.0 |

86.0469万美元的11 560吨钢铁构件;但这不是正常情况下的贸易。钢铁贸易每年的波动幅度非常大,但是在这一时期的后期,中国对这些产品的需求就相当稳定,贸易额通常占到美国出口总额的10%～12%①。

接下来,面包原料特别是小麦粉占据了美国对华出口贸易第五名的位置。19世纪最后几年里,美国每年出口的小麦粉和其他面包原料不超过10万美元,但20世纪初开始,许多中国人开始使用外国面粉,美国人很快抓住了这一扩大其贸易的良机。1907年,美国分别向中国出口631.2万美元的小麦粉、143.3万美元的其他面包原料,两者合计占到当年美国对华出口总额的28%。这一短暂的成功使华盛顿和俄勒冈州的小麦种植业者产生这样的想法:这是为他们生产的面粉创造一个有利可图的,巨大市场的良机。但是,中国对美国面粉的需求没有什么变化,不久就能够由自己的面粉厂为民众供应面粉。所以,自1907年开始,美国对华面包原料出口大幅下滑。

其他商品,如汽车、马车和皮革制品的出口也在增长。木板及其他木制品的贸易也有一定的份额。铜贸易的规模涨落不定,有些年份零成交,而1905年高达994.1万美元。自19世纪中叶起,美国就开始向中国出口水果和坚果,但是如此大距离地运输这些易腐产品,成本非常高,因此这一贸易从未有任何实质的增长,这一时期没有超过10万美元。对于肉类和乳制品而言,情况也是如此,但浓缩奶和其他一些罐装食品除外。

除了表3-4所列的这些商品,还有其他一些物资由美国出口到中国,如时钟、手表、科学仪器、化工产品、药品和染料,以及电力机械和电器用具、图书和其他纸制品,等等。这些产品的年贸易额通常都不足10万美元。

由表3-4可见,美国对华出口贸易的一个明显趋势是,简单形式制造业的产品总体上是下降的,而制造复杂度高的产品则保持增长。小麦粉和棉布属于前者,中国已经可以通过自己建造良好的工厂从而实现自给,所以它们在中国的市场份额快速缩小。相反,钢铁机器及其他制品、汽车和火车等产品必须依靠发展水平较高的大型企业才能完成,而这类企业短期内无法在中国建立;相应地,这些产品在中国的市场就扩大。

美国对华出口贸易的另一个特点是美国的生产资料开始扮演重要角色。在此之前,所有向中国出口的美国商品实际上都是消费品,机器、建筑材料、汽车、机车等的出口微不足道。但是,随着中国的工业化渐露端倪,对生产资料的需求越来越大。

但是,美国对华出口贸易的这两个趋势在下一时期表现得更为全面。本时期,只能算是一个逐渐过渡期。

**2. 美国从中国进口的主要商品**

这一时期,美国从中国进口的商品类目见表3-5。其中,丝绸最为重要,占据首

---

① 后见第十三章《工业机器与设备》(译注:应为第十四章)。

位。仅生丝一项的年贸易额就超过美国对华进口总额的 1/3。尽管日本丝绸在美国市场具有强大的竞争实力,但中国丝绸出口的数量和贸易额都保持稳定增长。其原因在于美国丝绸业的快速发展,扩大了生丝需求量。然而,还是可以从后文[1]看到,中国丝绸失去了其在美国的大部分市场。

茶叶以前是美国从中国进口的商品中最为重要的品种,但在这一时期,茶叶的进口数量、贸易额及相对份额都逐渐下降。1895,美国从中国进口价值 750 万美元的茶叶,二十年后进口额只剩下一半,而茶叶贸易在美国进口总额中的份额则由 36.8% 下降到仅有 8.2%,后文将予以说明[2]。

表 3-5 中位居第三的是羊毛,其贸易量增长,在这一时期扮演非常重要的角色。1895 年,美国从中国进口的羊毛价值 1 700 万美元[3],在美国对华进口总额中占 8.3% 的份额。十年后的 1905 年,羊毛进口额超过 300 万美元,占比 11.2%,1913 年进口额 470 万美元,占比 11.8%。

生皮排名第四。这类商品的贸易只是最近才变得重要起来,植物油、猪鬃、锑矿石和锑块等产品同样如此,这类贸易很不起眼,但其重要性在这一阶段末期开始上升。

这一时期前半段,化工产品和药品的进口额每年都相当大,通常在 100 万～200 万美元间浮动。但是,进口"药品"的大部分是精制鸦片,仅其一项在某些年份就超过 100 万美元。然而,1911 年,美国政府发布鸦片禁令,因此其在进口总额中的份额迅速下降到稍多于 1%。

单从表 3-5 的一般观察难以发现这样重要的事实:进口的一大部分是支撑美国工业进一步生产的原材料或半成品。除了为数不多的产品如茶叶、鞭炮、发网、绸缎和木制品处,美国进口的大部分商品是无法即期消费的。随着时间的推移,原材料进口增长、制成品进口下降的趋势越发明显。1895 年,制成品几乎占据了一半份额(化工产品、药品 4.9%,炸药、鞭炮 1.8%,地席 2.7%,丝制品 1.1%,木制品 0.3%,蔬菜 0.2%,茶叶 36.8%)。但是,它们的份额随着时间的流逝持续下降,1905 年共同占据了 1/3 稍强的进口份额,到 1913 年则不足美国进口总额的 1/5。这一下降趋势在两国贸易史的下一时期将更加明显。

## 五、1895—1913 年间的贸易差额

在长达一个半世纪时期的中美贸易历史中,中国的贸易"顺差"在这二十年间是最小的。之前的三十年间,中国的年均顺差接近 1 500 万美元。那时,美国国内出口只

---

① 后见第七章。

② 后见第六章。

③ 译注:根据表 3-5 之 1895 年贸易数据判断,原文此处(64 页第一段)应为 170 万美元,疑为作者笔误。

### 表 3 - 5　1895—1913 年美国从中国(含租界)进口商品构成

出口额:万美元;占比:%

| 序号 | 名称 | 1895 年 进口额 | 占比 | 1898 年 进口额 | 占比 | 1901 年 进口额 | 占比 | 1903 年 进口额 | 占比 | 1905 年 进口额 | 占比 |
|---|---|---|---|---|---|---|---|---|---|---|---|
| 1 | 锑 | | | 0.8 | | 2.4 | 0.1 | 8.4 | | 4.3 | |
| 2 | 猪鬃,分选的、成束的 | 2.9 | 0.1 | 12.2 | 0.6 | 12.7 | 0.7 | 40.3 | 1.5 | 47.2 | 1.7 |
| 3 | 化工产品、药品、染料等 | 99.7 | 4.9 | 77.5 | 3.8 | 100.1 | 5.4 | 146.5 | 5.5 | 170.1 | 6.1 |
| 4 | 原棉 | | | | | | | | | | |
| 5 | 爆炸品、鞭炮 | 37.2 | 1.8 | 14.1 | 0.7 | 23.5 | 1.3 | 21.7 | | 31.2 | |
| 6 | 水果、坚果 | | | | | | | | | 2.3 | |
| 7 | 毛皮 | 27.6 | 1.3 | 20.5 | 1.0 | 4.2 | 0.2 | 33.7 | | 34.4 | |
| 8 | 头发和发网 | | | | | | | | | | |
| 9 | 帽子、头巾 | 56.5 | 2.8 | 63.2 | 3.1 | 55.3 | 3 | 66.5 | 2.5 | 81.5 | 2.9 |
| 10 | 皮张 | 48.1 | 2.3 | 121.1 | 6.0 | 145.3 | 7.9 | 267.0 | 10.0 | 253.5 | 9.1 |
| 11 | 黄麻、大麻及其他纤维 | | | | | | | | | 3.1 | |
| 12 | 席子 | 55.1 | 2.7 | 35.0 | 1.7 | 98.6 | 5.4 | 73.9 | 2.8 | 85.0 | 3.0 |
| 13 | 肉类及乳制品 | | | | | | | | | 3.2 | |
| 14 | 植物油 | 10.2 | 0.6 | 9.6 | 0.5 | 12.8 | 0.7 | 28.6 | | 41.2 | 1.5 |
| 15 | 米和米粉 | 50.4 | 2.4 | 56.1 | 2.8 | 48.9 | 2.7 | 47.3 | 1.8 | 51.3 | 1.8 |
| 16 | 生丝 | 551.2 | 26.9 | 750.6 | 37.0 | 630.4 | 34.4 | 889.4 | 33.2 | 884.9 | 31.6 |
| 17 | 废丝 | 9.5 | 0.4 | 10.6 | 0.5 | 6.3 | 0.3 | 3.9 | 0.1 | 7.6 | 0.3 |
| 18 | 绢丝 | 24.1 | 1.1 | 13.6 | 0.7 | 15.0 | 0.8 | 24.2 | 0.9 | 26.6 | 1.0 |
| 19 | 香料,碾磨的 | 8.5 | 0.4 | 2.2 | 0.1 | 12.3 | 0.7 | 19.3 | | 14.4 | |
| 20 | 香料,蒸馏的 | 1.9 | 0.1 | 1.1 | 0.1 | 2.4 | 0.1 | 2.5 | | 4.7 | |
| 21 | 茶叶 | 753.4 | 36.8 | 582.7 | 28.8 | 486.4 | 26.5 | 697.5 | 26.2 | 590.3 | 21.2 |
| 22 | 蔬菜 | 5.3 | 0.2 | 5.0 | 0.2 | 7.9 | 0.4 | 6.1 | | 7.8 | |
| 23 | 木材,已加工 | 6.3 | 0.3 | 7.0 | 0.3 | 11.7 | 0.6 | 12.2 | | 19.3 | |
| 24 | 羊毛,未加工 | 169.9 | 8.3 | 156.5 | 7.7 | 63.1 | 3.4 | 204.8 | 7.7 | 313.3 | 11.2 |
| 25 | 其他 | 137.0 | 6.7 | 90.0 | 4.4 | 91.1 | 5 | 73.5 | 2.8 | 111.5 | 4.0 |
| | 出口合计 | 2 054.6 | 100 | 2 032.6 | 100 | 1 830.5 | 100 | 2 667.3 | 100.0 | 2 788.7 | 100.0 |

（续表）

| 序号 | 名　称 | 1907年 | | 1909年 | | 1911年 | | 1912年 | | 1913年 | |
|---|---|---|---|---|---|---|---|---|---|---|---|
| | | 进口额 | 占比 | 进口额 | 占比 | 进口额 | 占比 | 进口额 | 占比 | 进口额 | 占比 |
| 1 | 锑 | 0.7 | | 15.6 | | 12.3 | | 14.0 | | 17.1 | 0.04 |
| 2 | 猪鬃,分选的、成束的 | 65.8 | 2.0 | 45.2 | 1.5 | 77.0 | 2.2 | 86.9 | 2.9 | 92.2 | 2.3 |
| 3 | 化工产品、药品、染料等 | 198.3 | 5.9 | 108.6 | 3.7 | 46.8 | 1.3 | 37.5 | 1.2 | 57.4 | 1.4 |
| 4 | 原棉 | | | 14.0 | | 105.3 | 3.0 | 73.1 | 2.4 | 128.2 | 3.2 |
| 5 | 爆炸品、鞭炮 | 51.6 | 1.5 | 30.9 | | 19.8 | | 18.8 | | 22.8 | 0.06 |
| 6 | 水果、坚果 | 3.9 | | 2.4 | | 14.4 | | 23.6 | | 10.9 | 0.3 |
| 7 | 毛皮 | 45.7 | 1.4 | 17.7 | | 26.6 | | 27.0 | | 59.5 | 1.5 |
| 8 | 头发和发网 | | | 16.5 | | 35.0 | 1.0 | 15.9 | | 33.6 | 0.8 |
| 9 | 帽子、头巾 | 179.6 | 5.3 | 55.3 | 1.9 | 68.7 | 1.9 | 70.7 | 2.3 | 42.1 | 1.0 |
| 10 | 皮张 | 405.3 | 12.1 | 261.3 | 8.9 | 370.3 | 10.5 | 220.1 | 7.2 | 527.1 | 13.3 |
| 11 | 黄麻、大麻及其他纤维 | 4.2 | | 8.5 | | 7.3 | | 14.6 | | 5.0 | |
| 12 | 席子 | 87.6 | 2.6 | 88.9 | 3.0 | 74.4 | 2.1 | 75.6 | 2.5 | 70.5 | 1.7 |
| 13 | 肉类及乳制品 | 5.5 | | 5.3 | | 6.9 | | 10.1 | | 11.4 | 0.3 |
| 14 | 植物油 | 81.5 | 2.4 | 83.1 | 2.8 | 298.1 | 8.5 | 236.5 | 7.8 | 289.7 | 7.3 |
| 15 | 米和米粉 | 81.5 | 2.4 | 45.7 | 1.6 | 50.7 | 1.4 | 64.5 | 2.6 | 93.0 | 2.3 |
| 16 | 生丝 | 1 037.5 | 30.9 | 1 234.2 | 42.0 | 1 366.7 | 38.6 | 1 139.9 | 37.4 | 1 357.5 | 34.0 |
| 17 | 废丝 | 16.4 | 0.5 | 16.0 | 0.5 | 39.1 | 1.1 | 50.3 | 1.6 | 101.2 | 2.6 |
| 18 | 绢丝 | 22.9 | 0.7 | 32.9 | 1.1 | 27.9 | 0.8 | 17.4 | 6.0 | 17.0 | 0.4 |
| 19 | 香料,碾磨的 | 23.2 | | 20.0 | | 21.4 | | 21.7 | | 22.5 | 0.6 |
| 20 | 香料,蒸馏的 | 8.1 | | 6.0 | | 8.9 | | 10.8 | | 8.9 | 0.2 |
| 21 | 茶叶 | 418.2 | 12.5 | 350.1 | 11.9 | 295.2 | 8.4 | 226.1 | 7.4 | 324.8 | 8.2 |
| 22 | 蔬菜 | 12.2 | | 8.0 | | 9.9 | | 11.5 | | 12.7 | 0.3 |
| 23 | 木材,已加工 | 17.7 | | 9.1 | | 10.9 | | 12.2 | | 8.3 | 0.2 |
| 24 | 羊毛,未加工 | 447.9 | 13.3 | 312.2 | 10.6 | 307.0 | 8.7 | 365.5 | 12.0 | 472.2 | 1.8 |
| 25 | 其他 | 142.3 | 4.2 | 206.5 | 7.0 | 227.4 | 6.4 | 201.5 | 6.6 | 190.0 | 4.8 |
| | 出口合计 | 3 357.3 | 100.0 | 2 944.3 | 100.0 | 3 528.0 | 100.0 | 3 046.0 | 100.0 | 3975.8 | 100.0 |

注:根据原文64页第1段文字及本表其他数据判断,该值应为11.8,疑为笔误-原文66页。

相当于美国从中国直接进口的 1/4。但是,"美国对中国货的需求更甚于中国对美国的需求"的老话在这一时期失去了力量,因为许多种美国产品已经逐步融入了中国人的日常生活。这一时期的前十年间,中国人对美国的棉花、矿物油、小麦粉、钢铁产品的需要如此之大,以至于中(含租界)美两国间的贸易差额好几年间都是有利于后者的。

至于香港方面,美国食品和其他产品的出口增长快于美国的进口,因此贸易差额一直对美国有利,年均近 600 万美元。这一时期的美国—香港贸易差额中,究竟有多少可视作中—美贸易差额的一部分,由于完全缺乏香港的贸易统计数据,并没有办法来确定。然而有一点是可以确定的:美国与南亚国家间的贸易增长时,香港的转口贸易必然也会增长,美国—香港贸易中能够归入美中贸易的部分必定是逐年减少的。除了这种概括外,不可能做任何精确的估计。

尽管有上述困难,通过美—中、美—港贸易差额之和(见表 3 - 6),还是可以得出这样一个有意思的结论:这一时期美中双方的贸易顺差、逆差之和彼此几乎完全平衡。所以,如果我们将美—港贸易看作对华贸易的一部分,美国将能够通过其工业成长及不断努力向东方销售而使其买卖账目平衡。

表 3 - 6　1895—1913 年美国对华贸易差额统计

单位:万美元

| 年份 | 美国—中国内地 | | 美国—中国租界 | | 美国—香港地区 | | 美国对华贸易合计 | |
|------|--------|--------|--------|--------|--------|--------|--------|--------|
| | 美国顺差 | 美国逆差 | 美国顺差 | 美国逆差 | 美国顺差 | 美国逆差 | 美国顺差 | 美国逆差 |
| 1895 | | 1 694.2 | | | 347.7 | | | 1 346.5 |
| 1896 | | 1 510.1 | | | 327.2 | | | 1 187.9 |
| 1897 | | 848.0 | | | 513.6 | | | 334.4 |
| 1898 | | 1 033.3 | | | 551.9 | | | 481.5 |
| 1899 | | 412.6 | | | 525.3 | | 112.8 | |
| 1900 | | 1 163.8 | 36.2 | | 723.0 | | | 404.6 |
| 1901 | | 789.8 | 37.7 | | 659.4 | | | 92.7 |
| 1902 | 366.7 | | 53.1 | | 675.2 | | 1 095.0 | |
| 1903 | | 775.1 | 68.7 | | 741.3 | | 34.8 | |
| 1904 | | 1 648.3 | 61.0 | | 893.9 | | | 693.3 |
| 1905 | 2 556.8 | | 17.0 | | 921.7 | | 3 495.6 | |
| 1906 | 1 524.3 | | 21.5 | | 521.6 | | 2 067.4 | |

(续表)

| 年份 | 美国—中国内地 | | 美国—中国租界 | | 美国—香港地区 | | 美国对华贸易合计 | |
|---|---|---|---|---|---|---|---|---|
| | 美国顺差 | 美国逆差 | 美国顺差 | 美国逆差 | 美国顺差 | 美国逆差 | 美国顺差 | 美国逆差 |
| 1907 | | 773.2 | 171.2 | | 559.2 | | | 42.8 |
| 1908 | 367.7 | 809.8 | | | 684.6 | | 1 126.7 | |
| 1909 | 937.9 | | | 11.5 | 549.9 | | | 399.5 |
| 1910 | 1 367.0 | | | 65.8 | 413.5 | | | 1 019.2 |
| 1911 | 1 494.0 | | | 11.8 | 503.8 | | | 1 002.0 |
| 1912 | 521.3 | | 4.0 | | 721.9 | | 204.6 | |
| 1913 | 1 768.4 | | 36.8 | | 641.2 | | | 1 090.5 |
| 合 计 | | | | | | | 8 136.7 | 8 094.9 |

## 六、硬币的航运

这一时期,尽管美国实际上并没有给美中贸易差额有什么支付,但美国自始至终一直在向东方输出硬币和金银。1895—1913 年,美国向中国内地和香港地区出口银币、银块达 1.24 亿美元,而黄金净出口仅值 50.4 万美元(见表 3－7)。在美国出口的数量庞大的白银中,中国直接获取的少得可怜;但是,按照中国海关的统计,中国每年从香港进口大量白银,而美国出口的白银则大部分通过香港运入英属印度、(英属)海峡殖民地①和其他南亚国家。

表 3－7  1895—1913 年美国对华(含香港地区)金银贸易统计

单位:万美元

| 年份 | 白银净出口 | 黄金净出口 | 黄金净进口 | 年份 | 白银净出口 | 黄金净出口 | 黄金净进口 |
|---|---|---|---|---|---|---|---|
| 1895 | 845.0 | 7.5 | | 1905 | 424.7 | | 18.6 |
| 1896 | 821.5 | 11.9 | | 1906 | 838.5 | 1.9 | |
| 1897 | 546.0 | 8.9 | | 1907 | 183.4 | 1.3 | |
| 1898 | 779.8 | 6.4 | | 1908 | 526.1 | | 12.6 |
| 1899 | 456.1 | | 16.8 | 1909 | 626.7 | 0.3 | |

---

① 译注:1826 年,英属东印度公司将新加坡、马六甲及槟城三地合并,组成“海峡殖民地”,华人称为“三州府”。1858 年 8 月 2 日,英国议会通过印度由英国女皇直接治理的法案,海峡殖民地移交给英政府殖民部直接管辖。1867 年 4 月 1 日海峡殖民地改称为“皇家殖民地”。

（续表）

| 年份 | 白银净出口 | 黄金净出口 | 黄金净进口 | 年份 | 白银净出口 | 黄金净出口 | 黄金净进口 |
|------|-----------|-----------|-----------|------|-----------|-----------|-----------|
| 1900 | 820.9 | 2.8 | | 1910 | 490.7 | 0.2 | |
| 1901 | 824.8 | 37.0 | | 1911 | 689.5 | 0.7 | |
| 1902 | 855.3 | | 3.1 | 1912 | 762.0 | | 2.8 |
| 1903 | 691.0 | 4.3 | | 1913 | 994.9 | 10.0 | |
| 1904 | 253.9 | 12.2 | | | | | |
| | | | | 合计 | 12 480.8 | 104.3 | 53.9 |

# 第四章

## 快速扩张期(1914—1922 年)

随着欧洲战争的爆发,美中贸易经历了根本性的变化。一方面,这一变化不仅体现在两国贸易的绝对量及对两国的相对重要性方面,还体现在参与进、出口的商品构成方面。当欧洲对中国的物资供应大部分被切断时,中国自然地就向美国寻求替代品。另一方面,美国工业为完成战争订单对原材料的需求非常迫切,而其国内供应严重不足,因此,美国被迫从远东购买各种原材料,而在此之前则从未或者极少从那里采购。这一状态导致过去十年间中美贸易发展极快。表 4-1 列出了各年的贸易额。

1914 年战争爆发后的数月里,世界各国面对新环境都开始进行自我调整,美中两国对那些与战争有关联的原材料,以及原由交战国给中立国供应但如今无法提供的产品的需求大大增加。所以,人们可以发现,一方面,美国对中国生产的锑、蛋白、苯胺染料、靛蓝糊、羊毛地毯、棉、蛋制品、植物油、油籽、兽皮、皮、毛皮、草编、羊毛和丝绸的需求增长;另一方面,中国需要更多的美国钢铁机器及其他制品,汽车、马车和其他交通工具,棉花和棉布,电力机械和其他电器,橡胶和皮革制品、纸制品、烟草、矿物油、和木材等。

除了两国快速增长的需求外,还有其他一些小的原因促使这一时期中美贸易的成长。按照 1913 年美国关税法案,许多原料和相当一部分产品的进口税大幅下降或完全取消,从而刺激了美国从中国的进口。同时,白银——当时中国使用的货币——与黄金的比价急剧升高,促进了中国从美国的进口。

然而,与自 1914 年起这些促使中美贸易超常发展的良好环境相反的是,还有一些势必抑制中美贸易成长的不利因素贯穿于战争及战后时期。

首先,越洋船舶短缺,运费上升。1914 年之后,世界 1/4 的商船运力因为战争不再从事普通贸易,运输问题立刻变得严峻起来。如此数量的航运业调整使太平洋上的吨位迅速显著下降,这一节骨眼上,商船的短缺极大地阻碍了中美贸易,不仅是因为运费持续上升,而且还多次发生大批中国货物无论出价多少都无法装船开往美国的情形。这一困难还被这样的事实所加剧:参与贸易的大部分商品都是体积庞大的物资,它们无法承受较高的运输成本,因此 300%～500% 的运费增幅对其造成了严重影响。

## 表 4 - 1　1913—1922 年美国对华贸易统计

单位:万美元

| 年度 | 美国—中国内地 | | | 美国—中国租界 | | | 美—中通过香港地区的转口贸易 | | |
|---|---|---|---|---|---|---|---|---|---|
| | 进口 | 出口 | 合计 | 进口 | 出口 | 合计 | 进口 | 出口 | 合计 |
| 1913 | 4 012.1 | 2 530.0 | 6 542.1 | 74.5 | 111.3 | 185.8 | 62.1 | 554.3 | 616.4 |
| 1914 | 3 631.4 | 2 036.8 | 5 668.1 | 92.9 | 164.7 | 257.6 | 40.0 | 462.9 | 502.9 |
| 1915 | 5 285.8 | 1 974.8 | 7 258.6 | 67.4 | 113.8 | 181.2 | 47.2 | 416.6 | 463.8 |
| 1916 | 8 004.2 | 3 151.6 | 1 1155.8 | 75.0 | 112.2 | 187.2 | 94.0 | 665.7 | 759.7 |
| 1917 | 12 510.6 | 4 029.2 | 16 539.8 | 1 481.8 | 495.7 | 1 977.5 | 155.8 | 787.9 | 943.7 |
| 1918 | 11 097.1 | 5 257.1 | 16 354.2 | 2 983.5 | 617.6 | 3 601.1 | 451.0 | 1 233.3 | 1 684.3 |
| 1919 | 15 415.4 | 10 551.5 | 25 966.9 | 1 549.2 | 1 273.5 | 2 822.7 | 331.7 | 1 104.6 | 2 436.2 |
| 1920 | 19 270.8 | 14 573.7 | 33 844.5 | 1 151.4 | 713.9 | 1 865.3 | 687.9 | 1 698.5 | 2 386.4 |
| 1921 | 10 113.6 | 10 829.0 | 20 942.6 | 128.0 | 531.5 | 659.5 | 153.6 | 936.3 | 1 089.9 |
| 1922 | 13 460.9 | 10 035.7 | 23 496.6 | 206.2 | 571.7 | 777.9 | 239.0 | 1 046.7 | 1 285.7 |
| 1923 | 16 961.9 | 9 685.2 | 26 647.1 | 381.9 | 608.9 | 990.8 | 303.3 | 1 410.6 | 1 703.9 |

| 年度 | 美—中贸易合计 | | | 美国—香港地区 | | | | | |
|---|---|---|---|---|---|---|---|---|---|
| | 进口 | 出口 | 合计 | 进口 | 出口 | 合计 | | | |
| 1913 | 4 138.7 | 3 195.6 | 7 344.3 | 347.5 | 1 108.6 | 1 456.0 | | | |
| 1914 | 3764.3 | 2 664.4 | 6 428.7 | 266.4 | 925.9 | 1 192.3 | | | |
| 1915 | 5 400.4 | 2 503.2 | 7 903.6 | 314.6 | 833.2 | 1 147.8 | | | |
| 1916 | 8173.2 | 3 929.5 | 12 102.7 | 626.4 | 1 331.4 | 1 957.8 | | | |
| 1917 | 14 148.2 | 5 312.8 | 19 461.0 | 1 038.4 | 1 574.7 | 2 613.1 | | | |
| 1918 | 14 531.6 | 7 108.0 | 21 639.6 | 3 006.8 | 2 466.5 | 5 473.4 | | | |
| 1919 | 17 296.3 | 12 929.6 | 30 225.9 | 2 211.9 | 2 209.3 | 4 421.2 | | | |
| 1920 | 21 110.1 | 16 986.1 | 38 096.2 | 4 586.0 | 2 597.1 | 7 176.7 | | | |
| 1921 | 10 395.2 | 12 296.8 | 22 692.0 | 1 024.2 | 1 872.6 | 2 896.8 | | | |
| 1922 | 13 906.1 | 11 654.1 | 25 560.2 | 1 530.4 | 2 093.4 | 3 623.8 | | | |
| 1923 | 12 647.1 | 11 704.7 | 24 351.8 | 2 021.7 | 2 821.1 | 4 842.8 | | | |

注 1：1913—1916 年"美国—中国租界"统计数据,1923 年各项数据均为以 6 月 30 日结束日的财年统计数据。

注 2："美国—香港地区"贸易中,美国进口的 15％、美国出口的 50％视为中美两国途经香港的转口贸易①。

---

① 由于存在途经英国殖民地香港的转口贸易,要确定中国的进口最初源于哪个国家、中国的出口最终流向哪个国家是非常困难的。如果检查中国海关统计、美国对外通商和航海统计,就会发现与香港之间的贸易是单独记载的。但是,来自香港的进口的最初来源,以及向香港出口的进一步去向是英国、(英属)海峡殖民地、菲律宾等以及中国沿海港口。再者,香港作为一个自由港,直到最近才开始发布其相关贸易的确切统计数据,而且即使现在也不公布细节情况,因此要相当准确地知道香港进出口量、货物的来源地或目的地都是不可能的。

1918 年,香港发布了《贸易和航运报告》,首次尝试提供香港贸易的完备记录。但是,没有更早年份的数据以作为对比。此外,报告还存在着一些在此之后不久就得到补救的缺陷。例如,报告所给的贸易数据基于商人的申报,而没有对其正确性做进一步的充分核查。(太平洋航运。1919 年 12 月,第 59 页)

香港 1918 年全年贸易总额是 12 799.1 万英镑,其中进口 6 093.4 万英镑、出口 6 705.7 万英镑。香港贸易的分布情况如下表所示。

**1918 年香港外贸分布情况**

| 国家或地区 | 进口到香港 | | 从香港出口 | | 合计 | |
|---|---|---|---|---|---|---|
| | 贸易额(万英镑) | 占比(％) | 贸易额(万英镑) | 占比(％) | 贸易额(万英镑) | 占比(％) |
| 中国 | 936.2 | 15.4 | 3701.1 | 5.5 | 4537.3 | 35.4 |
| 美国 | 834.8 | 13.5 | 541.7 | 8.1 | 1 376.5 | 10.7 |
| 英国 | 443.9 | 7.2 | 111.2 | 1.6 | 555.1 | 4.3 |
| 英联邦自治领和殖民地 | 813.1 | 13.4 | 754.9 | 11.3 | 1 568.0 | 12.3 |
| 日本和朝鲜 | 981.9 | 16.1 | 449.4 | 6.5 | 1 431.3 | 11.2 |
| 法属印度支那 | 1 528.9 | 25.0 | 585.4 | 8.5 | 2 114.3 | 16.5 |
| 其他 | 553.6 | 9.0 | 562.0 | 8.4 | 1 115.6 | 8.7 |
| 合计 | 6 093.4 | 100.0 | 6 705.7 | 100.0 | 12 799.1 | 100.0 |

**《香港贸易与航运报告》中发布的 1919 年香港与各国贸易情况**

| 国家或地区 | 进口到香港 | | 从香港出口 | | 合计 | |
|---|---|---|---|---|---|---|
| | 贸易额(万英镑) | 占比(％) | 贸易额(万英镑) | 占比(％) | 贸易额(万英镑) | 占比(％) |
| 中国 | 1 258.1 | 13.4 | 5 281.2 | 50.8 | 6 539.3 | 33.6 |
| 美国 | 1 775.9 | 19.6 | 487.7 | 4.7 | 2 263.6 | 11.6 |
| 英国 | 1 974.6 | 2.8 | 1 899.3 | 18.3 | 3 873.9 | 19.9 |
| 日本 | 965.8 | 10.7 | 983.7 | 9.5 | 1 949.5 | 10.0 |
| 法属印度支那 | 1 355.7 | 14.9 | 874.8 | 8.4 | 2 230.5 | 11.5 |
| 其他国家 | 1 735.1 | 19.1 | 867.5 | 8.3 | 2 602.6 | 13.4 |
| 合计 | 9 065.2 | 100.0 | 10 394.3 | 100.0 | 19 459.5 | 100.0 |

从美国进口商的角度看,第二个不利情况是银价的飙升。1916 年之后,美国黄金美元和中国银两之间的汇率变得对前者相当不利。一两白银可兑换的美国金元通常不超过 70 美分。但是 1916 年,一两白银的平均汇率是 79 美分,1917 年攀升到 1.03美元,之后两年又升到 1.26 美元和 1.39 美元。这种不利的汇率当然极大地束缚了美国对中国产品的进口。

## 一、中美贸易的实际增长(幅度)

但是,尽管存在高运费、金银汇率失调这两个严重影响两国贸易顺利发展的因素,美国对中国原料的需求还是增大到一个相当大的程度,以至于美国对华进口贸易的数量和贸易额在这十年间迅猛上升——只有 1921 年例外。1914 年,美国对华进口总额为 3 600 万美元,1915 年达 5 300 万美元,接下来先后上升至 8 000 万美元(1916 年)、1.25 亿美元(1917 年)、1.54 亿美元(1919 年),1920 年达到顶峰 1.93 亿美元。因为遭遇了全球商业萧条,1921 年的下降是必然的;不过,1922 年之后快速恢复,1923 财年(截至 6 月 30 日)美国对华进口总额达 1.7 亿美元。这些数字还应当加上美国从中国租界进口的货物价值,其中日本租借的(辽宁)关东地区最为重要。世界大战开始以后,美国从这些租界地区的进口数量相当可观。在 1917—1920 的四年间,美国每年从中国租界进口 1 000 多万美元,1918 年则几乎达到 3 000 万美元,这与战前美国从全中国进口的商品总额相当;1921 年两国贸易严重下滑,至今尚未完全恢复。

这些数字并不能说明全部问题。美国与香港间的贸易,大部分实际上是美中贸易

---

通过上述的统计,依然无法确定,从中国运达香港的货物最终有多少运到了美国和其他国家,以及从美国出口到香港的货物有多少最终到达中国内地。在缺乏其他证据的情况下,我们只能推断,美国经香港出口到中国的部分与美国直接出口香港总量之间的比例和香港出口中国内地的部分与香港出口贸易总量之间的比例相等。可用如下公式表示:

美国经香港出口中国 / 美国向香港总出口 = 香港向中国内地出口 / 香港总出口

关于美国通过香港从中国的进口,可以以此类推:

美国经香港中国进口 / 美国从香港总进口 = 香港从中国内地进口 / 香港总进口

按照表 14 统计,"香港向中国内地出口 / 香港总出口"之比值,1918、1919 年分别是 55.1%、50.8%;"香港从中国内地进口 / 香港总进口"分别是 15.4%、13.9%。如果忽略这些小的差异,就可以认为,香港出口的一半左右去了中国内地,而其进口的 15% 或近 1/7 则来自于中国内地。如果将同样的比例应用于美国与香港地区之间的进出口贸易,就可以粗略地确定美国—香港贸易中大概有多少实际上是中美贸易。

然而,对美国通过香港从中国内地进口货物估计的数字还是太小了。但是,任何试图计算这一贸易的真实数值都是徒劳的。统计数据的混乱状况因这样的实际情况(中国西南省份的产品首先出口到印度支那,然后进入香港,最终进入美国或其他国家)而加剧。香港与印度支那之间的赊销贸易很多都源自于中国的云南省。例如,1918 年美国从香港进口锡条、锡块、锡锭等,货值超过 1 000 万美元(Commerce and Navigation,1918),其中的大部分一定是源自云南并取道印度支那运入,但到底是多少,却无法弄清楚。

的一部分[①]。按照笔者的估计,战争期间,美国每年通过香港进口的中国物资达数百万美元。

就美国对华直接进口——包括从中国租界进口及途经香港的转口贸易——总额而言,每年都在增长(见表4-2之A栏)。

表4-2　1913—1923年美国对华进口贸易及其实际增幅

| 年份 | 美国对华进口总额(万美元) | 增长率 | 中国价格总指数(银基) | 汇率(美元/海关银) | 汇率指数 | 中国价格总指数(金基) | 进口总额的实际增长优选法 |
|---|---|---|---|---|---|---|---|
| | A | B | C(1913年=100) | D | E(1913年=100) | F=C×E | G=B/F |
| 1913 | 4 138.7 | 100 | 100 | 0.73 | 100 | 100 | 100 |
| 1914 | 3 764.3 | 91 | 107 | 0.67 | 92 | 98 | 93 |
| 1915 | 5 400.4 | 130 | 113 | 0.62 | 85 | 96 | 136 |
| 1916 | 8 173.2 | 198 | 122 | 0.79 | 108 | 132 | 150 |
| 1917 | 14 148.2 | 342 | 128 | 1.03 | 141 | 180 | 190 |
| 1918 | 14 531.6 | 351 | 136 | 1.26 | 173 | 235 | 149 |
| 1919 | 17 296.3 | 418 | 130 | 1.39 | 190 | 247 | 172 |
| 1920 | 21 110.1 | 510 | 128 | 1.24 | 170 | 218 | 324 |
| 1921 | 10 395.2 | 251 | 127 | 0.76 | 103 | 132 | 190 |
| 1922 | 13 906.1 | 337 | 140 | 0.83 | 114 | 160 | 210 |
| 1923 | 17 647.1 | 427 | 150 | 0.83 | 114 | 171 | 250 |

注1:1913—1921年之指数摘自笔者(即原书作者潘序伦)于1922年在哈佛大学完成的工商管理硕士学位论文《中国物价总指数的构建》(The Construction of a General Price Index Number for China)。1922、1923年之指数系用同样方法得出。

注2:1923年数据以6月30日为结束日的财年统计数据。

如果以1913年的进口额作为基数,将其后各年份的进口额转化为相应的指数(B栏),则1914年是91,表明与上年相比进口额下降了9%。但是,1915、1916年该指数分别130和198,1917年再次大幅升至342,此后稳定增长到1918年的351、1919年的418,1920年达到峰值510。这意味着在这八年中,美国从中国的进口增长了4倍。1921年有一个大的下挫,但这完全是由于美国的经济萧条使然,本质上是临时性的。

---

① 参见表4-1。

1922—1923 年间美国经营状况改善,进口贸易指数也回升至 427。但是,必须承认,这一增长率并不能完全代表贸易量的实际增长。为了核实真正的增长情况,还得根据战争期间的价格膨胀做一些修正。进口额是以货物起运港的货值计算的,因此价格修正必须以中国物价总水平的变化情况为基础。笔者去年(1922)建构的物价总指数可以在这里发挥作用[①]。但是该指数是建立在银价基础上的,如果要在此处采用,必须先将其转化为金基价格指数,这一转换在表 4-2 之 D、E、F 栏完成。从 F 栏可以看出,中国出口货物的金基价格指数上涨幅度与美元价格的上涨幅度相匹配。消除了通货膨胀引起的价格上涨因素,就可以得出美国进口贸易额的实际指数情况(见表 4-2 之 G 栏)。这样,就可以清晰地看到,这一时期美国从中国进口的实际增长远远低于按照进口总额计算的名义增长,1920 年美国的实际进口与 1914 年相比增加 2.5 倍,而 1922—1923 年则相当于 1914 年的 2.5 倍。

再看看美国对华出口。首先,出口远不及进口增长那么快,事实上在 1914—1915 年还有所下降。1918 年,美国对华出口比 1913 年增长 123%,而同期美国从中国的进口则增长了 251%。但是,在接下来的两年,出口增长率比进口增长率高 20 个百分点(530～510)(1920 年)。1921 年,美国对华出口总额的下降不及进口下降那么严重。如果消除了美国的价格上涨因素,就能修正美国对华出口贸易的名义增长,从而得出实际的增长情况。表 4-3 之 E 栏显示,1914—1917 美国对华出口的实际贸易额远低于 1913 年,其中,1914 年低 14%,1915 年低 23%,即便 1917 年仍然低 3%[②]。

**表 4-3 1913—1922 年美国对华出口贸易及其实际增幅**

| 年份 | 美国对华出口总额<br>(万美元) | 增长率<br>(1913 年＝100) | 美国批发价格<br>指数 | 美国对华出口贸易<br>的实际增长率(%) |
|------|------|------|------|------|
| A | B | C | D | E(＝C/D×100) |
| 1913 | 3 195.6 | 100 | 100 | 100 |
| 1914 | 2 664.4 | 84 | 98 | 86 |
| 1915 | 2 503.2 | 78 | 101 | 77 |
| 1916 | 3 929.5 | 123 | 127 | 97 |
| 1917 | 5 312.8 | 167 | 177 | 94 |
| 1918 | 7 108.1 | 223 | 194 | 115 |

---

① 见表 4-2 之 C 栏。该指数以中国最重要的出口商品——生丝、绢丝、皮张、茶叶、羊毛、棉花、豆、桐油、豆油、靛青——来构建。

② 译注:与 1913 年相比,美国对华出口实际增长率,1916 年下降 3 个百分点、1917 年下降 6 个百分点,原文此处(第 81 页)疑系作者笔误。

（续表）

| 年份 | 美国对华出口总额（万美元） | 增长率（1913 年＝100） | 美国批发价格指数 | 美国对华出口贸易的实际增长率（%） |
|---|---|---|---|---|
| A | B | C | D | E（＝C/D×100） |
| 1919 | 12 929.6 | 405 | 206 | 196 |
| 1920 | 16 986.1 | 530 | 226 | 234 |
| 1921 | 12 296.8 | 385 | 147 | 262 |
| 1922 | 11 654.1 | 365 | 149 | 245 |
| 1923 | 11 704.7 | 367 | 156 | 235 |

注：1923 年为以 6 月 30 日为结束日的财年数据。

　　美国对华出口贸易的这一缓慢增长态势可以用本章开头提到的几个背景原因来解释。首先，1915 年银/金比价大幅下滑，1916 年稍有回升，阻碍了中国对以金价结算的美国货的进口；其次，高运费进一步推高了价格，对中国买家造成了新的负担；最后，中国对美国货的需求不像对欧洲货那么迫切。然而 1918 年之后，实际贸易总额还是有了可观的增长。出口贸易实际增长指数从 1917 年的 97 上升到 1918 年的 115，1919 年攀升至 196，1920 年达到 234。1921 年，尽管世界大部分地区和美国陷入商业萧条，该指数仍然达到 262。1922—1923 年，中国的商业严重萧条，抑制了美国对华出口的进一步扩张，但该指数只有轻微下滑。出口贸易实际增长指数大幅提高同样归结于三个原因：第一，银/金比价的空前上涨自然刺激中国这样的银本币国家从金本币国家购买更多的货物；第二，美国从中国大量进口使得美元-银元的兑换更有利于中国，更加刺激美国产品向中国出口；第三，战争期间，中国出口繁荣，中国民众的购买力大大提高，所以能买得起更多的外国商品进行即期消费。此外，1918—1921 中国商业普遍繁荣，刺激了许多新兴行业，开始建设一大批工厂，这反过来使之对美国的生产资料如钢铁产品、机器、汽车、马车、电力机械和电器用具、建筑材料等产生了强烈需求。尽管 1921 年美国对华出口总额与上年相比严重下滑，但实际出口仍然在增长，这一事实是相当重要的。

　　总体来说，经过价格上涨因素修正后，在目前讨论的这十年间，美国对华进出口量增长 2.5 倍。这样就可以明白，战后新环境下美国对华贸易的重要性在提高。

　　美国对华贸易重要性的不仅体现在贸易额、贸易量的绝对数值，还体现其在两国各自外贸总量的相对份额。表 4-4 是美国与东方各国（地区）的贸易分布情况，显示了美国与各国（地区）进出口额在美国进出口总额中所占的份额。1913 年，来自中国的进口在美国进口总额中贡献了 2.19% 的份额，此后稳定增长，1919 年为 4.56%，

1922 年达 4.39％,约为战前的 2 倍。作为美国市场的供应者,1913 年中国在美国进口来源地中排名第九位[①],1918 年升至第七位[②],1920、1921、1922 年都是第六位[③]。

中国在美国产品买家名单中的排名从来没有像在美国进口名单上那么高过。1913 年,美国对华出口总额占美国出口总额的 6.91％[④],其排名(甚至包括香港在内)仅为第十四位[⑤]。这五年间,中国的排名上升了四位[⑥],但其实际份额仅提高了 0.05 个百分点(0.96－0.91)。1920 年,其排名位置未变,但所占份额几乎是 1918 年的 2 倍,从 1918 年的 0.96％升到 1920 年的 1.86％,1921、1922 年分别是 2.53％、2.77％。

表 4-4　1913—1922 年东方各国(地区)在美国外贸中的份额

单位:％

| 年份 | 中国(含租界) | | 香港 | | 日本 | | 英属东印度 | | 荷属东印度 | |
|---|---|---|---|---|---|---|---|---|---|---|
| | 进口 | 出口 | 进口 | 出口 | 进口 | 出口 | 进口 | 出口 | 进口 | 出口 |
| 1913 | 2.19 | 0.91 | 0.22 | 0.42 | 5.05 | 2.35 | 6.41 | 0.61 | 0.34 | 0.13 |
| 1914 | 2.13 | 1.11 | 0.16 | 0.45 | 5.67 | 2.17 | 5.91 | 0.66 | 0.28 | 0.01 |
| 1915 | 2.44 | 0.63 | 0.12 | 0.30 | 5.91 | 1.50 | 5.21 | 0.58 | 0.55 | 0.10 |
| 1916 | 3.29 | 0.60 | 0.25 | 0.28 | 6.72 | 1.72 | 8.07 | 0.57 | 1.26 | 0.17 |
| 1917 | 4.22 | 0.66 | 0.28 | 0.23 | 7.83 | 2.07 | 8.19 | 0.59 | 2.33 | 0.34 |
| 1918 | 4.66 | 0.96 | 0.99 | 0.40 | 9.96 | 4.45 | 9.87 | 0.84 | 2.47 | 0.38 |
| 1919 | 4.56 | 1.49 | 0.57 | 0.28 | 10.50 | 4.63 | 8.25 | 1.03 | 2.02 | 0.59 |
| 1920 | 3.87 | 1.86 | 0.87 | 0.32 | 7.85 | 4.59 | 7.60 | 1.48 | 3.17 | 0.72 |
| 1921 | 4.08 | 2.53 | 0.41 | 0.42 | 10.01 | 5.25 | 5.93 | 1.46 | 1.28 | 0.72 |
| 1922 | 4.39 | 2.77 | 0.49 | 0.55 | 11.39 | 5.70 | 6.61 | 0.97 | 1.10 | 0.21 |

---

　　① 按进口量排名,美国 1913 年最大进口来源地分别是:英国、德国、法国、古巴、巴西、墨西哥、英属东印度群岛、日本、中国(含香港)、比利时、意大利和加拿大。

　　② 按进口量排名,美国 1918 年最大进口来源地分别是:加拿大、英属东印度群岛、日本、古巴、阿根廷、英国和中国。

　　③ 1920—1922 年美国最大进口来源地:古巴、加拿大、英国、日本、英属东印度群岛、中国、巴西、阿根廷、荷属东印度群岛、法国。

　　④ 译注:按照表 4-4 及原文第 84 页其他文字,该处应为 0.91％,系作者笔误。

　　⑤ 1913 年美国商品最大出口去向地:英国、加拿大、德国、法国、荷兰、意大利、古巴、比利时、日本、墨西哥、阿根廷、澳大利亚、巴西、中国(含香港地区)、西班牙。

　　⑥ 1918 年美国商品最大出口去向地:英国、法国、加拿大、意大利、日本、古巴、俄罗斯、阿根廷、墨西哥和中国(含香港地区)。

与美国和其他东方国家的贸易增长相比,美国对华贸易的增长表现良好,尤其在最近几年。其份额增长差不多可以赶上日本在美国外贸中的份额增长,还稍微超过了英属东印度群岛。战争期间,美国只有与荷属东印度群岛间的贸易增长快于美国对华贸易的增长速度,但应当注意到,美国—荷属东印度群岛的贸易量的绝对值还远远低于美中贸易,美国—荷属东印度群岛贸易所占的份额在急剧下滑,而美中贸易仍然保持增长。

再将目光转回中国。对美贸易在中国外贸中所占的份额明显增长(见表 4 - 5)。1913 年,对美贸易仅占中国外贸总额的 7.6%,十年后上升至 17.0%。这十年间,除日本外,各国在中国外贸中的份额,都或多或少地有所下降,至多是保持稳定而已。即使日本,所占的份额也没有显著增长,仅从 1913 年的 19.7% 上升为 1922 年的24.3%,提高了 23%,与之相对应的是,对美贸易所占的份额从 1913 年的 7.6% 上升到 1922 年的 16.7%,提高了 120%。

表 4 - 5　1913—1922 年各国(地区)在中国外贸中的份额

单位:%

| 年份 | 美国 | 英国 | 德国 | 法国 | 日本 | 中国香港 | 英属印度 |
|------|------|------|------|------|------|----------|----------|
| 1913 | 7.6 | 11.4 | 4.5 | 5.3 | 19.7 | 29.1 | 5.5 |
| 1914 | 9.1 | 13.8 | 2.6 | 3.8 | 21.1 | 28.3 | 5.0 |
| 1915 | 11.4 | 11.5 | 0.1 | 4.8 | 23.4 | 28.2 | 5.4 |
| 1916 | 12.7 | 10.3 | | 3.4 | 28.3 | 26.8 | 3.8 |
| 1917 | 15.2 | 7.5 | | 3.0 | 33.4 | 26.3 | 3.2 |
| 1918 | 12.8 | 7.2 | | 3.1 | 37.8 | 26.3 | 1.3 |
| 1919 | 16.2 | 9.3 | | 3.0 | 33.9 | 21.9 | 2.8 |
| 1920 | 15.7 | 13.2 | 0.6 | 2.0 | 27.7 | 22.0 | 3.1 |
| 1921 | 17.3 | 11.8 | 1.3 | 2.2 | 24.9 | 25.0 | 2.9 |
| 1922 | 16.7 | 11.5 | 2.2 | 2.8 | 24.3 | 25.6 | 3.3 |

## 二、日本、英国及其他竞争对手

欧洲战争将许多强劲竞争者从东方市场上淘汰出去——至少在一段时间内是这样,只剩下两三个幸运的国家分享这个商机。战前与中国有贸易关系的国家中,贸易量及所占份额增长的有德国、比利时、法国、俄罗斯、意大利和英属东印度群岛。但是,1914 年战争甫一打响,德国、比利时就完全退出中国市场,稍后俄罗斯、意大利、法国、挪威和瑞典也发现与中国维持一定规模的贸易非常困难。英属印度与中国的贸易也在下滑，因为前者需要倾其全力服务宗主国。主宰中国外贸一个多世纪的英国，尽管也面临着许多困难，但仍然保持着优势地位。只有两个国家，即日本和美国，借助战争在与中国及其他国家的贸易中获取了巨大的利益。

与1914年之前中国外贸的多边竞争态势相反，现在是一个更加简化的美国与日本、英国（不那么强烈）间的三角竞争关系。为了揭示影响美国未来在中国外贸中所占份额的诸多重要因素，应当研究战前、战争期间及战后这三个国家参与的贸易竞争中重要而有趣的现象。可以将1909—1922年这十四年间——分成战前五年、以战争为主基调的五年及战后四年——美日贸易、中英贸易的比较作为前导。

多半是由于存在着途经香港口岸的商品转运情况，表4-5所示的中国外贸分布数据并不是很精确，没有显示各国贸易所占的实际份额。表中数据显示，这一时期中国内地与香港之间的贸易占到中国外贸总额的1/3，但是，中国内地从香港进口的货物的最初来源地以及出口香港的货物的最终目的地是与中国有贸易关系的英国、日本、美国及其他国家。所以，在得到最终的各国所占份额之前，应当为这些国家的对华贸易额做一个称为"香港折让"的处理。当然，也只能做一个粗略的估计，除此之外都是不可能的。但是这对于此处正在做的一般比较，已经可以符合要求。

这三个竞争国家对华贸易的较为详细的比较见表4-6。其中最为突出的特点是，与战前的五年相比，美、日两国对华贸易额在五年战争期间有明显的增长。日本对华贸易的增长率超过美国。战前，美国、日本对华贸易额（年均）分别为0.85亿两海关银元、1.78亿两海关银元；然而，战争期间，分别增长为1.49亿两海关银元、3.22亿两海关银元，增长率分别为75％和80％。此外，日本在中国外贸中所占份额的增长速度也超过美国。战前，日本所占份额的平均值是20.9％，战争期间升至32.8％，为战前的1.63倍。至于美国，其所占的份额由10.1％上升为15.2％，大约是1.5倍。通过这一比较可以总结，战争期间，即使在中国外贸中所占份额的增长方面，美国也被日本所超越。

然而，在接下来的战后四年里，情况发生了反转。尽管日本对华年均贸易额仍在3.22亿~4.62亿两海关银元之间，但所占份额从32.8％小幅下滑到32.5％。近年来，这一下降趋势越来越明显。相反，美国对华贸易在这一时期又一次大幅增长，年均贸易额从战前的1.49亿两海关银元上升至2.85亿两海关银元，所占份额从15.2％提高到20.0％以上。

世界大战的几年间，在那些研究日本对华政策的人眼里，日本竭力参与中国贸易竞争的意图非常明显。日本的贷款活动、政治活动是最明显的一种"金元外交"。表4-7、表4-8分别显示了日、美、英等国在华商人及商号的统计情况，从中可以捕捉到一些有关日本为争夺中国市场而精心准备的信号。

表 4-6 世界大战前后(1909—1922年)美、日、英三国在中国外贸中的份额

| 年份 | 中国外贸总额(万两海关银) | 中国内地—中国香港地区(万两海关银) | 中国—美国(含夏威夷、非律宾) | | | | 中国—英国(含所有殖民地) | | | | 中国—日本(含冲绳、台湾) | | | |
|---|---|---|---|---|---|---|---|---|---|---|---|---|---|---|
| | | | 直接贸易(万两海关银) | 香港中转(万两海关银) | 总额(万两海关银) | 在中国外贸中占比(%) | 直接贸易(万两海关银) | 香港中转(万两海关银) | 总额(万两海关银) | 在中国外贸中占比(%) | 直接贸易(万两海关银) | 香港中转(万两海关银) | 总额(万两海关银) | 在中国外贸中占比(%) |
| 1909 | 75 715.1 | 24 739.1 | 6 698.8 | 1 484.3 | 8 183.1 | 10.8 | 13 816.1 | 4 937.8 | 18 753.9 | 24.7 | 11 654.6 | 2 473.9 | 14 128.5 | 18.6 |
| 1910 | 83 479.8 | 28 018.9 | 5 777.8 | 1 681.1 | 7 458.9 | 9.0 | 14 631.2 | 5 603.8 | 2 0235.0 | 24.2 | 14 337.3 | 2 801.9 | 17 139.2 | 20.6 |
| 1911 | 84 884.2 | 25 191.9 | 7 535.1 | 1 511.5 | 9 046.6 | 10.7 | 16 692.3 | 5 038.4 | 21 730.7 | 25.6 | 14 755.6 | 2 519.2 | 17 274.8 | 20.3 |
| 1912 | 84 361.7 | 25 118.6 | 7 212.1 | 1 507.1 | 8 719.2 | 10.6 | 16 347.4 | 5 623.7 | 21 370.1 | 25.3 | 15 487.8 | 2 511.9 | 17 999.7 | 21.1 |
| 1913 | 97 346.8 | 28 876.5 | 7 523.3 | 1 732.6 | 9 255.9 | 10.5 | 18 804.7 | 5 775.3 | 24 580.0 | 25.2 | 19 523.1 | 2 887.7 | 22 410.8 | 23.0 |
| 战前年均 | 85 157.5 | 26 389.0 | 6 949.4 | 1 583.3 | 8 532.7 | 10.1 | 16 058.2 | 5 275.8 | 21 334.0 | 25.0 | 15 151.7 | 2 638.9 | 17 790.6 | 20.9 |
| 1914 | 92 548.8 | 26 242.2 | 8 454.0 | 1 574.5 | 10 028.5 | 10.8 | 18 256.6 | 5 248.4 | 23 505.0 | 25.4 | 20 124.8 | 2 624.2 | 22 748.0 | 24.6 |
| 1915 | 97 333.7 | 25 260.6 | 10 205.5 | 1 515.6 | 11 721.1 | 12.1 | 17 265.9 | 5 052.1 | 22 318.0 | 23.0 | 21 003.1 | 2 526.1 | 23 529.2 | 24.2 |
| 1916 | 99 820.4 | 27 283.3 | 12 927.2 | 3 274.0 | 16 201.2 | 16.2 | 16 310.9 | 5 456.7 | 21 767.6 | 22.0 | 28 842.9 | 2 728.3 | 31 571.2 | 31.6 |
| 1917 | 101 245.0 | 27 444.5 | 15 910.6 | 3 293.3 | 19 203.9 | 19.0 | 13 904.2 | 5 488.9 | 19 393.1 | 19.1 | 34 780.3 | 2 744.5 | 37 524.8 | 37.0 |
| 1918 | 104 077.6 | 27 918.0 | 14 116.7 | 3 350.2 | 17 466.9 | 16.7 | 12 279.8 | 5 583.6 | 17 863.4 | 17.1 | 42 639.5 | 2 791.8 | 45 431.3 | 43.5 |
| 战争期年均 | 98 005.1 | 26 829.1 | 12 322.8 | 2 601.5 | 14 924.3 | 15.2 | 15 603.5 | 5 365.9 | 20 969.4 | 21.4 | 2 9478.1 | 2 683.0 | 32 161.1 | 32.8 |
| 1919 | 127 780.7 | 28 512.6 | 21 589.3 | 3 421.5 | 25 010.7 | 19.6 | 20 388.0 | 5 602.5 | 26 090.5 | 20.4 | 47 399.6 | 2 851.3 | 50 250.9 | 39.4 |
| 1920 | 130 388.2 | 29 577.5 | 21 419.3 | 3 549.3 | 24 968.6 | 19.1 | 26 697.8 | 5 915.6 | 32 613.4 | 25.0 | 40 472.4 | 2 957.6 | 43 430.0 | 33.2 |
| 1921 | 150 737.8 | 38 410.3 | 27 112.6 | 4 609.2 | 31 721.8 | 21.0 | 26 864.1 | 7 681.2 | 34 545.3 | 22.9 | 40 952.2 | 3 841.0 | 44 793.2 | 29.7 |
| 1922 | 159 994.2 | 40 934.3 | 27 213.0 | 4 912.1 | 32 125.1 | 20.1 | 27 407.1 | 8 186.9 | 35 594.0 | 22.2 | 42 210.6 | 4 093.4 | 46 304.0 | 29.0 |
| 战后年均 | 142 225.2 | 34 358.7 | 24 333.6 | 4 123.0 | 28 456.6 | 20.0 | 25 339.2 | 6 871.6 | 32 210.8 | 22.6 | 42 158.7 | 3 435.8 | 46 194.5 | 32.5 |

注:中国内地—中国香港地区贸易额(第3栏)中,20%折算为途径香港的中—美中转贸易(第9栏)、10%归因于中—日转贸易(第13栏)、1915年前的6%,1916年后的12%计为中—英中转贸易(第5栏)①。

　　尽管日本精心筹划、布局,但美国仍在争夺中国贸易的竞争中占据优势的地位。中国的纺织厂、针织品、肥皂、眼镜及其他简单工业品正以惊人的数量增长,日本自然比其他出口国更加深切地感受到来自中国自身的这种竞争。如果日本不能在近期对其产业活动做大的提升,其产品将被中国本土产品逐出,理由很简单:日本对华出口的大部分是简单形式的工业产品,中国自己现在已经能够或很快就可以生产。然而,中国工业化的稳步推进对美国是一件好事。中国要达到美国已具优势的复杂工业活动

---

　　① 香港折让:在没有其他证据的情况下,可以假定,在中国内地—香港贸易(表4-6第3栏)中,目的地是美、英、日三国的部分所占的比例,与该国对香港直接贸易额在香港外贸总额中的比值相一致。用公式表达就是:

　　某国贸易在中(内地)港贸易中的份额 / 中(内地)港贸易总额=某国在香港外贸的份额 / 香港外贸总额

　　换句话说,在没有其他可靠证据的情况下,我们假定,某国与香港的贸易最终会按其他所有与香港有贸易关系的国家在香港外贸所占的份额分配给这些国家。在表4-1的注释中,笔者已经论证了1918—1919年各国在香港外贸中所占的份额,美、英、日三国的情况如下:

| 年份 | 美国 | 日本 | 英国 |
| --- | --- | --- | --- |
| 1918 | 10.7 | 11.2 | 16.6 |
| 1919 | 11.6 | 10.0 | 19.9 |
| 平均 | 11.2 | 10.6 | 18.3 |

　　在此基础上,可以粗略地估计出应当记入各国的香港折让。一般来说,中国内地—香港贸易的12%可折让给美国,10%归于日本,20%归于英国。但是,进一步的证据表明,战前,美国—香港贸易不太重要,12%的折让比例似乎太大了。据统计,1906年中国从香港进口1.16万美元,其中美国的货物为700万美元,占比6%(U.S.Com. Rel. 1906 "China")。既然1915年前美国与香港的贸易变化不大,可以假定在此之前,中国内地—香港间贸易的6%可以折让给美国。

　　即使按照最新的美元—海关银两平均汇率将一种货币计价贸易额转换为另一种时价单位,这样计算出的部分年份的香港折让(表4-6之第5栏)与按照同样方法以美国数据(参见表4-1之第4栏)为基础计算出的香港折让数据之间有很大的差异。当然,表4-6中的数字包括美国所有殖民地和未定地区,而表4-1则仅包括美国48个州的贸易数据。但是,即使对此做一些公平的折让,仍然还有些矛盾。就此,美国商务部做了如下评论(U.S.Com. Rel. 1880-81 P.201):

　　"由于中国、外国对同一贸易的统计存在本质上的差异,有必要对香港的外贸做一些评估,以使其与其他矛盾的统计数据相协调。即使对中国内地—香港贸易做最严密的分析,中国海关统计与英国、法国海关统计之间仍然有一些差异,这只能通过假设来解释:要么前者,要么后者,总有一个数据是错误的。"

　　"例如,按照中国海关统计,1880年中国出口欧洲大陆1 780万美元,而在法国的统计中,该年度法国从中国内地和香港进口3 061.6万美元,其中法国消费1 946.9万美元,其余部分过境到其他国家。在这里,仅法国一国的进口(法国统计数字)就接近中国统计中对整个欧洲大陆出口的2倍。由于缺乏官方的统计,其他欧洲国家来自中国的直接进口无法获知。"

　　"由此可见,即使对商品从一个国家出口到其作为进口商品进入另一个国家过程中的增值进行公平的折让,香港贸易、中国内地贸易的混杂仍然引起了很大混乱;就像要对欧洲、美国对华贸易关系做一个满意的评估时所做的那样。有必要就香港外贸与中国外贸关联作出声明。"

表 4 - 7　1913—1920 年各国在华侨民数

| 年份 | 美国 | 英国 | 日本 | 俄罗斯 | 法国 | 德国 | 合计 |
|------|------|------|------|--------|------|------|------|
| 1913 | 5 430 | 8 966 | 80 219 | 56 765 | 2 292 | 2 949 | 163 827 |
| 1914 | 4 365 | 8 914 | 84 948 | 56 319 | 1 864 | 3 013 | 164 807 |
| 1919 | 6 660 | 13 234 | 171 485 | 148 170 | 4 409 | 1 335 | 350 991 |
| 1920 | 7 269 | 11 082 | 153 918 | 144 413 | 2 753 | 1 013 | 326 069 |
| 1921 | 8 230 | 9 298 | 144 434 | 68 250 | 2 453 | 1 255 | 240 769 |
| 1922 | 9 153 | 11 855 | 152 848 | 96 727 | 2 300 | 1 986 | 282 491 |

注：1919、1920 年法国侨民中分别含 918 名、591 名传教士。

表 4 - 8　1913—1920 年各国在华公司数

| 年份 | 美国 | 英国 | 日本 | 俄罗斯 | 法国 | 德国 | 合计 |
|------|------|------|------|--------|------|------|------|
| 1913 | 131 | 590 | 1 269 | 1 229 | 106 | 296 | 3 805 |
| 1914 | 136 | 534 | 955 | 1 237 | 113 | 273 | 3 421 |
| 1919 | 314 | 644 | 4 878 | 1 760 | 171 | 2 | 8 015 |
| 1920 | 409 | 679 | 4 278 | 1 596 | 180 | 9 | 7 375 |
| 1921 | 412 | 703 | 6 141 | 1 613 | 222 | 92 | 9 511 |
| 1922 | 377 | 725 | 3 940 | 1 141 | 229 | 184 | 7 021 |

的水平尚需时日。在此期间,中国越是发展简单工业形式,对机器、钢铁产品、电器用具、化工产品及美国目前能够更好供应的其他产品的需求就越大,而目前日本还不能指望在这些产品方面与美国竞争。所以,除去战争的这几年,可能还包括战后的一两年外,日本并没有因欧洲突然停止向中国市场供应产品而长久获益。在许多钢铁制造领域、化学工业部门领域,日本没有获得任何显著的进步;其中的一些产品,还不能满足日本的国内供应。

此外,日本在其他许多方面与美国竞争也有不足。日本对中国采取侵略态度,1916 年强迫中国政府签订臭名昭著的《二十一条》,使中国民众对其充满了强烈的仇恨之情。直到最近,中国国内针对日本人的联合抵制仍然频繁发生,日本对华进出口贸易都受到相当大的影响。中日两国的政治关系仍很脆弱,人们可以想象出它们之间相互憎恶情绪继续延续的许多理由。如果日本对华政策在近期没有根本性的修正,日本与中国的商贸关系将仍然不能得到改善。中国民众对日本严重不满,反对日本一切事情的敌意还在继续上升。

　　除了这些不利因素处，日本最近又发生了地震①，使之在与美国的竞争中仍然处于弱势地位。不仅数以亿美元计的日本财产毁于地震，而且由于很多工厂在这场灾难中摧毁，日本的生产能力也遭到极大的破坏。震后的重建工作当然将吸纳日本国内的大部分资源，并在未来一段时间内吸引其国民全部的注意力和精力。

　　再将目光转向英国及其殖民地、自治领。战前，英国对华贸易额年均2.13亿两海关银左右，正好是中国外贸总额的1/4，在各国中占最大份额。战争五年间，中英两国年贸易额降为2.1亿两海关银元，降幅非常之小；但是考虑到物价膨胀因素，必须承认，两国间的贸易实际上下滑得相当严重。这一下滑也反映在英国在中国外贸中所占份额的下降——战前25％，战争期间21.4％。战争转移了所有英国民众的精力和注意力，对华贸易下滑是非常自然的结果。所以，日本和美国有了一个扩大其对华贸易的良机。

　　战争结束后，英国人自然要重返中国市场，美英两国在中国争夺商业利益的激烈竞争继续上演。战后五年间，英国对华贸易稳步增长，年均贸易额达3.22亿两海关银，而之前的五年平均为2.1亿两海关银元。英国在中国外贸中的份额也有所回升，尽管还没有达到战前水平。英国在华商贸企业的数量在增长，在中国经商的英国人远远多于美国人②。在满足中国工业化当前需求方面的能力方面，英国具有与美国同样强大的竞争力。所以，预测英美两国谁能在对华贸易中领先是相当困难的。

　　英国至少在一个方面仍然比美国更具竞争力。在华的英国商人经验丰富，对中国的市场环境和财务状况有着非常清晰的认识。他们已经在中国商界建立了非常良好的关系，相对来说美国商人经验较少。

　　战后初期，美国在中国市场仅有两个竞争对手，但它现在必须面对更多的竞争者，其中，德国更值得关注和思索。战前，德国与中国的贸易规模并不大，但一直在稳定增长。然而，战争期间，德国与中国间的贸易似乎消失了。最近几年，德国人重返东方，推动其贸易复兴。德国在华企业和居民数量迅速恢复到战前水平，其对华贸易从1919年的零数值增长到1922年的2 000万美元，并在当年中国外贸中占据2.2％的份额。

　　与美国及其他国家相比，德国在争夺中国市场的过程中会有一个比较好的前景。很明显，如果德国要从战争的惨重后果中恢复过来，其人民必须努力工作，践行克己理念，对微利感到知足。既然德国人在别处仍然或多或少地不受欢迎，他们就必须将注意力投向中国，在这里，较为便宜的德国产品将有很大机会以价格优势击败其他竞争对手。

---

　　① 译注：1923年9月1日11时58分，日本神奈川县发生7.9级大地震，共造成人员伤亡约25万人，房屋倒塌12万间，经济损失300亿美元，史称关东大地震。

　　② 见表4－7、4－8。

　　但是,现在德国可悲的政治、经济混乱状况使其优势受到了质疑,德国自身能否度过这一危机并步入复兴仍需拭目以待。即使德国的政治、经济环境改善,也可能还要因自身资金不足困扰数年。此外,战争废除了中国、德国之间所有的旧条约,现在德国的货物不能按其他保留条约的国家所享受的 5％关税进入中国。中国为新条约国开出了一份关税清单,按此规定,德国商品得支付 10％～100％不等的关税。在这方面,德国货将不能与美国货在同一水平上竞争。

# 第五章

## 快速扩张期（1914—1922 年）（续）

### 一、美中贸易构成的变化

随着美中贸易的快速扩张，进出口商品的构成也发生了许多明显的变化。一大批以前不怎么起眼的物资突然成了贸易的主打商品，而许多长期以来一直非常重要的货物的贸易量与/或贸易额却开始下降。这些变化，部分是因为受到了两国经济环境发生变化的影响，部分是由于受到了欧洲战争引起的短暂干扰影响。当然，当干扰不再发生作用时，受战争影响的那部分贸易已经或者很快将会恢复至原先的状态。而那些由于经济发展变化趋势而产生的影响因素将一直发挥作用，直到受到另一组相反方向的新影响。下文对这些变化分别评估。

#### 1. 美国从中国进口商品的构成变化

在美国从中国进口的商品中，商业地位上升最明显的有植物油、皮革、兽皮和毛皮、化工产品、蛋类和蛋产品、头发和发制品、羊毛。地位下降的商品中，茶叶是唯一值得关注的。在与美国对华进口发展趋势相当的商品中，丝绸最为重要。这些物资在两国贸易中占据非常重要的地位，在后面的两篇（第六至第十四章）将分别对其给予更为详细的描述和讨论，这里先予以简单叙述。

二十年之前，中国的植物油在美国还不为人所知。即使到 1910 年，美国每年从中国进口的植物油仍远远低于 100 万美元，在美国对华进口总额中占比 1%～3%①。然而，1911 之后，日本开始对南满地区——中国的大部分油籽产于此地的植物油产生兴趣，中美植物油贸易在世界战争爆发前前夕快速增长。1911—1915 年间，美国每年从中国进口植物油近 300 万美元，在美国进口总额中的份额也陡然升至 7%、8%。1917 年，植物油进口额跃升至 1 200 万美元，所占份额接近 11%。接下来的 1918 年，进口额冲高至 3 900万美元，在当年美国对华进口总额中所占的份额超过 2/3，地位最为重要。自 1919年开始，植物油贸易份额有所下降。1921—1922 年下降最显著，主要是由于美国重新制订的高关税壁垒、商业萧条，以及将植物油作为重要原料的许多工业活动的停止②。

---

① 见表 3-5。
② 后见第八章之《植物油》一节。

### 表 5 - 1　1914—1922 年美国从中国(含租界)进口商品统计

进口额:万美元;占比:%

| 序号 | 类别 | 1914 财年 进口额 | 占比 | 1915 财年 进口额 | 占比 | 1916 财年 进口额 | 占比 | 1917 财年 进口额 | 占比 |
|---|---|---|---|---|---|---|---|---|---|
| 1 | 锑矿石和精炼锑 | 16.6 | 0.4 | 56.3 | 1.4 | 379.6 | 5.3 | 153.7 | 1.4 |
| 2 | 艺术作品 | 6.4 | 0.2 | 15.3 | 0.4 | 27.0 | 0.4 | 56.2 | 0.5 |
| 3 | 猪鬃,分选的,成束的和预制的 | 93.4 | 2.3 | 161.3 | 3.9 | 161.2 | 2.2 | 172.8 | 1.5 |
| 4 | 化工产品、药品、染料 | 64.0 | 1.6 | 67.2 | 1.6 | 671.4 | 9.3 | 229.3 | 2.0 |
| 5 | 棉制品、花边 | 4.6 | 0.1 | 2.7 | 0.1 | 6.2 | 0.1 | 32.3 | 0.3 |
| 6 | 生丝 | 160.3 | 2.6 | 114.5 | 2.8 | 161.2 | 2.2 | 218.1 | 1.9 |
| 7 | 蛋、蛋黄及其他产品 | 26.1 | 0.6 | 77.8 | 1.9 | 65.9 | 0.9 | 169.9 | 1.5 |
| 8 | 水果和坚果 | 44.4 | 1.1 | 42.6 | 1.0 | 50.4 | 0.7 | 90.2 | 0.8 |
| 9 | 头发和发网 | 18.2 | 0.5 | 18.9 | 0.5 | 52.4 | 0.7 | 117.6 | 1.0 |
| 10 | 帽子、风帽、软帽材料 | 18.2 | 0.5 | 28.2 | 0.7 | 92.7 | 1.3 | 213.0 | 1.9 |
| 11 | 皮张(毛皮除外) | 431.7 | 10.7 | 534.9 | 13.1 | 960.4 | 13.3 | 2794.7 | 24.5 |
| 12 | 黄麻、大麻和其他纤维 | 16.4 | 0.4 | 21.1 | 0.5 | 65.2 | 0.9 | 47.4 | 0.4 |
| 13 | 席子和地席 | 61.9 | 1.5 | 38.8 | 0.9 | 18.3 | 0.3 | 34.0 | 0.3 |
| 14 | 肉类和乳制品 | 7.4 | 0.2 | 20.5 | 0.5 | 17.6 | 0.2 | 45.6 | 0.4 |
| 15 | 动物油及其他油脂 | 19.1 | 0.5 | 41.6 | 1.0 | 34.5 | 0.5 | 22.3 | 0.2 |
| 16 | 豆饼 | | | | | 1.1 | | 2.4 | |
| 17 | 油籽 | 2.5 | 0.1 | 1.1 | | 16.8 | 0.2 | 36.5 | 0.3 |
| 18 | 植物油 | 286.1 | 7.1 | 294.4 | 7.2 | 426.4 | 5.9 | 1 202.2 | 10.7 |
| 19 | 米及米粉 | 98.4 | 2.4 | 147.9 | 3.6 | 1 54.4 | 2.1 | 176.4 | 1.6 |
| 20 | 绢丝 | 26.0 | 0.6 | 45.1 | 1.1 | 89.6 | 1.2 | 176.5 | 1.6 |
| 21 | 生丝 | 1 571.9 | 39.0 | 1 145.9 | 28.1 | 1 870.7 | 25.8 | 2 785.1 | 24.8 |
| 22 | 废丝 | 80.6 | 2.0 | 108.6 | 2.7 | 182.2 | 2.5 | 213.1 | 1.9 |
| 23 | 香料(未磨的) | 20.6 | 0.5 | 14.9 | 0.4 | 24.1 | 0.3 | 25.3 | 0.2 |
| 24 | 烈酒(蒸馏的) | 11.3 | 0.3 | 10.7 | 0.3 | 9.2 | 0.1 | 18.1 | 0.2 |
| 25 | 茶叶 | 275.6 | 6.8 | 314.9 | 7.7 | 299.3 | 4.1 | 321.3 | 2.9 |
| 26 | 马口铁 | | | | | 43.5 | 0.6 | 197.5 | 2.0 |
| 27 | 蔬菜 | 14.2 | 0.4 | 14.1 | 0.3 | 22.5 | 0.3 | 30.4 | 0.3 |
| 28 | 羊毛制品 | 9.0 | 0.2 | 6.6 | 0.2 | 18.9 | 0.3 | 22.7 | 0.2 |
| 29 | 羊毛(已加工);地毯 | 7.5 | 0.2 | 9.8 | 0.2 | 28.1 | 0.4 | 82.8 | 0.7 |
| 30 | 羊毛(未加工的) | 444.8 | 11.0 | 544.0 | 13.3 | 1 023.3 | 14.2 | 1 109.2 | 9.9 |
| 31 | 毛皮及其制品 | 77.4 | 1.9 | 41.3 | 1.0 | 80.8 | 1.1 | 166.3 | 1.5 |
| 32 | 烟叶 | | | | | 0.1 | | 39.6 | 0.4 |
| 33 | 其他 | 173.1 | 4.3 | 142.0 | 3.5 | 192.4 | 2.7 | 276.9 | 2.5 |
| | 合计 | 4 031.2 | 100.0 | 4 083.0 | 100.0 | 7 240.5 | 100.0 | 11 202.2 | 100.0 |

（续表）

| 序号 | 类　别 | 1918 财年 进口额 | 占比 | 1919 财年 进口额 | 占比 | 1920 财年 进口额 | 占比 | 1921 财年 进口额 | 占比 | 1922 财年 进口额 | 占比 |
|---|---|---|---|---|---|---|---|---|---|---|---|
| 1 | 锑矿石和精炼锑 | 136.4 | 1.0 | 48.4 | 0.3 | 123.3 | 0.6 | 67.3 | 0.7 | 56.2 | 0.4 |
| 2 | 艺术作品 | 16.7 | 0.1 | 25.0 | 0.1 | 35.3 | 0.2 | 22.8 | 0.2 | 28.4 | 0.2 |
| 3 | 猪鬃、分选的、成束的和预制的 | 338.1 | 2.4 | 275.0 | 1.6 | 616.8 | 3.0 | 383.1 | 3.7 | 296.9 | 2.2 |
| 4 | 化工产品、药品、染料 | 116.4 | 0.8 | 727.1 | 4.3 | 834.3 | 4.0 | 210.5 | 2.1 | | |
| 5 | 棉制品、花边 | 46.5 | 0.3 | 138.6 | 0.8 | 211.8 | 1.0 | 303.9 | 3.0 | 284.6 | 2.1 |
| 6 | 生丝 | 428.2 | 3.0 | 222.4 | 1.3 | 817.9 | 4.0 | 35.7 | 0.3 | 169.9 | 1.2 |
| 7 | 蛋、蛋黄及其他产品 | 256.0 | 2.0 | 706.1 | 4.2 | 632.2 | 3.1 | 254.6 | 2.5 | 316.0 | 2.3 |
| 8 | 水果和坚果 | 66.3 | 0.5 | 152.8 | 0.9 | 283.1 | 1.4 | 91.9 | 0.9 | 112.1 | 0.8 |
| 9 | 头发和发网 | 142.0 | 1.0 | 286.4 | 1.7 | 740.9 | 3.6 | 908.6 | 8.9 | 599.4 | 4.4 |
| 10 | 帽子、风帽、软帽材料 | 454.3 | 3.5 | 471.0 | 2.8 | 857.8 | 4.2 | 139.6 | 1.3 | 160.2 | 1.2 |
| 11 | 皮张(毛皮除外) | 1 197.5 | 8.5 | 1 708.5 | 10.1 | 3 080.5 | 15.1 | 419.5 | 4.1 | 696.6 | 5.1 |
| 12 | 黄麻、大麻和其他纤维 | 53.4 | 0.4 | 26.3 | 0.2 | 31.5 | 0.2 | 24.8 | 0.2 | 18.0 | 0.1 |
| 13 | 席子和地席 | 7.7 | 0.1 | 22.8 | 0.1 | 123.0 | 0.6 | 24.9 | 0.2 | 31.7 | 0.1 |
| 14 | 肉类和乳制品 | 112.3 | 0.8 | 113.8 | 0.7 | 182.2 | 0.9 | 77.9 | 0.8 | 31.7 | 0.2 |
| 15 | 动物油及其他油脂 | 142.1 | 1.0 | 39.5 | 0.2 | 23.4 | 0.1 | 11.4 | 0.1 | 27.3 | 0.2 |
| 16 | 豆饼 | 86.0 | 0.6 | 22.6 | 0.1 | 67.9 | 0.3 | 20.8 | 0.2 | | |
| 17 | 油籽 | 23.2 | 0.2 | 86.8 | 0.5 | 67.4 | 0.3 | 36.1 | 0.4 | 39.8 | 0.3 |
| 18 | 植物油 | 3 936.1 | 27.9 | 3 095.5 | 18.2 | 1 946.0 | 9.5 | 280.6 | 2.7 | 836.4 | 6.1 |
| 19 | 米及米粉 | 275.3 | 2.0 | | | 49.2 | 0.2 | 2.2 | | 0.7 | |
| 20 | 绢丝 | 275.3 | 2.0 | | | 49.2 | 0.2 | 2.2 | | 0.7 | |
| 21 | 生丝 | 2 528.2 | 18.0 | 5 460.8 | 32.2 | 5 395.2 | 26.4 | 4 807.3 | 47.0 | 5 661.0 | 41.5 |
| 22 | 废丝 | 567.7 | 4.0 | 436.3 | 2.6 | 884.4 | 4.3 | 233.7 | 2.3 | 224.8 | 1.6 |
| 23 | 香料(未磨的) | 19.1 | 0.1 | 16.4 | 0.1 | 17.0 | 0.1 | 6.1 | 0.2 | 35.8 | 0.3 |
| 24 | 烈酒(蒸馏的) | | | | | | | | | | |
| 25 | 茶叶 | 322.0 | 2.3 | 273.0 | 1.6 | 240.3 | 1.2 | 206.6 | 2.0 | 212.8 | 1.6 |
| 26 | 马口铁 | 322.0 | 2.3 | 273.0 | 1.6 | 240.3 | 1.2 | 206.6 | 2.0 | 212.8 | 1.6 |
| 27 | 蔬菜 | 14.2 | 0.1 | 20.2 | 0.1 | 13.0 | 0.1 | 4.9 | | 20.5 | 0.2 |
| 28 | 羊毛制品 | 17.0 | 0.1 | 9.1 | 0.1 | 32.4 | 0.2 | 36.8 | 0.4 | 68.9 | 0.5 |
| 29 | 羊毛(已加工);地毯 | 40.7 | 0.3 | 44.2 | 0.3 | 201.2 | 1.0 | 139.3 | 1.4 | 270.0 | 2.0 |
| 30 | 羊毛(未加工的) | 1 423.5 | 10.1 | 1 298.7 | 7.6 | 539.4 | 2.6 | 545.8 | 5.4 | 984.5 | 7.2 |
| 31 | 毛皮及其制品 | 310.3 | 2.1 | 732.7 | 4.3 | 1 249.4 | 6.1 | 482.0 | 4.7 | 1 384.7 | 10.1 |
| 32 | 烟叶 | 145.5 | 1.0 | 129.1 | 0.8 | 96.1 | 0.1 | 11.7 | 0.1 | 2.5 | |
| 33 | 其他 | 725.2 | 5.1 | 558.6 | 3.3 | 903.6 | 4.4 | 253.9 | 2.5 | | |
| | 合计 | 14 080.6 | 100.0 | 16 964.6 | 100.0 | 20 422.2 | 100.0 | 10 241.6 | 100.0 | 13 667.1 | 100.0 |

注：1914—1917 年各财年均以 6 月 30 日为结束日；1918 年后为日历年统计数据。

与植物油贸易相比稍显逊色的是皮革和兽皮进口贸易。在前一时期,皮革和兽皮已经在美国对华进口贸易中占据了重要的地位,年进口额250万~400万美元,在对华进口总额中约占10%的份额。1913年,皮革和兽皮进口贸易蹿升,到1915年贸易额增至500万美元以上,在美国进口总额中占有13%的份额。1917年,皮革和兽皮成为美国从中国进口的最重要的两种商品之一(另一种为丝绸,两者各占约1/4的份额),进口额创下2 750万美元的新纪录。1920年,进口额再次增长至3 100万美元,但是由于来自中国的进口普遍增长,其份额下降到15%。然而,1921—1922年,由于美国皮革业萧条,贸易出现了急剧下降。尽管这一时期进口贸易起伏波动巨大,但还是增长了数倍,在美国对华进口贸易总额中的份额总体上是增长的①。

中国毛皮只是在最近才成为美国重要的进口商品。1916年之前,年均进口额不足50万美元,在美国对华进口总额中的份额稍多于1%;但是,1917年之后的增长非常明显,从当年的170万美元上升至1918年的310万美元、1919年的730万美元、1920年的1 250万美元,此后,由于商业萧条,1921年下降到480万美元。不过,1922年,再次急剧上升至将近1 400万美元。毛皮进口在1917年美国对华进口总额中的份额是1.5%,1920年升至6.1%,1921年回落至4.7%,1922年回升到10.1%。这是中国毛皮正在成为美国市场上一种主要进口物资的有力证明。

与之地位同等重要的还有1916年之后的"化工产品、药品和染料"大类。应当指出,本世纪初,化工产品和药品进口量非常大,年均进口150万美元,占美国对华进口总额的6%。该大类中的2/3是精制鸦片,但美国从1910年开始禁止进口鸦片;其他化工产品和药品,如樟脑和甘草精,进口数量和进口额都相当小。所以该大类产品的年均进口额下降到50万美元左右,所占份额稍多于1%。但是,1916年,美国突然非常需要中国的染料。战前,中国是德国颜料和染料的重要买家,战争初期,中国贮存了大批颜料和染料,现在又重新出口到美国。当年(1916年),美国从中国进口价值460万美元的颜料、染料,其中仅靛青一项就达300万美元。归入"化工产品、药品和染料"大类的进口总额为670万美元,占美国进口总额的9.3%;1919年,进口额增长到730万美元,1920年又增至830万美元,约占美国进口总额的4%。美国进口的化工产品中,最为重要的是当时美国化学工厂广泛使用的蛋白,1919年美国进口蛋白760万磅、价值560万美元,1920年进口蛋白850万磅、价值450万美元。其他比较重要的化工产品还有樟脑、甘草等。

蛋类和蛋产品是美国进口商品清单上的新品种。在前一时期,它们的进口额实际上可以忽略不计,但其地位在1915年之后开始上升。1917年,美国从中国进口了大约1 000万磅的干蛋、冰蛋,价值170万美元。1919—1920年,年均进口额上升到接近

---

① 后见第九章之《皮革和兽皮》一节。

700万美元,此后两年下降到每年300万美元左右。1918年前,这类商品在美国对华进口总额中所占份额不足2%,但1919年上升到4.2%,此后一直保持在3%左右。

在美国商业活动活跃的这一时期,草编、制帽材料的进口也显著增长。美国从中国的山东省进口草编已近半个世纪,进口额长期维持在每年50万美元左右。为作战士兵提供草帽而形成的战时需求使美国的草编进口突然增大,在1917—1919年的三年里,美国每年从中国进口超过10亿码的草编,年进口额约400万美元。1920年,进口额增长到上年的近2倍,而其数量增长不足一半。

毛发和发制品贸易的增长来得最晚,但也可能让人最感兴趣。1916年前,它仅占美国进口总额的0.5%,1918年前也仅为1.0%,而1920年的进口额达740万美元,所占份额上升到3.6%,1921年进口额为910万美元,所占份额为8.9%,1922年稍有下降[1]。

另一个更新的成长领域是中国棉制品——其中大部分是花边和刺绣,它们在其贸易额于1917年首次超过100万美元大关后才开始引人注意。棉制品进口增长迅速,即使在美国陷入商业萧条低谷年的1921年,美国也从中国进口了大约1800万码、价值300万美元的花边和刺绣滚边,其中的90%为手工制作[2]。

原棉也是新近才进入美国对华进口商品目录。1910年之前,美国实质上没有从东方进口这种物资。1911—1916年,美国每年进口大约1000万磅原棉,进口额稍多于100万美元。1917—1919年间,实际进口量并没有太大增长,但由于价格膨胀,进口额上升较多。1920年,由于价格飙升,将近3000万磅中国棉进口到美国,其价值达820万美元,占对华进口总额的4%。1921年商业萧条来临时,美国自己生产的棉已经绰绰有余,中国原棉的进口贸易实质上就全部停止了。原棉进口贸易前些年的增长大多是由于对廉价棉的临时性需求,今后,很难期望会有庞大数量的棉从中国进口到美国。

另外一种商品只在1918—1920年间引人关注,那就是烟叶。几个世纪以来,美国一直是烟草出口国,极少进口。美国向中国出口烟丝和制成烟草已有一个半世纪。但是,欧洲战争爆发后,美国对烟丝的需求非常强烈,因此从中国进口了大量烟叶,并继续向中国运送其成品。1916年,美国仅仅从中国进口了价值349美元的2030磅烟叶;次年则增长至300万磅、39.6万美元;此后两年的进口量都超过500万磅,进口额分别为150万美元和130万美元。然而,与原棉的情况一样,烟叶的需求最近也停止了,未来也不会恢复进口。

锑和马口铁曾经一度是美国对华进口贸易的重要商品,但战后,对它们的需求大大降低。

---

① 后见第八章之《头发和发网》一节。
② 后见第八章之《棉制品》一节。

　　本时段之初开始在进口贸易中占据重要地位的所有商品中,只有少数几种似乎还能在美国对华贸易中保持其份额。植物油、兽皮、毛皮、蛋产品、棉花边、可能还包括头发及毛发制品,是美国不大可能在近期压缩需求的物资;然而,锑、马口铁、原棉、烟叶、靛青和其他一些物资被大量进口只是为了满足战争引发的临时性的急迫需求,难以期望它们未来还会有什么发展。

　　在美国对华进口中,重要程度下降的唯一商品是茶叶。前一时期,茶叶是对华进口商品中最重要的;20世纪之初,茶叶在美国对华进口总额中仍能占有 1/4 的份额,但在本时期开始,其份额就掉头向下,一直降到 7% 左右,年进口额 300 万美元。1917年之后,茶叶贸易的份额持续下降,到 1920 年仅有 1.2%[1]。

　　还有一些商品,其在美国对华进口贸易中的相对地位与美国对华进口贸易的总体发展基本保持一致,它们是:丝和丝制品、猪鬃、羊毛,及其他一些不那么重要的商品如水果、坚果、稻米和蔬菜等。19 个世纪末期以来,丝绸一直是美国进口的最重要的中国商品,生丝、废丝和丝制品三项合计占到美国对华进口总额的 35%~40%;但是,1915—1918 年,尽管其贸易量、贸易额都大幅增长,但所占份额大约下降了 10%。不过,1919 年起,丝绸完全恢复了其之前的重要地位,1921—1922 年的贸易额份额为 45%[2]。

　　未加工的羊毛在很长一段时间里都是美国从中国进口的最重要的物资。在前一时期,它的贸易份额平均为 10%;这一数据一直保持到所讨论的最后十年。1916—1921 年间,美国每年从中国进口四五千万磅未加工的羊毛,平均价值 1 250 万美元。1920 年,进口量、进口额双双大幅下降,但在 1921—1922 年,羊毛进口量恢复到先前水平,进口额则由于价格偏低稍有下降[3]。

　　一般来说,美国从中国进口的商品,与从其他东方国家和南美洲进口的一样,大部分是原材料和半成品,其目的在于进一步生产而非即时消费。几乎所有最重要的商品类目,如生丝、植物油、兽皮、羊毛、草编等,都是如此。从未来趋向看,这类进口还是会逐步增长的,这是因为,一方面,美国各个工业领域对这些原材料的需要将会增加,另一方面,中国农业和初级工业的逐步发展使中国能够供应更多的原材料和半成品。相反,美国对制成品或消费品的进口呈下滑趋势。首先,茶叶贸易绝对数量和相对份额的最新下滑清楚地表明,中国在这种商品上几乎不可能重享其昔日的荣光。丝制品贸易的绝对数量还在保持着,但相对份额也在下降。羊毛制品——大多是地毯——也已经不重要了,其份额通常不超过 1%,而木制品之类的物资所占的份额仅为 0.1%~0.2%。

---

① 后见第六章。
② 后见第七章。
③ 后见第九章《羊毛》一节。

　　尽管如此,中国还是能够向美国出口一些相对份额正在上升的制成品。这些物资总是需要大量的人工劳动,而在这方面,中国比世界上其他任何国家都有更强的竞争力。这类制成品以花边、刺绣、发网以及其他产品为典型代表,战前均由欧洲国家向美国供应。

　　**2. 美国对华出口商品的构成变化**

　　没有什么能比下面所列的近年来两国交易品种的变化情况更能清楚地表明美国对华出口贸易的趋向:

　　(1) 出口数量、相对份额双双下降的品种:棉布;面包原料(包括小麦粉)。

　　(2) 出口数量增加、但相对份额下降的品种:矿物油。

　　(3) 出口数量增加、相对份额基本保持稳定的品种:木材;水果和坚果;肉、乳制品和其他食物。

　　(4) 出口数量、相对份额双双增加的品种:皮革制品;烟草(制成品及未制成的);钢铁产品和机器;其他金属。

　　(5) 其贸易地位最近才上升的品种:汽车和马车;电力机械;纸制品和图书;化工产品和药品;橡胶制品。

　　在前两个时期,棉布都是美国对华出口的最重要物资,其次是精炼矿物油;再下来是面包原料——其中大部分是小麦粉。制成烟草也占据了重要地位,尽管其重要性远不如前述这几类商品。机器、汽车、马车的出口实际上是可以忽略不计的,但其他钢铁制品在前一时期的后半段开始大量出口中国。

　　美国的出口自1914年起发生了很大的变化。1915年前,棉布贸易在美国对华出口总额占有1/2～2/3的份额,但在1915年之后下滑到不足1/4;战争爆发后,下滑速度更快。现在,棉布贸易在美国对华出口总额中的份额已不足5%,战争期间甚至曾下降到1%、2%。因此,美国对华棉布出口贸易的现状就是茶叶进口贸易的翻版。两种物资都曾在过去占据重要地位,而现在已下滑到几乎无可挽回的地步,其原因将在后面的章节中给出[①]。

　　前一时期的多个年份里,美国曾向中国大量出口面包原料,其中小麦粉贡献了将近90%的出口额。通常,面包原料占美国对华出口总额的3%～4%。但1907年是个例外,出口到中国的面粉和其他面包原料达770万美元,占美国出口总额的28%。在现在正讨论的这一时期[②],这类食品的出口量非常小,实质上已经退出了美国出口贸易行列。1921、1922年,出口额达到畸高的280万美元、840万美元,分别相当于当年美国对华出口总额的2.4%和7.9%。但是,这些食品中的大部分运往中国华北

---

　　① 后见第十章。

　　② 译注:原文此处(第108页第2段第8行)之 persent,疑为 present 一词之笔误。

地区以救济饥民,而不是商业交易的结果。所以,可以说这类商品已经退出了中美贸易。

矿物油摘取了棉布曾经拥有的美国对华出口榜第一商品之位置。上世纪末以来,矿物油的年贸易量、贸易额稳步增长,在美国对华出口贸易中贡献了 1/4 的份额。最近十年间,矿物油的出口额仍在增长,但在美国对华出口中的份额下降到 1/8 左右[①]。

烟草,包括原烟和制成烟草,都是美国对华出口的最重要的两、三种商品中的一种,出口数量和所占份额的成长都很明显。上一时期的初期,实际上还没有原烟出口到中国,运往中国的制成烟草也只有很少一点。本时期初,制成烟草、原烟的贸易额为三四百万美元,所占份额 15%。现在,原烟、制成烟草的出口量都在增加,出口额通常超过 1 000 万美元,占出口总额的 1/10。原烟的出口增速高于制成烟草,通常是后者的 2 倍[②]。

在本时期之前,皮革制品在美国对华出口贸易中并不引人注目,实际出口额最大为 13.5 万美元,份额不足 0.5%。但在本时期,特别是 1917 年以后,皮革异军突起,其对华出口额在 1917、1918 年两次达到 300 万美元关口,在美国对华出口总额中所占的份额分别为 7.1% 和 4.9%。1919—1922 年,出口额维持在 150 万美元左右,所占份额约为 1%。

这一时期最重要的出口增长属于钢铁机器及其他制品领域。十年前的 1913 年,这类物资的出口不足 300 万美元,在对华出口总额中占 13.2%。在过去的几年间,出口额上升了好几倍,每年超过 3 000 万美元,在出口总额中占比 1/4～1/3[③]。

其他金属制品如铅、马口铁、铜、锌、黄铜、铝等的出口,也在快速增长。以前,出口中国的铜数量大,而且起伏不定;其他金属及其制品的出口微不足道,以至于无法单独区分,所以在表 5-2 中作为组合出现。但是,近年来,这些金属产品的出口以惊人的速度增长,1921—1922 年,每年出口额超过 600 万美元,在出口总额中贡献了 6% 的份额。

汽车和马车、电力机械和电器用具仅仅在最近几年才参与中美贸易。十年前,每一类产品的出口额不足 25 万美元,现在则达到四、五百万美元。十年前,它们各类的份额几乎都不到美国对华出口总额的 1%,现在则可达 3%、4%。

与此类贸易同样上升的另一组产品是包括图书在内的纸制品贸易。外国的纸张和图书仅仅在二十年前才开始运往中国,且仅仅是为了在华外国人使用,因此贸易量可以忽略不计。现在,这类物资已经被中国的学童普遍使用。1918 年之后,美国每年向中国出口纸张和图书价值 200 万～500 万美元,所占份额为 2%～5%。

①后见第十一章。
②后见第十二章之《烟草》一节。
③后见第十三章。

### 表 5 – 2　1914—1922 年美国对华出口商品构成

出口额：万美元；占比：%

| 序号 | 类　别 | 1914 财年 | | 1915 财年 | | 1916 财年 | | 1917 财年 | |
|---|---|---|---|---|---|---|---|---|---|
| | | 出口额 | 占比 | 出口额 | 占比 | 出口额 | 占比 | 出口额 | 占比 |
| 1 | 面包原料（含面粉） | 121.1 | 4.6 | 9.7 | 0.5 | 5.5 | 0.2 | 4.5 | 0.1 |
| 2 | 汽车、马车及零件 | 23.3 | 0.9 | 23.2 | 1.3 | 30.8 | 1.2 | 89.2 | 2.1 |
| 3 | 化工产品、药品、染料 | 14.1 | 0.5 | 28.1 | 1.6 | 130.6 | 5.0 | 97.2 | 2.3 |
| 4 | 棉布 | 609.6 | 23.1 | 119.5 | 6.8 | 86.3 | 3.3 | 40.6 | 1.0 |
| 5 | 棉制品和服装 | 9.1 | 0.3 | 6.6 | 0.4 | 10.5 | 0.4 | 32.0 | 0.8 |
| 6 | 原棉 | 58.8 | 2.2 | 73.4 | 4.2 | 72.9 | 2.8 | 40.3 | 1.0 |
| 7 | 电力机器和电器用具 | 23.9 | 0.9 | 24.2 | 1.4 | 41.7 | 1.6 | 114.3 | 2.7 |
| 8 | 水果和坚果 | 7.8 | 0.3 | 8.9 | 0.5 | 10.9 | 0.4 | 18.3 | 0.4 |
| 9 | 玻璃和玻璃制品 | 2.1 | 0.1 | 4.9 | 0.3 | 27.0 | 1.0 | 16.1 | 0.4 |
| 10 | 印度橡胶制品 | 7.4 | 0.3 | 4.9 | 0.3 | 8.3 | 0.3 | 8.7 | 0.2 |
| 11 | 钢铁制品 | 212.0 | 8.0 | 242.2 | 13.8 | 494.4 | 18.8 | 743.1 | 17.8 |
| 12 | 钢铁机器 | 114.0 | 4.3 | 56.4 | 3.1 | 98.5 | 3.7 | 182.1 | 4.4 |
| 13 | 皮草、鞣制兽皮和其他、 | 14.5 | 0.6 | 13.6 | 0.8 | 35.8 | 1.4 | 296.8 | 7.1 |
| 14 | 金属（不含钢铁）及其制品 | 13.6 | 0.5 | 26.3 | 1.5 | 76.9 | 2.9 | 59.6 | 1.4 |
| 15 | 肉类、乳制品和其他食品 | 14.4 | 0.6 | 32.2 | 1.8 | 33.0 | 1.3 | 96.1 | 2.3 |
| 16 | 精炼矿物油 | 717.3 | 27.2 | 641.1 | 36.5 | 676.5 | 25.8 | 584.3 | 14.0 |
| 17 | 纸、纸制品、图书 | 19.2 | 0.7 | 23.4 | 1.4 | 68.3 | 2.6 | 134.2 | 3.2 |
| 18 | 石蜡和蜡 | 33.3 | 1.3 | 57.2 | 3.3 | 58.3 | 2.2 | 58.3 | 1.4 |
| 19 | 烟草，制成的 | 178.2 | 6.7 | 120.6 | 6.8 | 251.1 | 9.6 | 915.4 | 22.0 |
| 20 | 烟草，未制成的 | 200.5 | 7.6 | 61.2 | 3.5 | 123.3 | 4.7 | 171.3 | 4.1 |
| 21 | 木材、木板等 | 114.7 | 4.3 | 55.5 | 3.2 | 35.3 | 1.3 | 27.2 | 0.6 |
| 22 | 其他木制品 | 36.8 | 1.4 | 23.4 | 1.3 | 25.1 | 1.0 | 63.6 | 1.5 |
| 23 | 其他 | 84.3 | 3.3 | 102.6 | 5.8 | 224.6 | 8.5 | 373.3 | 9.0 |
| | 合计 | 2 634.6 | 100.0 | 1 759.1 | 100.0 | 2 652.3 | 100.0 | 4 166.5 | 100.0 |

（续表）

| 序号 | 类 别 | 1918 财年 | | 1919 财年 | | 1920 财年 | | 1921 财年 | | 1922 财年 | |
|---|---|---|---|---|---|---|---|---|---|---|---|
| | | 出口额 | 占比 | 出口额 | 占比 | 出口额 | 占比 | 出口额 | 占比 | 出口额 | 占比 |
| 1 | 面包原料（含面粉） | 3.6 | 0.01 | 19.2 | 0.2 | 30.2 | 0.2 | 277.8 | 2.4 | 837.3 | 7.9 |
| 2 | 汽车、马车及零件 | 169.8 | 2.9 | 493.6 | 4.2 | 496.6 | 3.3 | 334.6 | 2.9 | 332.5 | 3.1 |
| 3 | 化工产品、药品、染料 | 182.5 | 3.1 | 434.8 | 3.7 | 861.3 | 5.6 | 151.5 | 1.3 | 246.9 | 2.3 |
| 4 | 棉布 | 91.5 | 1.5 | 641.0 | 5.4 | 770.1 | 5.0 | 228.2 | 2.0 | 194.0 | 1.8 |
| 5 | 棉制品和服装 | 34.0 | 0.6 | 90.9 | 0.8 | 152.3 | 1.0 | 30.0 | 0.3 | 34.3 | 0.3 |
| 6 | 原棉 | 55.8 | 0.9 | 178.6 | 1.5 | 209.2 | 1.4 | 1005.1 | 8.8 | 359.4 | 3.4 |
| 7 | 电力机器和电器用具 | 149.3 | 2.5 | 190.4 | 1.6 | 437.7 | 2.9 | 446.4 | 3.9 | 165.5 | 1.6 |
| 8 | 水果和坚果 | 21.8 | 0.4 | 52.4 | 0.4 | 59.8 | 0.4 | 41.5 | 0.4 | 51.3 | 0.5 |
| 9 | 玻璃和玻璃制品 | 36.4 | 0.6 | 58.8 | 0.5 | 75.6 | 0.5 | 27.4 | 0.2 | 12.9 | 0.1 |
| 10 | 印度橡胶制品 | 19.7 | 0.3 | 55.7 | 0.5 | 82.8 | 0.5 | 31.5 | 0.03 | 19.1 | 0.2 |
| 11 | 钢铁制品 | 1 314.8 | 22.2 | 2 052.8 | 17.3 | 2 498.0 | 16.3 | 1 075.2 | 9.5 | 607.4 | 5.7 |
| 12 | 钢铁机器 | 322.0 | 5.4 | 1 686.4 | 14.2 | 1 821.7 | 11.9 | 1 965.2 | 17.3 | 1 113.6 | 10.5 |
| 13 | 皮草、鞣制兽皮和其他、 | 289.4 | 4.9 | 195.0 | 1.6 | 155.3 | 1.0 | 77.3 | 0.7 | 105.9 | 1.0 |
| 14 | 金属（不含钢铁）及其制品 | 44.3 | 0.7 | 102.4 | 0.9 | 402.0 | 2.6 | 574.6 | 5.0 | 684.0 | 6.5 |
| 15 | 肉类、乳制品和其他食品 | 65.2 | 1.1 | 111.2 | 0.9 | 101.1 | 0.7 | 95.6 | 0.8 | 87.6 | 0.8 |
| 16 | 精炼矿物油 | 457.3 | 7.7 | 2 056.9 | 17.2 | 1 946.9 | 12.7 | 1 426.2 | 12.5 | 2 171.2 | 20.5 |
| 17 | 纸、纸制品、图书 | 231.8 | 3.9 | 350.3 | 3.0 | 527.2 | 3.5 | 283.0 | 2.5 | 161.8 | 1.5 |
| 18 | 石蜡和蜡 | 61.4 | 1.0 | 90.9 | 0.8 | 81.9 | 0.5 | 105.5 | 0.9 | 74.8 | 0.7 |
| 19 | 烟草，制成的 | 1 153.7 | 19.5 | 1 014.6 | 9.7 | 1 608.6 | 10.5 | 1 169.9 | 10.3 | 1 708.4 | 16.1 |
| 20 | 烟草，未制成的 | 586.4 | 10.0 | 632.8 | 5.3 | 1 331.6 | 8.7 | 840.6 | 7.4 | 1 072.1 | 10.1 |
| 21 | 木材、木板等 | 42.5 | 0.7 | 160.1 | 1.4 | 420.6 | 2.8 | 194.7 | 1.7 | 221.7 | 2.1 |
| 22 | 其他木制品 | 84.6 | 1.4 | 149.4 | 1.3 | 178.9 | 1.2 | 43.8 | 0.4 | 317.0 | 3.0 |
| 23 | 其他 | 495.7 | 8.4 | 1 029.3 | 8.7 | 1 038.2 | 6.8 | 937.2 | 8.2 | | 0.3 |
| | 合计 | 5 913.5 | 100.0 | 11 827.5 | 100.0 | 15 287.6 | 100.0 | 11 360.5 | 100.0 | 10 607.4 | 100.0 |

注：1914—1917年各财年均以6月30日为结束日；1918年后为日历年统计数据。

从上述冗长、枯燥的事实列举中，可以得到如下结论：

（1）在过去数十年间，简单形式的工业产品一直是美国对华出口的商品主体，但现在其出口的绝对数量及所占份额都在下降，而且这一趋势似乎还将在未来延续。棉布和小麦粉可以看作是这类产品的两个代表。前已述及，中国正在快速发展它的简单工业，每年有很多面粉厂、棉纺厂等投入生产。外国要在这些领域与中国本土企业进行竞争，似乎是不太可能的。

制成烟草似乎是一个例外。尽管它也是一种简单制造业，但对华出口的数量还在增长。中国烟草制造业的发展不如面粉业、棉纺业那么快，其原因仅仅是由于这样的事实：抽吸香烟的习惯在中国蔓延的速度超过了中国烟草业的发展速度，因此需要从美国进口大量的制成烟草。但是，目前美国向中国出口未制成烟草的增长速度高于制成烟草的趋势清楚地表明，中国正在发展这一产业，美国制成烟草的对华出口迟早将下降，就像棉布和小麦粉的出口一样。

至于矿物油，中国到目前为止还没有能力开发、利用自己的油田，因此其供应很大程度上要依赖美国。然而，电气照明已经开始在中国的许多城镇流行起来，就很难指望这类照明油的贸易会一直增长下去。这一时期的矿物油的出口数字清楚地显示其原有的份额在下降。

（2）那些复杂工业、大型工业的产品的出口贸易的绝对数量、相对份额都呈现出决定性的增长趋势。

钢铁机器和其他设备出口贸易的增长速度最快；汽车、马车、电器用具、化工产品和药品等的出口也在增长，但增幅较小。美国在这些领域里不只对中国有比较优势，对世界其他竞争国家也有优势，因为它拥有许多可从事大规模生产的非常发达的工业。

## 二、美中贸易的差额

与前一时期一样，中美两国的贸易差额在这一时期也是一直有利于中国，只有1921年例外。这种情形在美国与东方各国的贸易中非常普遍。1915年美国首次从欧洲抢回战争订单后，它对许多原材料的需求就变得非常急迫，而中国恰好能够予以供应。这一状况一直持续到美国对华贸易差额达到创纪录的1917年。贸易差额大幅增长的原因在于，一方面美国扩大了从中国的进口，而另一方面美国对华出口发展缓慢。

美中贸易差额首次由升到降的趋势变化发生于欧战结束、恢复和平的1918年。停战协议签署后，原来由欧洲转向美国的战争订单大部分逐渐停止了，这促使美国尽可能地扩大对中国的出口。所以，尽管从中国的进口还在继续扩大，但两国之间的贸易差额越来越不利于中国。

贸易差额转向的另一个因素与美国1921年的商业萧条有关。这一年，美国几乎所有的工业领域都收缩了生产活动,对原材料的需要也因之减少。许多种曾在美国有大量需求的中国原材料突然之间在美国市场上卖不动了。另一方面,由于战争刺激,中国一直在持续快速发展其工业化,对美国机器及其他设备的需求增加。这导致两国贸易差额自 1906 年以来首次向相反方向转化(见表 5-3)。

表 5-3　1913—1922 年美国对华贸易差额

单位:万美元

| 年份 | 美国—中国内地 | | 美国—中国租界 | | 美—中经香港转口贸易(估计) | | 美中贸易差额总计 | |
|---|---|---|---|---|---|---|---|---|
| | 美国顺差 | 美国逆差 | 美国顺差 | 美国逆差 | 美国顺差 | 美国逆差 | 美国顺差 | 美国逆差 |
| 1913 | | 1482.1 | 36.8 | | 492.2 | | | 953.1 |
| 1914 | | 1 594.6 | 71.8 | | 422.9 | | | 1 100.0 |
| 1915 | | 3 308.9 | 46.4 | | 369.3 | | | 2 894.2 |
| 1916 | | 4 852.6 | 37.2 | | 571.7 | | | 4 243.7 |
| 1917 | | 8 481.4 | | 986.1 | 632.1 | | | 8 835.4 |
| 1918 | | 5 840.0 | | 2 365.9 | 782.3 | | | 7 423.6 |
| 1919 | | 4 863.9 | | 275.7 | 772.9 | | | 4 366.7 |
| 1920 | | 4 697.1 | | 437.5 | 1 010.6 | | | 4 119.0 |
| 1921 | 715.5 | | 403.5 | | 782.7 | | 1901.7 | |
| 1922 | | 3 425.2 | 365.5 | | 807.7 | | | 2 252.0 |
| 1923 | | 7 276.7 | 227.0 | | 1 107.3 | | | 5 942.4 |

注 1:1913—1916 年"美国—中国租界"贸易差额为财年统计数据(以 6 月 30 日为结束日),其余各年为日历年统计数据;中国的租界地区中,英租界、法租界及原属德国的租界与美国之间的贸易量很小,自 1917 年起归入"美国—中国"贸易之中。因此,1917—1923 年的"美国—中国租界"贸易数据仅指(中国)关东地区。

注 2:通过香港的美国—中国转口贸易数据以前文第四章表 4-6 之"途经香港的转口贸易"估计值为基础。作者相信,通过《中国海关统计》的"中国—香港贸易"、美国《美国对外通商与船运》可以判断出,美国—中国途经香港的转口贸易对美国有利,但是,此表中的数值,尤其是 1918—1920 年,可能显得过大。但是,由于转口贸易混乱,准确的数字无法获得。

注 3:1923 年之所有贸易数据均按财年统计(以 6 月 30 日为结束日)。

但是,随着美国经济活动在 1922—1923 年逐渐恢复和中国经济陷入临时性萧条,美国很快恢复向东方大量采购,向中国出口则相对较少。所以,1922—1923 年的贸易差额重新对中国非常"有利"。

这些巨大的贸易差额至少部分是由白银、黄金支付,过去十年间美国曾向中国大量出口金银。在前面的章节里已经注意到,美国作为一个金、银生产国,一直在持续将这些财富运往东方。1913年之前,尽管部分黄金被运往香港,但实际上并没有直接向中国出口。1916年之后,美国向中国内地和香港大量出口黄金,部分支付美国的入超。金、银贸易的实际数据见表5-5。

### 三、战争期间的白银/黄金比价:美国、中国之间的财富移动

对这一时期黄金/白银比价变化做进一步的研究可能会很有趣。当然,银是美国贸易最重要的商品之一,金则在中国贸易中处于类似的地位。所以,如果忽视这两种商品,有关中美贸易的研究将是不完整的。

这两种金属贸易的统计数字中,最明显的一个特点是,在这短短的十年观察期内,两者之间的比价大幅变动。表5-4是1913—1922年海关银元与纽约即期市场美元之间的平均兑换汇率。

**表5-4 1913—1922年纽约即期市场的中国海关银元—美元汇率**

| 年 份 | 1913 | 1914 | 1915 | 1916 | 1917 | 1918 | 1919 | 1920 | 1921 | 1922 |
|---|---|---|---|---|---|---|---|---|---|---|
| 汇率(美元/两海关银) | 0.73 | 0.67 | 0.62 | 0.79 | 1.03 | 1.26 | 1.39 | 1.24 | 0.76 | 0.83 |

关于1915—1920年银价异常上升的原因,首先是因为全球产量的下降。战前,全世界平均每年生产白银2.2亿~2.26亿盎司;但1914年全球白银产量下降到2.11亿盎司,1915、1916年分别下降至1.79亿盎司和1.57亿盎司;1917、1918年回升至2.11亿盎司、1.77亿盎司,但1911年[①]重新跌落至1.75亿盎司,1920年估计还要低一些。美国的白银产量约占全世界产量的1/3。白银价格上涨的第二个原因是,1915年之后,交战各国对白银产生了特别的需求。黄金退出流通领域,被交战国的中央银行或民众所囤积。英、法、俄、意和其他国家开始大量铸造银币,以满足人民对"硬通货"的需求。白银上涨的第三个原因是,使用银币的东方国家,其增长的出口和贸易顺差都需要用白银来结算。所以,1915年后半年,白银价格持续上升,这一上行态势直到1920年后半年才停息。

白银价格于1915年上涨之前,曾于当年降至历史最低点。中国人从相反的角度看,并非白银贬值,而是黄金升值。于是,中国为换取更多的利润而把大部分盈余黄金(价值630万美元)出售给美国。这是美国除1920年[②]之外从中国直接进口黄金最多的年份(见表5-5)。

---

① 译注:根据文意分析,原文此处(第117页第1段第1行)之"1911年"为"1919年",疑为作者笔误。

② 译注:按照原文第119页之表6,美国直接从中国进口黄金最多的年份分别是1921年、1922年、1915年,因此,原文此处(第117页第2段第8行)之"1920"表述疑有误。

## 表5-5 1913—1922年美国对华金银贸易统计

单位:万美元

| 年份 | 中国内地·出口·金·国内 | 金·国外 | 银·国内 | 银·国外 | 总 | 内地·进口·金 | 银 | 合计 | 香港·出口·金·国内 | 金·国外 | 银·国内 | 银·国外 | 总 | 香港·进口·金 | 银 | 合计 | 净出口·银 | 金 |
|---|---|---|---|---|---|---|---|---|---|---|---|---|---|---|---|---|---|---|
| 1913 | 10.3 | 15.6 | 222.2 | 0.7 | 233.2 | 1.1 | 2.6 | 1.0 | 0.1 | 773.0 | | | | | 994.9 | 10.0 | | |
| 1914 | | | 131.6 | 9.7 | 141.3 | | | | 0.6 | | 805.8 | 5.1 | 811.5 | | | | 952.2 | 0.6 |
| 1915 | | | 22.5 | 0.2 | 22.7 | 626.8 | | 626.8 | 4.7 | | 579.7 | 2.1 | 586.5 | | | | 604.5 | −622.1 |
| 1916 | 480.6 | | 248.9 | 4.6 | 729.5 | 163.2 | 48.0 | 211.0 | 477.9 | 6.5 | 575.2 | 2.9 | 1 062.5 | | | | 779.1 | 801.8 |
| 1917 | 70.2 | | 756.4 | 84.0 | 826.6 | | 21.8 | 21.8 | 161.8 | | 489.1 | | 650.9 | | | | 1 228.3 | 232.0 |
| 1918 | 3 895.4 | | 1 486.9 | | 1 570.9 | | | | | | 1 200.7 | 22.7 | 1 223.4 | | | | 2 794.3 | |
| 1919 | 2 828.7 | | 5 693.2 | 2 065.1 | 11 669.3 | | | | 4 008.5 | 0.1 | 923.3 | 101.3 | 5 033.2 | 1 001.8 | 2.0 | 1 003.8 | 8 780.9 | 6 917.8 |
| 1920 | | | 4 559.7 | 1 575.1 | 8 963.5 | 0.1 | 129.5 | 129.6 | 3 148.7 | 1.0 | 1 828.8 | 658.5 | 5 637.0 | 3 019.2 | 0.2 | 3 019.4 | 8 492.3 | 2 959.0 |
| 1921 | | | 567.3 | 711.0 | 1 278.3 | 1 791.3 | 0.8 | 1 792.1 | 962.1 | | 581.8 | 459.0 | 2 002.9 | 566.1 | | 566.1 | 2 318.2 | −1 395.2 |
| 1922 | 10.0 | 25.0 | 900.7 | 1 156.9 | 2 092.6 | 893.8 | 1.2 | 895.0 | 358.2 | | 1 016.3 | 627.2 | 2 001.7 | 1.5 | | 1.5 | 3 700.0 | −502.1 |

*列组说明：美国—中国内地（美国出口：金〔国内、国外〕、银〔国内、国外〕、总；美国进口：金、银、合计）；美国—香港地区（美国出口：金〔国内、国外〕、银〔国内、国外〕、总；美国进口：金、银、合计）；美国对华净出口（负值为美国净进口：银、金）。*

注:1913—1917年为财年统计数据(以6月30日为结束日),1918年起为历年统计数据。

　　1916年,由于白银价格上涨,中国将其储备的一大笔超量白银以当时相当合算的价格售予印度和俄罗斯。然而,1917年,中国发现自己必须从美国市场补充自己的白银储备,并在那里多次大量购买白银。据说,中国对白银的这一新需求应为1917年下半年白银价格的进一步攀升负责。

　　由于美国向中国和其他东方国家大量购买原材料,必须支付大量的贵金属。但是,美国这个时候正在全力维持其黄金储备,因此不愿意用黄金支付。最终,美国有了一个好主意,即用美国国库储备的保证待付银元券安全的银元向中国支付。这一提议得到了通常称之为《皮特曼支付法案》的支持。该法案由威尔逊总统于1918年4月25日签署,简单地说,就是授权美国财政部长①可以熔化、售卖当时由财政部掌控的不超过3.5亿标准银币的白银,且每盎司获利不得低于1.00美元。截至1919年5月6日,共有2.6亿银元以此法案被熔化,并用于对外贸易。1918—1920年间,美国国内向中国内地出口白银价值11 739.8万美元,向香港出口3 952.8万美元。除了国内出口,这两年美国还从海外向中国内地出口白银3 700万美元,向香港出口782.5万美元。

　　白银价格随着时间的推移持续走高,美国与中国及其他东方国家之间的货币兑换关系、贸易关系受到了严重的影响。1919年,1两海关银元可以兑换1.39美元,汇率比1915年的两倍还要高。为了纠正这一状况,美国财政部和联邦储备委员会于1919年12月商定,将国库中的"自由"银元(即未用于银元券安全保证的银元)交由联邦储备委员会外汇局管理,用于调整美国与银本币国家特别是中国之间的汇率,具体实施由纽约联邦储备银行及美国银行在东方的分支机构完成。按照这一安排,约有1 300万美元的白银在1920年的前几个月间运往上海。此后几个月内,白银价格突然下跌,使得继续转运不再必要。

　　在战争期间及战后之际,美国不仅向中国运送了很多白银,也运送了大量的黄金。1919—1920年间,美国的白银供给非常吃紧,就向中国内地、香港分别运送价值670万美元和716万美元的黄金。但是,当白银供应改善、价格几乎下降到战前水平时,这些黄金中的一部分又于1920、1921年运回美国。

---

　　① 时任美国财政部部长小威廉·吉布斯·麦卡杜(William Gibbs McAdoo, Jr.,1863.10.31—1941.2.1),任职时间1913.3.6—1918.12.15。

# 第二篇

## 中国输美商品举要

# 第六章 茶 叶

## 一、中美茶叶贸易简史

### 1. 美中茶叶贸易的早期历史

茶叶在西方的早期历史与中国早期的对外贸易紧密相关。中国茶叶很可能最早由英国运达美国。自1711年开始,英属东印度公司实际上垄断着中美之间的茶叶贸易,从中获取了丰厚的收益。尽管现在无法准确地确定那一时期美洲殖民地进口的茶叶数量,但可以肯定的是,茶叶在这一地区的进口总额中占据了相当可观的份额。

相当有趣的是,早期的美国茶叶贸易与美国独立战争、美国建国有关。茶叶可以说是一种秉性极为平和的商品,但它却引发了几场战争和一系列政治问题。正是针对中国茶叶的三便士税[①],导致英属殖民地居民发动反对其母国的革命,并建立了美国;也正是茶叶,从所有商品中脱颖而出,成为强调"人人生而自由、平等"、"无代表、不纳税"原则的象征。回顾美国长期历史时,怎么可能会疏于关注带有美式幽默称呼的"1773波士顿茶党事件"呢?

恢复和平之后,美国、中国间的第一宗直接交易与茶叶有关[②]。1784年,美国商船"中国皇后号"被派往中国,次年返航时运回满满一船茶叶,赚取了相当可观的利润[③]。从那时开始,美国大力建造雨燕船以开展茶叶贸易,雨燕船是第一种公认为"快船"的轮船,输送能力有所下降,但速度得到了提升,从而使整个来回行程的航行时间平均减少二三十天。18世纪后十年,美国年均进口茶叶260万磅,其中的一小部分——通常不足5%——间接地经由英国进口。美国进口的茶叶仅仅够国内消费,只有很少的一部分重新出口。

随着美国商船业越来越发达,尤其活跃于中国水面[④],茶叶贸易量也随之增长。

---

① 译注:1773年,英国当局颁布茶叶税法,对美洲殖民地进口茶叶征税(一磅茶3便士),但免去东印度公司向殖民地销售茶叶的关税,同时禁止殖民地买卖走私茶。结果引发了著名的波士顿倾茶事件。

② 前见第一章。

③ 前见第一章。

④ 前见第一章。

1800—1810 年,美国每年进口茶叶约 540 万磅,比前十年间的两倍还要多。然而,美国轮船上的中国茶叶并不仅仅供应美国国内市场,其中很大一部分还要运往其他国家,或者从中国直接运送,或者从美国重新出口。拿破仑战争[1]期间,茶叶重新出口的比例很大,通常占到当年美国进口茶叶的 1/3。

1812 年英美战争使中国对美茶叶贸易严重下滑。但是战争结束后,这一贸易迅速恢复,茶叶一度成了美国进口的最重要的中国商品。早期茶叶贸易总额在美国对华进口总额中的份额(五年一期)列于表 6-1。可以看出,1814 年起,该份额持续增长,至 1840 年已达 82.0%;此后,缓慢下滑,二十年之后变为 65.5%。

表 6-1 1821—1960 年茶叶贸易在美国对华进口总额中的比例

| 年　　度 | 1821 | 1825 | 1830 | 1835 | 1840 | 1845 | 1850 | 1855 | 1860 |
|---|---|---|---|---|---|---|---|---|---|
| 比例(%) | 42.5 | 49.5 | 62.5 | 75.5 | 82.0 | 79.0 | 71.5 | 70.0 | 65.5 |

这一时期,美国茶叶进口的绝对数量非常稳定地增长,从 1821 年的 500 磅,增长为 1830 年的 900 万磅、1840 年的 2 000 万磅、1850 年的 3 000 万磅、1860 年的 2 600 万磅;但美国的人均茶叶消费量并没有明显增加。

19 世纪初期之后,美国茶商与英属东印度公司展开了激烈的竞争。英属东印度公司不仅失去了其在整个 18 世纪牢牢把持的茶叶贸易垄断地位,甚至其生存也受到了威胁,因为英国议会对该公司竞争失利非常不满。为此,英国议员 R. M. 马丁(Robert M. Martin)向议会提出了一份详细报告[2],为该公司辩护(以延续其贸易垄断地位)。然而,这一举措收效甚微,东印度公司的营业执照于 1833 年到期后未予换发。

美国茶商击败英国竞争对手可以说与英美两国迥异的政策有关,英国给茶叶贸易课以重税从而阻碍了贸易扩张,美国则几乎免除了所有的茶叶税收,这在 1832 年开始就成为事实[3]。

**2. 日本竞争的开始**

1856 年前,中国茶叶在美国及世界其他国家是独一无二的。但自 1856 年开始,

---

① 译注:拿破仑执政(1799—1804)和拿破仑一世帝国(1804—1814,1815)时期,法国资产阶级为了在欧洲建立法国的政治和经济霸权,同英国争夺贸易和殖民地的领先地位,以及兼并新的领土而发生战争。

② 译注:1830 年,东印度公司董事马丁,在他呈送给阁僚和上下两院议员的《英国与中华帝国关系》(British Relations with the Chinese Empire)中声称:只要中国广东贸易制度存在,那么东印度公司的垄断就是必需的。

③ 译注:1832 年 7 月,美国总统杰克逊签署《分类保护税则》,更改了 1828 年的保护关税法案,对南方作了某些妥协。次年 1 月,杰克逊要求国会授权在南卡罗来纳州执行关税法。同年 3 月,在他第二任正式就职的前两天,又签署了两项法令:一项是必要时可以使用陆军、海军强行收税,这就是所谓的"武力法令";另一项是亨利·克莱提出的分十年逐步减税的妥协税法。

中国茶叶的垄断地位被逐步打破,其优势受到挑战,并完全崩溃。所以,对笔者来说,回顾中国在美国茶叶市场上的失败历史是可悲的,首先是日本,接着是印度,最近则与爪哇有一定关联。然而,1856年之后中国对美茶叶贸易的失利仅仅是中日竞争中失败之一例而已。

1856年,一小批量日本茶叶,"约50半箱①",首次到达美国。由于日本茶叶"更加纯净、没有色料",因此很快在消费者中非常流行,这些消费者中的大部分对中国绿茶抱有偏见,认为中国茶叶多少有点人工着色。美国人对日本茶叶的需求稳定提升,次年进口400半箱,1859年则达1 100半箱。1860年左右,日本人改变了其茶叶烘焙方式,采用中国绿茶的烘焙方法,结果日本茶叶的颜色由深绿变为品绿,加入了高度麦芽风味。从那时起,日本茶叶在美国愈加风靡,这并不是因为日本茶在某些方面比中国茶更好,而仅仅是因为他们以这种方式满足美国人的喜好并控制了美国市场。日本茶叶在英国和其他欧洲国家没有找到合适的市场,因为那里当时仍然偏爱中国茶。

日本茶叶贸易的开端似乎是无关紧要的,然而,日本茶叶战胜中国的最终根源在于日本人竭尽全力使其产品满足美国人喜好这一铁的事实。"在销售市场上,买主是关键",卖家必须遵从他的选择。但中国人总是固守其旧有规则,对此似乎不以为意。中国茶叶败于此,丝绸贸易也是如此。现在无法获知1865年之前美国从日本进口茶叶的统计数据,但1865年以后的统计数据可以从美国统计局获取。从表6-2中可以看出,19世纪末期前,中日两国共同垄断了美国茶叶市场。尽管从这两个国家直接进口的茶叶通常占到美国进口茶叶总量的95%,但还是有一些中国茶叶继续经由英国间接进入美国,另外,印度和斯里兰卡的茶叶占很少的一部分,通常不足1%。表6-2揭示了19世纪最后三十年间中国、日本茶叶在美国进口市场上的此消彼长态势。

表6-2　1865—1894年美国茶叶进口来源统计

| 年份 | 美国年均进口茶叶总量(万磅) | 从中国进口 | | 从日本进口 | |
|------|------------------------|----------|--------|----------|--------|
| | | 进口量(万磅) | 占比(%) | 进口量(万磅) | 占比(%) |
| 1865—1869 | 3 478.9 | 2 667.4 | 77 | 667.4 | 19 |
| 1870—1874 | 5 664.2 | 3 799.7 | 67 | 1 412.0 | 25 |
| 1875—1879 | 6 233.0 | 2 981.0 | 48 | 2 543.3 | 41 |
| 1880—1884 | 7 478.4 | 3 892.7 | 52 | 3 407.6 | 46 |
| 1885—1889 | 8 160.6 | 4 107.8 | 50 | 3 569.2 | 43 |
| 1890—1894 | 8 800.0 | 4 515.5 | 51 | 3 833.5 | 44 |

① 译注:半箱为日本计量单位,1半箱=50磅。

在 1865—1894 年的三十年间，美国国土面积扩大、人口增长，茶叶进口量增加 2 倍之多，中国、日本茶叶的进口数量都在增加。然而，日本茶叶的份额越来越大，而中国则难挽颓势。在前五年，即 1865—1869 年，日本茶叶的份额不足 1/5，而中国则超过 3/4。仅仅十年之后，日本茶叶的份额超过 1/3，而后者则降至一半以下。1880 年之后，尽管中国茶叶受到了日本茶叶的激烈竞争，但所占份额保持了稳定。由于类似竞争，中国生丝对美出口下滑；这两类贸易的衰退就解释了为什么美国从中国的进口在其对华贸易史的第二个时期并没有任何明显的增长。

### 3. 中国对美茶叶贸易的衰退

中国对美茶叶贸易的下降可以回溯至三十年前。1895 年，美国从中国直接进口的茶叶达到最高的 5 500 万磅。从那时起，茶叶贸易持续严重下滑，中国似乎可能永远失去这一有利可图的贸易。其灾难性的下滑态势通过其五年一期的平均数字来体现。1895—1899 年，美国从中国进口茶叶 4 800 万磅，1900—1904 年下降为 4 700 万磅，接着先后下滑至 1905—1909 年的 3 400 万磅和 1910—1914 年的 2 300 万磅；甚至在欧洲战争爆发之后，来自中国的其他进口都受到刺激而增加，但 1915—1919 年的茶叶进口量却仍然下降到只有 1 900 万磅，1920 年为 1 100 万磅，1921 年略有回升。中国茶叶在同期美国茶叶进口总量中所占的比例分别是 54%（1885—1889 年）、49%（1900—1904 年）、35%（1905—1909 年）、24%（1910—1914 年）、17.5%（1915—1919 年）和 11.8%（1920 年）。至于中国在美国茶叶市场败落的原因，将在本章后文予以简单叙述。

**表 6-3　1895—1922 年美国茶叶进口来源统计**

进口量:万磅;占比:%

| 年份 | 美国茶叶进口总量 | 中国 | | 日本 | | 英国 | | 英属东印度 | | 荷属东印度 | | 加拿大 | |
|---|---|---|---|---|---|---|---|---|---|---|---|---|---|
| | | 进口量 | 占比 | 进口量 | 占比 | 进口量 | 占比 | 进口量 | 占比 | 进口量 | 占比 | 进口量 | 占比 |
| 1895—1899 | 8 962.9 | 4 331.0 | 54.0 | 3 503.7 | 39.0 | 348.9 | 4.0 | 164.7 | 2.0 | 0.0 | 0.0 | 142.9 | 1.0 |
| 1900—1904 | 9 434.2 | 4 656.0 | 49.6 | 3 622.2 | 38.5 | 438.0 | 4.6 | 495.3 | 5.3 | 0.1 | 0.0 | 173.5 | 2.0 |
| 1905—1909 | 9 835.3 | 3 427.3 | 35.0 | 4 308.4 | 44.0 | 956.8 | 9.7 | 773.4 | 7.9 | 0.5 | 0.0 | 271.2 | 3.0 |
| 1910—1914 | 9 512.6 | 2 293.4 | 24.1 | 4 624.6 | 48.7 | 1 159.5 | 12.2 | 1 031.9 | 10.9 | 16.2 | 0.1 | 278.8 | 2.9 |
| 1915—1919 | 1 0842.9 | 1 899.5 | 17.5 | 4 831.7 | 44.5 | 935.0 | 8.6 | 1 982.2 | 18.3 | 847.6 | 7.8 | 267.6 | 2.8 |
| 1920 | 9 024.7 | 1 062.5 | 11.8 | 2 975.0 | 32.9 | 1 390.0 | 15.4 | 2 468.6 | 27.4 | 669.6 | 7.4 | 164.5 | 1.8 |
| 1921 | 7 648.7 | 1 467.6 | 19.2 | 2 140.7 | 28.0 | 920.6 | 12.0 | 2 301.2 | 30.1 | 530.2 | 7.0 | 75.6 | 1.0 |
| 1922 | 9 709.7 | 1 464.9 | 15.0 | 3 638.8 | 37.4 | 1 453.4 | 15.0 | 2 003.1 | 20.6 | 716.6 | 7.4 | 67.4 | 0.7 |

注：中国茶叶之进口量、及所占比例关系不符。结合本表其他国家（地区）相应数值及原文第 129 页第 1 行之表述，推算该值应为 4 850 万磅左右。

中美茶叶贸易毁灭性下滑的原因主要有两个。第一个原因可以称之为内因,即中国茶叶的加工方法效率低下,质量没有提升;第二个原因可称为外因,即来自远东的几乎所有的中国近邻——首先是日本,接着是印度、斯里兰卡、爪哇,最后甚至包括原属中国的台湾地区——的强大竞争。这两个原因可以非常恰当地区分开来,但它们的合力却形成一个结果,即其他国家在茶叶种植、加工方面的进步超越了中国,使得美国人、欧洲人开始不再中意曾经非常满意的中国茶叶。

## 二、茶叶贸易下滑的原因——外部的激烈竞争

### 1. 日本竞争

尽管在欧洲茶叶市场上,东印度公司、中国都还没有强烈地感知到日本的竞争,但在美国市场上,却主要是日本茶叶侵蚀了中国茶叶的市场并几乎将之摧毁。欧洲战争后,这一局面有所改变,因为最近日本茶叶受到了英属东印度公司、荷属东印度公司的激烈竞争。1895—1914 年的二十年间,中国茶叶在美国进口市场上的份额下降了 30 个百分点(54.0%～24.1%),其中的 1/3 被日本所获取(39.0%～48.7%,9.7 个百分点)。

为了说明日本的这一胜利,笔者已经提请读者注意这样的事实:日本能够使其产品适合美国人的喜好。美国人想要的是大规模营销所需的大批量质量均匀的茶叶,这也正是日本试图供应的产品。下面是一名日本茶商有关日本人试图征服美国茶叶市场的描述。

在日本,机器较早地被引入茶叶加工,在很多县,机器作业很快代替了以往的手工作业。早在 1885 年,扎晃县的一个制造业主就采用了蒸青和炒干机器。随着劳动力越来越昂贵,机器运用更加普遍,产品也更加适合美国市场。机器的运用使茶叶的生产成本显著下降,进一步帮助日本在与中国竞争美国茶叶市场时取得胜利。据静冈茶叶制造商联合会的一份报告,目前手工茶的生产成本是每贯[①] 1.00～1.20 日元(50～60 美分)[②],而机制茶则仅为 35～45 钱(17.5～22.5 美分)。

日本茶叶制造业者认识到联合和合作的优势,长期坚持将其茶叶种植和制作从家庭作业转向大规模生产。1876 年起,一些公司建立起来了,其运营的直接目的就是最终完成茶叶出口。茶叶栽培者和小型个体制造业者建立了一套合作联盟体系,以降低生产成本,从而维系其国外市场,同时也希望引导统一生产、统一包装和统一表面加工的大批量茶叶生产。日本政府、地方当局和制造业者协会积极参与促进茶叶产业的发展,在这方面,建立了一套监管和保护体系。茶叶制造业者协会的职责是:在日本政府

---

① 译注:日本重量单位,1 贯(Kwan、kwamme)=3.75 公斤,即 8.267 磅。

② 译注:日本货币单位,1 日元(yen)=100 钱(sen)。

的指导下,防止制造、销售次品茶和掺假茶,提高和统一茶叶的包装和脱水干燥,对成员公司的茶叶产品进行强制检查。这些协会的代表被派往美国等地,以促进和保卫他们的海外利益。在日本重要的茶叶港口设有检查室,以防止可能会遭到美国及其他地方拒绝的次品茶、掺假茶和着色茶的出口。实验工厂和实验室也在茶叶生产中心建立起来。日本绿茶在美国市场的宣传工作也由这些协会承担。

考虑到日本试图促进其茶叶在海外市场销售的这些举措,日本在美国茶叶进口市场上占据一个还说得过去的份额有什么可以惊奇的呢? 事实上,日本所有促进茶叶出口的努力都直指美国市场,因为日本出口的绝大部分茶叶,通常是 90% 以上,都流向了美国。

### 2. 英属东印度群岛的竞争

除了日本之外,中国在对美茶叶贸易中还受到了东印度的竞争。半个世纪之前,茶叶工业和茶叶贸易在印度几乎不为人所知。但自那时起,茶叶迅速成为印度商业领域的一种物资,特别在英国市场。仅仅在三十年前,美国进口的印度茶叶还非常少,但中国茶叶已经感受到了其竞争。瓦尔士 (J. M. Walsh)(美国学者)先生在其论文《茶叶:历史及其秘诀》①中饶有兴趣地描述了印度茶和中国茶在美国市场竞争过程中的差异:

"印度茶的发酵和烧炒过程不像中国茶那么仔细、全面,印度种植业者的目的在于确保浓茶的成分性质,但对茶叶的口味和质量有损害。印度茶叶要普遍饮用还存在许多严重的不足,其中之一是丹宁(丹宁酸)含量太高,高达 14%～18%,这种茶叶口感苦涩,影响肠功能,墨黑色的茶叶能使水中含有铁盐。英国的医药权威为了反对饮用印度茶叶,发起了一场改革运动。相反,中国茶叶很少或根本没有丹宁酸(或其他破坏敏感的味觉或成分的元素)的痕迹;它们对那些最敏感的人来说也是适合和清爽的。"

由于印度茶叶质量低下,那时美国市场对其需求相当有限,按照瓦尔士先生的看法,似乎也看不出在未来会有什么增长希望。尽管英国茶商费尽心机,欲将之引入美国,但收效甚微。瓦尔士先生说:"(印度茶)煮熬后的形体、颜色、口感和香味等,与美国人已经习惯的中国茶、日本茶完全不同;因此,尽管印度茶叶到处布局,但很少或没有什么进步。"

然而,可以看出,这一预言被三十年的发展所逐步打破。19 世纪末,美国每年从英属东印度群岛进口的茶叶仅占美国茶叶进口总量的 2%,但 20 世纪初开始,这一比

---

① 译注:世界上大多数语言中有关"茶"的读音都源于中国,而世界上绝大多数的植物和历史学家,也都认同"茶发源于中国"这一观点。美国植物学家瓦尔士(J. M. Walsh),于 1892 年在其《茶的历史及其秘诀》中,也表述了相同的观点。在欧洲,最早确认这一点的是瑞典植物学家卡尔·冯·林内(Carl Von Linne),在其 1753 年出版的《植物种志》中,将茶树定名为"Tea Sinensis, L.",后来又改定为"Camellia Sinensis, L.",而"Sinensis"即为拉丁语"中国"之意。

例跳跃式提高,到 1920 年达到 27.4%,是中国茶叶所占份额的 2.5 倍,略低于日本茶叶。如果注意到美国从英国进口的茶叶现在几乎全都是印度茶叶这一事实,印度茶的实际份额必将大大提高。印度茶叶不仅把中国茶、也把日本茶驱离了美国市场。印度茶成功代替其他茶叶,很大程度上归因于英国茶商在美国市场上的积极销售方法。但是,美国人的味觉,如同数十年前他们的英国兄弟一样,开始逐步习惯于印度茶的浓烈。

### 3. 荷属东印度群岛的竞争

美国进口爪哇茶叶可以说始于 1905 年,当年有 8 000 磅茶叶运抵美国,但爪哇与美国间的直接贸易在 1918 年前都不重要。首次茶叶进口之后,直到 1911 年才有所提高,当年价值 3.6 万美元的 22.8 万磅爪哇茶叶运达美国。但在 1918 年,由于美国的战争需要,来自爪哇的茶叶进口大幅增长,飙升到 3 000 万磅,价值 561.5 万美元;同年,美国进口的中国茶叶仅有 2 100 万磅,价值 436.2 万美元,而爪哇茶要比其多出将近 1/3。战后,美国对爪哇茶叶的需求下降。尽管如此,爪哇茶叶已经在美国市场确立了自己的地位,其市场份额不会退回到战前无足轻重的状态,这一持久的提升对中国茶叶造成了损害。

据说,美国消费的荷属东印度的大量茶叶,是在选港提单的运送中购买,或在伦敦公开拍卖中成交。但是,荷兰的茶叶种植业者,对这样的非直接销售并不满意,正努力发展与美国的直接贸易。

## 三、茶叶贸易下滑的原因——中国茶叶自身因素

尽管美国茶叶市场上各方竞争非常激烈,但中国茶叶却并非因此被逐出美国市场;事实上是中国茶叶自身的几个原因,摧毁了曾经繁荣的市场。

### 1. 中国茶叶的栽培方法效率欠佳

中国茶叶种植的一般环境与印度、斯里兰卡和爪哇完全相反。在后几个地方,所有的茶叶实际上都生长在大农场。农场系统具有大批量生产质量统一的茶叶的优势,可以满足美国大规模交易的需求。而在中国,所有的茶都生长在只有几亩地大小的农户里;中国的茶期要比热带地区短,一年只有三四个月的采摘期。

### 2. 加工效率低下

日本、印度运用机器加工茶叶已有很长时间,而中国还在依靠手工方式,只有很少几台设备投入使用。中国人也多次尝试引入更好的加工方法,但没有取得明显的成功。关于机器的使用,中国的工业环境——特别是时令短及农户所有权使得运用昂贵设备的经济可行性成为疑问。1899 年,曾在一个茶叶中心尝试使用机器进行揉捻作业,但"收集足够数量的新鲜茶叶很困难"。

### 3. 茶叶掺假

可能没有什么能比不时发生的掺假行为更能毁坏中国茶叶在外国市场的形象了。甚至早在 1888 年，美国驻华公使①向美国政府报告中美茶叶贸易下滑的原因时，就提到"虚假样品、过大包装、茶叶掺杂、其他有害物质"②。

1899 年，美国采取了防止掺假茶叶进口的规程，并强制执行③。这些规则对于提高中国外销绿茶的质量具有决定性的作用。但是，绿茶的洁面或人工着色长期以来是中国茶叶工业的一个特点，在专供出口的茶叶加工中使用已有十年之久，其中着色最甚的品种至今仍出口至美国市场④。显然地，因为着色茶在土耳其和埃及找到另外市场，中国在适应（美国规则）这一新状况方面无所作为。然而，日本政府立即发布了一项禁止茶叶洁面的法令。

### 4. 茶叶出口重税

过去半个世纪里，中国政府对茶叶征收的出口重税妨碍了茶叶贸易，使其在与其他国家茶叶的竞争中难以获胜。

茶叶出口税最初在 1842 年《南京条约》中确定⑤，又被 1858 年《天津条约》所重申⑥，即每担（133.33 磅）2.5 两白银，相当于以 5% 按值计税。然而，茶叶价格从来没有达到每担 50 两银元这样高的数字，而每担 2.5 两银这样的出口税率被长期执行。后来，茶叶价格的下降使得出口税率由 5% 变成 40%。除了这一极端的出口税，中国政府还征收一种内地税——称之为厘金或战争税，加上其他小的壁垒性苛税，总的关税达到每担约 4.5 两海关银元。

与中国不同，印度、斯里兰卡、爪哇和日本都实行茶叶出口免税，因此中国茶叶被驱离世界市场也就不足为奇了。

### 5. 中国茶叶缺乏茶叶宣传

通常都认为，中国茶叶未能在美国及其他国家保住市场份额，很大程度上是由于广告的完全缺失。从最早到现在，我们都听到许多茶叶行家、出口商说，最好的茶叶仍然产自中国。此处只举一个例子，是笔者摘自美国人 J. M. 瓦尔士关于茶叶的论述：

---

① 译注：即田贝（Charles Denby），1885 年 5 月 29 日至 1898 年 7 月 8 日期间任美国驻清公使，1888 年到台湾观察洋务运动，认为台湾是大清帝国最进步的一省。

② Denby 在报告中引用。德国人 Paul Kransel 曾就中国茶叶掺假的方法做过描述，此处从略。

③ 规程有这样令人忍俊不禁的文字："被美国核查人员拒绝进入美国并返运至上海的寄售茶叶，在原有条件下重新装船，允许进口。"

④ S. E. Chanler 和 John McEwan 也提到过茶叶着色过程中使用过的几种物质，如石膏、普鲁士蓝、靛蓝和石墨。

⑤《南京条约》第 10 款。

⑥《天津条约》第 20 款。

"中国茶叶是唯一真正的茶叶。在构成和区分茶叶的特性和品质方面胜过其他所有国家的茶叶,拥有某些与众不同的、罕见的特点……印度茶叶含有大量的丹宁酸,长期饮用有害于健康,而中国茶几乎不含丹宁酸或根本没有丹宁酸的痕迹。与中国茶叶相比,印度和斯里兰卡茶叶主要的、唯一的优势据说是茶叶在水杯中的浓度更高,这主要是由于采用了发酵、蒸青或机械杀青等现代方法。中国茶叶在口味、香味方面更胜一筹,在与其他国家茶叶的竞争中占据着类似法国葡萄酒那样的地位。两者之间也有这样的差异,等量的印度和斯里兰卡茶叶,能比中国茶叶冲泡出更多的色深、味浓的茶汤,但不够高贵、精致。"

关于中国茶叶具有诸多优点的说法可能并没有违背事实真相,如同一位美国领事多年前所宣称的那样。一名英国的茶叶出口商同样承认,在质量方面,中国茶叶仍然是最好的。

尽管中国茶叶具有良好的广告卖点,但中国茶商似乎完全疏于在美国或其他国家进行任何广告活动。结果,许多美国人未能注意到中国茶叶的优良品质;又由于从中国进口的茶叶质量非常差,美国人以为中国没有什么好茶。关于这一点,中国海关总税务司的一个英国人[①]——有如下中肯的评论:"世界上最好的茶叶仍然产自中国,但不幸的是,被外国出口商带来的大量茶叶只能称之为垃圾。"

广告是现代商业的鲜血,无论何处的商业活动,只要有竞争元素,就需自由地借助于广告。"所谓印度、斯里兰卡茶叶更受欧洲、美国消费者欢迎,很大程度上是由于广告推动贸易的精神和坚持,茶叶被实实在在地强力推向市场。"[②]

此外,一般都会断定,使用机器加工茶叶会使其品质下降,所以日本政府不止一次努力阻止机器的使用。但是,日本的用工成本快速上升,而机械加工的成本要比手工制茶下降约 1/3,因此这一努力无法奏效。

过去六十年间,中国茶叶在美国市场上逐步被其他国家的茶叶所替代,除了上述这些基本原因外,还必须加上近期限制中美茶叶贸易的两个临时性原因:美国对中国茶叶进口强加临时性禁止和限制政策,世界大战期间及结束之际跨太平洋航运的吨位不足;这两个因素导致美国从中国进口的茶叶在 1917—1920 年严重下降。但是,这些因素消除后,尽管 1921、1922 年茶叶价格下降使得进口额波动较大,但进口数量在增长。

这些外部、内部因素共同作用,使得中国对美茶叶贸易的份额从六十年前的100% 下降到 1920 年的不足 12%。这一严重下滑引起中国人的长期关注,并评估如何消除内部原因。所以,当美国 1899 年采用规程以防止掺假茶叶进口时,中国茶商就

---

① 译注:英国人赫德(Robert Hart,1835—1911)于 1861—1908 年间,负责清政府"总司海关税务之事",全权负责管理海关事务,掌握中国海关实际管理权达半个世纪之久。

② 引自前述 J. M. 瓦尔士先生之文。

茶叶出口税问题向本国政府强烈呼吁;1902 年中国茶叶出口税下降一半至每担 1.25 两海关银元,因此向美国出口茶叶的费用没有随着数量的提高而增加。1905 年,中国的一个茶业考察团①访问印度、斯里兰卡的茶区,目的在于将印度种植体系引入中国。英国机器已经多次被引入中国,但这些努力至今尚未取得持续的好处。最近,中国政府命令在汉口、福州、上海及其他茶叶生产、出口中心设置茶叶调查局,并采取其他步骤以改进旧式的种植方法。中国政府和茶商已经给予茶叶贸易更多的关注,未来,中国茶叶在与其他国家的竞争中将会处于较为坚挺的地位。虽然如此,中国何时——如果有这一天的话——能够恢复其在美国茶叶贸易中原有的声望和优势是有疑问的,美国现在对中国茶叶的消费非常少;过去十年,中美茶叶贸易在中国茶叶出口中所占的份额不足 1/5,部分年份甚至只有 14.7%。

---

　　① 译注:1905 年,清政府南洋大臣、两江总督周馥派遣郑世璜等人赴印度、锡兰(即今之斯里兰卡)考察茶叶产制,这是中国最早出国的茶业考察团。考察团回国时购得部分制茶机械,宣传机械制茶方法和先进产制技术。回国后写出《考察锡兰、印度茶务并烟土税则清折》、《改良内地茶业简易办法》等禀文,结集为《乙己考察印、锡茶土日记》一书。

# 第七章 丝绸

中国向美国售卖的丝绸正在遭受激烈的竞争,但它仍然是中美贸易中最为重要的单一物资。最近数年间,美国每年从中国进口的生丝、绢丝的价值在美国对华进口总额的平均份额高达 40％[1]。

然而,中美丝绸贸易史,在许多方面与中美茶叶贸易史相似,是一段与日本(一定程度上还有欧洲)进行竞争、最终屈辱败落的历史。然而,丝绸贸易与茶叶贸易之间至少还有一个重大不同。在茶叶工业领域,中国已经失去了相对于其他国家的比较优势,因为后者已经在茶叶加工过程中引入了机器,而中国在使用机器方面并不处于有利的地位[2]、或者至少未来在这方面也不会比其竞争者处于更有利的地位;所以,尽管中国的茶叶工业不断进步,并积极推进茶叶贸易,但中国不可能完全恢复已经失去的市场份额。但丝绸业却非如此。养蚕需要大量的劳动力,而且由于这一产业的自然属性,无论规模多大,都不能引入机器,即便将来也未必可行。因此,养蚕依赖大量的廉价劳动力,这是蚕丝业在竞争性市场取胜的第一要素。毋庸置疑,中国在这方面比其他丝绸生产国处于更有利的地位。尽管中国过去对促进这一产业有所忽视,在将其丝绸贸易推向美国这样的丝绸消费大国方面较为松懈,但在丝绸的生产方面仍然保持着比较优势。如果中国像现在正在做的一样,继续对丝绸给予较多的关注,用不了多久她将恢复在丝绸贸易市场上曾经有过的辉煌地位。在下文中,笔者试图揭示中国如何在美国这个世界最大的丝绸市场上折戟沉沙,以及中国为夺回部分市场——至少在美国失去的份额——而正在进行的努力。

## 一、中美丝绸贸易的早期阶段

作为丝绸的原产地,中国向西方国家出口丝绸已经有几个世纪了。尽管无法通过现存的贸易记录来确定中国丝绸最早何时运往美国,但无疑在殖民时代就已经有一些中国丝绸到达美国。中美直接贸易之初,美国进口丝绸的数量与金额很少在早期美国政府和作家的资料中明确提及,这一点与茶叶有所不同。通过一些零星记录,可以清

---

① 1919 年,美国进口的中国丝绸类产品占美国进口总额的 39％;1920 年是 34％,1921 年是 52％。见后表。
② 前见第六章。

楚地知道,丝绸是早期贸易中除茶叶之外最重要的物资,当然丝绸进口的数量与价值均不及茶叶。随着时间的推移,丝绸贸易的地位日益重要;1820 年之后的几年间,美国每年进口的中国丝绸达数百万美元,贸易额多次超过当年美国对华进口总额的 40%。

## 二、丝织品贸易的下降

19 世纪上半叶,美国进口的所有丝绸几乎都是制成品——布匹、刺绣、花边等,很少进口生丝,因为美国的丝绸加工产业还没有成形。1873 年前,美国的丝绸需求实际上都通过进口外国制成品来满足,且这一需求在稳定增长,见表 7-1。不过,1883 年之后,美国丝绸产业发展良好,对外国绸缎的需求保持平稳。

表 7-1　1823—1913 年美国丝绸制品进口统计

| 年份 | 美国丝绸进口总额(万美元) | 从中国进口 | | 年份 | 美国丝绸进口总额(万美元) | 从中国进口 | |
| --- | --- | --- | --- | --- | --- | --- | --- |
| | | 进口额(万美元) | 占比(%) | | | 进口额(万美元) | 占比(%) |
| 1823 | 520.1 | 312.2 | 60.0 | 1873 | 2 912.6 | 13.0 | 0.5 |
| 1833 | 791.3 | 138.7 | 17.0 | 1883 | 3 396.7 | 35.0 | 1.0 |
| 1843 | 245.8 | | | 1893 | 3 895.9 | 36.2 | 1.0 |
| 1853 | 2 983.4 | 122.0 | 4.1 | 1903 | 3 399.5 | 26.9 | 0.8 |
| 1863 | 1 265.6 | 0.97 | 0.1 | 1913 | 3 530.8 | 17.3 | 0.5 |

19 世纪前七八十年间,美国对外国丝绸的需求快速增长,但中国丝绸所占的份额却显著下降。1823 年,中国绸缎占美国进口丝绸的 60% 左右,但在随后的四十年间,这一比例掉头下降为 1833 年的 17%、1853 年的 4.1% 和 1863 年的 0.1%,此后一直到欧洲战争爆发,都徘徊在 1% 左右。

中国丝绸份额下降的原因不难查找。第一,中国丝绸的生产并非出于出口目的,没有刻意去迎合西方人的品位和喜好,因此美国人更喜欢英国、法国的丝绸产品;第二,通过半个世纪的发展,美国已经成为全世界最大的丝绸制造国,现在完全能够自给自足;第三,自 19 世纪中期开始,美国对丝绸制品征收的保护关税几乎是禁止性的,中国丝绸无法承受这一重负,因此首先被逐出美国市场。

1914 年之后,丝制品贸易的情况没有发生变化。表 7-2 表示了 1913 年之后中国丝绸在美国丝织品进口中的份额。近年来,美国对华丝织品进口总额似乎是增长的,

表 7 - 2　1913—1922 年美国丝织品进口统计

| 年份 | 美国丝织品进口总额（万美元） | 从中国进口 | | 年份 | 美国丝织品进口总额（万美元） | 从中国进口 | |
|---|---|---|---|---|---|---|---|
| | | 进口额（万美元） | 占比（%） | | | 进口额（万美元） | 占比（%） |
| 1913 | 3 530.8 | 17.3 | 0.5 | 1920 | 7 532.8 | 148.5 | 1.6 |
| 1915 | 2 858.0 | 70.4 | 2.5 | 1921 | 4 824.9 | 172.5 | 3.6 |
| 1917 | 3 971.8 | 192.1 | 4.8 | 1922 | 3 673.2 | 158.7 | 4.3 |
| 1919 | 5 470.1 | 69.0 | 1.3 | | | | |

　　但是这一名义增长完全是由于物价膨胀,剔除价格因素后的进口量实际上可能是下降的。但是,由于法国、德国、英国、意大利等欧洲国家不能向美国市场供应丝织品,美国人自然将目光转向能满足其日常需求的东方市场,所以,中国收复了其原有份额中的一小部分;欧洲蚕丝业回归正常状态后,中国是否还能保住这一少得可怜的份额就非常令人怀疑。但是,只要前述三个原因继续存在,可以预期中美之间的丝织品贸易不大可能大幅增加。

## 三、生丝贸易的扩张

　　中美丝织品贸易下滑的同时,生丝贸易却反其道而行之,稳步扩大。19 世纪前七十年间,美国很少从国外购买生丝,进口数量如此之少以至于美国统计局甚至没有予以专门记录。但是,可以得到 1850 年之后的单独统计,五年一期的平均数据见表 7 - 3。美国进口的丝织品很大一部分直接来自中国,其余部分来自英国和法国。然而,1865 年之后,由于美国丝织产业的快速发展,对外国生丝的进口自然迅猛增长。事实上,美国多次试图养蚕,但均由于生产成本高昂而失败。美国蚕丝业的发展必然会对外国生丝产生更多的需求;在 1865—1784 年的二十年间,美国生丝进口增长超过 10 倍[①]。总体上来说,美国进口的中国生丝从绝对数量和金额上都是增长的,但其相对份额在大于 50～13% 之间剧烈波动。表 7 - 4 总结了这二十年间(1865—1884 年)美国生丝进口贸易的总体状况。

　　中国在美国对生丝需求的增长中未能充分受益,与茶叶贸易的失利一样,可以从两方面来解释,一是中国自己在提高蚕业质量、符合美国标准方面有疏失;二是其生丝贸易在与日本的激烈竞争中受挫。

---

① 1865 年美国进口生丝 25 万磅,1884 年进口 322.3 万磅。

表 7 - 3　1840—1864 年美国生丝进口统计(五年一期平均值)

| 年　份 | 美国年均生丝进口总额<br>(万美元) | 从中国进口 | |
|---|---|---|---|
| | | 进口额(万美元) | 占比(%) |
| 1840—1844 | 5.1 | | |
| 1845—1849 | 23.0 | | |
| 1850—1854 | 57.5 | 35.8 | 62.0 |
| 1955—1859 | 113.3 | 62.0 | 54.5 |
| 1860—1864 | 124.2 | 57.6 | 46.3 |

表 7 - 4　1865—1884 年美国生丝进口统计(五年一期平均值)

| 年　份 | 美国年均生丝总进口 | | 从中国进口 | | | | 从日本进口 | | | |
|---|---|---|---|---|---|---|---|---|---|---|
| | 进口量 | 进口额 | 进口量 | | 进口额 | | 进口量 | | 进口额 | |
| | (万磅) | (万美元) | (万磅) | (%) | (万美元) | (%) | (万磅) | (%) | (万美元) | (%) |
| 1865—1869 | 51.0 | 225.1 | 6.7 | 13.1 | 29.6 | 13.2 | 1.4 | 2.7 | 8.1 | 3.6 |
| 1870—1874 | 94.0 | 497.5 | 49.8 | 53.0 | 245.2 | 49.3 | 6.0 | 6.4 | 30.3 | 6.1 |
| 1875—1879 | 134.4 | 595.8 | 41.0 | 30.4 | 164.8 | 27.6 | 48.5 | 36.8 | 227.0 | 38.0 |
| 1880—1884 | 289.2 | 1 259.2 | 130.3 | 45.0 | 500.8 | 43.8 | 99.4 | 34.4 | 441.2 | 35.0 |

　　尽管养蚕业传入欧洲后,中国在丝绸领域的垄断地位被打破,但其在 19 世纪中期仍掌控着丝绸生产。欧洲、日本都没有大量生产生丝,美国被迫依靠上海、广州供应原材料,以满足本国织造厂不断增长着的原材料需求。中国的蚕丝业者几乎全是农户,对潜在的竞争一无所知,还天真地沉浸在虚幻的天堂世界里,认为自己手握着丝绸市场的唯一钥匙,对养蚕和缫丝越来越不上心。丝绸质量本已低劣,中国丝绸商还与当时的茶商一样开始掺假。这七十年间情况变得如此之糟,以至于美国丝绸协会(一个几乎由美国所有丝绸制造商所组成的组织)政府委员会于 1874 年发布一份正式决议,以反对这种做法。至于早期的日本丝绸,该协会秘书长于同年的报告中有如下评论:

　　"八年前(约 1865 年),日本人做着中国人目前正在做的事情;当时,中国人开始更加专心准备他们的丝绸——为美国市场重新缫丝和清洗,日本生丝则几乎要完全出局。但是,日本人已经认识到了自己的错误,正试图补救。近些年,我们已经购买了一些日本生丝、缫丝,表明日本能够按我们的需求向市场供应丝绸;如果日本人愿意,并决心恢复其失去的贸易机会,(目前正在实行错误做法的)中国人正好给他们提供了一个良机。"

　　除了日本丝绸质量提高、中国丝绸质量退化这一反差外,另一个大的差别是,日本人在美国丝绸贸易市场大力推广他们的产品,而中国人则在销售其丝绸产品时不够主动、行事懒散。尽管中国丝绸贸易在美国身陷危险的下滑境地,但中国却从未派出任何委员会或私人代表去调查、研究美国的市场环境,更不必说去努力做大量的广告或展览来进行市场宣传。另一方面,日本人则通过他们的政府机关为冲高销量做各方面的努力。如此一来,美国市场上的中国丝绸很快被日本丝绸替代就不足为奇了。事实上,如表 7-4 所示,在 1870—1874 年的五年间,美国平均每年从中国进口丝绸 245.2 万美元,而接下来的五年(1875—1879 年)则下降为 164.8 万美元;与之相反的是,同期美国对日本丝绸的进口由 30.3 万美元增至 227 万美元。这也是美国从日本进口的丝绸首次多于中国产品。

日本人的艰苦努力和中国人的粗心大意并行不悖数十年,一直没有中断或转变。19 世纪后几年,日本政府对保持、提高本国出口生丝的质量非常关注。1897 年,日本政府在横滨建立了一个生丝检验所,1900 年日本强制对生丝进行含水检查。另一方面,在中国进行革新则是困难重重。中国政府既提不出类似的可靠的计划意见,也没有行政机构去实施。据中国开放港口的报纸《中国海关》报导,美国、欧洲的丝绸商及其他对中国丝绸贸易感兴趣的人联合起来对中国的丝绸生产者提出警告。其中的一个例子载于 1904 年《中国海关》。报告称,过去三四担蚕茧可制造一担蚕丝,而现在则需要四到六担。"中国的养蚕人生活在愚昧无知的天堂乐园里。他们错误地认为蚕丝价格由自己确定,然而事实上价格是由美国、欧洲市场形成的"。世界上生丝的供应在增长,而中国的生产没有增长。世界对生丝的需求在增长,而中国的出口并没有增长。"只要没有科学方法,中国的养蚕方法就是最优秀的。"但是,一旦科学方法引入日本,中国无疑就要遭受竞争者的挑战。

中国丝绸生产者、丝绸商对这一危急状况的漠视或完全忽视,以及日本人抓住良机以扩大其美国丝绸市场所做的精心准备,在 1904 年密苏里州圣路易斯城世界博览会①上得到很好的体现。这次宏大的艺术、工业和科学博览会是为了庆祝美国从法国购买路易斯安娜 100 周年而举办的。丝绸是本次博览会上的一大特色。世界上所有重要的丝绸生产、制造国家,都懂得抓住这一良好机会展示自己的产品,纷纷派出会议代表、参展者和合作者,将最好的样品带到展览会场。在所有丝绸展品中,日本的样品超过了一半,包括 171 件生丝、绢丝展品和 95 件机织薄绢纱展品。据说,日本的这些展品远比之前在其他任何国际展览会中的展品都更为重要。相反,中国并没有派出任何专业丝绸代表团,仅有不多几件应付差事似的、质地一般的普通展品参展。本次博览会上,来自不同国家的 348 家参展商、224 家合作者获奖,其中,中国只有 7 家参展商获奖,但没有合作者获奖,而日本获得的奖牌数分别是 223 枚、25 枚。

中日两国对待丝绸贸易的态度差别如此之大,自然会出现中国丝绸在美国市场倒栽葱式衰退以及日本丝绸贸易超常扩张的局面。日本丝绸贸易的扩张情况以五年一

---

① 译注:本次世博会会期长达 8 个月(4 月 30 日至 12 月 1 日),有 60 个国家参加,参观者达 1969.5 万人次。

期的平均值列于表7-5。表中最早的数据来自1885—1889年,这五年间日本每年平均向美国出口230万磅、价值810万美元的生丝。接下来的五年(1890—1894年),这两个数字分别达到330万磅、1170万美元,与前一个五年相比增幅约为40%。此后,日本向美国出口的丝绸就呈爆发式增长,换句话说,就是几何比例增长,一直到战前的四年(1910—1913年),贸易量达1510万磅,贸易额为5180万美元。现在可以得到贸易统计数据的最后一年(1922年),美国从日本进口生丝4000万磅,价值高达2.9亿美元!在短短的可以进行比较的半个世纪中,日本努力提高其生丝质量并大力推销,其销售从无到有,成为国际贸易中最重要的物资之一。

表7-5  1885—1922年美国生丝进口来源统计(年均)

| 年 份 | 中国 | | 日本 | | 法国 | | 意大利 | | 其他 | | 美生丝进口合计 | |
|---|---|---|---|---|---|---|---|---|---|---|---|---|
| | (万磅) | (万美元) | (万磅) | (万美元) | (万磅) | (万美元) | (万磅) | (万美元) | (万磅) | (万美元) | (万磅) | (万美元) |
| 1885—1889 | 113.2 | 361.6 | 225.8 | 819.4 | 26.5 | 118.5 | 94.8 | 394.1 | | | 465.6 | 1 120.7 |
| 1890—1894 | 146.8 | 432.4 | 328.4 | 1 167.8 | 26.7 | 110.2 | 107.3 | 476.0 | | | 615.2 | 2 205.7 |
| 1895—1899 | 251.6 | 664.7 | 431.5 | 1 410.0 | 33.4 | 121.2 | 153.2 | 596.9 | 20.6 | 54.7 | 889.6 | 2 847.5 |
| 1900—1904 | 297.1 | 830.0 | 610.9 | 2 138.0 | 49.1 | 174.6 | 263.1 | 1 069.0 | 29.6 | 89.3 | 1 249.2 | 4 320.6 |
| 1905—1909 | 335.6 | 982.5 | 983.4 | 3 770.0 | 57.9 | 200.7 | 390.4 | 1 591.1 | 12.7 | 47.5 | 1 780.0 | 6 592.8 |
| 1910—1913 | 525.4 | 1 297.3 | 1 567.6 | 5 181.9 | 16.1 | 59.2 | 248.1 | 774.6 | 23.1 | 82.1 | 2 380.4 | 7 555.7 |
| 1914—1916 | 612.8 | 1 669.7 | 2 117.8 | 8 127.4 | 8.2 | 23.3 | 220.2 | 973.5 | 10.4 | 44.5 | 2 969.5 | 10 872.0 |
| 1917—1918 | 634.3 | 2 845.4 | 2 823.6 | 15 307.5 | 1.0 | 3.2 | 7.7 | 57.0 | 1.8 | 11.3 | 3 468.4 | 18 224.7 |
| 1919 | 909.9 | 5 447.6 | 3 372.7 | 25 611.3 | 5.0 | 33.6 | 186.6 | 1 788.9 | 7.5 | 52.4 | 4 481.7 | 32 933.9 |
| 1920 | 593.2 | 5 384.4 | 2 290.4 | 21 983.8 | 3.3 | 28.9 | 111.1 | 1 034.5 | 7.9 | 57.5 | 3 005.8 | 28 429.1 |
| 1921 | 958.7 | 4 805.0 | 3 170.4 | 18 806.2 | 68.6 | 374.6 | 308.5 | 1 754.5 | 29.3 | 165.1 | 4 535.5 | 25 905.4 |
| 1922 | 837.8 | 5 661.0 | 4 002.9 | 29 129.2 | 15.9 | 120.1 | 56.9 | 559.1 | 157.7 | 1 209.3 | 5 071.2 | 36 578.7 |

不过,中国与美国、欧洲间丝绸贸易将急转直下的预期似乎不会成为现实,因为即便美国人向中国丝绸商抱怨其产品质量低劣,向美国出口的中国丝绸的数量、金额实际上还是在持续稳定增长,当然也有一些异常的例外。1885—1889年间,中国每年向美国出口生丝110万磅、价值360万美元;这两个数字在后一个时期(1890—1904年)分别增长到150万磅和430万美元。此后,中美生丝贸易的增长并未中断,一直持续到战前四年期(1910—1913年),分别升至530磅、1300万美元。1922年,美国从中国进口丝绸840万磅、进口额5660万美元。

尽管中国丝绸越来越受到买家抱怨并遭受日本丝绸最激烈的竞争,但中美丝绸贸易继续扩张,其原因只是由于这一情况:美国绢织和纺织工业的快速发展导致对生丝的需求迅猛增长,而日本养蚕业即使连年增长、扩张也难以很好地满足这一需求。美国能从欧洲购买到的生丝向来相当有限。19 世纪末 20 世纪初,意大利供应了美国生丝总需求的 20%,而法国则供应了 4% 左右。但是,由于欧洲国家逐步发展绢织工业,不再情愿把他们的原料卖到国外,除非是高价。事实上,由于法国、意大利的人工成本高于东方国家,欧洲丝绸的价格比东方丝绸高出很多。如果美国的生丝需求不能完全通过日本得到满足,自然会被迫转向丝绸的原产地(中国),以满足其成长且无止境的需求。正是由于这些特殊情况,中国丝绸贸易得以从与日本激烈竞争的完全下跌态势中逃过一劫。

然而,如果因此而忽视中国丝绸原有的重要地位下滑这一事实,那我们对于丝绸贸易环境的分析将是不完整的。19 世纪中期(1850—1859 年),美国进口的生丝有 2/3 直接来自中国,而没有从日本进口。二十年之后(1875—1884 年),中国丝绸在美国市场的份额下降到 2/3 以下,而日本丝绸的份额与中国相当。此后,日本丝绸的市场占有率节节上升,1885—1904 年达到 1/2,1905—1913 年为 2/3,1914 年之后在 3/4～4/5 之间。相反,中国丝绸的市场份额从 1850—1859 年的 1/4 下降到 1905 年后的 1/5 左右。当我们提到中国丝绸在美国市场败落时,所指的就是其在美国市场的相对份额下滑(见表 7 - 6)。

表 7 - 6　1885—1922 年美国生丝进口来源统计(进口量百分比)

| 年　　份 | 中国 | 日本 | 法国 | 意大利 | 其他 |
|---|---|---|---|---|---|
| 1885—1889 | 24.3 | 48.3 | 5.7 | 20.4 | 1.3 |
| 1890—1894 | 23.8 | 53.4 | 4.3 | 17.4 | 1.1 |
| 1895—1899 | 28.3 | 48.5 | 3.1 | 17.2 | 2.3 |
| 1900—1904 | 23.8 | 49.1 | 3.9 | 21.5 | 2.4 |
| 1905—1909 | 18.8 | 55.2 | 3.3 | 21.9 | 0.8 |
| 1910—1913 | 22.2 | 65.6 | 0.8 | 10.4 | 1.0 |
| 1914—1916 | 20.6 | 71.2 | 0.3 | 7.4 | 0.4 |
| 1917—1918 | 18.3 | 81.5 |  | 0.2 |  |
| 1919 | 20.3 | 75.1 | 0.1 | 4.2 | 0.2 |
| 1920 | 19.7 | 76.2 | 0.1 | 3.7 | 0.3 |
| 1921 | 21.2 | 10.0 | 1.5 | 6.8 | 0.6 |
| 1922 | 16.5 | 79.0 | 0.3 | 1.1 | 3.1 |

通过上述给出的关于中日两国对待美国丝绸贸易的态度,可以立即看出,日本的成功很大程度上是由于其明智的政府政策,它为养蚕业的发展进行了严肃而科学的考量,而中国政府在这个重要问题上只不过是浅尝辄止而已。中国政府确实时不时为丝绸业者资助资金以完成其改革计划,但是业者对此并没有太多兴趣,只是要求自己的投入能有适当的利益回报。除了缺乏政府帮助外,还有另一个大的困难影响了中国养蚕业的实际进步。中国蚕虫的扩大继续依托于数以千计的小规模的农民及其家庭。丝绸商公会的任何改革都面临着非常大的困难,一是因为这些农户缺乏必需的资金,一是因为科学的养蚕方法在技术上、经济上都不适用于这种小规模的家庭生产方式。

## 四、中国丝绸与日本丝绸,美国市场与欧洲市场

根据前面的论述,人们可能很容易产生误解,以为中国丝绸品质低劣,不适合于现代丝绸业。这样的结论是不正确的,因为中国丝绸尽管在美国市场没有日本丝绸那么风光,但在很少需要日本丝绸的欧洲还是大有市场。通过研究中国、日本生丝的出口目的地,就能够对中国、日本丝绸在美国、欧洲市场上的相对优势做出更好的判断。当日本丝绸的地位开始上升时,中国的丝绸贸易已经很好地建立起来,与欧洲纺织业间的关系也更为紧密。很明显的是,日本生丝产品的增长与美国纺织业的发展紧密相关。日本的生丝出口可以说是和美国纺织业同时成长的,这可能是由于日本丝绸业者响应了美国人关于提升其丝绸产业的要求。总的来说,在欧洲战争之前的数年间,日本出口到美国的生丝要多于出口欧洲的 2 倍,战争期间日本 7/8～9/10 的生丝运往美国。中国生丝的情况则刚好相反。1913 年之前,中国出口欧洲、西亚的生丝是出口美国的 2 倍。欧洲、美国纺织业之间有所差异。"同一花样复制出大量廉价的普通丝绸,是美国机械工业的特点;而法国工业的典型产品是花样有限、质量纯正、服务于富人"。"中国生丝似乎更加适合法国和欧洲工业环境。如同中国的茶叶,中国生丝的质量要么非常优秀,要么就很差,而且这种状况已经持续了很长一段时间。通常,中国生丝比日本产品质量更好、纤维更粗。大批的原材料没有统一的标准,似乎使中国人很难轻松地将其产品销售到美国市场。日本丝绸或多或少地采用标准方法生产,质量更加统一,所以能更好地满足美国大规模机械工业的需要。但是中国最好的丝绸,如同其最好的茶叶一样,说起来还是要胜过日本产品。"所以,1913 年之前的整个时期,是日本而非中国收获了正在成长中的美国工业不断增长的需要所带来的利益。

然而,欧洲战争使这一状况发生显著变化。战争期间,欧洲纺织业非常混乱,对中国丝绸的需求也不确定了。所以,中国人被迫将其更多的丝绸产品输往美国。战前,中国仅将其出口丝绸的 1/3 发往美国,但在战后美国吸收了中国近一半的出口。美国市场对中国生丝的重要性提高,使得美国买家可以向中国人施加影响,使其产品更加满足美国人的需求,这也使得中国人更加愿意接受美国纺织业者的建议和要求。

## 五、近期中国养蚕业在满足美国需求方面的进步；中国丝绸对美贸易的未来预测

"多年来，日本丝绸的供应持续增加，能充分地满足美国丝绸制造商成长所需的大部分原料。但是，最近，丝绸在美国日渐流行，美国制造商开始感觉到了扩大原材料供应范围的必要性"。由于可栽种桑树的耕地不足，日本的丝绸生产已经接近其极限，而美国的丝绸工业仍在快速增长。

此外，美国丝绸制造业者最近也认识到将如此重要的原材料的全部供应系于单个国家的危险性。二十年来，日本供应了美国所需的绝大部分生丝，有时候超过美国进口生丝总量的 4/5。在这种垄断状况下，日本商人自然能够控制生丝市场，囤积居奇，将其价格抬升至"交易无法进行"的地步。这样的情形在 1920 年确实发生过，当时，一些日本丝绸公司控制丝绸产量，哄抬价格，结果丝绸市场不可避免地顷刻衰落，许多美国制造业者和日本商人破产。对美国人而言，防止这一惨剧重演的最好办法就是向不同国家购买丝绸，以免成为日本人垄断的牺牲品。但是，如同上文所指出的，美国寄希望于欧洲丝绸生产国以解决这一问题是不会有什么效果的。也正是因为这两个原因，美国必须向中国这个丝绸产业的故乡寻求解决办法。

另外，中国最近也认识到了与美国开展丝绸贸易的重要性，因此在这一商品的生产和销售方面更加尽心。丝绸在中国对外出口贸易中担当最重要的角色已近二十年，中国人觉得有必要进一步推进其国外贸易。此外，近期丝绸价格的稳定增长也使得丝绸贸易对中国非常有利，高回报强烈刺激着蚕业的进一步发展及在国外的积极销售。正是在这种情况下，中国这个曾经最优秀的丝绸生产者和最大供应者，已经开始向美国丝绸制造者寻求并接受合作，以促进丝绸工业发展和贸易。

中国丝绸进行改进的第一次认真尝试发生于 1909 年，美国丝绸协会在美国拈丝工协会的建议下，做出决议要求供应美国市场的广州缫丝厂提高质量。作为回应，广州人认真遵从了美国丝绸制造商关于制定标准束纱方法的建议。其直接效应是中美丝绸贸易在 1910 年后立马超过了之前的年份，如表 7-6[①] 所示。

为了进一步促进已经开始的改良活动，在上海外国丝绸商会的赞助下，中国合众蚕桑改良会于 1918 年在上海成立。美国是最大的生丝进口国，因此美国丝绸商会对这一活动非常关心，并积极协助。改良会承诺其首要工作是给中国丝绸产区的农户提供指导，为他们提供经科学选择的健康蚕种。以此为开端的中国生丝改良，得到了美国买家、中国政府及生产者的大力支持。美国捐赠者的基金用于改良会的工作，在南

---

① 译注：原文此处有未编号之表格，内容与表 7-6 中 1905—1909 年、1910—1913 年两时间段之数据完全相同，从略。

京和广州地区的大学里举办养蚕指导和研究工作的讲座，为这些大学的蚕业工作站提供场地和设备，为专家提供服务以通过实际示范和教育介绍广州和上海的美国标准养蚕束纱。改良会已经扩大其活动范围，目前在上海设有七个田间工作站和一个中央实验室，在山东北部的烟台有一个分支机构。

作为中国生丝生产进行科学改良的另一个步骤，美国丝绸商会为中国两所大学提供了建造两幢新的养蚕建筑物的全部资金。事实证明，资助大学是提高生丝质量的一个直接方法。

为了给美国丝绸贸易提供合适的水分检验设施，美国丝绸商会在纽约建立了水分检验站；美国测试公司的一个分公司于 1921 年 10 月在上海开业，是（为提高中国丝绸质量的）更进一步的补充措施。该分公司开业前，中国的纺线工通常依赖目视检查方法控制织造作业。上海分站按照公知的标准方法检测生丝，这一方法在应用中能被每一个操作人员和国际人士所理解。因此，该站的认证将对中国丝绸的卖家和买家起到实质性的帮助，其结论在美国消费市场也将很有分量。

## 六、美国消费者和中国生产者

除了中美两国为了提高中国生丝质量、产量所做的各种共同努力外，还有许多其他活动以促进美国消费者和中国生产者之间的相互理解和亲善关系。1920 年，一个由美国主要的丝绸制造、检验和研究机构的代表及美国丝绸商会组成的代表团用三个多月的时间对东方丝绸工业进行积极调研。代表团成员认真考察了增加产量，提高质量的可能性，以及消除瑕疵、级别确定等。美国丝绸商会主席查尔斯·切尼（Charles Cheney）在其提交的官方报告里，呼吁美国丝绸制造商关注，一种崭新、进步的精神在中国明显上升。报告说："商会发现，广州地区将近 85％的缫丝厂已经改变了他们的机器和方法，按照美国规格织造。据一位可靠的丝绸专家最新估计，广州今年 70％的丝绸将织成美国标准束纱。适合美国人消费的丝绸的数量增长很多（大约两倍），所谓的新型丝绸比旧法织造的丝绸价格更高……欣然而普遍地接受美国买家的指导意味着思想开明，该运动的成功对提供有利于继续进步的详细建议应当是很有价值的……中国已经抓住了将丝绸这一历史悠久的老行业发展、扩大到几乎无限空间的绝佳机会。"

1923 年 2 月，在美国丝绸协会主席詹姆斯·A·戈德史密斯（James A. Glodsmith）的领导下，第二个美国丝绸代表团前往东方，对丝绸生产环境做进一步研究。两国之间增加理解与合作确信是随之而来的事。

与以往漠不关心的态度相反，现在中国丝绸商人对与美国开展贸易表现出了浓厚的兴趣。1921 年，第一届国际丝绸博览会在美国举办，中国各地的丝绸相关方派去了一大批代表①，并带去了最好的丝绸产品。这些代表还参观了许多美国丝绸工厂，对美国消费者的需求有了更好的理解。1923 年的第二届国际丝绸博览会同样引起了这些中国丝绸巨头的关注。这些代表带回中国的，除了对美国市场更好的理解外，还有对美国更良好的感觉，以及与美国制造业者为了共同利益而进行合作的全面认识。

基于中美丝绸贸易的近期发展，可以对其未来扩张有一个非常好的期待。中国丝绸生产者现在越来越关注美国标准和规格要求，其产品也越来越符合美国人的用途。着眼于未来，可以有充分的理由预期，对中国生丝而言，美国将是比欧洲更好的消费者。

## 七、废丝

生丝是制造丝绸最主要的原料，但废丝也相当重要。废丝是不能缫丝的，必须通过一个与棉、麻纺织相似的工艺制成绢丝，它或多或少地混入了一定量的夹杂物。从这一点来说，"中国废丝尤其粗劣，因为其相当大部分的缫丝是在家庭的脏地板上完成的"。使用低等级废丝和生丝，要比使用优质材料耗费更多的时间和劳力，因此美国制造商普遍认识到有必要使用等级较高的欧洲废丝。20 世纪末以来，美国对中国废丝的进口、数量仍在稳定增长，但与中国生丝的进口数量相比，是非常少的。美国对中国废丝的进口统计见表 7 - 7。

表 7 - 7　1895—1922 年美国对华废丝进口统计

| 年　　份 | 1895 | 1900 | 1905 | 1910 | 1913 | 1915 | 1917 | 1918 | 1919 | 1920 | 1921 | 1922 |
|---|---|---|---|---|---|---|---|---|---|---|---|---|
| 进口量（万磅） | 21.3 | 69.7 | 11.4 | 54.6 | 190.5 | 235.9 | 359.3 | 783.1 | 437.9 | 558.2 | 363.6 | 331.6 |
| 进口额（万美元） | 9.5 | 18.9 | 7.6 | 25.3 | 101.2 | 106.8 | 213.1 | 567.7 | 436.3 | 884.4 | 233.7 | 244.6 |

欧洲战争期间，美国丝绸商业最显著的发展领域之一是绢丝工业。这很大程度上是因为战争对制造大炮药包所需的粗丝绸的需求。药包由丝绸制成，因为必须使用能快速完全燃烧且不留下闷烟的纺织品。选择使用绢丝绸而放弃生丝制品是因为前者更加便宜。这一特殊要求使得美国从中国进口的废丝数量和金额在 1917—1920 数年间异常上升，仅 1920 这一年的进口额就接近 900 万美元。但是这一特殊需要随着战争而终止，而且由于这样的制造业不大可能恢复，中国废丝的美国销售市场快速衰落。

---

① 译注：1921 年 1 月 7 日，上海丝绸行业应邀组团参加美国纽约举行的第一次世界丝绸博览会。丝厂业代表李佑仁、吴申伯和辑里丝业代表张鹤卿等人前往，丝绸业未参加。

# 植物油、棉制品

## 一、作为植物油市场的美国

植物油在美国工业中的广泛应用,以及中美植物油贸易的显著成长是过去十年间最有趣的商业现象之一;一些年来,由世界大战带来的植物油新用途的发展非常重要。战争的结果是,美国对植物油的依赖性在许多方面暂时性加大了——植物油新的功用被发现,原本微小的用途突然显现出极大的重要性。以前在美国几乎不为人所知的植物油如中国豆油现在被输入美国而普遍应用,是因为美国工业所需的一些油品的供应不足以满足大规模的军工生产,而其他地区的军用油品,如非洲棕榈油的供应在战争期间被部分切断。

到目前为止,战争对 1916—1920 年间植物油应用最重要的影响,可能是其作为食品的消费量大大增加。液体或固体形态的植物油替代动物脂肪,从而导致植物乳脂肪、猪油、调和油的消费大大增加,部分原因是由于战争期间畜产品短缺。但是,即使在战前,植物油在工业中的应用也已达到非常大的规模,一些非常有趣的、传奇的用途被开发出来,如制造装订用的人造革、生产人造橡胶产品及与赛璐珞相似的物质。然而,植物油的主要工业用途是制造色漆和清漆、蜡烛、油毯和油布及润滑油。

除美国南部产棉区以外,用于压榨植物油的种子和果实的最大来源地是远东地区。其中,中国是最大的生产者,其次是印度、日本、马来西亚和大洋洲。一些油籽从这些重点产区运送到美国,并被压榨。

美国本身也是一个植物油生产大国。然而,尽管其产量巨大,但除了棉籽油、玉米油外,其他品种都不能满足其庞大的消费。为了弥补这一缺口,美国只得每年进口相当数量的植物油,进口量在其工业活跃的年份特别大。表 8 - 1 即是美国在欧洲战争前后的主要油品进口情况。

当然,这些植物油来自世界不同的国家,例如桐油来自中国,花生油和豆油来自中国和日本,椰子油则来自菲律宾,棕榈油来自非洲,亚麻子油和橄榄油来自欧洲。

## 二、中国对美植物油贸易

中国植物油对美出口贸易并不是一件新鲜事,但直到最近才在两国贸易中占据一个重要的地位。19 世纪后半叶,桐油多次出现在美国从中国进口的商品名录之中,1900 年之前,桐油实际上也是美国从中国进口的唯一植物油产品。日本接替俄国租借南满时,产自中国的其他种类植物油,如豆油和花生油,开始通过日本商人在美国销售。直到 1911 年,中美植物油贸易才达到可观的规模。但是这一贸易一经启动,加之此后战争需要的刺激,贸易额在 1921 年锐减前一直保持快速扩张。表 8-2 是过去三十年美国从中国直接进口植物油的情况。

**表 8-1 1913—1922 年美国植物油进口分类统计**

单位:万磅

| 年 份 | 1913 | 1918 | 1919 | 1920 | 1921 | 1922 |
|---|---|---|---|---|---|---|
| 棉籽油 | 300 | 1 800 | 2 800 | 1 000 | 100 | |
| 花生油 | | 6 900 | 15 400 | 9 500 | 300 | 300 |
| 椰子油 | 5 100 | 35 600 | 28 100 | 21 600 | 19 000 | 22 700 |
| 豆油 | 1 200 | 33 600 | 19 600 | 11 200 | 1 600 | 1 700 |
| 亚麻子油 | 100 | | 1 600 | 3 500 | 6 100 | 14 400 |
| 桐油 | 4 500 | 4 300 | 5 400 | 6 800 | 2 700 | 7 900 |
| 橄榄油 | 3 900 | 100 | 7 000 | 3 100 | 5 400 | 8 800 |
| 棕榈油 | 5 000 | 2 100 | 4 200 | 4 100 | 2 300 | 5 800 |

**表 8-2 1896—1922 年美国从中国进口植物油统计①**

| 年 份 | 年均进口额(万美元) | 年份 | 进口额(万美元) |
|---|---|---|---|
| 1896—1900 | 11.0 | 1917 | 1202.1 |
| 1901—1905 | 26.2 | 1918 | 3936.1 |
| 1906—1910 | 78.3 | 1919 | 3095.5 |
| 1911—1913 | 274.8 | 1920 | 1846.0 |
| 1914—1916 | 339.8 | 1921 | 280.6 |
| | | 1922 | 836.4 |

可以确定无误的事实是,美国从中国进口的植物油快速增长。1906—1910 年,每年的进口额不超过 75 万美元,仅仅十年之后,就上升到每年 2 000 万～4 000 万美元。然而,这些数字只是中美间的直接贸易额,并非中美植物油贸易的全部。来自日本的

---

① 由于美国海关用不同的单位(加仑、磅)测量不同种类油的数量,故很难计算其总量。

大部分进口以及来自中国香港的几乎所有进口最初都源自中国。

表 8-3 是 1918—1922 年间美国植物油进口的来源分布统计情况。看起来,在欧洲战争进行的那几年,欧洲和非洲向美国的供应被临时切断,中国就在美国市场掌握了无可争议的控制地位。加上日本、中国香港地区部分,中国在 1918 年提供了进口美国植物油的 2/3 份额,而 1919 年也接近一半。

表 8-3　1918—1922 年美国植物油进口来源统计

| 年份 | 植物油进口总额（万美元） | （按进口额）各来源地所占比例（%） | | | | | | | |
|---|---|---|---|---|---|---|---|---|---|
| | | 中国（含中国香港） | 日本 | 菲律宾群岛 | 荷属东印度 | 意大利 | 西班牙 | 英国 | 其他 |
| 1918 | 11 090.9 | 36.8 | 26.0 | 27.7 | 3.9 | 0.7 | 0.3 | 0.1 | 4.5 |
| 1919 | 13 000.0 | 25.6 | 22.8 | 19.6 | 2.6 | 1.4 | 13.2 | 2.7 | 12.1 |
| 1920 | 11 349.0 | 20.2 | 20.7 | 21.2 | 7.0 | 5.0 | 6.5 | 9.8 | 9.6 |
| 1921 | 4 152.3 | 8.0 | 1.0 | 31.8 | 5.0 | 17.6 | 4.8 | 12.4 | 9.4 |
| 1922 | 5 904.2 | 14.8 | 1.2 | 27.4 | | 14.4 | 4.8 | 17.1 | 20.3 |

然而,1921 年,中国植物油失去了其重要的贸易地位。当年,中国向美国出口的植物油仅为 300 万美元,在美国植物油进口总额中的份额下降到不足 10%。当然,这一下降可以用每个商业人士都能理解的原因来解释:一是 1921 年的商业萧条使美国许多消费植物油的工厂关门倒闭;二是美国新的关税法案对植物油进口课以重税。第一个原因首先导致植物油供需失衡,价格跌至成本之下。但是,商业萧条只是一个暂时现象,它不可能持久地阻碍植物油贸易。只要 1922 年美国关税法案维持不变,第二个原因,即对植物油征收重税,会对植物油贸易的回升产生更为严重的阻碍。由表 8-4 可见,1909 年的美国关税法案对中国的各类植物油均予以免税。随后的 1913 年法案,也只对花生油征收每加仑六美分的税,其他品种仍然免税。所以,在 1911—1920年的十年间,这些法案极大地促进了植物油的进口。但是 1921 年商业萧条来临,美国的植物油生产者觉得有必要保护他们免受外国的竞争;当年,美国紧急关税法案对来自中国的各种植物油都课以重税,只有美国不能生产的中国胡桃油除外。1922 年的关税法案进一步提高税率,这样实际上把所有的中国应税品种逐出了美国植物油市场。这就解释了 1922 年为什么仅有中国胡桃油的进口有所恢复,而其他植物油均未恢复。

表 8 - 4　1909 年、1913 年、1921 年和 1922 年美国关税法案中关于进口中国油品的税率表

| 年　份 | 1909 | 1911 | 1921 | 1922 |
|---|---|---|---|---|
| 中国胡桃油 | 免税 | 免税 | 免税 | 免税 |
| 棉籽油 | 免税 | 免税 | 20 美分/加仑 | 3 美分/磅 |
| 花生油 | 免税 | 6 美分/加仑 | 26 美分/加仑 | 4 美分/磅 |
| 豆油 | 免税 | 免税 | 20 美分/加仑 | 2.5 美分/磅 |

注：1 加仑≈7 磅。

中国数年前在美国植物油市场拥有的重要地位的下滑表明,恢复中国植物油对美贸易的可能性仍然是一个非常严肃的问题。如上所述,中国的植物油,如豆油、花生油和棉籽油,在前些年的进口很大程度上是作为那些由于战争临时切断供应或由于需求过大而不能足量供应的那些品种的替代。自 1919 年开始,这些被替代的品种逐步返回美国市场,并排挤了其中国竞争产品。很大程度上是由于这个原因,美国从中国进口的各类植物油(除桐油外)在 1921—1922 年严重下滑,几乎触及战前水平。

### 1. 豆油

欧战及战后之际,美国从中国进口的所有植物油中,重要的只有四个品种,即豆油、中国胡桃油(或桐油)、花生油和棉籽油。其中,最为重要的是豆油。近年来,它已被认为是美国与东方贸易中最有标志性的发展。当时,其他品种供应不足、价格高企,因此豆油进口数量增加;它与棉籽油相似甚至更加优越,因此赢得了广大的市场。这些年,豆油是美国市场上一些猪油替代品和食用油脂的重要组成成分,此外还发现了与棉籽油相似的工业用途。那时,美国是最大的豆油买家,进口了国际市场近 90% 的豆油。

压榨豆油的大豆几乎仅在中国北方特别是满洲地区生长,那里的大豆闻名于世已经数个世纪。在远东,很少有蔬菜能有大豆那样的重要地位。对中国人来说,作为一个基本食品,大豆因其不寻常的营养价值,地位很高。除了豆腐这一常见食品、也是一种美味食品外,大豆制成品还有豆粉(制作意大利面条的原料之一)、腐乳、酱油、豆油和豆奶等。尽管美国农业部已经做了一些试验,但这些用途大多还不为美国人所知。大豆的食用价值被认识后,其贸易规模无疑将比现在大很多。表 8 - 5 是近年来美国从中国、日本进口大豆的情况。

世界大战爆发前,英国是向美国出口大豆油的一个重要国家,其中的一大部分是德国产品的再出口[①]。但是,战争期间,中国、日本成了美国豆油市场的唯一供应者,

---

① 1910 年,德国开始生产豆油,免除大豆关税,鼓励压榨;世界大战开始时,德国的豆油产业已经发展到相当规模。

而其最终来源都是中国。

战前,美国豆油市场对中国并不重要,中国的大部分产品都运往欧洲。但在战争期间,美国实际上是豆油产品的唯一消费者,出口到日本的大部分中国豆油被重新装运到美国。然而,欧洲恢复和平后,大量的中国豆油重新输入欧洲,对美贸易大大收缩。

表 8 - 5　1913—1922 年美国大豆进口统计

| 年份 | 美国大豆总进口 | | 从中国进口 | | 从日本进口 | |
|---|---|---|---|---|---|---|
| | (万磅) | (万美元) | (万磅) | (万美元) | (万磅) | (万美元) |
| 1913 | 1 234.0 | 63.6 | 117.2 | 6.1 | 797.9 | 37.9 |
| 1916 | 9 812.0 | 512.8 | 2 747.3 | 136.0 | 7 038.4 | 375.0 |
| 1918 | 33 682.5 | 3 282.7 | 24 998.8 | 2 457.1 | 8 683.1 | 825.5 |
| 1919 | 19 580.8 | 2 401.9 | 10 027.3 | 1 331.0 | 8 421.8 | 1 051.7 |
| 1920 | 11 221.4 | 1 372.1 | 5 991.1 | 724.4 | 5 230.1 | 649.7 |
| 1921 | 1 628.6 | 66.0 | 1 523.9 | 60.7 | 100.4 | 5.0 |
| 1922 | 1 729.4 | 101.3 | 1 252.1 | 72.4 | 374.5 | 22.2 |

### 2. 中国桐油(中国胡桃油)

按重要性排在豆油之后的是桐油,美国从中国进口桐油已有数十年。世界战争爆发后,桐油贸易得到进一步的促进。桐油从生长于中国、印度支那、(越南)东京和安南的两种树的坚果压榨而来。中国的四川、贵州、湖南和湖北是最重要的产地。这种油在中国广泛用于防水布、纸张,也用于油漆、油灰、亮漆和墨水。由于其快干特性,桐油在美国的应用主要是作为亚麻子油的替代品,用于油漆、防水粘合剂、油布(毯)和颜料。桐油比亚麻子油干得快,但其薄膜的弹性不如后者。温度高于 500 华氏度时,桐油会在短时间里固化成胶冻状的块体。这一特性构成桐油耐热试验的基础,这一点在检测其纯度时非常有用。

实际上,美国消费的所有桐油都来自于中国内地,详见表 8 - 6;有一小部分来自于香港,但它们也只是从华南、印度支那和安南转运而来。

即使在战前,美国也是桐油的最好市场,每年从中国进口 100 万美元左右的桐油。战争期间及战后之际,桐油贸易快速发展,1920 年的进口额达 1 100 万美元,其中约 900 万美元的桐油直接来自于中国。不过,进口额的增长很大程度上是由于物价膨胀,桐油的实际进口量并没有增长这么快。1922 年,进口量创下了 1 050 万加仑的新纪录。

表 8 - 6 1913—1922 年美国进口中国桐油统计

| 年份 | 从中国内地进口 | | 从香港地区进口 | | 美国进口中国桐油合计 | |
|---|---|---|---|---|---|---|
| | （万加仑） | （万美元） | （万加仑） | （万美元） | （万加仑） | （万美元） |
| 1913 | 585.8 | 265.9 | 4.5 | 2.6 | 599.7 | 273.4 |
| 1916 | 490.1 | 194.7 | 4.6 | 2.0 | 496.8 | 197.8 |
| 1918 | 464.9 | 389.6 | 11.1 | 10.3 | 481.6 | 403.8 |
| 1919 | 604.8 | 680.8 | 34.2 | 43.9 | 718.0 | 812.0 |
| 1920 | 743.6 | 869.0 | 89.7 | 135.0 | 906.1 | 1 107.7 |
| 1921 | 312.8 | 204.1 | 30.1 | 24.2 | 363.3 | 247.0 |
| 1922 | 1 016.2 | 759.1 | 25.5 | 18.6 | 1 054.5 | 789.1 |

在所有的中国植物油当中,目前美国只对桐油免征进口税。最近十年间其进口数量呈现决定性的上升趋势,因此可以预期,随着美国工业活动的恢复,桐油进口仍将进一步增长。

许多年来,美国大约吸纳了中国出口的桐油的 1/2～2/3,而到 1922 年该比例升至 4/5 以上。这充分显示了美国市场对中国桐油的重要性。

## 3. 花生油

战时及战争结束之际,中美贸易中另一种重要的植物油是花生油,通常称之为落花生油。这是美国大量生产所需的一种原料油。花生油被发现几乎适合所有其他重要植物油的应用,因此在南方一些州大量生产。但是,在欧洲战争之后经济繁荣的几年里,美国的花生油产量不能满足消费,缺口达 1/2～2/3,因此数年期间大量进口花生油就非常必要[①]。

出产花生的国家,除了美国外,还有中国、法属西非、尼日利亚和印度。战前,这些国家都向马赛这个几乎所有国际花生油贸易的唯一源头地航运去壳的、或带壳的花生。每年实际输出超过 3 000 万加仑,其中美国进口超过 100 多万加仑,主要来自法国,部分来自荷兰和德国。

欧洲战争或多或少地切断了花生向马赛的航运,结果致使贸易衰退。另外,日本、中国的压榨有了大的进步。但是由于前面提到的同样原因,即商业萧条、国内油品的

---

① 前见表 8-1。

替代、进口重税,美国从中国的直接进口实际上自 1921 年下降了;而且由于后两个原因,中美花生油贸易的未来也不乐观。多年来,中日两国在世界花生油出口中占据主导地位,美国从这两个国家进口了大量花生油。表 8 - 7 是 1913 年后美国花生油的进口情况。

表 8 - 7　1913—1922 年美国花生油进口来源统计

| 年份 | 美国花生油总进口 | | 从中国内地进口 | | 从中国香港地区进口 | | 从日本进口 | |
|------|--------|--------|--------|--------|--------|--------|--------|--------|
| | (万加仑) | (万美元) | (万加仑) | (万美元) | (万加仑) | (万美元) | (万加仑) | (万美元) |
| 1913 | 119.6 | 82.1 | 1.1 | 0.7 | 6.8 | 4.2 | | |
| 1916 | 147.5 | 81.8 | 27.7 | 11.9 | 10.8 | 5.4 | 70.8 | 31.2 |
| 1918 | 828.9 | 731.2 | 350.9 | 299.8 | 9.1 | 11.1 | 463.1 | 415.7 |
| 1919 | 2 054.0 | 2 201.0 | 703.0 | 733.9 | 106.2 | 146.1 | 1 235.4 | 1 305.8 |
| 1920 | 1 268.3 | 1 699.0 | 230.4 | 300.8 | 89.9 | 128.4 | 925.1 | 1 235.3 |
| 1921 | 40.2 | 31.4 | 0.4 | 0.3 | 21.2 | 14.5 | 0.1 | 0.1 |
| 1922 | 247.0 | 28.1 | 2.1 | 0.3 | 160.1 | 17.0 | 6.2 | 0.5 |

从表 8 - 7 中可见,即使在欧洲战争爆发、马赛的花生油贸易中止之后,中国也只供应了美国进口花生油总量的 1/4～1/2,这使人非常不解。实际上所有来自香港的进口都源于中国内地,美国从日本进口的花生油确信至少有一半来自中国。这被中国每年向香港出口大量花生油并被分发到美国、欧洲这一事实所证明。中国出口到日本并被重新装运到美国的花生油,甚至超过美国从中国的直接进口量。

#### 4. 棉籽油

棉籽油仅在中美植物油贸易中扮演过短暂的重要角色。美国是世界上主要的棉生产国,已然是棉籽油的最大生产者,所以其棉籽油能够自给自足。

然而,世界大战隆隆炮声的数年间,美国对棉籽油的需求增长很多,以至于从中国进口了相当数量的棉籽油以补充这种本土油料,平均每年超过 1 000 万磅,价值一二百万美元。中国出口的棉籽油 50％～80％ 被美国吸纳。但是,1920 年之后,美国的中国棉籽油市场突然下滑,一方面是因为美国的工业需求能轻松地被国内产品所满足,另一方面是 1921、1922 年的关税法案对进口棉籽油课以重税,终结了其与美国国内产品的竞争。自 1921 年开始,美国不再进口棉籽油,所以中国棉籽油未来在美国市场大批量销售的前景非常黯淡,除非美国出现异乎寻常的需求、本地产品价格攀升。

## 三、棉制品:花边

欧洲战争之前,美国很少进口中国棉制品。然而,如此描述时,我们当然不能忘记,在中美贸易的过去岁月,一种称作南京棉布的布料在数十年间都是美国从中国进口的主要商品之一。但是,随着19世纪的逐步发展,美国停止了对中国棉布的进口。最近,美国每年从中国进口的棉制品仅有几千美元,主要是居住在美国的中国居民的衣服和装饰。

然而,随着欧洲战争的爆发,一种新的棉纺织业被引入中国,并在美国进口贸易中扮演了非常重要的角色。最近,该产品的贸易份额不断成长,六年间从零成交上升到每年250万美元,这就是手工花边。

中国花边产业的成长是近期世界大战的间接结果。几年前,芝罘(今烟台)、上海、福州、厦门和汕头的外国女传教士就开始向中国妇女介绍花边制造术。1914年战争爆发时,对花边有大量需求的美国人与欧洲的花边来源国之间被完全切断。当时,中国的花边产业还仅仅处于萌芽阶段。但是,美国的巨大需求为中国人的崛起提供了良机。中国人似乎转瞬间就生产出了满足美国人需要的各种花边,这一发展花边产业的速度显示了中国人抓住商业良机的能力。

在《中国评论》杂志1923年3月号一篇关于中国花边贸易的文章中,纽约的中国著名商人彭先生(T. E. PUN)有如下论述:

"现在,中国花边完全可以与欧洲最好的花边媲美。美国妇女发现,中国花边在某些方面更加出色。由于中国支付的工资低,其生产的花边要比其他任何地方的产品都更便宜。

"中国的花边产业已经遍布全国,芝罘(烟台)、广州、上海、福州、宁波、厦门和汕头等城市是生产中心。传递给大量消费者的关于美国进口商在中国拥有自己的工厂或仓库,并可以直接控制工人的印象,是没有根据的。

"中国花边不仅用于各式各样的妇女服装,也广泛用于制造家庭用品。美国妇女们重新自裁自缝的情况在增加,自然会对手工花边有一些偏爱。"

战前,中国是一个花边进口国。只是最近几年,花边才成为中国的一种出口商品,其中约80%被美国所进口。

表8-8列示了1914年之后美国从中国进口花边及其他棉制品的情况。1918年之后,花边及其制品的贸易迅速扩大。1920年,美国花边产品的进口总额达200万美元;而在接下来的两年里,尽管有商业萧条和价格下滑因素,进口额仍然大幅增长,每年接近300万美元。似乎很明显的是,只要美国的花边流行风尚不减,中美花边贸易的前景必然是光明的,因为中国劳动力廉价,手工制作花边的成本便宜。

表 8 - 8　1914—1922 年美国从中国进口棉制品分类统计

| 年份 | 花边 | | 花边制品 | 其他棉制品(布匹、服装等) | 美国进口中国棉制品总额 |
|---|---|---|---|---|---|
| | （万码） | （万美元） | （万美元） | （万美元） | （万美元） |
| 1914 | | | | 4.6 | 4.6 |
| 1915 | | | | 2.7 | 2.7 |
| 1916 | | 0.9 | 0.9 | 4.3 | 6.1 |
| 1917 | | 15.0 | 1.1 | 16.3 | 32.4 |
| 1918 | | 39.5 | 4.1 | 3.0 | 46.5 |
| 1919 | 730.4 | 116.0 | 19.2 | 3.3 | 138.5 |
| 1920 | 715.5 | 147.7 | 54.2 | 9.9 | 211.8 |
| 1921 | 1 717.0 | 263.2 | 34.0 | 6.7 | 303.9 |
| 1922 | | 243.8 | 30.3 | 10.5 | 284.6 |

# 第九章　其他重要商品

## 一、羊毛

1914 年前的那几年,美国毛纺织产业每年大约消费 5 亿磅羊毛,其中美国国内生产的羊毛约占 3/5。然而,现在要确定战争期间增长的羊毛消费量中,多大比例将会永久持续下去,为时尚早;据估计,美国企业每年正常消耗的羊毛量略多于 6 亿磅。过去三十五年,美国国内羊毛产量都在 3 亿磅左右,因此超出的消费量必须通过增加进口来弥补。1914 年以后,美国每年进口各种羊毛 3.5 亿~4 亿磅[①]。

19 世纪后期数十年间,羊毛在美国对华进口贸易中占据了一个重要的地位。1891—1905 年的十五年间,美国每年从中国进口羊毛 2 000 万磅,进口额有时超过 150 万美元,在美国对华进口总额中的份额为 5%~7%,约占美国羊毛总进口的 10%。1906—1913 年间,美国从中国进口的羊毛年平均增长 50%,达到 3 000 万磅,年均进口额 350 万美元左右;其在美国对华总进口中的份额上升到 12%,在美国羊毛进口贸易中占比 16%。

表 9-1　1891—1922 年美国从中国进口(未加工)羊毛统计

| 年　　份 | 年均进口量(万磅) | 年均进口额(万美元) | 年度 | 进口量(万磅) | 进口额(万美元) |
|---|---|---|---|---|---|
| 1891—1895 | 1 631.1 | 133.9 | 1918 | 4 291.0 | 1 423.5 |
| 1896—1900 | 2 237.1 | 160.6 | 1919 | 3 898.5 | 1 298.7 |
| 1901—1905 | 2 051.8 | 191.4 | 1920 | 1 533.4 | 539.7 |
| 1906—1908 | 2 801.2 | 336.2 | 1921 | 4 680.4 | 548.3 |
| 1909—1913 | 3 328.4 | 380.7 | 1922 | 6 321.4 | 971.2 |
| 1914—1918 | 3 854.5 | 908.9 | | | |

---

① 美国羊毛进口总量:1909—1913 年,年均 2.11 亿磅;1914—1918 年,年均 3.63 亿磅;1918 年,4.54 亿磅;1919 年,4.46 亿磅;1920 年,2.6 亿磅;1921 年,3.21 亿磅。

　　战前,英国是美国的最大羊毛供应国①,其后分别是中国、阿根廷、澳大利亚,新西兰、乌拉圭和加拿大分享了其余份额②。尽管中国羊毛供应量的排名靠前,但那时中国的羊毛全部是地毯原料,它们比其他国家短梳毛、精梳毛的价格要低。

　　欧洲战争爆发后,美国对各种羊毛的需求突然增长,但原由英国大量供应美国的粗梳毛、精梳毛实质上停顿了好几年。来自阿根廷、澳大利亚、新西兰、乌拉圭、英属南非和加拿大的羊毛进口飞跃发展,但仍不能完全满足美国人的增长需求。

　　正是在这种特殊情况下,美国开始从中国进口短梳毛、精梳毛。五年战争期间,美国每年从中国进口粗梳毛 624.1 万磅,相当于美国粗梳毛进口总量的 2.34%。1918—1921 年间(除去美国毛纺工业、精纺工业萧条的 1920 年),美国每年从中国进口 850 万磅粗梳毛,在美国粗梳毛进口总量中的比例接近 3%(见表 9-2 之 A 栏)。

表 9-2　1909—1922 年美国从中国进口羊毛分类统计

| 年　份 | 粗梳毛 | | 精梳毛 | | 地毯毛 | | 合计 | |
|---|---|---|---|---|---|---|---|---|
| | (万磅) | A(%) | (万磅) | B(%) | (万磅) | C(%) | (万磅) | D(%) |
| 1909—1913 平均(财年) | 0.1 | | 0.1 | | 3 328.2 | 31.60 | 3 328.4 | 15.80 |
| 1914—1918 平均(财年) | 624.1 | 2.34 | 41.9 | 2.68 | 3 188.5 | 39.50 | 3 854.5 | 10.60 |
| 1918 | 1 050.6 | 2.82 | 120.6 | 12.08 | 3 119.8 | 44.90 | 4 291.0 | 9.45 |
| 1919 | 852.9 | 2.56 | 64.3 | 4.33 | 2 981.4 | 30.80 | 3 898.6 | 8.75 |
| 1920 | 52.5 | 0.25 | 286.4 | 25.22 | 1 176.3 | 32.80 | 1 515.2 | 5.85 |
| 1921 | 845.5 | 4.07 | 91.4 | 6.13 | 3 718.3 | 38.00 | 4 655.2 | 14.20 |
| 1922 | 18.6 | 0.49 | 149.5 | 0.96 | 6 153.3 | 35.60 | 6 321.4 | 17.20 |

　　注 1:A、B、C、D 各列分别为美国从中国进口的某类产品在美国该类产品进口总量中所占的百分比。

　　而美国从中国进口的精纺毛,自 1914 年起每年都在波动。五年战争期间,年均进口 41.9 万磅,占美国精纺毛进口总量的 2.68%。1918 年,进口量增至 120.6 万磅,占美国精纺毛进口总量的 1/8;1920 年,这两个数字分别增至 286.4 万磅、25%(表 9-2 之 B 栏)。1920 年的大幅增长相当异常,很大程度上是由于阿根廷精纺毛的短缺所致。1921—1922 年美国对华精纺毛进口恢复常态,来自中国的产品回落至每年 100

----

　　① 美国从英国进口的羊毛只不过是原产于澳大利亚的羊毛的转口船运。

　　② 1909 年—1913 年的五年间,美国每年从如下国家进口羊毛:英国,7348.6 万磅;中国,3328.4 万磅;阿根廷,2985.6 万磅;澳大利亚,1858.9 万磅,新西兰,453.3 万磅,乌拉圭,373.7 万磅,加拿大,116.3 万磅。

多万磅。

至于地毯羊毛，几十年来，中国都是美国最大的供应者。自 1909 年起，每年的进口量都相当稳定地保持在 3 000 万～3 500 万磅之间，约占美国地毯羊毛进口总量的 1/3～2/3(见表 9-2 之 C 栏)。

就上述各类羊毛的总量而言，1909—1920 年间，美国从中国的进口相当稳定，徘徊在 4 000 万磅左右。然而，由于战后数年物价异常膨胀，羊毛进口额的增长与进口量的增加不成比例。战前五年(1909—1913)，年均进口额仅为 380.7 万美元；接下来的 1914—1918 年，进口量仅有小幅增长，但年均进口额则高达 908.9 万美元。1918、1919 年，羊毛进口额再次大幅增长，但进口量没有任何增长。1921—1922 年，市场景气萧条，羊毛进口额大幅下挫，但进口量却分别创新高，分别达到 4 700 万磅和 6 300 万磅(见表 9-1)。

目前无法得到中国羊毛的确切生产数据，粗略估计每年约为 4 000 万磅。尽管中国羊毛被认为质量比不上美国、澳大利亚羊毛，但随着羊毛原料的需求持续增长，中国羊毛已经被认为是世界上最有前途的产品之一。

中国羊毛产自蒙古和西亚地区，大部分被运到天津，进行清洗、汽蒸、分类定级，并打包，为出口做准备。以前日本是中国羊毛最重要的买家，但是，现在美国进口商开始与日本人进行竞争。中国每年大约有 4 600 万磅羊毛装运出口，其中的 65%～70% 运往美国。

按照一位在东方的美国羊毛进口商的说法，中国羊毛品质次于美国或澳大利亚羊毛，很大程度上是因为中国的羊不是专用的毛用羊，养殖目的主要是食肉或取皮；然而，中国羊毛质量低劣更多的是由于其中时常混有泥土或其他杂质。所以，中国羊毛主要用于制造地毯、毛毯和针织物。尽管中国羊毛无法用于高质量的服装，但由于其价格低廉，仍被认为是一种重要的粗纺商品原料。

中国的另一种绒毛原料是骆驼毛，它来自蒙古草原，同样在天津港集中、出口。骆驼毛有多种用途，可以制造骆驼毛毯和小地毯。运往国外的最好部分据说用于制造纹理细密内衣，原因就在于其柔软性。中国每年出口骆驼毛 480 万磅，其中的 1/4～1/3 运往美国。

除了骆驼毛、羊毛，中国每年还出口 220 万磅的山羊毛，约占美国山羊毛进口总量的 1/3。

与国土面积相当的其他产毛国相比，中国产毛羊、牛的数量较少。中国(包括蒙古、西藏在内)比美国及其所有属地的领土还要大。中国的蒙古、西藏及其他内陆省份拥有延绵不绝的优质牧场，随着毛产品价格的上升、建设更好的运输设施、山区实施文明的警务系统，以及引进改良品种羊，可以预期中国的毛纺业无论在质量方面，还是数量方面都会有一个大的发展。所以，在不远的将来，中国可望成为一个更加重要的产毛国,在与南美、澳大利亚争夺美国市场的竞争中占据更为有利的位置。

至于羊毛制品的贸易,中国几乎都以地毯、毛毯形式出口。过去十年,中国的地毯、毛毯贸易有了明显发展[①]。羊毛制品的主要生产中心是与蒙古接壤的中国北方省份,用于出口的主要港口是天津。

仅仅在十五年前(1905年),美国才开始从中国进口地毯和毛毯。欧洲战争之前,尽管美国的进口量很少,但东方地毯在美国赢得了与其贸易量不相匹配的好名声。1905—1913年,美国每年的进口额不超过数千美元。

然而,1914年以后,中美地毯贸易快速发展,1920、1921年,美国每年从中国进口250万平方码,年均进口额150万美元。1922年,进口量、进口额均比上年增加1倍。1905—1922年美国从中国进口这类物资的情况见表9-3。

表 9-3　1905—1922 年美国从中国进口毛毯、地毯统计

| 时　　段 | (万平方码) | (万美元) | 年份 | (万平方码) | (万美元) |
|---|---|---|---|---|---|
| 1905—1908 平均(财年) | | 0.7 | 1918 | 8.5 | 40.7 |
| 1909—1913 平均(财年) | | 1.8 | 1919 | 9.0 | 44.2 |
| 1914—1918 平均(财年) | 6.3 | 33.8 | 1920 | 25.1 | 201.2 |
| | | | 1921 | 25.0 | 139.3 |
| | | | 1922 | 46.9 | 259.5 |

注:1905—1908 年、1909—1913 年的进口数量未见报道。

自地毯、毛毯贸易开展以来,美国就是中国此类产品最好的消费者[②]。战前,美国的进口占中国总出口量的一半还多,而 1914 年后,则达到 2/3。

---

① 下列 1913—1922 年中国地毯出口额及目的地统计数据摘自于中国海关年度贸易报告:

| 年份 | 中国毛毯、地毯总出口 | 出口美国 | | 出口日本 | |
|---|---|---|---|---|---|
| | (万两香港海关银元) | (万两香港海关银元) | (%) | (万两香港海关银元) | (%) |
| 1913 | 10.0 | 5.5 | 55 | 0.6 | 6 |
| 1915 | 16.5 | 10.2 | 62 | 5.0 | 30 |
| 1917 | 79.6 | 43.1 | 55 | 32.9 | 42 |
| 1919 | 46.1 | 29.5 | 64 | 7.0 | 15 |
| 1920 | 142.4 | 103.3 | 73 | 17.3 | 12 |
| 1921 | 97.5 | 64.8 | 66 | 8.7 | 9 |
| 1922 | 330.0 | 269.7 | 81 | 33.2 | 10 |

② 见前一脚注。

## 二、头发和发网

头发、发网这样不起眼的物资,在中国对外贸易、特别是对美贸易中不断提高的重要性,应该受到特别的注意。也就是十五年前,美国才开始从中国进口头发;1914 年前,并没有进口发网。但到了 1920—1922 年,美国每年从中国进口的头发、发网就已经接近 700 万美元。

1911 年(辛亥)革命后,剪辫子在中国南方变得非常普遍,并逐渐扩展到北方。因此头发的供应大为增加,其贸易也受到了刺激。后来妇女梳理的头发及理发店剪下的毛发也参与其中。世界大战前,中国的头发大部分直接运往欧洲,只有一小部分(不超过 4%～5%)销往美国。但是,1916 年后,美国市场开始扩张,1919、1920、1921 年,美国几乎吸纳了中国头发总出口的 50%。表 9-4 之 A1、A2 栏列举了美国从中国进口的头发的数量及金额。

表 9-4　1913—1923 年美国从中国进口头发及其制品统计

| 年份 | 未加工的头发（A） | | 头发制品（发网）（B） |
|---|---|---|---|
| | 进口量（万磅） | 进口额（万美元） | 进口额（万美元） |
| 1913 | 32.4 | 17.2 | |
| 1914 | 16.7 | 6.0 | 0.1 |
| 1915 | 26.2 | 7.0 | 0.5 |
| 1916 | 43.4 | 7.4 | 18.2 |
| 1917 | 31.9 | 8.5 | 48.7 |
| 1918 | 87.0 | 34.0 | 70.9 |
| 1919 | 110.0 | 46.3 | 203.1 |
| 1920 | 135.3 | 60.4 | 625.7 |
| 1921 | 62.3 | 19.3 | 835.4 |
| 1922 | 62.9 | 19.0 | 580.4 |
| 1923 | 19.9 | 7.9 | |

头发贸易的发展无法与发网贸易的异常成长相比较。也许中国没有哪个萌芽期的工业能比发网制造的扩张更加引人注目。这个产业尽管似乎无关紧要,但已提供了数千个就业岗位,为数百万美国妇女提供发网。德国人在十五年前才将该产业引入中国,但到了 1920 年,仅在中国的某一个城市就有 1.4 亿个发网运往美国,年出口总额超过 1 000 万美元。这些发网常被美国妇女用来定型头发。几年前,发网还是一种装

饰品或奢侈品,现在则是为了舒适,甚至成为一种必需品。

中国发网产业是另一个战争产物,并且是有持久性前途的一种。世界大战前,意大利、加力西亚与中国一道提供了大部分用于发网的头发,但生产集中在(法国)阿尔萨斯－洛林地区、(西班牙)加力西亚和(捷克)波希米亚。然而,在世界大战的敌对时期,发网产业逐渐转移到了中国,现在发网实际上是中国的一种独有产品。山东、直隶两省是最大的生产地。1 磅预制头发——成本几美元、取决于长度和质量——可以制成 2 000 多个发网,一个发网的总重量仅为 1 盎司①左右。发网由手工制作,女工制作一个发网可获得 1 美分的劳动报酬,每个人每天制作的发网不会超过 10 个。

中国人的头发色泽深黑,不适合头发通常为浅色的美国人使用,因此,头发在织成发网前要用化工产品进行漂白和复染。以前,头发从中国航运到欧洲或美国,完成化学作业后再运回中国制作发网。但是,随着工业的发展,头发的预加工也大多移往中国进行。现在中国出口的发网,可能有 90% 是在中国国内完成头发预加工的。中国化工厂完成的漂白、复染工作,效果令人满意。已有一家美国企业签署协议,将在老练的美国化学家的指导下,在中国完成其头发预制工作。

美国妇女对这些发网似乎非常满意,而且看起来将来会更加频繁地使用。表 9 - 4 之 B 栏表示了美国从中国进口发网的成长情况。令人十分惊奇的是,在不足十年的时间里,发网贸易额从不足 1 000 美元增长到 800 万美元以上。值得注意的是,在几乎各行各业都陷入萧条的 1921 年,物价总水平严重下挫,但中美两国发网贸易额仍然持续增长。一旦发网市场在美国建立起来,只要戴发网的风尚在美国保留,中国就依靠它为其数千女工谋取了工作机会。发网贸易也是中国不担心其他国家竞争的行业之一,因为中国有丰富的廉价劳动力,而这在其他任何国家都是不存在的。一个发网需要手工完成多达 1 000 甚至更多的结,而为这一辛勤劳动所支付的报酬,在过去数年间一直在 2～2.5 个铜板(约合 1 美分)左右。

## 三、猪鬃

猪的鬃毛是制造刷子的主要原料。猪鬃根据长度、颜色、硬度、形状、质地和弹性确定等级,最好的猪鬃要从生长在寒冷气候地区的猪身上获取;所以,俄罗斯和西伯利亚的猪鬃以其品质优良而闻名。俄罗斯和中国提供了美国毛刷业所需的大部分猪鬃。俄罗斯产量第一,其后是中国、德国和印度。中欧的一些国家也生产、出口数量可观的猪鬃。猪鬃在美国是屠宰场的副产品。由于猪的品种原因,加之屠宰时尚未成年,美国猪鬃较短,质量等级较差。美国猪鬃主要用于制造价格较低的刷子,如鞋刷和尘刷。

中国猪鬃进入美国市场是毛刷工业的一个重要事件。反对中国猪鬃替代俄罗斯

---

① 译注:1 盎司＝1 英两,约 28.35 克。

猪鬃的声浪逐步消退,很大程度上是因为发现了恰当的处理中国猪鬃的方法。中国猪鬃必须要采用不同于俄罗斯猪鬃的独特的预加工方法,这是影响其使用的主要原因。中国猪鬃通常为黑色,长度2.5～7英吋。中国猪鬃的弹性与俄罗斯猪鬃一样,但据说不够坚韧、耐用。然而,19世纪后期,美国还是从中国进口了猪鬃;进口量、进口额在过去均有很大的增长。三十年前的1894年,美国进口的中国猪鬃仅为7.4万磅,价值2.7万美元。十年后的1904年,进口量增至92.1万磅,进口额达47.5万美元。在接下来的十年里,这两个数字都接近于1904年的2倍。过去的十年间,中国平均每年出口800万磅鬃毛[①],其中约2/3输往美国,从战前的不足150万磅(进口额不足100万美元),上升至1920年的近350万磅(见表9-5之A栏)。现在,已经分选、成束、预加工的猪鬃在中美贸易中占据着重要的地位,超过两国贸易总额的3%。

表9-5　1894—1922年美国从中国进口猪鬃及其他动物毛发统计

| 年份 | 猪鬃(分选、成束、预加工的) | | 马毛(未加工的) | | 其他动物毛发 | |
| --- | --- | --- | --- | --- | --- | --- |
| | (万磅) | (万美元) | (万磅) | (万美元) | (万磅) | (万美元) |
| | A | | B | | C | |
| 1894 | 7.4 | 2.7 | | | | |
| 1899 | 38.9 | 17.0 | | | | |
| 1904 | 92.1 | 47.5 | | | | |
| 1908 | 136.3 | 80.0 | | | | |
| 1912 | 148.8 | 86.9 | | | 32.1 | 8.0 |
| 1913 | 143.9 | 92.2 | | | 41.8 | 16.8 |
| 1914 | 141.0 | 93.4 | 14.3 | 12.0 | 1.0 | 0.1 |
| 1915 | 235.9 | 162.3 | 19.4 | 9.5 | 17.0 | 1.7 |
| 1916 | 235.9 | 161.2 | 47.1 | 17.8 | 76.8 | 9.0 |
| 1917 | 238.5 | 172.8 | 99.5 | 50.9 | 65.6 | 9.6 |
| 1918 | 317.3 | 338.1 | 67.8 | 32.1 | 8.7 | 5.1 |
| 1919 | 215.9 | 275.0 | 63.6 | 35.1 | 6.4 | 3.4 |
| 1920 | 335.7 | 616.8 | 64.3 | 48.9 | 9.3 | 5.8 |
| 1921 | 254.0 | 383.1 | 78.2 | 50.0 | 8.1 | 3.8 |
| 1922 | 272.1 | 296.9 | 73.5 | 49.0 | 27.4 | 9.4 |

注:1912年,"马毛(未加工的)"未单列,数据包括在"其他动物毛发"之中。

① 据中国海关贸易报告,文中所述时段内中国平均每年出口猪鬃6万担(1担=133.33磅)。

　　战前,英国与中国共同分享对美猪鬃贸易。战争期间,英国的份额下降到很小的数字,而中国几乎独享该种贸易;这种情况在战后没有发生改变。中国目前供应着美国约80%的猪鬃进口需求(见表9-6),而且由于英国猪鬃价格比中国猪鬃高出很多[1],中国将能在未来继续控制美国猪鬃市场。

　　为了制造软毛刷,美国从中国进口的马毛及其他兽毛的数量也在增长(见表9-5之B、C栏),但它们的贸易地位尚不重要。

表9-6　1913—1922年美国进口猪鬃来源统计

| 年份 | 美国进口猪鬃总量 | | 从中国内地 | | 从中国香港 | | 从英国 | |
|---|---|---|---|---|---|---|---|---|
| | (万磅) | (万美元) | (万磅) | (万美元) | (万磅) | (万美元) | (万磅) | (万美元) |
| 1913 | 355.9 | 349.2 | 143.9 | 92.2 | 4.2 | 3.0 | 105.0 | 116.9 |
| 1918 | 411.9 | 564.0 | 311.5 | 336.9 | 35.7 | 55.8 | 18.2 | 74.7 |
| 1919 | 308.1 | 593.2 | 212.6 | 272.7 | 5.1 | 11.8 | 55.8 | 146.8 |
| 1920 | 482.1 | 1 010.2 | 332.2 | 602.0 | 3.9 | 5.8 | 88.2 | 229.9 |
| 1921 | 341.4 | 534.1 | 252.9 | 377.8 | 10.2 | 12.0 | 52.8 | 76.1 |
| 1922 | 408.5 | 534.6 | 272.1 | 296.9 | 1.5 | 1.5 | 82.7 | 128.6 |

## 四、兽皮

　　美国是世界上最重要的皮革制造国之一,它拥有大量的牲畜,能供应数量庞大的兽皮。然而,其无数个皮革工厂对兽皮原料的需求如此之大,以至于在正常的商业情况下,美国每年需从世界各地进口超过1亿美元的各类兽皮。世界大战期间及战后之初的几年里,美国每年进口的兽皮超过2亿美元。

　　19世纪末期以来,兽皮在中美贸易中长期占据着重要地位。1891—1913年的二十年间,中美兽皮贸易扩大了近10倍(见表9-7最后一栏)。1891—1895年,美国从中国进口兽皮的数量未见报告,每年进口额不足40万美元。1911—1913年,美国从中国进口的兽皮增加至每年1 550万磅,进口额达350万美元。这一增长的部分原因是1909年的美国关税法案将所有兽皮都列入免税名录[2]。1914—1920年期间,受战争及战后需求的刺激,兽皮的进口数量,尤其是进口额再次巨幅增长。因此,仅1917

---

　　[1] 英国猪鬃的进口数量少,但进口额相当大,可以推知英国猪鬃的价格通常比中国猪鬃的价格高出2倍以上。

　　[2] 1909年前,牛皮按价值的15%计征进口关税,其他兽皮免税。

年,美国就从中国进口了 5 900 万磅兽皮,价值 2 750 万美元;而 1920 年则分别为 2 900万磅、3 100 万美元。1921—1922 年,兽皮进口几乎下降到战前水平,但随着美国工业活动的逐步恢复,如今兽皮贸易再次回升。

表 9 - 7　1891—1922 年美国从中国进口兽皮分类统计

| 年　　份 | 牛皮、水牛皮 | | 山羊皮 | | 绵羊皮、牛犊皮、马皮、马驹皮等 | | 兽皮进口合计 | |
| --- | --- | --- | --- | --- | --- | --- | --- | --- |
| | （万磅） | （万美元） | （万磅） | （万美元） | （万磅） | （万美元） | （万磅） | （万美元） |
| 1891—1895 | | | | | | | | 37.9 |
| 1986—1900 | | | | | | | 769.1 | 119.8 |
| 1901—1905 | | | | | | | 1097.8 | 241.3 |
| 1906—1910 | | | | | | | 1344.7 | 347.2 |
| 1911—1913 | 442.8 | 95.3 | 938.2 | 252.8 | 149.8 | 24.6 | 1 530.8 | 372.7 |
| 1914—1915 | 1 089.3 | 251.6 | 760.1 | 200.6 | 176.2 | 34.9 | 2 025.6 | 487.0 |
| 1916—1917 | 2 285.8 | 658.2 | 1 828.1 | 987.6 | 735.1 | 208.8 | 4 849.0 | 1 854.6 |
| 1918 | 587.6 | 192.3 | 1 381.2 | 875.3 | 352.6 | 129.9 | 2 321.4 | 1 197.5 |
| 1919 | 1 105.0 | 372.0 | 1 521.7 | 1 094.2 | 712.9 | 248.7 | 3 339.6 | 1 714.9 |
| 1920 | 766.6 | 285.4 | 1 906.2 | 2 663.4 | 210.0 | 131.2 | 2 882.8 | 3 080.6 |
| 1921 | 149.9 | 26.3 | 1 058.6 | 360.8 | 88.8 | 32.5 | 1 297.3 | 419.5 |
| 1922 | 465.5 | 82.4 | 1 340.8 | 570.8 | 128.8 | 43.4 | 1 935.1 | 696.6 |

注 1:1895 年前的进口量未见报道。

注 2:1911—1913 年之"牛皮、水牛皮"数据中不包括水牛。

　　尽管中国兽皮被大量进口到美国,但其在美国兽皮总进口中的份额并不很大。战前,美国制革厂、皮革厂主要从德国、俄罗斯的欧洲部分、英国、法国和其他中欧国家、英属印度、加拿大、墨西哥、阿根廷、巴西、哥伦比亚、智利、乌拉圭、英属非洲、新西兰和澳大利亚进口原材料;那时美国从中国进口的兽皮数量已经非常大,但 1911—1913 年的中美兽皮贸易额在美国兽皮进口总额中的平均份额还不到 4%。战争及战后时期,欧洲供应源几乎完全切断,美国对兽皮增长的需求只得由中国及其他亚洲、美洲国家来满足。所以,1916—1920 年间,中国兽皮的份额上升到 10% 左右,1921—1922 年稳定在 6.5%,与战前相比有了大幅增长(见表 9 - 8)。

表 9 - 8　1911—1922 年美国对华进口兽皮统计

| 年　　份 | 美国进口兽皮总额(万美元) | 从中国进口 | |
|---|---|---|---|
| | | 进口额(万美元) | 在美国市场占比(%) |
| 1911—1913 年均 | 9 678.9 | 372.7 | 3.9 |
| 1914—1915 年均 | 11 121.1 | 487.0 | 4.4 |
| 1916—1917 年均 | 18 533.4 | 1 854.6 | 10.0 |
| 1918 | 10 804.4 | 1 197.5 | 11.1 |
| 1919 | 30 651.0 | 1 714.9 | 5.6 |
| 1920 | 24 387.8 | 3 080.6 | 12.6 |
| 1921 | 6 756.1 | 419.5 | 6.2 |
| 1922 | 10 703.6 | 696.6 | 6.5 |

中国国内出产的大批动物长期服务、并将继续更好地服务于美国的皮革工业,成为其原材料的备用来源。大皮来源于牛、水牛、马和驴;而小皮则来源于山羊、绵羊、牛犊、马驹等。重皮用于生产鞋底革、机器皮带、衣箱、行李箱等,而轻皮则用于轻便鞋和鞋面。绵羊皮、山羊皮用于制造最轻的鞋类、手套、小工艺品、钱包、室内装饰品等。在从中国进口的各种兽皮中,山羊皮最为重要,其在美国进口中国兽皮的总额中通常占到 80% 以上;排在其后的是牛皮,其他各种兽皮的进口规模都不太大。但是,当所有兽皮都能在美国免税进口时,中国没有理由不能在与其他国家竞争的基础上增加对美输出、提高本国各种兽皮在美国市场的份额。

## 五、毛皮

与兽皮进口紧密相关的是中国毛皮的进口。1875—1890 年,受本国毛皮需求大增的压力,美国毛皮商开始寻求新的供应源,并在中国找到了答案。美国皮毛商从东方进口了大量的用山羊皮和狗皮制作的皮褥子和皮袍,它们可以轻松地加工成划船、赶雪橇时穿的温暖、耐用的长袍。"起初中国毛皮价格很低,进口商获利丰厚,但不久,由于市场竞争使其价格抬升,美国的利润下降。美国对山羊皮、狗皮的消费量仍然很大,但是,这两种动物在中国仍然繁盛,数量充足,能满足美国的需求。"

但毛皮贸易在 1891—1913 年实际上停滞不前,年贸易额约在 30 万美元。事实上,当中美贸易年复一年地增长时,中国毛皮在美国市场的相对重要性在持续下降。这一时期,向美国供应毛皮的出口大国是英国、德国、加拿大、澳大利亚和阿根廷,中国的份额只有 1%～2%。

但在 1914 年后,由于战争的影响,毛皮贸易发生了很大变化。战争滋扰使美国从欧洲进口的毛皮大幅下降;而加拿大、南非和澳大利亚的毛皮不能满足美国增长的需求,与半个世纪前一样,美国再次将目光投向中国,寻求补充的供应。在此情形下,中国毛皮被东方的美国企业大量购买,贸易额从 1914 年的 50 万美元上升到 1918 年的 300 万美元、1919 年的 700 万美元、1920 年的 1 200 万美元。1921 年,由于美国商业萧条,毛皮贸易有所回落。1922 年收复了上一年丢失的失地,贸易额达到创纪录的 1 400万美元。中美毛皮贸易的重要性同样明显提高,中国毛皮在美国毛皮进口总额中的占比,1914 年仅为 4.7%,1918—1921 年各年平均超过 10%,1922 年达到 20%,中国第一次成了美国毛皮进口的第一大来源地(见表 9-9)。

表 9-9 1891—1922 年美国从中国进口毛皮统计

| 年 份 | (未鞣的)毛皮 进口额 (万美元) | (已鞣的)毛皮 进口额 (万美元) | 毛皮制品 进口额 (万美元) | 美国从中国进口毛皮合计 | |
|---|---|---|---|---|---|
| | | | | 进口额 (万美元) | 在美国毛皮总进口 中占比(%) |
| 1891—1895 | | | | 38.9 | |
| 1896—1900 | | | | 28.1 | |
| 1901—1905 | | | | 26.1 | |
| 1906—1910 | | | | 30.2 | |
| 1911—1913 | 12.4 | 25.4 | | 37.7 | 1.5 |
| 1914—1915 | 4.8 | 40.9 | 13.6 | 59.3 | 4.7 |
| 1916—1917 | 37.6 | 76.4 | 9.6 | 123.6 | 5.3 |
| 1918 | 237.3 | 46.7 | 26.2 | 310.1 | 9.01 |
| 1919 | 525.8 | 22.3 | 184.5 | 732.6 | 10.2 |
| 1920 | 1 073.1 | 23.1 | 153.2 | 1 249.4 | 13.4 |
| 1921 | 404.7 | 9.3 | 67.9 | 481.9 | 11.9 |
| 1922 | 1 212.5 | 27.3 | 144.7 | 1 384.7 | 20.0 |

中国毛皮以未鞣的、已鞣的、毛皮制品三种形态进口到美国。1917 年之前,已鞣毛皮及毛皮制品的进口远多于未鞣的毛皮。但是 1918 年后,未鞣毛皮的进口额增至十年前的 100 倍以上,毛皮制品只增长 10 倍,而已鞣毛皮实际上在减少。增长幅度的差异主要是由于已鞣毛皮和毛皮制品被课以沉重的进口关税,而所有的未鞣毛皮则免除了进口税。中国对美毛皮贸易将会有一个非常光明的未来。美国人现在越来越富有,他们对毛皮这样的奢侈品的需求相应提高。由于大量出产皮毛动物,中国能够向美国鞣皮厂和毛皮商供应许多种毛皮原料。

## 六、禽蛋和蛋产品

很久之前,禽蛋就已经是中国人日常饮食的重要食品,并在中国大量生产,但是,直到二十年前才进入中国的对外贸易领域。但是,最近十年间,禽蛋贸易快速发展,并占据了一个重要地位;目前中国每年出口的禽蛋和蛋产品达一二千万美元,其中大部分输往美国,美国近90%的禽蛋来自中国。表 9 - 10 表明了中美两国之间禽蛋贸易的超常成长。1912 年,贸易额勉强超过 1 万美元,但到 1919 年则增长为近 1 300 万美元,1920 年为 1 100 万美元。1921—1922 年美国商业萧条,中美禽蛋贸易大幅回落,但每年的贸易额仍保持在 400 万～500 万美元。

表 9 - 10  1911—1922 年美国从中国进口禽蛋、蛋产品统计

| 年　　份 | 禽蛋 | | 蛋黄(冷藏、干制等) | | 蛋白 | | 进口总额 |
|---|---|---|---|---|---|---|---|
| | (万磅) | (万美元) | (万打) | (万美元) | (万磅) | (万美元) | (万美元) |
| 1911—1913 | 11.1 | 1.1 | 25.0 | 1.6 | | | 2.7 |
| 1914—1915 | 196.6 | 22.9 | 371.8 | 29.0 | | | 51.9 |
| 1916—1917 | 39.3 | 6.1 | 648.2 | 111.9 | | | 118.0 |
| 1918 | 49.0 | 10.5 | 673.6 | 245.5 | 135.3 | 46.9 | 302.9 |
| 1919 | 47.5 | 11.7 | 2 216.8 | 694.4 | 755.7 | 560.3 | 1 266.4 |
| 1920 | 84.7 | 22.8 | 2 564.7 | 609.3 | 852.6 | 445.3 | 1 077.4 |
| 1921 | 113.2 | 24.6 | 1 532.6 | 230.0 | 449.8 | 111.9 | 366.5 |
| 1922 | 38.3 | 6.1 | 1 756.6 | 309.9 | 644.1 | 199.5 | 505.5 |

注 1:1917 年前,蛋白进口统计数据未单列。

中国出口到美国的禽蛋通常是腌制方式加工的。中国人用泥土和食盐、或者石灰包裹禽蛋,以使其保味、保质数月之久。它们还以蛋黄或蛋白的加工形式出口,前者用于制造饼干和其他蛋糕,而后者是糖果的生产原料。中国的禽蛋及蛋制品能以相当低的价格购买到,因此被美国面包店和糖果工厂广泛采用。

1919 年前,美国从中国进口的蛋产品数量还不是很大,因此进口活动没有受到美国政府的限制。但在该年之后,美国的禽蛋生产者充分认识到了中国冰蛋和粉状蛋的竞争,太平洋沿岸各州的法律不断企图排斥这些中国产品。以前,中国的干蛋粉生产者通常使用锌制容器。美国卫生部由此认定,中国蛋产品含有锌,因此是有毒的。美国卫生部要求蛋产品中可检出的锌含量不得超过 1‰,并发布了一项针对中国进口产品的非常严格的规定,这一技术壁垒导致中国向美国出口的蛋产品自 1920 年开始减

少,中国商人遭受了严重的损失。预制过程中需把蛋黄倒入锌盘的制作方法,无法保证锌的含量下降到如此之低的水平。中国人试用过其他加工方法,并曾使用过瓷器,但由于一些原因,产品质量不如原有的加工方法。按照一位在华的美国调查人员的说法,就中国蛋产品的公共卫生影响而言,几乎没有什么可担心的。

不只是这样相当严格的规定阻碍着中国禽蛋向美国市场的出口,美国最近修订的进口关税法案也构成了对这一贸易的第二个壁垒。因此,中国海关贸易报告评论说,"美国市场上,来自中国的冻蛋和干蛋要承受美国 1922 年 9 月 22 日实施的关税提高法案①中所征收的更高的进口关税。当年早些时间,满载禽蛋的重型货船都来自中国,但到当年八月,中国的禽蛋出口几乎都停止了。"所以,在美国政府撤销这些严格限制之前,中美禽蛋贸易的前景不会很乐观。

---

① 下表摘自美国 1909、1913、1922 年关税法案,表明禽蛋和蛋产品的关税在 1922 法案中有了很大提高。

| 项　　目 | 1909 年 | 1913 年 | 1922 年 |
|---|---|---|---|
| (干)蛋白 | 3 美分/磅 | 3 美分/磅 | 18 美分/磅 |
| (冰冻或其他方法保藏的)蛋白 | 3 美分/磅 | 1 美分/磅 | 6 美分/磅 |
| (干)蛋黄 | 25% | 10% | 18 美分/磅 |
| (冰冻或其他方法保藏的)蛋黄 | 25% | 10% | 6 美分/磅 |
| (带壳的)禽蛋 | 5 美分/打 | 免税 | 8 美分/打 |

在美国关税历史传统中,计税方法由从价计税改为从量计税,实际税率通常会大幅增长。

# 第三篇

美国输华商品举要

# 第十章 棉织品

## 一、作为棉织品市场的中国

19 世纪中叶以来,棉制品一直是中国进口贸易中最大的单一物资;中国是世界上仅次于印度的第二大布匹市场。在过去的半个世纪里,布匹进口约占中国总进口的 1/3。布匹进口额几乎与中国进口总额同步大幅增长。1880 年,中国布匹进口仅为 3 200 万美元,而 1900、1920 年则分别达到 5 100 万美元、3.06 亿美元;战前十年间,年均进口超亿美元,而从那时起,进口额已经翻番。人们可以从这些数字得出明显的结论:现在中国为棉织品提供了一个潜藏着巨大前途的广阔市场。

中国丰富的天然资源的开发、能使国内运输设施更加完美的铁路建设、人民经济社会的进步,将无可争议地使消费进一步稳定增长,无疑将极大地刺激中国本土工厂尚不能充分供应的各种外国棉制品的大量进口。

## 二、美国对华布匹贸易的早期繁荣——英国竞争

美国棉纺业自建立以后,就一直在中国这一布匹大市场中占据着相当重要的地位。早在 19 世纪 30 年代,美国的布匹就在其对华国内出口中贡献了可观的份额[1]。19 世纪 50 年代,布匹成为美国最重要的对华出口物资。1850—1853 年间,仅布料一项就占到美国国内对华出口的近 90%,同时中国成了美国布匹的最好消费者,其进口占美国布料总出口的 1/3 强[2]。透过这些数字,可以容易地认识到中美两国棉制品贸

---

[1] 参见第一章。

[2] 1850—1853 年美国对华布料出口情况如下:

| 年份 | 美国国内对华出口总额 (A)（万美元） | 美国布料出口总额 (B)（万美元） | 美国对华布料出口 | | |
|---|---|---|---|---|---|
| | | | 出口额（C）（万美元） | 在美国对华总出口中占比（＝C/A）（%） | 在美国布料总出口中占比（＝C/B）（%） |
| 1850 | 148.6 | 377.4 | 120.3 | 81 | 32 |
| 1851 | 215.6 | 557.2 | 189.4 | 88 | 34 |
| 1852 | 248.0 | 613.9 | 220.2 | 89 | 36 |
| 1853 | 321.3 | 692.6 | 280.1 | 87 | 40 |

易在早期是多么地繁荣,布料在其中扮演着多么重要的角色。

但是,由于美国内战使运送大宗棉布物资所依赖的商船队遭到破坏,加之英国、印度激烈竞争,美国在 1860 年后失去了与东方的大部分棉制品贸易。19 世纪 70 年代,美国恢复了一些失去的份额,但无论在美国出口榜单抑或中国进口榜单上,美国棉制品都没有恢复到它原有的地位。棉制品的出口量、出口额有时会高于 1850 年代,但所占份额则从来回升到曾有的荣光。

当然,美国棉制品在中美贸易中的份额相对萎缩,有美国其他产品对华出口增长,以及美国棉制品向南美和欧洲的出口大幅增长的原因。但是,棉制品贸易相对份额下降的主要原因似乎是,美国棉制品刚刚在中国展开国际竞争,就遭遇了制造成本偏高的困难,从而导致其布匹售价较高。价格因素在中国一直相当敏感,因为大多数中国人的收入通常都较低。为了满足低价需要,英国人很大程度上被迫在布匹中掺杂泥土和其他杂质。美国厂商抵制了这种诱惑,"完全用棉制作诚实的衣服",所以价格肯定要比英国人的服装高一些,有时还高出很多。"尽管中国人从来不吝夸赞美国棉制品的质量,但由于购买标准的斜纹布和帆布要比其他布料贵,掺杂的英国便宜货满足了中国人不能忽视、而美国人必定反对的低价愿望"。所以,在 19 世纪 80 年代中国进口的棉制品中,6/7 是英国货,美国货不足 1/12。

通过一名美国驻华领事[①]的另一份报告,人们可以初步认识到美国在棉制品贸易方面曾经遭受、未来仍可能延续的严重障碍:

"这里有几家大的美国棉制品贸易商号;但是,说来奇怪,出售的大部分货物来自伦敦而非美国城市。对此有各种不同的解释,但最为可信的理由是,堆放在这里的货物,伦敦产品要比美国其他城市的更为便宜。贸易很少能由爱国原则来支配,利益才是其指路明灯。"

这位领事先生认为,在早期竞争中国棉制品市场的过程中,英国人战胜美国人还有其他一些原因:①美国商人对航运到外国的货物包装并不在意,而英国人与之相反;②美国在中国没有足够的金融机构以支持其进口业务,实际上没有商船队从事棉制品运输业务,而中国的银行和轮船公司大多由英国人控制。

尽管有这些不利条件,19 世纪末期及 20 世纪初,美国布匹仍在美国对华贸易中占据了非常重要的地位。如同表 10-1[②] 所示,在 1891—1905 年这十五年间,美国对棉布出口量、出口额每五年增长 1 倍;整个这一时期,美国对华布匹出口总额在美国对华出口总额中所占的比例接近 60%(表 10-1 之最后一栏)。1902 年,美国产品在中国布匹进口总额中所占的比例为 27%,1905 年则高达 36%(见表 10-2)。

---

① 指时任美国驻福州总领事的 J. T. Campbel。
② 译注:原文此处(第 208 页第 3 段第 5 行)为表号错误,疑为作者笔误。

表 10-1　1891—1922 年美国对华(含租界)棉布出口统计

| 年　　份 | 美国(年均)对华总出口 | 美国对华棉布总出口 | | |
| --- | --- | --- | --- | --- |
| | (万美元) | (万码) | (万美元) | 在美国出口总额中占比(%) |
| 1891—1895 | 554.6 | 5 218.2 | 308.2 | 56.0 |
| 1896—1900 | 1 171.8 | 14 638.9 | 701.9 | 60.0 |
| 1901—1905 | 2 406.9 | 24 973.1 | 1 329.5 | 55.0 |
| 1906—1910 | 2 551.3 | 12 397.6 | 1 035.8 | 41.0 |
| 1911—1915 | 2 093.8 | 7 516.4 | 512.6 | 25.0 |
| 1916—1918 | 4 554.8 | 730.8 | 72.8 | 1.6 |
| 1919 | 11 827.5 | 3 921.6 | 641.0 | 5.4 |
| 1920 | 15 287.6 | 2 862.4 | 770.1 | 5.1 |
| 1921 | 11 360.5 | 2 456.0 | 228.2 | 2.0 |
| 1922 | 10 607.4 | 1 588.4 | 194.0 | 1.8 |

表 10-2　战前(1902—1913 年)中国布匹进口来源分布比例(进口额百分比)

| 年份 | 英国 | 香港地区 | 日本 | 俄罗斯 | 美国 |
| --- | --- | --- | --- | --- | --- |
| 1902 | 55.3 | 8.1 | 2.7 | | 26.8 |
| 1905 | 49.2 | 7.3 | 2.5 | | 35.5 |
| 1907 | 72.2 | 11.7 | 4.7 | | 5.7 |
| 1909 | 54.7 | 12.8 | 8.3 | 1.7 | 18.1 |
| 1911 | 61.3 | 10.5 | 13.8 | 1.4 | 9.5 |
| 1913 | 53.3 | 10.1 | 20.2 | 3.3 | 7.9 |

美国输往中国的大部分棉织物是平纹布,如被单料、衬衫衣料、牛仔布、帆布,还有非常少量的染色布料。实际上中国的所有染色布料都来自英国,在这一领域美国无力挑战英国在中国市场的强势地位。

1905 年之前美国布匹对华贸易繁荣的理由,是不难理解的。那个时候,除了英国,事实上没有哪个国家能与美国织品商进行任何强有力的竞争。日本向中国出口平纹棉织物已有数年,但其在中国市场的份额与美国相比可以忽略不计,因为它的棉业还没有很好地发展起来。那时,中国自己的棉纺制造还仅仅是一个"新鲜的产业"。中国的第一家纺织厂建立于 1891 年,此后的十二年,数量也仅增加到 12 家。作为一个新生产业,这些数量不多的工厂难以向中国消费者提供充足的布料;另一方面,进口总量的快速上升证明中国人对这种布匹的需求在年复一年地增长。正是这一市场态势,美国棉织商更加从中受惠。

美国对华布匹贸易在 1905、1906 年达到顶峰,中国从美国进口 5 亿码、约 3 000 万美元,(美国产品)所占的份额几乎与英国相当。但这是由于满洲地区的(俄日)战争需求而形成的两个相当例外的年份。

**1. 布匹贸易的近期下滑**

1906 年后,美国棉织商迅速失去了其在中国的战场,美国输往中国的布匹持续下滑。表 10－1 清晰显示,年均贸易量从 1901—1905 年的 2.2 亿码,缩减至 1906—1910 年的 1.24 亿码,再到 1911—1915 年的 7 500 万码,最后滑落至 1916—1918 年三年战争期间的 700 万码。中美布匹贸易额同样以惊人的速度下降,从 1901—1905 年的年均 1 300 万美元以上,下降到 1906—1910 年的 1 000 万美元、1911—1915 年的 500 万美元,最终到 1916—1918 年不足 75 万美元。布匹贸易在中美贸易中的份额也显现同样的下降趋势。20 世纪前五年,布匹出口在美国对华出口中占比 55％,而在第二个五年下降到 41％,第三个五年则只有 25％,而到 1916—1918 年的三年间,更是跌落到只有 3％。1919 年之后,布匹贸易量、贸易额均有所恢复,但仍远低于几年前的情况。1921 年,美国对华布匹出口稍多于 200 万美元,在美国对华出口总额中的比例也仅为 2％多一点。另一方面,美国布匹在中国布匹进口中所占的份额也在下降。如表 10－2、表 10－3 所示,1905 年前,美国布匹(加上通过香港转运的折算部分)在中国布匹进口总额中所占的比例在 2/5～1/3 之间;但是在此之后,这一比例急剧下降至 10％左右,欧洲战争爆发后,更是直线下降到不足 5％(见表 10－3)。

美国对华布匹出口贸易的严重下滑首先是由于日本人的新竞争,最近则是由于中国纺织厂的竞争,其优势是使用更加低廉的中国、印度原材料,生产成本更低。

**表 10－3　1911—1922 年中国进口布匹来源分布**

| 年份 | 中国布匹总进口 | 从美国 | | 从英国 | | 从日本 | | 从其他地区 | |
|------|------|------|------|------|------|------|------|------|------|
| | (万匹) | (万匹) | (％) | (万匹) | (％) | (万匹) | (％) | (万匹) | (％) |
| 1911 | 1 616.0 | 198.8 | 12.3 | 1 131.8 | 70.0 | 283.3 | 17.5 | 2.2 | 0.2 |
| 1913 | 1979.5 | 228.1 | 11.5 | 1 170.5 | 58.0 | 591.7 | 30.0 | 9.2 | 0.5 |
| 1914 | 1 935.9 | 104.0 | 5.4 | 1 047.3 | 54.0 | 772.8 | 40.0 | 11.8 | 0.6 |
| 1915 | 1 414.8 | 63.8 | 4.5 | 759.1 | 53.6 | 571.7 | 40.5 | 20.2 | 1.4 |
| 1916 | 1 180.3 | 41.5 | 3.5 | 545.5 | 46.2 | 558.9 | 47.3 | 34.7 | 3.0 |
| 1917 | 1 316.4 | 7.2 | 0.5 | 439.7 | 33.4 | 804.6 | 61.0 | 65.0 | 5.0 |

（续表）

| 年份 | 中国布匹总进口 | 从美国 | | 从英国 | | 从日本 | | 从其他地区 | |
|---|---|---|---|---|---|---|---|---|---|
| | （万匹） | （万匹） | （%） | （万匹） | （%） | （万匹） | （%） | （万匹） | （%） |
| 1918 | 1 042.1 | 10.1 | 1.0 | 263.4 | 25.3 | 700.7 | 67.2 | 67.9 | 6.5 |
| 1919 | 1 411.6 | 62.2 | 4.5 | 459.2 | 32.5 | 889.9 | 63.0 | | |
| 1920 | 1 343.8 | 56.4 | 4.3 | 578.4 | 43.0 | 703.5 | 52.3 | 5.5 | 0.4 |
| 1921 | 1 038.0 | 62.6 | 6.0 | 348.9 | 33.6 | 581.6 | 56.0 | 44.9 | 4.4 |
| 1922 | 1 242.5 | 38.1 | 3.0 | 496.1 | 40.0 | 649.7 | 52.3 | 58.6 | 4.7 |

注1：本表所指布匹含衬衫衣料、被单料、斜纹布、牛仔布、T恤布。

注2：本表中1911、1913年两个年度的百分比数据与表10－2有所差异，原因是：(1)本表数据源于中国海关按布料的类别统计加总，而表10－2则是按货物的来源港口统计；例如，美国的布料可能途经加拿大或日本航运到中国，这部分货物在表10－2中没有归因于美国，而在本表中则认为是来源于美国；(2)表10－2是货值比例，而本表是数量比例；(3)香港作为一个中转港口，剔除于本表之外；所以，在某些品种棉布的进口来源分布方面，本表比表10－2更加准确。

(1) 日本竞争

首先看看日本棉织品的竞争及其对美国对华棉织品出口的影响。在美国出口贸易的繁荣期，出口到中国的布匹大部分在满洲地区销售。俄-日战争之后，日本确立了在该地区的永久利益和特权。各种工业，包括棉纺业和棉织业，立刻在日本及其租借地满洲发展起来。原材料可以容易地从英属印度或中国南方及中部地区获得，同时由于满洲地区劳动力廉价，日本很快就能生产出比美国、欧洲产品更加便宜的棉布。日本商人抓住价格诉求在中国市场上的效力，大力推进其销售业务，很快为其棉制品开发出一个巨大的市场，首先是满洲地区，后来是整个中国。日本棉制品的崛起使美国损失惨重，英国及其他欧洲国家的棉制品也在中国受挫。

美国产品现在面临的日本竞争，与19世纪后数十年间遭受的英国竞争相同，因为美国产品的价格通常要比日本产品高出不少。表10－4所列两国价格的对照，为美国棉制品出口贸易的持续下滑及日本棉制品出口贸易的快速扩张提供了一个充分的理由。美国产品的价格通常比日本产品高出12%。像棉布这样的主要产品，两国产品价格的差额比棉布商人期望获取的利润还要高出不少。据一位美国特约代理1914年对这一情况的调查，中国某工厂的管理者宣称他只是因为客户想要一点质量更好的美国货而偶尔做了几笔美国棉布生意，更多的时候都是经销数量大得多的日本货。美国许多以前知名的被单料、斜纹布品牌已被日本货所替代。日本人模仿外国的畅销产品，并试图制造出实用性与原商品非常相似的廉价替代品。

表 10 - 4　日本、美国棉布价格比较(1914 年 2 月)

| | 灰色被单布料 | 灰色斜纹布 | 灰色衬衫布衫 | 灰色牛仔布 | 白色衬衫布料 |
|---|---|---|---|---|---|
| 日本产品价格(美元/匹) | 2.71 | 2.89 | 3.09 | 2.19 | 3.49 |
| 美国产品(美元/匹) | 3.29 | 3.34 | 3.59 | 2.39 | 3.98 |

注 1:表中价格是尚未征收关税时的大连港口到岸价。

战前的竞争态势现在仍然还在持续。这对美国棉布出口贸易的影响大于其他任何国家,因为美国出口的棉布主要局限于粗平布和粗斜纹布,而日本企业对此类产品给予了特别的关注,在这方面也最为成功,原因在于原材料成本是构成这些产品总成本的一个重要因素。

这一竞争的结果可用表 10 - 1、表 10 - 2 的数字清晰地表示出来。1906 年之后,美国对华棉布出口在数量、金额两方面都持续下滑(见表 10 - 1),这必然引起美国棉织商和专家的严重关切。英国对中国的出口品种主要是精细织物,而日本尚未成功模仿,因此英国产品在中国棉布进口贸易中的份额在战前十年并没有受到日本竞争的影响。相反,美国产品的份额由 1902 年的 26.3% 下降到 1913 年的 7.9%(见表 10 - 2),大约 19 个百分点的下降份额几乎全部由日本获得,因此其份额由 1902 年的 2.7% 上升到 1913 年的 20.2%。

欧洲战争爆发后,海洋运费突然上涨至一个令人不敢问津的水平。这为美国对华棉布贸易增添了一个新的不利因素;作为一种廉价的大宗商品,棉布无法在如此长距离的运输中承担高额的运费。1916—1918 年的三年间,美国的布匹贸易几乎全部停止,而正是日本再一次把握了这一良机。战争期间,日本提供了中国进口布匹的 2/3 还多,而美国只提供了 1%。战后,在中国进口的布匹中,日本产品仍超过 50%,美国尽管恢复了战争期间丢失的一些份额,但仍然少得可怜、不足 5%。

(2) 中国的竞争

然而,一定不能理解为日本竞争是美国布匹贸易下滑的唯一原因。十年前可以这么认为,但是,现在市场状况已经发生很大变化。事实上,日本遭遇因中国棉业崛起而产生的新竞争也已经有好几年了。

中国在非常古老的时代就开始利用手织机纺织棉花,现在这个产业还很兴旺。据一名美国特别调查员估计,中国手织机生产的产品在价值、数量方面都超过进口的布匹。用织布机织出的布在中国人当中非常普遍。尽管市面上销售的手织布的价格有时候与类似的进口货同样昂贵,但应该记住,大部分手织布是人们闲暇时在家里为他们自己使用而织的。手工纺织继续保持的另一个因素是一种与爱国主义类似的精神,因此国民被敦促购买自己国家制造的布料。

随着最近手工纺织业的发展,中国一定程度上不再受制于外国布匹。战争期间,外国棉布价格攀升,遍布全中国的手工纺织就增加供给,以满足人民的需要。这种条件下,高价的美国布料与中国手工布料进行竞争是完全做不到的。

中国的手工纺织不是外国布料所要面对的唯一严重竞争。联想到近期的发展,中国的机织工业现在正以异乎寻常的步伐进步。现代棉纺工艺引入中国的时间,据说最早只能回溯至 1890 年;但在此后的三十年间,这一产业快速扩张。表 10 - 5 显示了过去三十年间中国棉纺企业数量逐步增长的情况。此外,还有 28 家企业的 91.8 万个纱锭在建设之中。

表 10 - 5　1891—1921 年中国纺织企业及纱锭数

| 年份 | 企业数 | 纱锭数(万) | 年份 | 企业数 | 纱锭数(万) |
|------|--------|------------|------|--------|------------|
| 1891 | 2 | 6.5 | 1916 | 41 | 114.5 |
| 1896 | 12 | 41.7 | 1918 | 49 | 120.0 |
| 1902 | 17 | 56.5 | 1921 | 63 | 174.7 |
| 1911 | 32 | 83.1 | | | |

起初,这些工厂主要局限于纺纱业务;1905—1906 年俄-日战争期间及随后,布匹贸易大量进行,到 1907、1908 年,织布机才开始大范围安装。现在,许多工厂添置了动力织布机,开始制造被单布和斜纹布。

促进中国棉纺产业建立和成长的主要因素有:①中国本国可以供应用于制造纺、织粗布的质量上乘的棉花;②企业生产存在巨大的国内需求;③充足的廉价劳动力,使得中国的生产成本比世界其他任何地方都要低。由于这些明显的优势,中国国内棉布能够轻松胜过美国甚至日本产品。棉布业内人士有一个共识:不远的将来,中国将能够在自己国内制造出其众多人口消费所需的大部分粗布。所以,美国棉布制造商将没有希望赢得这场竞争的胜利,重获曾经掌控的棉布贸易。

## 三、美国对华布匹贸易的前景

尽管美国的对华粗布贸易(如被单布、斜纹布)注定要衰落,但这并不意味着美国将永远游离于中国棉布市场之外。还有其他许多布匹产品并不被日本或中国所制造,但却被众多的中国人口所消费,例如,平纹细布、涤棉、印花棉布、锦缎、直贡呢、平绒和其他花式棉线、染色棉线。战前,这些商品几乎全由英国独家供应,1915 年后日本参与了一些贸易。现在,这些细棉贸易的绝大部分仍然控制在英国商人手中。中国市场广阔,潜藏着商机,相信美国企业能在竞争基础上提供许多类似产品。美国具有大规模机械化纺织工业的优势、且其国内可以大量供应棉花,因此美国棉织品商没有理由不能生产出与英国产品成本相当、甚至更低的产品。如果美国人能够坚持不懈地努力生产所需的这类物资,支持培育持久市场的庄严决定,美国的对华棉制品出口无疑将会有一个相当大的扩张,使美国人能够——至少在某种程度上——恢复其在中国外贸中曾有的重要地位。

## 四、原棉

尽管美国在对华布匹贸易中失去了很大的份额,但在向中国出售原棉方面收获颇丰。1921 年,美国向中国直接出口的原棉价值高达 1 000 万美元。中国棉纺工业的快速成长将极大地提高中国消费棉花的能力,因此,有必要对吸纳美国原棉的中国市场进行研究。

中国拥有无垠的肥沃土地和无限的廉价劳力,是世界最大的棉花生产者之一,仅次于美国和英属印度。尽管不可能精确估计中国的棉花生产总量,但粗略估计也应当在 100 万~500 万包(500 磅/包)之间,而 200 万~250 万包似乎是更为合理的数字。拥有 200 万个纱锭的中国棉纺企业每年消耗各种原棉 100 万包[①],手织机每年的棉花消耗量为 140 万包。这些数字表明,就原棉而言,中国总体上是一个自给自足的国家。

事实上,中国棉纺厂很大程度上——如果不是全部的话——依赖于本国的原料供应。然而,使用外国棉花的比例正在提高。此外,本地歉收、国外低价、汇率优惠等,都导致某些时期外国棉的大量进口。有时,精纺需要的高等级棉花也需要向外国、特别是美国购买,因为中国棉花的纤维较短,不适合精纺。最近,特别是 1920 年以后,中国纺织工业突然剧烈扩张,对原棉的进口也稳步增加,由中国棉纺织业者协会(Chinese Cotton Mill Owners' Association)摘编的相关数字如表 10－6 所示。

1920 年,有 9 000 万磅(或 18 万个 500 磅的包)原棉进口到中国;1921、1922 年的进口量分别是 2.24 亿磅(44.8 万包)、2.37 亿磅(47.5 万包)。最近两年的进口实际上供应了中国棉纺厂所需原棉总量的一半。

表 10－7 是中国方面给出的过去二十年间中国进口原棉统计情况。

按照表 10－6、表 10－7 所示,中国从好几个国家进口原棉,但供应中国原棉市场的真正来源只有英属印度和美国,很小程度上还有日本。来自香港的这部分进口主要是美国和印度的棉花,而从英国进口的大部分棉花,以及从日本进口的一部分棉花,实际上是美国棉花。所以,表 10－7 中有关从美国进口棉花的数量或多或少地要低于实际数量。1901—1922 年间从美国直接出口到中国的原棉数量见表 10－8。

除了这些直接出口,还有一部分出口到日本的美国原棉,以及相当大一部分出口到香港的美国原棉,以非直接方式出口到中国,在表 10－8 中都没有包括在内。

---

① 1915 年,R. M. Odell 称,中国企业有 100 万个纱锭,每年消耗 53.3 万包棉花。

表 10 - 6  1921—1923 年中国棉纺企业棉花消耗量

单位:包(1 包＝500 磅)

| 财　　年 | 中国本土棉花 | 美国棉花 | 东印度棉花 | 埃及及其他地区棉花 | 合计 |
|---|---|---|---|---|---|
| 1921 | 728 292 | 29 122 | 119 029 | 649 | 877 092 |
| 1922 | 744 076 | 154 926 | 298 365 | 1 213 | 1 199 115 |
| 1923（截至 1.31 的半财年） | 492 162 | 58 115 | 135 330 | 4 019 | 689 626 |

表 10 - 7  1902—1922 年中国原棉进口来源统计(年均)

| 年　份 | 中国原棉总进口（万磅） | 从美国（万磅） | （%） | 从日本（万磅） | （%） | 从英国（万磅） | （%） | 从香港地区（万磅） | （%） | 从英属印度（万磅） | （%） |
|---|---|---|---|---|---|---|---|---|---|---|---|
| 1902—1905 | 1 653.8 | 120.1 | 7.3 | 13.5 | 0.8 | 109.0 | 6.6 | 454.9 | 27.5 | 830.4 | 50.2 |
| 1906—1910 | 1 673.7 | 0.3 | | 69.7 | 4.2 | 5.5 | 0.3 | 259.1 | 15.5 | 1 256.0 | 75.0 |
| 1911—1913 | 2 105.4 | 773.1 | 36.7 | 159.0 | 7.6 | 24.8 | 1.1 | 214.2 | 10.2 | 854.5 | 40.5 |
| 1914—1916 | 4 071.8 | 600.9 | 14.8 | 412.1 | 10.1 | | | 265.9 | 6.5 | 2 741.1 | 67.4 |
| 1917—1919 | 3 399.7 | 371.4 | 11.1 | 1 697.5 | 50.8 | | | 226.6 | 6.8 | 885.9 | 26.6 |
| 1920 | 9 177.7 | 453.9 | 4.9 | 2 159.2 | 23.4 | | | 300.3 | 3.3 | 5 584.8 | 60.8 |
| 1921 | 22 529.5 | 6 886.5 | 30.5 | 1 889.6 | 8.4 | | | 406.0 | 1.8 | 13 078.5 | 58.0 |
| 1922 | 24 765.7 | 2 070.4 | 8.1 | 4 037.6 | 16.3 | | | 252.8 | 1.0 | 18 286.4 | 74.0 |

　　如表 10 - 7 所见,在某些时期,美国原棉在中国原棉进口中占据了相当可观的份额,然而,中国原棉进口贸易大部分仍然掌握在英属印度人手中。印度棉花通常价格便宜,更适合在中国棉纺厂制造粗支纱;美国原棉质量更好,但要支付比印度棉花更长运距的航运、铁路运输费用,因此在东方市场的销售价格较高。

　　从表 10 - 8 可以清楚地看出美国原棉价格与出口中国的原棉数量之间的关系。美国原棉正常供应时,价格高于印度棉花,向中国出口的数量通常较小,甚至下降到零。但当美国棉花丰收、价格回落时,就马上开始向中国大量出口。因此,1912 年,中国就因美国棉花价格偏低而向美国大量采购[①];1921 年,美国原棉价格落入历史最低谷时,就有超过 7 700 万磅的原棉被销往中国。所以,中国不是美国棉农的固定消费者,但可以在丰收年或工业萧条时充当其富余棉花的补充销路。

――――――――――

　　① 据 R. M. Odell 计算,1912 年,在东方市场,美国棉花的价格是每磅 12.48 美分,印度棉花的价格为每磅 11.77 美分;前者只是略高于后者,因此中国棉纺厂认为从美国进口棉花更加有利可图。

### 表 10-8  1901—1922 年美国原棉对华直接出口统计

| 年份 | （万磅） | （万美元） | 年份 | （万磅） | （万美元） |
|---|---|---|---|---|---|
| 1901 | | | 1912 | 2 529.8 | 259.1 |
| 1902 | 305.5 | 29.1 | 1913 | 363.5 | 46.4 |
| 1903 | 130.7 | 12.3 | 1914 | 449.0 | 58.8 |
| 1904 | | | 1915 | 761.7 | 73.4 |
| 1905 | 212.0 | 17.6 | 1916 | 617.9 | 72.9 |
| 1906 | 35.0 | 4.0 | 1917 | 240.3 | 40.3 |
| 1907 | 14.5 | 1.6 | 1918 | 195.8 | 55.8 |
| 1908 | | | 1919 | 581.4 | 178.6 |
| 1909 | 22.1 | 2.2 | 1920 | 569.0 | 209.2 |
| 1910 | | | 1921 | 7 728.5 | 1 005.1 |
| 1911 | 5.3 | 0.8 | 1922 | 1 860.1 | 359.5 |

　　最近几年里，美国对华棉花出口贸易额达数百万美元。然而，中国似乎并不是美国棉花未来最好的市场。现在，中国的细支纱产量相对而言毫不起眼，也没有很快地提高。然而，在不远的将来，中国棉花工业可能发展到一个能生产更细的棉纱的新阶段，所以需要更多品质更高、种植方法更优的棉花；经过中国各类农业院校、棉花种植实验园的从业人员的努力，中国国内棉花的质量将得到提升，并极大地满足国内需要。

# 第十一章　矿物油

## 一、作为矿物油市场的中国

不少地理学家很早就报道过,中国具有很多富含矿物油的矿床。然而,这些资源的开采活动尚未取得成功。近些年,纽约美孚石油公司、一家日本公司先后在中国北方的几个省份开钻油井,但这些试验的效果都不令人满意[①]。与过去一样,中国现在不得不依然完全依赖一些产油国,特别是美国和荷属东印度,以获得其数百万个城乡家庭照明所需的石油。

大约五十年前或更早时候,矿物油在中国还不是普通的商业物资,1867 年仅进口 3 万加仑煤油,供在华的外国侨民使用。然而,自 1870 年开始,煤油被中国人快速接受,普遍使用,但是,直到 19 世纪末期,煤油才被一些大的外国公司分支机构带入中国内陆地区。

现在,美国的纽约美孚石油公司、德克萨斯石油公司,荷兰的亚洲石油公司在中国的经营规模较大,特别是纽约美孚石油公司、亚洲石油公司在中国的许多地方都有设备。没有一种进口物资——可能棉布例外——能像煤油那样在中国民众之中有如此的基础。煤油进入每一个与条约港口相距甚远的乡村,被那些可能从来不曾使用过其他任何外国货的人们所使用。后面的数字清楚地表明,在过去的半个世纪里,中国人如何变得习惯于使用煤油。1870 年,中国进口的煤油仅仅超过 28 万加仑,到 1900 年上升到 8 400 万加仑,1914 年则升至 2.25 亿加仑,三十五年间增长了 805 倍。

1914 年以后,中国的煤油进口额增长迅猛,但进口数量有所回落,这其中有两个原因。首先,电灯作为石油照明的成功竞争者,最近十年里在中国逐步普遍使用。其次,欧洲战争期间及之后,照明用油的价格攀升阻碍了中国石油消费的正常扩张。过于高昂的油价使中国人认为,在城市甚至更多的小城镇建造照明发电厂更为经济划算。电力对煤油的替代最终将阻止石油贸易的进一步扩张,但是这样的一个时间点在遥远的未来才可到来。对于中国这样一个地域宽广、人口众多的国家,其今天的石油

---

[①] 后见第 16 章。

贸易规模可以说是仅仅象征性的点缀而已。不少内地省份与几个世纪之前一样,仍然用动物脂肪油和植物油来照明;进口的矿物油还没有到达那里,因为中国缺乏长距离的运输设施,运费高不可攀。一旦中国国内的运输水平改善、能力提高,一个新的石油市场必然浮现出来,并导致中国石油进口量的再次猛烈增长。

必须注意到中国石油进口贸易的另一个重要变化,即,过去十年间其他矿物油的进口比煤油增长更快。大约十年前,煤油实质上是中国进口并消费的唯一一种矿物油;尽管中国自二十多年前开始进口其他一些石油品种,如燃料油和柴油、润滑油、汽油及其他石脑油,但进口量、进口额(甚至两者合起来)相当小;20世纪前十年间,它们在中国进口的石油中所占的比例不足2%,煤油的比例则超过98%。但是,由于战争的刺激,中国自身已由农业阶段向工业阶段转变;随着工业的逐步发展,中国对润滑油、石脑油和燃料油、柴油的利用也自然快速增长。1914年,这类油在中国石油进口中的份额仍然不足2%,但在此后短短的八年里,增长惊人,所占比例于1922年达到25%,而进口量、进口额仍然在高速增长。

中国石油贸易的新时代正在初见端倪。以前,中国只购买用于即期消费即采光、照明的石油品种,但现在则越来越多地为了进一步生产用途——即机械车间的使用——而大量购买石油。通过目前中国机器进口贸易的增长状况,人们可以容易看出哪些石油品种是中国机器用油进口贸易的未来。

## 二、中国市场上的美国石油

读者可能认为,上述有关中国作为矿物油市场的一般描述,在这样一部专门论述中美贸易的专著里是不恰当的。笔者确信,如果将1890年前中国进口的每一加仑石油都来自美国、而中国现在进口的石油中仍有80%左右来自美国这一事实告知读者,这种批评将会有所减轻。美国是世界上石油资源最为富集的国家之一,发展石油工业的历史也早于其他石油资源国。因此,直到19世纪末,美国不仅事实上垄断着中国的石油贸易,实际上也垄断着整个世界的石油贸易。

但是,美国石油在中国的超级地位并非不受挑战地长期维持。19世纪最后几年间,俄罗斯成功地开采了其西伯利亚的石油资源,很快成为一个重要的石油出口国。数年后,在苏门答腊岛和婆罗洲①拥有富集油矿的荷属东印度群岛步其后尘,也成为重要的石油出口国;其石油产量高居第二位,除美国外没有哪个国家能出于其右。最近,日本也开采了一些石油,当然数量还较小。这些国家都是中国的近邻,其优势是比美国更加接近中国市场;所以,尽管美国商人使出浑身解数、试图通过竞争将他们驱逐出去,但他们还是成功地将其石油引进到中国。

---

① 译注:苏门答腊岛,现属印尼;婆罗洲,现一半属马来西亚,一半属印尼。

俄罗斯石油于 1889 年首次进入中国,其后是苏门答腊石油 1894 年、婆罗洲石油 1901 年,日本石油只是在欧洲战争之前几年才进入中国。从 1890 年开始,中国的石油贸易不再仅仅掌控在美国人手中,所以必须将美国对华石油贸易连同其他竞争对手分别描述。表 11-1 显示了过去三十年间美国对华矿物油贸易的总体状况。

**表 11-1　1891—1922 年美国矿物油对华(含租界)出口统计**

| 年　　份 | (万加仑) | (万美元) | 年度 | (万加仑) | (万美元) |
|---|---|---|---|---|---|
| 1894—1895 | 2 617.3 | 185.4 | 1916—1918 | 8 085.4 | 577.2 |
| 1896—1900 | 3 380.4 | 271.1 | 1919—1920 | 16 578.1 | 1 993.4 |
| 1901—1905 | 4 773.1 | 449.0 | 1921 | 13 635.7 | 1 925.6 |
| 1906—1910 | 8 482.7 | 659.8 | 1922 | 18 698.6 | 2 171.2 |
| 1911—1915 | 9 479.5 | 642.7 | | | |

表 11-1 所示的石油贸易的显著特点是,尽管有了俄罗斯、荷属东印度石油的激烈竞争,美国对华石油出口量还是在稳步增加。当然,这三十年间,每年的数字显现出许多不规则的起伏。例如,在俄日战争期间及之后的 1905—1908 年那几年超常发展。而欧洲战争激战正酣的 1917—1919 年间则不正常收缩。但是,临时性的逐年波动被五年均值消除后,其长期趋势仍是有规律地上升。

但是,这并不意味着俄罗斯、荷属东印度的竞争是可以忽略的。事实上,从 19 世纪末到欧洲战争爆发这一时期,中国石油市场的竞争非常激烈,并贯穿于那一时期中国石油贸易的始终。俄罗斯石油进入中国市场后,立刻得到了一个大的贸易份额。因此,1890 年,中国石油市场 24.5% 的份额属于俄罗斯,76.5% 属于美国(见表 11-2),而仅仅两年前,俄罗斯石油还未在中国市场现身,美国占据着 100% 的中国市场。19 世纪 90 年代,不只俄罗斯的份额大大增加,苏门答腊也开始与美国石油强力竞争。结果,美国人的超级地位立刻受到严重的威胁,1900 年,在中国石油市场上,美国的份额仅为 41.5%,而俄罗斯是 39.1%,苏门答腊是 19.4%。

但俄罗斯在 1904—1905 年间被日本击败后,随即失去了其在中国的商业、政治地位,其建立不久的石油工业在与强大的美国、荷兰公司的竞争中立即变得软弱无力。其在中国石油市场的份额由 1900 年的 39.1% 下降到 1905 年的 8.3%、1910 年的 1.4%,欧洲战争爆发后实际上成了空白(见表 11-2)。

尽管荷属东印度石油公司晚于俄罗斯数年之后才进入中国市场——首先是苏门答腊、其后是婆罗洲,但它比俄罗斯更加长期地经受着美国人的严重竞争。荷兰石油于 1869 年进入中国后,由德国商人协理的皇家荷兰石油公司就在香港地区及中国其他沿海港口强力推进。所以,自 20 世纪早些时间开始,中国煤油的销售就排他性地落入两家竞争公司之手：一家是美国的美孚石油公司，另一家是荷属东印度群岛的亚洲石油公司。以前，后者也处置一些俄罗斯石油。随着时间的推移，竞争变得非常激烈，削价就成了双方经常使用的手段。1910年前后，双方的关系变得非常紧张，对抗实际上相当于战争。有这样一个事例，1910年上半年，美国煤油在南满地区击败了苏门答腊石油。美国石油打了一场硬仗，在该地区的销售量比上一年提高了29%，但是价格却下降了12%，美国石油业和荷兰出口商之间发生了价格竞争。1912年之后，据说这一竞争受到一种大家熟悉的协议和谅解的影响，市场与之前相比变得平静下来。

表 11 - 2　1870—1922 年中国煤油进口来源分布①

| 年份 | 中国进口煤油总量 | | 各来源地所占份额（%） | | | | | | | | | |
| | 进口量（万加仑） | 进口额（万美元） | 美国 | | 婆罗洲 | | 苏门答腊 | | 俄罗斯 | | 其他 | |
| | | | 按量 | 按价 | 按量 | 按价 | 按量 | 按价 | 按量 | 按价 | 按量 | 按价 |
| 1870 | 28.1 | | 100.0 | 100.0 | | | | | | | | |
| 1880 | 342.9 | | 100.0 | 100.0 | | | | | | | | |
| 1890 | 3 082.9 | 518.9 | 76.5 | 80.0 | | | | | 24.5 | 20.0 | | |
| 1900 | 8 358.0 | 1 038.2 | 41.5 | 45.0 | | | 19.4 | 18.0 | 39.1 | 37.0 | | |
| 1905 | 15 347.2 | 1 481.0 | 52.2 | 56.0 | 7.2 | 5.4 | 31.6 | 29.3 | 8.3 | 8.4 | 0.7 | 0.9 |
| 1910 | 16 139.0 | 1 436.0 | 59.6 | 53.0 | 11.8 | 13.0 | 26.5 | 30.5 | 1.4 | 2.9 | 0.7 | 0.8 |
| 1913 | 18 398.4 | 1 854.4 | 61.0 | 56.5 | 12.8 | 13.6 | 22.8 | 25.3 | 3.2 | 4.6 | | |
| 1914 | 22 546.4 | 2 306.9 | 71.2 | 69.4 | 10.0 | 10.1 | 16.3 | 17.0 | 2.3 | 3.2 | 2.0 | 0.3 |
| 1918 | 11 020.2 | 3 558.2 | 43.7 | 45.3 | 10.6 | 9.7 | 44.0 | 43.2 | | | 1.8 | 2.0 |
| 1920 | 18 958.9 | 6 735.5 | 74.0 | 74.7 | 5.1 | 4.7 | 19.7 | 19.3 | 0.5 | 0.6 | 0.6 | 0.6 |
| 1921 | 17 522.0 | 4 416.8 | 76.8 | 77.0 | 4.7 | 4.6 | 18.4 | 18.4 | | | | |
| 1922 | 20 919.1 | 5 265.7 | 84.0 | 83.5 | 2.1 | 2.1 | 9.0 | 9.7 | | | 4.9 | 4.7 |

　　美国石油业在这一时期的激烈竞争中遭受的巨大损失在表11-2中清晰可见。正常情况下，在中国煤油进口总量中，美国石油的份额为2/3～4/5。而竞争达到顶峰的1900—1910这十年间，美国的份额下降到稍多于50%。

　　从表11-2中不同年份的进口量、进口额之份额的差异可以看出，在整个竞争时段里，贸易会流向或趋向于能比对手提供更低价格的竞争者。假定总的进口量份额、进口额份额均为100%，那么，如果一个国家的进口量份额高、而进口额份额低，则其价格必然低于竞争对手；如果其进口额份额高于进口量份额，情况则刚好相反。利用

---

　　① 本表中的份额以石油种类、而非按进口来源地计算得出。这可以根据中国海关有关石油是美国油、俄罗斯油等的分类来完成。所以，此处显示的份额要比按进口来源国统计的数据更为准确，因为很多输往中国的石油是取道新加坡、中国香港转运的。

这一竞争价格评估规则,可以立刻从表11-2看出,俄美竞争之初,美国石油的价格要比俄罗斯高出不少,因为前者相当于76.5%的进口量分享了80%的贸易额。而对俄罗斯而言,相当于24.5%的数量份额只卖了20%的贸易额份额。俄罗斯石油的廉价在中国的下层民众中是一个非常好的卖点,因此此后十年间贸易大大扩张。1900年,美国石油价格仍然高于俄罗斯和苏门答腊石油,这很大程度上导致了美国石油销量的下滑及俄罗斯石油、苏门答腊石油贸易的强劲成长。这个价格规律贯穿着整个时期,例如,1905年俄罗斯的贸易额份额高于其贸易量份额,即它的石油价格高于其他国家时,其石油贸易立刻下滑。从那时起,俄罗斯石油的价格一直高于其他竞争对手,可能就是这个原因使得俄罗斯再也未能恢复其二十年前丢失的份额。

1900—1905年,苏门答腊和婆罗洲的油价均低于美国。结果,这段时间,它们在中国的石油贸易兴旺起来。但1910年是个转折点,当时它们的油价都开始高于美国这个强劲的竞争对手,后者立刻得到了一个更大的市场份额。似乎可以确信,1913—1915年这一时间段,美国对华石油贸易的恢复只是因为削价竞争。美国石油在跨太平洋运输时开销更大,因此一般情况下不可能卖得比俄罗斯、荷兰的石油低;所以,1910年左右美国的低油价主要是由于强大的美孚石油公司的低价策略。1914年之后,美国人、荷兰人的石油价格几乎保持在其贸易额份额、贸易量份额大体相当的同等水平。这可能就是各竞争公司于1912年达成的协议和谅解的结果。

由于运费高企,美国煤油贸易在1916—1918年的三年战争期间下滑到不足中国煤油总进口的一半,甚至于1918年被苏门答腊所超越。当然,这一下滑实质上是临时性的。战后,航运状况改善,美国获得了比以前更多的份额,现在中国市场供应的石油中,80%以上来自美国油井。

## 三、中美在其他矿物油领域的贸易

除了煤油,美国现在还向中国输送数量巨大、且继续增多的其他矿物油,主要用于中国成长的工业。1913年前,煤油实质上是唯一具有重要商业意义的矿物油;向中国出口的其他矿物油数量非常小,以至于美国国内外商务局的统计报表似乎都认为不值得将其单独记录。列名于"其他矿物油"之下的出口量只是稍多于100万加仑。

但是,欧洲战争爆发后,中国的工业化进展神速,为煤油之外的美国其他矿物油开创了一个新市场。它们在美国商务局的报告中被区分为燃料油和柴油、润滑油、石脑油、汽油等。过去十年间这些矿物油的对华出口量、出口额情况见表11-3。

先说说燃料油和柴油。1918年之前,中国进口的燃料油和柴油几乎全都来自于荷属东印度群岛。由于高运费、远距离的限制,美国无法与荷兰竞争。但是1919年这些障碍被消除,中国市场上美国石油的份额上升。中国进口的燃料油中,1920—1921年有1/2、1922年有2/3来源于美国。

表 11－3　1913—1922 年美国对华出口其他精炼矿物油统计

| 年份 | 燃料油和柴油 | | 润滑油 | | 石脑油、汽油等 | |
|---|---|---|---|---|---|---|
| | （万加仑） | （万美元） | （万加仑） | （万美元） | （万加仑） | （万美元） |
| 1913 | 132.8 | 21.0 | | | | |
| 1914 | 22.9 | 0.6 | 147.2 | 28.1 | 28.4 | 5.4 |
| 1915 | 177.7 | 9.6 | 292.1 | 41.9 | 47.2 | 7.9 |
| 1916 | 5.5 | 0.3 | 332.6 | 54.4 | 18.0 | 3.7 |
| 1917 | 284.6 | 11.7 | 213.9 | 41.5 | 24.5 | 5.8 |
| 1918 | 316.3 | 15.4 | 409.6 | 104.8 | 24.5 | 9.3 |
| 1919 | 396.0 | 15.7 | 563.0 | 148.3 | 114.8 | 38.6 |
| 1920 | 1 713.1 | 85.6 | 352.0 | 134.0 | 84.0 | 35.2 |
| 1921 | 2 000.1 | 77.0 | 419.2 | 123.6 | 149.8 | 52.9 |
| 1922 | 1 943.4 | 69.5 | 509.8 | 130.8 | 144.7 | 47.0 |

注：1913 年的"燃料油和柴油"数据包括照明油（煤油）之外的所有其他矿物油。

　　石脑油和润滑油的情况则与此有所不同。1914—1918 年，中国进口的 461.2 万加仑石脑油中，有 142.6 万加仑（约 30％）源自美国，进口的 2 196.2 万加仑润滑油中，有 1 395.4 万加仑（64％）来自美国。1919—1921 年，中国进口石脑油 993.6 万加仑，其中 348.6 万加仑即 35％产自美国；同一时期，中国进口润滑油 1 836 万加仑，其中 1 333.2 万加仑（72％）为美国产品。与竞争对手荷兰相比，美国的相对份额增长缓慢，但这两种矿物油的绝对贸易量增长迅猛。

# 第十二章 烟　草

## 一、作为外国烟草市场的中国

抽吸外国烟草的习惯进入中国也就是几十年前的事。1867 年前，中国只有本土烟草，香烟还不为人所知①。即使现在，本地烟草及与其配套的老式中国烟斗仍在中国各地、特别是内陆地区广泛使用。不过，香烟进入中国市场后，中国吸烟者发现它更加方便取用，因此使用香烟的习惯逐步增加。然而，香烟贸易量起初相当小，以至于香烟及未制成烟草的进口在 1901 年前并未被中国海关单独记录，而是一并列入"未分类的杂项"。1902 年，"香烟"从杂项中单列出来，当年中国香烟总进口额 125.9 万美元；次年，"烟草"数据首次予以单列，进口额仅为 32.5 万美元。

但在最近二十年间，抽吸香烟的习惯以令人吃惊的速度在整个中国蔓延。1912 年，中国进口香烟 44 亿支，价值 649.3 万美元；1922 年，进口量达 100 亿支，价值 2 361.4万美元。

战前，烟叶的进口未能与香烟贸易的增长保持同步。1904 年，中国进口烟叶 1 200万磅、价值 106.5 万美元，十年后增长为 1 600 万磅、183.4 万美元。烟叶贸易增长缓慢的原因是中国的香烟工业当时仍不发达，不需要很多烟叶。然而，烟叶贸易在最近十年间有了显著发展，1922 年，烟叶进口量超过 3 500 万磅，价值 1 146.1 万美元。

各种烟草的进口量、消费量的增长使一些中国人相信，这是削弱中国国家及人民力量的第二种鸦片祸端。然而，与无处不在的革新人士对抗的居然是爱国公民，他们确信烟草不仅能使个人产生无害的愉悦感，而且对刺激国内商业繁荣有利。这其中有已故的中国现代重要的实业家、南洋兄弟烟草公司的创办者简照南先生。创业先锋取得成功，加之外国资本在中国建立工厂，中国烟叶贸易和烟草工业实力加强，更多的中国本土烟草工厂也开办起来。

---

① 据中国海关的统计资料，外国烟草的进口首次出现于 1867 年；而美国资料显示，1850 年后，每年都有一些烟草出口到中国。

## 二、中国市场的美国烟草

随着中国不断大量进口外国烟草和香烟,美国对华烟草贸易在过去二三十年间有了明显的进步。由表 12 - 1 可见,美国对华烟叶、香烟出口总额在三十年前仅为数千美元,而到 1920 年则高达 3 000 万美元。1914 年以后,烟草贸易的增长特别迅速,一方面是因为中国社会寻求舒适生活、购买奢侈品的经济能力提高,另一方面是因为美国烟草制造业在战前最为强大的竞争对手英国很大程度上被淘汰了。

表 12 - 1　1891—1922 年美国烟草对华出口统计(年均)

| 年份 | 未制成烟草 | | | 香烟 | | |
|---|---|---|---|---|---|---|
| | (万磅) | (万美元) | 占中国烟草总进口之比(%) | (亿支) | (万美元) | 占中国香烟总进口之比(%) |
| 1891—1895 | 1.4 | 0.1 | | | 8.0 | |
| 1895—1900 | 27.9 | 2.1 | | | 32.0 | |
| 1901—1905 | 82.5 | 11.5 | | | 83.2 | |
| 1906—1910 | 414.0 | 52.2 | 31 | 5.84 | 108.5 | 16 |
| 1911—1913 | 627.2 | 92.3 | 35 | 5.23 | 82.2 | 11 |
| 1914—1916 | 794.4 | 128.6 | 52 | 10.88 | 183.3 | 18 |
| 1917—1919 | 1 300.9 | 463.5 | 56 | 58.54 | 1 028.9 | 70 |
| 1920 | 1 852.5 | 1 331.6 | 63 | 85.09 | 1 609.6 | 90 |
| 1921 | 1 938.9 | 840.6 | 63 | 64.44 | 1 169.9 | 90 |
| 1922 | 3 241.8 | 1 072.1 | 92 | 85.80 | 1 703.5 | 88 |

注 1:1891—1895 年之未制成烟草的进口数据实为 1894—1895 年两年之均值。

注 2:1906—1910 年之香烟进口数量实为 1908—1910 年三年之均值。

1914 年前,美国烟草在中国烟草贸易中已经比较重要,但还没有占据主导地位。英国制造的香烟在中国烟草进口中占据着非常大的份额,而位居次席的美国所占份额很小。据中国海关统计,1913—1914 年间中国进口的外国香烟中,每十支就有七支来自英国,只有一支来自美国,其余两支则来自日本、朝鲜和俄罗斯。英国的超级地位一直保持到 1905—1906 年,之后其首席位置被美国取代。由于美国的原材料质量上乘,加之欧洲竞争对手因世界大战而回撤,美国香烟制造商迅速抢占了东方贸易的制高点;如表 12 - 2 所示,现在中国人购买的每十支外国香烟中,就有九支来自美国。

在原材料方面,英国当然无法与美国进行竞争,因为它也不得不依赖美国提供烟叶以满足工厂的需求。日本、朝鲜、俄罗斯和菲律宾时不时地、或多或少地分享中国烟叶贸易,但这些国家对中国的烟叶出口从未威胁到美国的老大地位。1914 年前,美国烟叶在中国烟叶进口中占 1/3,1914—1916 年则占到一半左右,1917—1921 年为 2/3,1922 年超过 90%。

大多数中国人的购买力还很低,买不起高级烟草。因此,运往中国的美国产品自然都是价位较低的,通常低至每支 0.25 美分。这一超低价格已为中国的烟草行业所普遍采用。为了利用中国的廉价劳动力向中国市场提供产品,外国烟草公司在中国的几个开放港口建造了很多工厂。英美烟草公司①雄霸中国市场将近二十年。

中国工厂使用美国烟草,很大程度上是用来制造与外资产品相抗衡的高级香烟,中国市场上的一些高级香烟实际上纯由美国原料制造而成。也有一些美国烟叶被混合在中国烟斗所使用的中国细切烟丝之中。

中国现在还算不上是美国烟叶的大买主(1920—1921 年仅占美国烟草总出口的 4%),但多年来它已经在美国香烟出口业务中占据最重要的地位。表 12-2 列示了美国对华香烟出口情况。1915—1920 年,中国吸纳了美国香烟出口总量的 2/3,1921—1922 年则上升至 3/4。

**表 12-2　1915—1922 年美国对华香烟出口统计**

| 年份 | 美国香烟总出口 | 美国对华香烟出口 | | 年份 | 美国香烟总出口 | 美国对华香烟出口 | |
|---|---|---|---|---|---|---|---|
| | (亿支) | (亿支) | (%) | | (亿支) | (亿支) | 占比(%) |
| 1915 | 20.76 | 10.85 | 52 | 1919 | 162.12 | 61.92 | 38 |
| 1916 | 42.59 | 25.52 | 60 | 1920 | 158.34 | 85.07 | 54 |
| 1917 | 70.20 | 49.49 | 70 | 1921 | 85.44 | 64.44 | 75 |
| 1918 | 121.46 | 67.92 | 56 | 1922 | 114.70 | 85.80 | 75 |

## 三、中国烟草工业的最新发展及其未来与美国贸易的关系

近年来,中国从美国进口的烟草(包括未制成的烟叶和制成的香烟)数量在大量增加,但在不远的未来将发生一个大的变化。威胁美国对华烟草贸易进一步成长的并非竞争对手英国或日本,而是更多的难以对付的、快速发展的中国本土产业。早在战前许多年,与外国产品等级、风格相似的香烟就已经在设立于中国开放港口、城市的无数个小企业中制造出来,这类本土产品的销量已经相当可观。

---

① 1902 年 9 月 29 日,为平息激烈的贸易战,英国的帝国烟草公司与美国的美国烟草公司联合创办合资企业——英美烟草公司(British-American Tobacco,简称 BAT),总部设于英国伦敦。

所以,美国驻华领事1915年在报告中称,"中国国内烟草企业的竞争已经成为美、英两国烟草公司面临的一大难题。许多中国人更愿意选择本地产品,不只是因为其口味更加习惯、价格更为便宜,还因为每个人都认为,购买烟草这样的奢侈品时,选择本国产品似乎有一种爱国情结⋯⋯正是在烟草贸易中,尤其能感受到中国人对本国产品的偏爱在不断增加。"

战前就已存在的这一偏好状况在现在更为真切,因为中国烟草工业受战争期间的高价刺激而快速发展,使得中国企业能够充分保证国内市场需求的增加。南洋兄弟烟草公司于1906年开业,1914年后快速发展,之后许多其他本土公司也组建起来,从而使中国恢复了对以前先后被英、美公司所掌控的烟草工业和烟草贸易的控制。现在,超过95％的烟草工业已经掌握在中国人手中,中国人消费的香烟中超过70％的是国产货。有这样一个有利的环境,加之偏爱本国产品的爱国精神高涨,一旦中国工厂的生产供应能充分满足中国社会的需要,美国对华香烟出口将停止增长。

美国烟叶贸易的未来似乎要比香烟光明一些,这是因为,一方面,中国烟草工业的增长需要使用更多的原料,另一方面,在制造一些能与美国产品竞争的高等级香烟时特别需要美国原料。然而,中国烟草生产在烟草世界中的重要性在上升。提高本土烟叶质量的各种努力,如进口美国种子、由训练有素的美国专家培养种植和示范等,都被证明是相当成功的。大型本土公司对小型生产者的奖励扶持使得烟草产量增长、质量提高,"现在中国烟草已经在色泽、形态上与美国产品相媲美,只是口味略显温和。"

中国烟草种植的进步自然对中国市场上的美国烟草形成了激烈的竞争态势。数年前,中国本土卷烟厂所使用的原料几乎全部是进口的,主要是来自美国。而现在,中国卷烟工厂所需的烟叶通常有60％为本国生产,进口烟叶只占40％。所以中国烟草不仅供应本国市场,供应外国工业使用的出口也在增加。1918—1920年,中国每年向美国出口的烟草就达500万磅。

由于中国人偏爱国产货的缘故,甚至于以前只使用美国原料的英美烟草公司(BAT)现在也被迫越来越多地购买中国国内烟草,用于其在华工厂生产香烟。美国驻华领事在同一份报告中说:"中国人渴望支持本国工业,此时购买国产烟草甚至香烟特别对中国人有吸引力。"

另一方面,中国的快速工业化使民众的生活水平提高,无疑增大香烟这种物质的消费量。中国本土增加的产量不能满足新增的需求,加之对进口货的需求在每个国家都是会存在的,因此,外国香烟对华贸易的规模继续不减并非没有可能。

# 第十三章　木材和木制品

　　美国木材在中国的历史肇始于外国人在上海的置业。代理商把俄勒冈松木带到这个港口城市,并卖给中国木材行。1860年,美国早期对华贸易的最大公司上海拉塞尔公司(Russell and Company)不只进口木材,还进口预制房。1890年,该公司倒闭,这一业务中止;直到20世纪初,美国木材贸易一直完全把持在掮客和中国商行手中。这一时期中国进口的木材大部分是来自俄勒冈州、华盛顿州的松木,但是相当数量的加利福尼亚红木也有一定的市场,英属哥伦比亚的木材也是如此。

　　美国波特兰的太平洋木材出口公司组建于1900年,其主要目的是跨太平洋销售木材。该公司特许汽船业务,成功地携带了一些木材。

　　美国太平洋沿岸的超大型的船东和船舶运商营罗伯特·大赉公司也于20世纪初在上海开设了一个办公室。现在该公司在上海、天津、汉口和南京拥有自己的办公楼和花园,并在中国的其他港口设有代理和代表处。

　　表13-1列示了美国1891年之后向中国出口木材的数量与金额、及木制品的金额。可以注意到,19世纪90年代,美国每年向中国出口的木材仅为1 000万平方英尺,出口额不足10万美元。十年之后,木材贸易量增长五倍多;1920—1922年间,出口量增长到平均每年1.14亿平方英尺,出口额达221.7万美元。

　　除了木材,美国向中国出口木制品也已经有三十多年的历史。这一领域贸易的增长同样是确定无疑的,年均贸易额从1891—1900年的5万美元左右增长到1920—1922年的200多万美元。

　　表13-2列示了美国木材在中国木材市场上所占的份额。欧洲战争之前,中国进口的软木一半来自美国,另一半来自于日本和朝鲜。与此同时,俄罗斯和西伯利亚向中国供应其他木材产品,但数量并不很大。世界大战期间,美国木材在中国市场上的份额从1/2下降到1/4。这一暂时性下降仅仅是由于战争期间航海运费过高、木材这样的大宗货物无力承受。中国市场上的美国木材被日本、朝鲜替代,仅此一次。1920年以后,太平洋运输的费用大幅下降,美国对华木材贸易恢复到其失去的原有份额之上,目前中国进口的软木有2/3以上来自美国的俄勒冈州和华盛顿州。

　　至于中国的硬木进口,美国实际上没有参与,所有贸易都被日本和英属海峡殖民地控制。

表 13 - 1　1891—1922 年美国木材、木制品对华出口统计

| 年　份 | 木板、木模板和木料 | | 木制品 |
|---|---|---|---|
| | 年均出口量(亿英尺) | 年均出口额(万美元) | 年均出口额(万美元) |
| 1891—1895 | 50.01 | 4.8 | 2.6 |
| 1896—1900 | 147.92 | 12.4 | 7.2 |
| 1901—1905 | 243.26 | 28.5 | 25.6 |
| 1906—1910 | 539.83 | 68.4 | 26.6 |
| 1911—1913 | 713.43 | 77.6 | 26.4 |
| 1914—1916 | 659.01 | 68.5 | 28.5 |
| 1917—1919 | 297.08 | 76.6 | 99.2 |
| 1920 | 1 170.65 | 420.5 | 178.9 |
| 1921 | 987.73 | 194.7 | 43.8 |
| 1922 | 1 172.55 | 221.7 | 317.0 |

表 13 - 2　1911—1922 年中国软木进口来源分布(数量百分比)

| 年份 | 中国软木进口总量 (万平方英尺) | 从美国 | | 从加拿大 | | 从日本、朝鲜 | | 从俄罗斯、西伯利亚 | |
|---|---|---|---|---|---|---|---|---|---|
| | | (万平方英尺) | (%) | (万平方英尺) | (%) | (万平方英尺) | (%) | (万平方英尺) | (%) |
| 1911—1913 | 11 575.0 | 5 376.9 | 46.5 | 0.8 | | 5 746.2 | 49.5 | 292.1 | 2.5 |
| 1914—1916 | 16 909.3 | 4 686.7 | 27.8 | 159.2 | 0.9 | 10 966.9 | 64.9 | 575.6 | 2.4 |
| 1917—1919 | 10 175.0 | 2 337.3 | 23.0 | 1 027.2 | 10.1 | 6 076.3 | 59.8 | 699.1 | 7.0 |
| 1920 | 20 940.2 | 12 050.4 | 57.5 | 1 501.1 | 7.2 | 6 923.4 | 33.1 | 131.4 | 0.6 |
| 1921 | 12 638.0 | 8 834.8 | 70.0 | 1 007.7 | 8.0 | 2 476.7 | 19.5 | 266.2 | 2.1 |
| 1922 | 23 368.5 | 14 201.3 | 61.0 | 2 717.8 | 11.6 | 4 254.6 | 18.3 | 2 097.9 | 9.0 |

　　尽管木材目前还没有成为中国主要的进口商品,但美国对华木材贸易的未来应该是非常有希望的。中国东部几乎没有大片森林,国内木材供应量非常有限。目前,中国各种不同的工业建设快速发展,为此必须进口大量木材、而且正在不断增加。造林活动是能使中国最终实现木材自给自足的一种方法,但生产出足够多的木材以满足国内需求、进而对国外进口形成冲击至少需要几代人的时间。

# 工业机器和设备

## 一、作为美国钢铁机械市场的中国

中国由农业国向工业国转进的进展速度,可以通过其逐年增长的各种机械进口数量很好地反映出来。大约三十年前,中国海关报告的各类机械进口总额为每年 50 万美元左右①。此后十年间,这一微不足道的数字仅仅增长一倍②。即使在欧洲战争前夜,中国各类机械的进口也不是很多,通常为每年三四百万美元③。但在最近十年,这类进口增长十倍,如此显著的增长清楚无误地显示了年轻的工业化中国的爆发式进程。

一名美国驻华商务专员说:"这种情况下,有些事情强烈地吸引着外国商人的想象力。中国广袤的国土面积、众多的人口资源、丰富的自然资源——包括矿产资源和农业资源、潜在的水力发电,如果都掌握在智慧、聪明、勤劳、可靠、可爱的人民手中,无疑将使中国成为世界上最先进的工业化帝国之一。"

但是,中国在发展到较高工业阶段之前,绝对有必要从其他较发达国家进口机器和设备,来装配自己的车间和工厂。现在,中国只能生产那些仅靠简单工业形式制造的产品,其工业要发展到欧洲、北美那样的水平、并制造自己的机器和设备尚需时日。就不远的将来而言,外国机械的进口必将随着中国的工业化进程而增加。

在中国,比较重要的企业有棉纺织厂、豆油厂、钢铁工厂、冶炼厂(锑、马口铁、锌和其他矿石)、缫丝厂、火柴厂、肥皂厂、蜡烛厂和卷烟厂、白酒厂、啤酒厂、罐头厂和蛋白厂、造船工程业、水泥厂和造纸厂。过去两年里,面粉厂、米厂、玻璃厂和地毯厂的业务量也有了很大的提高。

中国最近开办了许多企业,值得提及的有机动织袜厂、甜菜制糖厂和甘蔗糖厂、橡胶厂和油漆厂、电镀厂、羊毛纺织厂、饼干厂和果酱厂、纽扣厂、伞厂和玩具厂。几乎在

---

① 1890 年,中国机械进口总额 41 万两海关银元,约合 52.1 万美元(1 两海关银元=1.27 美元)。

② 1900 年,中国机械进口总额 145 万海关银元,折合 108.8 万美元(1 两海关银元=0.75 美元)。

③ 见表 14－1 之 1912—1913 数据。

中国的每一个大城市,现代工厂如雨后春笋般涌现出来,并生产出越来越多的以前只能从外国进口的物资,并带动了对外国机械、工具和其他设备的需求增长。

　　过去十年间中国机械市场的发展,可以通过表14-1的进口统计数据予以展现。1918年后,中国工业受到世界范围内的价格膨胀和商业繁荣刺激,进口增长特别明显。中国各类机械产品的进口额,从1918年的1 000万美元上升到1919年的2 200万美元、1921年的3 100万美元;1922年,尽管全球商业萧条波及中国,但进口额仍达到4 400万美元。虽然中国的工业发展因近期国内的政治混乱环境而受到很大的扰乱、阻滞,但1922年的机械进口仍然保持增长态势,表明中国的工业发展仍在继续。一旦中国的政治环境改善,必将修建新的公路和铁路,开设新的工厂和商店,外国机械的进口量必将再次冲高。"中国人现在是一个大买家。但是,他们今天正在购买的(机械设备的数量),与未来将要采购的相比只是微不足道的一小部分。"

**表14-1　1912—1922年中国钢铁机械①进口统计**

| 年份 | 银元计价进口额 | 汇率 | 美元计价进口额 | 来源分布比例(%) | | | | |
|---|---|---|---|---|---|---|---|---|
| | (万两香港海关银元) | (美元/银两) | (万美元) | 美国、加拿大 | 英国 | 中国香港 | 日本 | 其他地区 |
| 1912 | 462.4 | 0.70 | 323.1 | 11.4 | 34.5 | 15.6 | 10.8 | 22.7 |
| 1913 | 577.8 | 0.73 | 421.8 | 9.8 | 37.2 | 10.3 | 10.2 | 32.5 |
| 1914 | 875.6 | 0.67 | 586.8 | 8.2 | 40.0 | 10.5 | 10.3 | 31.0 |
| 1915 | 495.4 | 0.62 | 307.1 | 15.4 | 41.3 | 11.1 | 17.8 | 14.4 |
| 1916 | 665.5 | 0.79 | 525.7 | 18.7 | 37.2 | 3.9 | 30.8 | 9.4 |
| 1917 | 654.0 | 1.03 | 673.6 | 22.3 | 25.6 | 4.5 | 39.3 | 8.3 |
| 1918 | 833.9 | 1.26 | 1 050.7 | 31.8 | 15.8 | 4.9 | 44.3 | 3.2 |
| 1919 | 1 548.2 | 1.39 | 2 152.0 | 47.0 | 13.4 | 5.0 | 24.1 | 10.4 |
| 1920 | 2 460.8 | 1.24 | 3 051.4 | 55.0 | 21.4 | 2.8 | 16.8 | 6.0 |
| 1921 | 5 780.5 | 0.76 | 4 393.2 | 43.7 | 36.8 | 2.1 | 13.4 | 4.0 |
| 1922 | 5 154.1 | 0.83 | 4 277.9 | 24.0 | 43.2 | 2.5 | 18.0 | 12.3 |

　　在这个发展潜力巨大的东方市场,美国机械已经在最近十年里获取了相当大的份

---

　　① 在中国海关统计中,"钢铁机械"包括如下类目:农业机械;动力机械(牵引)(锅炉、涡轮机等);纺织机械;酿造机械、蒸馏机械、制糖机械等;刺绣机械、编织机械、缝纫机械;其他机械;机械部件;机械工具。

额、而且还在增大。按照美国的统计,战前中国每年仅进口价值不超过 50 万美元的美国机械,而 1919、1920、1921 年的进口额则分别为 1 700 万美元、1 800 万美元和 2 000 万美元(见表 14－2)。反过来,在美国机械的全球市场中,1913 年中国排第 28 位,1919 年则大步前进到第 7 名,1921 年更进一步至第 5 位。1913 年,在中国的进口机械中,美国只供应了其中的不到 10%,当时这一业务大多被英国和中欧所控制。但到 1919—1921 年,中国超过一半的需求由美国机械来满足。最令美国制造商高兴的是,现在中国的机械市场按价值计算已经接近十年前的 40 倍;对美国人来说,在中国之外寻找另外一个能使其机械销售的数量、排名和市场份额有更好记录的地方将会是困难的。

表 14－2　1908—1922 年美国钢铁机械对华(含租界)出口统计

| 财　　年 | 年均出口额(万美元) | 日历年 | 出口额(万美元) |
| --- | --- | --- | --- |
| 1908—1910 | 44.2 | 1918 | 322.0 |
| 1911—1913 | 42.5 | 1919 | 1 686.4 |
| 1914—1915 | 82.1 | 1920 | 1 821.7 |
| 1916—1917 | 140.3 | 1921 | 1 965.2 |
|  |  | 1922 | 1 113.6 |

多年来,纺织机械在中国从美国进口的各类机械中是最为重要的。前文已经提及①,中国的棉纺织工业在最近十年里取得了显著的进步,因此纺织机械的进口在 1919—1921 年这三年间有了很大增加,主要是从美国进口。

战后,美国机械主导了中国市场,但市场还是从过渡期回复到战前状况。1916 年前,英国在中国机械进口市场中占据着最大的份额。但在接下来的五年里,在美国、日本和英国这三个最为强劲的竞争对手之中,英国先后退至第二、第三的位置。1921 年,英国明显恢复,1922 年重新居于领先地位(见表 14－1)。至于中欧地区的其他竞争国家中,德国、比利时在战前占有较大的份额;但在战争及战后的数年里,这些国家的对华机械贸易完全消失,不过它们现在恢复市场份额的努力已经有了一定成效。借助于货币贬值和低廉的制造成本(按照金价与美国相比),它们现在能够以低于美国产

———————

① 从加拿大运达中国的机械中,有很大一部分源于美国。Walter H. Rastall 在其著作《Asiatic Markets for Industrial Machinery》(美国商务部 1922 年印行)中如此阐述:

单单依靠中国海关统计中的表面数字,不能准确反映美国制造业主在中国市场的规模;海关统计中,货物装载量通常归因于所经最后一个港口所在的国家,因此,在中国香港、或加拿大和日本的港口转运的机械都会被统计到这些地方的贸易额中,即使它们起运于美国。例如,1919 年,中国海关将价值 190 万美元的纺织机械归因于加拿大,但很可能这些设备全部是在美国的新英格兰州制造、途经温哥华船运而来。美国提供了日本不同年份 30%~80% 的机械进口,经船运到达香港的机械有 30%~47% 也由美国提供。因此,这一点非常清楚,即,在上述中国海关严格意义上的统计数据外,美国还向中国提供了更多的机械。

品的价格向中国销售许多种机械。

这样,英国和中欧国家在这一竞争中取胜,美国现在似乎正在让出其在中国机械市场的地盘。1920 年,美国供应了中国机械采购总量的 55%,但是 1921 年这一比例降至 44%,1922 年更是降至只有 24%。这一下滑非常严重,1922 年的中美钢铁机械贸易额仍保持在战前的 20 倍之上,但在中国机械贸易中的份额则收缩至不超过战前水平的两三倍。

面对这一严重局面,美国机械出口商应当尽其所能,竭力保住中国这一前景非常看好的市场;如第五章所述,工业机械将是中国未来必然扩大进口的主要领域——如果不是唯一的话。美国一旦失去,要想重新恢复会更加困难。

现在由于黄金和汇率的原因,美国机械的价格高于一些中欧国家甚至英国的产品,因此,美国人能够在中国市场上击败其他竞价者的唯一制胜办法是为新的中国工业融资、扩大他们的长期信贷。以前,中国进口工业设备的订单常常伴随着国外贷款,因为外国在与中国的协议中加入一个借贷条款、要求使用该资金购买的原材料和设备必须向该国采购,这已经成了一个惯例。一名在华的美国调查人员说:"这一点对我来说似乎是非常清楚的,至少在东方,融资与贸易结伴而行、密切相关;没有金融活动做坚实的后盾,营业利润不能充分享受,贸易利益也不能完全维护。"尽管中国人对贷款协定中的限制性条款非常反感,然而中国工业的进一步发展还是需要外国资本。每一个人都能感觉到,目前大多数欧洲国家和日本不能满足中国增加贷款的要求,这对于美国贸易商获得中国业务市场似乎是一个良机。如果其他国家能以低价策略胜出,美国则能够通过向中国企业家提供更多的、条件宽松的贷款击败竞争对手。贸易一旦掌握在手,它对进一步的扩张会有相当大的累积效应,美国人将不止能保持住他们原有的份额,而且还能加以扩大。

## 二、其他钢铁产品

早在成为钢铁机械市场之前,中国就已经成了其他钢铁产品,如工具、条棒、片材、结构件、筒材、线材、钉子和其他各种五金材料的大买家。战前十年间,中国每年进口这类物资多达 1 000 万美元,美国获得了其中 12~15%[①]的份额。中国进口的大部分——约 80%——来自欧洲,主要是英国、德国、比利时、法国和奥地利。美国钢铁业发展成熟、产量巨大,但美国在中国此类贸易中的份额相当小,这主要是由于美国产品价格较高所致。

随着欧洲战争的爆发,如同前面所述影响机械贸易的变化一样,出现了两个对中国五金贸易产生影响的大的变化。其一是,中国工业的快速发展使得这些五金产品的

---

① 按中国海关统计数据的归因于香港的贸易中,有一定比例已经调整给了美国。

进口迅速增加;其二是,由于欧洲竞争对手的回撤,美国在中国五金贸易中的份额有了明显的增加。表14-3所列战前及战后数年间中国与主要镀锡伙伴之间的五金贸易总额及来源分布比例佐证了这些变化。可以看出,中国五金贸易年均进口额从战前的1 000多万美元上升到1918—1921年间的4 000万～5 000万美元,与此同时,美国的市场份额也从12%升至40%以上。

**表14-3　1913—1922年中国钢铁产品①进口来源分布**

| 年份 | 银两计价进口额 | 汇率 | 美元计价进口额 | 来源分布比例（%） | | | | | |
|---|---|---|---|---|---|---|---|---|---|
| | （万两香港海关银元） | （美元/银两） | （万美元） | 美国 | 加拿大 | 香港 | 英国 | 日本 | 其他 |
| 1913 | 1 737.4 | 0.73 | 1 268.3 | 11.2 | | 14.7 | 32.9 | 6.0 | 35.1 |
| 1914 | 1 583.5 | 0.64 | 1 013.4 | 12.1 | | 14.0 | 33.0 | 6.2 | 34.7 |
| 1918 | 2 907.5 | 1.26 | 3 663.5 | 40.0 | 7.5 | 11.4 | 8.8 | 29.0 | 3.3 |
| 1919 | 3 623.7 | 1.39 | 5 036.9 | 43.8 | 7.6 | 10.1 | 12.1 | 20.8 | 5.6 |
| 1920 | 4 166.3 | 1.24 | 5 166.2 | 39.4 | 4.3 | 9.1 | 26.4 | 17.5 | 3.2 |
| 1921 | 3 837.6 | 0.76 | 2 916.6 | 39.1 | 0.9 | 11.8 | 25.2 | 10.4 | 12.6 |
| 1922 | 2 967.8 | 0.83 | 2 464.0 | 24.6 | | 15.2 | 25.0 | 11.6 | 23.6 |

注1:中国机械进口来源分布(见表14-1)的脚注在此处同样适用。加拿大所占份额的大部分、中国香港所占份额的一部分实际上应当归因于美国。

注2:在"其他"所占份额中,比利时、德国和法国拿走了其中的90%左右。

表14-4呈现了1891年之后美国对华出口五金产品的稳定增长情况,这一领域贸易的上升趋势,除了特殊的1921年外从没有改变过。美国对华五金产品出口额从1891—1895年的每年10万美元增长到1919—1920年的每年1 200万美元。

**表14-4　1891—1922年美国钢铁产品②对华(含租界)出口统计**

| 年　　份 | 年均出口额（万美元） | 年份 | 出口额（万美元） |
|---|---|---|---|
| 1891—1895 | 10.9 | 1917 | 743.1 |
| 1896—1900 | 35.5 | 1918 | 1 314.8 |
| 1901—1905 | 63.1 | 1919 | 2 052.8 |
| 1906—1910 | 145.1 | 1920 | 2 498.0 |
| 1911—1913 | 175.9 | 1921 | 1 075.2 |
| 1914—1916 | 316.2 | 1922 | 607.4 |

---

① 包括工具、条棒、线材、板材、片材、筒材、管材、箍件、托梁、角析、路轨、钉子、结构件、螺钉、枕木、铸件、其它钢铁制品和未制成的钢铁材料;但不包括钢铁机械、机床、钢铁设备和家具。

② 不包含钢铁机械。

但是,由于欧洲产品逐步返回中国市场,美国产品因价格高于竞争对手再次陷入曾有的不利状况,其结果必然是市场份额下降。前面谈过的美国制造业者应当如何保住其在东方机械市场的做法,在这里同样适用,因为中国进口的钢铁产品的一大部分就是用于建设和工业。

不过,话虽如此,中国的机械市场与其他钢铁产品市场的未来前景之间还是有一个根本的差别。就机械领域而言,中国仍在依赖国外进口、并将继续依赖数年甚至数十年,因此美国及其他出口国有望在中国维持基本的贸易;但是,其他简单形态的钢铁制品并非如此,至少情况很快将与此不同。

截至目前,中国钢铁产品大多还是从美国、欧洲进口。但是,如同棉制品、香烟,以及大约十五年前的小麦粉一样,新生的共和国希望使钢铁产品成为另一个最终不再依赖进口的部门。几乎没有办法来精确估算中国的矿产资源,但已有足够证据让人确信,中国蕴含的铁——可能还有煤——比世界其他任何国家都要多。能满足中国数百年工业化发展需求的丰富的铁矿、煤矿已经在铁路、通航河道可及的范围内开采。坐落于长江中游的汉阳钢铁厂为中国有望在路轨、结构件及类似钢铁制品方面达到自给自足提供了一个很好的例证。在美国,一个技术工人每天的产出为 6～10 美元(相当于欧洲标准的 2/3～1/2),可获得 50～100 美分的报酬,无特殊条件要求的非熟练工人每天到手的报酬是 20～30 美分,而中国的工厂则能使制造钢铁的劳动成本只相当于美国、欧洲钢铁厂成本的一小部分。一旦中国开办更多这样的工厂——有了外国资本的帮助,似乎任何时候都有可能出现这种情况——中国将能制造出本国需要的大部分简单钢铁制品。所以,有关钢铁制品贸易的结论是:在不远的未来,中国在五金产品方面可能仍将非常依赖美国和欧洲,但在未来的十年或二十年之内,对进口货的需求相对来说可能会有实质性的下降——如果不是绝对量下降的话。

## 三、电力机械、电器用品和其他物资[①]

电力机械、电器用品和其他物资是美国在不久的未来能在中国极大成长的另一个贸易领域。现在,这一领域的贸易规模已经非常大,1920—1921 年的贸易额已超过400 万美元,1922 年有所下降。前面一节关于"中国今天正在购买的与未来将要采购的相比只是微不足道的一小部分"的引语用在这里也很精准。

最近二十年间,古老的中国城市对电气材料和电力机械的需求以令人吃惊的速度增长。也就是 1903 年,中国海关统计才首次将电气材料单列为一个类目,当年进口额仅有 36.8 万美元[②]。战前,中国的电气材料进口总额略低于 250 万美元;但在最近十

---

① 汽车将在下一部分论述,此处不包含。
② 约合 57.46 万两香港海关银元(当年,1 两海关银元＝0.64 美元)。

年里,持续增长,1919—1922 年进口总额增长至 1 000 万美元左右(见表 14 - 5)。这
一巨大增长是由于为其他工厂提供照明和运转、现有工厂的运行与扩张、新建工厂而
产生的对电气设备的热切需要。用于照明目的、小型电动装置的电力建设在中国增长
很快。这些小型电动装置主要由美国供应。中国正在运营的大量的小型工厂实际上
尤其适合以电力作为动力,它可以很好轻松地控制、不需要时就可以切断。

但是,现在有一个倾向,那就是中国较为重要的设施中安装大型电力机组;几年前
200、400 千瓦就已经相当大了,而现在安装 1 000 千瓦及以上的机组变得很普通;最近
几年间签订了一大批私人电站订单,其目的在于为棉纺厂、面粉厂提供动力。当然,这
种对安装机械的增长,刺激了电气附件、配件和其他各种电气材料的需求。

1922 年,电气产品的贸易似乎有所回落。无疑,过去两年间的超购行为导致这类
物资市场饱和,加之贸易的普遍萧条以及汇率下跌,共同导致了 1922 年电气用品贸易
额的收缩。尽管有这样的挫折,也无需在这里强调,中国用于动力和照明目的的电厂
的使用确信会持续成长,各种电气用品会有一个光明的未来。

美国及其竞争对手在这一贸易领域的市场份额情况见表 14 - 5。战前,美国的电
气用品在中国销售得并不好,而德国、比利时和日本的产品则有大量进口。1915 年之
后,德国和比利时暂时退出这一领域,英国的商业活动大大收缩,美国电气厂商开始迎
来了东方市场的机会。按照美国的统计,美国对华出口的电力机械、电气设备和电气
材料,与钢铁机械的数量一样非常巨大。1913 年,美国对华出口仅为 12 万美元,到
1920 年增至 437.7 万美元。1921 年,尽管价格膨胀、银价下跌,出口额仍进一步增至
446.4 万美元(见表 14 - 6)。1913 年,美国在中国电气用品进口的份额中仅占 6.3%,
而 1920、1921 年则分别上升到 27.6% 和 35.2%(见表 14 - 5)。

表 14 - 5　1913—1922 年中国电气材料及配件进口来源统计

| 年份 | 银两计价进口额（万两香港海关银元） | 汇率（美元/银两） | 美元计价进口额（万美元） | 中国进口来源分布比例（%） | | | | |
|------|------|------|------|------|------|------|------|------|
| | | | | 加拿大、美国 | 英国 | 香港 | 日本 | 其他国家 |
| 1913 | 315.9 | 0.73 | 230.6 | 6.3 | 27.2 | 6.8 | 15.2 | 44.5 |
| 1914 | 336.3 | 0.67 | 225.3 | 4.4 | 23.6 | 10.1 | 22.8 | 39.1 |
| 1915 | 255.0 | 0.62 | 158.1 | 9.4 | 22.6 | 13.4 | 35.6 | 19.0 |
| 1916 | 419.7 | 0.79 | 331.6 | 18.0 | 18.9 | 8.4 | 49.6 | 5.2 |
| 1917 | 504.5 | 1.03 | 519.6 | 21.4 | 8.2 | 9.8 | 58.8 | 1.8 |
| 1918 | 480.8 | 1.26 | 605.8 | 25.3 | 4.6 | 7.9 | 56.1 | 6.2 |

（续表）

| 年份 | 银两计价进口额 | 汇率 | 美元计价进口额 | 中国进口来源分布比例（%） | | | | |
|------|------|------|------|------|------|------|------|------|
| | （万两香港海关银元） | （美元/银两） | （万美元） | 加拿大、美国 | 英国 | 香港 | 日本 | 其他国家 |
| 1919 | 611.0 | 1.39 | 849.3 | 34.4 | 5.8 | 7.5 | 34.2 | 8.1 |
| 1920 | 940.4 | 1.24 | 1 166.1 | 27.6 | 13.9 | 3.6 | 40.1 | 14.8 |
| 1921 | 1 512.9 | 0.76 | 1 149.8 | 35.2 | 25.0 | 3.6 | 22.8 | 13.4 |
| 1922 | 1 126.1 | 0.83 | 933.8 | 18.5 | 29.6 | 5.7 | 28.1 | 18.1 |

　　注1：该名称之下包括了中国海关统计之"电气材料和配件"、"电话和电报用品"两大类目之下的所有电气用品和配件。不包括汽车、及其他大部分电力机械。不幸的是，海关统计没有预留一个专门的栏目，因此没有电力机械的准确数字。大部分输入品可能在"推进机械"、"其他机械"和"电气材料和配件"等类目之下。所以，此处的数据并不完整。

　　注2：中国归因于加拿大的大部分进口最初源于美国。参见本章前文表14-1、表14-3之脚注。

　　注3：美国国内外商务局1918年发布的报告称，"考虑到美国进口商的总部大多设在上海、与华南没有太多业务的事实，以及只有少数几家美国电子制造商在香港表现抢眼的事实，很可能1913年及以后从香港进入中国的商品中，最初来源于美国的部分比例并不大。"战争开始之后，这一情况已经发生了变化。

　　注4：战前，德国（比利时也有少部分）实际上分享了该列数据的90%份额；战后，许多中欧国家也参与了该贸易。

表 14-6　1913—1922 年美国电力机械、电气用品及电气材料对华出口额

| 年份 | 出口额（万美元） | 年份 | 出口额（万美元） |
|------|------|------|------|
| 1913 | 12.0 | 1918 | 149.3 |
| 1914 | 23.9 | 1919 | 190.4 |
| 1915 | 24.2 | 1920 | 437.7 |
| 1916 | 41.7 | 1921 | 446.3 |
| 1917 | 114.3 | 1922 | 165.5 |

　　然而，这种快速增长在1922年未能延续，美国当年对华出口仅为165.5万美元，（在中国同类产品总进口额中的）份额下降到18.5%。这一剧烈下滑，部分是由于中国普遍的商业萧条、其电气用品的进口突然收缩。但是，美国份额下降的主要原因是，欧洲国家在战争期间濒临凋敝的商业活动的恢复、英国对战争的巨大投入，以及英国

向中国市场推销其产品的不懈努力。像其他机械、设备一样，美国电气用品的价格也高于欧洲产品，所以在战后的竞争中受到挫折。但是之前已经提及的授信期限延长的方法也能被美国电气用品制造业者所采用，以冲抵高价之不利因素。

## 四、汽车

中国为美国扩张其汽车贸易提供了最大的市场，其集中表现是：过年几年间，中国的道路建设在各地铺开，从美国进口的汽车日益增加。最近一份市场报告披露，在广阔的中国大地，处处都有异乎寻常的、因商业目的而开建新的交通线路的活动，每年有数千辆汽车和运货卡车被运往中国以满足其增长的需要。

中国汽车市场的发展来得相当突然。仅仅在十年前，一位驻华领事还向其政府报告说汽车在中国的大多数地方都没有什么市场。报告称："在中国的农村，许多地方的道路仅仅是一些乡村小路，没有一点改善；而城市的街道实在过于狭窄，根本无法行驶任何轮式车辆。"那时，只有很少的汽车作为身份象征被中国的富豪所拥有，其他人不使用汽车，对此也不关心。

但是，最近十年间，中国的道路状况发生了非常大的变化。中国人现在认识到良好的公路作为一种开发本国丰富资源的辅助手段极其必要。许多私营道路公司、汽车运输公司已经成立或正在筹建当中；截至目前，已建成长达数百英里的、供汽车通行的优质公路。汽车在中国原先被视作为奢侈品，现在则已被认为是城市高速运输、郊区与城市间交流的需求，也是将铁路与水路连接、作为铁路和水路支线所必需的。如果道路持续建设和养护的资金能有保证，开发各种汽车巨大市场的未来看起来是光明的。中国的这一发展阶段很大程度上可以从如下事实看出端倪：数十年来，中国的铁路建设实际上已经陷入停顿、几无希望从国外引入大量资金以恢复铁路工程建设。中国内陆地区的城镇不能期望通过铁路连接，正在将注意力转向更便宜的道路交通。如果外国资本可以找到协助中国道路建设的方法，其对华汽车贸易必将得到很大的推动。

远东市场的重要性已经打动了美国汽车制造商的心；1922年春，美国商务部向中国派出了一名汽车专家以研究那里的市场环境，并协助美国汽车制造商扩大出口。

表14－7展示了美国汽车在中国市场的增长情况。战前，中国的汽车进口非常少，几乎可以忽略不计。1912年，中国汽车进口总额为28.2万两海关银元，仅合19.7万美元（1两海关银元＝0.7美元）。当时，中国市场上欧洲汽车的销售是美国的2倍。战争期间，中国的汽车进口上升到每年超过100万美元，其中的2/3由美国商人供应。现在中国道路上行驶的汽车约有一半来自美国。美国人的成功据说是由于美国人总体上与中国人保持着亲善关系这一事实，另一个优势是最近在中国市场上销售的美国汽车质量上乘。

中国对美进口总额平均每年超过 1 亿美元,但它从美国进口的汽车却连续数年仅仅维持在 200 万美元左右,这一点也许并不令人吃惊,但对那些了解中国实际状况的人来说,这可能就是中国汽车销售业务快速发展的前兆。必须记住这一点,就在数年前,中国还不是一个大的汽车买家。如果能想象出中国省际的碎石公路网络图,就可以在大脑中估计出来中国每年可能的汽车销量。

表 14 - 7　1912—1922 年中美汽车、摩托车贸易统计

| 年份 | 中国汽车、摩托车进口 (数据来自《中国海关统计》) | | | 美国对华汽车及零配件出口 (数据来自《美国通商航海统计》) | | | |
| --- | --- | --- | --- | --- | --- | --- | --- |
| | 总进口 | 从美国进口 | | 汽车 | | 汽车零件 | 出口总额 |
| | (万两海关银元) | (万两海关银元) | (%) | (辆) | (万美元) | (万美元) | (万美元) |
| 1912 | 28.2 | 8.8 | 31 | | | | |
| 1913 | 53.6 | 11.9 | 22 | | | | |
| 1914 | 60.8 | 15.1 | 25 | 144 | 14.4 | | |
| 1915 | 43.1 | 24.9 | 58 | 123 | 12.2 | | 12.2 |
| 1916 | 75.4 | 49.3 | 65 | 314 | 28.4 | 2.2 | 30.6 |
| 1917 | 95.7 | 58.8 | 62 | 645 | 43.2 | 5.6 | 48.8 |
| 1918 | 137.4 | 65.6 | 48 | 1 058 | 98.6 | 7.2 | 106.1 |
| 1919 | 245.0 | 146.1 | 60 | 1 722 | 209.7 | 23.9 | 233.6 |
| 1920 | 387.7 | 223.1 | 58 | 2 245 | 287.6 | 31.4 | 319.0 |
| 1921 | 386.8 | 184.4 | 48 | 646 | 70.3 | 16.0 | 86.3 |
| 1922 | 249.5 | 94.9 | 38 | | | | |

# 第四篇

## 美国的对华商业政策及其在华利益

# 第十五章 美国的对华商业政策与对华通商条约

对外贸易政策是贸易发展的原动力,反过来,外贸政策也是现有贸易状况的反映。我们经常借助于各国商业政策间的相互作用来诠释国际贸易历史;反过来,我们也能通过追踪各国贸易在不同发展阶段的特点,来理解这些国家之间为什么彼此会遵循这样那样的政策。所以,为了理解美国对华贸易的现状并预测其未来前景,最好是对这两个国家彼此间的商业政策加以研究。而这些政策大多具体体现在两国陆续签订的通商条约和协议之中。所以,在审视两国商业政策的同时,也要对其通商条约加以检视。

美国自 1784 年开展对华贸易起,在不同发展阶段,对中国这个与其隔海相望的姐妹国家采取过各种各样的商业政策。起先是贯穿于整个非条约交往期的不干涉政策;其后有顾圣于 1844 年和中国签订中美第一个通商条约[1]时的最惠国政策;有帕克[2]于 1858 年向美国政府建议在台湾建立"保护国"的抢占土地政策;还有蒲安臣于 1868 年带领中国使团出访欧洲、美国时提出的完全主权政策;最后是海伊[3]于 1899 年再度发表,并一直为美国所沿用的"门户开放"政策。无论这些政策如何不同,但有一条清晰的主线贯穿其中。换句话说,中美开始外交往来以来,美国在调整其在华商业及对华贸易方面,事实上只有一个政策——最惠国条约政策。美国认识到中国是全世界潜在的最大市场,因此希望有一个公平的机会,通过公平的竞争在中国获得合理的商业份额。这是最惠国待遇的基本原则。

为此,中国的主权和领土完整必须得到保护,但其门户则必须向所有有意进入者开放。因此,顾圣条约对最惠国待遇做了清楚表述,后来的蒲安臣完全主权政策、海伊"门户开放"政策都先后对此予以重申。甚至,帕克前些年提出的抢夺土地政策、塔夫

---

① 译注:即中美《望厦条约》。

② 译注:Peter Parker(1804—1888),也译作伯驾、巴驾或派克,美国传教士、医生兼外交官、美国利用宗教侵略中国的代表人物。1844 年,作为美国特使的助手和翻译,参与《望厦条约》的谈判。1855 年 8 月 16 日至 1857 年 8 月 25 日任美国驻华公使。曾屡次建议美政府武装夺取台湾。

③ 译注:John Milton Hay(1838—1905),又译海约翰。美国作家、记者、外交家、政治家,于威廉·麦金莱和老罗斯福等总统时期任国务卿(1898—1905)。在对华事务方面,反对列强划分势力范围,主张"门户开放政策",要求"中国开户开放,各国利益均沾"。清光绪三十年至三十一年(1904 年至 1905 年),认为庚子赔款赔款过多,希望减免。

脱总统[①]于 1908 年推出的"美元外交"也都丝毫没有偏离这一基本原则。19 世纪后半叶，欧洲列强相继从中国攫取土地或其他特权，美国的一些政治家自然不甘落后。丹涅特[②]先生在其为人称道的《十九世纪美国人在远东》一书的前言中写道：

"美国政策的主轴并非博爱、仁慈而是要求最惠国待遇。人们常常臆想，门户开放政策由海伊发明，并于 1899 年首次提出。事实上，门户开放政策与我们和亚洲之间的关系一样古老。在中国，这一政策早在 1844 年就宣布了，当时顾圣将最惠国条款纳入到望厦条约之中；当蒲安臣使团代表中国和美国缔结 1868 年条约[③]、从英国获得克拉兰敦照会时，这一政策得到了全面发展。从那时起，再也没有引入什么新的原则。似乎不能认为海伊先生或许士[④]先生创造了什么新的原则。"

所以，中美之间或美国与其他涉华国家之间的所有通商条约和协定，以及其他协议都是以最惠国待遇为基础的。

## 一、顾圣的最惠国政策

1840 年之前，美国政府对在华美国公民的态度和中国政府对从事外贸活动的中国商人的态度没有什么不同。美国早期的商业政策可能以"自由放任"[⑤]——"让其自我调整"为原则，这也没有不合适。所以，广州的美国商人就自我调适，总体来说，他们的贸易也比较成功。但是，中英两国 1842 年签署《南京条约》的消息，使美国政府清楚地认识到，如果美国人要在东方市场上与竞争对手保持平等地位，就有必要在中、美之间签订一份类似的条约。1843 年，美国国会通过一个特别法案，以组建第一个交涉对华通商条约事务的美国使团。

使团最终于 1843 年年底前组建起来，由凯莱布·顾圣任特使。美国使团于 1844 年 2 月 24 日到达澳门。使团向广州署理总督递交了公函，说明其访华理由。总督衙门向朝廷禀报，清廷任命耆英为钦差大臣，负责与美国特使谈判。条约的实际谈判很简单，1844 年 7 月 3 日，美中之间的第一份通商条约在澳门附近的望厦签订。

该文件中最重要的条文当然是最惠国条款，如下文规定：

---

① 译注：William Howard Taft(1857—1930)，1909.3.4～1913.3.4 任美国总统。

② 译注：Tyler Dennett(1883—1949)。其著作《Americans in eastern Asia; a critical study of the policy of the United States with reference to China, Japan and Korea in the 19th century》于 1922 年由纽约 Macmillan 公司出版。

③ 译注：即《中美续增条约》。

④ 译注：Charles Evans Hughes(1862—1948)，美国政治家，曾任纽约州州长、美国国务卿(1921 年 3 月 5 日至 1925 年 3 月 4 日)和美国首席大法官。1921 年组织了华盛顿会议来调谐列强的海军力量。

⑤ 译注：源自法语的"laissez-faire"，又称自由放任主义或无干涉主义，意思就是政府放手让商人自由进行贸易。这一词首先在 18 世纪由重农主义在字典里使用，以反对政府对贸易的干涉。这一词到了 19 世纪早期和中期成为了西方自由市场经济学的同义词。

"……合众国来中国贸易之民人所纳出口、入口货物之税饷,俱照现定例册,不得多于各国。……如另有利益及于各国,合众国民人应一体均沾,用昭平允。"[①]

另一个重要的条款,即在中国建立美国的治外法权[②],也应当予以特别关注。即:

"嗣后中国民人与合众国民人有争斗、词讼、交涉事件,中国民人由中国地方官捉拿审讯,照中国例治罪;合众国民人由领事等官捉拿审讯,照本国例治罪。……"

条约还进一步规定,美国公民和其他国家的国民或公民在中国境内发生所有争议,必须依据美国与相关国家政府之间的条约办理,中国官员不得过问[③]。

除了上述条款,望厦条约还要求中国的广州、福州、厦门、宁波和上海等五个港口——它们之前按 1842 年(中英南京)条约已向英国开放——向美国开放通商[④],准许美国公民及家眷居住、经商,其船只和货物可以任意往来[⑤]。这些港口的各种杂费规定被正式废除,进、出口关税在条约所附的关税表中加以规定[⑥],还规定了船舶吨税[⑦]。洋行商人的独占贸易,以及其他的垄断行为或不法限制行为都被废除[⑧],条约还给予美国正式任命驻华领事的权利[⑨]。

外国人认为,作为贸易管控的基础,美国 1844 年条约比两年前英中条约的条款更加优厚。事实上,也正因此,该条约立刻成了数周后开始谈判的法国条约,以及挪威和瑞典于 1847 年签订的条约[⑩]的范本。的确,顾圣条约已成为中国建立国际关系的基础,直至它于 1858 年被天津条约[⑪]所替代。可以确信,美国从来没有仿效欧洲列强,使用武力;但同样可以确信的是,美国常常欣赏欧洲列强利用暴力所获取的果实,因为其他国家通过武力获得的贸易特权按照最惠国条款会自动适用于美国。

## 二、美国修订 1844 年条约的企图

随着中美之间正式条约关系的建立,两个国家间的贸易迅速扩张——这在第二章已有描述。但是,外国列强和中国政府之间的关系很快达到了一个关键阶段,并于太

---

① 《望厦条约》第 2 款。

② 望厦条约》第 21 款

③ 《望厦条约》第 25 款。

④ 《望厦条约》第 3 款。

⑤ 《望厦条约》第 5 款。

⑥ 《望厦条约》第 13 款。

⑦ 《望厦条约》第 6 款。

⑧ 《望厦条约》第 15 款。

⑨ 《望厦条约》第 4 款。

⑩ 译注:1844 年 10 月,中法签订《黄埔条约》;1847 年 3 月,中国与瑞典、挪威分别签订《五口通商章程》。

⑪ 译注:1858 年(咸丰八年)5 月,英法联军侵入天津,并扬言进攻北京。清朝廷派大学士桂良、吏部尚书花沙纳为钦差大臣,赴天津议和,被迫先后与俄(6 月 13 日)、美(6 月 18 日)、英(6 月 26 日)、法(6 月 27 日)签订《天津条约》。

平天国运动 1853 年取得第一次胜利时达到了顶峰。

太平天国运动为外国列强扩大其在华利益提供了良好的机会,并被美国、英国、法国、俄罗斯发挥到了极致。1854 年,美国政府派遣罗伯特·M·麦莲[1]访华,以保证清廷"对顾圣条约做一些重要的修订"。清朝政府意识到,如果给予美国人任何优惠,法国人、英国人必然也会提出新的特权,因此严词拒绝其提议。

顾圣条约第 34 款规定,条约届满十二年后可以磋商修订,因此 1856 年该条约进入修订期。中国拒绝任何修约提议的坚定态度给美国政府留下了深刻印象,因此美国驻华公使彼得·帕克被派往伦敦、巴黎,与英法政府进行协商以便采取协调一致的对华政策。在美国对华政策的演变过程中,这是唯一一次与欧洲合作压制中国。

美、英、法三国公使在广州请求会谈,但遭到执拗的叶总督的拒绝[2],他们决定诉诸武力。1856 年 10 月下半月[3],英国海军进攻广州,城墙被毁;11 月 15 日,美国海军摧毁了一个中国港口,理由是一艘美国船只在该港口遭到攻击。时任美国驻华商务公使的彼得·帕克甚至向美国政府提出建议,声称如果三国的代表仍然不受欢迎,"法国旗帜将在朝鲜升起,英国旗子将在宁波岸外的舟山升起,而美国的旗子将在台湾升起"。

## 三、帕克的抢夺土地政策

第二章提到,美国政府曾考虑开办太平洋邮件和货运业务。要完成这样一个计划,在东方提供充足的煤炭供应是不可缺少的。基于这个目的,台湾——当时中国的一个省——吸引了在华的一些有野心的美国官员的注意。1847 年,英美两国的海军官员赴台调查其煤炭资源;1849 年,美国双桅帆船"海豚号"赴台湾进行更深入的勘察。美国海军准将佩里(Matthew C. Perry)于 1854 年对台湾的访问,再次刺激了美国对台湾的兴趣,美国组建了一个商业公司以进行相关开发。这对雄心勃勃的帕克是一个好机会,他于 1857 年 2 月致信美国国务院[4]:

---

① 译注:Robert Milligan McLane(1815—1898 年),美国政治家、军官、外交家,曾任美国驻华专员(1853—1854 年)。在华期间,曾于 1854 年(太平天国甲寅四年)乘军舰至南京,访问太平天国,太平天国答复为"准年年来贡",逐对太平天国没有好感,建议美国政府支持清政府。

② 译注:叶名琛(1807—1859 年),字昆臣,清朝中后期的政治人物,湖北汉阳人,官至两广总督擢授体仁阁大学士。第二次鸦片战争爆发后,叶名琛对英法联军不战、不守、不议和,后被俘往印度绝食而卒。

③ 译注:1856 年 10 月 23 日(九月二十五日)英国海军上将西马縻各里率军舰 3 艘、划艇 10 余只、海军陆战队约两千人进攻广州,第二次鸦片战争正式爆发。11 月 15 日(十月十八日),美国两艘军舰驶往广州,误被炮台轰击。1856 年 12 月 12 日(十一月十五日),帕克致书美国务卿,主张与英法分占台湾、舟山、朝鲜,再与中国交涉。此建议遭到拒绝。

④ 译注:帕克于 1857 年 2 月 12 日向美国国务院呈送美国商人的建议;1857 年 3 月 10 日,再次向国务院报告。

"非常希望美国政府在与台湾的关系中,不吝于将人道主义、文明和商业强加于它。目前,这个岛屿居住着野蛮之人,因其邪恶、残酷,我们有理由相信许多欧洲人——其中有我们自己的朋友和同胞——已经深受其害。"

当年 3 月,他又向美国国务院建议:

"如果建立了连接加利福尼亚、日本和中国的轮船航线,(台湾的)煤炭供应将是最有优势的。该岛不再留在(大清)帝国之内是有可能的;如果它在政治上与帝国割裂——在地理上是这样的,作为对列强均势这一基本原则的尊重,美国显然应当领有该岛。"

对于帕克这些要求获得授权以完全攫取台湾的激进建议,国务卿没有给予任何答复。但是对于其最初有关(法英美)三国暂时占领朝鲜和舟山、台湾的建议,国务卿马西①回复说总统不相信"我们与中国的关系需要采取您所说的'最后手段';即使需要,美国的陆、海军部队也只有得到国会授权方可动用。"

## 四、天津条约

1857 年,美国首任驻华全权公使列卫廉②与俄、法、英三国公使一起抵达中国,谋求完成期盼已久的对南京条约、望厦条约的修订工作。他们率领由军舰和轮船组成的强大舰队联袂来到中国,为公开战争做足了准备。这次,四国公使要求中国政府完全接受曾被拒绝的所有条件,别无选择。5 月 20 日,英法舰队进攻并最终占领天津大沽炮台,中国政府被迫让步。在列强的军事压力下,谈判进展很快。中美天津条约于 6 月 18 日签订,中国与俄罗斯、英国、法国间的天津条约也陆续签订。

天津条约最重要的条款是在通商、通航、政事或其他交往等方面全面保证最惠国待遇③;美国获得的其他特权有:与中国政府建立外交往来,清政府承诺若准许其他国家公使驻京,应准美国一律照办④;条约港口数从 5 个立即增加到 8 个⑤,并准许美国人与嗣后向其他国家开放的中国港口市镇通商⑥;准许美国官员镇压、惩罚海盗、抢劫

---

① 译注:William Learned Marcy(1786—1857),曾任美国美国国务卿(1853 年 3 月 7 日至 1857 年 3 月 6 日),时任总统福兰克林·皮尔斯。

② 译注:William Bradford Reed(1806—1876),著名律师。首任美国驻华特命全权公使(1857 年 4 月 18 日至1858 年 11 月 11 日),时任总统詹姆斯·布坎南(James Buchanan)。

③ 中美《天津条约》第 30、6、15 款。

④ 中美《天津条约》第 48 款。

⑤ 译注:按中美《天津条约》条约第 14 款,除《望厦条约》规定之广州、福州、厦门、宁波和上海五个港口外,增开潮州(设在汕头)、台南为通商口岸。原文此处(第 277 页)之"8 个"疑为作者笔误。

⑥ 中美《天津条约》第 14 款。

和暴乱行为①；对吨税做了修订；允许自由传教②。中国的进、出口关税，除因与其他国家订立条约而改变者外，均沿用 1944 年（望厦）条约的规定。由于这类关税变化非常多，中美两国于 1858 年 11 月签订了一个补充条约，明确规定了适用于美国贸易的关税和税则。

中国作为一方，美、英、法、俄作为另一方订立的这些天津条约，对美国在华商业利益产生了非常大的影响。约前时代的旧广州贸易传统③在美国商人当中荡然无存。一种新的国际贸易秩序形成了，其他国家的商人可以寻求政治和军事支持。接下来的十年里，德国、葡萄牙、丹麦、西班牙、荷兰和意大利等 6 个国家也与中国签订条约，使得美国商业不得不面对激烈的国际竞争和贸易冲突。

## 五、蒲安臣的完全主权政策和 1868 年条约

美国首任留驻北京的美国公使安森·伯林格姆（即蒲安臣）于 1862 年来到中国。这位能干、富有远见、高尚正直的政治家，对中国人抱着深切的同情。他于 1867 年辞去美国公使职务，以大清帝国全权特使的身份，出使与中国有条约关系的西方各国。

蒲安臣接受这一新职务的原因不难理解。无论是为了中国利益，还是为了美国和世界利益，远东问题都必须得到公正、和平的解决。如果西方人现在"抢夺土地"的政策继续下去，中国之被瓜分似乎是相当可能的。但是，如果出现这样不幸的事件，世界政治的失控局面将不可避免；尽己所能、避免出现这样一场世界性灾难是任何人都会有的原动力，蒲安臣完全明白其使团是否完成使命所产生的巨大影响。

蒲安臣使团的主要目的是劝说西方列强承认大清帝国的主权，以完全平等原则对待中国人。这个政策归根结底是美国的对华政策，这可以从如下事实证明：蒲安臣作为中国使团的领队到达美国时受到民众的热烈欢迎，且不久之后，他又与自己的政府签订了一份通常称作"蒲安臣条约"的《中美续修条约》，其中的所有八个条款都体现了中国完全主权及平等对待中国人的原则。

蒲安臣使团在美国完成了使命之后，转道伦敦，在那里得到英国政府的一个照会④，照会声称"中国政府完全有权仰赖外国的自制，英国政府无需、也无意向中国施加不友好的压迫。"

---

① 中美《天津条约》第 9 款。

② 中美《天津条约》第 29 款。

③ 译注：1784 年美国商船中国皇后号（The Empress of China）抵达广州，开启了中美直接通商的历史。此后直至 1844 年中美两国签订第一个不平等条约《望厦条约》，双方共有 60 年的交往过程。这段期间常被称为"早期中美关系时期"，一些美国学者或称其为"约前时代"（Pre-treaty Ear），或是旧广州贸易时期（Old Canton Trade Period）。

④ 1868 年 12 月 26 日，英国外交大臣克拉兰敦会见了蒲安臣等人。28 日，克拉兰敦发表一份自制性的照会，通常称克拉兰敦照会。

蒲安臣受到与美、英成功谈判的鼓舞,继续向欧洲大陆前进,先后访问了巴黎、柏林,并于 1870 年到达彼得格勒。不幸的是他在那里突然亡故,留下了未竟之功。

蒲安臣使团是美国第一次试图以中国领土完整原则建立门户开放政策。尽管其即时效应并不很大,但美国后来的数次政策很可能在某种程度上得益于该使团的成就。

## 六、通商条约于 1880、1903、1920 年的三次修订

总体来说,1858 年条约和 1868 年增订条款已经很好地解决了美中两国间的通商关系问题。这些已经达成的条约从缔结之日起就只是不断进行增补,而不是被直接替代。1880 年 11 月 17 日,中美两国在北京签订《管制和限制华工赴美条约》[①],由于"条约尚有未备之外"[②],还一并缔结了一个关系到两国贸易往来和审判程序的补充通商条约[③]。条约在如下方面提供了更加具体的互惠承诺:涉及吨税、进/出口税、或沿岸贸易的最惠国待遇[④];两国间绝对禁止鸦片贸易;国民或其他任何国家不得要求与本规定相抵触的最惠国条款[⑤]。条约还赋予明确美国治外法权,即中国人、美国人在中国发生争议时,应由被告所在国的官员按本国法律审理,但原告所在国的官员可以前往观审[⑥]。

20 世纪初,义和团运动在中国华北地区兴起,与中国有着商业及其他利益关系的国家又有了一个修订已有条约、扩大其在华商业权利和特权的机会。涉及此事件的 11 个国家[⑦]于 1900 年 12 月 22 日、1901 年 1 月 16 日两次就与中国重新建立正常关系的条件发出联合照会,声称"中国政府将承诺就对各国认为非常有益的通商行船条约的修订问题,以及与商业关系相关的其他议题进行谈判,以促进其发展"。鉴于这一规定,美国政府与中国签订了 1903 年条约[⑧]。可以这样理解,这个条约与 1880 年条约相似,是对以前缔结的条约进行增订而非替代。原条约的所有条款仍然完全有效,只有那些由增订条约、及以美国作为缔约一方的其他条约所明文修改的部分除外[⑨]。下

---

① 这其实不是通商条约,只能间接影响中美贸易。见前第三、第四章之中国移民问题部分。

②《中美续修条约》之前言。

③ 译注:光绪六年(1880)十月十五日,美国驻华公使安吉立(J. B. Angell)与清总理衙门大臣宝鋆在北京签订《中美续修条约》。共四款,另有"续增附款"。规定:对华工赴美,美国"可以或为整理,或定人数、年数之限"。光绪七年(1881)六月二十四日在北京互换条约批准书。

④《中美续修条约》第 3 款。

⑤《中美续修条约》第 2 款。

⑥《中美续修条约》第 4 款。

⑦ 即奥匈、比利时、法国、德国、意大利、英国、日本、荷兰、俄罗斯、西班牙、美国。

⑧ 译注:即《中美通商行船续订条约》。

⑨《中美通商行船续订条约》第 17 款。

面就是条约文件的概要：

（1）在最惠国待遇方面保证：

（a）一国给予对方外交代表所有的特权、特许权和豁免权（第1款）。

（b）一国的领事官员在对方国家的特许权、豁免权和审判权（第2款）。

（c）美国公民居住在向外国人开放居住贸易的中国港口或其他地点时，在人身、财产方面的权利、特许权和豁免权（第3款）。

（d）关于货物进口的关税，他国公民可在本国缴纳（第5款）。

（e）美国公民、企业和公司在中国内河通航水域上经营旅客和合法商品运输的权利（第12款）。

（2）中国保证，关于矿场租用、专利权税的国民待遇和最惠国待遇的规定和条件，将及于期望从事采矿工作及其他与此有关的商业活动的美国公民（第7款）。

（3）在关税方面，中国政府同意废除厘金和其他行货税捐；为了补偿，将征收不超过进口正税1.5倍的进口附加税，出口税（含附加税）不得超过货值的7.5％（第4款）。美国公民在中国缴纳的进口货物税则也在条约中加以规定。但是无论如何，都不得另征关税或比最惠国更高（第5款）。

（4）明确扩大了美国贸易权利和贸易特许权：

（a）准许美国人在向外国人开放居住、贸易的中国港口及其他地方定居、贸易或从事其他合法活动，外国人在其地界内可以租住或购买房屋，也可以租赁或永租地基并在其上自建房屋（第3款）。

（b）美国公民在开放港口设立保税仓库的权利（第6款）。

（c）开放奉天府、安东县①供外国人居住、贸易（第12款）。

除了1920年10月20日补充条约之附件②对进口关税进行修订外，上述所有条款及其他一些条款直到现在仍然全部有效，中国进口的各种货物的关税都列于该补充条约之税则表之中。因此，与进口商品海关估价有关的规则也在1920年条约中予以修订，以适应现在价格水平的变化。

## 七、海伊的门户开放政策——最惠国待遇政策的重申

中国的"瓜分利权"时期之后，1899年美国政府宣布了"门户开放"政策。这个政策就是为各列强在中国开辟"势力范围"，各"势力范围"主权仍归中国所有，列强在"势力范围"内享受同等的贸易、政治机会以保持各国在远东地区的稳定平衡。事实上，该

---

① 译注：即今沈阳、丹东。

② 译注：即1920年签订于华盛顿的《修改通商进口税则：善后章程》，其基本内容与1918年12月20日修改税则委员会讨论通过的《修改各国通商进口税则：善后章程》一致，两个文件的税则部分完全相同。

政策并没有意味着打开中国的大门,因为1839、1858年及1860年三次战争之后,中国已经门户洞开。截至1898年,中国已有30多个港口开放对外通商,各个国家都在中国享受着最惠国待遇。因此所谓"门户开放",其真正意义并不在于中国的门户需要开放,而是在中国拥有特别优先权、设立"势力范围"的各个列强。

　　19世纪末,列强在远东地区的平衡状态非常不稳定。欧洲列强都想在中国立足,但又担心竞争对手超越自己。因此,一方面,为了保护自身利益制衡、反制衡,另一方面,保障自己的"优先权"以便击败其竞争对手。为了给本国发展建立坚实的基础,列强们相互排斥,在自己的"势力范围"内不允许他人建造工业企业。列强除了不断重复要求中国政府发布所谓"不得让与的声明"外,还相互协商、以确定各自的"势力范围"。然而,这并不能平息列强间的利益冲突,反而使之更为加剧。美国认识到这种不加节制的竞争和效仿行为的严重危险性,立即推出其远东政策,在消除国际冲突、维护世界和平方面发挥了显著作用。

　　然而,美国宣布门户开放政策并不仅仅是基于维护文明世界的道义责任,以及避免正在迫近的世界大战的发生。除了其他考虑因素外,这一声明的动机还在于美国的自身利益。美国无意涉入远东政治事务,但对在中国进行贸易有着浓厚的兴趣。美国购买阿拉斯加、占有菲律宾、计划开掘巴拿马运河之后,进行远东贸易的前景更加光明。如果准许西方国家殖民中国,美国将首当其冲、在其未来广阔的贸易中遭受损失。约翰·巴诺特[1]于1899年声称,美国应当毫不延迟地宣布将门户开放政策作为保护美国在华商业利益的唯一手段:

　　"……目前的趋势是将中国划分为外国的势力范围,这只是实际最高治权地区的另一种说辞,它将意味着旧天津条约的废除,而该条约确保我们在全中国与其他国家进行绝对自由的贸易。如果允许势力范围存在并成为普遍行为,这个庞大帝国里可能就没有可供美国与其他国家平等竞争的地方了。在每个势力范围内,我们可能会发现特惠关税和优惠费率对特定土地的产品有利,而对我们不利;同样的原则运用于其他势力范围,这就实际上把我们排除出一个公平参与中国这样一个拥有3亿人口、400万平方英里面积的国家之无限[2]增长的需求之外。

　　"如果把中国划分为各国的势力范围,我们将失去所有一切,而不会有任何收获。现在,市场的发展取决于我们对于与世界各国平等竞争的努力程度。如果中国被瓜分,我们必须面对新的环境和条约下的各种各样的诸个障碍和集体屏障。

　　"一旦我们须臾显露出对抢劫这个天朝帝国的默许,就会出现对中国富裕地区的争夺和冲突,因为全世界都会惊羡于其繁华。……毫无疑问,原本属于我们美国的巨大机会将被其他国家夺取、占有和利用,最终使我们国家沦为太平洋上的一个二流

---

① 译注:John Barrett,时任美国驻泰国公使。

② 译注:此处原文为immeasurble,疑为immeasurable拼写之误,更正。

国家。"

在这份报告中,美国欲将门户开放政策作为确保其在华最惠国待遇的一种手段的意图表露无遗。很大程度上是由于这一潜在动机,美国被迫采取行动。这项政策在海伊1898年就任国务卿后开始实施,尽管其最早可溯源到1844年。

"英国、日本政府正式地、且不断重复发出声明,要求中国确保世界各国自由贸易",因此,海伊于1899年9月6日训令美国驻伦敦、柏林、巴黎和圣彼得堡的大使,要求英、德、法、俄四国正式答复美国提出的在中国实施门户开放政策的要求。数月后,海伊将同样的指示传送到意大利和日本。美国在照会中提出了如下三项原则:

(1)对于在中国的所谓利益范围或租借地内的任何条约口岸或任何既得利益,一概不加干涉。

(2)中国现行条约税则适用于所有势力范围内一切口岸(自由港除外)所装卸的货物,不论其属何国籍。此种税款由中国政府征收。

(3)在各自势力范围内的任何口岸,对他国入港船舶所征收的入港费,均不得高于本国船舶;在各自势力范围内修筑、管理或经营的铁路,对他国臣民运输的货物,不得高于对本国臣民运输同样货物、经过同等距离所征收的铁路运费。

英国首先表态接受。接下来依次是法国、日本、意大利和俄罗斯,德国的回应最晚。这样,至少在名义上,海伊的政策被相关的各国所接受①。

海伊照会的原则,有三个明显的特点。首先,承认列强已经在中国建立的"利益范围",决不允许干涉"范围"内的既得利益。其次,确立了中国在这些"范围"内征收关税的主权。最后,废除了一国向他国臣民征收较高入港税和铁路运费的经济歧视。因此,它把各国置于平等地位,与美国在华商业利益完全一致。

然而,为了使该政策基础坚实、具有可操作性,必须要求有一个最基本的条件,即,中国的主权独立和领土完整必须得到保证。但是,恰在此时,义和团运动在中国北方省份爆发,外国军队纷纷涌入北京,中国的独立陷入危机之中。美国为了支持门户开放政策,首先向其他国家提出明确要求,在达成和平条约前必须尊重中国的领土完整和政治独立。

义和团运动后,除俄罗斯外的所有欧洲国家表面上都遵守门户开放原则。俄罗斯向美国及世界保证,俄罗斯帝国政府已经"表明了遵从这一政策的坚定立场",但无意用语言来保证。义和团运动期间及之后,俄罗斯千方百计试图在满洲地区获取特别优先权,而将其他国家拒于其外。针对俄罗斯的侵略,海伊于1902年2月向日本和几乎所有欧洲国家发出措辞严厉的照会。但俄罗斯对此毫不在意,反而更加积极地推进其

---

① 译注:1899年11月30日,英国索尔兹伯里复函;法国继英国之后,于12月16日复照接受美国照会;日本和德国分别于12月26日和1900年2月19日复照表示接受;俄国于1899年12月30日作了回答,但并未完全接受,实际上是拒绝的。1900年1月7日,意大利政府表示"欣然赞成"美国的建议。

帝国政策;这样就危及到了日本的地位。日本为了维护自身利益,于1904年向俄罗斯宣战。俄罗斯的战败一度消除了其对中国北方的侵略。但不幸的是,日本作为俄罗斯的后继者进入满洲,成了中国门户开放政策的挑战者。

## 八、鲁特–高平协议

此后,美国关于远东政策的正式声明只是继续和重申海伊政策。每当中国的门户开放受到威胁,美国似乎都不会忘记重申其政策——即中国门户开放或美国的最惠国待遇。所以,日本战胜俄罗斯并接收了后者在满洲地区拥有的所有特权之后,重申门户开放政策对美国来说似乎就有必要了。第一次重申发生于海伊换文第九年之后,美国国务卿伊莱休·鲁特[①]和日本驻美大使高平小五郎于1908年11月(30日)在华盛顿以另一次换约的形式完成。协议承认了日本在远东地区上升的影响力,以及美国在太平洋地区的利益。鲁特–高平协议的实质是鼓励太平洋地区贸易的自由、和平发展,维护上述地区"现有状况"[②],保护中国商业、工业的均等机会原则,保护列强的公共利益——支持用所有和平手段维护中国的独立和完整、捍卫所有在华列强机会均等的原则。

## 九、蓝辛–石井协定[③]

鲁特–高平协议之后第九年,美国国务院于1917年发表了第三份声明。此次与以前的声明有所不同。日本以英国同盟国的身份参与世界大战,从德国手中抢走山东,控制了远东的局面。日本要求美国特别承认其在亚洲的主导地位,这一目的在《蓝辛—石井协定》中得以实现,该协定由美国国务卿和日本特使在华盛顿签订,于1917年11月对外公布。协定明确宣称,领土的相邻会在国家之间造成特殊的关系,因此,(美国承认)日本在中国拥有特殊利益[④]。

当然,中国不愿在事关自己主权和独立的事件中被完全忽视。北京政府"为免除误会起见",就《蓝辛—石井协定》的签署公开发表照会[⑤],强调"中国政府不因他国文书互认,有所拘束"。

----

① 译注:Elihu Root(1845—1937),美国著名律师、政治家,1905年7月19日至1909年1月27日期间担任美国国务卿,时任总统西奥多·罗斯福。1912年诺贝尔和平奖获得者。

② 译注:即美国将尊重日本在朝鲜的利益,而后者也不会干涉菲律宾。

③ 译注:1917年11月2日,日本外务大臣石井菊次与美国国务卿兰辛就分割在华殖民权益达成协定,故名。1922年秋,美国政府以与《九国公约》的精神相悖为由,向日本提议并在日本的反对中于1923年4月废除了"蓝辛–石井协定"。

④ 译注:该协定称"合众国和日本两国政府承认领土的接近造成两个国家之间的特殊关系,因而合众国政府承认日本在中国,特别是在它的与之接近的部分,有特殊的利益"。

⑤ 译注:中国政府8号照会两国、9号公开照会,对此表示反对。

### 十、战后远东问题及华盛顿会议上门户开放政策的重申

世界大战使远东地区陷入极度不稳定的状态。然而,远东问题的基本情况在1920年本质上与1898年时相同。首先,中国的软弱给列强在中国领土内建立各种特权的机会。其次,比其他国家更具侵略性的某一强国——1898年是俄罗斯、1920年是日本——拥有更大机会的优势,并因此在中国建立了使其他国家处于劣势的地位。1898年,这样的局势因美国通过宣布海伊的门户开放政策而挽回;而到了1920年,美国显然应当与对此有兴趣的欧洲国家联手完成此事。

此外,解决远东问题事实上是要求各国限制军备的必要条件。凡尔赛和会之后,各国军备继续大幅增长、并没有下降,因此限制军备对有效防止第二次世界大战是很必要的。哈定(Harding)总统认识到这一问题的重要性,于1921年8月11日向主要的协约国和参战国发出参加军备限制和太平洋及远东问题会议的正式邀请。会议于1921年11月11日召开,美国、英国、法国、意大利、日本、荷兰、比利时、葡萄牙和中国等九个国家参加。人们对这一会议的成果记忆犹新,此处无需详细描述。只要说其最重要的成果是与会九国签订了一份关于中国问题原则和政策的条约①就足够了。门户开放政策首次在一个以中国作为一方的条约里加以规定。

条约第一款包含了缔约各国在处理中国事务时应当遵循的四个基础原则,如下规定:

"除中国外,缔约各国协定:

(1) 尊重中国之主权、独立及领土与行政之完整。

(2) 给予中国完全无碍之机会,以发展并维持一有力巩固之政府。

(3) 施用各种之权势,以期切实设立并维持各国在中国全境之商务实业机会均等之原则。

(4) 不得因中国状况,乘机营谋特别权利,而减少友邦人民之权利,并不得奖许有害友邦安全之举动。"

条约第二款强调了上述原则:

"缔约各国协定,不得彼此间及单独或联合与任何一国或多国,订立条约、或协定、或协议、或谅解,足以侵犯或妨害第一款所称之各项原则者。"

第三款则对门户开放政策做了详细的定义:

"为适用在中国之门户开放,或各国商务实业机会均等之原则,更为有效起见,缔约各国除中国外,协定不得谋取或赞助其本国人民谋取:

(1) 任何办法,为自己利益起见,欲在中国任何指定区域内,获取关于商务或经济

---

① 译注:即1922年2月6日签订的《九国关于中国事件应适用各原则及政策之条约》,又称《九国公约》。

发展之一般优越权利。

（2）任何专利或优越权，可剥夺他国人民在华从事正当商务实业之权利，或他国人民与中国政府或任何地方官共同从事于任何公共企业之权利，抑或因其范围之扩张、期限之久长、地域之广阔，致有破坏机会均等原则之实行者。"

第四款对势力范围做了说明：

"缔约各国协定，对于各该国彼此人民间之任何协定，意在中国指定区域内设立势力范围，或相互设有独立之机会者，均不予以赞助。"

第五款与铁路相关：

"中国政府约定，全国铁路不施行或许可何种不公平之歧视待遇。……缔约各国除中国外，对于上述之中国铁路基于任何让与、或特别协约、或他项手续，各该国或各该国人民得行其任何管理权者，负有同样之义务。"

这些条款，确保了中国的门户开放和美国的最惠国待遇。

## 十一、中国贸易法案

门户开放政策，就其目前状态而言，只是加强在华美国商人力量的一种消极措施。最近，美国政府采取一个积极措施，以提高美国在华商业经营的竞争实力，促进对华贸易的进一步发展，这就是美国国会 1922 年通过的、通常称之为中国贸易法案的联邦贸易法案。

美国国内外贸局局长朱利叶斯·克莱因博士说："这一法案的目的是对从事对华贸易事务的美国商人予以紧急救济。欧洲战争之前，在中国的美国重要企业仅有三四家……但是在华美国企业的数量，按照位于上海的中国美国总商会的会员数计算，已从 1915 年的 48 家增加到 1920 年的 313 家。……为了使美国进入这个扩大的贸易市场成为可能，需要做一些法律修改；正是为了满足这样的需求，制定了中国贸易法案。"

这一中国贸易法案意欲克服的困难在美国众议院司法委员会戴尔先生（Mr. Dyer）的报告中做了概括：

"中国是一个治外法权国家，其含义是，所有在中国从事贸易活动的外国人，按照条约，必须遵从其原在国的法律和规则。……实际上，每个对中国贸易有兴趣的国家，特别是我们强大的竞争对手，都已经颁布了管控、促进其在华业务的特别法。美国尚未这么做，结果，在中国经商的美国公司必须接受 48 个州政府和美国领地的各种相互抵触的商业规程。这一事实使我们在如下方面特别困难：

首先，法律没有统一，也没有哪个州的法律能满足外贸需要；而且其中几个州立公司组建法不够严谨，准许创办的公司可能会给我们在中国商人中的声誉造成很大损害。

其次，我们在中国的主要竞争对手，英国、日本和法国都已经通过了管理其在华公司的特别规定,使其豁免国内所得税、利润税。这使美国企业明显处于劣势,因为它不能为萧条、不确定的年份建立必要的储备。年景繁荣时,美国企业尚能应对竞争,但在商业淡季它会破产,而我们的竞争对手却能够持续经营。

第三,在中国的美国公司按各州的不同规章缴纳国内所得税、超额利润税,对中国商人与美国商人建立合资企业形成了阻碍。中国人正在致力于发展其本国工业,渴望与对现代工业有着丰富管理经验的美国商人进行合作。既然进入美国公司的中国资本在税收方面与美国资本同等对待,中国人就不愿与我们合作。

为了补救这些困难,促进美、中以国民合作,如今的中国贸易法案做了如下规定:

(1)法案使在中国经商的美国企业可以遵循一套单一的联邦级的公司组建规程。这消除了由于域外法权而使美国48个州、领地和属国的相互矛盾的公司规程同时应用于中国而引起的混乱。

(2)法案提供了中、美资本进行商业合作、发展企业的机制,允许中国人在此类公司中的股份达到49%,并以对中国资本投资收益免除全部所得税和超额利润税的方式鼓励此类合作。

(3)其他国家的竞争企业已经享受本国政府的税收豁免,本法案力图对美国在华企业做类似的豁免。税收豁免只惠及各公司在中国(含满洲、西藏、蒙古和英国直辖殖民地香港、葡萄牙属澳门省)经营的部分,豁免比例按照美国侨民在依中国法案组建的公司中所拥有的股份确定。

(4)法案对依照该法案运营的公司的各种活动提供了严格的规范,违者需受惩罚。所有这些严格的规章用于指导在华美国企业,确保商业管理按照美国法律和中美条约进行。"有一点得到了保证,即,这些在华公司的商业活动,遵循一套标准;整体来看,这些条款为美国公司本身带来荣光。"

尽管这一立法的益处如此之多,但现今的中国贸易法案即使在美国人自己看来也并非没有可议之处。其中有些人的批评意见较为积极,他们对有限的免税不满意。他们支持这样的观点:尽管该法案为通过美国政府许可在中国组建美国公司提供了更多的必要管理机制,但政府在激励对华外贸方面仍然不够。这一法案可以说仅仅是一个开始、一个铺路石而已。下面的一段评论文字,可以用来解释这一批评观点。

"中国贸易法案意欲对在华美国企业在联邦所得税方面的困难给予救济。不幸的是,无论如何,与该类公司联邦税相关的法案第12条的局限性相当大,以至于就承诺减免而言,法案无能为力。只有在华美国公民的投入资本可以免税,而中国之外的美国公民的投入资本则不可以豁免美国税。因此,只有纯粹的本土企业才能享受这一条款的好处。但是,事实上,大量的美国资本必然来自于美国的金融中心。由美国国内和工业负担费用的分公司、子公司将不能从该法案获得任何救济;因此,这样的法案不能吸引大量资金投资中国。"

还有一种反对中国贸易法案的负面声音。它出于对美国制造业的担心而对这个法案加以"全盘"指责,该观点认为,依照此法案组建的公司中的中国资本会利用美国公民身份获得保护,并在中、美两国豁免税收,因此美国工业可能遭遇中国资本的竞争。

其实,对于该法案的反感,中国人更甚于美国人。当然,中国愿意在发展本国工业和商业时与美国资本合作。然而,该法案承诺给予美国创办人以优惠,而完全牺牲中国人的利益。该法案以治外法权为武器,使美国人免于缴纳中美两国的税收,从而将中国资本置于美国人的控制之中。人们一旦明白,按照这一法案,中国将被剥夺在自己的领土上对本国资本征税的权利,从政治、金融两方面的观点看,就再没有什么比该法案更加对中国不公了。中美资本之间这样的"合作"越多,中国的公共财政就越发局促。

此外,如果一些美国制造商担心依照该法案组建的免税工业、商业与美国国内同类出口企业相比享有太多优待的话,那么,依照中国法律组建、接受中国税制监管的中国公司就有十倍的理由担心:依照该法案组建的中国贸易法案公司借助大幅豁免税收,将能在中国以最不公平的方式竞争。把一部分中国资本转移至美国人手中,并使其以一种不公平的方式与中国公司竞争,这对中国人来说是自杀性的行为。这样的"合作"越多,中国人发展本国工业、商业的机会就越少。

当然,美国人可能会辩解说,这项立法(在保持本国企业方面)并不比其他许多国家走得更远。作为中国的好朋友,美国总是希望去做其他国家不大情愿去做的事——帮助中国解决商业困难而不是使其加剧。英国、日本、法国和其他一些大国,为了促进本国的贸易发展,不断地向中国要求租约和特权,创建势力范围,推行其他殖民政策。美国没有追随这些不公正的侵略行为,而是紧紧抱定其传统的"门户开放"政策,作为维持美国在内的各个国家在对华贸易中享有平等机会的手段。在目前的情况下,美国意在确保其商人在税收豁免方面享受到与其他竞争对手相同的特权。但是,这一目的也可以通过倡导全面废除中国现有的所有治外法权来达到,从而使各国贸易,无论是征税还是豁免,都以同样的中国法律条文为基础。如此行事,美国将不仅能保持其传统的宽容政策,同时还有机会巩固1/4世纪前美国宣布"门户开放"之时,中国人心里留存的对美国人的亲善。如果中国商人、资本家和政府看到这样的合作不会带来伤害而只有利益,就会更愿意与在华投资的美国资本合作。然而,中国贸易法案之下的任何"合作"都会伤及中国现有的金融、司法、工业及商业利益,有爱国心的中国公民无疑将不愿染指这样的"合作"。

# 第十六章　美国在华投资

　　毋庸置疑,拥有大量待开发资源的中国是一个非常良好的投资场所。中国自身缺乏资金,自然欢迎外国资本的流入。半个世纪之前,美国的开发很大程度上借助于欧洲资本;美国现在除了有一些正在偿还的外债外,已经是世界上最富有的国家。南美地区近期的发展也得益于国外投资;如果没有欧洲、美国资本介入,南美国家自身不可能为铁路建设和土地开发提供如此快捷、充裕的资金,其对外贸易也达不到目前的规模。中国目前的情况与数十年前北、南美洲的情形完全相同。笔者提出了一些有关外资在中国抓住投资机会的想法,认为中国对外贸易的扩张有赖于其农业、矿产和工业资源的开发;如果中国不能得到外部的金融支持,这些极为丰富的资源显然难以在不久的将来得到开发。

　　大家都愿意看到中国对外贸易规模增大,因为这对于和中国有外贸关系的国家以及中国自身都是有利的。但是,很明显,除非中国首先完成了内部发展,否则中国的对外贸易不可能有显著增长。所以,任何有意扩大对华贸易的国家,只能通过扩大对中国的金融援助来实现这一目的。

　　现在,美国拥有最丰富的国外投资手段。美国工业已经进入成熟期,资本的进一步投资将因收益递减法则而产生障碍;所以,美国资本家被迫在国外寻求更好的机会。过去数十年间,南美提供了这样一个良好投资机会的场所。但是,对美国投资者和商人来说,投资这块大陆不再那么乐观,因为其工业、农业和商业已经非常发达。

　　欧洲战争摧毁了中欧大部分地区,美国似乎可以在许多欧洲国家的重建工作中为其过剩的资本找到大量投资机会。但是,德国、俄罗斯和许多巴尔干国家极度动荡的社会、政治状态在眼下似乎难以结束,这对美国金融家的判断产生了负面的影响。此外,欧洲已经对美国严重负债,考虑到未来的偿还问题,美国加大贷款是非常不安全的。所以,美国投资者为寻找最有发展前途的投资场所,而将注意力转向远东地区,是非常自然的。

　　另一方面,中国自然更愿意优先向美国而不是其他国家寻求金融支持以发展自己的工业和商业。长期以来,欧洲国家竞相向中国贷款,彼此间经常激烈竞争;但是,战争以来,这一情况完全得到改变。现在,所有欧洲大国——可能只有英国例外——都有艰巨的重建任务,既没有过剩资本,也没有多余的精力投向中国以促进其工业化发展。日本刚刚在一场前所未见的大地震中遭受了空前的大灾难,损失惨重,其目前状况不比刚刚脱离战争的法国、比利时更好。可以确定的是,日本自身的重建工作将动用本国国民的全部精力和资源,并将持续多年。所以,即使日本乐意援助,中国也不能指望从日本得到任何帮助。

所以,在不能获得其他国家金融支持的情况下,中国至少得在近期指望美国为其开掘未开发的财富,这不是很自然吗?

自从美国、中国商务交往的早期阶段,美国人就非常看好中国市场的大好机会,并在不同时间、多次尝试利用这些优势,但是到目前为止,几乎没怎么成功。中国未来发展中的融资问题将长期成为一个非常混乱的国际政策话题,而不是一个简单的商业利益事件。笔者非常遗憾地指出,美国已经深深陷入财政问题,其结果是,尽管美国过去和现在在中国有一定优势,但其在金融支持工业化中国方面不比其他国家有更多的进展。希望美国能够摆脱国际政治对于美国及其他国家和中国之间融资方式的羁绊和束缚。笔者认为,如果这些束缚和羁绊继续存在,就没有希望能成功完成任何能促进美国对华贸易明显扩张的融资。

笔者将在下文对美国在中国进行投资的各种尝试进行简单概括。本章称为美国在华投资失败史可能更为合适。从这些文字不难看出,为什么美国迄今为止的努力都归于失败,而使中国、甚至美国自己深感遗憾。基于过去的经历,笔者非常真诚地希望,为了促进中美两国互惠互利的在华投资的未来发展,美国应当对其对华金融政策做一定的修正。

## 一、中国铁路的早期融资

### 1. 粤汉铁路[①]租让权

在中国的各种投资机会中,铁路建设首先引起了外国投资者的注意。从中日(甲午)战争结束一直到1900年义和团运动,争夺在华铁路租让权是许多欧洲国家之间展开的"利权掠夺战"的主要特征之一。在中国特定地区修建铁路的租让权被列强看作是一个建立和确保其各自"势力范围"的有效手段。也就是不久前,美国人才意识到,如果不能在中国铁路建设中分得一杯羹,其在中国的贸易将不能均衡发展。所以,他们与中国政府展开协商,以确保粤汉铁路的租让权。该租让权按照中国驻美公使代表

---

① 译注:光绪二十二年(1896),清政府决定决定修建粤汉铁路,各国争相谋求入股。是年,美商华士宾、毕来斯即创立了合兴公司,以图夺取粤汉路建筑权。1898年4月14日,清政府驻美大使伍廷芳代表邮传部大臣盛宣怀与美国合兴公司代理人柏许,在华盛顿签订《粤汉铁路借款合同》共15条,借款额英金为400万镑。后来由于美国卷入了与西班牙的战争,合兴公司无法履行合同借款。1900年7月13日,由伍廷芳代表盛宣怀在华盛顿与合兴公司签订《粤汉铁路借款续约》,共26款,改借美金4 000万元,将路权出卖。

清廷核准执行的协议,于1898年4月被授予给美国资本家。这条铁路连接了华南地区最大的商业中心广州和华中地区最大的内陆商业中心汉口,长约600英里,纵贯于富庶的重要农业区,所覆盖的人口与当时美国的人口数相当,其沿线形成了一个重要的钢铁工业区。这个项目可以说是至今为止唯一由美国资本真正控制的铁路租让权。

事实上,粤汉铁路项目几乎不能看作是路权租让,更像是中国政府的一份铁路贷款与建设协议。但是,由于美国承包商开展工作并不积极,中国政府接管了该项目。从美国人的角度看,该项目未能完工无疑是非常可惜的。

**2. 哈里曼和诺克斯的满铁计划**

1905年,已故美国铁路大王爱德华·H·哈里曼[①]做出了美国资本参与中国铁路建设的第二次融资努力。俄日战争后,日本扩张了其在满洲地区的势力,损害了中国及其他和平国家的利益。美国希望维护中国对满洲的主权、保护门户开放,于是向列强建议,满洲铁路应当在国际监督下"商业中立化"。这一建议的理由非常清楚,就是美国企图扩大其在中国、特别是美国已拥有重要贸易利益的满洲地区的工业、金融利益。就在俄日1905年9月签署朴次茅斯条约之后没几天,哈里曼先生与日本代表桂太郎首相达成了一项备忘录[②],将俄国移让给日本的南满铁路转租给美国。这条铁路是哈里曼的环球铁路计划中的一部分。但是,由于日本国内普遍反对,直到1908年谈判没有取得任何成果,也没有关于哈里曼方案的任何信息。

1908年12月,关于中东铁路——俄罗斯政府欲将其售与美国金融家——的谈判在纽约举行,双方要求日本应当同意出售南满铁路。但是,1909年哈里曼去世,购买铁路之事不再有效。

然而,接下来的1909年,美国国务卿诺克斯[③]先生在事先没有获得俄罗斯、日本认可的情况下,同时向英国、德国、俄罗斯、日本和中国政府提出满洲铁路中立化计划。该方案建议上述列强组建国际财团,收买日、俄两国在满洲经营的铁路。诺克斯还进一步建议,如果列强不愿参加这一全面中立化计划,也至少应当在锦州—瑷珲铁路的筹资与建设方面进行联合。这一计划的政治意味更浓于工业和商业意味,所以引起了俄罗斯、日本的疑虑,并最终被两国拒绝。如果哈里曼或诺克斯的计划投入实施,美国资本就会在满洲、华北和朝鲜扮演重要角色,很可能会导致美国、日本在太平洋地区进行合作,远东地区的态势也可能与现在所看到的完全不同。

**3. 锦州—瑷珲铁路项目**

1907年,中国政府通过美国驻奉天总领事与美国就创办满洲银行事宜进行谈判。

---

①译注:Edward H. Harriman(1848—1909),时任美国联合太平洋铁路公司董事长。

②译注:即"桂·哈里曼备忘录"。

③译注:Philander C. Knox(1853—1921),于1909年3月6日至1913年3月5日期间任美国国务卿,时任总统威廉·霍华德·塔夫脱。

这个由美国资本资助的银行,是满洲政府的财务代理人,与英国金融家一起,承担锦州—瑷珲铁路以及其他用于开发满洲商业和工业的重要企业的建设。此后,1909 年,代表中国政府的东三省总督、位于纽约的 J·P·摩根公司、库恩-洛布公司、第一国民银行和国民城市银行[①]等组成的美国银行集团,和英国承包商宝林公司就该铁路筹资、建设和运营事宜达成初步协议[②]。但此后,并未达成过任何最终协议。

## 二、为运河疏浚、河川保护筹资

1910 年,江苏省北部的淮河流域洪水泛滥,损失惨重,中国政府在美国红十字会的建议下,试图通过现代科学方法改善航道、特别是淮河及与之相连的大运河的航道,以便洪水更加有效地下泄,防止新的洪灾。在美国红十字会的努力下,中国(北洋政府)全国水利局和美国国际公司于 1916 年早些时候协商一项用于疏浚大运河(包含于淮河治理之中)的 300 万美元借款事宜。借款草约于 1916 年 5 月 13 日签署。同时(1916 年 4 月 19 日),山东省政府也草拟了疏浚运河北段河道的计划,并与美国红十字会签署了另外一个 300 万美元的借款草约。但此后,再没有听到过这些草约的消息。

1917 年 11 月 20 日,在一系列复杂、艰难的谈判后,双方又签署了另一份借款合约[③],发行价值 600 万美元的债券,用于疏浚山东省、及直隶省境内的天津南运河。1918 年 9 月,一批美国工程师抵达中国,立即勘测、收集必要的工程数据。现在这些工程师返回美国已有三年多时间,还没有迹象表明该工程即将动工。中国未能得到美国人的援助,据说很大程度上是由于中国混乱、不稳定的政治状况,这不利于外国投资。

## 三、为中国其他产业融资

### 1. 关于含油区的勘探和经营的提议

直隶、陕西两省境内蕴含石油,早就为人所知。为了开采这一宝贵资源,中国政府和纽约美孚石油公司于 1914 年就这些油田的勘探和经营事宜签订合同。按照这份协议,美孚石油公司将派专家对这些油田进行详细调查,如果确实具有值得开采价值,双方将组建中美合资公司以开展运营。

---

① 译注:1927 年后,纽约国民城市银行的中文名称改为花旗银行。

② 译注:1909 年 10 月 2 日,美国银行团代表司戴德在沈阳与东三省总督锡良、奉天巡抚程德全签订《锦瑷铁路借款草合同》,规定在东北修筑由锦州经齐齐哈尔到瑷珲的铁路,资金由美国银行团提供,工程由英国宝林公司承包,中、美、英三方联合组成铁路公司,详细办法另行商订。同时东北地方路政局与宝林公司还订立了《锦瑷铁路包工草合同》,具体规定有关工程的事宜。

③ 译注:即《导淮借款合同》。

1914 年在多个地方进行了调查,但美孚石油公司的专家认为含量不大。连续钻开 7 口井,尽管看到了油苗,但没有发现油泉。1916 年春天停止了这种乏味(而无收获)的钻探;相应地,以前的协议也中止了。

### 2. 无线电台建站合同

1921 年 1 月 8 日,中国交通部和美国费得拉尔电报公司签署了一份协议①,由中国政府与美国公司成立一家合资公司,专事无线通讯电台的建设和经营业务。协议规定,在上海建立一座甚高功率无线电台,在北平、汉口、广州和哈尔滨建立较低功率的电台。事有凑巧,中国政府早些年与日本三井公司、英国马克尼无线电电话电报公司签订了在中国建立无线电台的合同,并给予两家公司一定时间的独占权②。因此,日英公司通过各自国家政府向中国政府提交抗议书,反对中国政府与美国公司签订协议,宣称如果允许美国公司参与建设,那他们在之前签订的合同中规定的权利将受到侵犯。然而,美国政府以此类声明与在华美国公民的条约权利及"门户开放"原则相抵触而拒绝承认其合法性,并全力支持费得拉尔无线电公司。争执持续了两年多,目前(1924)仍悬而未决。美国无线电公司目前隐身于该项活动,所以,这表明美国人对发展由美国国务院支持的跨太平洋通讯方面有强烈的兴趣。

## 四、美国参与对中国的国际融资

各个国家独自向中国企业融资时,中国和外国金融家频繁遭遇到由于各国争取"利益范围"和国家"控制"而引起的国际金融竞争所造成的困难。由于相互猜忌,不同列强的资本利益经常发生冲突,许多融资计划最终并未成功。与中国有商业关系的那些大国认识到这样的问题,于 20 世纪早些年达成共同谅解,即,应当用国际合作而非竞争手段作为向中国融资的指导原则。诺克斯先生的满洲铁路国际化计划是美国人乐意参与类似合作的最早证明。

### 1. 湖广铁路③借款

中国政府和英-德银行财团于 1908 年签署了第一份国际铁路协议,用于建设天津—浦口铁路。1908—1909 年冬春之际,英、德、法三国财团及各自政府展开谈判,以期就作为未来向中国提供借贷前提的"控制"程度达成谅解。这些谈判的目标指向是广州—汉口铁路、汉口—四川铁路——这两段铁路合称为湖广铁路——的建设借款。

---

① 译注:该协议为无线电台借款合同,涉及金额 462 万美元。

② 译注:1918 年,中国海军部与日方三井洋行订立无线电正副合同,规定日本在华无线电事业有 30 年独占权;中国陆军部与马可尼公司订立借款购买军用电台 200 部。

③ 译注:清朝末年预备修建的"湖北、湖南省境内粤汉铁路"和"湖北省境内川汉铁路"两线都在湖广总督辖区的范围内,故有此称。湖广铁路借款的计划线路是:前者由武昌起经岳阳、长沙而至宜章,与广东商办粤汉铁路衔接;后者以汉口为起点,经应城、钟祥、当阳至宜昌,由此抵达四川夔州(现称奉节)。

此时,美国政府进行了干涉,理由是美国金融家已于 1904 年获得中国政府保证,如果川汉铁路湖北段的建设需要国外借款,中国应当首先考虑美国和英国。鉴于美国并没有正式放弃其参与权,美国政府就要求美国银行财团分享该项目。时任国务卿的诺克斯先生对此表示支持,指出:"对维护商业机会均等原则非常有兴趣之列强之间,若缺乏真正的同情①,可能会对国际贸易产生威胁",并称"美国政府把全面、坦诚的合作视之为保持中国门户开放和领土完整的最好打算,……建立一个强势的美国、英国、法国和德国财团会推动这一目标的实现。"

由于塔夫脱总统的个人干预,英法德"三国银行团"于 1910 年 5 月邀请美国财团加入其中。美国接受了这一邀请,四国银行团于 1910 年 11 月签订了一份协议。湖广铁路借款的最终协议于 1911 年 5 月 20 日由中国与四国银行团的代表签订。该协议向中国提供借款 600 万英镑,以清朝政府发行湖广铁路五厘利息递还金镑借款债券的方式获得②。然而,由于随后中国(辛亥)革命期间的政治、财政状况,湖广铁路的建设没有什么大的进展。

### 2. 货币改革借款

声名狼藉、混乱不堪的中国银元货币体系使得中外商人进行贸易往来时异常艰难。为了使交易易于进行,一些美国商人表达了他们通过扩大对华金融援助推动早期币制改革的愿望。1910 年,中国政府和美国四大银行组成的财团草签一份协议,向美国发行、出售高达 5000 万美元的中国政府递还金镑借款公债。但稍后不久,应美国财团的提议和美国政府的恳请,中国政府同意英国、法国和德国银行参与其中,从而形成所谓的"四国银行团"。1911 年 4 月 15 日,中国政府和该国际财团签订正式协议,授权四国银行团发行五厘利息递还金镑借款债券,募集资金 1 000 万英镑。然而,协议所约定的借贷募集尚未得到妥善安排,中国就于 1911 年 8 月③爆发了反对满清王朝的(辛亥)革命。既然环境发生了变化,"四国银行团"就延缓了该项目的进一步行动,以便按新成立的共和政府的要求承担善后大借款。

### 3. 善后大借款

1911 年(辛亥)革命爆发后,中华民国政府面临着严重的银根短缺问题,被迫向国外求援。1912 年 2 月 27 日,时任中国民国政府总理的唐绍仪先生与四国银行团商议

---

① 译注:原文此处(第 308 页第 2 段倒数第 4 行)之"proper sympathy"之译法参考自《道德情操论》(亚当·斯密著,商务印书馆,1997.11)。

② 译注:1911 年 5 月 20 日,清廷代表盛宣怀与英国汇丰银行、法国汇理银行、德国德华银行、美国花旗银行四国银行团签订的《粤汉川铁路借款合同》举借英金 600 万镑,利息五厘,九五折扣(扣除债券发行成本按借款额 95%付给清政府),借款期 40 年(1911—1951 年),自第 11 年起分 30 年(60 期)归还本金;债券在英、法、德、美四国各发行 150 万镑债券,面额两种:20 镑(发行 140.3 万镑),100 镑(发行 459.7 万镑)。

③ 译注:农历辛亥年八月十九日(公元 1911 年 10 月 10 日),武昌起义爆发。

善后借款事宜。四国银行团为使中国借款尽可能国际化,马上决定邀请俄罗斯、日本银行家进行合作①,以加强银行团的地位。但是,六国向中国政府提出的作为借贷基础的条件,遭到了中国的强烈反对。这些条件主要有:

(1) 中国应建立一套审计制度,并聘用外国人在其中任职,这些洋员不是仅仅充当顾问,而应有行政权力,借以保证为特定目的而举借的"外债得以有效使用"。

(2) 作为借贷担保的中国盐税,应当由外国监管。

(3) 中国应当任命六国银行团的金融代表协助其管理善后工作,为期五年。

也就是这个时候,强烈反对类似外国监管这样难以容忍的条款的浪潮几乎遍及全中国,以至于美国银行不再参与借款,因此六国财团缩减为五国财团。美国退出善后借款的另一个原因是威尔逊新政府对塔夫脱政权所谓"金元外交"持同样的反对态度。威尔逊总统在一份弥漫着对中国人民同情、敬佩精神的宣言中,非常清晰地宣布,美国政府不再参与中华民国的六国借贷,也不再与此有任何官方关联。威尔逊总统认为,美国政府以官方甚至半官方形式参与这样的借贷都是不正当的。他对六国借贷的一些条件进行了批评,主要观点在如下文字之中:

"应当要求银行家明白,美国银行如若参与这个借款,则势将使美国政府承担责任,在万一发生某些不愉快的情况时,要对刚刚觉悟到对其权力和人民具有义务的伟大的东方国家的财政事务、甚至政治事务强行干预。……美国政府如若支持如此担保和管理之借款,其所应承担之责任即十分明显,同美国所依据的原则是不相容的"。

因此,美国财团于 1913 年 3 月正式退出通货贷款和善后大借款②;尽管如此,美国政府对中国币制改革项目继续保持着兴趣。

### 4. 日本提议与美国合作

1914 年世界大战爆发后,日本接管了原属德国的势力范围,逼迫中国政府签订了臭名昭著的《二十一条》,从而使其在华影响力快速增长。日本试图控制中国工业发展的未来并垄断全部利益,但是这需要大量的资金,而日本可以供应的头寸并不宽裕。所以,日本人提出了一个与美国资本合作的计划。1915 年秋,日本金融领袖涩泽荣一男爵③作为(巴拿马博览会的)国家发言人被委派到美国。这位日本金融家在美期间反复告诫美国人,称他们应当与日本合作以"和平开发"中国。他还向美国资本家指

---

① 六国银行集团于 1912 年 6 月 18 日就借款事宜签订协议。

② 善后大借款条约最终于 1913 年 4 月 26 日由中国政府和五国财团在北京签订。

③ 译注:Shibusawa Eiichi(1840—1931),原名渋沢栄一,日本现代企业制度——株式会社的创始人,后人称赞他的头衔有"日本企业之父"、"日本企业创办之王"、"日本资本主义之父"、"日本产业经济的最高指导者"、"儒家资本主义的代表"等。1915 年出席巴拿马万国博览会期间以及会后,涩泽向美国人屡屡陈述自己的日美合作开发中国论。他曾向美国纽约商会极力鼓吹此事,当一些美国财界人士访日之时,又不失时机地推销自己的观点。

出，美国资本和日本管理进行合作非常重要、绝对有必要。他不客气地对美国人说，如果美国不采纳这个计划，"日、美两国在中国市场的活动可能导致恶性竞争、互不信任、反目成仇，从而使双方损失惨重"。言下之意是，如果美国今天想在中国投资，就不能绕开日本；如果美国试图单独进入中国，麻烦将随之而来。

但是，美国人、中国人对这份建议不感兴趣，认为日本之意不在合作，而更像是独占。日本认识到中国的发展绝对需要外国资本，但是如果允许美欧洲资金自由流入中国，将削弱日本对中国正在增长的控制力。然而，日本无力提供足量资金，也充分认识到自身地位还不足以能坚定而快速地对西方企业家关上大门。所以，它既向美国提出建议，也向欧洲提出建议，如果美欧希望参与到中国伟大的经济转型，则其投资应当置于日本人的控制之下。

**5. 美国主导的新国际银行团**

美国虽然拒绝了日本的建议，但也认识到放手日本给中国借款同样是不明智的。美国退出后，"六国银行团"变成为五国集团；随着世界大战的爆发和沙皇政府的衰落，德国、俄罗斯资本也淡出银行团，只剩下英国、法国和日本。

但是，大战期间及战后初期，英法两国财政拮据，无力向中国扩大借贷。事实上，日本作为出借方垄断了特权，它向中国国内各敌对派系提供许多贷款，不仅伤害了中国利益，也不利于其他投资者。

因此，当中国需要外部资金协助以向同盟国宣战时，美国即想改变日本的垄断局面。1918 年 7 月，华盛顿政府批准了一项美国银行团与英、法、日银行家的对华借款案，以使中国能够"装备自己、在战争中起到特殊的协助作用"。美国银行家们与美国国务院之间签署了一份协议，国务院向这些金融家们保证，如果借款条款被美国、中国所接受，美国政府愿意以尽可能的方式予以协助，进行迅速而强有力的交涉，采取任何可能的步骤确保本国公民在其他国家以诚实原则签订的公平合同的执行，以鼓励和促进美国公民和外国公民双方互利的自由交往。这是美国政府对私营投资企业进行援助的最明确保证，当时被认为其中蕴含着对在战后严重的贸易竞争情况下，扩大美国对华贸易和投资、确保在中国市场占有一席之地的深切期望。

为了永久地保持门户开放政策，确保"大国"在中国有平等的机会，美国政府进一步提议组建所谓的新国际银行团。1913 年，威尔逊总统曾以前文提及的理由宣布退出六国银行团；仅仅五年之后，威尔逊政府自己采取了一个与曾被威尔逊总统义正词严批判过的计划本质上相同的方案。

美国于 1919 年提出新国际银行团计划，英国、法国和日本受到美国邀请，并最终同意该方案。这一新机构的目的是承揽中国未来的所有工业贷款及政治贷款业务，如同美国银行家宣称的，是要"帮助中国建设庞大的公共设施，如铁路、运河等，从而帮助中国稳定经济和金融，使中国成为美国公民在商业、工业等领域创设私营企业的安全之地"。美国银行家要求的条件之一是"旧银行团成员现有的借款优先权,应当让与中国或新银行团,所有经由他们进入中国的贷款都应当作为新四国集团的业务。"

关于政府支持方面,各国赞成美国关于保证"各国政府对本国银行团支持,而不是支持四国银行团整体"的提议。

这份对华国际援助的方案看上去似乎美丽动人,但新银行团自 1920 年成立之后实际上就一直处于濒死状态,它还没有为中国任何大型企业成功达成过一项谈判。协议最初约定的银行团五年存续期很快将要届满,在此或许可以做一些确定性的预言:这一方案如同其他大多数国际建议一样,将会以完全失败而告终。

这一国际方案的失利,可能很大程度上是由于中国反对筹资方式、拒绝向国际财团提出任何借贷要求;这一点不能理解为,中国拒绝与任何国际财团交往,是不领情于意欲帮助中国的美国。中国人民真诚地相信,由美国领导建立的新金融机器可能最终会效力于中国的利益,但也不必惊讶于中国人民会有这样的担心:这样一种由世界上四个政治大国幕后操控的筹资方法可能(给中国)带来严重后果。通过最新分析得知,他们反对更多的,并不是国际财团,而是这样的事实:中国的公共财政置于外国监管之下,用国家的土地税作为贷款担保,从而使中国主权受到侵犯。只要外国投资的政治意味大于商业意味,中国人就不愿意接受贷款,从情感上讲宁愿国家贫穷也不愿忍受外国的金融枷锁。

另外,中国人民强烈反对国际财团的垄断角色。国际财团在不受外交压力或政治胁迫的自由、公平、友好竞争的基础上,制订了金援中国的游戏新规则,用新国际银行团中英国银行团代表查尔斯·爱迪爵士的话说,它不失为"一个可能的好手段"。不同的银行集团将他们掌握的所谓"既得权利"汇入四国银行团,但却损害了对其他国家的开放门户;这样一个公共池能够确保四国的银行集团具有同等的特权,但却是以中国的自由议价权为代价的。此外,通过中国政府排他性的"公共性质贷款",国际财团有效地用财政领域的利益取代了区域范围的利益。这个专制的银行联合体、信贷垄断者如此无懈可击、势不可挡,以至于给作为借款者的中国没有留下多少自由。

所以,实际的商业状况是,世界新生的全部有前途的、有益的商业都在中国陷于停顿,未能大规模发展。许多中国企业焦急地等待国外投资以开展业务,但没有中国人愿意看到自己的政府接受上述国际财团的借款。New York Globe(日报)就这一情况做了如下简短而中肯的评论:

"美、英、日、法四国政府将新国际银行团置于中国门前,把守着中国的大门。由于中国人不喜欢它们开门的方式,因此大门无法开启。我们看到的是,财团像是守门人,而门快速地关上了。"

在考虑这一困难状况时,该文还提出了如下的问题:

"如果美国摆脱这一理论上非常美丽、但实际上显然无用的金融国际化主义,携带自己的金融资源进入中国,在不对其他国家构成不公的情况下,本着有力而迅速发展美中利益的愿望,施展美国自己的金融手段,是不是对美国有利、对中国有利、同时也对世界有利呢?"

## 五、美国在华投资私营企业的近期前景:边缘法案在远东的机会

到现在为止,向中国提供大规模借贷的尝试几乎都具有公营性质;合作通常在中美两国政府之间或中国政府与美国银行集团之间进行,很少有美国个体工商业者在中国资助或兴建私营工业企业。(民间投资)停滞不前的原因有两个。

首先,美国国民在外国建立工业企业有悖于美国的传统政策。中国根据 1880 年条约给予英国在中国领土建造制造企业的特权,但美国却拒绝通过引用最惠国条款主张同样的权利。阿瑟总统①在其 1883 年 12 月 4 日的年度咨文中阐述了理由:

"让我们的公民全面分享各种受条约保护的利益是政府的职责所在,但我怀疑,强迫中国允许这种我们仅有非直接的条约权利的(资本)相互渗透仅仅是权宜之计。美国资本向中国转移并在那里雇佣中国劳动力,会对目前由我们国内工业供应的市场形成竞争。"

其次,美国缺乏促进、鼓励在外国进行私营投资的机制。直到最近的 1914 年,美国仍不准许其国内银行在国外建立分支机构,经营外国银行业务的美国银行不能在美国国内发售债券,也不能在联邦储备银行贴现其商业票据。结果,美国个人投资者发现将其资金投向外国私营企业非常困难,特别是当后者规模较小,在世界股票市场上不为人所知时尤为如此。

但最近,在中国投资私营企业的必要性凸现出来。英国人、日本人,以及战前的德国人都在中国的私营工业大量投资,美国被迫步其后尘,否则它将在中国贸易的国际化竞争中失利。另外,中国的私人投资与美国本土工业大多是非竞争性的。

为了促进私人在国外投资、借款,美国国会于 1919 年通过了一部被称为《边缘法案》的特别法案②,为组建经营国外银行业务和金融运营业务的银行做准备。该法案意在创建一套银行体系作为美国联邦银行机制的组成部分,该银行体系具有与参与外贸的金融家同等重要的职能,还将被授权经营外国证券。边缘法案银行需在中国履行

---

① 译注:ChesterAlan Arthur(1829—1886 年),1881—1885 年任美国总统。
② 译注:1919 年,美国国会通过边缘法案(The Edge Act),以增强美国银行业在国际贸易中的竞争地位。该法案规定,银行可在联邦当局特许下成立所谓边缘法案银行公司(Edge Act Corporations),专营国际银行业务。边缘法案银行公司可以吸收外国居民的存款,亦可吸收本国居民用于对外贸易方面的存款。这些存款同样需要缴纳存款准备金并加入联邦存款保险系统。边缘法案银行公司可以从事国际贸易方面的信贷业务、外汇交易的业务以及其他诸多的国际银行业务。不过,这类银行不能从事国内商业信贷业务及吸收与国际业务无关的一般性居民存款。边缘法案银行公司的一大特权是其开设分支机构不受地域限制。因此,许多大银行便在边缘法案的规定下组建子公司。

类似于投资银行或债券市场的功能,因此这样的美国银行在中国显然有必要存在,其发展机会也是明显的。

"可以有两种投资方法,银行可以购买中国债券,并直接销售给美国投资者,或者将中国证券作为抵押品进行担保,发行自己的公司债券。"

"法案允许外国个人或公司可以持有边缘法案银行不高于49%的股份,使得美国联邦政府设立的这种银行有可能成为一个国际合作企业。法案允许中国的银行、制造商、出口商、进口商在为中国的工、商企业提供资金时,享有与美国人同样的利益,并成为股东,也允许中国资本分享本国工业发展的成果。"

这种私营借贷方法是最受中国人欢迎的一种方式。然而,这种投资机制的成功程度还有待于证明。当然,中国资本家一直渴望与美国人合作,以开发本国资源。但是,只要治外法权在中国继续存在,有思想的、谨慎的中国人就不愿意外国伙伴自由参与其业务。按照中国大多数工业企业的规章,即使向非中国公民出售一份公司股权也是被严格禁止的,因为中国人经常担心,这一点并非毫无缘由,任何无关紧要的借口都可能招致外国政府和官员的干涉,从而使中国的民法、商法丧失效力,自身利益受到损害。

本章内容结束之际,作者还准备就美国在华公共投资、私营投资计划发表一些个人观点。关于公共借款,程序应当清楚、简洁,不带有任何政治意味或垄断特性。如果中国铁路建设的贷款事项由外国政府而非外国资本家和企业主导,则使中国人担心此举可能会对中国的主权和独立构成严重损害而心生顾虑、犹豫不决,最终不能达成协议。正是由于这一原因,即使中国人认识到外国援助的巨大必要性,但公众舆论通常还是强烈反对任何外国贷款。中国发展的延宕确实不利于中国人,但中国公共财政被国际控制的危害将更是其十倍之巨,所以他们(对外国借款)毫不犹豫地选择了抵触。

对于私营投资,中国人秉持更为欢迎的态度;然而,只要在华美国人所受的法律管控体系与其不同,并置于美国政府代表的司法权之下,在中国人看来他们简直可以说是"不法之徒"。中国人因担心外国干涉经营,决不会接受美国人自由进入他们的企业。那么,美国企业在19世纪后期是怎样接受欧洲资本的贷款呢?南美洲又是如何由美国、欧洲资本开发的呢?中国人不愿意受到的待遇与美国人曾经得到的及美国人施与他人的方式有所不同。如果针对中国的所有歧视都被消除,美国在私人投资方面像对待南美洲一样对待中国,无疑立刻将会有大量的美国资本被吸纳到中国,反过来,中国也能给予美国资本相当可观的收益。此外,由于中国人民的购买能力日益增长,中国对美国机器和设备需求在增加,而美国对此类物资有大量的出口需求;如果美国资本成功地应用于促进工业化中国,美国对华贸易的扩张将会无可限量。

# 第十七章　美国银行业在中国

美国人积极开展对华贸易已有 150 年的历史,但美国银行业在中国的发展却仍然比较落后。即使现在,在中国的美国金融机构数量"与美国在中国国内贸易及对外贸易中所占的份额相比是如此之小,也与美国在世界银行业中所占的份额完全不成比例"。"近年来,美资银行的重要性日益提高,但是,除了汇兑银行外,中国的美资银行仍然只处理美国在华商业业务中的很小一部分。美国的商业利益尚未得到金融机构提供的服务,而其他国家的竞争对手已经具备了这一点。总体上说,中国的美资银行都是外汇兑换机构;它们也做一般银行业务,但主要还是从事外汇业务,少有例外。"

正是由于缺乏足够的金融机制、融资机制,美国在与其他国家争夺中国市场时已经多次失利。已在中国建立起来的这样的美资银行不能进行融资业务;另外,如上所述,中国的工业发展主要由欧洲资本控制,因此美国在俄日战争前后就已落败于中国市场①。这一点在中国的铁路建设的合同方面特别明显。"中国在 1898 年 12 月 1 日之前获准建造的铁路总里程约为 7 500 英里,而美国人已经拿到或能够拿到合同的只有 300 英里;他们数次因为根本无力按可以接受的条款提供资金而失利。"

美国人认识到金融机构在远东地区进行贸易、投资活动中的重要性,已在 1890 年代多次试图在中国组建美资银行,但均告失败。最早的一次发生于外国投资者在中国非常活跃的 1887 年;费城财团(Philadelphia Syndicate)规划的中美银行项目是一个大型投资计划,但不幸的是,该计划未能实现。

直到 20 世纪初,才在中国建立起第一家美资银行。1901 年,纽约花旗银行(International Banking Corporation of New York)在上海设立分行,开启美资银行在华之先河。几乎与此同时,纽约保证信托公司(Guaranty Trust Company of New York)也在上海开设办事处,但运营不久即由花旗银行接收。

同年,花旗银行在香港设立分行,一年后又在广州设立分行。但此后的五年间,却没有进一步的发展。1907 年,花旗银行在北平、汉口设立两家分行。当人们了解到,就是花旗银行的这五家分行在为中国内地、香港地区和美国之间不断成长的进出口贸

---

① 前见第三章之"第三时期"。

易(这一时期中美年均贸易额超过 1 亿美元)提供贷款时,立刻就能明白中国的美国金融机构是如何地不够充足。

由于欧洲战争爆发后中美贸易快速扩张,加之利用在华的其他外资银行进行贸易融资的难度增大,美国人自 1917 年起大力扩展其在华金融机构。当年,美丰银行(American Oriental Banking Corporation)在上海成立。1918 年,纽约美国运通银行(American Express Company of New York)通过在上海、香港开设两个分行的方式进入远东的银行领域。次年,友华银行(Asia Banking Corporation)设立七家分行,中美合办的中华懋业银行(Chinese-American Bank of Commerce)经中国政府特许组建。此后两年,更多的美资银行成立;现在,包括中美合办银行在内,中国国内已经有 28 家美资银行。这些银行属于六个组织,而五年前只有其中的一个组织,即花旗银行进入中国市场。这些银行的情况列于表 17-1[①]。

### 表 17-1 美资银行在华情况

| 序号 | 银行名称 | 总部所在地 | 组织形式 | 业务范围 | 在华分支机构(设立时间) |
|---|---|---|---|---|---|
| 1 | 花旗银行 | 纽约 | 大陆法系 | 专营国际汇兑 | 上海(1901)、香港(1901)、广州(1902)、汉口(1907)、北京(1907)、天津(1918)、哈尔滨(1919)、大连(1923)<br>(花旗银行在香港亦称万国宝通银行) |
| 2 | 美国运通银行 | 纽约 | 大陆法系 | 银行、航运和旅行 | 上海、香港(1918)<br>北平、天津(1921) |

① 以下为各家银行概况,均引自于同一来源——1921 年 5 月 3 日纽约出版的《远东》(双周刊)第 5 页之"远东美资银行一览表",所涉数字均为 1921 年度数据:在中国,花旗银行(资本和盈余 1 000 万美元,未分配的利润 320 万美元)和友华银行(资本 400 万美元,盈余和未分配利润 148.9362 万美元)的外汇业务最强;这两家公司,尤其是花旗银行,主要从事外汇业务竞争的国际化。这两家银行的业务不限于外汇,但这是其主要的业务。

美国运通在中国是一个银行组织,它是作为一家全球性航运、旅行、银行组织的美国运通的一个分支。很大程度上是由于美国运通经由其旅行部门发展商业的原因,该公司做了大量的金融业务,特别是汇总业务。

美丰银行公司是美国企业在中国附设的一系列银行,与其他在华美资银行集团不同,其业务更多定位于中国的国内银行结售汇和内部汇兑(实收股本 40.995 万美元,未分配利润 3.7454 万美元)。位于长江航道起点之重庆的四川美丰银行因其是所有在华美资银行中最为靠近内陆的一个,被认为地处前沿位置。

大通银行上海分行(资本 400 万美元,盈余和未分配利润 75.4 万美元)在银业务方面特别突出。航运的大量白银通过这家银行买卖。

中华懋业银行(额定资本 1 000 万美元,实收 500 万美元)相当年轻。它进入这个领域的目的是支持和促进在华的美资企业、中美合办企业的发展,帮助中国在美国发售股票。按照管理者的公告,该行试图通过分行将业务扩展到全世界。

（续表）

| 序号 | 银行名称 | 总部所在地 | 组织形式 | 业务范围 | 在华分支机构（设立时间） |
|---|---|---|---|---|---|
| 3 | 友华银行 | 纽约 | 纽约法律 | 专营国际汇兑 | 上海、香港、汉口、天津、北平、广州（1919）（友华银行于 1923 年 12 月被花旗银行吸收合并） |
| 4 | 美丰银行（美东银公司） | 上海 | 大陆法系 | 一般银行业务 | 上海（总行，1917）重庆、福州（1922） |
| 5 | 大通银行 | 纽约 | 纽约法律 | 专营国际银行 | 上海（1921） |
| 6 | 中华懋业银行 | 北平 | 中国政府1919年4月12日特许 | 商业银行业务 | 北平（总行，1919）上海、汉口、天津、济南（1920）哈尔滨、石家庄（1921） |

　　可以预料,如果中国的政治、商业环境改善到足以保证美资银行健康发展的程度,中国的美资银行有望在近期得到进一步的发展。已经进入中国的美资金融机构已经为开设新的分支机构、拓宽业务领域勾画了蓝图,其他金融组织则正在思考如何进入中国市场。

　　美国国会通过《边缘法案》后,一个新的时代已经向在华的美国银行业露出了曙光。依照该法案组建的所谓边缘法案银行,意在建立一个属于美国联邦银行机制的银行体系。这类银行的设计目的是促进美国对外贸易的发展,这与联邦储备银行在促进美国国内贸易发展中的作用一样。边缘法案银行的汇票可由联邦储备银行承兑,其股票可望由美国的国内银行认购。

　　远东的进口商、制造商通常缺乏资金,长期信贷的展期是他们从国外购买物资的一个先决条件。那些能为他们提供长期信贷的国家可以获得他们的贸易合同,反之则不能。日本、英国和战前的德国银行在这一点上胜过美资银行,因为它们为中国进口商提供的信用贷款有时可长达一年,而美资银行提供的信贷不超过 3 个月。中国的美资银行将其大部分资金用于汇兑业务,同时由于法律或其局限于短期贷款的业务特点,还没有涉及中国工业企业经常需求的那种长期信贷融资。边缘法案的颁布恰恰满足了这一需要。按照该法案组建的边缘银行不能吸收存款,但享有发行一年期承兑汇票的特许权利,因此,在为出口、进口贸易融资方面有了更加宽广的余地。

# 概述和结论

## 一、中美贸易的历史背景：要点复述

在美国独立建国之前，古老的中华帝国和新世界之间非直接的商业关系已经存在了很长时间。殖民地时代，美国经常通过英国进口中国的茶叶。但是，直到值得纪念的1784年，美国的"中国皇后号"轮船抵达广州，中美贸易才正式开始。这两个濒临太平洋的大国之间的直接贸易已经历时一个半世纪，其成长实际上是与美国国民生活的发展同步进行的。

中美两国贸易发展的各个阶段有不同的趋势和特点，整个中美贸易史据此可以分为四个时期。

中美贸易的第一个时期是1784—1844年的非正式或非条约交往阶段。这一时期，有魄力的美国水手在中国外贸中非常活跃，没有哪个国家的水手能比得上他们的重要性。摆脱英国殖民体系禁锢的许多美国船只不停往返于亚洲、美洲两岸，从中国购买茶叶和丝绸，起先他们用花旗参和硬币支付，后来用毛皮、檀香木和美国商人从南太平洋获得的其他物品交换。

1820年之后，早期的毛皮贸易寿终正寝，檀香木贸易也达到其顶峰，但一个新情况使中美贸易得以继续稳定增长。由于美国这个新生的西方共和国人口、财富逐步增长，结果对那些东方奢侈品的需求也不断提高，因此中国的茶叶和丝绸畅销于此；另一方面，由于在东方贩卖英国鸦片，美国能够很好地用伦敦汇票完成中国商品的货款支付。美国国内对华出口也逐渐增加，其中，棉制品成为新的重要出口商品。本时期末，美国政府趁中英发生鸦片战争之机，效仿英国，派顾圣出使中国，并与中国签订了第一份中美通商条约。

中美贸易的第二个时期是一个短暂增长之后的持续下滑。这一时期始于美、中两国依据望厦条约开始正式交往的1845年，终于中日爆发甲午战争的1895年。这一时期以美国内战为界分为两个阶段。在第一时段，这些活跃商人的贸易活动达到高潮。拥有全世界最大规模的船舶装备的美国，在19世纪五六十年代期间的中国外贸中拿走了非常大的份额。但是，由于这两个国家的政治混乱及内战，中美贸易的这一异常扩张匆匆中断。美国内战期间,其对外贸易中起关键作用的强大航运业陷入衰退,美国商人逐渐从中国市场中消失,因为他们被美国国内发展的迷人前景吸引而踏上了返家之途。与此同时,银价对金价的贬值,使中国向美国增加采购的计划受阻,在茶叶、丝绸方面,日本新的激烈竞争极大地阻止了美国进一步从中国进口。除了这些原因外,中美两国人民由于中国移民问题产生了普遍的反感情绪。这一反感情绪可能是中美贸易在 1890 年代缓慢发展的最主要原因。1860—1894 之间为期三十四年的第二个时段里,美国从中国的进口总额仅从 1 350 万美元增长至 1 700 万美元,而其对华出口则从 900 万下降到 600 万美元。

中美贸易的第三个时期是一个激烈的国际竞争阶段,始于 1895 年,终于 1913 年。日本于 1895 年轻松击败中国,这对远东的商业及政治态势造成了严重影响。最为强大的西方殖民帝国,如英国、德国、俄罗斯和法国等,很快抓住这一良机,扩大其在华商业、政治影响。日本自身也跻身于工业国家行列,使出浑身解数将其产品进入中国市场。中国领土内的强占和租借变得非常普遍,势力范围接二连三地建立起来。这一时期,各国争夺中国贸易市场的竞争非常激烈,尽管美国重新关注对华贸易的发展,但中美贸易的发展仍然远远落后于美中两国各自对外贸易的增长速度。当然,这近二十年中,尽管中美贸易的增长并不稳定,但绝对数量仍然增长近 2 倍。1895 年,美国从中国(含香港)进口价值 2 300 万美元,向后者出口 1 200 万美元。1905 年,美国对华进出口额分别为 3 000 万美元和 6 400 万美元,1913 年则分别是 4 400 万美元和 3 800 万美元。

这一时期,美国对华出口贸易增长非常缓慢可以用两个原因来解释。首先,美国政府官员处理中国移民问题时的狭隘方式极大地伤害了中国人民的民族自尊心,迫使后者于 1905 年发起一场针对美国人的激烈抵制运动作为报复。其次,欧洲战争之前,中国的工业发展主要控制于欧洲资本之手;欧洲通过对华贷款"垄断"中国贸易,使美国对华出口贸易发展受阻。至于这一时期美国从中国的进口,则相当稳定,令人关注。然而,首先,由于日本人在美国丝绸市场强大的竞争力,以及东印度在美国茶叶市场的竞争,其次,由于中国丰富的矿产、农业资源迟迟未能开发,导致中国缺乏适合美国市场所需的商品,这一时期美国对华进口基本上也在削弱。

中美贸易的第四个时期是一个快速扩张期,自然以欧洲战争爆发作为起始时间点。战争期间,欧洲国家无力参与对华贸易,原属欧洲的贸易大部分转向了美国。美国对中国物资的需求大增,中国对美国物资的需求也在提高。所以,可以看到,一方面,美国从中国进口的锑、蛋白、胺苯、染料、靛青、羊毛、棉花、蛋产品、植物油和油籽、兽皮、毛皮、草编和生丝大幅增长;另一方面,美国向中国出口的钢铁机器及其他产品、各种车辆、化工产品和染料、电力机械和电工器材、橡胶制品、皮革制品、纸制品、矿物油、烟草、木材和木制品等也在相应增加。在前一时期,这些物资尚未参与中美贸易或数量非常小,但在这一时期,每一种类的年贸易额都达到数百万美元。

整个这一时期,金、银比价的混乱,航海运力的不足以及由此引发的运费上涨,对中美贸易造成了严重破坏。但在后来,两国对对方物资的需要,克服了这些不利因素,十年间中美贸易的绝对数量及相对份额都增长了3～5倍。1914年,美国对华进口总额3 800万美元,1923年达到1.76亿美元;这两年美国对华出口分别为2 700万美元和1.7亿美元。即使扣除了战争及战后的价格膨胀因素,实际贸易额仍然增长了2～3倍。

## 二、中美贸易的总体趋势

在前一部分,笔者简单概述了中美贸易开端、扩张、衰减和恢复等各个阶段,以及隐藏于贸易涨落现象之后的一些重要的经济因素。然而,如果把中美贸易的各个阶段联结起来,对其发展趋势加以研究,就会发现中美贸易总体上是逐年持续繁荣、扩张的。如图18-1[①]所示,呈现了一个明确的向上移动趋势,其上升并不仅仅是算术级的,而是几何级数的[②]。

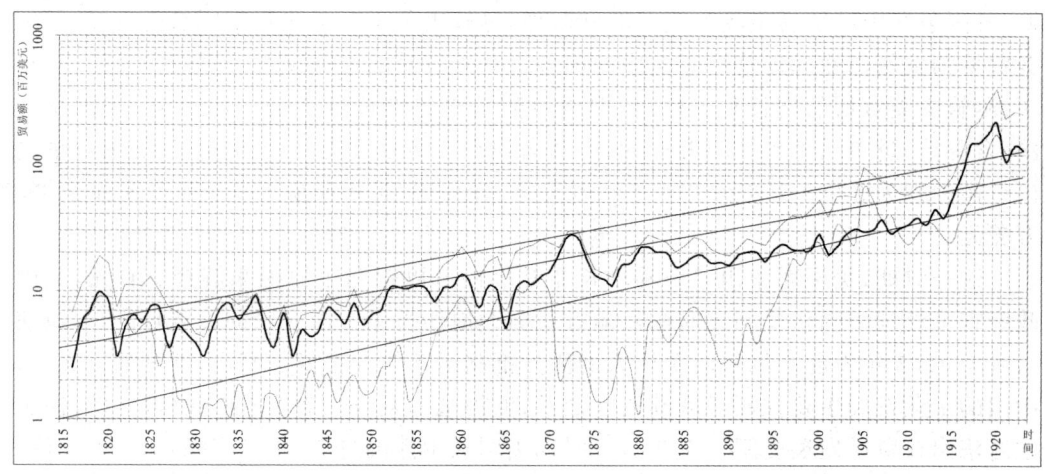

**图 18 - 1**

19世纪,美国对华进口始终大于对华出口,只有少数几个年份例外。但总的趋势是,贸易差额与贸易总额之比越来越小,因为美国对华出口的增速总体上比对华进口增长更快。

---

① 译注:原文此处(第334页)示意图不清晰,译者按照文中两国之间贸易数据及图注重新绘制,以供参考。

② 图18-1中的三条曲线自下向上分别代表美国对华出口额、进口额及进出口贸易总值,它们按对数坐标绘出,因此分别代表年度之间的百分比变化。这些曲线的拟合线按最小二乘法绘制,但并不意味着可以以数学精度测定它们的趋势,因为不可能对长达一个世纪的时段做单一的定量趋势。它们只是试图简单地表明中美贸易的逐步增长,粗略而又清晰地显示中美贸易开端、扩张、衰退和复兴等四个阶段(的总体发展变化情况)。

### 三、中美贸易的前景

我们可以根据过去,对未来作出一些判断。首先,美国对华贸易一定会随着时间的推移而增长,尽管在任何时候都会有一些不期而遇的问题干扰其顺利进行,正如过去已经发生过的那样。但是,无论中美贸易以与19世纪相同的速度扩张,或是以世界大战引发的近期剧变而加速发展,现有的观察期都过于短促,致使无法正确预测未来。然而,有一件事似乎是相当确定的,那就是,从现在起中美贸易将在一个比以前更高的水平上波动,维持、并且可能是永久性地停留在这一较高水平上。如同图18-1中所见,现在的进口、出口都远高于其各自趋势线显示的正常数值。如果没有世界大战,之前的趋势可能仍代表正常的贸易交往状况。但是,现在,世界贸易关系按照新的国际需求平衡进行了重新调整,美国、中国的价格水平都有上升,而且可能是永久性的;因此,美国对华贸易额回到战前水平似乎是极不可能的。

### 四、美国进口的中国商品

在分析了中美贸易的一般趋势后,再对曾经或现在构成进出口贸易主体的重要商品做一下盘点。

在从老牌的中华帝国进口到美洲新大陆的各种物资中,茶叶是传统的重要物资之一。美国独立使得对华直接贸易成为可能,大批茶叶就年复一年地从东方运来,通常占到美国对华进口总额的一半,有时甚至达到80%。但是,19世纪中期,中国茶叶的垄断地位被打破,先是遭遇日本人的竞争,其后是英国东印度和荷兰东印度。与日本、东印度种植主、加工商相比效率低下的中国种植、加工茶叶方式,早些年发生过的中国茶叶掺假的丑恶行为,中国政府之前对茶叶征收的高额出口关税,部分中国茶商缺乏销售技巧,这些因素共同发挥作用,这一时间或那一时间,使中美茶叶贸易下滑。但是,按照茶叶行家的说法,中国茶依然是世界上最好的茶叶,不过中国茶叶的质量不统一,不大适合美国大规模市场化方法。然而,认识到美国茶叶市场的重要性之后,中国茶商、中国政府多次尝试改善其茶叶种植方法,以期挽回在对美贸易中丢失的市场份额。

按照时间点,在茶叶之后进入美国市场的是丝绸,现在它已成为美国从中国进口的商品中最重要的单种物资。19世纪早期,美国进口的所有丝绸都是绢丝,其中大部分直接来自中国。但是,从那时起,绢丝贸易在绝对数量、相对份额两方面都开始下降。*丝绸贸易下滑的原因有三个*:首先,中国丝制品只是为国内市场加工,不适合西方人的口味和喜好;其次,美国自身成为世界最大的丝绸制造国家之一已有半个世纪,能够自给自足;第三,美国的保护性关税,在丝织品方面,几乎是禁止进口的。

与绢丝贸易早期衰退相对照的是,美国生丝进口贸易成长稳定。1865年前,美国很少购买生丝,但此后,由于美国绢织工业的快速发展,对外国生丝的进口自然也飞速提高。在过去的半个世界里,美国对华生丝贸易绝对数量的增长相当稳定,但是,未能与美国丝绸进口保持同步。其相对弱势的原因有两个。一方面是由于中国的养蚕方法没有改进,未能守住这一新市场;另一方面是由于日本生丝工业的激烈竞争和快速成长。然而,最近,丝绸在美国风靡一时,美国感到有必要扩大其原材料来源,于是再次将目光投向中国,向其寻求更加充分的生丝供应。中国的蚕农也开始认识到美国市场的重要性,做出各种努力,以提高产量,适应美国的大规模加工。过去几年间,这方面已经取得了非常明显的成功,中国丝绸无疑正在重新获得其丢失的地位。

接下来的重要进口商品是兽皮和毛皮,它们在超过三十年的时间里在美国对华贸易中占据显著的地位。19世纪末,中国的牛皮和水牛皮、山羊、绵羊、牛犊和马的皮都以年均数百万磅的数量进口到美国。欧洲战争前,贸易额增加了1倍还多,战后则翻了4倍。毛皮(包括已处理的、未处理的)及毛皮制品的进口贸易额从战前的年均30万美元上升到战后的数百万美元。众所周知,中国拥有广大的牧场地区,能很好地向美国供应这类产品;所以,此类商品的贸易一定会随着中国的畜牧业发展而扩大。

与生皮和毛皮贸易相关的有羊毛(包括制成地毯的及未加工的)及猪鬃和其他动物毛发的进口贸易。由于生皮、毛皮、毛发是同一种动物的产品,用于同样的目的,所以,这些领域的贸易也将在未来得到扩大。

还有几种手工制作的中国产品,如发网、花边和刺绣,最近在中美两国贸易中扮演着重要角色。

除了刚刚列举的这些中国商品,还有几种产品,它们也都在战争及战后数年间的美国对华进口贸易中占据大的份额。

其中,首先得提到植物油。植物油在美国工业中的广泛应用,以及中美植物油贸易的大幅增长,是过去十年间最有兴趣的商品现象之一。但是,美国本身就是世界上一些植物油(特别是棉籽油)的最大生产者,正常情况下能够自给自足。因此,自1921年起中国植物油贸易大幅下滑,尽管我们期望其在中美贸易中保持一定地位,但似乎不大可能达到几年前的进口量和进口额。

还有一些商品在大战及战后初期的中美贸易中,扮演着与植物油有点相似的作用,它们是锑、蛋白、靛青、原棉、烟草、蛋产品和草编。1915—1920年间,美国商业发展繁荣,从中国大量进口这些物资,贸易额都以数百万美元计。1921—1922年间,这些物资的进口量、进口额双双严重下滑。由于这些物资是美国工业用于进一步生产的原材料,可以预期,只要美国商业环境恢复正常,对这些产品的进口必将或多或少地恢复。

一般来讲,美国从中国进口的商品,与其从其他东方国家、南美洲进口的一样,主要是原材料和半成品。其中,最重要、最有希望的是生丝、兽皮、毛皮、草编、羊毛、猪鬃、植物油等,其贸易的未来趋势必然是稳步增长。这是因为,一方面,美国工业的活力增强将导致对这些物资的需求量提高,另一方面,由于中国的农业及简单工业正在稳定发展,它将有能力为美国提供大量的这类物资。与之相反,制成品或消费品的进口在中美贸易中的地位呈现下降趋势,此类物资包括茶叶、丝织品等。虽然如此,中国还是能够向美国出口一些比较重要的手工制品,拥有丰富的廉价劳动力的中国,能够在花边、刺绣、发网等手工制作的商品方面超越世界上任何国家。

## 五、美国对华出口商品

再来关注一下美国对华出口的主要商品。可以看到,仅仅在二十年前,最重要的出口物资还是棉布。19 世纪 50 年代,棉制品贸易曾在一些年份中占到美国国内对华出口总额的 90%,年贸易额超过 200 万美元。但是,1860 年之后,这一贸易受到了抑制,部分原因是运输大量棉花所必需的美国商船队在美国内战期间遭受残损,部分原因是因为英国产品的激烈竞争。但是,尽管有这些不利因素,棉布依然在 19 世纪后期几十年,以及 20 世纪初的美国对华出口清单上占据重要的地位。棉布贸易在美国对华出口总额中所占的份额接近 60%,每年的贸易额达数百万美元。但是,自1906 年开始,由于日本、中国先后加入竞争,美国棉布出口遭受重挫,目前在美国对华出口总额中的份额不足 5%。美国不大可能在未来重新获取其在棉布出口领域失去的地位。

但是,绝对不能因此理解为,美国将永远放弃中国棉制品市场。还有许多其他类型的、在中国有大量消费的细棉产品,目前尚不能被日本或中国企业制造。现在,这类棉布的贸易几乎全由英国垄断,但没有理由说美国棉品商不能生产这类精细物资,并通过竞争将它们卖给中国。

棉制品之后就是煤油和烟草。近年来,中国从美国进口的烟草增长明显,其在中国烟草进口贸易中的份额,20 世纪初尚不足 1/5,最近几年已超过 4/5。中国多年来都是美国香烟的最大买主,现在购买美国烟丝的数量也相当大。尽管这几年美国对华烟草贸易有这样大的发展,但不能期望它未来仍会以最近几年那样的惊人速度进一步扩张。中国的烟草行业像棉花工业一样,进步很快,中国如果没有对外国烟草的巨大需求,其本国产品完全能够满足烟草市场。近期,中国努力提高烟草质量、增加产量,并取得了明显的成功;最近几年,中国烟草已经开始批量出口。中国对美国烟叶的购买量无疑在不远的将来仍将持续增长,中美烟草贸易的未来发展将最终取决于中国国内烟叶生产的发展进程。

就矿物油而言,古老的中华帝国是美国产品的优良市场,尽管俄罗斯、荷属东印度的竞争使得美国的贸易起伏很大。1890 年前,中国进口的每一滴油都来自美国,中美矿物油贸易从 19 世纪 60 年代的几乎空白扩张到 1891—1900 期间年均 3 000 万加仑的水平,战前增长到近 1 亿加仑,最近几年达到每年 1.6 亿加仑。19 世纪末、20 世纪初,美孚石油公司在东方先后遭遇俄罗斯、荷兰的阻击,但美国挟其巨大力量,战而胜之,目前仍掌控着东方石油贸易。

据地质专家报道,中国本身就有丰富的油藏。但是,这些资源还未能成功开发。与以前一样,中国的照明现在仍然依赖于外国石油;只要这一需求持续,美国与中国之间的石油贸易一定会增长。

此外,当中国的工业化开始成型时,会需要越来越多的燃料油和汽油、润滑油、石脑油等,以及以往最重要的进口品种——照明油。美国拥有非常丰富的石油资源和发展成熟的炼制工业,在分享中国这一扩张的石油市场时,自然处于非常有利的位置。

木材是 19 世纪 90 年代从美国进口到中国的另一种重要产品。中国自己没有大森林,因此其用于建设和制造的木材需求增长,必须通过增加进口来满足。事实上,中国的木材进口自 1900 年起实际上已经增长 10 倍,现在每年超过 1 000 万美元,其中超过一半来自美国。但是,木材还没有进入中国主要进口商品的行列,其贸易将会有一个辉煌的未来。美国太平洋沿岸各州拥有丰富的木材资源,因此必然能在增长的中国木材贸易中获益。

近来,美国皮革制品、橡胶制品和纸制品等各类产品的对华出口贸易额,每年都能达到数百万美元。

接下来关注的几类其他产品,它们的出口贸易在十年前还微不足道,但现在已经在两国贸易中扮演了非常重要的角色,实际上在美国对华出口中占据了较大份额。它们是钢铁机器和其他制品、电器用具和电工器材、汽车和其他车辆、化工产品和药品、及美国高度发达的其他精细产品。这些产品出口贸易快速扩张的原因可以从以下两方面很好理解:中国近年来发展工业,因此对这些工业设备和设施的需求增加很大;自世界大战起,美国各种工业品的产量增加,而东方市场的竞争有所减缓,因此美国能够更好地向中国提供这些产品。

综上所述,可以对美国对华出口贸易的一般趋势有所认识。首先,在过去数十年间,简单工业品构成了美国对华出口的最大部分,但现在其重要性在下降,这在绝对数量、相对份额两方面都有体现,而且这一趋势将在未来延续。需要再次声明的是,近来,中国的工业化进步显著,每年都新建大批的面粉厂、棉纺厂、钢铁厂、皮革厂等。在1906 年之前的一段时间里,美国面粉在中国销路很好,但是由于中国现在能够加工面粉,面粉出口贸易量已经到了可以忽略不计的地步。对美国棉布、制成烟草来说也是这样,像皮革、纸制品等其他简单工业品将来也会是这种情形。

到目前为止,中国的大部分钢铁产品,如铁路、钢铁构件、钢筋、钢丝、薄钢板、钢铁板材、钢管等,都来自于美国、欧洲进口,贸易量快速增长。但是,这是中国这个新生共和国又一类具有潜力、最终将不再依赖进口的产品。中国拥有许多具有丰富储藏的煤矿、铁矿,如果能够获得足够资金的资助,将能在本国制造出简单钢铁产品。

由于中国拥有原材料资源,美国或其他任何外国在简单制造的产品出口方面与中国建立永久的贸易是不太可能的,此处将不再列举实例来论证。中国人民能够成功扩大、并正在扩大各种原材料其具有丰富的天然储藏的供应,所以,将不利于外国尤其是美国在这些产品领域与中国发展贸易。美国制造商暂时可以向中国出售面粉、棉织品、香烟、金属、皮革制品和纸制品,但不久,他们将会面对需求下降的局面,这在前面提到的很多商品中都发生过。

现在再分析一下美国向中国出口的产品中,哪些能够拥有更好、更持久的效益。

过去,美国工厂的产品立足于美国市场,针对工资收入相对较高的人群设计,因此质量较高,其价格在个人收入水平较低、支付能力相对较弱的东方市场没有竞争力。因此,那些国内对廉价物资有更大需求的国家,在向东方市场供应方面比美国处于更为有利的地位。美国在 1921—1923 中国进口贸易中的份额下降清晰地诠释了这一状况。这一状况将一直持续到中国经济条件改善,中国大众的收入水平和购买能力得到提高为止。当中国人的购买能力提高到能够为更昂贵的美国商品提供销售市场时,美国的对华贸易无疑将会一直扩大到一个更大的规模。

再注意这样一个事实:中国工业化的最新发展给美国贸易带来的利益将多于其他任何国家。如前面所指出的,中国在非常适宜的自然条件及低工资水平下,其简单产品逐年增加。在洋务运动的影响下,这些产品被生产出来以满足价格低廉的需求,所以对那些在中国市场贱卖美国产品的国家产生了比销售高档美国产品的国家更严重的竞争。接下来的十年或二十年,中国将发展成一个制造大国,同时,其对各种质量优于本国制造的产品的需求将显著增加。涉及高机械技能、标准化流程的物资将越来越多地由美国向中国供应,美国在这些领域目前没有、将来也不会有任何强劲的对手。

美国向中国出口工业机器、机车和高等级铁道车辆、汽车和电气铁路设备、各种农业机械和其他一系列产品,如打字机、收银机、缝纫机等的良好时机已经存在,并肯定将继续增长。这些产品充分体现了美国人的创造力,是保证美国未来在中国市场获得永续成功的最容易的、实际上也是最主要的产品线。

## 六、美中贸易的特点

美国、中国贸易关系发展过程中,有几个明显的特点值得关注。

中美贸易的第一个特点是"动机单纯",自从中美开始商业交往伊始就具备这一特点。双方彼此没有不可告人的目的,也不猜疑对方,这一点和中国与其他国家的交往相反。中美两国开展贸易只为赚取合法的利润,而没有其他因素考虑。中国人完全是具有敏锐商业意识的平和的商人。他们感知、领会与美国人建立密切商业关系的意愿,并毫不犹豫地反复重申。

中美贸易"利益一致"是中美贸易关系的第二个明显特点。中国、美国的利益特别一致、平行发展,没有根本性的冲突或矛盾来损害两国商业交往的发展。事实上,没有哪两个国家能像美国、中国那样,在认识太平洋贸易的无限可能性、努力推动互惠互利的东亚经济发展方面彼此充分合作。

中美贸易的第三个特点是双方的"相互依赖"。每个人都认识到,美国对外贸易的进一步发展很大程度上要依赖其在中国市场的扩张,因为,中国作为具有丰富资源和大量人口的中国,是世界上最有潜力的市场。反过来,如果中国期望开发其丰富的资源,使其人民富裕,也必须向美国寻求其创办资本、大部分机器和设备,美国还可为其提供一个几乎与中国一样无限的互惠市场,以消化处置其原材料及半原料——发展中的中国工业不久将能生产出来,而美国制造商将对此有大量需求。

## 七、美国进一步扩张贸易对中国市场的依赖

过去五十年里,中国的进口增加非常明显。然而,尽管中国进口总额增长惊人,但人均进口贸易额目前仍不足 2 美元,其中美国商品的份额接近 40 美分。这一数字似乎并不引人注目,但是,世界大战刚刚结束之际,美国每年向中国销售的商品价值就超过 1.5 亿美元。现在,日本人均每年购买价值 18 美元的美国货,如果中国对美进口在不远的将来达到这样的水平,意味着中国的市场容量将比现在大 10 倍。

美国广泛运用水利电力,并将省力机器和科学管理应用于各种物资制造过程,极大地增加、并还在继续增加美国矿山、农场和工厂的产量。为了解决这些产品的出路,美国将其注意力更多地投向欧洲和南美洲,而不是远东地区。世界大战前,欧洲市场通常能消化美国对外出口的 60% 份额。世界大战期间及结束之际,欧洲对美国产品来说几乎是一个无限的市场。但是,现在这一状况已经变得、或正在变得与过去完全不同。现在,欧洲对美国负债累累,按照国际贸易的一般理论,欧洲向美国销售多于从那里购买是迟早的事;只有这样,欧洲、美国间的国际支付——无论其资本账目还是利息账户,都才能平衡。所以,未来美国不可能期望欧洲像战前或战争期间那样,仍然是一个好的市场,美国必须在欧洲之外为其增长的产量寻找出路。

美国出口商普遍的看法是,南美洲是美国商品在欧洲之外的最大市场,其次是东亚。世界大战之前,与美国土地相连的南美大陆自然最受美国制造业者和商人的青睐,而东亚地区当时的国际政治环境对美国出口贸易扩张极为不利。然而,随着中国"门户开放"政策在华盛顿会议上的重申,环境现在越来越对外国商业和投资有利。为了显示中国将在不远的未来成为对美国商品来说与南美洲一样、甚或更好的市场,下文将对中国、南美洲进行一个综合观察。

1914 年,南美洲总进口 6.71 亿美元,人均 11.92 美元,总出口 8.82 亿美元,人均

16.7 美元;1923 年①进出口分别增长为 12.74 亿美元和 14.1 亿美元,人均分别为
20.45 美元、24.24 美元。将这些数字与东方的主要市场(也就是中国)做比较,1914 年
中国的进出口额分别是 3.81 亿美元和 2.39 亿美元,人均分别是 95 美分、60 美分。
1922 年,中国进出口额分别是 7.84 亿美元和 5.45 亿美元,人均分别是 1.96 美元和
1.37 美元。在过去十年间,南美洲人均进口额从 11.92 美元上升到 20.45 美元,增长
71％,人均出口额从 15.70 美元上升到 24.24 美元,增长 54％。而中国的人均进口额
从 95 美分上升到 1.96 美元,增长了 106％,人均出口额从 60 美分上升到 1.37 美元,
增长了 128％。比较而言,中国进口贸易的增长速度是南美洲的 1.5 倍,而其出口增
长速度接近南美洲的 2.5 倍。

同样,可以对这两个地区与美国之间的贸易状况进行更加清晰的比较。1914
年②,美国对南美洲国家出口额为 1.16 亿美元,在南美国家进口总额中的份额为
17.3％,美国从南美洲进口 2.22 亿美元,占南美国家出口总额的 25.2％。1922—
1923 财年,这四个数字分别是 2.59 亿美元、20.4％、4.7 亿美元和 33.4％。1914 年,
美国对华出口总额 2 469.9 万美元,占中国进口总额的 6.4％,美国从中国进口
2 694.3 万美元,占中国出口总额的 11.3％。1922 年,这些数字分别变为 1.40 亿美
元、18％、8 099.1 万美元和 16.5％。这再次证明,美国对华贸易的增长速度要快于美
国与南美洲之间的贸易增长速度。

从这一贸易统计的具体分析,可以得出结论:如果美国期望国外贸易有进一步的
扩张,就不能在欧洲或南美洲投入太多;它必须关注东方,特别是中国——“世界上最
具潜力的市场”。

美国不仅需求一个适应其现有生产、制造能力的市场,还需要一个能随其产量增
加而扩大的市场,中国就是这样一个能够满足其工业发展的市场。

## 八、中国进一步发展和贸易对美国的依赖

再考虑一下中国依赖其对美贸易的发展作为其工业发展、商业成功的指数的问
题,这同样需要一些解释。

首先,在某种意义上,中国的对美贸易在过去的一个世纪里非常必要,中国在很大
程度上依赖对美贸易顺差去支付与其他国家之间的贸易逆差。中国的贸易逆差,起先
只是由于大量进口昂贵的鸦片;后来则很大程度上是由于自身工业缺乏发展所致。结
果,中国近一百年间的外贸状况总是不利于自己。这种单边差额对中国资源构成了长
期的严重消耗,外债大量聚积,人民日益贫困。

---

① 以 6 月 30 日为最后一日的财年。

② 以 6 月 30 日为最后一日的财年。

但是,幸运的是,自 1784 年中国与美国建立直接贸易后,除少数几个年份外,中国在对美贸易中一直获取着贸易顺差的好处。按照美国的官方贸易统计,19 世纪的后四十年间,中国对美贸易的顺差年均为 1 500 万美元。20 世纪前十四年里,中国对美贸易顺差下降到 720 万美元,但在接下来的九年(1914—1922)时,再次上升到 4 200 万美元。中美贸易的顺差极大地帮助中国平衡了其他逆差,因此缓解了中国长期遭受的外国剥削的严重程度。然而,中国的顺差对美国来说,也并不是一件非常不好的事情。美国从中国进口的商品大多是美国无数工厂所需要的原材料或半成品,当它们以成品形态出售时,其价值将成倍或 3 倍增加。

其次,具有无限购买力的美国庞大市场,正是中国在不远的将来为其快速发展的工业生产出的大量矿产品、农产品寻找一部分出路时所指望的。中国的蒙古、西藏、新疆和一些内陆省份拥有数百万英亩的牧场,能够养活几千万只的绵羊、山羊、奶牛、马、猪等。这些动物可以生产出大量的兽皮、毛皮、猪鬃和羊毛,而它们正是美国制造皮革、衣物和其他商品所大量需要的。中国东北地区的农用土地超过 1 200 万英亩,如果耕种得法,将可以生产出超过 1 亿蒲式耳①的大豆和其他豆子,而豆油最近在美国工业中扮演了一个非常重要的角色。中国还可以提供无数的廉价劳动力,可以生产出大量的生丝(采用最新改进的养蚕法),以及高等级茶叶、手工花边、发网等,而这些都是美国所急于购买的。一句话,中国也必须反过来将美国看作其由于本国工、农业快速发展而生产出的越来越多的各种产品的市场。

简单地说,中国需要的产品,即各种机器、钢铁制品、电器用具、化工产品、药品等,恰好是美国能很好供应的;这些产品通常是大规模生产、需要有高度发达的工业,在这些方面世界上没有哪个国家能超过美国。另一方面,美国需要的物资,即生丝、兽皮、毛皮、植物油、羊毛和其他手工产品如地毯、发网、花边等,也恰好是中国的优势产品;它们大多数是简单工业产品。在中国大量廉价劳动力供应的支持下,这些简单工业品快速兴起时,无论美国的关注点移到哪个领域,中国都将能够满足美国对这些材料、产品不断成长的需求。

所以,中国工业的稳步推进对美国来说是一件好事。中国要达到美国占据优势的复杂工业活动那样的高度尚需时日;但是,在此期间,中国的简单工业活动越发展,其对美国商品的需求也越大。同时,中国这些简单形式工业的发展将为美国提供一个更加充足的、而且可能更便宜的原料供应地。这反映了中美两国之间商业利益的一致性,也反映了它们之间的相互依赖。

除了已经提到的这些因素,中美两国之间还有着自两国开始贸易以来就存在的强烈的、诚挚的友谊。这个友谊当然是双方最宝贵的财产,是无法用金钱买来的,而且是

---

① 译注:容积单位,1 蒲式耳=36.368735 升,1 蒲式耳大豆、小麦约合 27.216 千克。

双方贸易成功的强有力的保证。

## 九、中美贸易关系的改善

那么，如何改善这两个太平洋大国之间的贸易关系，以使双方互惠互利？在笔者看来，对中美贸易发展最有效的促进办法是美国在中国投资应秉持真正的美国公正精神。老话"商随财走"在现在的东方特别符合事实，因为在中国的现代工业意识达到一个相当先进的阶段之前，中国贸易矿藏的大门最多只是被轻叩几下而已。但是，什么是中国工业进步最迫切的需求呢？对中国发展来说，没有什么比无私的外国资本和专家援助更加不可或缺。本书第十六章，对中国为什么是美国资本现在最好的投资地，以及中国为什么主要向美国寻求资金的原因进行了深入的分析。对此，美国资本家有一定的认知，并在铁路建筑、运河疏浚、矿产资源勘察、创办新实业方面与中国有过合作。但是，不幸的是，双方的这些努力大多数——如果不是全部所有的话——到目前为止还没有结出硕果，这在前文回顾美国对华投资史的过程中有所论述。完全失利的原因可能有很多，但其中两个相当明显，首先是美国资本家政策失误，将其投资与国内、国际政治相混淆，其次是中国目前的势态不稳定。

就第一个原因而言，作者相信，除非对中国有兴趣的美国或其他国家的商人，愿意在不(将纠纷、矛盾)诉诸外交事务大臣的纯商业基础上进行投资，否则，中国民众难免会以援助可能引起严重后果的疑虑来看待外国的投资。这样的事情过去确实已经发生过，并对中国的政治主权和经济独立造成损害。

至于第二个原因，中国势态目前的不稳定状态是中国正在经历的这样一个过渡期内不可避免的问题，没有理由对此绝望。中国内部困难的快速解决已经有了令人鼓舞的迹象。人们只要回想一下，美国自与英国的独立战争取胜之际起，国内事态连续几十年间令人沮丧的状态，以及法兰西共和国建立之后的困难期，更不用说世界其他地区民主国家的兴起过程，就可以认识到，崭露头角的中华民国在跨越艰难的民主道路上已经取得了显著的进步。

中国社会、经济的基本面是健康的。她现在不幸的困境不完全是由于自身的错误，外国要为此承担一定责任。中国问题今天已经成为世界和平问题的组成部分，对外国尤其美国来说，在其解决方案中扩大与中国富于同情心的合作是明智的。中国工业的正常发展将不只要求外国资本的合作，外国科技专家诚恳合作参与中国工业化进程也是必不可少的。美国过去在教育领域给予中国慷慨的援助，中国在其发展过程中向美国寻求金融合作的同时，还必须寻求美国专家的技术援助。以现代工业化为引导，对中国金融进行改组、对本国丰富的资源进行有效调度，中国当前过渡期内普遍存在的混乱状况——它很大程度上是一个经济问题，即人民为了能在拥挤的人群和未开发的资源引起的恶劣环境下生存而斗争——同样会在某一个太阳初升的早晨消失。

美国政府和美国金融界对中国近年来渴望外国资本的迫切需求并非毫无察觉。为此,设计了各种促进中美合作的措施。所以,在美国主导下组建了国际银行财团,美国国会通过了中国贸易法案和边缘法案,一些中美合资商业、工业企业也通过了立项。不幸的是,国际银行财团未能完成其预期的目标,目前显得有心无力,而中国贸易法案、边缘法案由于前面章节所讨论的原因,不容易变成中美合作的工具。

再次申明,中国目前急切需要的是外国人与中国人进行公平的金融、技术合作,以促进这个亚洲大国工业发展,合作双方都能获利。尽管外国金融界更愿意以他们自己的特殊条件——然而这常常对中国造成伤害——在中国投资,但还有一个急迫的问题需要解决,以使该合作不会损害中国主权和独立、而能被中国人民所接受,也能为外国投资者的资金安全提供必要的保障。

目前,美国政府和人民有一个非常大的机遇。基于两国人民之间传统的友好关系,以合适的方法解决中美两国间的金融、工业和商业合作问题,对于中国国内问题及世界未来和平,的确是有价值的。

附录　英　文　原　稿

解 説 文 献 ・ 辞 典

# THE TRADE
# OF THE UNITED STATES
# WITH CHINA

BY

SHÜ-LUN PAN, M.B.A., Ph.D.

CHINA TRADE BUREAU, INC.,
New York.

Dedicated

TO THE MEMORY OF THE LATE

KAN CHIU-NAM

1872—1923

A pioneer of modern industry in China and a firm believer
in Chinese-American commerce and cooperation,
whose moral encouragement and financial
support made this study possible
in the United States
of America

and to

KAN SAT-HING

upon whose shoulders the mantle of his illustrious
father has descended.

## FOREWORD

It is with great pleasure that I accede to the request of Dr. Pan to write a few words of introduction to his very excellent book. In China we have one of the oldest and one of the greatest civilizations—a civilization which from the point of view of literature, of art, and of æsthetics is in many respects superior to ours, a civilization which in some ways has taught the world what really is the worth of life. Yet China is now faced by the stupendous problem of rejuvenation, of making herself young again. Because she has failed in one particular, namely in her effort to utilize the powers of nature and in the command of science over nature, China is still in the position in which Europe was a few centuries ago.

The transformation of industry and the application of science to economic conditions in the western world have brought about a revolution not alone in the foundations of life, but all the way up to the very top of the pinnacle. Now we see the growing pains of a youthful China. If China is wise, it will perhaps discover a short cut to the solution which is awaiting the East and West alike. After all we are not much more than a century ahead of China, and perhaps in a great part of the world not more than half a century ahead. In Germany the industrial revolution took place only fifty years ago; in Japan it began only a generation ago; in parts of the United States the transition is going on even at present; so perhaps when history is being written one thousand years from now we shall find that China was

vii

viii                FOREWORD

only a little behind the rest of the world and that perhaps it will by then have even surpassed the rest of the world.

This development will naturally mean great changes in the future foreign trade of China. Dr. Pan has given us a painstaking and accurate account of its rise and development. Perhaps his most helpful contribution consists in the detailed story of each of the most important exports of China to the United States and of the use and distribution of the more significant articles of import from the United States. Singularly interesting are the account of American commercial policy and the story of the comparative failure of the recent banking consortium. Stimulating above all is the last chapter in which the interdependence of these two great empires, China and America, is analyzed and illumined and in which a sober and scientific appeal is made to the government and the people of the United States to do their share in making mutual cooperation possible.

Edwin R. A. Seligman,
*McVickar Professor of Political*
*Economy, Columbia University.*

# INTRODUCTION

It is with great pleasure that I accept the invitation of Nanyang Brothers, Inc., to write a few introductory words to the scholarly treatise on "The Trade of the United States with China," written by Mr. Shü-lun Pan, one of the scholarship students of the Nanyang Brothers Tobacco Company of China.

It has seemed to me for many years that more intimate intercourse of all kinds should be developed between China, the great republic of the East, and the United States, the great republic of the West. No other factor can tend more strongly in this direction than the preparation of treatises on subjects of common interest to the two countries, prepared by qualified scientific representatives of one of these countries, working in hearty cooperation with one of the great universities of the other country and with the assistance of their scholars and business men. It is of especial importance at the present time that questions of business and trade be given particular prominence.

My own first personal connection with China came indirectly through the initiative of the Chinese Government in requesting the Government of the United States to give whatever assistance might be practicable toward the establishment of a gold monetary standard in China. The request originated on the one side from the growing desire of Chinese business men and of the Chinese Government for closer trade relations with the Western world. On the part of the United States it arose from the recognition of the fact that if a gold standard could be established, it would both greatly stimulate the trade and promote the friendly relations in politics between the two countries.

Although it was not found practicable for the Chinese Government at that time (1903 and 1904) to carry out its

purpose, nevertheless the influence of the effort has been strongly marked in various ways since that date. In many other aspects of international life, there have grown up steadily increasing relationships between the two countries. During later years the growth of commerce between the two countries has been characterized by the strengthening of the natural community of interests between them, as shown by the interchange of goods, and particularly perhaps by the rapidly increasing investments of the United States in China. This is true not only in the trading field but also in banking and manufacturing.

These relationships, while marked by the reasonable business desire for mutual profit, have been accompanied by other motives. In the minds of the American people and of the American Government there has existed the feeling that our trade with the peoples of the Far East should be carried on with no purpose on our part of territorial aggrandizement or of any other means of exerting a selfish political interest. We have believed that a policy of friendship and fair treatment based on our enlightened self-interest and not upon one-sided selfish advantage would be in the long run the wisest policy.

The strengthening of this intercourse has doubtless served on the whole to promote greater respect on the side of both peoples for the admirable qualities of the other; and, in spite of occasional unfortunate misunderstandings, the friendliest of feelings have been promoted.

In my own earlier relations with the Chinese, I thought that I noticed certain likenesses of character and personal qualities between the two peoples that would normally further their mutual respect and friendship. The same characteristics I have often heard emphasized by other people of both nations better qualified by experience and long observation than I. The habit of individual initiative on which Americans often pride themselves is equally characteristic in many respects of the Chinese. One notices this

even among the servants, most of whom desire to be given a task and allowed to think out their own way of performing it. So also the native American ideal of fair dealing, even though characterized by shrewdness, has long been known as a prime characteristic of the Chinese business man. Moreover, as a foreigner's knowledge of the Chinese and of Chinese culture increases, the greater becomes his respect for the artistic qualities of the Chinese, for their love of learning, and for their practical common-sense as well as the lofty idealism of their moral characteristics. One feels that while we may have much to give in the way of technical knowledge, or modern methods of trade on a large scale, and of the use of capital, we have opportunities for receiving knowledge and benefits no less important than those we give.

Since the revolution in China in 1911, and perhaps especially dating from the Great War of 1914-1918, there have been various new conditions affecting deeply the relations between the two countries. China's governmental difficulties have left her political situation chaotic, so much so that at the present time our intercourse with China has been very greatly hampered and we are finding ourselves compelled to look for measures of relief.

Again, the increasing extent of American vested interests in China, the loans that we have made to the central government, to the provincial governments and to private business, our investments in banks and industries, and perhaps even more the extent to which our missionary enterprises have expanded, have all led us to feel that internal disorder would so jeopardize our interests that it would be likely to interfere seriously with our good relations. Chinese "politics," in the derogatory sense in which that word is sometimes used both in China and the United States, on account of delinquencies of individual politicians, have seriously interfered with good trade and good feeling. In consequence, the injury done to our material interests has

led our people to adopt an attitude that appears at times less idealistic and even perhaps less sympathetic toward China and her needs, because these practical problems are pressing both our business men and our Government for a solution. We are continually feeling the urgency of the need for relief. Many people who perhaps are not so far-sighted or so patient as they should be, become inclined at times to listen to the suggestions, more or less direct, of our adopting what we have been in the habit of characterizing as "the grab policy" of other nations. My own feeling, however, is that the more thoughtful, the more far-sighted American have implicit faith that if the Chinese people are not too seriously interfered with, but are given the opportunity of working out their own problems without too much pressure from the outside, the sound judgment and honorable instincts of the Chinese people, as well as their practical vision, will lead them themselves gradually to purge the country of its grossest evil doers and thus to promote in the not too distant future better and more harmonious relations.

Momentous changes in China's international outlook seem to be indicated by the economic revolution in China's own relations to the world. In this treatise is demonstrated the fact that the trade currents are distinctly changing. Relatively speaking, the exports of Chinese luxuries are lessening, while the exports of the great staples of world industry such as raw cotton, silk, vegetable oils, wool, not to mention antimony, hides and skins, etc., are increasing. China is, of course, a great reservoir of raw material, not only in these fields but also in coal and iron ore. Apparently, also, the country is rather rapidly becoming organized along industrial lines. The growth of the cotton textile industry is a noteworthy indication of what we may anticipate in the near future.

The studies of so many able Chinese in foreign countries along engineering, industrial and banking lines, as well as in the fields of philosophy and government, are beginning to show a strong influence. There is every reason to believe that as this influence rapidly strengthens, as it certainly will in the near future, we shall find in China a stronger determination on the part of her citizens to shape her destiny themselves. In previous decades they have been largely subjected to international dictation. If they can make themselves more nearly independent financially, they will achieve a greater degree of political independence. It is, beyond any question, the desire and hope, and in many instances even the determination, of many of China's ablest thinkers to build up for their country a great economic position in the world, believing that in this way they can most safely and most certainly become the arbiters of their own destiny along political and social lines. If this work is carried on wisely and temperately—not with any idea of hostility toward foreigners but with the idea of independent, fair cooperation for mutual interests—Americans will be ready to welcome that attitude. This work of mutual cooperation and mutual respect can in no way be better furthered than by such studies on both sides, carried out in the spirit of accurate, scholarly, and friendly cooperation shown in the preparation of this book.

Jeremiah W. Jenks,
*Research Professor of Government and Public Administration; Director of the Division of Oriental Commerce and Politics, New York University.*

## AUTHOR'S PREFACE

In this treatise an attempt is made to discuss rather fully the economic forces underlying the origination, expansion, decline, and revival of the trade of the United States with China during the last hundred and fifty years. This discussion is based largely upon historical facts and statistical data now available from both Chinese and American sources and deals only slightly with current business practices. The author has endeavored to interpret the future trend of Chinese-American trade in the light of the past as well as to express his opinions regarding constructive measures that may help to increase the trade of the two great republics bordering on the Pacific to their mutual benefit.

In the preparation of this treatise, the author desires to make grateful acknowledgment of his indebtedness to Professors Edwin R. A. Seligman, Wesley C. Mitchell, Theodore H. Brown, of Columbia University; Professor Charles Hodges, Assistant Director of the Division of Oriental Commerce and Politics, New York University; Mr. Ernest K. Moy, Director of China Trade Bureau; and Mr. Alfred S. Lee, Secretary of Nanyang Brothers, Inc., New York; all of whom read the whole or a part of the manuscript, made many invaluable criticisms and suggested many important corrections.

The author is also under heavy obligations to Mr. Tsze E. Pun, Vice-President and General Manager of Nanyang Brothers, Inc., for making all the necessary arrangements in connection with the publication of this book.

Shū-lun Pan.

Columbia University,
City of New York,
May, 1924.

xiv

## TABLE OF CONTENTS

# TABLES

# TABLES

# PART I

## Historical Sketch

# CHAPTER I

## THE PERIOD OF INFORMAL OR NON-TREATY INTERCOURSE, 1784-1844

### 1. General Statement

Trade between the United States and China has run its course for nearly one and a half centuries. Its whole history naturally divides itself into four periods. Disregarding the indirect commercial relations before American independence we shall begin our historical account with the establishment of the United States. The first period of this history is one of informal or non-treaty intercourse, extending from 1784, when the first American ship reached Canton, to 1844, when the first American commercial commissioner, Caleb Cushing, concluded with the Chinese authorities the first Sino-American commercial treaty. During this period the enterprising American seamen played a very active part in China's foreign trade, second in importance to that of no other country. This period may in turn be sub-divided chronologically as follows: (1) the beginning of the trade, 1784-1790, (2) trade expansion and the British-American War, 1791-1814, (3) quietness in the trade from the close of the war of 1812 to the outbreak of the opium trouble and the treaties of Nanking and Whanghia, 1815-1844.

The second period of our trade history naturally begins with the year 1845 when formal intercourse between the United States and China under the provisions of the Treaty of Whanghia began, and ends with the Sino-Japanese War in 1895. The reason for choosing this latter year as a line of demarcation between this and the later periods is that before this time American business men encountered less competition from Japan and from European Powers in the Oriental market, although the development of Sino-American trade had been comparatively slow. This period natur-

3

ally falls into two subperiods with the American Civil War as their dividing line. In the first subperiod American business men were still active in carrying on Oriental trade, but owing to the rapid decline of the American marine during the Civil War and the rapid internal development after that event, American brains and capital became more and more occupied with their domestic enterprises and their Oriental trade was therefore allowed to wane.

The third period begins in 1895 and ends with 1913—a period of disturbances and severe competition. During this period, there were the Sino-Japanese War, the Russo-Japanese War, the Chinese boycott of 1905 against American goods, the Chinese Revolution of 1911, and the creation of the Chinese Republic. All these disturbing factors exerted a great influence on the trade between the United States and China. The easy victory of Japan over China radically altered the political situation in the Far East. The most powerful colonizing empires of the Occident, such as Great Britain, Germany, Russia and France, were quick enough to take advantage of this opportunity to expand their political and commercial influence in China. Japan, also, had made herself an industrial nation and exerted her entire energy to make China the market for her products. Occupations and leaseholds within Chinese territory became very common, and "spheres of influence" were viciously established. It was in this period that competition for Chinese trade was the severest, and although the United States had renewed her interest in the development of her trade in China, she made little headway in this direction.

The fourth period—a period of rapid expansion—is naturally set off by the outbreak of the European War. Because of the inability of European nations to carry on trade with China during the war, most of their trade was diverted to America, resulting in a tremendous increase in the trade between these two nations. During this period China and the United States became much more intimately related in their commercial interests. In former periods China played a

passive part in the trading, but she now began to play an active part in buying and selling as well as in the carrying trade. Since 1914, therefore, we have entered a new era in the trade between China and the United States.

### 2. The beginning of trade

American commerce with China was the result of influences reaching back over an extensive period. It may be said that at the very discovery of the New World a connection existed with the Celestial Empire, for it was to find Cathay and the Indies that Columbus sailed westward. Indirect trade had existed between China and America long before the establishment of the United States. Tea was imported from Canton by the East India Company by way of Great Britain; since 1718 ginseng, the drug which formed a large part of the cargoes of the first Chinese ship, had been known to be native to North America,[1] and it is probable that the East India Company had shipped some of it to Canton.[2] These early activities naturally led the way to direct trade when America became an independent nation.

Another influence leading to American commerce with China was the development of shipping in the colonies. Many of the American ports, especially Boston, Salem, Philadelphia, and New York were distinguished for their ship owners and for their excellent ships. It was only natural that these enterprising seamen should have found their way not only on the Atlantic but also on the Pacific. Still another influence was the loss to the Americans of the trade with the British West Indies after the Revolution. Before the Revolution the colonies had, of course, been included in the British colonial system, but independence, by placing them outside the system, made it necessary for them to look elsewhere for the investment of their commercial

[1] "Jesuit Relations and Allied Documents," Cleveland, C., 1900, 66:333.
[2] William Speer: The Oldest and the Newest Empire: China and the United States, 1870, p. 140.

capital. Independence, therefore, while shutting the door of the West Indies to the Americans, opened the portals of Asia and the East Indies.

In the light of these causes we are not surprised to find in the United States widespread movements right after independence was established to take advantage of Chinese trade. The first definite effort to establish direct trade with the old Empire of the East was made in 1783, when in December a little fifty-five ton sloop, the *Harriet*, sailed from Boston with a cargo of ginseng for China.[1] "Putting in at the Cape of Good Hope, she met with some British East-Indiamen, who, alarmed at this portent of Yankee competition, bought her cargo for double its weight in Hyson tea."[2] Her captain made a good bargain, but lost the honor of hoisting the first American ensign in China to another ship, the *Empress of China*.

It was in the next year, 1784, that this epoch-making vessel, fitted out by a New York merchant, first reached China.[3] Ginseng formed the main part of her cargo. After rounding the Cape of Good Hope the vessel reached Canton, anchoring on August 28 at Whampoa, the harbor of that city. As a beginning this voyage may be considered to have been most auspicious. Samuel Shaw, the supercargo of that ship, says in his *Journal*: "The Chinese were very indulgent toward us. They styled us the new people; and when by the map we conveyed to them an idea of the extent of our country with its present and increasing population, they were highly pleased at the prospect of so considerable a market for the product of theirs." The Americans disposed of their ginseng to advantage, and purchased a cargo of teas and Chinese goods of various kinds. The returning voyage of the ship ended on May 10, 1785, when she arrived safely in New York, bringing home a cargo that proved America need pay no further tribute for teas and silks to the British or the

[1] S. E. Morrison: *The Maritime History of Massachusetts*, p. 44.
[2] *Ibid.*
[3] S. E. Morrison: *The Maritime History of Massachusetts*, p. 45.

Dutch. The net profit of the voyage was estimated at $30,727, or about 25% on the capital invested.[1]

The news of this successful voyage created much interest and added incentive to the plans which were already projected. Shaw reported the result of the voyage to John Jay, United States Secretary of State; and received soon afterward by order of Congress a reply telling of that body's "peculiar satisfaction in the successful issue of this first effort of the citizens of the United States to establish a direct trade with China."[2] Soon afterward another ship, the *Alliance*, was sent out from Philadelphia, and returned with a cargo said to have been worth half a million dollars.[3] After this, several voyages were undertaken and in 1786 Shaw went out again from New York as supercargo of the ship *Hope* carrying with him a commission from the Congress of the United States as Consul at Canton.[4] This was the first American Consulate beyond the Cape of Good Hope and was the only one in China until after 1844.

The Canton trade thus started had become firmly established by the year 1790. Merely running over such names of the ships engaged in it as have come down to us gives us some idea of its extent.[5] There were the *Asia* and the *Canton*, whose voyages were not very successful;[6] the *Jenny*, the brig *Eleonora*;[7] the *Massachusetts*,[8] the *Astrea*,[9] the *Columbia*,[10] the *Light Horse*,[11] the *Atlantic*,[12] the brig *Three Sisters*,[13] and the brigantine *Hancock*.[14]

[1] Shaw's *Journal*.
[2] Shaw's *Journal, Appendix*, p. 337.
[3] For Accounts of this voyage, see A. Ritter, *Philadelphia and Her Merchants as Constituted Fifty to Seventy Years Ago*, Philadelphia, 1860.
[4] Shaw's *Journal*, p. 150.
[5] For the early history of the shipping trade between America and China, see Morison, Samuel E., *The Maritime History of Massachusetts, 1783-1860*; Boston, 1920.
[6] Shaw's *Journal*, pp. 295-296.
[7] *Ibid.*, p. 297.
[8] Delano: *Voyages*, pp. 21-25.
[9] *Journal of Brig Astrea to China.*
[10] Morison: *op. cit.*, p. 47.

In order to aid the development of direct Oriental trade as well as that of the American marine, early tariff provisions were enacted by the American Congress.[1] A moderate duty was imposed on tea imported direct from China, in American vessels, ranging from six to twenty cents per pound; but on tea imported from Europe in American bottoms, the duty ranged from eight to twenty-six cents, and on tea brought in foreign vessels, from fifteen to forty-five cents per pound.[2] Likewise, all other Oriental products imported in foreign vessels were obliged to pay a duty of 12.5 per cent. *ad valorem*, or almost twice the rate levied on imports brought in American vessels.[3] Largely because of these tariff provisions, Oriental trade rapidly became an important factor in the commerce of Salem, Boston, New York, Providence, Philadelphia, and Baltimore, and "laid the foundation of those great fortunes which constitute the origin of the wealth of so many of the older New England families."[4] They "brought back immense quantities of tea, spices, sugar, coffee, silks, nankeen and other cloths—all of them of great value in proportion to their bulk and therefore yielding heavy profits in the carrying trade; and whatever failed to find a market at home was reshipped from New England ports and sold in Hamburg or Northern Europe."[5]

American trade with China was then confined to the port of Canton, and was from the first compelled to fit into the Canton commercial system of what has been well known as "Co-hong." Co-hong was a mercantile organization, comprising a certain number of Chinese merchants to whom was granted by the Chinese Government a loose monopoly of

[1] Johnson, E. R., *History of Domestic and Foreign Commerce of the United States*, Vol. II, p. 336.
[2] *Ibid.*
[3] *Ibid.*
[4] Soley, "Maritime Industry of America," in Shaler, *The United States of America*, Vol. I, p. 525.
[5] *Ibid.*

dealing with foreign merchants. The members of the "Hong" were responsible to the Chinese authority for the "control" of foreigners and the enforcement of trade regulations. All trade transacted between China and foreign countries was handled by this organization.

### 3. The Expansion of trade and the effects of the European Wars and the Anglo-American War of 1812, 1791-1814

In the first flush of success America felt that her trade with Canton was destined to expand indefinitely. It soon became apparent, however, that a limit would speedily be reached. The chief article of importation from China was tea, and its consumption in America was limited. In addition, there was great difficulty in getting commodities with which to purchase cargoes in Canton. Through the centuries, Europeans had gone to China, as to the rest of the East, in quest of its teas and silks, while but few Western products could be found for which there was a return demand. The balance of trade had been met by heavy shipments of specie, a drain which had long been a cause of concern. From the very first the Americans had faced this same difficulty. For a time they had hoped that in ginseng they had a product which would supply the need.[1] Before long, however, it became apparent that the demand for the root in China was limited, since it served only for some curative purposes and was not commonly consumed by the Chinese people. Its quantity and value fell far short of those of silk and tea which the Americans bought of the Chinese. It was therefore necessary to export specie extensively to make up the deficit.

During the period, 1805-1815, the export of specie from the United States to Canton amounted in value to $22,719,000, 70% of the total exports, while the value of merchandise exports was only $10,239,688, 30% of the total.[2]

[1] Shaw's *Journal*, pp. 229-236.
[2] Pitkins: *Statistical View of the Foreign Trade of the U. S.*, 1835 ed., p. 303.

Specie was of all commodities the one which the United States could least spare at that time as they then had no silver or gold mines of importance. Specie was hard to get to exchange for such luxuries as tea and silk, and the prospects of American trade with Canton appeared to become extremely limited.

At about this time, however, two widely separated groups of events partially removed both of these hindrances, and gave Chinese-American trade an impetus which resulted in its rapid expansion. The effect of the first group of these events, the European wars following the French Revolution, is too well known to require detailed treatment here. The United States was made the common carrier of the whole world as well as of Europe. The effect on the trade with China was to give a wider market for tea. Between 1800 and 1812, from a fourth to a half of each year's imports of tea were re-exported from the United States.[1] In addition American bottoms took many cargoes directly from China to Europe. The second group of events, the opening of new sources of supply of goods for the Chinese market, resulted in new demands of the Chinese for furs, for sandal wood and for various products which the American traders got from the South Seas, and for which they exchanged the Chinese silks and teas. The fur trade, it was estimated, became of even greater importance in the Chinese market than ginseng during this period. This trade falls easily into three classifications: the furs which were brought from the interior—from the region of the Great Lakes and the Mississippi Valley—to the Atlantic Ports and then shipped as part of the regular cargoes to Canton; the sealskin trade with the Falkland Islands and the South Pacific, and the trade with the northwest coast of America in both land and sea skins. The sealskin trade developed more rapidly, and was carried on almost exclusively by the Americans in small vessels with relatively small crews. While the trade lasted, that is, until the seals were nearly extinct, it was probably the most profitable branch of the Canton trade. It was, however, both

ruthless and reckless, and within a generation the seals had become so scarce that it was no longer profitable.[1]

As to the extent of the fur trade, it was estimated that from the Island of Massafuero alone three and a half million fur seals were taken and sold at Canton.[2] Another estimate put the number of fur seals brought to Canton from all the South Pacific during the two decades, 1805-1834 at nearly 1,800,000, the valuation of which may be placed "most conservatively" at $3,500,000.[3] Sea otter pelts from the northwest coast during the same period amounted to 160,000 valued at not less than $4,000,000. The value of the land skins shipped directly from Atlantic ports was probably less than either of these items.

The sandalwood trade was vigorously carried on with the native Hawaiian chiefs, leading to the visits of Hawaiians to the United States, to the missionary efforts of 1820, and eventually to annexation.[4] Although the exact extent of the trade with China is not known today, it can safely be stated that it was second only to that of the fur trade in importance.

In addition to the trips to the northwest coast of America and the South Seas for furs and sandalwood, the Canton ships took other roundabout routes, many of them opened to them by European wars. These wars, resulting in the opening of new avenues of trade and the establishment of an efficient merchant marine, caused a phenomenal growth in the Chinese-American trade. In 1789 Shaw mentions four American vessels at Canton;[5] in the season of 1804-5 there were thirty-four, in 1806-7 there were forty-two and in 1809-10 there were thirty-seven. The imports to Canton in these

[1] For a more detailed account of the Fur Trade see S. E. Morison, *The Maritime History of Massachusetts*, 1774-1860, p. 52 ff.
[2] Benjamin Morell, *A Narrative of Four Voyages to the South Sea, from 1822-1831*, New York, 1832, p. 130.
[3] Fur trade statistics may be found in Pitkins' *Commerce of the United States* (editions 1816 and 1835).
[4] S. E. Morison, *Maritime History of Massachusetts*, p. 59.
[5] Shaw's *Journal*, p. 297.

last three seasons were $3,555,818, $5,127,000 and $5,715,000 respectively.[1] While the total commerce of the United States had more than quadrupled in a decade and a half,[2] that with China had nearly kept pace with it, averaging each year four and five percent of the total.

The costs of doing business at Canton in these early days were said to be very heavy.[3] In addition to the usual charge of commissions and duties, there were "presents and grafts that must be yielded at every step to the hoppo (an official taking charge of the harbour), the compradore, or the linguist."[4] The *Columbia's* first lading, we are told, of one thousand and fifty sea-otter skins was sold for $21,400; but after fees, expenses and repairs were deducted, only $11,242 remained to invest in a homeward cargo.[5] Yet the American demand for Chinese goods increased so fast that the trade grew by leaps and bounds.

The War of 1812 brought about a distinct break in the trade between the United States and China. Here, as in other branches of commerce, fear of capture by the British kept American ships at home. The total commerce of the three seasons from 1812 to 1815 was barely half that of the year before the War, and less than a third of that for the season of 1809-11.[6]

### 4. A period of Peaceful trade—from the close of the Anglo-American War of 1812 to the conclusion of the first commercial treaty between the United States and China, 1815-1844

The close of the War of 1812 between Great Britain and

[1] U. S. Sen. Docs. No. 31, 19th Congress, 1 Sess., also see *supra*, table on p. 8.
[2] American State Paper, *Commerce and Navigation*, Washington, 1832; 1,927, 928, Exports from the United States, 1791-92, $20,753,-088; 1806-7, $108,343,150.
[3] S. E. Morison, *op. cit.*, p. 66.
[4] *Ibid.*
[5] *Ibid.*
[6] See Table I.

the United States brought with it a stimulus to American commerce with China. The high prices of tea and silk caused by the war stimulated the natural increase due to the resumption of trade and for the first few years many new American firms were established, and both the United States and Europe were flooded with teas, nankeens, and silks. The first season showed a decided increase, the second nearly equaled the largest one before the war, and the three succeeding ones all greatly surpassed it. But after 1821 trade returned to a normal condition, and its volume became fairly steady year after year. Table 1 compiled from several different sources presents a view of the total American-Chinese trade during the whole period under discussion.

A change came in the Chinese-American commerce: the fur trade had nearly reached its end because of the gradual disappearance of the fur seals from the northwest coast of America; and the sandalwood trade had passed its zenith. There were new conditions, however, which led to the steady growth of the Canton trade. Teas carried in American bottoms still had a market in Europe, and because the population of the United States was more numerous and wealthier than in 1790 there was at the same time a growing market for Chinese goods. Hence, in spite of the removal of the principal causes of earlier prosperity, the years between 1814 and 1844 were, on the whole, successful ones for the Canton trade, even though they were, for the most part, quiet and lacking the fervor and the romance of the two decades before 1814.

However, in 1821 there came an exciting episode—the Terranova affair. The complete lack of diplomatic intercourse and treaties between foreign nations and China, and hence of a mutually recognized means of adjusting international difficulties caused a temporary suspension of trade relations. Terranova was an Italian sailor on board the American ship *Emily*, and was accused by the Chinese of having killed a Chinese woman on a boat. The Chinese authorities demanded his surrender, which the captain of the ship refused. An embargo was thereupon laid upon all American trade in Canton as a means of bringing pressure to bear upon the Americans to consent to his surrender. After repeated conferences between the Americans and the Chinese Co-hong merchants, the sailor was surrendered to the Chinese authorities for punishment. American trade was by an edict of the Canton viceroy at once reopened after the Americans had eventually admitted respect for the Chinese legal right over this case.[1] Aside from this episode, Chinese American relations during this period were quite uneventful, the traders of both countries living together peacefully and amicably.

With a review of the accompanying table, we can see some remarkable changes in the trade itself. During the first five years, 1816-1820, the total amount of the value of imports from Canton to America was $33,266,936, while the American exports thereto, including $25,779,000 of bullion and specie, amounted to $33,930,107, thus nearly balancing each other. But in the following decade, 1821-30, the total imports amounted to $52,954,994 while the exports were only $35,477,581, leaving a discrepancy of $17,477,013. The discrepancy between exports and imports in the second decade was much greater, the total imports from China being increased to $61,223,223, while exports decreased to only $12,749,203, leaving a balance of $48,474,020. One may well wonder at the enormous sums of these balances of trade, and ask what had become of them. To clear up this point of doubt, one must realize the fact that America paid off these balances not by credit borrowing from the Chinese, but by exchange bills on England. Before 1826, all balances of trade favorable to China were paid in bullion and specie, so there remained no appreciable discrepancy between the values of exports and imports. From 1805 to 1826 the exportation of precious metal by America to Canton reached

[1] For details of this case, see T. Dennett, *Americans in the Far East*, Ch. on Terranova case.

TABLE 1

TRADE BETWEEN THE UNITED STATES AND CHINA, 1810-1844

| Years ending Sept. 30 | Exports from U. S. to China | | | Imports to U. S. from China | Whereof there was in Bullion and Specie | |
| --- | --- | --- | --- | --- | --- | --- |
| | Domestic in $1,000 | Foreign in $1,000 | Total in $1,000 | Total in $1,000 | Exports to China in $1,000 | Imports from China in $1,000 |
| 1810a | .... | .... | 5,715 | 5,745 | 4,723 | |
| 1816b | .... | .... | 4,220 | 2,528 | 1,922 | |
| 1817 | .... | .... | 5,703 | 5,610 | 4,545 | |
| 1818 | .... | .... | 6,777 | 7,077 | 5,601 | |
| 1819 | .... | .... | 9,057 | 9,867 | 7,414 | |
| 1820 | .... | .... | 8,173 | 8,186 | 6,297 | |
| 1821c | 389 | 3,902 | 4,291 | 3,112 | 3,391 | .. |
| 1822 | 429 | 5,506 | 5,935 | 5,243 | 5,075 | 1 |
| 1823 | 288 | 4,348 | 4,636 | 6,511 | 3,584 | 22 |
| 1824 | 330 | 4,971 | 5,301 | 5,619 | 4,464 | .. |
| 1825 | 160 | 5,410 | 5,570 | 7,533 | 4,523 | . |
| 1826 | 242 | 2,324 | 2,567 | 7,422 | 1,652 | .. |
| 1827 | 291 | 3,574 | 3,864 | 3,617 | 2,525 | .. |
| 1828 | 230 | 1,252 | 1,481 | 5,339 | 456 | 24 |
| 1829 | 261 | 1,094 | 1,355 | 4,681 | 602 | .. |
| 1830 | 156 | 586 | 742 | 3,878 | 80 | 9 |
| 1831 | 245 | 1,046 | 1,291 | 3,083 | 367 | .. |
| 1832 | 339 | 924 | 1,261 | 5,345 | 452 | 26 |
| 1833 | 538 | 896 | 1,434 | 7,542 | 290 | 6 |
| 1834 | 256 | 755 | 1,010 | 7,892 | 379 | .. |
| 1835 | 336 | 1,533 | 1,869 | 5,987 | 1,392 | .. |
| 1836 | 342 | 853 | 1,194 | 7,325 | 414 | .. |
| 1837 | 319 | 312 | 631 | 8,965 | 155 | .. |
| 1838 | 656 | 861 | 1,517 | 4,765 | 729 | 4 |
| 1839 | 430 | 1,103 | 1,534 | 3,679 | 993 | .. |
| 1840 | 469 | 541 | 1,010 | 6,641 | 477 | .. |
| 1841 | 715 | 485 | 1,201 | 3,095 | 427 | .. |
| 1842 | 738 | 707 | 1,444 | 4,935 | 607 | .. |
| 1843d | 1,755 | 664 | 2,419 | 4,386 | 572 | .. |
| 1844 | 1,110 | 647 | 1,757 | 4,931 | 567 | .. |

a and b. The figures for year 1810 and for 1816-1820 were taken from U. S. Senate Doc. 31, 1 Sess., 19th Congress.

a This was the largest before the War of 1812.

c From 1821-1844, the figures are taken from Homan's, I. S.; "A Historical and Statistical Account of the Foreign Commerce of the United States," 1857.

d Nine months to June 30, and the fiscal year after 1844 changed to begin July 1.

e These figures are taken Pitkins; Statistical View (1835 ed.), p. 303.

a large total of $58,707,891. Until replaced by bills of exchange it formed half and even three-fourths of the total export to China amounting in one year to nearly seven and one-half millions of dollars.[1] The drain, while necessary, was heavy, and American merchants found it profitable to import teas, even when paying for them with so expensive a commodity. Most of it was in the form of Spanish milled dollars obtained from the Spanish West Indies, South America, Portugal, and Gibraltar. About 1827, however, bills of exchange on England began to take the place of specie. The rapidly increasing importation of the nineteenth century had turned the general balance of trade against China and made it cheaper for America to buy exchange with American products shipped to England than to get silver from the Spaniards. During the seven years, 1827-1833, nearly nine million dollars of these English bills were used by Americans to pay off their unfavorable balance of Canton trade.[2] How much was paid after 1833 can not be ascertained from the available statistics of Chinese-American trade, but it is safe to assume that the sum was on the increase, as the amount of the exported specie was rapidly on the decrease.

The period between 1815 and 1839 was also marked by noticeable changes in the composition of exports and imports to and from China. Of American exports to China, cotton had assumed a new importance. It is true that America purchased nankeens (Chinese domestic cotton cloths) at Canton, but later the increased quantity and cheapness of the coarser cottons of the Occident won for them a market in the East. For American raw cotton there was little demand, since the product of China herself and that of India were cheaper.[2] Other goods, such as quicksilver, copper, lead, rice, and a little steel were also exported to China. All of these products America got from places other than her own

[1] Year 1819, see Table 1.

[2] Cf. Pitkm, *Statistical View* (1835 edition), p. 303.

country. Ginseng still continued to be shipped from America, but its quantity was not large.[1]

Another article imported into China was opium. During the early years of the nineteenth century, the importation of opium into China by Americans was always much less than that by the British, and most of it was of the inferior kind obtained in Turkey. It is, however, quite impossible to determine with any precision the amount of Turkish opium thus imported into China by American merchants, for it was a contraband article after 1791,[2] and therefore smuggling was great. It was asserted by one who traded in it extensively that from 1827 to 1830 Americans disposed of from twelve to fourteen hundred piculs annually.[3] The share in the importation by Americans of opium from India is even more difficult to determine as American ships carried cargoes freely from British India to Canton, and in these consignments opium eventually appeared. At the time of the surrender of stored opium to Commissioner Lin in 1839, out of a total of 20,283 chests, there were in the possession of Americans 1540 chests.[4]

Although at no time did the American importation of opium form a very considerable part either of the total import of the drug to China or of the total of American imports the existence of the trade itself conferred on the Americans a direct benefit, for it reduced the necessity for the importation of specie. As the supply of furs began to diminish after 1820, and while the American cotton trade was in its infancy, the increased importation of opium was a very important transaction.

Of the exports from China to America, tea was always predominant. We shall come in Chapter VI to a more detailed discussion of tea trade during this early period, but

[1] Documents 35, 3 session, 27 Congress. Executive Report.

[2] Foster: *American Diplomacy in the Orient*, pp. 64-73.

[3] Forbes: *China Trade*, p. 27. One picul = 133.3 lbs.

[4] Hunter: *Fan Kwai*, p. 146.

here suffice it to say that in value the proportion of tea to the total American imports from China during these years was for 1822, 36%; 1828, 45%; 1832, 52%; 1837, 65%; 1840, 81%. It may readily be seen from these percentages that in the years following 1815 the relative proportion of tea to other Chinese imports constantly increased.

Besides tea, silks were also an important article of import from China to the United States. In the fifteen years after 1820, they were of great importance, several times amounting to more than one-third of the total imports from China.[1] Later, however, owing possibly to changing fashions, the importation of silk declined, until in 1841, it was scarcely eight per cent of the whole.[1] Somewhat similar was the fate of cotton cloths or nankeens, because the Americans had at that time reached a stage where they were able to manufacture their own cottons with their newly established domestic cotton industry. Other articles such as cassia, chinaware, a little sugar, and a number of minor articles such as fire screens, fire crackers, camphor, rhubarb, and fans were also imported to the United States.

The last important set of incidents in the history of Chinese-American intercourse before 1844 cluster around the first British-Chinese War, commonly known as the Opium War, because it was caused by the determination of the Chinese Government to exterminate this demoralizing trade and the equally strong determination of the British Government to maintain it. It does not seem necessary to describe here the intricate relations between Great Britain and China which led to this notorious occasion, which falls rather in the realm of Sino-British political history than in that of the history of Chinese-American trade. Suffice it to say that the Americans, though having been involved in the opium trade to a certain extent, were much less involved in it than the British. So they seemed to have little to do

[1] See Chapter VII, infra.

with this incident, except that its result affected the future of the Chinese-American trade more than anything else. It closes an old chapter and opens a new one in the history of their trade, when, as an aftermath of the war, the United States concluded with China the first "treaty of peace, amity and commerce" in 1844.[1] We now emerge from a period of informal intercourse into one of diplomatic relations.

Owing to the disturbances of the intermittent warfare from 1839 to 1842 at the mouth of Canton River, American trade with China suffered a noticeable decrease during this short period. For a time the port of Canton was blockaded by the British fleet, and the freight for conveying goods from the seacoast to the city of Canton was higher than that from America to China. The Americans, however, made large profits in transporting goods between the two places. With the return of peace in 1843 Chino-American trade resumed its normal magnitude with a rush, and in Table 1 we notice that in 1843, when the fiscal year consisted of only nine months, the total American imports from China amounted to $4,385,566 in value, and exports to China to $2,418,958, while the corresponding figures for the previous year (of twelve months) were $4,934,645, and $1,444,397.

[1] See Chapter XIV, infra.

## CHAPTER II

### The Period of Temporary Expansion and Steady Decline, 1845-1894

Although commercial relations had existed between the United States and China for more than half a century, it was not until the treaty of 1844 that a beginning was made in formal treaty intercourse. But when formal relationship had once been established there immediately followed a rush of commercial activities on the part of Americans in China. The United States was taking a very big share in China's foreign trade during the first decade and a half of this period, and it seemed as if a very rapid and unlimited increase would be our normal expectation.

But this phenomenal trade expansion came at the beginning of a stage characterized by great confusion both in China and in the United States. Within a generation China was to pass through her Taiping Rebellion which devastated thirteen of her twenty-one provinces and destroyed twenty million people. This is said to be the greatest civil conflict the world has ever had so far as loss of lives and property is concerned. This greatly reduced the purchasing power of the Chinese people and delayed at least for a generation their national improvements. In the United States, on the other hand, the Civil War came, during which her magnificent shipping, the vital element of her foreign trade, fell into decay, while high tariff walls were established, first, for revenue purposes, and later, for protection of American industry, and thus seriously blocked the way to further growth of imports from China. With these disturbing factors in full swing, it was only natural that the development of her Oriental trade should have been unavoidably slow.

The tardiness in the development of Chinese-American
20

trade would have been even more significant had there been no favorable influences stimulating at the same time the commercial intercourse of the two peoples. During the latter part of the period, the preeminently favorable characteristic was the shortening of distances. Communication between Asia and America became quicker and cheaper; it was as though the globe suddenly contracted to a quarter of its former size. Following rapidly upon the clipper ship with its quicker and cheaper transportation came the extended development of steam motive power; the transcontinental railway lines of America were constructed; and the transoceanic steamers were first put into regular passenger and freight service. The overland and submarine telegraph was introduced into general use. These inventions were accompanied by the perfection of labor-saving machinery and the multiplication of the uses of steam power in manufacturing processes in the United States. All these industrial and commercial changes exerted their influence to an immeasurable extent in promoting the trade between the United States and China.

### 1.—The period of temporary trade expansion, 1845-1860

Table 2 presents in a compact mass the entire statistics of Chinese-American trade during this short period of phenomenal trade expansion.

The outstanding fact of the trade of this sub-period is the rapid though irregular increase of both imports and exports, as indicated in the amount of total annual trade. The total trade for 1845 was greatly in excess of that of the previous years, indicating a quick recovery from the disturbing effects of the opium troubles in China; yet in the following years it steadily increased from a value of nine million dollars to about fourteen and a half millions in 1853, in spite of the fact that the Taiping Rebellion was just on its high tide in China. In 1858, when the Rebellion was quelled and the country again became peaceful, both imports and exports between the countries received great stimulation and leaped to the high water mark of twenty-two and a half millions in 1860.

TABLE 2

AMERICAN TRADE WITH CHINA, 1845-60

| Year ending June 30 | Exports from U. S. A. to China | | | Imports into U. S. from China | Whereof there was in bullion and specie | | Total trade in $1,000 |
|---|---|---|---|---|---|---|---|
| | Domestic in $1,000 | Foreign in $1,000 | Total in $1,000 | Total in $1,000 | Export in $1,000 | Import in $1,000 | |
| 1845 | 2,079 | 197 | 2,276 | 7,286 | 159 | 27 | 9,562 |
| 1846 | 1,178 | 154 | 1,332 | 6,594 | 113 | .. | 7,926 |
| 1847 | 1,709 | 124 | 1,833 | 5,583 | 33 | .. | 7,416 |
| 1848 | 2,064 | 126 | 2,190 | 8,083 | 72 | .. | 10,273 |
| 1849 | 1,461 | 122 | 1,583 | 5,514 | 10 | .. | 7,087 |
| 1850 | 1,486 | 119 | 1,605 | 6,593 | 25 | .. | 8,199 |
| 1851 | 2,156 | 329 | 2,485 | 7,065 | 147 | .. | 9,550 |
| 1852 | 2,480 | 183 | 2,663 | 10,594 | 20 | .. | 13,257 |
| 1853 | 3,213 | 524 | 3,737 | 10,574 | 489 | .. | 14,311 |
| 1854 | 1,294 | 104 | 1,398 | 10,506 | 156 | 108 | 11,904 |
| 1855 | 1,533 | 186 | 1,719 | 11,049 | 675 | .. | 12,768 |
| 1856 | 2,048 | 510 | 2,558 | 10,454 | 634 | 1 | 13,013 |
| 1857 | 2,020 | 2,375 | 4,395 | 8,360 | 1,898 | .. | 12,755 |
| 1858 | 3,008 | 2,690 | 5,697 | 10,571 | 2,016 | .. | 16,258 |
| 1859 | 4,233 | 2,894 | 7,127 | 10,791 | 2,050 | .. | 17,919 |
| 1860 | 7,171 | 1,735 | 8,906 | 13,567 | 3,156 | .. | 22,493 |

Data from U. S. Bur. of Statistics (Treasury Dept.) : *Commerce of Asia and Oceania*, 1898.

Throughout this period the flow of specie had been steadily from America to China, although during the first ten years the flow was slight, averaging about $100,000 annually. In 1849, the net exportation of bullion and specie from the United States to China was only $9,967, an almost negligible sum. This gives evidence of the fact that the big balances of imports against exports were nearly all paid by bills of exchange on London, which originated from British opium trade. But after 1855, heavy exports of specie were again

resumed, because America had found its gold and silver mines in California and Mexico. From that time the flow of specie, especially silver, has been going on without interruption up to the present.

In 1860, China was seventh in supplying American imports, following the United Kingdom, France, Spanish West Indies, British North American Provinces, Brazil and Germany, in the order of their importance.[1] Although the percentage of United States exports to China was only 1.78 of the total American exports in the same year, yet China held the same rank among the best customers for American goods as that held among the suppliers. She was exceeded only by the United Kingdom, France, the British North American possession, Germany, and Spanish West Indies in the order of their relative importance.[2]

*Growing American Shipping, a cause of trade expansion*

Among the several causes which underlie the expansion of trade during this period must be first mentioned the growth of American shipping. In the previous period the tonnage of shipping between these two countries had never exceeded the 10,000 ton mark except during the two years, 1843-4.[3] But within a period of ten years, it increased to more than one hundred thousand tons, and by the perfection of the American type of clipper ships, which appeared in 1840, they were able for a time to monopolize the transportation of tea even to England, for they could carry larger cargoes and deliver the tea in shorter time and in fresher condition than could their competitors.[4] Since in those early days ship owners and mariners were themselves traders, it is no sur-

[1] See U. S. Bureau of Commerce, *Commerce and Navigation of U. S.*, 1860.

[2] *Ibid.*

[3] See I. S. Homans: *A Historical and Statistical Account of the Foreign Commerce of the United States*, 1857, Sec. on China.

[4] Nye: *Tea and Tea Trade*, Part I, 1850.

prise that the import and export trade with China should have come with a big rush.

*The Lowering of American Tariff, a Cause for the Increase of Imports from China*

Just at the beginning of this period American imports from China, as well as those from other parts of the world, were greatly facilitated by another factor—the lowering of American import duties. A new tariff act was passed by the United States Congress in 1846 "with the avowed intention of putting into operation, as far as possible, the principles of free trade."[1] Tea, formerly a pure revenue article, was now admitted free of duty, and this liberating measure at once caused a rapid expansion of its imports from China. The duty on many other articles and manufactures were also reduced to an average of thirty per cent,[2] and this reduction also exerted a great stimulating influence upon the ensuing growth in such imports of Chinese commodities like raw and manufactured silks, spices, wool and woolens, sugar, etc. "The tariff act of 1857 took away still more from the restrictive character of the American tariff legislation, and until her Civil War the United States had a tariff, which, though not arranged completely or consistently on the principle of free trade, was very moderate in comparison with the later system after 1860."[3] It is partly due to this moderation of the previous American tariff restrictions that imports from China increased during this sub-period from seven million dollars in 1845 to eleven million in 1852, and to fourteen million in 1860.

*The Establishment of a Low Chinese Tariff by Treaty, a Cause for the Increase of American Exports to China.*

Nearly at the same time when the reduction of American

[1] F. W. Taussig: *Tariff History of the U. S.*, 1922 ed., p. 156.

[2] *Ibid.*

[3] *Ibid.*, p. 157.

import duties promoted American import trade with China, the establishment of a low Chinese conventional tariff by the Treaties of Nanking and of Wanghia, and thus the elimination of all the irregular exactions of the Chinese customs officers, also reduced greatly the cost of American and other foreign merchants in importing their commodities into Chinese ports. In the preceding chapter the writer has already given his readers some idea about the heavy cost of doing business that the foreign importers at Canton were formerly compelled to bear in such items as duties, "commissions," "presents," and grafts, to the Chinese Government, harbor officials, compradores and linguists.[1] Even worse, perhaps, than the mere heaviness of the levy was its uncertainty and inconvenience. It is said that before a foreign vessel was allowed to land its cargo at Canton, the Chinese customs officials usually took days and even weeks to survey its loading capacity and to decide the amount of dues.[2] Bribes in order to lessen the official duty were common. Once a vessel was said to have been levied a duty of 1,500 taels, of which 1,300 taels went to the private pocket of customs officials "for the expenses of survey," and only 200 to the government treasury.[3] Under such a corruptive tariff system, any great increase of American exports to China was naturally impossible.

But the Treaties of Nanking and Whanghia concluded between China on the one hand, and Great Britain and the United States on the other, put an end to all such vicious practices, and marked a turning point in the tariff history of China. The import tax on all foreign commodities was now strictly limited to the rate based on a uniform five per cent levy, specified in a tariff, which formed an integral part of these treaties,[2] and it was also definitely stipulated in the documents that no "presents" or commissions whatsoever

[1] Chapter 1, p. 21, *supra*.

[2] C. Chu: *The Tariff Problem in China*, New York, 1916; p. 22.

[3] *Ibid.*

should hereafter be paid by the British and American importers.[1] These stipulations actually meant a substantial reduction of the duties to be paid by foreign merchants, and, therefore, acted as a strong impetus to further the growth of American exports to China. Thus, we had, in 1845-7, an annual average value of American exports to China of less than two million dollars, but the value increased to three million dollars in 1851-3, and again to eight million dollars in 1858-60.

### The "Coolie Trade"

During this period we had an important incident to the history of American trade with China in the so-called "coolie trade." In this hideous "trade" the Americans, as well as the British, Portuguese and Spanish had taken no small share, giving many thousands of innocent Chinese laborers the most trying treatment and originating for themselves the very unpleasant problem of Chinese immigration. During the fifties of the last century, swift clipper ships carried across the Pacific the news of the gold discovery and of the demand at San Francisco for cheap labor. American vessels, as well as those of some other nations, were drawn into the transportation of Chinese laborers to these various destinations, and the "trade" was in full swing by 1854. At Swatow in 1855, out of a total of twelve ships carrying 6,388 coolies, five were American, taking 3,050 of the total.[2] The Hongkong returns for the coolie trade for 1857 showed that out of a total of seventy vessels employed twenty-two were American, while nine American vessels brought coolies to Havana.[3]

The evils of the "coolie trade" were numerous and far-reaching. As the demand for cheap labor increased in

[1] *Ibid.*, p. 26.
[2] Marshall: *Correspondence*, p. 78; Report of House of Commons, 84, 116-7, 106.
[3] *Ibid.*

America artificial methods of stimulating recruiting were employed and large numbers of ignorant Chinese laborers were decoyed to the vessels where they were detained by force and became practically slaves. They were crowded into ships which were sometimes not even seaworthy, and supplied with insufficient food and water. The mortality *en route* was, therefore, naturally very high.[1] At their destination the laborers were often transferred or practically "sold" to contractors, and were miserably treated and subjected to all the customary evils of the contract labor system so that at the expiration of the term they were unable to return to China. The legal and moral outrages of these "traders" at once aroused the deepest resentment on the part of the Chinese people against all foreigners, because the Chinese could not very well distinguish who were the real evil doers. A general uprising against foreigners was threatened at various southern ports in China. Finally the abuses of the "trade" aroused the conscientious action of some western governments. In 1855, the English Parliament passed the so-called British Passengers Act, which forbade British vessels to carry such contract laborers except to British ports, and subjected them to close inspection. American vessels continued to share the "trade" until 1862, when it was prohibited by Act of Congress in the same spirit that settled the American slave question. The American representatives in China had also made some effort to check evils of the traffic, even before they got the support of legislation. "Reputable firms withdrew entirely from the trade, but individuals brought much disgrace upon the American flag and added to the anti-foreign sentiment in China."[2]

The result of this "coolie trade," so far as the United States and China are concerned is the most unpleasant problem of Chinese immigration, a problem which led the Americans to deal unfairly with the Chinese, and also caused much

[1] Parker: *Correspondence*, p. 625.
[2] *Cf.* Tyler Dennett: *Americans in the East*, N. Y., 1922.

political strife in America itself. To enter into a detailed discussion of this problem, falls perhaps outside the scope of the present treatise. Yet it has such an important bearing on the trade between these two peoples that we shall have to give it at least a passing notice in a later section.

### Composition of Imports and Exports

During this period the composition of imports from China to the United States did not show much change, while that of exports to China underwent a constant alteration. As has been indicated above, the Chinese in previous years wanted few American products while the demand in America for Chinese products was much greater. The Americans had to procure goods outside their own country to pay for their Chinese imports. So the value of foreign exports was usually greater than that of domestic exports.[1] But during the middle of the nineteenth century the industrial revolution was taking full effect in America and developing some manufactures which were to have a good market in China. As a result the share of American domestic goods in the total exports to China had been increasing rapidly. In 1842 the total value of foreign exports was $706,888, while that of domestic exports was $737,509, the first year in which domestic exports to China exceeded foreign exports. Three years later in 1845, domestic exports amounted to $2,079,341, constituting ninety-two percent of the total exports, while foreign exports decreased to the negligible sum of $196,654 or eight percent of the total. In 1853 the domestic exports amounted to $3,212,574, or eighty-six percent, as against $524,418 of foreign exports, or fourteen percent of the total, and in 1860 domestic exports leaped to the figure of $7,170,784.

Of American domestic exports to China cotton manufactures now held a place far outranking other products. In

[1] See Table I.

1860 the United States exported to China painted, printed or dyed cloths to the value of $591,185, white and other duck cloths $262,424, and other cotton manufactures $3,043,753. The total of all cotton manufactures was $3,897,362, which is fifty-four percent of the total domestic exports $7,170,784. From that time on American cotton goods constantly increased in importance in Chinese markets until the beginning of the present century when they were supplanted by Japanese and Chinese domestic cottons.

Other big items composing the total domestic exports in the same year (1860) were as follows:—

| | |
|---|---:|
| Cotton manufactures | $3,897,362 |
| Meats, dairy products and other provisions | 269,032 |
| Wheat flour (37,328 bbls.) | 302,304 |
| Coal (29,023 tons) | 117,969 |
| Drugs and medicines | 51,010 |
| Ginseng (395,909 lbs.) | 295,766 |
| Iron and steel manufactures | 87,731 |
| Manufactured tobacco (664,289 lbs.) | 97,957 |
| Gold and silver bullion and coins | 1,545,914 |
| Other articles | 508,043 |
| | $7,170,784 |

Of the foreign exports during this period practically all were silver coins, which were transported from Mexico and the Spanish West-Indies. In 1860 such silver coins amounted to a value of $1,556,828, which is ninety percent of the total foreign export.

Among the imports from China to the United States tea still retained the preëminent position it held in the previous period, varying in different years between sixty to eighty per cent of the total imports therefrom. But its relative importance now shows a tendency to decline. Silk came next, and then sugar, spices, and wool. The composition of 1860 imports is shown in the following table:

| | |
|---|---|
| Tea ........................................... | $8,799,141 |
| Silk, raw.................................... | 1,020,496 |
| Silk piece goods and other manufactures...... | 906,929 |
| Clothing .................................... | 108,205 |
| Matting ..................................... | 273,709 |
| Oils, essential, or volatile expressed........... | 99,056 |
| Spices (mostly Cassia)........................ | 296,743 |
| Brown sugar (13,143,376 lbs.)................. | 628,668 |
| Wool, manufactures of....................... | 204,352 |
| Other articles............................... | 1,229,305 |
| | $13,566,587 |

## 2. The Period of Slow Development, 1861-1894

At no time throughout the last one and a half centuries was the development of Chinese-American trade so slow as in the last four decades of the nineteenth century. Throughout the first six decades of that century, the magnitude and importance of the trade had been on the increase both absolutely as well as relatively, and there was every reason to expect a continual rapid increase both in imports and in exports. But in spite of this, there was no noticeable increase of trade between these two countries for a period of nearly forty years. During this same period, American trade with Japan increased from nearly nothing in 1860 (imports to United States $138,274; exports from United States $55,091) to $28,330,674 in 1894 (imports to United States $23,695,957; exports from United States $4,634,717), while American trade with China increased from $22,472,705 in 1860 to only $22,997,000 in 1894. In 1860 China had a share of 3.15% of the total foreign trade of the United States. In 1880 its relative share decreased to only 1.86%, and in 1894 to 1.75%. At the beginning of this subperiod, China was the seventh best foreign source of supply for American demands, and the sixth best customer for American products. But fifteen years later, in 1885, she was relegated to the eighth place as source of supply and to the fourteenth as a customer.

Even viewing the question from the other side, the declining relative importance of the American share in the total foreign trade of China is also clearly indicated in the following percentages: in 1872 the share of the United States in China's foreign trade was 8.46%; in 1877, 6.33%; 1881, 6.5%; 1887, 6.5%; 1889, 5.2%; in 1893, 6.4%, while China's trade with Japan was 3.01%, 3.76%, 3.4%, 4.10%, 6.2%, and 6.4% respectively in these same years.

The first half of Table 3 presents the complete statistics of American trade with China during the period under discussion. From the figures in the "total trade" column it is evident that trade was merely marking time on its way to later development.

These figures, however, do not represent the total volume of Chino-American trade because of the use of Hongkong as a port of transshipment between China and America as well as between China and all other European countries.[1] In those early years, American trade with the British and Dutch East Indies, and Indo-China was yet small in volume; a very large portion, if not all, of the American imports from Hongkong must have originated in South China, and an equal portion of exports thereto must have gone ultimately to China. We are sure not to commit any serious error, if we treat all the American Hongkong trade as Chinese trade. This has been done even in American Governmental reports; down to 1874, the American statistics for the China trade included all those for Hongkong.

The second half of the above table shows American trade with Hongkong since it was reported separately, and the last column, showing the total of American trade with China and Hongkong combined, certainly gives a more complete view of Chino-American trade.

Even after this correction of the trade statistics for China the trade still showed no material increase, but fluctuated be-

[1] For further discussion on this point, see Chapter IV on Hongkong allowance of trade, infra.

### TABLE 3
#### TRADE OF THE UNITED STATES WITH CHINA AND HONGKONG.
1861-1894 a. UNIT: $1,000

| Year ending June 30 | Value of Imports from China | Value of Exports to China b | Total | Value of Imports from Hongkong | Value of Exports to Hongkong | Total | Total Trade with China and Hongkong Combined |
|---|---|---|---|---|---|---|---|
| 1861 | 11,352 | 6,917 | 18,269 | | | | |
| 1862 | 7,459 | 5,499 | 12,958 | | | | |
| 1863 | 10,961 | 6,142 | 17,103 | | | | |
| 1864 | 10,165 | 8,733 | 18,898 | | | | |
| 1865 | 5,131 | 7,105 | 12,236 | | | | |
| 1866 | 10,133 | 10,150 | 20,283 | | | | |
| 1867 | 12,112 | 9,768 | 21,880 | | | | |
| 1868 | 11,385 | 11,691 | 23,077 | | | | |
| 1869 | 13,209 | 12,376 | 25,585 | | | | |
| 1870 | 14,628 | 9,040 | 23,669 | | | | |
| 1871 | 20,066 | 2,068 | 22,135 | | | | |
| 1872 | 26,754 | 2,936 | 29,690 | | | | |
| 1873 | 26,353 | 3,394 | 29,748 | | | | |
| 1874 | 18,159 | 2,543 | 20,703 | | | | |
| 1875 | 13,480 | 1,458 | 14,938 | 1,203 | 2,102 | 3,305 | 18,243 |
| 1876 | 12,361 | 1,383 | 13,744 | 494 | 3,240 | 3,733 | 17,478 |
| 1877 | 11,141 | 1,697 | 12,838 | 1,171 | 3,230 | 4,401 | 17,239 |
| 1878 | 15,895 | 3,597 | 19,492 | 2,233 | 3,263 | 5,495 | 24,988 |
| 1879 | 16,566 | 2,517 | 19,083 | 1,653 | 3,291 | 4,944 | 24,027 |
| 1880 | 21,770 | 1,101 | 22,871 | 2,251 | 2,877 | 5,128 | 27,199 |
| 1881 | 22,318 | 5,448 | 27,765 | 2,400 | 2,917 | 5,117 | 33,082 |
| 1882 | 20,214 | 5,896 | 26,110 | 2,424 | 3,429 | 5,852 | 31,962 |
| 1883 | 20,141 | 4,080 | 24,222 | 1,919 | 3,778 | 5,697 | 29,918 |
| 1884 | 15,617 | 4,627 | 20,243 | 1,505 | 3,082 | 4,586 | 24,830 |
| 1885 | 16,292 | 6,397 | 22,689 | 984 | 4,149 | 5,133 | 27,822 |
| 1886 | 18,973 | 7,521 | 26,494 | 1,072 | 4,056 | 5,129 | 31,622 |
| 1887 | 19,077 | 6,247 | 25,323 | 1,436 | 2,984 | 4,421 | 29,744 |
| 1888 | 16,691 | 4,583 | 21,273 | 1,446 | 3,352 | 4,798 | 26,071 |
| 1889 | 17,028 | 2,791 | 19,820 | 1,480 | 3,686 | 5,167 | 24,986 |
| 1890 | 16,260 | 2,946 | 19,207 | 970 | 4,439 | 5,408 | 24,616 |
| 1891 | 19,322 | 2,710 | 28,023 | 563 | 4,769 | 5,232 | 33,355 |
| 1892 | 20,488 | 5,663 | 26,152 | 763 | 4,894 | 5,657 | 31,809 |
| 1893 | 20,367 | 3,900 | 24,537 | 878 | 4,217 | 5,095 | 29,632 |
| 1894 | 17,135 | 5,862 | 22,997 | 893 | 4,210 | 5,102 | 28,100 |

a Before 1874, inclusive, Hongkong trade was included under China.
b Gold and silver included until 1870 inclusive.

tween $20,000,000 and $30,000,000. It is an undeniable fact, therefore, that American trade with China was declining in importance to both countries.

### Tardiness of trade development

One may well ask why, despite so many favorable conditions for trade expansion, such as shortening of distances, development of industry, etc., the trade failed to expand as it should have done. This pertinent question is answered by the reasons enumerated in the following sections.

(a) Decline of American Shipping Interest in China. The decline of the American merchant marine, which became so marked after the Civil War, naturally had an adverse effect upon the further expansion of American trade in the Orient. During the time of bitter strife between the South and the North, American vessels were exposed to the gravest danger of attack by the naval force of the opposite parties. Many of them were sold to other countries and many left to remain idle and to decay in their harbors. Within a few years, the magnificent American merchant marine, which had been second to none before the war, suddenly dwindled in importance and activity. Large quantities of exports and imports to and from China, which formerly were carried in American bottoms, now had to be transported by the people of other countries. In 1860, of the $7,170,781 domestic exports from the United States, goods to the value of $6,774,422; and of the $13,566,587 imports, goods to the value of $13,135,340; were carried by America's own vessels.[1] But in 1893 these vessels carried only 12.6% of her total exports to China and only 13.2% of her total imports therefrom.[2]

[1] Commerce and Navigation of the U. S., 1860.
[2] In 1893 American imports from China were valued at H. K. Taels 5,443,569; exports to China, at H. K. Taels 4,138,000. In this year value of goods carried by American ships to and from China were H. K. Taels 688,000 and H. K. Taels 1,412,000 respectively. Data from Chinese Customs Returns 1893, Part I.

*(b) The Re-establishment of Restrictive Tariff Systems by the United States after 1862.* The American Civil War retarded the natural expansion of American trade with China, not only by ruining the magnificent American shipping, but also by turning the American liberal commercial policies of the preceding sub-period into a system of extreme protection and thus shackled the American import trade with China as well as that with other countries. When the Civil War broke out, the American Government immediately felt the need of additional revenue for carrying on the struggle, and by the tariff acts of 1862 and of 1864, a great increase in the rates of import tax was brought about. Those acts "raised the duties so greatly and indiscriminately that the average rate on dutiable commodities, which had been 37.2 per cent under the act of 1862, became 47.1 per cent under that of 1864. It established protective duties more extreme than had been ventured on in any previous tariff act in American history." [1] These high duties were first considered as a temporary war measure, but they were retained, increased, and systematized in succeeding acts of 1872, 1875, 1883, and 1897, and not even partly removed until 1909. Not only manufactured articles were subject to heavy import taxes, but also many kinds of raw materials such as wool and hides. Under these restrictions there is no wonder that imports from China have been stunted to a certain extent.

*(c) The Inactivity and Failure of American Business Concerns in China.* It was also during this sub-period that the active American pioneer traders in China disappeared from the market. "It is probably no injustice to those who came later to the market to state that the American mercantile community in the East reached its zenith of development and vigor before the outbreak of the American Civil War. Dry-rot was already setting in and the domestic development of the United States was such that men of ability and character

[1] Taussig, *op cit.* p. 167.

equal to that of the pioneers in Asia could now find ampler rewards at home in the fields of manufacturing, banking, and transportation." [1] As a result of this condition the period of 1860-95 was characterized by the decay, withdrawal or failure of all the American mercantile houses famous before the treaties of Tientsin, and by the entrance of no new merchants who rose to equal eminence. [2] The failure of Elyphant and Company in December, 1878, and of Russell and Company in June, 1891, eliminated two of the most famous of the older American firms in China, and surrendered to British and German competitors a prestige and commercial leadership in China which the Americans have never regained even since the European War. [3] The new firms which had appeared after the Civil War were, with very few notable exceptions, not well supplied with capital, and sometimes inclined to speculations and methods which brought little credit to American trade.

*(c) Japan's competition in tea and silk market.* A more obvious reason for the slow increase of American trade with China is found in the severe competition which China began to suffer from Japan in her tea and silk trade with America. Before Commodore Perry's expedition to Japan to open this heretofore isolated country to international commerce in 1860, all the teas and a large part of all the silks imported into the United States came from China. So long as China held the monopoly of these two articles, and so long as there was a growing demand for them in this rapidly growing country, American imports therefrom could not fail to increase greatly. And increase of importation would in turn stimulate exportation thereto. But when Japan came into the American market, she at once became the strongest competitor of her Oriental sister; and in a comparatively short

[1] Tyler Dennett, *Americans in the Far East*, p. 348.

[2] *Ibid.*

[3] *Ibid.*

time her American silk and tea trade encroached tremendously upon that of China and almost completely ruined it. [1]

*(d) Depreciation of the value of silver.* There was another reason why the relative status of Chinese trade had been becoming constantly more and more insignificant to the United States. (The value of trade with China dropped steadily from 1860 to 1894 from three to less than two per cent of the total American trade.) It was the consistent shrinkage in the value of silver in terms of gold. Although the volume of trade with China indicated a fairly steady, though slow, increase after the American Civil War, its value in American currency showed an actual shrinkage due to the declining gold value of silver. The increase in volume was not even sufficient to offset the decrease in value. While the trade was valued at $22,472,605 in 1860, thirty years later it was only $19,206,680.

The first column of the following table shows the rapid decline of the average annual dollar exchange of Haikwan Tael, the Chinese standard silver money for foreign trade. In 1871, one H. K. Tael was exchanged for $1.58. Only twenty-four years later the gold value of the H. K. Tael dropped to $0.77, not even half of its former value. As a result of this unfavorable exchange for China, purchases by the Chinese from America were naturally discouraged. That is the reason why American exports to China failed to show any increase in value and actually decreased during this period.

That American trade with China did make some irregular increase from the viewpoint of the Chinese, though not from that of the Americans, may be seen from the following table in which the trade is recorded in terms of the silver Haikwan Taels, and then converted into American dollars:

[1] For further information and discussion on Japanese competition, cf. Chs. on Tea and Silk, *infra.*

TABLE 4

| Year | Rate of each 1 HK Tl | U. S. Imports from China | | U. S. Exports to China | | Total Direct Trade | |
|---|---|---|---|---|---|---|---|
| | | In HK T 1000 | In $1000 | In HK T 1000 | In $1000 | In HK T 1000 | In $1000 |
| 1871 | $1.58 | 10,358 | 16,366 | 449 | 710 | 10,807 | 17,067 |
| 1876 | 1.45 | 7,259 | 10,526 | 739 | 1,071 | 7,998 | 11,597 |
| 1881 | 1.37 | 10,222 | 16,867 | 3,300 | 4,505 | 13,523 | 21,372 |
| 1886 | 1.22 | 9,686 | 11,816 | 4,647 | 5,670 | 14,333 | 17,486 |
| 1891 | 1.20 | 9,034 | 10,840 | 7,732 | 9,278 | 16,765 | 20,188 |
| 1894 | .77 | 9,264 | 7,133 | 16,443 | 12,661 | 25,706 | 19,794 |

Data from Chinese Maritime Customs Returns.

In the last two columns, those of total direct trade, we notice that the trade as recorded in silver value jumped from 10,807,000 HK Taels in 1871, to 25,706,000 HK Taels in 1894, an increase of nearly 120%. But when we value the same trade in gold the increase is only from $17,067,000 to $19,794,000, hardly twenty percent.

*(e) The ill-feeling between Americans and Chinese as a result of the problem of Chinese Immigration.* But in addition to all the causes enumerated above, there is still another which for the most part accounts for the dry-rot of Chino-American trade during this period. It is the consensus of opinion in business circles that good-will between buyers and sellers is the most effective agent for trade expansion. But during the later decades of the last century, China's good-will toward the United States was at least temporarily marred by a very unpleasant problem which resulted in the exclusion from the United States, of Chinese, not only laborers as provided in the Treaty of 1880, but very frequently discrimination against merchants and travelers. This exclusion was followed some years later by a Chinese boycott against American goods as a measure of retaliation. How could the Sino-American trade have had any rapid increase under such conditions?

Chinese immigration has been such a big problem in the United States that it has seriously engaged the attention of American economists, politicians, legislators, unionists, and writers for nearly thirty years. To give any full description of the question here is out of the scope of this treatise, but it concerns the history of American trade with China to such an extent that we must give it at least a passing notice in order to understand one important cause which deferred the rapid development of trade between these countries for at least one generation.

The root of Chinese immigration had been planted in the hideous "coolie trade," which we have already touched upon in a previous section. During the first few years of their coming, the Chinese, mostly in California, were welcomed, and looked upon with favor. But gradually a feeling of opposition to them began to grow up, fomented by the jealousy and race prejudice of the native miners.[1] Their different appearance and customs began to make them the objects of suspicion and hatred and the scapegoats for all the ills that afflicted these communities, and in time an anti-Chinese declaration came to be essential for the success of any political party or candidate. In such a state of public opinion it was inevitable that their lot should be a hard one. "They were robbed, beaten, murdered, and persecuted in a variety of ways. The foreign miners' license tax was used against them in a discriminating way which amounted to quasi-legal plunder."[2]

In response to the repeated demands of the coast states for some federal action to debar the Chinese, the United States Congress in 1876 appointed a special committee on Chinese immigration, which made what purported to be a thorough investigation of the matter, and reported thereupon. The report was wholly anti-Chinese. But this was inevitable, as it is apparent from a careful study of the testimony, that the

[1] Fairchild: *Immigration*, New York, 1913, p. 99.
[2] *Ibid.*, p. 101.

committee "came to its task committed to an Anti-Chinese conclusion and that it had no judicial character whatever."[1] "The evidence was willfully distorted to produce the desired result."[2]

During all this time the relations between the United States and China had been nominally subject to a series of treaties, including the famous Burlingame treaty of 1868,[3] by which the right of voluntary emigration was definitely recognized as between the two countries on the basis of the most favored nation clause, though "it was not to be interpreted to include the privilege of naturalization." It became evident that no federal legislation, satisfactory to the politicians of the western states could be secured under the existing treaties. After much conference between the representatives of the United States and China, a new treaty was signed in 1880, the most important feature of which was the right conferred upon the government of the United States reasonably to regulate, limit, or suspend, but not prohibit, the coming or residence of Chinese laborers, whenever it deemed that the interests of the country demanded such action. It is under this treaty that the various Chinese exclusion acts have been passed by the United States Congress. The first of these acts was passed in 1882, and provided for the exclusion of Chinese laborers for a period of ten years. The strictness of the exclusion was increased by the second act of 1888, and the terms were extended for another ten years by the act of 1892, and again indefinitely extended in 1902.

From the initial negotiations of the treaty of 1880, it is evident that the object of the American Government was to secure the prohibition of Chinese laborers only, and no other class, and to this the consent of the Chinese Government was given. "But as the exclusion law stood at the end of the

[1] Coolidge, Mary R., *Chinese Immigration*, p. 107.
[2] Fairchild, *op. cit.*, p. 102.
[3] See Chapter XIV, *infra.*

last century, aside from the four classes named in the treaty of 1894, viz., students, merchants, travellers, and officials, the following classes could not enter the United States, to wit: bankers, lawyers, journalists, priests, and the clergy, physicians, dentists, insurance agents, brokers, and travelling commercial agents. . . . In fact, the laws on the subject seemed to be in such a state of hopeless confusion that "different Attorney-Generals of the United States rendered conflicting opinions as to the meaning of certain requirements, with the result that the Chinese immigrants whether resident merchants or travelling agents, were made to suffer great hardship in their attempt to land in the United States, and after being admitted, they were incessantly harassed by immigration agents of the Government with domiciliary visits and unreasonable interruptions while pursuing their lawful business in this country."[1]

The bad effects which the immigration problem entailed on the Chino-American trade may be briefly enumerated as follows:

First, it hurt the tender feelings of the Chinese and for a long time nullified their good will toward the Americans which they had entertained since direct trade was established between these two peoples. This resulted otherwise in antagonism to the use of American goods, which culminated in a violent boycott movement against everything American.

Secondly, the unreasonable hampering of the coming to this country of such Chinese as bankers, journalists, lawyers, insurance agents, brokers, travelling commercial agents and other professional men naturally debarred the Chinese from taking active part in the import and export trade of the United States. This fact, coupled with the declining interest of American business men in trade with China owing to the

[1] See "boycott" in the following chapter.
[2] *Commercial Relations between the U. S. and China*, by Sir Chantung Liang Cheng, Chinese Minister to Washington, *Harper's Weekly*, Dec. 23, 1905, p. 1860 and p. 1877.

internal development of the United States, accounts largely for the tardiness in the growth of Chino-American trade.

### Composition of the Trade

During this sub-period, the composition of the Chinese-American trade experienced one important change, viz., the introduction of many new articles which were to play important rôles in later periods. Drugs, dyes, chemicals, straw materials for hats and bonnets, vegetable oils, hides and skins, furs and wool, one after another entered into the list of imports from China while to the exports from the United States were added tobacco and mineral oils. Tea and silk, nevertheless, retained their leading positions among the imports, and cotton goods among the exports. This period may be looked upon as one of transition. Table 5 shows the annual value of some important items of the trade at five-year intervals.

### Balance of Trade and Specie Shipment

Beginning with 1871, when the exportation of specie and bullion from America to China and Hongkong was separately reported, we can calculate the balance of trade down to 1894 as shown in Table 6. The interesting features of this table are: first, that the trade of China as a whole was still consistently in favor of China as it had been in previous periods; second, that the condition is just the reverse with the Hongkong trade whose balance was then, as now still is, consistently against Hongkong. If we assume the Hongkong trade as largely a part of the trade of China and offset the two opposite balances in corresponding years we get a net balance amounting to $300,467,239 for a period of twenty-four years.

The consistent exports of silver and gold from America to the Orient as shown in the last column were doubtless for the part payment of this enormous trade balance. From 1875 on, when separate statistics for China and for Hongkong have become available, specie imports from and exports to China showed great fluctuations; sometimes a net import, as

TABLE 5

COMPOSITION OF AMERICAN TRADE WITH CHINA

| Article | 1870 $1,000 | 1875 $1,000 | 1880 $1,000 | 1885 $1,000 | 1890 $1,000 |
|---|---|---|---|---|---|
| Imports from China: | | | | | |
| Tea | 9,796 | 8,746 | 9,995 | 8,039 | 6,858 |
| Silk, raw and mfrs. | 477 | 682 | 6,937 | 3,787 | 4,466 |
| Drugs, dyes, opium | 650 | 540 | 1,089 | 346 | 407 |
| Hats, bonnets, material of | 216 | 446 | 829 | 980 | 892 |
| Vegetable oils | 95 | 200 | 162 | 189 | 140 |
| Hemp, jute, and mfrs. of. | 375 | 409 | 529 | 37 | 5 |
| Rice and rice flour | 520 | 931 | 980 | 730 | 603 |
| Spices, sugar, and fruits.. | 859 | 574 | 311 | 181 | 150 |
| Hides and skins | .... | .... | 70 | 380 | 130 |
| Furs | .... | .... | .... | 222 | 292 |
| Wool | .... | .... | .... | 103 | 814 |
| Wool and cotton clothing. | 75 | 80 | 77 | 156 | 86 |
| Other articles | 1,566 | 872 | 1,620 | 1,142 | 1,417 |
| Total | 14,629 | 13,480 | 21,770 | 16,292 | 16,260 |
| Exports to China: | | | | | |
| Cotton mfrs. | 626 | 553 | 339 | 3,443 | 1,231 |
| Coal | 620 | 53 | 10 | 3 | 1 |
| Iron and steel mfrs. | 114 | 134 | 41 | 802 | 74 |
| Mineral oil | 142 | 411 | 366 | 1,455 | 1,301 |
| Tobacco | 39 | 11 | 5 | 14 | 41 |
| Wheat and flour | 839 | 35 | 66 | 46 | 59 |
| Other articles | 667 | 268 | 274 | 743 | 243 |
| Total | 3,047 | 1,466 | 1,101 | 6,396 | 2,944 |

in 1875 and 1876, usually extremely small, but amounting in 1887 to half a million dollars. When combined with Hong-kong, however, a net export of considerable quantities is shown. In this table it is indicated that $207,320,000 worth of specie and bullion was sent to Hongkong and China, which amounts to little more than two-thirds of the net trade balance during the same period. How the remaining one-third was paid by the Americans we have no way of know-ing. A fair guess is that it was paid, as formerly, by bills

on London, or on continental countries, because the balance of Chinese-European trade was, contrary to the present case, invariably against China to a very considerable amount.

TABLE 6

BALANCES OF AMERICAN TRADE WITH CHINA AND HONGKONG AND NET SPECIE SHIPMENTS THERETO, 1871-94

Unit = $1,000

| Year | Balance in Favor of China | Balance against Hongkong | Net Balance in Favor of China and Hongkong | Specie (Net) Exported from U. S. A. to China and Hongkong |
|---|---|---|---|---|
| 1871 | 17,994 | * | 17,994 | 3,570 |
| 1872 | 23,816 | * | 23,816 | 5,999 |
| 1873 | 25,291 | * | 25,291 | 7,154 |
| 1874 | 17,276 | * | 17,276 | 9,341 |
| 1875 | 12,009 | 899 | 11,110 | 6,596 |
| 1876 | 10,964 | 2,446 | 8,118 | 7,923 |
| 1877 | 9,423 | 2,059 | 7,364 | 15,420 |
| 1878 | 12,283 | 1,030 | 11,253 | 16,205 |
| 1879 | 13,780 | 1,637 | 12,142 | 7,297 |
| 1880 | 20,668 | 626 | 20,042 | 6,422 |
| 1881 | 16,870 | 517 | 16,353 | 3,437 |
| 1882 | 14,318 | 804 | 13,515 | 4,414 |
| 1883 | 16,061 | 1,859 | 14,202 | 6,948 |
| 1884 | 10,990 | 1,579 | 9,411 | 9,336 |
| 1885 | 9,896 | 3,165 | 6,230 | 14,572 |
| 1886 | 11,450 | 2,984 | 8,469 | 10,245 |
| 1887 | 12,830 | 1,548 | 11,283 | 10,713 |
| 1888 | 12,108 | 1,906 | 10,202 | 7,552 |
| 1889 | 11,237 | 2,206 | 9,031 | 14,035 |
| 1890 | 13,314 | 3,469 | 9,845 | 10,421 |
| 1891 | 10,621 | 4,205 | 6,415 | 4,646 |
| 1892 | 14,825 | 4,131 | 10,794 | 7,430 |
| 1893 | 16,731 | 3,339 | 13,398 | 8,535 |
| 1894 | 11,273 | 3,317 | 7,955 | 9,111 |
| Total of 24 yrs. | 34,034 | 41,527 | 300,467 | 207.320 |

* Before 1874, inclusive, American-Hongkong trade was included in American-Chinese trade.

CHAPTER III

THE PERIOD OF DISTURBANCES AND SEVERE COMPETITION, 1895-1913

For at least two reasons the close of the Sino-Japanese War in 1895 may serve as a clear line of demarcation be-tween the previous and the present period. First, the war led to a series of more or less connected disturbances in the Orient, which had a great effect upon American trade over there as well as upon that of other countries. The defeat of China awakened the Chinese and resulted in the phenomenal reorganization of the Chinese Government by the pro-gressives in 1898. This in turn had its reaction in the re-storation of political power to the conservatives. The Boxer trouble followed in immediate succession in 1899, and then the Russo-Japanese War in 1904-5. As a final issue of the unpleasant problem of Chinese immigration in this country, a violent Chinese boycott movement arose in 1905 against American trade. Five years later, the Chinese Revolution marked a complete upset of old Chinese tradition, socially, politically and economically. On the other side of the Pacific the purchase of Alaska, the annexation of the Hawaii Islands, the occupation of the Philippines and the excavation of the Panama Canal gave the United States a new commercial status in the Pacific. All these disturbances had their respective effects in shaping American trade with China.

Secondly, the Sino-Japanese War marks the beginning of an era in which the severity of international competition for Chinese trade was to attain its zenith. Although China's lack of military strength had become well known since her defeat in the Opium War in 1842, it was still not so completely revealed to the Western World as after her war with Japan. Led by Japan, to which Formosa was ceded, and Russia, to

which Southern Manchuria was leased, Great Britain, France, Germany, and even at one time, Italy, all rushed into this vast empire with a common land-grabbing policy. Permanent leases were granted and spheres of influence were at once created in various places. All of them, with the single exception of the United States, wanted nothing less than complete colonization of the Far East.

Moreover, the rapid expansion of the privileges of foreigners in China dates from the Treaty of Shimmonosiki between Japan and China in 1895 [1] as a result of this import-ant war. This was followed by another Sino-Japanese com-mercial treaty in the following year.[2] The important feat-ures of the two treaties were that they opened the waters of the Chinese rivers and canals to citizens of other nations, giving the foreigners the right to purchase goods or produce in the interior of China, to rent warehouses without the payment of special taxes, and to engage freely in all kinds of manufacturing industries in the treaty ports; also to import all kinds of machinery, paying only the stipulated import duties thereon, and upon products manufactured by them in China, paying only such inland transit dues as are leviable on imported merchandise. (The latter provision having been somewhat modified, however, by commercial treaty.) While the Sino-Japanese treaty specifically conferred these privi-leges only upon Japanese subjects, they at once became appli-cable to the peoples of other nations having full treaty relations with China under the "most favored nation" prin-ciple. The prompt result of this complete opening of China, so ruinous to her own industry and commerce, was a move-ment from all parts of the business world in the direction of the East.

In fact, business competition in China had become so keen that the complete opening of China, hitherto so much desired

[1] MacMurray, Treaties and Agreements with and Concerning China, No. 1895/3, p. 18 ff.
[2] Ibid., No. 1896/4, p. 68 ff.

by foreigners, now turned out to be the chief element in their dissatisfaction. Each of the western powers attempted to close the door of certain provinces in China in the face of others, in order that they might exterminate competition by preferential rights. In such a state of affairs it is no wonder that the United States, with no intention of colonizing any part of China, should have been handicapped in her trade with that country. It was to remove this handicap that the United States, through Secretary Hay's able speech, declared her policy of the Open Door of China.[1]

It has been noted that the decline of American trade with China in the later years of the nineteenth century was partly due to the internal development of America, which absorbed all her capital and engaged the full energy of her people. But with the close of the last century, her internal development had attained almost full completion, and therefore both capital and capability could be partly released from domestic enterprises and put back again into the development of foreign commerce. In addition it was necessary that the huge home industry of America should find an outlet for its products outside its own territory. It also needed such raw materials as could not be adequately supplied by its own soil. Foreign trade, therefore, now came to attract its attention. But for the United States both as a buyer and a seller, South America was then a better market than the Far East. The Americans did not fail to see, however, that the Orient would in the near future come out as one of the biggest markets in the world. For this reason, their interest in foreign trade was diverted towards the East. That they now had an intense interest in the Far Eastern trade was evidenced not only by the declaration of the Open Door Policy in China but also by the acquisition of the Philippines and the proposed excavation of the Panama Canal. With the increasing trade interest there was also the gradual increase in the quantity of Chino-American trade. Table 7 gives the complete trade

[1] See Chapter 14, infra.

statistics for this period of twenty years. The absolute volume of trade was decidedly on the increase, although the increase was quite irregular. In 1896 the total Chino-American trade amounted to a value of $29,000,000. In the following five years, trade increased rather consistently until in 1900 it reached a total of $42,156,000. But in the next year, 1901, the value suffered a severe decline of 32%, which might have been due to the disturbing effect of the Boxer trouble in the northern provinces of China, although there has been no detailed and accurate estimate of the loss in trade which the United States suffered from this anti-foreigns uprising. The American Consul of Chefoo reported in 1901[1] that in his estimation the loss to the American cotton trade alone was over $3,000,000.

But the temporary disturbance passed over quickly and American trade with China had fully recovered in 1902. In 1905 and 1906 due to the Russo-Japanese War the trade attained its high water mark, the great demand for war materials and provisions in Manchuria being the cause of this phenomenal expansion.

As soon as the war demand in Manchuria for food and provisions dwindled, the volume of American trade again decreased to a pre-war figure, and remained around the $50,000,000 mark, making no substantial increase until 1914.

### The Comparative Importance of the Trade

Although the absolute volume of trade in this period shows some increase, its comparative importance did not change, so far as China is concerned. Table 8 shows the distribution of China's foreign trade by countries:

In 1896 the American share was 6.7%. This increased to 15.0% in 1905 and then again declined to 7.6% in 1913. Its variations year after year represent a fairly normal bell-shaped curve; the end does not much exceed the beginning.

[1] U. S. Bureau of Statistics (Treas. Dept.) Commercial China 1901, p. 2827 ff.

TABLE 7

VALUE OF AMERICAN IMPORTS FROM AND EXPORTS TO CHINA AND HONGKONG, 1895-1913. Unit = $1,000.

| Year ending June 30 | China Imports | China Exports | China Total | China, Leased Territories Imports | China, Leased Territories Exports | China, Leased Territories Total | Hongkong[1] Imports | Hongkong[1] Exports | Hongkong[1] Total | Total Imports | Total Exports | Total Total |
|---|---|---|---|---|---|---|---|---|---|---|---|---|
| 1895 | 20,546 | 3,604 | 24,150 | | | | 776 | 4,253 | 5,029 | 21,322 | 7,857 | 29,179 |
| 1896 | 22,023 | 6,922 | 28,945 | | | | 1,416 | 4,691 | 6,110 | 23,442 | 11,613 | 35,055 |
| 1897 | 20,404 | 11,924 | 32,328 | | | | 924 | 6,060 | 6,984 | 21,328 | 17,984 | 39,312 |
| 1898 | 20,326 | 9,993 | 30,319 | | | | 747 | 6,265 | 7,012 | 21,073 | 16,258 | 37,331 |
| 1899 | 18,619 | 14,493 | 33,112 | | | | 2,479 | 7,733 | 10,212 | 21,098 | 22,226 | 43,325 |
| 1900 | 26,897 | 15,259 | 42,156 | | 5 | 5 | 1,256 | 8,486 | 9,742 | 28,158 | 24,112 | 52,270 |
| 1901 | 18,304 | 10,406 | 28,710 | | | | 1,416 | 8,010 | 9,426 | 19,720 | 18,793 | 38,513 |
| 1902 | 21,056 | 24,723 | 45,779 | 372 | 8 | 372 | 1,278 | 8,030 | 9,308 | 22,342 | 33,292 | 55,634 |
| 1903 | 26,649 | 18,898 | 45,547 | 377 | | 377 | 1,360 | 8,772 | 10,132 | 28,033 | 28,381 | 56,414 |
| 1904 | 29,345 | 12,862 | 42,207 | 547 | 8 | 547 | 1,519 | 10,459 | 11,978 | 30,872 | 23,939 | 54,811 |
| 1905 | 27,685 | 53,653 | 81,338 | 735 | 24 | 711 | 1,360 | 10,770 | 12,322 | 29,439 | 64,395 | 93,834 |
| 1906 | 28,531 | 43,774 | 72,305 | 626 | 8 | 626 | 1,552 | 7,049 | 8,674 | 30,396 | 51,070 | 81,466 |
| 1907 | 33,437 | 25,705 | 59,141 | 174 | 2 | 172 | 1,829 | 8,332 | 11,073 | 36,378 | 35,590 | 72,328 |
| 1908 | 26,021 | 22,344 | 48,365 | 287 | 36 | 251 | 2,741 | 8,975 | 11,104 | 28,729 | 39,996 | 68,825 |
| 1909 | 28,799 | 19,420 | 48,219 | 2,113 | 200 | 1,913 | 2,129 | 7,268 | 9,037 | 31,212 | 27,217 | 58,439 |
| 1910 | 29,990 | 16,321 | 46,311 | 9,266 | 579 | 8,677 | 1,769 | 7,756 | 10,474 | 33,630 | 23,438 | 57,068 |
| 1911 | 34,228 | 19,288 | 53,516 | 1,173 | 644 | 529 | 2,332 | 6,467 | 8,799 | 37,999 | 27,979 | 65,978 |
| 1912 | 29,574 | 24,361 | 53,935 | 1,958 | 1,308 | 650 | 2,718 | 10,334 | 13,449 | 33,575 | 35,621 | 69,195 |
| 1913 | 39,011 | 21,327 | 60,338 | 1,988 | 1,053 | 935 | 4,020 | 10,431 | 14,451 | 43,776 | 32,871 | 76,647 |
| | | | | 1,812 | 886 | 925 | | | | | | |
| | | | | 1,858 | 745 | 1,113 | | | | | | |

[1] See Ch. II, p. 17, supra, and Ch. IV, footnote on Hongkong Allowance, infra.

TABLE 8

DISTRIBUTION OF THE FOREIGN TRADE OF CHINA TO THE FOLLOWING COUNTRIES IN PERCENTAGES

| Year | U. S. of America | Great Britain | British India | Europe except Russia | Russia and Siberia | Germany | France | Japan | Hong-kong |
|---|---|---|---|---|---|---|---|---|---|
| 1896 | 6.7% | 16.5% | 7.4% | 8.0% | 5.0% | | | 8.4% | 42.5% |
| 1899 | 9.5 | 11.7 | 7.8 | 10.2 | 2.2 | | | 11.5 | 41.6 |
| 1902 | 10.5 | 12.8 | 6.8 | 10.8 | 8.1 | | | 12.2 | 40.8 |
| 1905 | 15.0 | 14.9 | 5.5 | 9.8 | 4.3 | | | 14.0 | 31.4 |
| 1908 | 9.9 | 12.7 | 5.1 | | 5.4 | 3.1% | 5.8% | 15.3 | 36.1 |
| 1911 | 8.7 | 12.4 | 4.9 | | 4.8 | 4.2 | 5.4 | 17.1 | 29.3 |
| 1913 | 7.6 | 11.4 | 5.5 | | 6.0 | 4.5 | 5.3 | 19.7 | 29.1 |

Data computed from the China's Maritime Customs Returns.

The share of Great Britain, including that of British India, shows a downward trend while Japan's share represents a consistent increase, more than doubling in twenty years. The share of Continental Europe was also increasing, especially that of Germany.

Turning to the other side, we notice a downward trend in the importance of Chinese trade to the United States. During this period American trade with the Far East as a whole expanded, especially trade with Japan and the British East Indies. But the reverse is the case with Chino-American trade.

TABLE 9

Percentages of total values of imports from and exports to the Oriental countries computed on the total values of imports and exports of the United States as bases.

| Year | China | | | Hongkong | | | Japan | | |
|------|------|------|-------|------|------|-------|------|------|-------|
|      | Imp. | Exp. | Total | Imp. | Exp. | Total | Imp. | Exp. | Total |
| 1895 | 2.81 | 0.45 | 1.57 | 0.11 | 0.53 | 0.33 | 3.24 | 0.57 | 1.84 |
| 1900 | 3.18 | 1.10 | 1.88 | 0.15 | 0.62 | 0.43 | 3.84 | 2.08 | 2.74 |
| 1905 | 2.51 | 3.52 | 3.08 | 0.14 | 0.71 | 0.47 | 4.64 | 3.40 | 3.92 |
| 1910 | 1.92 | 0.94 | 1.40 | 0.15 | 0.37 | 0.26 | 4.26 | 1.26 | 2.68 |
| 1913 | 2.15 | 0.87 | 1.48 | 0.22 | 0.42 | 0.33 | 5.05 | 2.35 | 4.00 |

| Year | British East Indies | | | Dutch East Indies | | |
|------|------|------|-------|------|------|-------|
|      | Imp. | Exp. | Total | Imp. | Exp. | Total |
| 1895 | 2.90 | 0.35 | 1.57 | 1.06 | 0.14 | 0.58 |
| 1900 | 5.34 | 0.34 | 2.24 | 3.28 | 0.11 | 1.31 |
| 1905 | 4.80 | 0.50 | 2.32 | 1.65 | 0.11 | 0.76 |
| 1910 | 4.53 | 0.54 | 2.43 | 0.68 | 0.13 | 0.39 |
| 1913 | 6.41 | 0.61 | 3.28 | 0.34 | 0.13 | 0.25 |

In 1900 American imports from China amounted to 3.18% of the total imports of the United States; ten years later it dropped to 1.92% recovering only slightly in 1913, when it reached 2.15%. In the former year exports to China were

1.10% of the total American exports; in the latter year its percentage decreased to 0.94% and again to 0.87% in 1913. As a whole, the trade with China diminished from 1.57% in 1895 to 1.40% in 1910 and 1.48% in 1913, while that with Japan increased in the same period from 1.84% to 4.00%, and that with British East Indies from 1.57% to 3.28%. (See Table 9.)

The decline in the relative importance of Chinese trade to the United States may be expressed in another way: In 1900 China was the tenth best customer for American goods, in 1913 her rank dropped to the thirteenth. In 1900 she ranked sixth among the countries importing goods from the United States, but in 1913 her place was again relegated to ninth.

So marked a decline naturally attracts attention and requires explanation. But if we explain the development of the trade in the early half of the period by the renewal of commercial interest of the Americans in the Far East, by the complete opening of China, not only to foreign traders, but also to foreign manufacturers, and also by the temporary war demand for food and clothing in Manchuria, how shall we explain its decline in the latter half?

*Decline of American Exports to China after 1905*

The decline of American trade with China after 1905 was especially marked in the exports to China and it may be graphically pictured in the successive dropping of figures. In 1905 American exports to China, including Hongkong, were valued at sixty-four million dollars, the first drop was from this figure to fifty-one millions in 1906, then to thirty-six millions in 1907. It rose a little to forty millions in 1908,[1] only to drop again to twenty-nine millions in 1909, and finally to twenty-three millions in 1910, only a little more than one-fourth of the maximum figure of five years

[1] This unusual rise was due to heavy exports of railroad materials and equipment to South Manchuria.

previous.[1] After 1910 it gradually recovered, but in 1913 it still did not exceed thirty-three millions.[2]

*Reasons for the Decline*

*(a) Foreign Competition in China.* The first and the most obvious reason for this serious decline was the very keen competition among manufacturers and traders of various countries seeking a market in that country for their growing output. As to the degree of keenness of such competition we get a vivid impression from the following passages graphically presented by Mr. F. McCormick, an expert in the trade of the Far East thirteen years ago:[3]

"Previous to the beginning of the present century foreign goods were laid down on the seaboard docks in China, and, it might be said, left for the Chinese to carry away as they chose. . . . . Now the foreign trader has been forced by competition to go into the highways and byways himself. Today over China's highways plod the consular official, compiling trade reports, the civilian inspector, as well as the foreign trader himself; and even the foreign itinerant vendor hawking patent medicines, etc. In Manchuria, foreign traders are surprised to find Japanese hucksters. Even the unadvanced Russia has come into trade conflict with China in Mongolia. It is an active question with England and Russia as to how to deal with the Japanese match trade in Tibet; while under the shadow of the Long White Mountain, on the Korean frontier, Osaka knives are contending with Solingen blades for the favor of the Yalu lumbermen. . . . ."

In this new state of competition American trade failed to discover its true position. America, which had the flower of the Russo-Japanese war trade in 1905, was the only country that did not share the post-bellum prosperity in the Far East. Japan and Germany reaped the profit of this prosperity, Great Britain held her own, while America fell behind.

Of all the countries whose commerce with China was either outstripping or beginning to outstrip America's share,

[1] 1905.
[2] See Table 7.
[3] *American Defeat in the Pacific*, by F. McCormick. The *Outlook*, Vol. 97, p. 68, Jan., 1911.

Germany and Japan were the most strenuous in their efforts to gain a victory in the trade tournament of the Far East. The former made a large investment in her general commerce in China, where her efforts were more strenuous, perhaps, than those of any other power. She minutely and efficiently organized the entire commercial field of China by extending her official system while her traders made what was then admitted to be a "successful conquest of the market" through extensive credits.

The commerce of Japan in China was also formidable at that time since it was most elaborately supported by subsidies, loans, and official encouragement. Japan, with Manchurian coal, successfully competed not only with American coal but also with the Chinese mines. Japanese flour mills in Darien, financed by Government money loaned at four percent, also met all competition.[1] This cut into the American flour trade, losses in which were not compensated by the additional trade in American milling machinery extensively used in Manchuria. The development of the Hokkaido and the Yalu River timber zones by Japan also diminished American timber exports from the Pacific Coast. In 1907, the Japanese even built certain kinds of rolling stock for the South Manchurian Railway of better finish and material at less cost than that supplied by American builders.[1] Although Americans were great steel producers, Japan had even entered the warship competition and many contracts for the construction of smaller-sized Chinese gun-boats were granted to the Japanese builders.[1]

It was chiefly in cotton goods and mineral oils that American trade with China declined during this period. The falling off of cotton goods was caused by the fact that cotton production had been stimulated in China and that large quantities of cotton yarn were secured from India owing to advances in the price of American raw cotton. The latter reason is important because it is related to the rise of

[1] *Ibid.*

Japanese cotton industries and Japanese invasion of the commerce and trade of all nations in Eastern Asia. Japan, therefore, with her formidable tools of trade competition, such as the national assistance to all her important industries after the Russo-Japanese War, the subsidizing of her merchant marine, the investment of imperial funds in industries, the extension of state monopolies of salt, camphor, tobacco, and the railways might be regarded as having made a formidable onslaught upon American trade in China in the lines of cottons, timber, flour, and some other manufactures.

It was not only Japan, however, that "slaughtered" American trade in China. In the two items where the decline was most significant—namely, cottons and oil—India, Russia, and the Dutch East Indies had profited by nearly the whole of America's loss. In steel and machinery, Great Britain, Germany, France, and Belgium had taken the trade.

(*b*) *Boycott in China Against America.* In such a state of keen competition, the good-will of the customer would naturally count a great deal in determining to whom his trade should go. But just at this juncture, China's good-will was lost to America, because of the latter's unjust treatment of the problem of Chinese immigration. The severity of the terms of the Exclusion Act and of the rules regulating the admission of Chinese to the United States was for a time so intolerable to the Chinese that they decided in 1905 to boycott the Americans as a measure of protest and retaliation.

The immediate cause of this boycott movement appears to have been the impending negotiation for a renewal of the Chinese immigration treaty of 1894. The treaty had been denounced in 1904 by the Chinese Minister at Washington because of the mistreatment of Chinese merchants, students, and travelers, such action having become peculiarly "flagrant" after 1899. In May, 1905, the leading merchant guilds and the gentry of Shanghai held a meeting at the Chamber of Commerce, and decided to request Chinese

merchants throughout the empire to stop ordering goods from the United States as a protest against the severe terms of the proposed new Chinese exclusion treaty. In a few days the movement had the endorsement of the gentry, merchants and school teachers of twenty-five treaty ports in China, while Chinese all over the world telegraphed their approval of the action.[1]

But under the enthusiastic guidance of the more violent elements of the society, the movement began to take on the aspect of a general anti-foreign agitation. Remembering the Boxer outbreak, foreigners were more alarmed by this dangerous anti-foreign complexion than by the danger of trade interests. The Chinese Government also feared that the movement might get beyond control and become an excuse for another uprising by the revolutionary elements of the society.

In compliance with the request of the American Government, the Chinese Government issued an imperial edict, warning the people to respect every treaty stipulation under penalty of severe punishment, and pacifying them by the statement that the friendship with the United States was of long standing and that the American Government had promised to discuss the immigration treaty on friendly terms.[2] The viceroys and governers of the various provinces were ordered to issue similar proclamations and were held responsible for "any disorders" and directed to arrest violent agitators. But it was not until President Roosevelt was prompted to take action toward remedying to a certain extent the grievances complained of in the new treaty with China that the movement became quiet on the surface.

The effect of this rather short-lived movement was, however, far-reaching. Although American exports to China reached their greatest value in the very year of the boycott, it should be noted that the demand for American food and

[1] *North China Herald,* July 7, 1905.
[2] U. S. Cong. Doc., 1905-6, S. N. 4641, 225.

clothing came largely from the Japanese and Russian soldiers in Manchuria. The successive decline of American exports to China in the following years, while those of other countries were on the increase, is a clear indication that China did not prefer American goods to those of other countries, because of the ill-feeling toward the Americans. This ill-feeling did not completely disappear until the refunding by the United States of the Boxer Indemnity to China in 1908 and her early recognition of the Chinese Republic in 1912. Since then China has realized that the United States is after all her best friend, and the recovery of good will is directly expressed in the gradual increase of American exports to China since 1910.

(*c*) *The Control of Industrial Development in China by European Capital.* Coupled with the above two main causes is a third cause which explains the stationary status of American trade with China after the Russo-Japanese War: that is, the control of industrial development in China by European capital. American trade was checked by the "monopolizing" of China's trade by foreign nations through their loans to China. It is customary, in making loans to China, for the lenders to benefit by the expenditure of the money. In this way for several years China's orders for steel and railway machinery, mining machinery, arsenal equipment, woolen, cotton, and silk spinning and weaving machinery, leather machinery, minting machinery, and also equipment for steel plants and iron works, were placed in Europe. America during these years could secure only orders for insignificant quantities of electrical supplies, fine printing materials, etc., which could not be obtained elsewhere. The capitalistic nations of Europe were benefited by the Chinese industrial development and by America's losses.

*Steady Increase in American Imports from China*

Having mentioned the causes of the comparative decline

of American exports to China and noted some of its features, we shall now investigate the reasons why American imports from China had also been stationary in the face of expected expansion. These reasons are not difficult to perceive. First, the strong Japanese competition in the American silk market, and the no less strong competition of the British East Indies in the American tea market had blocked the entrance of the two articles which had hitherto occupied the most important position among the articles imported from China. Second, the delay in the development of the vast mineral and agricultural resources of China was also a serious check to further development of American imports therefrom, because the Chinese had few things which were in great demand in America.

In spite of these unfavorable conditions, American imports from China did show some steady increase during this period. In 1895, the total imports from China including Hongkong were valued at twenty-one million dollars; ten years later, they were twenty-nine millions; and in 1913, forty-four millions. Even making allowance for the nominal increase during the upward movement of the general price level, the real increase of the trade is still apparent. But this is nothing more than a normal increase, keeping in nearly even pace the total volume of American imports and Chinese exports.

*Composition of the Trade*

Table 10 is a condensed list of some important articles exported from America to China. Not more than a score of these items exceed in annual value one hundred thousand dollars.

Among all exports, cotton cloth had held the greatest share until the end of the period. Before 1905, it usually amounted from a half to two-thirds of the value of the total exports. China was then the second largest market for cotton piece goods, second only to British India.[1] In 1905, the sale of American cotton goods had attained its zenith in China, amounting to $27,761,000. This market occupied the first rank in American cotton-goods export trade. But since that year, cotton goods export have rapidly declined both in absolute value and in relative importance, as is clearly shown in the table. The loss of this trade, as has been already briefly stated above and will be discussed more fully in a later chapter on cotton goods, was primarily due to the competition of Japanese and Chinese cotton mills, which secured an advantage in the use of cheaper raw material from China and India and in the lower cost of production.

The second important item of American exports was refined mineral oils. Although competition in the oil market in China was very keen, the United States had been able to hold its own throughout the whole period. Oil trade had been steadily increasing in its absolute volume, although its relative importance fluctuated widely from thirty-eight percent of the total exports (1907) to twenty percent (1912).[2]

Tobacco, both manufactured and unmanufactured, held the third place. The increase in its absolute and relative importance as an article of American-Chinese trade was very significant. In 1895, the value of tobacco exports was only a little more than one hundred thousand dollars, and this amount is less than three percent of the total American exports to China. Very rapidly the Chinese were getting the habit of using American tobacco, and in less than twenty years the total value of American tobacco exported to China amounted to more than two million dollars, being nearly ten percent of the total exports.[3]

The fourth place in importance was held by iron and steel machinery and other products. Before 1895, very little

[1] U. S. Bureau of Foreign and Domestic Commerce, Special Agents Series No. 107, Cotton Goods in China, p. 5.
[2] See Chapter 11 on Mineral Oil, infra.
[3] See Chapter 12 on Tobacco, infra.

TABLE 10

COMPOSITION OF AMERICAN EXPORTS TO CHINA, INCLUDING LEASED TERRITORIES, 1895-1913

| No. | Article | 1895 $1,000 | % | 1898 $1,000 | % | 1901 $1,000 | % | 1903 $1,000 | % |
|---|---|---|---|---|---|---|---|---|---|
| 1 | Bread Stuff, excluding wheat flour | 9 | 0.2 | 21 | 0.2 | 144 | 1.3 | 30 | 0.2 |
| 2 | Bread Stuff, wheat flour | 104 | 2.9 | 89 | 0.9 | 334 | 3.1 | 564 | 2.9 |
| 3 | Cars, carriages and parts | | | | | | | | |
| 4 | Copper, ingots, bars, plates, etc. | | | | | | | | |
| 5 | Cotton cloth | 1,703 | 47.3 | 5,196 | 52.0 | 4,553 | 42.5 | 13,690 | 69.6 |
| 6 | Cotton, manufactured | 14 | 0.4 | 371 | 3.7 | 81 | 0.8 | 123 | 0.3 |
| 7 | Fruits and nuts | | | 32 | 0.3 | 284 | 2.6 | 56 | 0.3 |
| 8 | Iron and steel, machinery | | | 121 | 1.2 | 554 | 5.1 | 25 | 0.1 |
| 9 | Iron and steel, other mfrs. | 118 | 3.3 | 244 | 2.4 | 427 | 4.0 | 538 | 2.8 |
| 10 | Meat, dairy products and other provisions | | | 76 | 0.8 | 166 | 1.5 | 166 | 0.8 |
| 11 | Leather and tanned skins | 35 | 1.0 | 5 | 0.1 | 28 | 0.3 | 24 | 0.1 |
| 12 | Oils, mineral, refined | 1,181 | 32.8 | 2,865 | 28.7 | 2,445 | 22.7 | 1,866 | 9.5 |
| 13 | Paraffin and wax | | | | | | | | |
| 14 | Tobacco, unmanufactured | 105 | 2.9 | 328 | 3.3 | 522 | 4.9 | 701 | 3.6 |
| 15 | Tobacco, manufactured | 1 | | 18 | 0.2 | 25 | 0.2 | 11 | 0.1 |
| 16 | Wood, boards and planks | 65 | 1.8 | 120 | 1.2 | 138 | 1.3 | 314 | 1.6 |
| 17 | Wood, manufactures of | 24 | 0.7 | 48 | 0.5 | 304 | 2.7 | 304 | 1.5 |
| 18 | Other articles | 242 | 6.7 | 450 | 4.5 | 957 | 8.9 | 1,178 | 6.0 |
| | Total American exports to China | 3,604 | 100.0 | 9,993 | 100.0 | 10,783 | 100.0 | 19,610 | 100.0 |

TABLE 10—Continued

| Item No. | 1905 $1,000 | % | 1907 $1,000 | % | 1909 $1,000 | % | 1911 $1,000 | % | 1912 $1,000 | % | 1913 $1,000 | % |
|---|---|---|---|---|---|---|---|---|---|---|---|---|
| 1 | 293 | 0.5 | 1,433 | 5.0 | 32 | 0.2 | 44 | 0.2 | 57 | .02 | 50 | 0.2 |
| 2 | 318 | 0.6 | 6,312 | 23.0 | 266 | 1.3 | 1,089 | 5.4 | 2,900 | 11.4 | 493 | 2.2 |
| 3 | | | 279 | 1.0 | 166 | 0.8 | 71 | 0.3 | 116 | 0.5 | 233 | 1.0 |
| 4 | | | 270 | 1.0 | | | | | 164 | 0.6 | 1 | |
| 5 | 27,761 | 51.6 | 5,714 | 20.7 | 8,004 | 40.0 | 5,293 | 26.2 | 7,372 | 29.0 | 5,585 | 24.8 |
| 6 | 9,941 | 18.5 | 301 | 1.1 | 22 | 0.1 | 46 | 0.2 | 2,591 | 10.1 | 464 | 2.1 |
| 7 | 176 | 0.3 | 90 | 0.3 | 49 | 0.2 | 481 | 2.4 | 65 | 0.2 | 78 | 0.3 |
| 8 | 287 | 0.5 | 145 | 0.5 | 303 | 1.5 | 1,715 | 8.5 | 580 | 2.3 | 786 | 3.5 |
| 9 | 1,000 | 1.9 | 1,736 | 6.3 | 97 | 0.5 | 62 | 0.3 | 2,175 | 8.5 | 2,195 | 9.7 |
| 10 | 1,016 | 1.9 | 197 | 0.7 | 81 | 0.4 | 93 | 0.5 | 134 | 0.5 | 143 | 0.6 |
| 11 | 135 | 0.3 | 133 | 0.5 | 85 | 0.4 | | | 100 | 0.4 | 123 | 0.5 |
| 12 | 8,527 | 15.9 | 6,154 | 22.3 | 7,552 | 38.0 | 7,300 | 36.1 | 5,182 | 20.3 | 6,699 | 29.8 |
| 13 | | | 197 | 0.7 | 964 | 4.8 | 377 | 1.9 | 824 | 3.2 | 419 | 1.9 |
| 14 | 1,439 | 2.7 | 1,428 | 5.2 | 274 | 1.4 | 576 | 2.8 | 937 | 3.7 | 1,065 | 4.7 |
| 15 | 460 | 0.9 | 358 | 1.3 | 357 | 1.8 | 764 | 3.8 | 338 | 1.3 | 1,067 | 4.7 |
| 16 | 414 | 0.8 | 976 | 3.5 | 37 | 0.2 | 1,019 | 5.0 | 166 | 0.6 | 864 | 3.8 |
| 17 | 275 | 0.5 | 606 | 2.0 | | | 261 | 1.3 | | | 230 | 1.0 |
| 18 | 1,523 | 2.8 | 1,388 | 5.0 | 714 | 3.6 | 1,032 | 5.1 | 1,162 | 4.6 | 1,317 | 5.8 |
| Total | 53,625 | 100.0 | 27,517 | 100.0 | 19,949 | 100.0 | 20,223 | 100.0 | 25,287 | 100.0 | 22,512 | 100.0 |

American machinery was sold in China; her demand for machinery had been largely supplied by Great Britain, Germany, and Belgium. The reason has been stated in a previous section as the control of China's industrial development by European capital.[1] But as their merits gradually became known in China, trade in American machinery was the inevitable result. Other products such as iron plates, wires, nails, tools, etc., had had a wider market since the closing years of the last period. In 1908 Manchuria alone bought from America one hundred and ninety-eight locomotives valued at $3,059,873; 31,454 tons of steel rails, valued at $1,121,199; and 11,560 tons of iron and steel structure materials, at $860,469. But this was not a normal condition of the trade. Fluctuations in the iron and steel trade were violent from year to year, but at the end of the period China's demand for these products became fairly steady. The volume of their sales usually amounted to from ten to twelve percent of the total exports.[2]

Then came bread stuffs, especially wheat flour, as the fifth item in importance. During the closing years of the nineteenth century the annual exports of American wheat flour and other bread stuffs amounted to scarcely more than $100,000 in value, but since the beginning of the new century most Chinese were beginning to use foreign flour and the Americans were quick to grasp the chance to extend their trade. In 1907 the sales of wheat flour alone amounted to $6,312,000, and of other bread stuffs, to $1,433,000. Combined they reached a total amounting to twenty-eight percent of the total American exports to China in that year. This temporary success suggested to the wheat men of Washington and Oregon that here was an opportunity of developing a large and profitable market for the product of their mills.[3] But China's demand for American flour was any-

[1] See page 92, supra.
[2] See Chapter 13, infra.
[3] American Trade with China, by L. R. Freeman, Engineering Magazine, Jan., 1914, p. 502.

thing but constant, and in a short time she was supplying her people with flour from her own mills. Exports of breadstuffs to China had therefore declined rapidly since 1907.

Other articles of export such as cars, carriages, and leather goods were also on the increase. Wood boards and planks and other manufactures had a fair share in the trade. Trade in copper had been extremely irregular, ranging from nothing in some years to $9,941,000 in 1905. Fruits and nuts had been exported from America to China since the middle of the nineteenth century, but the expensiveness of trade in such perishable products over so long a distance had never warranted any substantial increase in the trade, which had never exceeded the $100,000 mark in any year of the period. This was also true in the case of meat and dairy products, except condensed milk and some other canned goods.

Besides these items enumerated in the list, there were several other articles of export, such as clocks, watches, instruments for scientific purposes, chemicals, drugs, and dyes; electrical machinery and appliances, books and other paper products, etc., for each of which the annual value of trade usually stood below $100,000.

One significant tendency in the American export trade with China as revealed by a general survey of the above table is that products of a simpler form of manufacturing industry were as a whole tending to decrease while those of the highly complex industry were on the increase. Wheat flour and cotton cloth are things of the former type, and China could well develop her own mills and factories to supply them; therefore, their markets in China were rapidly declining. On the other hand, iron and steel machinery and other products, cars, and carriages, etc., are things whose production must be carried on by highly developed large-scale industries such as cannot be installed in China at a

moment's notice. Consequently, their market in China was expanding.

Another characteristic is that American exports of producer's goods to China were just beginning to play a very important role in their trade. Before this time, practically all exports from America to China consisted of consumers' goods. Trade in machinery, materials for construction work, cars, and locomotives, etc., was insignificant. But with the dawn of industrial China her demand for producers' goods became more and more important.

Both these tendencies will express themselves more fully in the next period. The present period, however, is a period of gradual transition.

The composition of American imports from China during the period is shown in Table 11. Among all the items, silk held the first place and was by far the most important. The annual trade in raw silk alone constituted more than one-third of the total American import trade with China. Although Japanese silk competed most formidably in the American market, yet Chinese silk exports had been steadily increasing in both quantity and value. This is due to the rapidly growing silk industry in the United States and the resulting expansion in her demand for raw material. Yet, as we shall see later,[1] China has lost much of her share in the American silk market.

Tea, formerly by far the most important article of American import from China, was steadily losing its importance throughout this period, declining both in absolute quantity and value, and in relative share. In 1895, seven and a half million dollars worth of tea was imported from China; two decades later only half of that sum was imported. In the former year tea constituted 36.8% of the total imports; in the latter, it declined to only 8.2%. This decline will be accounted for later.[2]

[1] See Chapter 7, infra.
[2] See Chapter 6, infra.

The third place in the list is held by wool, whose increasing volume of trade played an important part in this period. In 1895, imports of this article were valued at seventeen million dollars, constituting 8.3% of the whole American imports from China. They increased one decade later to more than three million dollars, 11.2% of the total, and to 4.7 million dollars, with a share of 11.8% in 1913.

Hides and skins are ranked fourth in the list. This only recently came into importance. This is also true regarding such products as vegetable oils, bristles, antimony ore and regulus, all of which had been very insignificant but had been growing in importance towards the end of the term.

The annual importation of chemicals and drugs during the early half of the period had been fairly large in value, usually fluctuating between one to two million dollars. But a substantial part of the "drugs" consisted of prepared opium, which alone amounted in some years to more than one million dollars. The United States Government, however, ordered its prohibition in 1911 and the volume under this item suddenly contracted to a little more than one per cent of total imports.

With a general survey of the list one cannot fail to realize the significant fact that a very great part of the imports consisted of raw or semi-raw materials to supply American industries for further production. With the exception of a few articles such as tea, firecrackers, hairnets, silk piece-goods, and wood manufactures, most of the products were not for immediate consumption. The increasing importation of raw materials and the decreasing importation of finished goods was a trend which had shown itself more and more clearly with the advancement of time. In 1895, finished products constituted nearly half of the total (chemicals, drugs, 4.9%; explosives, firecrackers 1.8%; mats 2.7%; silk manufactures 1.1%; wood manufactures 0.3%; vegetables 0.2%, and tea 36.8%). But as time went on their relative share steadily declined; in 1905 they altogether con-

TABLE II — COMPOSITION OF AMERICAN EXPORTS FROM CHINA, INCLUDING LEASED TERRITORIES, 1895-1913

| Article | 1895 $1,000 | 1895 % | 1898 $1,000 | 1898 % | 1901 $1,000 | 1901 % | 1903 $1,000 | 1903 % | 1913 $1,000 | 1913 % |
|---|---|---|---|---|---|---|---|---|---|---|
| 1. Antimony, ore and regulus | 29 | 0.1 | 8 | | 24 | 0.1 | | | 84 | 0.3 |
| 2. Bristles, sorted and bunched | | | 122 | 0.6 | 127 | 0.7 | | | 403 | 1.5 |
| 3. Chemicals, drugs, dyes, etc. | 997 | 4.9 | 775 | 3.8 | 1,001 | 5.4 | | | 1,465 | 5.5 |
| 4. Cotton, raw | | | | | | | | | | |
| 5. Explosives, firecrackers | 372 | 1.8 | 141 | 0.7 | 235 | 1.3 | | | 217 | 0.8 |
| 6. Fruits and nuts | 276 | 1.3 | 205 | 1.0 | 42 | 0.2 | | | 337 | 1.3 |
| 7. Furs | | | | | | | | | | |
| 8. Hair and hair nets | 565 | 2.8 | 632 | 3.1 | 553 | 3.0 | | | 665 | 2.5 |
| 9. Hides, boards, material of | 481 | 2.3 | 1,211 | 6.0 | 1,453 | 7.9 | | | 2,670 | 10.0 |
| 10. Hides and skins, other than furs | | | | | | | | | | |
| 11. Jute, hemp, and other fibers | 551 | 2.7 | 350 | 1.7 | 986 | 5.4 | | | 739 | 2.8 |
| 12. Matting and mats | 102 | 0.5 | 96 | 0.5 | 128 | 0.7 | | | 286 | 1.1 |
| 13. Meats and dairy products | 504 | 2.4 | 561 | 2.8 | 469 | 2.7 | | | 473 | 1.8 |
| 14. Oil, vegetable | | | | | | | | | | |
| 15. Rice and rice flour | | | | | | | | | | |
| 16. Silk, raw | 5,512 | 26.8 | 7,506 | 36.9 | 6,304 | 34.4 | 8,394 | 33.2 | 6,975 | 26.2 |
| 17. Silk, waste | | | 106 | 0.5 | 63 | 0.3 | | | 242 | 0.9 |
| 18. Silk, manufactures of | 241 | 1.1 | 136 | 0.7 | 150 | 0.8 | | | 193 | 0.7 |
| 19. Spices, unground | | | 22 | 0.1 | 123 | 0.7 | | | 25 | 0.1 |
| 20. Spirits, distilled | 19 | 0.1 | 11 | 0.1 | 24 | 0.1 | | | | |
| 21. Tea | 7,534 | 36.8 | 5,827 | 28.7 | 4,864 | 26.5 | | | 2,187 | 8.2 |
| 22. Vegetable | 95 | 0.2 | 50 | 0.2 | 117 | 0.6 | | | | |
| 23. Wood, manufactures of | 63 | 0.3 | | | 79 | 0.4 | | | 61 | 0.2 |
| 24. Wool, unmanufactured | 1,699 | 8.3 | 1,565 | 7.7 | 631 | 3.4 | | | 3,147 | 11.8 |
| 25. Other articles | 1,370 | 6.7 | 900 | 4.4 | 911 | 5.0 | | | 733 | 2.8 |
| Total American imports from China | 20,546 | 100.0 | 20,325 | 100.0 | 18,304 | 100.0 | | | 26,673 | 100.0 |

stituted a little more than a third and in 1913 even less than one-fifth of the total. This tendency will become still more marked in the next period of our trade history.

### Balance of Trade

Throughout the whole period of one and one-half centuries of Chinese-American trade, the "favorable" balance to China in this period of twenty years was the smallest. In the previous thirty years, the average balance in favor of that country was nearly fifteen million dollars a year. American domestic exports to China was then only one-fourth to one-third of what the United States directly imported from China. But during this period, the old saying, "America needs what China has to sell more than China needs what America has to sell" was losing strength because many kinds of American manufactures gradually came into general use by the Chinese. During the first ten years, the demand of the Chinese for American cottons, mineral oils, wheat flour, and iron and steel products was so heavy that, taking together China and Chinese Leased Territories, the balances of quite a few years were in favor of the United States.

As regards Hongkong, the exports of American foodstuffs and other manufactures to that port increased at a more rapid rate than the American imports therefrom, and the balance was consistently in favor of the United States, averaging nearly six million dollars a year. How much of the American Hongkong balance in this period should be deemed as a part of the Chinese-American balance, we have no way of determining because of the complete lack of trade statistics in Hongkong. One point, however, is sure, that is, as American trade with the South Asiatic countries was now growing, their trade through transshipments at Hongkong was also growing, and the portion of the American Hongkong trade which can be ascribed to China must contract year by year. Besides this generalization any accurate estimate is impossible.

Disregarding the above difficulty and taking a total of the Chinese and Hongkong balances (see table 12), we get an interesting result that the sums of favorable and unfavorable balances during this period almost exactly balance each other. If, therefore, we consider Hongkong as a part of commercial China, the United States was enabled by her growing industry and increasing effort to sell the Orient to square her buying and selling accounts.

### Shipments of Specie

Throughout this period the shipment of specie and bullion was still consistently on the way from the United States to the East, despite that the trade balance left actually nothing to be paid by the United States. From 1895-1913, the total net American export of silver coin and bullion to China and Hongkong combined was $124,000,000, and the net gold export only $504,000. (See Table 13). Of this huge export of silver China received only a little directly from the United States, but, according to the Chinese Customs returns, she imported every year much of this metal from Hongkong, while a large part of this American silver export went on from Hongkong to British India, Straits Settlements, and other south Asiatic countries.

TABLE 13

VALUE OF NET EXPORTS OF GOLD AND SILVER COIN AND BULLION
FROM THE UNITED STATES TO CHINA AND HONGKONG
Unit = $1,000

| Year | Silver | Gold | Net Import of Gold into U. S. Therefrom |
|---|---|---|---|
| 1895 | 8,450 | 75 | ... |
| 1896 | 8,215 | 119 | ... |
| 1897 | 5,460 | 78 | ... |
| 1898 | 7,798 | 64 | ... |
| 1899 | 4,561 | ... | 168 |
| 1900 | 8,209 | 28 | ... |
| 1901 | 8,248 | 370 | ... |
| 1902 | 8,553 | ... | 31 |
| 1903 | 6,910 | 43 | ... |
| 1904 | 2,539 | 122 | ... |
| 1905 | 4,247 | ... | 186 |
| 1906 | 8,385 | 19 | ... |
| 1907 | 1,834 | 13 | ... |
| 1908 | 5,261 | ... | 126 |
| 1909 | 6,267 | 3 | ... |
| 1910 | 4,907 | 2 | ... |
| 1911 | 6,895 | 7 | ... |
| 1912 | 7,620 | ... | 28 |
| 1913 | 9,949 | 100 | ... |
| Total | 124,808 | 1,043 | 539 |
|  |  | 539 |  |
|  | Net gold exp. | 504 |  |

CHAPTER IV

THE PERIOD OF RAPID EXPANSION, 1914-1922

With the outbreak of the European War, trade between the United States and China underwent a complete change, not only in its absolute and relative importance to both countries, but also in the character of the imports and exports. Naturally, when most of the supply of European goods was cut off in China, the Chinese looked for substitutes in the United States. On the other hand, the demand of American industries for raw material to provide for war orders was so urgent and the supply of them became so scarce in the United States, that Americans were compelled to buy many kinds of materials from the Far East which they had never or very seldom bought before. This situation has led to an enormous expansion of Chinese-American trade during the last decade, of which Table 14 presents the annual value.

A few months after the outbreak of the war in 1914 when the nations of the world had begun to readjust themselves to the new conditions, demands began to spring up in the United States as well as in China, for materials to be used in connection with the war, and for products formerly supplied to neutral nations by belligerents who were no longer able to furnish them. Thus one finds, on the one hand, increased demands of the United States for China's antimony, albumen, aniline dyes, indigo paste, woolen carpets, cotton, egg products, vegetable oils, oil seeds, hides, skins, furs, straw braids, wool and silks; and on the other, increased demands in China for more American iron and steel machinery and other manufactures; cars, carriages, and other vehicles; cotton and cotton cloth; electrical machinery and other appliances; rubber and leather manufactures, paper products, tobacco, mineral oils, and lumber.

In addition to this greatly increased demand on both sides,

71

there were other minor causes which helped the growth of the trade during this period. The American import duties on many kinds of raw materials and quite a few manufactures were either greatly reduced or entirely removed by the provisions of the American Tariff Act of 1913, thus stimulating the growth of American imports from China; while silver, the currency in use in China, rose sharply in gold value and thus facilitated China's imports from the United States.

Opposing these favorable conditions under which American trade with China has made extraordinary progress since 1914, there were, however, also a few adverse conditions which tended to check its growth throughout the war and post-war period. First, there was the shortage of trans-oceanic ships and the rise in freight rates. Immediately after 1914 the question of transportation became a serious one, since one-fourth of the world's mercantile tonnage was taken from ordinary trade channels because of the war.[1] The re-adjustment in shipping on this account soon reduced very materially the tonnage in the Pacific, and the shortage of ships at this juncture operated greatly to hinder the Chinese-American trade not only because freight rates had risen continuously but also because there had been times when a large quantity of cargo in China could find no space at any price on ships bound for America.[2] The difficulty was much aggravated by the fact that the greater part of the commodities entering into the trade consisted of cheap and bulky materials; they could not bear a high cost of transportation and were, therefore, seriously affected by the increase in freights from 300 to 500 per cent.[3]

Second of the adverse conditions, from the viewpoint of American importers, was the enormous rise in the price of silver. After 1916 the rate of exchange between the Amer-

[1] U. S. Bur. of For. & Dom. Com., Misc. Series. No. 44, Trans-pacific Shipping, 1916, p. 13.
[2] Ibid., p. 44.
[3] Ibid.

ican gold dollar and the Chinese silver tael became extremely unfavorable to the former. In normal times a tael has been exchangeable for less than seventy cents of American money. But in 1916 the average rate was 79 cents for one tael; in 1917 it went up to $1.03; then to $1.26 and $1.39 in the two successive years. This unfavorable exchange, of course, greatly hampered the growth of American imports from China.

*Actual Increase of the Trade*

But in spite of these two serious disturbing elements against the smooth expansion of trade—the high freight rate and the dislocation of gold-silver exchange—the American demand for Chinese materials increased to such an enormous degree that the quantity and value of American import trade with China actually rose by leaps and bounds throughout this ten-year period, with the exception of the year 1921. In 1914 the total value of American imports from China was thirty-six million dollars; in 1915 it was fifty-three millions, then it rose to eighty millions, to one hundred and twenty-five millions, to one hundred and fifty-four millions, and culminated at one hundred and ninety-three millions in 1920. The drop in 1921 was inevitable because of the business depression in the whole world; yet the trade has speedily recovered since 1922 and in the fiscal year 1923 (ending June 30) the total stood at one hundred and seventy millions. To these figures should be added the value of goods imported from China's leased territories, among which Kwantung, a Japanese lease, was by far the most important. Since the war goods imported from these territories have attained considerable sums. During the four years, 1917-20, they averaged much in excess of ten million dollars a year, and in 1918 the annual figure nearly reached the mark of thirty millions, which equals the value of imports from all China before the war. In 1921, a severe

TABLE 14

VALUE OF AMERICAN TRADE WITH CHINA, 1913-1922.
Unit = $1,000

| Calendar Year | China | | | China Leased Territories | | | Estimated U. S.-China Trade through the port of Hongkong[b] | | | Total | | |
|---|---|---|---|---|---|---|---|---|---|---|---|---|
| | Imports from China | Exports to China | Total | Imp. | Exp. | Total | Imp. | Exp. | Total | Imp. | Exp. | Total |
| 1913 | 40,121 | 25,300 | 65,421 | 745 | 1,113 | 1,858 | 621 | 5,543 | 6,164 | 41,387 | 31,956 | 73,443 |
| 1914 | 36,314 | 20,368 | 56,681 | 929 | 1,647 | 2,576 | 400 | 4,629 | 5,029 | 37,643 | 25,644 | 64,287 |
| 1915 | 52,858 | 19,748 | 72,586 | ᵃ674 | 1,138 | 1,812 | 472 | 4,166 | 4,638 | 54,004 | 25,032 | 79,036 |
| 1916 | 80,042 | 31,516 | 111,558 | 750 | 1,122 | 1,872 | 940 | 6,657 | 7,597 | 81,732 | 39,295 | 121,027 |
| 1917 | 125,106 | 40,292 | 165,398 | 14,818 | 4,957 | 19,775 | 1,558 | 7,879 | 9,437 | 141,482 | 53,128 | 194,610 |
| 1918 | 110,971 | 52,571 | 163,542 | 29,835 | 6,176 | 36,011 | 4,310 | 12,333 | 16,643 | 145,316 | 71,080 | 216,396 |
| 1919 | 154,154 | 105,515 | 259,669 | 15,492 | 12,735 | 28,227 | 3,317 | 11,046 | 14,363 | 172,963 | 129,296 | 302,259 |
| 1920 | 192,708 | 145,737 | 338,445 | 7,139 | 11,514 | 18,653 | 6,879 | 16,985 | 23,864 | 211,101 | 169,861 | 380,962 |
| 1921 | 101,136 | 108,290 | 209,426 | 1,280 | 5,315 | 6,595 | 1,536 | 9,363 | 10,899 | 103,952 | 122,968 | 226,920 |
| 1922 | 134,609 | 100,357 | 234,966 | 2,062 | 5,717 | 7,779 | 2,390 | 10,467 | 12,857 | 139,061 | 116,541 | 255,602 |
| 1923ᶜ | 169,619 | 96,852 | 266,471 | 3,819 | 6,089 | 9,908 | 3,033 | 14,106 | 17,039 | 176,471 | 117,047 | 243,518 |

ᵃ These figures were for fiscal year ending June 30.
ᵇ See table and note on the following pages.
ᶜ Fiscal year ending June 30.

TABLE 14—Continued

| Year | American Imports from Hongkong in $1,000 | 15% of figure in former column is considered as originated from China. In $1,000 | American exports to Hongkong in $1,000 | 50% of figures in former column considered as ultimately re-shipped to China | Total American Hongkong trade in $1,000 | Estimated total Chino-American trade through Hongkong in $1,000 |
|---|---|---|---|---|---|---|
| 1913 | 3,475 | 621 | 11,086 | 5,543 | 14,560 | 6,164 |
| 1914 | 2,664 | 400 | 9,259 | 4,629 | 11,923 | 5,029 |
| 1915 | 3,146 | 472 | 8,332 | 4,166 | 11,478 | 4,638 |
| 1916 | 6,264 | 940 | 13,314 | 6,657 | 19,578 | 7,597 |
| 1917 | 10,384 | 1,558 | 15,747 | 7,879 | 26,131 | 9,437 |
| 1918 | 30,068 | 4,510 | 24,665 | 12,333 | 54,734 | 16,843 |
| 1919 | 22,119 | 3,317 | 22,093 | 11,046 | 44,212 | 14,363 |
| 1920 | 45,860 | 6,879 | 25,971 | 16,985 | 71,767 | 23,864 |
| 1921 | 10,242 | 1,536 | 18,726 | 9,363 | 28,968 | 10,902 |
| 1922 | 15,304 | 2,390 | 20,934 | 10,467 | 36,238 | 12,857 |
| 1923ᵃ | 20,217 | 3,033 | 28,211 | 14,106 | 48,428 | 17,039 |

ᵃ Fiscal year ending June 30.

drop was witnessed and now the trade has not as yet fully recovered.

Nor do these figures tell the whole story. A large part of the trade between the United States and Hongkong is, in fact, a part of the trade between the United States and China.[1] According to the writer's estimate the United States imported each year several million dollars' worth of Chinese goods by way of Hongkong during the war.

[1] See Table 14.

Because of transshipment through the British colony of Hongkong, it is very difficult to determine the true origin of the imports and exports of China from and to any individual country. If the Chinese Maritime Customs returns and the American Foreign Commerce and Navigation statistics are examined it will be found that the Hongkong trade is separately recorded. But the imports from Hongkong come originally from and exports to that colony are further carried on to, Great Britain, the Straits Settlements, the Philippines, etc., and the coast ports of China. Again, Hongkong, being a free port, did not publish actual statistics of its trade until very recently, and even at present it does not publish them in any detail, so it is impossible to know with exact accuracy the amount of its trade, originating in or destined for any particular country.

In 1918 the colony issued Trade and Shipping Returns, representing the first attempt to furnish a complete record of the trade of the colony. But no comparison with earlier years is possible. There are, moreover, certain defects which will no doubt be remedied after a short time. The values given, for instance, are based upon merchants' declarations without further adequate checks as to their correct uses. (Trans-Pacific, Dec., 1919, p. 59.)

The total value of Hongkong's trade during 1918 was £127,991,000, of which £60,934,000 represented imports and £67,057,000 exports. The distribution of the bulk of this trade is indicated by the following table (Ibid.).

Note continued from the preceding page.

YEAR 1918—DISTRIBUTION OF THE FOREIGN TRADE OF HONGKONG

| Countries | Imports into Hongkong | | Exports from Hongkong | | Total Imports and Exports | |
|---|---|---|---|---|---|---|
| | £1,000 | % | £1,000 | % | £1,000 | % |
| China | 9,362 | 15.4 | 37,011 | 55.1 | 45,373 | 35.4 |
| United States | 8,348 | 13.5 | 5,417 | 8.1 | 13,765 | 10.7 |
| United Kingdom | 4,439 | 7.2 | 1,112 | 1.6 | 5,551 | 4.3 |
| British Dominions and Colonies | 8,131 | 13.4 | 7,549 | 11.3 | 15,680 | 12.3 |
| Japan and Korea | 9,819 | 16.1 | 4,494 | 6.5 | 14,313 | 11.2 |
| French Indo-China | 15,289 | 25.0 | 5,854 | 8.5 | 21,143 | 16.5 |
| Other countries | 5,536 | 9.0 | 5,620 | 8.4 | 11,156 | 8.7 |
| Total | 60,934 | 100.0 | 67,057 | 100.0 | 127,991 | 100.0 |

The distribution of Hongkong trade in 1919 by countries as reported in the Trade and Shipping Returns of Hongkong is as follows:

| Countries | Imports into Hongkong | | Exports from Hongkong | | Total Imports and Exports | |
|---|---|---|---|---|---|---|
| | £1,000 | % | £1,000 | % | £1,000 | % |
| China | 12,581 | 13.4 | 52,812 | 50.8 | 65,393 | 33.6 |
| United States | 17,759 | 19.6 | 4,877 | 4.7 | 22,636 | 11.6 |
| British Empire | 19,746 | 21.8 | 18,993 | 18.3 | 38,739 | 19.9 |
| Japan | 9,658 | 10.7 | 9,837 | 9.5 | 19,495 | 10.0 |
| French Indo-China | 13,557 | 14.9 | 8,748 | 8.4 | 22,305 | 11.5 |
| Other countries | 17,351 | 19.1 | 8,675 | 8.3 | 26,026 | 13.4 |
| Total | 90,652 | 100.0 | 103,943 | 100.0 | 194,595 | 100.0 |

From the above statistics it is still impossible for us to determine what part of Chinese goods imported into Hongkong were ultimately transshipped to the United States and other countries, and what part of American goods imported into Hongkong were ultimately destined for China. We can only infer, in the absence of other evi-

*Note continued from the preceding page.*

dence, that the proportion of American exports through Hongkong into China to the total American exports directly to Hongkong is the same as the proportion of Hongkong exports to China to the total exports of Hongkong. Expressing this statement in the form of an equation, we have:

$$\frac{\text{U. S. exports through Hongkong to China}}{\text{Total U. S. exports to Hongkong}} = \frac{\text{Hongkong exports to China}}{\text{Total Hongkong exports}}$$

In connection with American imports from China through Hongkong, we may ascertain their proportion by analogy:

$$\frac{\text{U. S. imports from China through Hongkong}}{\text{Total U. S. imports from Hongkong}} = \frac{\text{Hongkong imports from China}}{\text{Total Hongkong imports}}$$

According to the statistics shown in the above tables, $\frac{\text{Hongkong Exports to China}}{\text{Total Hongkong Exports}}$ were 55.1% in 1918 and 50.8% in 1919; and $\frac{\text{Hongkong Imports from China}}{\text{Total Hongkong Imports}}$ were 15.4% in 1918, and 13.9% in 1919. Neglecting the small differences, we may assume that about half or 50% of Hongkong's exports goes to China and about 15% or nearly one-seventh of Hongkong's imports comes from China. If we apply these same proportions to the Imports and Exports of the United States from and to Hongkong we can roughly ascertain what part of the American Hongkong trade is really American trade with China.

The estimated figures of the American imports of Chinese goods through Hongkong, however, are too small. But any attempt to calculate the real value of the trade would be futile. The confusion is aggravated by the fact that the products of the Chinese southwestern provinces are exported first to Indo-China, then to Hongkong and then finally to the United States as well as to other countries. Much of the trade of Hongkong credited to Indo-China really originated in the Yunnan Province of China. For instance, in 1918 the United States imported from Hongkong tin in bars, blocks, pig, etc., to the value of more than ten million dollars (Commerce and Navigation, 1918), most of which must have originated in the Province of Yunnan by way of Indo-China, but actually how much could never be known.

Taking the total American imports directly from China, both through Chinese leased territories and by transshipment through Hongkong, we have the following annual figures representing the increase in the value of imports (Table 15, Column A).

If we take the value for the year 1913 as a base, and convert the values for succeeding years into index numbers (Column B) we get ninety-one for 1914, representing a drop of nine percent from that of the preceding year. But the index rose suddenly to 130 in 1915, to 198 in 1916, and again made a huge stride to 342 in 1917, then increased steadily to 351 in 1918, to 418 in 1919, and attained its zenith of 510 in 1920. It means that the American import trade with China quintupled in a period of eight years. In 1921 there occurred a big drop; but this drop was entirely due to the business depression in this country and was only temporary in nature. As American business conditions were picking up in 1922-23, the index of the import trade followed the same trend, recovering to 427. But this rate of increase in value, we must admit, does not truly represent the real increase in the volume of trade. In order to ascertain the real increase, we have to make certain allowances for price inflation during the war. As the valuation of imported goods is made at the port of origination, the price allowance here to be made must be based upon the changes in the general price level in China. A general price index number constructed by the writer last year becomes available here.[1] But this index is constructed on silver prices and if we want to use it here we must first convert this silver price index into a gold price index. This is done in columns D, E, F of Table 15. We see from the index in column F that the rise of gold prices of Chinese exports nearly kept pace with the rise in Amer-

[1] See column C in Table 15. This index number was constructed with the prices of the most important exports of China: Raw silk, manufactured silk, hides and skins, tea, wool, cotton, beans, wood oil, bean oil, indigo.

TABLE 15

STATISTICS SHOWING THE REAL INCREASE OF THE VOLUME OF AMERICAN IMPORTS FROM CHINA, 1913-1923

| Year | Total American imports from China in $1,000 (A) | Rate of increase 1913=100% (B) | Index of Gen. Price in China 1913=100 Silver stan. (C) | Av. rate of gold-silver exchange J HK Tael (D) | Column D converted into Index 1913=100 (E) | Convert. silver-price index (C) into gold price index C × E (F) | Real index of vol. of imports (G) |
|---|---|---|---|---|---|---|---|
| 1913 | 41,387 | 100 | 100[c] | $0.23 | 100 | 100 | 100 |
| 1914 | 37,643 | 91 | 107 | 0.67 | 92 | 98 | 93 |
| 1915 | 54,004 | 130 | 113 | 0.62 | 85 | 96 | 136 |
| 1916 | 81,732 | 198 | 122 | 0.79 | 108 | 132 | 150 |
| 1917 | 141,482 | 342 | 128 | 1.03 | 141 | 180 | 190 |
| 1918 | 145,316 | 351 | 136 | 1.26 | 173 | 235 | 149 |
| 1919 | 172,963 | 418 | 130 | 1.39 | 190 | 247 | 172 |
| 1920 | 211,101 | 510 | 128 | 1.24 | 170 | 218 | 234 |
| 1921 | 103,952 | 251 | 127 | 0.76 | 104 | 132 | 190 |
| 1922 | 139,061 | 337 | 140[c] | 0.83 | 114 | 160 | 210 |
| 1923[b] | 176,471 | 427 | 150[d] | 0.83 | 114 | 171 | 250 |

*This is a part of the Index number constructed by the writer in his thesis "The Construction of a General Price Index Number for China," submitted in partial fulfilment of the requirements for the degree of Master of Business Administration at Harvard University, 1922.

[b] Fiscal year ending June 30.
[c] Index constructed according to the same method as above.

ican prices. After we eliminate that part of the increase of trade due to this inflation of price, we come to the real index of the volume of import trade which is shown in column G. Now it becomes clear that the real increase during this period is far less phenomenal than the nominal increase in terms of total value, yet the volume of imports became almost two and a half times as large in 1920 as in 1914, and in 1922-23, it was two and a half times as large.

Let us now turn our attention to American exports to China. The total value of exports increased at first much less rapidly than that of imports, in fact, there was a decline between 1914 and 1915. But in 1918, the total value is 123% over that of 1913 while that of American imports in the same year showed an excess of 251%. But in the next two years, the increase of exports overtook that of imports by twenty points (530-510). In 1921 the drop in the total export value was much less severe than the drop in the total import value. By eliminating the element of the rise due to price inflation in this country, we can again correct the rate of the nominal increase to show the real increase of the export trade of the United States with China. As column E of Table 16 shows us, the actual volume of American exports to China during 1914-17 were much below that of 1913. In 1914 it was fourteen percent below, in 1915 twenty-three percent below, and even in 1917, still three percent below. This tardiness of expansion is explained upon several grounds which we have touched upon at the beginning of this chapter. First, the heavy drop of the price of silver in terms of gold during 1915 with only a little recovery in 1916 discouraged the Chinese from importing American goods which are expressed in terms of gold; second, the high rate of freight added to the high price, another heavy burden to the Chinese buyer; and third, China's demand for American goods was not so urgent as that of Europe. After 1918, however, the real volume of trade had increased considerably. The index rose from 94 in 1917 to 115 in 1918, climbed to 196 in 1919, and to 234 in 1920, and in spite of business depression in most parts of the world and in America again increased to 262 in 1921. In 1922-23, the severe business depression in China checked the further expansion of American exports to that country, yet the index dropped only slightly. This

TABLE 16

STATISTICS SHOWING THE REAL INCREASE OF THE VOLUME OF AMERICAN EXPORTS TO CHINA, 1913-1922

| Year | Total American Exports to China in $1,000 | Rate of increase 1913 = 100 | Index No. of American wholesale prices [1] | Real increase of volume of trade |
|------|------|------|------|------|
| 1913......... | 31,956 | 100 | 100 | 100 |
| 1914......... | 26,644 | 84 | 98 | 86 |
| 1915......... | 25,032 | 78 | 101 | 77 |
| 1916......... | 39,295 | 123 | 127 | 97 |
| 1917......... | 53,128 | 167 | 177 | 94 |
| 1918......... | 71,080 | 223 | 194 | 115 |
| 1919......... | 129,296 | 405 | 206 | 196 |
| 1920......... | 169,861 | 530 | 226 | 234 |
| 1921......... | 122,968 | 385 | 147 | 262 |
| 1922......... | 116,541 | 365 | 149 | 245 |
| 1923 [2]...... | 117,047 | 367 | 156 [3] | 235 |
| (A) | (B) | (C) | (D) | (E) |

enormous increase can be accounted for also upon three grounds: first, the unprecedented rise in the price of silver in terms of gold naturally stimulated a silver-standard nation like China to buy more from a gold standard nation; second, the enormous value of the imports from China into this country made the dollar-tael exchange rate more favorable to China and this again stimulated the exportation of American products to China; third, due to the exportation boom in China during the war, the purchasing power of the Chinese people had enormously increased, and they could therefore afford to buy more foreign goods for immediate

[1] U. S. Bur. of Labor Statistics.
[2] Fiscal year ending June 30.
[3] For fiscal year ending June 30.

consumption. Furthermore, there prevailed in China during 1918-1921 a business prosperity that promoted many new industries and started a great number of plants and factories which in turn created a strong demand for American producers' goods such as iron and steel manufactures, machinery, cars, carriages, electrical machinery and appliances, building materials, etc. It is a rather significant fact that although the value of American exports to China dropped heavily in 1921 from that of the previous year, yet the actual volume had actually increased.

To conclude this section let us say in general that during the ten-year period under present discussion, both the American imports from China and the exports thereto have increased in volume two and a half times, when allowance for price inflation has been made. We see, therefore, the increasing importance of American trade with China as created under the new conditions arising from the war.

This increase of importance shows itself not only in the absolute value and volume of the trade, but also in the comparative share in the foreign trade of both countries. Table 17 presents a view of the distribution of American trade with the Oriental countries, showing the percentage of total values of imports therefrom and exports thereto, computed on the total values of imports and exports of the United States as bases. In 1913 American imports from China constituted 2.19% of the total American imports. This share was steadily expanding; in 1919 it became 4.56% and in 1922, 4.39%, about double that of pre-war times. As a supplier of the American market, China ranked ninth in 1913 among those countries from which America bought its imports,[1] while in 1918 her rank was advanced to seventh place,[2] and

[1] The large importers from the U. S. were in 1913 in order of their importance: the United Kingdom, Germany, France, Cuba, Brazil, Mexico, British East Indies, Japan, China including Hongkong, Belgium, Italy, and Canada.
[2] In the order of their importance, the countries importing from the U. S. were in 1918: Canada, British East Indies, Japan, Cuba, Argentina, United Kingdom, China.

TABLE 17

PERCENTAGES OF TOTAL VALUES OF IMPORTS FROM AND EXPORTS TO THE ORIENTAL COUNTRIES, COMPUTED ON THE TOTAL VALUES OF IMPORTS AND EXPORTS OF THE UNITED STATES AS BASES, 1913-1922

| Year | China together with leased territories | | Hongkong | | Japan | | British East Indies | | Dutch East Indies | |
|------|------|------|------|------|------|------|------|------|------|------|
| | Imp. | Ex. | Imp. | Ex. | Imp. | Ex. | Imp. | Ex. | Imp. | Ex. |
| 1913 | 2.19 | 0.91 | 0.22 | 0.42 | 5.05 | 2.35 | 6.41 | 0.61 | 0.34 | 0.13 |
| 1914 | 2.13 | 1.11 | 0.16 | 0.45 | 5.67 | 2.17 | 5.91 | 0.66 | 0.28 | 0.01 |
| 1915 | 2.44 | 0.63 | 0.12 | 0.30 | 5.91 | 1.50 | 5.21 | 0.58 | 0.55 | 0.10 |
| 1916 | 3.29 | 0.60 | 0.25 | 0.28 | 6.72 | 1.72 | 8.07 | 0.57 | 1.26 | 0.17 |
| 1917 | 4.22 | 0.66 | 0.28 | 0.23 | 7.83 | 2.07 | 8.19 | 0.59 | 2.33 | 0.34 |
| 1918 | 4.66 | 0.96 | 0.99 | 0.40 | 9.96 | 4.45 | 9.87 | 0.84 | 2.47 | 0.38 |
| 1919 | 4.56 | 1.49 | 0.57 | 0.28 | 10.50 | 4.63 | 8.25 | 1.03 | 2.02 | 0.59 |
| 1920 | 3.87 | 1.86 | 0.87 | 0.32 | 7.85 | 4.59 | 7.60 | 1.48 | 3.17 | 0.72 |
| 1921 | 4.08 | 2.53 | 0.41 | 0.42 | 10.01 | 5.25 | 5.93 | 1.46 | 1.28 | 0.72 |
| 1922 | 4.39 | 2.77 | 0.49 | 0.55 | 11.39 | 5.70 | 6.61 | 0.97 | 1.10 | 0.21 |

in 1920, 1921 and 1922 to sixth.[1] Among the buyers of American goods, China has never ranked so high as in the export list of the United States. In 1913 total American exports to China amounted to 6.91% of total American exports, while China's position, even including Hongkong, was fourteenth.[2] Yet in the course of five years her rank was advanced four places,[3] although her actual share had increased only by one-twentieth of one per cent (0.96-0.91). She held in 1920 the same place in the list, but her share had increased to nearly twice that of 1918, viz. from 0.96% in

[1] Cuba, Canada, the United Kingdom, Japan, British East Indies, China, Brazil, Argentina, Dutch East Indies, France.
[2] United Kingdom, Canada, Germany, France, Netherlands, Italy, Cuba, Belgium, Japan, Mexico, Argentina, Australia, Brazil, China, including Hongkong, and Spain in the order of their importance.
[3] The United Kingdom, France, Canada, Italy, Japan, Cuba, Russia, Argentina, Mexico and China including Hongkong.

1918 to 1.86% in 1920, to 2.53% in 1921, and to 2.77% in 1922.

As compared with the increase of American trade with other countries in the Orient, the increase of Chinese trade has presented a favorable aspect especially in the recent years. It has nearly kept pace with the growing share of Japan in American foreign trade, and has somewhat exceeded that of the British East Indies. Trade with the Dutch East Indies alone increased during the war at a rate more rapid than that of China, although it must be noted that the absolute volume of trade with the Dutch East Indies is now much below that with China, and that in recent years the American-Dutch Indies trade declined enormously in its relative share, whereas American-Chinese trade is still on the increase.

TABLE 18

DISTRIBUTION OF CHINA'S FOREIGN TRADE BY COUNTRIES IN PERCENTAGES, 1913-1922

| Year | U. S. of America | Great Britain | Germany | France | Japan | Hongkong | British India |
|------|------|------|------|------|------|------|------|
| 1913 | 7.6% | 11.4% | 4.5% | 5.3% | 19.7% | 29.1% | 5.5% |
| 1914 | 9.1 | 13.8 | 2.6 | 3.8 | 21.1 | 28.3 | 5.0 |
| 1915 | 11.4 | 11.5 | 0.1 | 4.8 | 23.4 | 28.2 | 5.4 |
| 1916 | 12.7 | 10.3 | ... | 3.4 | 28.3 | 26.8 | 3.8 |
| 1917 | 15.2 | 7.5 | ... | 3.0 | 33.4 | 26.3 | 3.2 |
| 1918 | 12.8 | 7.2 | ... | 3.1 | 37.8 | 26.3 | 1.3 |
| 1919 | 16.2 | 9.3 | ... | 3.0 | 33.9 | 21.9 | 2.8 |
| 1920 | 15.7 | 13.2 | 0.6 | 2.0 | 27.7 | 22.0 | 3.1 |
| 1921 | 17.3 | 11.8 | 1.3 | 2.2 | 24.9 | 25.0 | 2.9 |
| 1922 | 16.7 | 11.5 | 2.2 | 2.8 | 24.3 | 25.6 | 3.3 |

When we turn to China we at once notice the remarkable increase of the relative share taken by American trade as shown in Table 18. In 1913, the share of the United States was only 7.6% of the total foreign trade of China; ten years later it became 17.0%. During this ten-year period, the shares of all countries trading with China, except Japan, have more or less dwindled, or at best remained stationary.

Even in the case of Japan the increase of her share has been far less phenomenal, from 19.7% in 1913 to 24.3% in 1922, an increase of 23%, as compared with the increase of the American share from 7.6% in 1913 to 16.7% in 1922, an increase of 120%.

### Japanese, British and Other Competition

The European War eliminated, for a time at least, many strong competitors from the markets in the Orient, and left only two or three fortunate countries to avail themselves of this opportunity. Among those whose commerce with China before the war had been growing in volume and importance were Germany, Belgium, France, Russia, Italy, and British East Indies. But immediately after the outbreak in 1914, German and Belgian competition was completely removed from the field, and a little later, Russia, Italy, France, Norway and Sweden, also found it extremely difficult to carry on any considerable amount of trade with China. The trade between British India and China also declined, because the former had to serve its mother country to the utmost of its capacity. Only Great Britain, for more than a century the dominating country in China's foreign trade, succeeded in preserving its place, though with a great deal of difficulty, in the Oriental market. There were only two countries, viz., Japan and America, that profited enormously by the war in their trade with China as well as with others.

As contrasted with the multi-sided competition for the trade of China before 1914, we now find a much simplified mesh of triangular competition—America versus Japan, and, with less keenness, Great Britain. In order to reveal many important considerations which will throw much light on the future tendency of the share of the United States in the foreign trade of China, we should investigate the important as well as interesting phenomenon of the competition entered into by these three countries before, during and after the European War. Our examination may be guided by a com-

parison of the American with Japanese and British trade with China during the fourteen years, 1909-1922, a period which consists of an ante-bellum quinquennium, another quinquennium the chief factor in which was the war, and a post-bellum quadrennium.

The distribution of China's trade as shown in Table 18 is to a certain extent inaccurate, because it does not indicate the real share of each country, largely owing to the transshipment of commodities through the open port of Hongkong. It is shown by this table that the share credited to Hongkong has been for the whole period about one-third of the total foreign trade of China, but the imports from Hongkong come originally from, and exports to that colony are carried to, Great Britain, Japan, America as well as many other countries which have trade relations with China. Therefore before arriving at a final percentage for each nationality there should be made to each of these countries what is called a Hongkong allowance. It is impossible, of course, to make the allowance anything more than a rough estimate. But for a general comparison such as we are making now, it will serve our purpose.

A somewhat detailed comparison of the trade of these three competitors with China is presented in Table 19. The most striking thing in this table is that during the war quinquennium both American and Japanese trade increased considerably in value over that in the ante-bellum quinquennium. The rate of increase of Japanese trade outstripped that of America. The average annual trade before the war was eighty-five million Haikwan taels for the United States and one hundred and seventy-eight millions for Japan; while during the war it increased to one hundred and forty-nine millions for the former and three hundred and twenty-two millions for the latter. The increase in the case of the United States was seventy-five percent, and in the case of Japan eighty percent. Furthermore, the increase of the relative share of Japan also exceeded that of the United States. Before the war the average share of Japan was

**TABLE 19**

**COMPARATIVE SHARES OF THE UNITED STATES, JAPAN, AND GREAT BRITAIN IN THE FOREIGN TRADE OF CHINA, BEFORE, DURING, AND AFTER THE EUROPEAN WAR, 1909-1922**

| | Total foreign trade of China in 1,000 H.K. Tls. | Total China trade with Hongkong 1,000 H.K. Tls. | Direct trade in 1,000 H.K. Tls. | Hongkong allowance 6% before war and 12% since 1916 | Trade of China with the United States including Hawaii and Philippines — Corrected total trade 1,000 H.K. Tls. | % of total China's total foreign trade |
|---|---|---|---|---|---|---|
| 1909 | 757,151 | 247,391 | 66,988 | 14,843 | 81,831 | 10.8 |
| 1910 | 834,798 | 280,189 | 57,778 | 16,811 | 74,589 | 9.0 |
| 1911 | 848,842 | 251,919 | 75,351 | 15,115 | 90,466 | 10.7 |
| 1912 | 843,617 | 251,186 | 72,121 | 15,071 | 87,192 | 10.6 |
| 1913 | 973,468 | 288,765 | 75,233 | 17,326 | 92,559 | 10.5 |
| 5-year average. | 851,575 | 263,890 | 69,494 | 15,833 | 85,327 | 10.1 |
| 1914 | 925,488 | 262,422 | 84,540 | 15,743 | 100,285 | 10.8 |
| 1915 | 973,337 | 252,606 | 102,055 | 15,156 | 117,211 | 12.1 |
| 1916 | 998,204 | 272,833 | 129,272 | 32,740 | 162,012 | 16.2 |
| 1917 | 1,012,450 | 274,445 | 159,106 | 32,933 | 192,039 | 19.0 |
| 1918 | 1,040,776 | 279,189 | 141,167 | 33,502 | 174,669 | 16.7 |
| 5-year average. | 980,051 | 268,297 | 123,228 | 26,015 | 149,243 | 15.2 |
| 1919 | 1,277,807 | 285,126 | 215,893 | 34,215 | 250,107 | 19.6 |
| 1920 | 1,303,882 | 295,775 | 214,193 | 35,493 | 249,686 | 19.1 |
| 1921 | 1,507,378 | 384,103 | 271,126 | 46,092 | 317,218 | 21.0 |
| 1922 | 1,599,942 | 409,343 | 272,130 | 49,121 | 321,251 | 20.1 |
| 4-year average. | 1,422,252 | 343,587 | 243,336 | 41,230 | 284,566 | 20.0 |

Data compiled from Chinese Maritime Customs Returns.

**TABLE 19—Continued**

| Year | British Empire, including all colonies — Total direct trade in 1,000 H.K. Tls. | Hongkong allowance 20% | Corrected total trade | % of total foreign trade in China | Japanese Empire, including Chosen and Formosa — Total direct trade in 1,000 H.K. Tls. | Hongkong allowance 10% | Corrected total trade in H.K. Tls. | % of total foreign trade of China |
|---|---|---|---|---|---|---|---|---|
| 1909 | 138,161 | 49,378 | 187,539 | 24.7 | 116,546 | 24,739 | 141,285 | 18.6 |
| 1910 | 146,312 | 56,038 | 202,350 | 24.2 | 143,373 | 28,019 | 171,292 | 20.6 |
| 1911 | 166,923 | 50,384 | 217,307 | 25.6 | 147,556 | 25,192 | 172,748 | 20.3 |
| 1912 | 163,474 | 56,237 | 213,701 | 25.3 | 154,878 | 25,119 | 179,997 | 21.1 |
| 1913 | 188,047 | 57,753 | 245,800 | 25.2 | 195,231 | 28,977 | 224,108 | 23.0 |
| 5-year average. | 160,582 | 52,758 | 213,340 | 25.0 | 151,517 | 26,389 | 177,906 | 20.9 |
| 1914 | 182,566 | 52,484 | 235,050 | 25.4 | 201,248 | 25,242 | 227,490 | 24.6 |
| 1915 | 172,659 | 50,521 | 223,180 | 23.0 | 210,031 | 25,261 | 235,292 | 24.2 |
| 1916 | 163,109 | 54,567 | 217,676 | 22.0 | 288,429 | 27,283 | 315,712 | 31.6 |
| 1917 | 139,042 | 54,889 | 193,931 | 19.1 | 347,803 | 27,445 | 375,248 | 37.0 |
| 1918 | 122,798 | 55,836 | 178,634 | 17.1 | 426,395 | 27,918 | 454,313 | 43.5 |
| 5-year average. | 156,035 | 53,659 | 209,694 | 21.4 | 294,781 | 26,830 | 321,611 | 32.8 |
| 1919 | 203,880 | 56,025 | 260,905 | 20.4 | 473,996 | 28,513 | 502,509 | 39.4 |
| 1920 | 266,978 | 59,156 | 326,134 | 25.0 | 404,724 | 29,576 | 434,300 | 33.2 |
| 1921 | 268,641 | 76,812 | 345,453 | 22.9 | 409,522 | 38,410 | 447,932 | 29.7 |
| 1922 | 274,071 | 81,869 | 355,940 | 22.2 | 422,106 | 40,934 | 463,040 | 29.0 |
| 4-year average. | 253,392 | 68,716 | 322,108 | 22.6 | 421,582 | 34,358 | 461,945 | 32.5 |

Data compiled from the Chinese Maritime Customs Returns.

Note to Table 19:

*Hongkong Allowance.* In the absence of other evidence, we may assume that, of the total China-Hongkong trade (figures in the third column of Table 19) the ratio of that portion whose destination is some part of any of the three countries under comparison is proportionate to the ratio between the amount of the direct trade of any one of those countries with Hongkong and the total amount of foreign trade of Hongkong. Expressed in an equation it means:

$$\frac{\text{A's share in China's trade with Hongkong}}{\text{Total Chinese trade with Hongkong}} = \frac{\text{A's share in the total trade of Hongkong}}{\text{Total trade of Hongkong}}$$

In other words, we assume in the absence of other reliable evidence country A's trade with Hongkong is ultimately and evenly distributed to all other countries having trade relations with Hongkong in a proportion according to their relative share in Hongkong trade. In the footnote on p. 72, we have already demonstrated the distributive shares of the various countries in the Hongkong trade during the two years 1918 and 1919. In connection with the United States, the British Empire and the Japanese Empire, they are as follows:

| Year | United States | Japanese Empire | British Empire |
|---|---|---|---|
| 1918 | 10.7% | 11.2% | 16.6% |
| 1919 | 11.6 | 10.0 | 19.9 |
| Average | 11.2 | 10.6 | 18.3 |

With these ratios as our bases, we may roughly estimate the Hongkong allowance which should be credited to each of these countries. Generally speaking, we may allow 12% of China-Hongkong trade to the United States; 10% to Japan and 20% to the British Empire. But from further evidence we notice that before the war American trade with Hongkong was comparatively unimportant and a 12% allowance seems too big. Of the total imports from Hongkong to China in 1906, $116,000,000, there were American goods to the value of $7,000,000, a share of about 6%. (U. S. Com. Rel. 1906 under "China.") Since the American trade with Hongkong did not alter very much before 1915, we may assume that 6% of the China-Hongkong trade may be allowed to the United States before that year.

The Hongkong allowance thus computed (column 5, Table 19) for some years differs quite a good deal from that computed according to a similar rule but from American data (cf. column 4, Table

20.9% ; during the war it became 32.8% which is 1.63 times the previous figure. As regards the United States, the increase was from 10.1% to 15.2%, or 1.5 times. From this comparison we come to the general conclusion that during the war America had been outstripped by Japan even as far as comparative increase is concerned.

In the next four-year post-bellum period, however, the

*Note continued from the preceding page.*

14) even though one standard of value is converted into the other according to the current average rate of dollar-tael rate of exchange. Of course in Table 19 the figures include all the American colonies and territories while the figures in Table 14 consist of the trade of forty-eight states of the United States. But even if a liberal allowance is made for this, there still remains some discrepancy. In this connection the United States Department of Commerce made the following comment (Com. Rel. 1880-81, p. 201) :

"Owing to the material difference between Chinese returns of foreign trade and the returns of the same trade as given in the returns of foreign countries, an estimate of the foreign trade of Hongkong is necessary for the harmonization of what would otherwise appear as contradictory statistics. Even with the closest possible analysis of the trade of China and Hongkong there will remain some discrepancies between the Chinese customs returns and those of England and France which can be explained only upon the hypothesis that either the former or the latter are erroneous.

"For instance: The Chinese returns give the exports to the continent of Europe during the year 1880 as $17,800,000; the French returns for the same year give the general imports into France alone from China and Hongkong as amounting to $30,616,000, of which France consumed to the value of $19,469,000, the remainder passing on to other countries. Here is an import into France alone nearly double that which is credited to the whole continent in the Chinese returns. How much direct imports were received by the other continental countries cannot be given in the absence of official returns.

"It will be seen that even after liberally allowing for the increased value of merchandise, from their export from one country until they are entered as imports in another, there is considerable confusion caused by the intermixing of the trade of Hongkong with that of China, and that to arrive at anything like a satisfactory estimate of the trade relations of Europe and the United States with China, it is necessary to give a statement of the foreign commerce of Hongkong in connection with that of China."

above condition was reversed. Although Japanese trade with China has gained in absolute values from an average of three hundred and twenty-two million Haikwan Taels to four hundred and sixty-two millions, its relative share has slightly declined from 32.8% to 32.5%. This tendency toward decline has become more and more obvious in recent years. The trade of the United States, on the other hand, has made another huge increase during this period from an average value of one hundred and forty-nine million in the war period to two hundred and eighty-five million Haikwan taels, and relatively from a share of 15.2% to exactly 20.0%.

That Japan had intended to compete very strongly for the trade of China has been evident to all who have studied her policy in that country during the several years of the World War. Her loans and her political activities were of the most marked kind of "dollar diplomacy." Some indications of her strenuous preparations for capturing the Chinese market may also be gathered from Table 20 and 21 which show the number of her firms and merchants doing business in China so contrasted with those of the United States and Great Britain.

TABLE 20

FOREIGN RESIDENTS IN CHINA

| Year | American | British | Japanese | Russian | French | German | Total |
|---|---|---|---|---|---|---|---|
| 1913 | 5,340 | 8,966 | 80,219 | 56,765 | 2,292 | 2,949 | 163,827 |
| 1914 | 4,365 | 8,914 | 84,948 | 56,319 | 1,864 | 3,013 | 164,807 |
| 1919 | 6,660 | 13,234 | 171,485 | 148,170 | 4,409a | 1,335 | 350,991 |
| 1920 | 7,269 | 11,082 | 153,918 | 144,413 | 2,753b | 1,013 | 326,069 |
| 1921 | 8,230 | 9,298 | 144,434 | 68,250 | 2,453 | 1,255 | 240,769 |
| 1922 | 9,153 | 11,855 | 152,848 | 96,727 | 2,300 | 1,986 | 282,491 |

a Including 918 proteges.
b Including 591 proteges.
Data from Chinese customs returns.

TABLE 21

FOREIGN FIRMS IN CHINA

| Year | American | British | Japanese | Russian | French | German | Total |
|---|---|---|---|---|---|---|---|
| 1913 | 131 | 590 | 1,269 | 1,229 | 106 | 296 | 3,805 |
| 1914 | 136 | 534 | 955 | 1,237 | 113 | 273 | 3,421 |
| 1919 | 314 | 644 | 4,878 | 1,760 | 171 | 2 | 8,015 |
| 1920 | 409 | 679 | 4,278 | 1,596 | 180 | 9 | 7,375 |
| 1921 | 412 | 703 | 6,141 | 1,613 | 222 | 92 | 9,511 |
| 1922 | 377 | 725 | 3,940 | 1,141 | 229 | 184 | 7,021 |

But in spite of Japan's strenuous preparations the United States is now in a highly advantageous position in its competition for Chinese trade. Spinning mills and factories, knitted goods, soap, glass, and other simpler forms of industries are now springing up at a really remarkable pace in China. Japan, naturally, feels more keenly the effect of all this competition from China itself than any other exporting country. Unless the industrial activities of Japan take a tremendous forward step in the near future, Japanese exports to China will be gradually crowded out by the native products of China, for the simple reason that the large proportion of Japan's exports to China are products of the simpler forms of manufacturing industry—the very kind which China can herself produce now or very soon. The steady advance of industrial China is, however, a good thing for America. It will be some time before China attains the height of complex industrial activity which prevails in the United States. Meanwhile the more China develops her simpler forms of industrial activities, the greater will be her demand for machinery, steel and iron products, electrical appliances, chemical products and such other things as the United States is better able to furnish, and these are the very articles in which Japan cannot now hope to compete with the United States. Therefore, except for the few years of war, and possibly the year or two immediately succeeding it, Japan has not gained much permanent benefit from the sudden stoppage of European supplies to China. In many departments of iron and steel manufactures and in chemical industries, Japan had not attained any marked advance; she could hardly supply her own needs in some of these products.

Moreover, Japan is handicapped in many other ways in competing with the United States. Since Japan has taken an aggressive attitude toward China and in 1916 forced upon her the notorious "Twenty-one Demands," she has created for herself an immeasurable quantity of ill-will on the part of the Chinese people. Even recently boycotts have been frequently instituted in China against everything Japanese and Japanese trade both import and export has been substantially affected. The political relations between China and Japan are still very delicate and one can conceive of a number of causes likely to continue the ill-will between them. If the Japanese policy toward China is not radically modified in the near future Japanese commercial relations with China will suffer rather than improve. The Chinese have serious grievances against Japan, and the animus against everything Japanese is steadily on the increase.

In addition to these handicaps Japan is now, because of the recent earthquake, in a still weaker position in competing with America. Not only hundreds of millions of dollars worth of her national wealth was destroyed, but her producing power has been immensely damaged, as not a few industrial plants and factories were demolished in this calamity. The re-construction work will certainly absorb the greater part of her national resources and engage the whole attention and energy of her people for some time to come.

Now let us turn our attention to Great Britain and her colonies and dominions. Before the War, the trade of the British Empire with China averaged about two hundred and thirteen million Haikwan Taels a year which is just one-fourth of China's total foreign trade, the largest share enjoyed by any one nation. During the quinquennium of war, her trade dropped to a yearly average of two hundred and ten million Haikwan Taels, rather a small decline, but when

taking into consideration the element of price inflation, it must be admitted that the real volume of British-Chinese trade had declined rather severely. This severe drop is also reflected in the decreasing share of China's trade Britain was then enjoying. It was 21.4% as contrasted with 25% in the ante-bellum period. This decrease was a natural result of the distraction, due to the war, of the energy and attention of all the British peoples. Japan and the United States, therefore, had a better chance to extend their trade in China.

With the close of the war the British naturally came back and now the keenest competition between American and British trade interests is carried on in the Chinese markets. During the five year post-bellum period, British trade has been steadily on the increase, the annual average being three hundred and twenty-two million Haikwan Taels as against two hundred and ten millions in the previous quinquennium. Her share has recovered somewhat, although it has not as yet attained its pre-war percentage. The number of her firms trading in China is increasing and that of her residents in China carrying on trade greatly exceeds that of the American residents.[1] As regards her ability to supply what the growing industrial China now needs, her competing power is just as strong as that of the United States. It is, therefore, rather difficult to predict whether British or American trade is to come out ahead.

In one direction at least Great Britain still has an advantage over the United States in the competition. British merchants in China have long experience and a clear insight of the market and financial conditions. Their connections are exceedingly well established, while the American traders have had comparatively little experience in China's commerce..

Although in the immediate past America had only two competitors in the Chinese market, she must now reckon

[1] See Tables 20 and 21.

with more, among which is Germany whose return has attracted much attention and speculation. German trade with China before the war, though not large, was steadily growing. It disappeared, however, during the war. But in recent years Germany has come back to the Orient and pushed her trade with renewed effort. Her firms and residents in China are resuming their pre-war number with remarkable rapidity. Her annual trade increased from nothing in 1919, to twenty million dollars in 1922 and her share was 2.2% in the latter year.

In competing with America as well as with other countries, German trade has in one way good prospects in China. It is obvious that if Germany is to recover from the disastrous results of the war, her people must work very hard, practice immense self-denial and be content with small profits. Still more or less unwelcome elsewhere, they must turn their attention to China, where their manufactures, produced with comparative cheapness, will have a great opportunity in outselling and underbidding other competitors.

But the deplorable political and economic chaos now prevailing in Germany makes her advantages doubtful and it still remains to be seen whether Germany will be able to pass the crisis and rehabilitate itself. Even though her political and economic condition may improve, she is likely to be handicapped for years by inadequate capital of her own. Furthermore, the war cancelled all the old treaties between Germany and China, and her goods cannot now enter China at the five per cent rate enjoyed by countries whose treaties stand. China has prepared a tariff for the new-treaty countries, under which German goods will have to pay rates varying from ten to one hundred per cent. In this respect German goods will be unable to compete with American goods on the same basis.

## CHAPTER V

The Period of Rapid Expansion, 1914-1922 (continued).

### Changes in the Composition of the Trade

Along with the rapid expansion of the trade between the United States and China are many significant changes which have taken place in the composition of both imports and exports. A great many articles which were insignificant in former days have come suddenly to be the principal commodities of the trade. On the other hand many articles which had long been important have declined either in quantity or in share or in both. These changes have been effected partly by the changing force of the economic conditions in both the buying and selling countries, and partly by the temporary disturbing influence of the European War. Of course, those affected by the temporary disturbances of the war have already resumed, or will soon resume, their original status when the disturbances cease to work. But those which have been due to the changing trend of economic development will run their course as time goes on until they are checked by another set of new influences working in the opposite direction. Let us, therefore, examine these changes separately.

*1. Changes in the composition of American imports from China.* Among the articles imported from China which have increased in commercial importance, vegetable oils, hides, skins and furs, chemicals, eggs and egg products, human hair and hair products, and wool, are the most significant. Among those decreasing in importance, tea is the only one deserving attention. Among those which has kept an even pace with the total imports from China to America, silk is by far the most important. Owing to the considerable share these articles have played in the trade, the writer will endeavor to give each of them a more detailed description and discussion in the next two parts. Here let us run over them in a very brief manner.

Only two decades ago Chinese vegetable oils were practically unknown in this country. Even down to 1910 imports of vegetable oils were still far less than one million dollars a year, constituting from one to three percent of the total imports from China.[1] After 1911, however, when Japan had become interested in the oil industry in South Manchuria, where most of China's oil seeds are produced, the trade had greatly increased even before the war broke out. From 1911 to 1915 the United States imported every year nearly three million dollars' worth of this commodity from China, and their share in the total import trade suddenly increased to seven or eight percent. During 1917, the value of imports soared upward to twelve million dollars, being nearly 11% of the total. In the next year, 1918, another headlong dash was made to a figure of thirty-nine million dollars, being more than two-thirds of the total and by far the most important article of all the imports from China in that year. Since 1919 the part played by this product has been declining. The serious drop in oil imports in 1921-22 was due mainly to the re-enacted high tariff walls, the business depression and the stoppage of many industrial activities which use these vegetable oils as one of their important raw materials.[2]

Less phenomenal than the increase of trade in vegetable oils was the increase in the imports of hides and skins. In the preceding period, hides and skins had already assumed an important place in the import trade, the imports amounting to between two and a half to four million dollars a year, which constituted about one-tenth of the total import from China. In 1913 trade in these articles came with a rush, and from 1913 to 1916 its value increased to more than five million dollars a year, and its share to 13% of the total. In 1917 hides and skins became one of the two most important articles of import from China, the other being silk, each

[1] See Table 11.
[2] See Ch. 8 on Vegetable Oils, infra.

sharing about one quarter of the whole. The value of the former attained the mark of twenty-seven and a half million dollars. In 1920, another increase was effected, totaling thirty-one million dollars, although owing to the general increase of Chinese imports, its share declined to fifteen percent. In 1921-22, however, a sharp decline occurred because of the following business depression in American leather industry; yet, in spite of its wide annual fluctuation, the trade has increased many times during this period, and the general trend of its comparative share in the total imports from China tends to rise.[1]

Chinese furs are imports which have assumed importance only recently. Before 1916 the annual value did not average more than half a million dollars, constituting a little more than one percent of the total value of imports. But since 1917 the increase has been remarkable, from 1.7 million dollars to 3.1 in 1818, 7.3 in 1919; and 12.5 in 1920, and then, owing to business depression, the figure dropped to 4.8 millions in 1921. Yet in 1922 it suddenly increased to nearly 14 millions. Its share of 1.5% in 1917 was raised to 6.1% in 1920, dropped to 4.7% in 1921, and recovered to 10.1% in 1922. This is rather strong evidence that Chinese furs are coming to stay in the American market as a principal article of import.

No less important was the growth of imports under the heading of "chemicals, drugs and dyes" since 1916. It should here be noted that at the beginning of the century, chemicals and drugs were imported in rather large quantities valued at an average of one and one half million dollars a year, and constituting six per cent of the total imports. About two-thirds of the imports under this item consisted of prepared opium. Since 1910 the importation of opium has been prohibited. Imports of other chemicals and drugs, such as camphor and licorice, were rather small in quantity and value and therefore the share of this item dropped to about

[1] See Chap. 9 on Hides and Skins, infra.

TABLE 22

COMPOSITION OF AMERICAN IMPORTS FROM CHINA, INCLUDING LEASED TERRITORIES, 1914-22

| No. | Fiscal year ending June 30 | 1914 | | 1915 | | 1916 | | 1917 | |
|---|---|---|---|---|---|---|---|---|---|
| | | $1,000 | % | $1,000 | % | $1,000 | % | $1,000 | % |
| 1 | Antimony, ore and regulus | 166 | 0.4 | 563 | 1.4 | 3,796 | 5.3 | 1,537 | 1.4 |
| 2 | Art works | 64 | 0.2 | 153 | 0.4 | 270 | 0.4 | 562 | 0.5 |
| 3 | Bristles, sorted, bunched and prepared | 934 | 2.3 | 1,613 | 3.9 | 1,612 | 2.2 | 1,728 | 1.5 |
| 4 | Chemicals, drugs, dyes | 640 | 1.6 | 672 | 1.6 | 6,714 | 9.3 | 2,293 | 2.0 |
| 5 | Cotton goods: Laces... | 46 | 0.1 | 27 | 0.1 | 62 | 0.1 | 323 | 0.3 |
| 6 | Cotton, raw | 1,603 | 2.6 | 1,145 | 2.8 | 1,612 | 2.2 | 2,181 | 1.9 |
| 7 | Eggs, egg yolk and other products | 261 | 0.6 | 778 | 1.9 | 659 | 0.9 | 1,699 | 1.5 |
| 8 | Fruits and nuts | 444 | 1.1 | 426 | 1.0 | 504 | 0.7 | 902 | 0.8 |
| 9 | Hair and hair nets | 182 | 0.5 | 189 | 0.5 | 524 | 0.7 | 1,176 | 1.0 |
| 10 | Hats, hoods, bonnets, materials of | 182 | 0.5 | 282 | 0.7 | 927 | 1.3 | 2,130 | 1.9 |
| 11 | Hides and skins, other than furs | 4,317 | 10.7 | 5,349 | 13.1 | 9,604 | 13.3 | 27,947 | 24.5 |
| 12 | Jute, hemp and other fibres | 164 | 0.4 | 211 | 0.5 | 652 | 0.9 | 474 | 0.4 |
| 13 | Matting and mats | 619 | 1.5 | 388 | 0.9 | 183 | 0.3 | 340 | 0.3 |
| 14 | Meats and dairy prod. | 74 | 0.2 | 205 | 0.5 | 176 | 0.2 | 456 | 0.4 |
| 15 | Oil, animal, and other grease | 191 | 0.5 | 416 | 1.0 | 343 | 0.5 | 223 | 0.2 |
| 16 | Oil cakes | ... | ... | ... | ... | 11 | ... | 34 | ... |
| 17 | Oil seeds | 25 | 0.1 | 11 | ... | 168 | 0.2 | 265 | 0.3 |
| 18 | Oil, vegetable | 2,861 | 7.1 | 2,944 | 7.2 | 4,264 | 5.9 | 12,022 | 10.7 |
| 19 | Rice and rice flour... | 984 | 2.4 | 1,479 | 3.6 | 1,544 | 2.1 | 1,764 | 1.6 |
| 20 | Silk, manufactures of | 260 | 0.6 | 451 | 1.1 | 896 | 1.2 | 1,765 | 1.6 |
| 21 | Silk, raw | 15,719 | 39.0 | 11,459 | 28.1 | 28,707 | 25.8 | 27,851 | 24.8 |
| 22 | Silk, waste | 806 | 2.0 | 1,086 | 2.7 | 1,822 | 2.5 | 2,131 | 1.9 |
| 23 | Spices, unground | 206 | 0.5 | 149 | 0.4 | 241 | 0.3 | 353 | 0.3 |
| 24 | Spirits, distilled | 113 | 0.3 | 107 | 0.3 | 92 | 0.1 | 181 | 0.2 |
| 25 | Tea | 2,756 | 6.8 | 3,149 | 7.7 | 2,993 | 4.1 | 3,213 | 2.9 |
| 26 | Tin | ... | ... | ... | ... | 435 | 0.6 | 1,975 | 2.0 |
| 27 | Vegetables | 142 | 0.4 | 141 | 0.3 | 225 | 0.3 | 304 | 0.3 |
| 28 | Wood, manufactures of | 90 | 0.2 | 66 | 0.2 | 189 | 0.3 | 227 | 0.2 |
| 29 | Wool, manufactured; carpets | 75 | 0.2 | 98 | 0.2 | 281 | 0.4 | 828 | 0.7 |
| 30 | Wool, unmanufactured | 4,446 | 11.0 | 5,440 | 13.3 | 10,233 | 14.2 | 11,092 | 9.9 |
| 31 | Furs, and manufactures of | 774 | 1.9 | 413 | 1.0 | 808 | 1.1 | 1,663 | 1.5 |
| 32 | Tobacco leaf | ... | ... | ... | ... | 1 | ... | 396 | 0.4 |
| 33 | Other articles | 1,731 | 4.3 | 1,420 | 3.5 | 1,924 | 2.7 | 2,769 | 2.5 |
| | Total | 40,312 | 100.0 | 40,830 | 100.0 | 72,405 | 100.0 | 113,022 | 100.0 |

TABLE 22—Continued

Calendar Year

| No. of Item | 1918 | | 1919 | | 1920 | | 1921 | | 1922 | |
|---|---|---|---|---|---|---|---|---|---|
| | $1,000 | % | $1,000 | % | $1,000 | % | $1,000 | % | $1,000 | % |
| 1 | 1,364 | 1.0 | 484 | 0.3 | 1,233 | 0.6 | 673 | 0.7 | 562 | 0.4 |
| 2 | 167 | 0.1 | 250 | 0.1 | 353 | 0.2 | 228 | 0.2 | 284 | 0.2 |
| 3 | 3,381 | 2.4 | 2,750 | 1.6 | 6,168 | 3.0 | 3,833 | 3.7 | 2,969 | 2.2 |
| 4 | 1,164 | 0.8 | 7,271 | 4.3 | 8,343 | 4.0 | 2,105 | 2.1 | ... | ... |
| 5 | 465 | 0.3 | 1,386 | 0.8 | 2,118 | 1.0 | 3,039 | 3.0 | 2,846 | 2.1 |
| 6 | 4,282 | 3.0 | 2,224 | 1.3 | 8,179 | 4.0 | 357 | 0.3 | 1,699 | 1.2 |
| 7 | 2,560 | 2.0 | 7,061 | 4.2 | 6,322 | 3.1 | 2,546 | 2.5 | 3,160 | 2.3 |
| 8 | 663 | 0.5 | 1,538 | 0.9 | 2,831 | 1.4 | 919 | 0.9 | 1,121 | 0.8 |
| 9 | 1,420 | 1.0 | 2,864 | 1.7 | 7,409 | 3.6 | 9,086 | 8.9 | 5,994 | 4.4 |
| 10 | 4,543 | 3.5 | 4,710 | 2.8 | 8,578 | 4.2 | 1,196 | 1.3 | 1,602 | 1.2 |
| 11 | 11,975 | 8.5 | 17,085 | 10.1 | 30,805 | 15.1 | 4,195 | 4.1 | 6,966 | 5.1 |
| 12 | 534 | 0.4 | 363 | 0.2 | 315 | 0.2 | 248 | 0.2 | 180 | 0.1 |
| 13 | 77 | 0.1 | 228 | 0.1 | 1,230 | 0.6 | 249 | 0.2 | 317 | 0.1 |
| 14 | 1,123 | 0.8 | 1,138 | 0.7 | 1,822 | 0.9 | 779 | 0.8 | 317 | 0.2 |
| 15 | 1,421 | 1.0 | 295 | 0.2 | 234 | 0.1 | 114 | 0.1 | 273 | 0.2 |
| 16 | 860 | 0.6 | 226 | 0.1 | 679 | 0.3 | 208 | 0.2 | ... | ... |
| 17 | 232 | 0.2 | 868 | 0.5 | 674 | 0.3 | 361 | 0.4 | 398 | 0.3 |
| 18 | 39,361 | 27.9 | 30,955 | 18.2 | 13,460 | 9.5 | 2,806 | 2.7 | 8,364 | 6.1 |
| 19 | 2,753 | 2.0 | ... | ... | 492 | 0.2 | 23 | ... | 7 | ... |
| 20 | 1,098 | 0.7 | 786 | 0.5 | 1,765 | 0.9 | 1,961 | 2.0 | 1,587 | 1.2 |
| 21 | 25,282 | 18.0 | 54,608 | 32.2 | 53,952 | 26.4 | 48,073 | 47.0 | 56,610 | 41.5 |
| 22 | 5,677 | 4.0 | 4,363 | 2.6 | 8,844 | 4.3 | 2,337 | 2.3 | 2,248 | 1.6 |
| 23 | 191 | 0.1 | 164 | 0.1 | 170 | 0.1 | 61 | 0.1 | 358 | 0.3 |
| 24 | ... | ... | ... | ... | ... | ... | ... | ... | ... | ... |
| 25 | 3,220 | 2.3 | 2,730 | 1.6 | 2,403 | 1.2 | 2,066 | 2.0 | 2,128 | 1.6 |
| 26 | 2,090 | 1.5 | 35 | ... | 399 | 0.2 | 15 | ... | 320 | 0.2 |
| 27 | 142 | 0.1 | 202 | 0.1 | 120 | 0.1 | 49 | ... | 205 | 0.2 |
| 28 | 170 | 0.1 | 91 | 0.1 | 324 | 0.2 | 368 | 0.4 | 689 | 0.5 |
| 29 | 407 | 0.3 | 442 | 0.3 | 2,012 | 1.0 | 1,393 | 1.4 | 2,700 | 2.0 |
| 30 | 14,235 | 10.1 | 12,987 | 7.6 | 5,394 | 2.6 | 5,458 | 5.4 | 9,845 | 7.2 |
| 31 | 3,103 | 2.1 | 7,327 | 4.3 | 12,494 | 6.1 | 4,820 | 4.7 | 13,847 | 10.1 |
| 32 | 1,455 | 1.0 | 1,291 | 0.8 | 961 | 0.1 | 117 | 0.1 | 25 | ... |
| 33 | 7,252 | 5.1 | 5,586 | 3.3 | 9,036 | 4.4 | 2,539 | 2.5 | ... | ... |
| | 140,806 | 100.0 | 169,646 | 100.0 | 204,232 | 100.0 | 102,416 | 100.0 | 136,671 | 100.0 |

half a million dollars a year, a little more than one percent of the total. But in 1916 there came an abnormal demand for dyes from China. Before the war China has been a heavy buyer of colors and dyes from Germany and at the beginning of the war she had accumulated a big stock of these products which she now re-exported to this country. In that year the United States imported colors and dyes from China to a value of 4.6 million dollars, of which indigo alone was valued at three million. The total value credited under this heading "chemicals, drugs and dyes," amounted to $6,700,-000 in value, constituting 9.3% of the total. The value credited to this latter item increased to $7,300,000 in 1919 and to $8,300,000 in 1920, constituting about four percent of the total. Of the chemicals imported by far the most important was albumen which was then extensively used in American chemical plants. In 1919, 7,600,000 pounds of this chemical, valued at $5,600,000, and in the next year 8,500,000 pounds valued at $4,500,000 were imported. Other articles such as camphor, licorice root, etc., came next.

Eggs and egg products constitute a new item in the list of imports. In the preceding period, they were practically negligible in annual value but since 1915 they have begun to assume importance. In 1917 about ten million pounds of eggs both dried and frozen, valued at $1,700,000, were imported. Their value increased to an annual average of a little less than seven million dollars in 1919-20, and then dropped to about three millions a year in the next two years. Before 1918 this item amounted to less than two percent, but in 1919 it rose to 4.2% and since then amounts to about three percent of the total imports from China.[1]

The increase in the imports of straw braids, materials for making hats and bonnets, was also remarkable during the period of business activity in this country. Straw braid has been imported from the Shantung province of China for nearly half a century, yet its annual import value was around the half-million dollar mark for a long time. The war demand for straw braids to provide the soldiers in the battle-fields with hats suddenly increased the American importation of this article and in the three years, 1917-1919, the United States imported from China more than one billion yards of braids a year at an annual value of about four million dollars. In 1920 the value of imports of this article increased to

[1] See Ch. 9 on Eggs and Egg Products, *infra*.

nearly double the figure for the previous years, although the quantity increased by not more than one-half.

A very recent and perhaps the most interesting growth is noticed in hair and hair products. Sharing only a half of one percent of the total imports before 1916, and only 1.0% before 1918, it rose to 3.6% at a value of $7,400,000 in 1920 and 8.9% at $9,100,000 in 1921, with a slight setback in 1922.[1]

Another more recent growth is the importation of cotton goods from China, mostly laces and embroideries, which came into notice only after 1917 when the annual imports exceeded for the first time the mark of one million dollars. The increase was rapid and even in 1921, the trough year of American business depression, America imported about eighteen million yards of laces and embroidery edging, ninety percent of them handmade, and valued at more than three million dollars.[2]

Raw cotton is also an article which has only recently entered the list of American imports from China. Before 1910 there was practically no importation of this material from the Orient. From 1911 to 1916 the United States imported about ten million pounds of raw cotton yearly, valued at a little more than one million dollars. In 1917-1919, the actual quantity imported had not much increased although, due to price inflation, the value rose to much higher figures. In 1920 owing to extremely high prices nearly thirty million pounds of Chinese cotton was imported into this country at a value of $8,200,000, four percent of the total Chinese imports. But when depression came in 1921, the United States had more than enough cotton of her own and practically all trade in this material stopped. The increase in the several previous years was due largely to the temporary demand for cheaper cotton, and henceforth we can hardly expect any substantial quantity of cotton imports from China to the United States.

[1] See Ch. 8 on Hair and Hair Nets, *infra*.
[2] See Ch. 8 on Cotton Goods, *infra*.

Another article which came into significance only in 1918-20 is tobacco leaf. For centuries the United States has been a tobacco exporting country, but imported little of it. She had been exporting tobacco to China for more than a half century, both in raw and in manufactured condition. But when the European War broke out, the demand for raw tobacco in America was so intensified that she imported large quantities of leaf tobacco from China, while still sending her own product over there. In 1916, however, the import was only 2,030 pounds of tobacco leaf at a value of three hundred and forty-nine dollars. It increased in the next year to three million pounds at $396,000 and in the following two years to more than five million pounds at $1,500,000 to $1,300,000 respectively. The demand, however, has, as was the case with raw cotton, ceased recently and there can be no recovery in the import of this article in the future.

Antimony and tin had each for a time been important articles of Chinese imports, but the demand for them has also greatly lessened after the war.

Of all the articles which have come into importance since the beginning of the present period, only a few seem to be able to retain their important share in the American import trade with China. Vegetable oils, hides and skins, furs, egg products, cotton laces, and perhaps hair and hair products are things for which the United States has a demand which is not likely to dwindle away in the near future; while antimony, tin, raw cotton, tobacco leaf, indigo and a few others were imported in large quantities to meet only the most urgent but temporary demand caused by the war, and therefore future development in them can hardly be expected.

The only article which is dwindling in importance is tea. In former periods tea was by far the most important article of import from China. At the beginning of this century, it still constituted one-fourth of the total, but at the beginning of the present period, its share dropped headlong to about seven percent with a value of three million dollars a

year. Since 1917 its share has suffered successive drops and in 1920 it constituted only 1.2% of the total.[1]

Among those articles whose relative importance in the trade has kept a nearly equal pace with the growth of the total Chinese imports are (1) silk and silk manufactures, (2) bristles and (3) wool, omitting some other relatively unimportant articles such as fruits and nuts, rice, vegetables, etc. Since the end of the last century silk has been the most important article of import from China. Taking raw silk, silk waste and silk manufactures together, they usually constituted thirty-five to forty percent of the total Chinese imports, but from 1915 to 1918 this share had decreased by about ten percent, although both the quantity and value increased greatly. But since 1919 silk has fully recovered its former importance and in 1921-22 its value constituted forty-five percent of the total value of imports.[2]

Unmanufactured wool has for a long period been one of the most important imports. In the preceding period it constituted an average share of ten percent. This share it has retained in the last decade under discussion. In 1916 to 1921 the United States imported from China some forty or fifty million pounds of unmanufactured wool each year at an average value of $12,500,000. In 1920 a big drop both in quantity and value occurred, but in 1921-22 the quantity of wool imports resumed its former size, though the low price somewhat depressed its total value.[3]

Generally speaking, America's imports from China, like her imports from other Oriental countries and South America, are composed largely of raw and semi-raw materials. They are imported for the purpose of further production and not for immediate consumption. This is true of nearly all the most important items, such as raw silk, vegetable oils, hides and skins, wool, straw braids, etc. The tendency in the future will be a gradual increase of this kind of imports,

[1] See Ch. 6, *infra*.
[2] See Ch. 7, *infra*.
[3] See Ch. 9 on Wool, *infra*.

as, on the one hand, various branches of American industry will require more of these raw materials, and, on the other, China will be able to supply more as her agriculture and simpler forms of industry are gradually developing. The importation of finished or consumers' goods, on the contrary, shows a tendency toward decreasing importance. First, the recent decline of the tea trade, both in absolute quantity and relative share, shows clearly that in this article China will hardly be able to recover her old prestige. Silk manufacture has also declined in its relative share, although in absolute quantity it has held its own. The share of manufactured wool, mostly in the form of carpets, is also insignificant, usually less than one per cent, while the imports of such articles as manufactures of wood constituted only one- or two-tenths of one percent.

China has nevertheless been able to export some kinds of manufactured products to the United States whose relative importance is on the rise. These articles invariably require a great deal of hand labor, and in this respect China has a stronger competing power in the market than any country in the world. This class of manufactures is typified by laces, embroideries, hair-nets and other products, all of which were before the war supplied to the United States by European countries.

*2. Changes in the composition of American Exports to China.* Nothing is clearer as an indication of the tendency of American export trade with China than an examination of the changing composition of the trade during recent years as summarized in the following list:

1. Declining both in absolute volume of trade and relative share:
    (a) cotton cloth
    (b) breadstuffs including wheat flour
2. Declining in relative shares, but gaining in absolute quantity:

    (c) mineral oils.
3. Gaining in volume of trade, by keeping nearly constant shares:
    (d) timber and lumber
    (e) fruits and nuts
    (f) meat, dairy products and other provisions
4. Gaining in importance both in absolute values and in relative shares:
    (g) leather goods
    (h) tobacco, both manufactured and unmanufactured
    (i) iron and steel products and machinery
    (j) other metals.
5. Articles newly coming into importance:
    (k) cars and carriages
    (l) electrical machinery
    (m) paper products and books
    (n) chemicals and drugs
    (o) rubber manufactures.

In the two previous periods cotton cloth had been by far the most important article of American export to China; second came refined mineral oils, then bread stuffs, of which a great part was wheat flour. Tobacco in manufactured condition occupied an important place in the list though it was far less important than those just enumerated. The exportation of machinery, cars, and carriages was practically negligible, though other manufactures of iron and steel began to be exported to China in large quantities in the latter half of the previous period.

Since 1914 considerable changes have taken place in the exports from the United States. Cotton cloth, which constituted from one-half to two-thirds of the total value of exports before 1905, had already declined to no more than

one-fourth after that year, and since the outbreak of the war, its decline has proceeded with an even greater rapidity. At present it constitutes no more than five percent of the whole export trade and in some years during the war its share even went down to one or two percent. Cotton cloth in the American export trade is, therefore, the counterpart of tea in the import trade. Both articles had been of prime importance in the past, and both are now, for reasons given in the following chapters, diminishing in importance to an almost irrecoverable degree.[1]

Breadstuffs, of which wheat flour constituted nearly nine-tenths of the value, was for some years in the preceding period heavily exported to China. Usually they amounted to between three and four percent of the total value of exports. But in 1907, which was of course an exceptional year, the value of flour and other stuffs exported to China rose to $7,700,000 or twenty-eight percent of the total. During the persent period these foodstuffs have practically dropped out of the trade, amounting to a small fraction of one percent. In 1921 and 1922 the export value was abnormally high, standing at $2,800,000 and $8,400,000 respectively or 2.4% and 7.9% of the total. But a large part of all these stuffs were sent to the North China famine-stricken districts for relief purposes and were not the result of commercial transactions. This item, therefore, may be said to have dropped out of Chino-American trade.

Mineral oils attained first place in the list when cotton cloth lost its hold. Since the end of the last century the annual quantity and value of this export has been steadily on the increase and has on the average constituted one-fourth of the total exports. During the last decade its aggregate value has been increasing, but its share in the total has decreased to about one-eighth.[2]

Tobacco, both in raw and finished state, has come to be one

of the two or three most important articles of export to China, and its growth both in absolute quantity of trade and in relative share has been a remarkable phenomenon. At the beginning of the last period, practically no raw tobacco and only very little in manufactured form was sent to China. Until the beginning of the present period the value of both finished and raw tobacco was three or four million dollars, constituting an aggregate share of fifteen percent. Now each kind is exported in increasing quantities, usually valued at more than ten million dollars, and representing nearly one-fifth of the total exports. The export of raw tobacco has increased at a higher rate of speed than manufactured tobacco, the former usually doubling that of the latter.[1]

Leather manufactures were insignificant in the trade prior to the beginning of the present period, amounting to not more than a half of one percent at a maximum actual value of $135,000. But during this period, and especially after 1917, this item has come to be an important one among the exports to China. The total value of this commodity exported to China had twice reached the three million dollar mark in 1917 and 1918, and its share amounted to 7.1% and 4.9% respectively. In 1919-22 it stood around one and a half million dollars, constituting about 1% of the total exports to China.

The most significant increase during this period was in the export of iron and steel machinery and other manufactures. Ten years ago, in 1913, trade in these articles amounted to nearly three million dollars, or 13.2% of the total exports to China. During the last few years, it rose several times to more than thirty million dollars a year, constituting from one-fourth to one-third of the total exports.[2]

Manufactures of other metals, such as lead, tin, copper, zinc, brass, aluminum etc., are also rapidly increasing. In former years copper only had been exported to China in large but spasmodic quantities. Trade in other metals and

[1] See Ch. 10, *infra*.
[2] See Ch. 11, *infra*.

[1] See Ch. 12 on Tobacco, *infra*.
[2] See Ch. 13, *infra*.

TABLE 23

COMPOSITION OF AMERICAN EXPORTS TO CHINA, INCLUDING LEASED TERRITORIES, 1914-22

| June 30 Fiscal year ending | 1914 | | 1915 | | 1916 | | 1917 | |
|---|---|---|---|---|---|---|---|---|
| Article | $1,000 | % | $1,000 | % | $1,000 | % | $1,000 | % |
| 1 Breadstuffs, incl. flour... | 1,211 | 4.6 | 97 | 0.5 | 55 | 0.2 | 45 | 0.1 |
| 2 Cars, carriages and parts | 233 | 0.9 | 232 | 1.3 | 308 | 1.2 | 892 | 2.1 |
| 3 Chemicals, drugs, dyes | 141 | 0.5 | 281 | 1.6 | 1,306 | 5.0 | 972 | 2.3 |
| 4 Cotton cloth | 6,096 | 23.1 | 1,195 | 6.8 | 863 | 3.3 | 406 | 1.0 |
| 5 Cotton goods and wearing apparel ... | 91 | 0.3 | 66 | 0.4 | 105 | 0.4 | 320 | 0.8 |
| 6 Cotton, raw | 588 | 2.2 | 734 | 4.2 | 729 | 2.8 | 405 | 1.0 |
| 7 Electrical machinery and appliances | 239 | 0.9 | 242 | 1.4 | 417 | 1.6 | 1,143 | 2.7 |
| 8 Fruits and nuts | 78 | 0.3 | 89 | 0.5 | 109 | 0.4 | 183 | 0.4 |
| 9 Glass and glassware | 21 | 0.1 | 49 | 0.3 | 270 | 1.0 | 161 | 0.4 |
| 10 Indian rubber, mfs. of | 74 | 0.3 | 49 | 0.3 | 83 | 0.3 | 97 | 0.2 |
| 11 Iron and steel, mfs. of | 2,120 | 8.0 | 2,422 | 13.8 | 4,944 | 18.8 | 7,431 | 17.8 |
| 12 Iron and steel mach'y | 1,140 | 4.3 | 564 | 3.1 | 985 | 3.7 | 1,821 | 4.4 |
| 13 Leather, tanned skins and mfs. of | 145 | 0.6 | 136 | 0.8 | 358 | 1.4 | 2,968 | 7.1 |
| 14 Metals, other than iron and steel, and mfs.of | 136 | 0.5 | 263 | 1.5 | 769 | 2.9 | 596 | 1.4 |
| 15 Meat, dairy products and other provisions | 144 | 0.6 | 322 | 1.8 | 336 | 1.3 | 961 | 2.3 |
| 16 Oils, mineral, refined... | 7,173 | 27.2 | 6,411 | 36.5 | 6,765 | 25.8 | 5,843 | 14.0 |
| 17 Paper, paper products, books | 192 | 0.7 | 234 | 1.4 | 683 | 2.6 | 1,342 | 3.2 |
| 18 Paraffin and wax... | 333 | 1.3 | 572 | 3.3 | 583 | 2.2 | 583 | 1.4 |
| 19 Tobacco, manuf'd | 1,782 | 6.7 | 1,206 | 6.8 | 2,511 | 9.6 | 9,154 | 22.0 |
| 20 Tobacco, unman'f'd | 2,005 | 7.6 | 612 | 3.5 | 1,233 | 4.7 | 1,713 | 4.1 |
| 21 Wood, timber boards, planks, etc. | 1,147 | 4.3 | 555 | 3.2 | 353 | 1.3 | 272 | 0.6 |
| 22 Wood, other mfs. | 368 | 1.4 | 234 | 1.3 | 251 | 1.0 | 636 | 1.5 |
| 23 Other articles | 843 | 3.3 | 1,026 | 5.8 | 2,246 | 8.5 | 3,733 | 9.0 |
| Total | 26,345 | 100.0 | 17,591 | 100.0 | 26,523 | 100.0 | 41,665 | 100.0 |

their manufactured products was so trifling as not to justify listing them separately. They are therefore given as a combined item in Table 23. But during recent years export of these metal products is increasing at a remarkable rate and in 1921-22 it amounted to more than six million dollars a year and constituted six percent of the total export trade.

Cars and carriages, and electrical machinery and appli-

TABLE 23—Continued

| Calendar year | 1918 | | 1919 | | 1920 | | 1921 | | 1922 | |
|---|---|---|---|---|---|---|---|---|---|---|
| No. of Item | $1,000 | % | $1,000 | % | $1,000 | % | $1,000 | % | $1,000 | % |
| 1 | 36 | .01 | 192 | 0.2 | 302 | 0.2 | 2,778 | 2.4 | 8,573 | 7.9 |
| 2 | 1,698 | 2.9 | 4,936 | 4.2 | 4,966 | 3.3 | 3,346 | 2.9 | 3,325 | 3.1 |
| 3 | 1,825 | 3.1 | 4,348 | 3.7 | 8,613 | 5.6 | 1,515 | 1.3 | 2,469 | 2.3 |
| 4 | 915 | 1.5 | 6,410 | 5.4 | 7,701 | 5.0 | 2,282 | 2.0 | 1,940 | 1.8 |
| 5 | 340 | 0.6 | 909 | 0.8 | 1,523 | 1.0 | 300 | 0.3 | 343 | 0.3 |
| 6 | 558 | 0.9 | 1,786 | 1.5 | 2,092 | 1.4 | 10,051 | 8.8 | 3,594 | 3.4 |
| 7 | 1,493 | 2.5 | 1,904 | 1.6 | 4,377 | 2.9 | 4,464 | 3.9 | 1,655 | 1.6 |
| 8 | 218 | 0.4 | 524 | 0.4 | 598 | 0.4 | 415 | 0.4 | 513 | 0.5 |
| 9 | 364 | 0.6 | 588 | 0.5 | | | 574 | 0.2 | 129 | 0.1 |
| 10 | 197 | 0.3 | 557 | 0.5 | 828 | 0.5 | 315 | .03 | 191 | 0.2 |
| 11 | 13,148 | 22.2 | 20,528 | 17.3 | 24,980 | 16.3 | 10,752 | 9.5 | 6,074 | 5.7 |
| 12 | 3,220 | 5.4 | 16,864 | 14.2 | 18,217 | 11.9 | 19,652 | 17.3 | 11,136 | 10.5 |
| 13 | 2,894 | 4.9 | 1,950 | 1.6 | 1,553 | 1.0 | 773 | 0.7 | 1,059 | 1.0 |
| 14 | 443 | 0.7 | 1,024 | 0.9 | 4,020 | 2.6 | 5,746 | 5.0 | 6,840 | 6.5 |
| 15 | 652 | 1.1 | 1,112 | 0.9 | 1,011 | 0.7 | 956 | 0.8 | 876 | 0.8 |
| 16 | 4,573 | 7.7 | 20,569 | 17.2 | 19,469 | 12.7 | 14,262 | 12.5 | 21,712 | 20.5 |
| 17 | 2,318 | 3.9 | 3,503 | 3.0 | 5,272 | 3.5 | 2,830 | 2.5 | 1,618 | 1.5 |
| 18 | 614 | 1.0 | 902 | 0.8 | 839 | 0.5 | 1,055 | 0.9 | 748 | 0.7 |
| 19 | 11,537 | 19.5 | 10,146 | 9.7 | 16,086 | 10.5 | 11,699 | 10.3 | 17,084 | 16.1 |
| 20 | 5,864 | 10.0 | 6,328 | 5.3 | 13,316 | 8.7 | 8,406 | 7.4 | 10,721 | 10.1 |
| 21 | 425 | 0.7 | 1,601 | 1.4 | 4,206 | 2.8 | 1,947 | 1.7 | 2,217 | 2.1 |
| 22 | 846 | 1.4 | 1,494 | 1.3 | 1,789 | 1.2 | 438 | 0.4 | 3,170 | 3.0 |
| 23 | 4,957 | 8.4 | 10,293 | 8.7 | 10,382 | 6.8 | 9,372 | 8.2 | ... | 0.3 |
| Total. | 59,135 | 100.0 | 118,275 | 100.0 | 152,876 | 100.0 | 113,605 | 100.0 | 106,074 | 100.0 |

ances are items which entered into the realm of Chino-American trade only in the past few years. Ten years ago, the value of exports was no more than one-quarter of a million dollars for each of the items; now, it reaches four or five million dollars. Ten years ago each of them constituted scarcely one percent of the total exports. Now they amount to three or four percent.

Another group of products whose rising importance is tantamount to that of the preceding items is paper products, including books. Only twenty years ago foreign paper and books were sent to China solely for the use of foreigners residing in China, so the volume of trade in them was necessarily negligible. Now these articles have come into gen-

eral use among the Chinese school boys. Since 1918 America alone has exported to China papers and books to a value of two to five million dollars a year or two to five percent of the total.

From the above tedious enumeration we may draw the following conclusion:

1. The simpler forms of manufactures, which formed the most important part of American export to China in the past decades, are now decreasing in importance both in absolute quantity and in relative shares, and it seems that this tendency will persist in the future. Cotton cloth and wheat flour may be taken as two examples of this class of products. As already stated, China is developing her simpler forms of industry with remarkable rapidity and she is adding every year a great many flour mills, cotton factories, etc., to the host of those already in existence. It is unlikely that foreign countries can compete with her in such lines within her own territory.

Manufactured tobacco might seem to be an exception to this general conclusion. Although this article is also a simpler form of manufacture it is being exported to China in increasing quantities. Yet the tobacco manufacturing industry is developing in China no less rapidly than the flour and cotton industries. It is owing only to the fact that the spread of the cigarette habit among the Chinese has outstripped the development of the cigarette industry in China, that she still has to import a great part of her manufactured tobacco from this country. But, nevertheless, the present tendency that American exports of unmanufactured tobacco to China have increased at a more rapid rate than those of manufactured tobacco, clearly shows that this form of industry is developing in China, and American exports of manufactured tobacco will decrease in amount sooner or later as has been the case with cotton cloth and wheat flour.[2]

[1] See Ch. 11, infra.
[2] See Ch. 12 on Tobacco, infra.

As to mineral oils, China has so far not been able to utilize her own oil fields, so she still depends largely upon the United States for its supply. Yet as electric lighting becomes more prevalent in most of the towns and cities in China any unlimited increase in the trade of these lighting oils can hardly be expected. The export figures during this period clearly indicate a decline of the share that this item formerly held.

2. Those articles which are the products of complex and large-scale industry show a decided tendency to increase both in absolute quantities and in relative share in the export trade. Iron and steel machinery and other manufactures, have increased at a most rapid rate, and in like manner, but to a less extent, cars, carriages, electrical appliances, chemicals and drugs, etc. The United States has a comparative advantage in these articles not only over China but also over other competing countries in the world because she is in possession of a great many highly developed industries engaged in a large scale production.

### Balance of Trade

With the exception of the single year 1921 the balance of trade between China and the United States has been, as in former periods, consistently in favor of China. This condition prevails rather generally in American trade with the Oriental countries. Beginning in 1915, when America was first pressed with war orders from Europe, her demand for many sorts of raw materials became more urgent, and China was just in a position to furnish them. This condition continued to 1917, a year which showed a record balance in the history of American trade with China. The huge increase in the balance was due, on the one hand, to the rapid expansion of imports from China, and on the other, to the slow development of export trade thereto.

A change from a rising to a falling trend in the balance was first evident in 1918 when peace was restored in Europe.

TABLE 24

THE BALANCE OF AMERICAN TRADE WITH CHINA, 1913-22

| Calendar year | China + Excess of American exports to | China — Excess of American imports from | China, Leased Territories + | China, Leased Territories — | China through Hongkong (estimated) — | Total (algebraic) + | Total (algebraic) — |
|---|---|---|---|---|---|---|---|
| 1913 | | 14,821 | 366 | | 4,922 | | 9,531 |
| 1914 | | 15,946 | 718 | | 4,229 | | 11,000 |
| 1915 | | 33,080 | 464 | | 3,693 | | 28,942 |
| 1916 | | 48,526 | 372 | | 5,717 | | 42,437 |
| 1917 | | 84,814 | 9,861 | | 6,321 | | 88,354 |
| 1918 | | 58,400 | 23,639 | | 7,823 | | 74,236 |
| 1919 | | 48,639 | 2,757 | | 7,729 | | 43,667 |
| 1920 | | 46,971 | 4,375 | | 10,106 | | 41,190 |
| 1921 | 7,155 | | | 4,035 | 7,827 | 19,07 | |
| 1922 | | 34,252 | | 3,655 | 8,077 | | 22,320 |
| 1923 d | | 72,767 | | 2,270 | 11,073 | | 59,424 |

a Fiscal year ending June 30.
b Only Kwantung; other English, French and former German Leased Territories, because of the small size of their trade with America, are included in "China" since 1917.
c Based on the estimated Chinese trade through Hongkong," as shown in Table 19, Chapter IV, supra. Although the writer is of the opinion that, judging from the composition of the China-Hongkong trade as reported in the Chinese Customs Returns and of the American-Hongkong trade as reported in the Foreign Commerce and Navigation of the U. S., the balance of American-Chinese trade through Hongkong must be in favor of America, yet these balances we have given, especially those in 1918-1920, might be too large. But owing to the conclusion of this transshipment no accurate figure can be obtained.
d Fiscal year ending June 30.

After the armistice was signed a greater part of the war orders which had been coming with a rush from Europe to America were gradually stopped. This enabled the latter to increase her exports to China enormously. Therefore, in spite of the continuous expansion of imports from China the balance became less and less favorable to her.

Another turn of the trade balance came with the business depression in America in 1921. In this year, nearly all branches of American industry curtailed their activities and thus diminished the demand for raw materials. Many kinds of Chinese raw materials which were in great demand in America suddenly ceased to move in the American market. On the other hand, the rapid development of industrial China, stimulated by the war, is continuing its course and requires American machinery and other equipment in increasing quantities. This condition turns the balance for the first time since 1906 in the opposite direction (See Table 24).

But with the gradual recovery of business activities in America in 1922-23 and the temporary depression in China, the United States soon resumed its large amount of purchases from the Orient, offset by comparatively small sales thereto. Therefore, the balance in 1922-23 was again highly "in favor" of China.

These huge balances were paid in part at least by silver and gold which during the last decade were exported in huge quantities from America to China. In previous chapters, we noted that the United States, being a silver and gold producing country, has consistently shipped those treasures to the Orient. But before 1913 there was practically no direct export of gold to China, although some of this metal was sent to Hongkong. Since 1916, heavy exports of gold have been sent to China and Hongkong as part payment of the excess of American imports over exports. Silver has also been sent there in even greater quantities. The actual figures of these gold and silver movements are shown in Table 26.

*Silver-Gold Situation During the War: Treasure movements between the United States and China.*

It may be interesting to make a further and brief study of the gold-silver situation during the period under discussion. Of course, silver is one of the most important commodities in American commerce, gold occupying a similar position in the trade of China. Our study of Chino-American trade will, therefore, be incomplete, if we overlook these two commodities.

One of the most striking features of the trade statistics of these two metals is the wide variation in their relative price, which they have undergone during the comparatively short period of ten years. The following table shows the Annual Average exchange of the Haikwan Tael in American dollars at average sight rate on New York 1913-1922.

TABLE 25

| Year | AVERAGE RATE OF EXCHANGE One HK. Tael = Am. Dollar |
|---|---|
| 1913 | $0.73 |
| 1914 | 0.67 |
| 1915 | 0.62 |
| 1916 | 0.79 |
| 1917 | 1.03 |
| 1918 | 1.26 |
| 1919 | 1.39 |
| 1920 | 1.24 |
| 1921 | 0.76 |
| 1922 | 0.83 |

As to the causes of the phenomenal rise in the price of silver from 1915 to 1920 we may first mention the declining world output of this metal. Before the war, the world's production of silver averaged between two hundred and twenty and two hundred and twenty-six million ounces per year; but in 1914 it dropped to two hundred and eleven million ounces; in 1915 to 179,000,000; in 1916 to 157,000,000; rising to 211,000,000 in 1917 and to 177,000,000

in 1918, but again falling to 175,000,000 ounces in 1911, and to an amount estimated at slightly less than that in 1920.[1] The United States porduces about one-third of the whole output.[2] A second cause was the extraordinary demands of the belligerents for silver after 1915. Gold had disappeared from circulation, being hoarded either by the central banks or by the people of the warring nations. England, France, Russia, Italy and other nations began to coin silver in large amounts so as to supply the needs of the people for "hard" money. Thirdly, the Oriental silver-using countries, with their increasing exports and favorable balance of trade demanded silver in squaring their account. In the latter half of 1915, therefore, the price of silver rose steadily and this upward swing did not stop its course until the latter part of 1920.

Before the rise in the price of silver in 1915 it first dropped in 1915 to the lowest figure it ever reached. The Chinese looking from the opposite angle saw not a drop in silver but a rise in gold. So they disposed for the sake of profit of much of their surplus gold to America, an amount worth $6,300,000. This was the biggest importation of gold the United States had ever received directly from China in any one year except 1920. (See Table 26).

In 1916, owing to the rising price of silver, China disposed of a large amount of her surplus silver to India and Russia at prices that, at the time, were considered most satisfactory.[3] In 1917, however, she found herself forced into the American market to replenish her stock, and made many heavy purchases there. This new demand for silver in China is said to have been responsible for the further advance of the price of silver in the latter half of that year.[4]

Owing to the heavy American purchases of raw materials in large quantities from China and other Oriental countries,

[1] Cross, I. B. Domestic and Foreign Exchange, 1923, p. 427.
[2] Ibid.
[3] See Chinese Customs Returns and Trade Reports, 1916.
[4] Cross, op. cit., p. 431.

it was necessary to pay a large quantity of hard metals for them. But the Americans disliked to pay in gold at this juncture inasmuch as they were doing all within their power to conserve their gold holdings. They finally arrived at the happy idea of paying China out of the large supply of silver dollars which the United States Treasury had stored away as security for the outstanding silver certificates. This was provided for by what is known as the Pittman Bill, signed by President Wilson on April 25, 1918. This Act, in brief, authorized the United States Secretary of the Treasury to melt and sell as bullion not over 350,000,000 standard silver dollars, then being held by the Treasury, and to sell the bullion thus obtained at not less than $1.00 per ounce. Up to May 6, 1919, 260,000,000 silver dollars had been melted down under the provisions of the act for use in foreign trade. During 1918 and 1920, the domestic silver exports to China amounted to a value of $117,398,000, and those to Hongkong to $39,528,000. Besides these domestic exports, there were during these two years, foreign silver exports to China valued at $37,000,000 and exports to Hongkong at $7,825,000.

With the price of silver going still higher, as the time went on, American exchange and trade relations with China and some other Oriental countries were seriously menaced. In 1919 one Haikwan Tael exchanged for $1.39 American currency, which is more than two times the exchange rate in 1915. In order to correct the situation to some extent, the United States treasury and the Federal Reserve Board arranged in December, 1919, to deliver the "free" silver dollars in the Treasury (viz., silver dollars not used as security for silver certificates) to the Division of Foreign Exchange of the Federal Reserve Board, which would, acting through the Federal Reserve Bank of New York in cooperation with the branches of American banks in the Orient, employ such dollars in regulating American exchanges with silver stand-

TABLE 26

AMERICAN EXPORTS AND IMPORTS OF GOLD AND SILVER COINS AND BULLION TO AND FROM CHINA AND HONGKONG, 1913-1922

Unit = $1,000

| Year | China Exports to Gold Dom. | For. | China Exports to Silver Dom. | For. | Total | China Imports from Gold | Silver | Total | Hongkong Exports to Gold Dom. | For. | Hongkong Exports to Silver Dom. | For. | Total | Hongkong Imports from Gold | Silver | Total | Net Exports of silver to China and Hongkong | Net Exports of gold to China and Hongkong | Net Import of gold from China and Hongkong |
|---|---|---|---|---|---|---|---|---|---|---|---|---|---|---|---|---|---|---|---|
| 1913* | 103 | | 2,222 | | 2,332 | 7 | 11 | 26 | | 1 | 7,720 | | 7,741 | | | | 9,949 | 100 | |
| 1914 | | 97 | 1,216 | | 1,413 | | | | | 6 | 8,058 | | 8,115 | | | | 1,522 | 6 | |
| 1915 | | 2 | 225 | | 227 | 8,268 | | 6,268 | | 47 | 5,797 | | 5,865 | | | | 6,045 | | 6,221 |
| 1916 | 4,806 | | 2,489 | | 7,295 | 1,623 | 480 | 2,110 | | 63 | 5,752 | | 10,625 | | | | 7,791 | 8,018 | |
| 1917* | 702 | | 7,564 | | 8,940 | 1,566 | 218 | 211 | 1 | 29 | 4,991 | | 6,509 | | | | 12,283 | 2,326 | |
| 1918 | | 156 | 14,849 | 15,720 | 20,651 | 14,603 | | 12,007 | 227 | | 12,007 | | 12,234 | | 10,038 | 10,038 | 27,943 | | |
| 1919 | 58,932 | 15,751 | 45,397 | | 99,651 | 16,693 | 1,295 | 80,981 | 11,913 | 10 | 97,233 | | 50,323 | 10,018 | | 39 | 97,895 | 69,178 | |
| 1920 | 28,357 | 7,110 | 5,671 | 12,783 | | 17,921 | 17,288 | 39,259 | | 56,370 | 36,352 | 56,372 | 36,194 | 84,952 | 25,830 | | | | |
| 1921 | | | 5,671 | | | 7,913 | 9 | 9,401 | 4,598 | 26,029 | 5,661 | 5,661 | 32,393 | 25,830 | 13,952 | | | | |
| 1922 | 100 | 250 | 9,807 | 11,569 | 20,926 | 5,538 | 12 | 8,550 | 3,592 | 10,163 | 6,273 | 20,017 | 15 | 17,000 | | 5,021 | | | |

* From 1913 to 1917, fiscal year ending June 30.
** Since 1938, calendar year.

ard countries, especially China.[1] About $13,000,000 of silver was shipped to Shanghai under this arrangement during the early months of 1920.[2] The sudden decline in the price of silver which occurred within a few months made further shipments unnecessary.

The United States had shipped not only much silver to China during the war and immediately after it, but also a huge quantity of gold. During 1919 and 1920, when the drain on the American silver supply was most oppressive America sent to China gold to the value of $67,000,000 and to the value of $71,600,000 to Hongkong. But when the silver situation eased up and the price of silver dropped almost to its pre-war level, a portion of this gold was sent back to America in 1920 and 1921.

[1] Cross, op. cit., p. 434.
[2] Ibid.

# PART II

## Some Important American Imports from China

## CHAPTER VI.

### TEA.

*1. Early History of Tea Trade between the United States and China.* The early history of tea in the West is intimately bound up with that of the foreign trade of China. In all probability Chinese tea first reached America from England.[1] Since 1711 the British East India Company practically monopolized the tea trade between China and the United States, and it is said that the company reaped a handsome profit therefrom.[2] Although it is impossible now to determine the exact quantity of tea imports into the American Colonies in those days, yet it is fairly certain that this article took a quite significant share of the total colonial imports.

It is quite interesting to note the early American tea trade in connection with the American Revolution and the establishment of the United States. Although tea is an article which may be said to have connotations eminently peaceful, yet it has been the cause of several wars and a number of political problems. It was the three-penny tax on Chinese tea that led the English colonists to revolt against their mother country and to establish the United States. It was Chinese tea that was chosen above all others to emphasize the principles that "All men are born free and equal" and that "taxation without representation is tyranny." Who, in looking back over a long range of events in American history, can fail to have his attention attracted to what has been termed, with a characteristic touch of American humor, "The Boston Tea Party of 1773"?

After the reestablishment of peace the first direct commercial transaction between the United States and China was

[1] Walsh, J. M.; *Tea; Its History and Mystery,* p. 23. Philadelphia, 1892.
[2] Day, Samuel Phillips; *Tea, Its History and Mystery,* p. 59. London, 1878.

123

concerned with tea.[1] In 1784 the American ship *Empress of China* was sent to China, and in the following year brought back a full cargo of the herb, reaping a handsome profit.[2] Since that time swift ships have been expressly built in the United States for the tea trade. They were the first of the class of vessels known as "clippers" in which speed was sought at the expense of carrying capacity, and by which the average passage was reduced twenty or thirty days for the round trip.[3] During the last ten years of the eighteenth century, the American importation of tea averaged about 2,600,000 pounds each year, a small part of which—usually less than five per cent—was imported indirectly by way of England. Very little was re-exported because the quantity imported was just enough for home consumption.

As the American merchant marine became more developed and especially active in Chinese waters,[4] tea trade accordingly increased in volume. From 1800 to 1810 the annual import was about 5,400,000 pounds, being more than double the figure of the preceding decade. The exportation of teas from China in American ships, however, was not to supply the home market alone. There were also large shipments of tea to other countries, both directly from China and by re-exportation from the United States. During the Napoleonic wars the proportion of re-export was large, amounting usually to a third of the year's imports.[5]

The American war with England in 1812 caused a serious decline in the Chinese tea trade with America. But after the close of the war the recovery was rapid, and in a few years tea had almost become the sole important article of import from China. In value the proportion of tea to the total American imports from China during the early years is

[1] See Ch. I.
[2] *Ibid.*
[3] Walsh, J. M.; *Tea; Its History and Mystery,* p. 6.
[4] See Chapter I.
[5] Pitkins: *Statistic View of the Commerce of the United States,* ed. 1836, pp. 246-247.

shown quinquennially in Table 27. It can be readily seen that in the years following 1814 the relative proportion of tea to other Chinese imports constantly increased, until in 1840 it amounted to eighty-two per cent. of the total. After this year the ratio declined, though slowly, and in another score of years it became 65.5 per cent.

### TABLE 27

#### THE PROPORTION OF TEA IMPORTS TO THE TOTAL AMERICAN IMPORTS, FROM CHINA

| Year | Per cent. | Year | Per cent. |
|------|-----------|------|-----------|
| 1821 | 42.5 | 1840 | 82.0 |
| 1825 | 49.5 | 1845 | 79.0 |
| 1830 | 62.5 | 1850 | 71.5 |
| 1835 | 75.5 | 1855 | 70.0 |
|      |      | 1860 | 65.5 |

During this early period the absolute increase in the quantity of tea imported was fairly steady, from five million pounds in 1821, to nine millions in 1830, twenty millions in 1840, thirty millions in 1850, and twenty-six millions in 1860; but the per capita consumption in this country did not show any regular increase.

After the beginning of the nineteenth century the American tea traders entered into very keen competition with the British East India Company. Not only was the monopoly in tea trade which the company had enjoyed throughout the eighteenth century ruined, but the very existence of the Company was threatened, because the English Parliament felt dissatisfaction over the company's defeat. This led R. M. Martin, a member of the English Parliament, to make an elaborate report to the legislature for the purpose of defending the company.[1] This, however, had little effect, and

[1] Martin, R. Montgomery: *The Past and Present State of the Tea Trade of England, and of the Continent of Europe and America.* London, 1832.

the charter of the East India Company was not renewed at its expiration in 1833.

The success of American tea traders in their competition with the British concern is said to be that in striking contrast with the British policy in applying a heavy duty to tea trade and thus checking trade extension, the United States exempted tea almost entirely from duty. This has been the case since 1832.[1]

*2. The beginning of Japanese Competition.* Up to 1856 Chinese tea was the only tea used in the United States as well as in all other countries. But since that year China's tea monopoly has been gradually shattered, her supremacy challenged and then utterly ruined. It is sad, therefore, for the writer to review the history of China's defeat in the American tea market first at the hands of Japan, then at those of India and recently, to a lesser extent, of Java. Yet the whole history of China's tea trade with America after 1856 is nothing more than a chapter of defeat in this competition.

In 1856 a small quantity of Japanese teas—"consisting of about fifty half chests"—was first received in the United States.[2] "Being found pure and free from coloring-matter," it soon became very popular with consumers, a large number of whom were prejudiced against Chinese green teas at the time, under the impression that they were more or less artificially colored. The demand steadily increased, four hundred half-chests being imported the following year and one thousand one hundred chests in 1859.[3] About 1860 the Japanese changed their mode of curing, adopting that of the Chinese as applied to green teas, with the result that the color was altered from a dark to a light green, and a high malty flavor was imparted.[4] Since that time Japanese teas

[1] Nye, Gideon: *Tea and Tea Trade.* Canton, 1850. Part II, p.
[2] Walsh, J. M., *op. cit.,* p. 99.
[3] *Ibid.*
[4] *Ibid.,* p. 100.

have continued to grow in popular favor, not because Japanese teas were in any sense of the word better than the Chinese teas, but simply because they were prepared in such a way as to suit the American fancy and command a market in America. They found little market in England and other European countries, where the consumers in those days still favored Chinese teas.[1]

Insignificant as the beginning of the Japanese tea trade might seem to be, yet the root of the victory of Japanese teas over the Chinese lies in the very fact that the Japanese whether for good or for ill can make their product suit the American fancy. "In the selling market the buyer holds the key." With his choice the seller must comply. Always sticking to her good old rule, China did not seem to care for this. Her tea trade failed in this, in the same way that her silk trade failed. No regular separate statistics for the imports of Japanese teas into the United States for the period before 1865 can now be obtained. Since then, however, complete statistics may be compiled from the data supplied by the United States Bureau of Statistics. From Table 28 we notice that down to the end of the nineteenth century China and Japan together held the monopoly of the American tea market. Though the direct imports from these two countries were usually ninety-five per cent of the total American tea imports, some Chinese teas still continued to be shipped here indirectly by way of England while Indian and Ceylon teas took an insignificant part, usually less than one per cent. The following table shows the decline of Chinese tea imports into America on the one hand, and the expansion of Japanese on the other during the last three decades of the nineteenth century.

From 1865 to 1894, a period of three decades, the imports of tea into the United States had been more than trebled in consequence of the expansion of the nation and the increase of population, both the Chinese and the Japanese imports

[1] *Ibid.*

having increased in absolute amounts. Yet the Japanese share became larger and larger, while China's suffered an irrecoverable decline. In the first five years, 1865-69, Japan had a share of less than one fifth of the American tea, while China's share was greater than three fourths. In only a decade the former increased to more than one third and the latter diminished to less than one half. Since 1880 Chinese teas have been able to hold their own even though they have felt keenly the severe competition of Japan. This, together with the diminishing importance of raw silk exports to the United States due to similar competition, explains why the total American imports from China did not make any appreciable increase during the second period of our trade history.

TABLE 28

THE DISTRIBUTION OF AMERICAN TEA TRADE
1865-1894

| Years | Total Annual Average Import in 1,000 lbs. | Total % | China in 1,000 lbs. | % of the total | Japan in 1,000 lbs. | % of the total |
|---|---|---|---|---|---|---|
| 1865-69 | 34,789 | 100 | 26,674 | 77% | 6,674 | 19% |
| 1870-74 | 56,642 | 100 | 37,997 | 67 | 14,120 | 25 |
| 1875-79 | 62,330 | 100 | 29,810 | 48 | 25,433 | 41 |
| 1880-84 | 74,784 | 100 | 38,927 | 52 | 34,076 | 46 |
| 1885-89 | 81,606 | 100 | 41,078 | 50 | 35,692 | 43 |
| 1890-94 | 88,000 | 100 | 45,155 | 51 | 38,335 | 44 |

*3. The Decline of Chinese Tea Trade with America.* The beginning of the decline of Chinese tea trade with America dates back thirty years. In 1895 the total American direct imports of tea from China attained their highest mark, being fifty-five million pounds. Since then the drop has been consistent and heavy, and China appears to have lost perhaps for all time her profitable trade with America. The disastrous drop in tea imports can be graphically presented in the following average quinquennial figures. It

dropped first from forty-eight million pounds in 1895-99 to forty-seven millions, in 1900-4, then to thirty-four millions in 1905-9, to twenty-three millions in 1910-14, and even after the outbreak of the European War when other imports from China were greatly stimulated and increased, tea imports dropped again to nineteen million pounds, in 1915-19, and to eleven millions in 1920 with only a little recovery since 1921. The percentages of these figures, computed on the total American tea imports in the corresponding periods as bases, are 54%, (1895-99), 49%, 35%, 24%, 17.5% (1915-19) and 11.8% respectively. (See Table 29.) To the causes which underlie this decisive defeat of China in the American tea market, the rest of the chapter will be chiefly devoted.

*Causes of the Decline*

There are two main causes of the final ruinous decline of Chinese tea trade with America. The first, which we may term as the internal cause, is the inefficiency in the method of tea manufacture and the non-improvement of the quality of teas in China; and the second, which we may term as external, is the strong competition from nearly every country in the Far East—first, Japan, then India and Ceylon, Java, and finally even Formosa, formerly a part of China's own territory! These two causes, though properly so distinguished, combine to produce a single result that the improvement in the culture and in the manufacture of tea in other countries outstripped that of China and made the Americans as well as Europeans dissatisfied with Chinese teas with which they had formerly felt contented. Now let us consider the external competition.

*(1) Japanese Competition.* Although in the European tea market, Japanese competition has not been strongly felt by either the East Indies or China, in America it is mainly Japanese teas that have encroached upon China's market and nearly ruined it. The case has been somewhat altered since the War, because recently Japan's teas have been subjected

TABLE 29

THE DISTRIBUTION OF AMERICAN TEA IMPORTS BY COUNTRIES IN
QUINQUENNIAL AVERAGES IN 1,000 LBS. AND PERCENTAGES

| Year | China 1000 lbs. | % | Japan | | England | | British East Indies | |
|---|---|---|---|---|---|---|---|---|
| 1895-99 | 43,310 | 54.0 | 35,037 | 39.0 | 3,489 | 4.0 | 1,647 | 2.0 |
| 1900-04 | 46,560 | 49.6 | 36,222 | 38.5 | 4,380 | 4.6 | 4,953 | 5.3 |
| 1905-09 | 34,273 | 35.0 | 43,084 | 44.0 | 9,568 | 9.7 | 7,734 | 7.9 |
| 1910-14 | 22,934 | 24.1 | 46,245 | 48.7 | 11,595 | 12.2 | 10,319 | 10.9 |
| 1915-19 | 18,995 | 17.5 | 48,317 | 44.5 | 9,350 | 8.6 | 19,822 | 18.3 |
| 1920 | 10,625 | 11.8 | 29,750 | 32.9 | 13,900 | 15.4 | 24,686 | 27.4 |
| 1921 | 14,676 | 19.2 | 21,407 | 28.0 | 9,208 | 12.0 | 23,012 | 30.1 |
| 1922 | 14,649 | 15.0 | 36,388 | 37.4 | 14,534 | 15.0 | 20,031 | 20.6 |

| Year | Dutch East Indies | | Canada | | | | Total | |
|---|---|---|---|---|---|---|---|---|
| 1895-99 | 0 | 0.0 | 1,429 | 1.0 | | | 89,629 | 100 |
| 1900-04 | 1 | 0.0 | 1,735 | 2.0 | | | 94,342 | 100 |
| 1905-09 | 5 | 0.0 | 2,712 | 3.0 | | | 98,353 | 100 |
| 1910-14 | 162 | 0.1 | 2,788 | 2.9 | | | 95,126 | 100 |
| 1915-19 | 8,476 | 7.8 | 2,676 | 2.8 | | | 108,429 | 100 |
| 1920 | 6,698 | 7.4 | 1,645 | 1.8 | | | 90,247 | 100 |
| 1921 | 5,302 | 7.0 | 756 | 1.0 | | | 76,487 | 100 |
| 1922 | 7,166 | 7.4 | 674 | 0.7 | | | 97,097 | 100 |

to the keen competition of teas from the British and Dutch
East Indies. From 1895 to 1914, a period of two decades,
China lost a share of thirty per cent. of the total American
imports (54.0%—24.1%) (See Table 29). Japan got about
one-third of China's loss (48.7%—39.0%—9.7%). To
account for this victory of Japan, the writer has already
called the reader's attention to the fact that Japan can make
her product fit the American fancy. What America wants
is a large quantity of tea of a uniform quality such as her
large scale marketing methods demand. This is the very
thing Japan has tried to supply. The following is a descrip-

tion of the Japanese attempt at the conquest of the American
tea market as described by a Japanese tea trader.[1]

Machinery was early introduced in Japan into tea manufacturing, and in many prefectures mechanical processes are
rapidly replacing the old manual ones. As early as 1885
steaming and firing machines were adopted by a manufacturer in Saitama Prefecture.[2] As labor becomes more expensive, however, machinery becomes more popular and the
output more adaptable to the American market. The use of
machinery again helps Japan to compete successfully with
China in the American tea market in that it materially re-
duces the cost of production. A report from the Shizuoka
Tea Manufacturers' Association gives the present cost of the
production of hand-made tea as being 1.00 to 1.20 yen
(fifty to sixty cents) per kwamme as against only thirty-five
to forty-five sen (17.5 to 22.5 cents) for machine made tea.[3]

Becoming aware of the advantages of combination and
co-operation, the Japanese manufacturers have long turned
their tea culture and manufacture from a household industry into one of large scale production. Since 1876 a number
of companies have been established and are directing their
operations towards the finishing of the leaves for export.
Tea growers and small individual manufacturers adopted a
system of cooperation and combination to lower the cost of
production for the purpose of maintaining their foreign
market and also in the hope of leading to the production of
uniform goods in large quantities, together with uniform
packing and finishing. Government, municipalities and
manufacturers' associations are also actively engaged in the
promotion of the industry, and in this connection a system
of supervision and protection has been perfected. It is the
duty of manufacturers' associations, under the guidance of

[1] Japan's Tea Industry and Trade. The Trans-Pacific, Tokio;
Jan., 1920, p. 73.
[2] Ibid.
[3] Ibid.

the Japanese Government, to prevent the manufacture and
sale of inferior or adulterated tea, to improve and unify the
packing and drying of teas, and to make a compulsory inspection of the products of a member manufacturer. Agents
of these associations are despatched to America and elsewhere for the purpose of promoting and guarding their
oversea interests. Inspection houses are maintained in the
important tea ports of Japan to prevent the export of inferior, adulterated, or colored tea which might be rejected
by inspectors in America or elsewhere. Experimental
plantations and laboratories are also established in tea producing centers. The propaganda work for Japanese green
tea in America is also undertaken by these associations.

In view of these attempts which Japan has made to promote her tea sales in foreign markets, is there any wonder
that Japan should get a fair share in the tea imports of this
country? In fact, all Japan's efforts in promoting her exports of tea are directed toward the American market, because by far the greater part of Japanese tea exports, usually
more than 90 percent, comes to the United States.

(2) The Competition of the British East Indies. Besides
Japanese competition, China has also suffered from East
Indian competition in her tea trade with America. Tea
industry and trade were almost unknown in India half a
century ago. Since that time tea is fast becoming an important article in her business, particularly in the English markets. Only thirty years ago imports of Indian teas into
America were very small, although Chinese teas had already
felt their competition. Mr. J. M. Walsh, in his interesting
essay, Tea, Its History and Mystery described the difference
between Indian and Chinese teas in their competition in the
American tea market as follows:—

"In India the process of fermenting and firing the tea are
not as detailed or complete as in China, the India planter
aiming to secure the component properties of a strong tea
at the expense of flavor and qualities. There are many

serious objections to the general use of India Teas, one of
which is the great excess of "tannin" (tannic acid) which
they contain, ranging from thirteen to eighteen per cent.,
and to which property tea owes its astringency, constipating
effect on the bowels and the ink-black color which it imparts
to water containing salts of iron. In England a crusade is
being preached against their use by medical authorities. On
the other hand, China teas possess little or no trace of tannic
acid, or elements offending the most sensitive palate or con-
stitution. They are both pleasing and refreshing to the
most sensitive natures."[1]

Owing to the inferiority of Indian teas, the demand for
them in the United States was at that time very limited, and
according to Mr. Walsh, there appeared little hope of any
increase in the future. Though strenuous efforts had been
made by the British tea traders to introduce them to this
country, they met with little success. This was accounted
for by Mr. Walsh as "the character of the beverage after
infusion being so entirely foreign in body, color, flavor, and
aroma from that of China and Japan sorts to which the
people in the United States have become accustomed, so
deeply is it set, that little or no progress can be made in these
attempts."

Yet from thirty years' experience we have come to see
this prediction gradually disproved. Although at the end of
the last century, the average annual tea imports into the
United States from the British East Indies amounted to only
two per cent. of the American total tea imports, the ratio
has advanced by leaps and bounds since the beginning of the
present century, until in 1920 it came to 27.4%, which is
two and a half times the percentage of China, and only a
little smaller than that of Japan. The significance of this
share will be greatly increased, if one notices the fact that tea
imports from England now consist mostly of Indian teas.
These teas are not only driving away Chinese teas but also

[1] Page 111.

Japanese teas, from America. The success of Indian teas in replacing other teas is largely ascribable to the aggressive selling method of British tea traders in the United States. But the taste of Americans, like that of their English brothers a few decades ago, has gradually become accustomed to the strong infusion of Indian teas.

*(3) Competition of the Dutch East Indies.* Although the importation of Java tea into the United States may be said to have commenced in 1905, when eight thousand pounds was shipped to America, the direct business done with the United States was unimportant until 1918.[1] After the first importation little improvement was made until 1911, when 228,000 pounds of Java tea valued at $36,000 was shipped to America. But in 1918, due to war demands in the United States, a big increase was made, the figure being thirty million pounds of tea at a value of $5,615,000. In the same year Chinese teas imported into the United States amounted to only twenty-one million pounds valued at $4,362,000, imports of Java tea exceeding these figures by nearly one-third. Since the close of the War, the demand for Java tea in this country is decreasing. It has, nevertheless, already established itself in the American market, and its share will not return to its pre-war insignificance. This permanent advance has been made at the expense of China.

It is said that a large quantity of Dutch East Indian teas is consumed in the United States, being purchased either in transit under optional bills of lading or at the London public auctions. But the Dutch planters, not content with such indirect selling, are making efforts to develop a direct trade with America.

Although the competition from all directions has been so keen in the American tea market, Chinese teas would not have been driven out had it not been for some internal causes

[1] Java, Division of Industry and Commerce of the Department of Agriculture, Industry, and Commerce. *Java Tea.* 1917.

which have actually ruined the once flourishing market. These internal causes may be enumerated as follows:—

*(1) The inefficiency of the Chinese methods of cultivation.* The general circumstances of Chinese tea cultivation contrast strongly with those of India, Ceylon and Java. In the latter places, practically all teas are grown on large plantations. The plantation system has the advantage of raising a large quantity of tea of a uniform quality as required by the large-scale marketing of the United States. But in China, practically all tea is raised on small peasant holdings of a few acres. The tea season is short as compared with that in the tropical regions, having but three or four pluckings a year.

*(2) The inefficiency of manufacturing.* While machinery has long been used in Japan and India in the manufacturing of teas, the manufacture in China is still carried on by hand, only very simple appliances being used. Many attempts have been made by the Chinese to introduce better methods of manufacturing, but with no appreciable success. In regard to the use of machinery it is a question whether the circumstances of the Chinese industry—notably the short season and peasant proprietorship—do not render the use of expensive appliances economically impossible.[1] Machinery was once tried for the rolling of the leaves in one center in 1899, but there was "difficulty in obtaining fresh tea leaves in sufficient quantity."[2]

*(3) The adulteration of tea.* Perhaps nothing has done more toward destroying China's tea market in foreign countries than the occasional exportation of adulterated teas. Even as early as 1888 the American Minister at Peking reported to the United States Government the causes of the decline of Chinese tea trade with America as "false samples,

[1] Chandler, S. E., and McEwan, John; *Tea: Its Cultivation, Manufacture, and Commerce;* Great Britain, Imperial Institute Bulletin, Vol. II, 1913, p. 295.
[2] *Chinese Maritime Customs, Returns and Trade Reports,* 1899, p. 4.

muster packages, the admixture of lie tea, and other deleterious substances."[1] In 1899 the United States adopted regulations to prevent the importation of adulterated tea and took steps to secure their enforcement.[2] These regulations, we are told, had a decided effect in improving the quality of the Chinese green tea offered for export. But the facing or artificial coloring of green teas had long been a feature of the Chinese tea industry and continued for another decade in the manufacturing of teas intended solely for export, of which the most highly colored kinds had hitherto been sent to the American market.[3] In 1911, however, the American market was again officially closed to all faced teas.[3] Apparently no action was taken in China to meet the new situation because a market for the colored teas was found elsewhere in Turkey and Egypt. The Japanese Government, however, immediately issued an order forbidding the facing practice.[2]

*(4) Heavy export duties on tea.* The heavy export duties imposed by the Chinese Government on tea have done a great deal in the past half century to handicap Chinese tea

[1] *U. S. Com. Rel.,* 1888, p. 862. Report of Minister Denby. The methods of adulterating Chinese teas are described in Paul Kränsel, *Entwicklung und gegenwärtiger Stand des Chinesische Theehandels* (Berlin, 1902, p. 24-5), as follows: "Die Fälschungen des Thees deschehen im allgemeinen auf zwierlei Arten und zwar: (1) durch künstliche Färbung der Blätter geringer Theeorten, um diesen das Aussehen besser Qualitäten zu geben, und (2) durch Vermischung und Zusatz von Blättern anderer Pflanzen, welche gar nicht zur Theegattung gehören."
[2] *Chinese Maritime Customs, Returns of Trade,* 1889, p. 4. The comment on the American regulations contains this amusing touch: "A consignment of tea, which was rejected by the American inspectors and sent back to Shanghai, was reshipped in its original condition and was allowed to be imported."
[3] Chandler, S. E., and McEwan, John, *op. cit.,* p. 297. Mr. Chandler and Mr. McEwan also mentioned the several substances used in the coloring process as gypsum, Prussian blue, indigo, and plumbago.

and to prevent its competing successfully with the teas of other countries. The export duty was originally fixed by the Treaty of Nanking, 1842[1] and again by the Treaty of Tientsin, 1858[2] at two and one-half taels per picul (133 ⅓ lbs.), which was to represent the rate of five per cent *ad valorem.* Tea, however, had never reached so high a figure as fifty taels per picul, and this rate of two and one-half taels per picul had long been held to be excessive.[3] Later on the diminishing value of teas resulted in the export duty representing forty instead of five per cent.[4] In addition to this excessive export duty, the Chinese Government has imposed an inland duty, called likin, or war tax, together with other minor barrier exactions, making a total impost of about four and one-half taels per picul.[5]

Unlike this system of taxation the teas of India and Ceylon, Java, and Japan are exported free of all duties. Is there any wonder that these latter teas should drive Chinese teas out of the markets of the world?

*(5) The complete lack of advertising.* It is generally conceded that the failure on the part of China to maintain her tea market in America as well as in other countries is to a very great extent due to the complete lack of advertising. From the earliest time down to the present, we have heard many tea connoisseurs and exporters maintain that the best tea in the world is still produced in China. To mention only a single example the writer extracts the following quotation from an American on tea.

"China tea is the only true tea, surpassing that of all other countries in every property and quality constituting and distinguishing tea, and possessing certain distinctive characteristics peculiar to and contained in no other variety

[1] Article X.
[2] Article XX.
[3] *U. S. Com. Rel.,* 1888, p. 862. Report of Minister Denby.
[4] *Tea Trade of China,* Sci. Am. (N. Y.) Suppl. No. 1411. Jan. 17, 1903, p. 22612.
[5] *U. S. Com. Rel., op. cit.*

grown or known.[1] . . . While the great excess of tannic acid in Indian teas make them unwholesome for constant use, China teas possess little or no trace of this acid.[2] The chief and only advantages that India and Ceylon teas possess over those of China are said to be their great strength and thickness in the cup, which are due mainly to the modern methods of fermentation and firing by steam and machinery. Chinese teas excel them in flavor and aroma, occupying a position analogous to that of French wines in comparison with those of other countries. There is also this difference between them, that while a given quantity of India and Ceylon teas will yield a larger amount of a dark-colored liquor and stronger in taste than that of a similar quantity of China, they still lack the richness and delicacy of the latter."[3]

Likewise it was stated by an American consul in China some years ago that a dozen virtues of China teas might be claimed without overstepping the bounds of truth.[4] An English tea expert also conceded that as to the quality of teas, those of China are still held to be the best of all.[5]

In spite of the good advertising points of the China teas the Chinese tea merchants seem to have completely neglected to conduct any kind of advertising either in the United States or in other countries. As a consequence most Americans have overlooked the good qualities of Chinese teas, and because many tea imports from China were of an extremely poor quality, they concluded that China produced no good tea. Regarding this point the Inspector General of Chinese Customs, an Englishman, made the following pertinent comment: "While the finest teas in the world are still produced

[1] J. M. Walsh, op. cit., p. 70.
[2] Ibid., p. 111.
[3] J. M. Walsh, op. cit., p. 121.
[4] Tea Trade of China, Sci. Am. (N. Y.) Suppl. No. 1411, Jan. 17, 1903, p. 22612.
[5] Chandler, S. E., and McEwan, J., op. cit., p.

in China, it is unfortunately true that a large quantity of what can only be described as rubbish is brought by foreign exporters."[1]

Advertising is the lifeblood of commerce at the present day, and is freely resorted to in all business wherever there is an element of competition. "The so-called great favor with which India and Ceylon teas are said to be regarded by some European and American consumers is due largely to the energy and persistency with which the trade has been pushed by means of advertising, the teas being literally forced on the market."[2]

Moreover, it is generally conceded that the use of machinery in the manufacturing of tea causes great deterioration in its quality, and more than once the Japanese Government has made efforts to prevent its use. But as the cost of labor in Japan rapidly advances the use of machinery cannot be prevented owing to the great reduction in cost of production to about one-third of that of hand-made tea.[3]

To these fundamental causes which have been at work in the gradual replacing of Chinese teas in the American markets by those of other countries during the last sixty years, we must add two temporary causes which have recently restricted Chinese tea trade with America. The temporary prohibitions and restrictions imposed by the United States on tea imports from China and the lack of tonnage in the trans-Pacific service during and immediately after the War combined to bring about a serious drop in Chinese tea imports from 1917 to 1920. But as soon as these causes were removed, the quantity of tea imports began to increase though their value has shown wide fluctuations due to price drops in 1921 and 1922.

Due to the combined working of these external and internal causes, China's tea trade with America has dropped

[1] Chinese Customs Returns, 1913, Pt. II, Vol. 3, p. 553.
[2] Walsh, op. cit., p. 120.
[3] Tea Industry and Trade of Japan, The Trans-Pacific, Tokio, Japan, Jan., 1920, p. 73.

from one hundred per cent sixty years ago to less than twelve per cent in 1920. This serious drop has been attracting the attention of the Chinese for a long time and measures toward removing the internal causes have been taken up. Thus, when the United States adopted regulations to prevent the importation of adulterated tea in 1899, vigorous representations were made by the Chinese tea traders to their own government upon the subject of the taxation of tea exports, and in 1902 the export duty was reduced by a half to one and a quarter tael per picul, so that the cost of tea exportation to the United States would not increase with the required improvement in the quality. In 1905 a Chinese commission visited the tea districts of India and Ceylon, with a view to adopting the Indian plantation system in China. English machinery has also been repeatedly introduced into the country, though no permanent good has hitherto attended these efforts. Recently the Chinese Government ordered the establishment of tea investigation bureaus at Hankow, Foochow, Shanghai, and other tea producing and exporting centers, and has taken other steps to improve the old-fashioned methods of cultivation. Hereafter, owing to the greater attention that both the Chinese Government and tea merchants have been giving to the tea trade, Chinese tea will be in a stronger position to meet the competition of other countries. It is, nevertheless, problematical when, if ever, China will be able to regain her former prestige and supremacy in the tea trade of the United States, which has become a very poor customer for Chinese teas, taking less than one-fifth of the total Chinese tea exports during the last ten years, and in some years as little as 14.7%.

## CHAPTER VII

### SILK

Although China is now suffering from keen competition in the sale of her silk to the United States by far the most important position in Chinese-American trade is still held by this single article. In the last few years the total value of imports of Chinese raw silk and manufactured silks into the United States amounted on the average to no less than forty percent of the total value of all imports from that country.[1]

Yet the whole history of China's silk trade with America, in many respects like that of her tea trade, is a chapter of humiliating defeat in her competition with Japan and, to a less extent, with Europe. There is, however, at least one important difference between China's trade in silk and her trade in tea with America. In the tea industry China has lost her comparative advantage over other countries, because they have introduced machinery into the manufacturing processes of tea while she is still not in an advantageous position to use machinery,[2] or at least will not be in a better position than her competitors to use it in the future. She will, therefore, not be able to recover the whole of her lost share even though the tea industry is much improved and the tea trade energetically pushed. But this is not the case with silk. Sericulture requires a good deal of labor and because of the nature of the industry, the use of machinery can not, and perhaps will not, be introduced into the culture of silk worms on any extensive scale. The development of sericulture, therefore, depends upon a huge supply of labor which can be commanded at a rather low price as the first requisite for its success in a competitive market. It goes without saying

[1] In 1919 the value of China silk and silks imported into the United States was 39% of the total imports; in 1920, 34%; in 1921, 52%. See following table.
[2] See Chapter 6, supra.

that in this respect China is in a better position than any other silk producing country. Although in the past she neglected to make improvements in this industry, and was also slack in pushing her trade in large silk-consuming countries such as the United States, she still retains her comparative advantage in the production of this article. If China continues to pay more attention to silk, as she is now doing, it will not be long before she resumes the predominant position that she had once held in the silk trade world. It is the writer's purpose to show in the following pages how China has been defeated in the American silk market, the largest market in the world, and what effort she is now making to get back some part, at least of her lost share in America.

### China's early trade with America.

As the original home of silk China has been for centuries exporting silk to the western nations. Some Chinese silks no doubt reached this country in the early colonial days, although the exact date of their first coming can not be ascertained from the records of trade extant today. In the beginning of the direct trade between China and the United States the quantity and value of silk imports, unlike tea, were much less clearly stated in the records of the early American Government and writers. Judging from some sporadic records,[1] we are fairly sure that aside from tea, silks were the most important article of trade in those early years, though the silk imports were smaller in quantity and value than tea. Yet silk trade became more and more important as time went on, and during the several years after 1820 the value of imported Chinese silks ran into several million dollars a year, several times amounting to more than two-fifths of the total imports from China.

### Decline of trade in Manufactured Silks

During the early half of the nineteenth century nearly all

[1] S. E. Morison: *The Maritime History of Massachusetts* (Boston, 1922), pp. 44, 62, 87.

American silk imports were in the form of manufactured silks—piece goods, embroideries, ribbons, etc. Very little raw silk was imported, because the silk manufacturing industry in this country had not as yet taken shape. Prior to 1873, practically all the demand for silks in America was met by the importation of foreign manufactures. And this demand was growing steadily as is shown in Table 30. Since 1883, however, the American silk industry has become well developed, and the demand for foreign silk goods has remained stationary.

TABLE 30

| Year | Total Imports of Manufactured Silks into the U. S. | Imports from China | China's % of the total |
|---|---|---|---|
| 1823 | $5,201,000 | $3,122,000 | 60.0 |
| 1833 | 7,913,000 | 1,387,000 | 17.0 |
| 1843 | 2,458,000 | .......... | ... |
| 1853 | 29,834,000 | 1,220,000 | 4.1 |
| 1863 | 12,656,000 | 9,700 | 0.1 |
| 1873 | 29,126,000 | 130,000 | 0.5 |
| 1883 | 33,967,000 | 350,000 | 1.0 |
| 1893 | 38,959,000 | 362,000 | 1.0 |
| 1903 | 33,995,000 | 269,000 | 0.8 |
| 1913 | 35,308,000 | 173,000 | 0.5 |

Although the increase in America's demand for foreign-made silks was fairly rapid during the first seven or eight decades of the nineteenth century, the decline of China's share in this trade was nevertheless marked. In 1823 Chinese silk goods constituted sixty percent of the total silk imports into the United States. During the forty years following, her share dropped headlong to 17% in 1833, to 4.1% in 1853, to 0.1% in 1863. Since then and until the outbreak of the European War, it fluctuated around 1% of the total.

The reasons for this decline are not difficult to seek. In the first place Chinese silk goods have never been manufac-

tured for the purpose of exporting, and thus have never been made to suit the taste and fancy of westerners. Americans, therefore, preferred to have their silk goods made in England or France. Secondly, America has in the course of half a century developed into the largest silk manufacturing country in the whole world, and can today easily supply her own needs. Thirdly, the American protective tariff as applied to silk goods has been almost prohibitive since the middle of the last century, and Chinese silks, being unable to bear the burden, were the first to be excluded from the market.

Since 1914, the situation in the manufactured silk trade has not greatly altered. Table 31 shows the share of China in American imports of silk textiles. The total imports seem to have increased in value in recent years, but this apparent increase is entirely due to price inflation, and when price allowance is made it may be shown that trade has practically decreased in quantity. But, owing to the fact that some European countries—France, Germany, England, Italy —were unable to send manufactured silks to the American market, Americans naturally turned to the Orient for a supply which would meet their usual demand for foreign silks. China has, therefore, recovered a little of her old share, but it remains in doubt whether she will be able to retain even this humble share when the European silk industry has come back to its normal condition. But as long as the three conditions mentioned above remain unaltered, we can expect no huge increase in the trade of manufactured silks between China and the United States.

### Expansion of the Raw Silk Trade

Along with the decline of the Sino-American trade in manufactured silks, but opposite in direction, has come the steady expansion in the raw silk trade. During the first seven decades of the last century, America bought little raw silk from outside, so little that the United States Bureau of

TABLE 31

| Year | Total imports of silk textiles to U. S. in $1,000 | Imports of silk textiles from China in $1,000 | % of the whole |
|---|---|---|---|
| 1913 | 35,308 | 173 | 0.5 |
| 1915 | 28,580 | 704 | 2.5 |
| 1917 | 39,718 | 1,921 | 4.8 |
| 1919 | 54,701 | 690 | 1.3 |
| 1920 | 75,328 | 1,485 | 1.6 |
| 1921 | 48,249 | 1,725 | 3.6 |
| 1922 | 36,732 | 1,587 | 4.3 |

Data from *Annual Reports* of Am. Silk Assoc.

Statistics did not even take the trouble to record the quantities imported. But after 1850 separate quantities can be obtained and they are shown in Table 32 in five-year averages. More than half of these imports came directly from China and the rest from England and France.[1] Since 1865,

TABLE 32

| Average of 5-year period | Value of total imports of raw silk in $1,000 | Value of raw silk imported from China | China's % in the total |
|---|---|---|---|
| 1840-44 | 51 | ... | ... |
| 1845-49 | 230 | ... | ... |
| 1850-54 | 575 | 358 | 62.0 |
| 1855-59 | 1,133 | 620 | 54.5 |
| 1860-64 | 1,242 | 576 | 46.3 |

however, due to the rapid development of the silk weaving industry in this country, the importation of foreign raw silk has naturally increased by leaps and bounds. In fact, silk culture was many times attempted in this country, but failed because of its high cost of production.[2] Consequently, any development in the American silk industry has resulted

[1] See U. S. Bureau of For. and Dom. Commerce, *Commerce and Navigation*, 1850-1864.
[2] See Brockett, L. P., *Silk Industry in America*, 1876.

in a greater demand for foreign raw silks; and in the two decades 1865-1884, the imports of raw silk increased more than ten fold.[1] The absolute quantity and value of Chinese raw silks imported, of course, increased as a whole, yet her relative share fluctuated violently from more than 50% to 13%.

Table 33 presents in a summary form the situation of the American raw silk trade during the two decades mentioned above:

TABLE 33

PERCENTAGE DISTRIBUTION OF THE RAW SILK IMPORTS OF THE UNITED STATES TO CHINA AND JAPAN, 1865-1884

| 5-year Average | China | | Japan | | Total American imports of raw silk | |
|---|---|---|---|---|---|---|
| | Qty. in 1,000 lbs. | Value in $1,000 | Qty. in 1,000 lbs. | Value in $1,000 | Qty. in 1,000 lbs. | Value in $1,000 |
| 1865-69 | 67 | 296 | 14 | 81 | 510 | 2,251 |
| 1870-74 | 498 | 2,452 | 60 | 303 | 940 | 4,975 |
| 1875-79 | 410 | 1,648 | 485 | 2,270 | 1,344 | 5,958 |
| 1880-84 | 1,303 | 5,008 | 994 | 4,412 | 2,892 | 12,592 |
| | % of the total | % | % | % | % | % |
| 1865-69 | 13.1 | 13.2 | 2.7 | 3.6 | 100.0 | 100.0 |
| 1870-74 | 53.0 | 49.3 | 6.4 | 6.1 | 100.0 | 100.0 |
| 1875-79 | 30.4 | 27.6 | 36.8 | 38.0 | 100.0 | 100.0 |
| 1880-84 | 45.0 | 43.8 | 34.4 | 35.0 | 100.0 | 100.0 |

The failure of China to get full benefit of the growing American demand for raw silk is, like her tea trade, to be explained on the one hand by her own neglect to improve her sericulture and to conform to the American standard, and on the other to push her silk trade with vigor to offset the severe competition of Japan.

Although China's silk monopoly was broken down when

[1] Imports of raw silk into the United States: 1865, 250,000 lbs.; in 1884 total 3,223,000 lbs. See *Annual Reports* of American Silk Association.

sericulture was introduced into Europe, she still held control of silk production in the middle of the nineteenth century. No great volume of raw silk was produced in Europe or in Japan, and America was forced to rely upon Shanghai and Canton for a supply of material to feed an increasing number of her weaving factories. The Chinese silk producers being nearly all peasant farmers, ignorant of the existence of potential competition and living in a fool's paradise, thought that they held the only key to the silk market, and were growing more and more careless in rearing the worm and reeling the fibre. In addition to furnishing a poor quality of silk, Chinese silk merchants began to practice adulteration, just as the tea traders did at the same time. The condition became so bad in the seventies that the Board of Government of the American Silk Association—an organization comprising in its membership nearly all the silk manufacturers in this country—adopted in 1874 a formal resolution against such practice.[1] As regards early Japanese competition, the Secretary of the Association reported in the same year in the following words:

"Eight years ago (about 1865), the Japanese did as the Chinese began to take more care in preparing their silk—re-reeling it and cleaning it for this market, thus the use of Japanese raw silk went out almost entirely. But the Japanese have seen their error and are now trying to remedy it. During recent years, we have some Japanese raw silk, filature reel, which shows what the Japanese can do in the way of supplying this market with the silk which we need; and if the Japanese are willing and determined to get back their lost trade, the Chinese are offering them a good opportunity to do so." [2]

In addition to the difference between the improving quality of Japanese and the deteriorating quality of Chinese

[1] *Annual Report of Silk Association of America,* 1874, p. 27.
[2] *Ibid.,* p. 46.

silks there was another great contrast between the energetic pushing by the Japanese of their silk trade in America and the inactive and indolent method of selling on the part of the Chinese. In spite of the threatened decline of her silk trade in America, China never sent any commission or even any private agent to investigate the market conditions here, to say nothing of making an effort at extensive advertising or exhibition. On the other hand, the Japanese, through their governmental organs, were exerting their full efforts to push their sales here.[1] In such a state of affairs, there is no wonder that Chinese silk was rapidly supplanted by Japanese silk in the American market. In fact, as shown in the above table, American imports of Chinese silk declined from an annual average value of $2,452,000 during the five-year period 1870-74, to an average of $1,648,000 during the next five-year period, 1875-79. On the other hand, sales of Japanese silks increased from an annual average of $303,000 in the first five-year period, to $2,270,000 in the second. This was the first time that America imported more silk from Japan than from China.

The strenuous efforts of the Japanese and the carelessness of the Chinese went on side by side for some decades without interruption or alteration. During the latter years of the nineteenth century the Japanese Government took a lively interest in maintaining and improving the quality of the raw silk exported from that country. In 1897 the Japanese Government established a silk-conditioning house at Yokohama and in 1900 the examination of silk for watering was made compulsory in Japan.[2] In China on the other hand, reforms proved much more difficult. The Government had neither the point of view nor the administrative machinery to make the carrying out of such proposals feasible. The Chinese customs reports, the newspapers of the open ports of China, the silk merchants in America as

[1] For a typical case, cf., *Ibid.,* p. 22.
[2] *Encyclopedia Sinica,* p. 515.

well as those in Europe, and all who were interested in the silk trade of China, united in admonishing the Chinese silk producer. An example of this sort of admonition is to be found in the Chinese customs report for 1904.[1] It used to take, we are told in this report, three or four piculs of cocoons to make a picul of silk; now it took from four to six. "The silk men of China are living in a fools' paradise. Their error consists in thinking that they make the price, whereas the fact is that the price is made in the market of the United States and in Europe. The world's supply of raw silk is going up; China's production is not. The world's demand for raw silk has increased; China's export has not. "The Chinese methods of breeding the silk-worm were excellent as long as no scientific methods were available." But as soon as scientific methods were introduced into Japan China was soon to suffer in the competition.

The indifference of the Chinese silk producer and merchant towards this critical juncture, or, rather their complete ignorance of it, and the Japanese preparedness to make the most of the excellent opportunity to extend their silk trade in America can not be better described than by depicting their respective parts in the International Exposition at St. Louis, Missouri, in 1904. This great International Exposition of Art, Industry and Science was inaugurated for the celebration of the centenary of the Louisiana Purchase from France by the United States. The silk section was made a special feature of the Exposition. All the important silk producing and manufacturing countries in the world, being fully aware of the excellent opportunity for advertising their products, sent hosts of delegates, exhibitors, and collaborators, together with their best samples to the exhibition.[2] Japan

[1] Chinese Maritime Customs: *Returns of Trade and Trade Reports,* 1904, pp. 7-9.
[2] For a full report of the silk section of the Exposition, cf. *Annual Report of Silk Assoc. of America,* 1904, p. 24 ff.

contributed more than one-half of all the silk exhibits, there being one hundred and seventy-one exhibits of raw silk, spun silk, etc., and ninety-five exhibits of woven tissues. These exhibits were said to be by far the most important of any exhibits ever made by Japan at any previous international exposition.[1] China, on the other hand, sent no special silk delegation and only a few perfunctory and commonplace exhibits to the Exposition. Out of a total of 348 awards to exhibitors and 224 to collaborators of the different countries, China got seven of the first kind and none of the second; while Japan was awarded 233 exhibitor's medals and twenty-five collaborator's.

With so great a difference in the attitudes of China and Japan toward the silk trade, we naturally expect to see a headlong downfall in the Chinese silk trade with the United States, and an unusual expansion of Japanese silk trade. The expansion of the Japanese silk trade is shown by the five-year annual average figures in Table 34. The table starts with the period 1885-89, in which Japan exported annually 2.3 million lbs. of raw silk to the United States at an average value of $8,100,000. For the next five year period the quantity of silk thus exported increased to 3,300,000 pounds valued at $11,700,000, an increase of about 40% over the figures for the last period. Since that time the increase has been cumulative or, in other words, in geometrical progression until the four-year pre-war period, 1910-13, when the quantity was 15,100,000 lbs. at a value of $51,800,000.[2] In the latest year for which trade statistics are now available, America imported 40,000,000 pounds of Japanese raw silk at a value of $291,292,000! During the comparatively short period of half a century, Japan has, through her strenuous effort to improve the quality of her silk and to push the sale of this commodity, raised the position of

[1] Ibid., p. 36.
[2] See Table 34.

her silk from nothing to one of the most important articles of international commerce.

Our expectation that China's silk trade with the United States, as well as with Europe, would fall headlong seems to have been disproved, because ever since the Americans began to complain to the Chinese silk producers of the poor quality of their product, the actual exports to this country constantly and steadily increased both in quantity and value disregarding, of course, a few abnormal exceptions. During the period of 1885-89, China exported to the United States annually 1,100,000 pounds of raw silk, valued at $3,600,000. In the next period both the quantity and value increased to 1,500,000 pounds and $4,300,000 respectively. The increase went on without interruption until in the four-year pre-war period, 1910-13, the quantity became 5,300,000 pounds with a value of $13,000,000. In 1922 American silk imports from China were recorded as 8,400,000 pounds at a value of $56,600,000.

This expansion of Chinese silk trade with America, in spite of much complaint from buyers and the most formidable competition of Japan, is solely due to one condition—the rapid development of the silkweaving and knitting industry in America and the resulting tremendous expansion of the demand for raw silk, which Japan has never been quite able to meet even with the yearly improvement and extension of her sericulture. The quantity of raw silk the United States can buy from Europe has long since become extremely limited. At the end of the last century and the beginning of the present, Italy supplied about twenty percent of the total demand of the United States for raw silk; France, about four percent. But as the silk weaving industry in Europe also tends to expand, these countries cannot well afford to sell their raw materials abroad except at a higher price. In fact the price of European silk is much higher than that of Oriental silk, owing to the high cost of labor in France and Italy as compared with the wage scale in the Orient. If the United States cannot get all that she needs from Japan she

### TABLE 34
#### AMERICAN IMPORTS OF RAW SILK BY COUNTRIES

| Year average | China Quantity in 1,000 lbs. | China Value in $1,000 | Japan Quantity in 1,000 lbs. | Japan Value in $1,000 | France Quantity in 1,000 lbs. | France Value in $1,000 |
|---|---|---|---|---|---|---|
| 1885-89 | 1,132 | 3,616 | 2,258 | 8,194 | 265 | 1,185 |
| 1890-94 | 1,468 | 4,324 | 3,284 | 11,678 | 267 | 1,102 |
| 1895-99 | 2,516 | 6,647 | 4,315 | 14,100 | 334 | 1,212 |
| 1900-04 | 2,971 | 8,300 | 6,109 | 21,380 | 491 | 1,746 |
| 1905-09 | 3,356 | 9,825 | 9,834 | 37,706 | 579 | 2,007 |
| 1910-13 | 5,254 | 12,973 | 15,676 | 51,819 | 161 | 592 |
| 1914-16 | 6,128 | 16,697 | 21,178 | 81,274 | 82 | 233 |
| 1917-18 | 6,343 | 28,454 | 28,236 | 153,075 | 10 | 32 |
| 1919 | 9,059 | 54,476 | 33,727 | 256,113 | 50 | 336 |
| 1920 | 5,932 | 53,844 | 22,904 | 219,838 | 33 | 289 |
| 1921 | 9,587 | 48,050 | 31,704 | 188,062 | 686 | 3,746 |
| 1922 | 8,378 | 56,610 | 40,029 | 291,292 | 159 | 1,201 |

| Year average | Italy Quantity in 1,000 lbs. | Italy Value in $1,000 | Other Countries Quantity in 1,000 lbs. | Other Countries Value in $1,000 | Total Quantity in 1,000 lbs. | Total Value in $1,000 |
|---|---|---|---|---|---|---|
| 1885-89 | 948 | 3,941 | ... | ... | 4,656 | 11,207 |
| 1890-94 | 1,073 | 4,760 | ... | ... | 6,152 | 22,057 |
| 1895-99 | 1,532 | 5,969 | 206 | 547 | 8,896 | 28,475 |
| 1900-04 | 2,631 | 10,690 | 296 | 893 | 12,492 | 43,206 |
| 1905-09 | 3,904 | 15,911 | 127 | 475 | 17,800 | 65,924 |
| 1910-13 | 2,481 | 7,746 | 231 | 821 | 23,804 | 75,557 |
| 1914-16 | 2,202 | 9,735 | 104 | 445 | 29,695 | 108,720 |
| 1917-18 | 77 | 570 | 18 | 113 | 34,684 | 182,247 |
| 1919 | 1,866 | 17,889 | 75 | 524 | 44,817 | 329,339 |
| 1920 | 1,111 | 10,345 | 79 | 575 | 30,058 | 284,291 |
| 1921 | 3,085 | 17,545 | 293 | 1,651 | 45,355 | 259,054 |
| 1922 | 569 | 5,591 | 1,577 | 12,093 | 50,712 | 365,787 |

is naturally compelled to turn to the original home of silk to meet her growing and almost insatiable demand. It is due to these special conditions that the Chinese silk trade has been saved from a complete downfall through the fierce onslaught of Japanese competition.

Our presentation of silk trade conditions will be incom-

plete, however, if we neglect to mention the decline of the relative importance of Chinese silk from its position in former days. During the middle of the nineteenth century (1850-59) two-thirds of the American raw silk import came directly from that country, and nothing from Japan. Two decades later (1875-84) China's share declined to less than

### TABLE 35
#### QUANTITY DISTRIBUTION OF AMERICAN SILK IMPORTS IN PERCENTAGES

| | China | Japan | France | Italy | Other Countries | Total |
|---|---|---|---|---|---|---|
| 1885-89 | 24.3 | 48.3 | 5.7 | 20.4 | 1.3 | 100.0 |
| 1890-94 | 23.8 | 53.4 | 4.3 | 17.4 | 1.1 | 100.0 |
| 1895-99 | 28.3 | 48.5 | 3.1 | 17.2 | 2.3 | 100.0 |
| 1900-04 | 23.8 | 49.1 | 3.9 | 21.5 | 2.4 | 100.0 |
| 1905-09 | 18.8 | 55.2 | 3.3 | 21.9 | 0.8 | 100.0 |
| 1910-13 | 22.2 | 65.6 | 0.8 | 10.4 | 1.0 | 100.0 |
| 1914-16 | 20.6 | 71.2 | 0.3 | 7.4 | 0.4 | 100.0 |
| 1917-18 | 18.3 | 81.5 | ... | 0.2 | ... | 100.0 |
| 1919 | 20.3 | 75.1 | 0.1 | 4.2 | 0.2 | 100.0 |
| 1920 | 19.7 | 76.2 | 0.1 | 3.7 | 0.3 | 100.0 |
| 1921 | 21.2 | 10.0 | 1.5 | 6.8 | 0.6 | 100.0 |
| 1922 | 16.5 | 79.0 | 0.3 | 1.1 | 3.1 | 100.0 |

two-thirds while Japan shared equally with China in the American trade. Since that time Japan has secured a constantly increasing share, one-half of the whole during the period 1885-1904, two-thirds during 1905-13, and about three-fourths to four-fifths since 1914. China's share, on the other hand, has contracted from one-fourth during 1885-1904 to about one-fifth since 1905. It is the decline of the comparative importance of China's silk trade with the United States that we refer to when we speak of the defeat of China in the American market. (See Table 35.)

From a cursory reading of the examples given above of the attitude toward the American silk trade in China and in Japan one may readily see that the success of Japan has been due largely to wise governmental policies which gave to the

development of sericulture serious and scientific consideration while the Chinese Government had shown little more
than a passing interest in this important question. It is true
that from time to time the Chinese Government has assisted
the silk producers with funds to carry out their reform plans,
but beyond that even the producers took no more interest in
the matter than to assure themselves of the return of their
money with suitable interest. Besides the lack of governmental aid, sericulture in China had another great handicap
in effecting improvements. The raising of silkworms in
China is carried on on a small scale by thousands of peasant
farmers and their families. Any reform in their methods by
guilds of silk merchants is faced with great difficulties, either
because these farmers lack the capital necessary to carry out
the reform or because scientific methods are not suited to
such domestic small-scale production either technically or
economically.

### Chinese Silk vs. Japanese Silk: American Market vs. European Market

From what has been said above, one might easily fall into
the error of assuming that Chinese silk is not of good
quality and therefore unfit for use in the modern silk industry. This conception is erroneous for Chinese silk, though
not so desirable in the American market as Japanese silk, had
a larger market in Europe, where little Japanese silk was
in demand. By taking into account the destination of the
raw silk exports from China and Japan, therefore, we can
form a much better judgment of the relative merits of the
Chinese and Japanese silks in their connection with the
American and European markets. The Chinese silk trade
was already well established and its relation with the weaving industry of Europe was close when the Japanese industry began to grow in importance. It is significant that
the growth of the production of raw silk in Japan has been
connected with the growth of the weaving industry in the

United States. The export of raw silk from Japan and the
weaving of silks in the United States may be said to have
grown together and this may have been due to the response
on the part of the Japanese silk producers to American suggestions for the improvement of the industry.[1] In general
during the years before the European War more than twice
as much Japanese raw silk was sent to the United States as
was sent to Europe, and since the war nearly seven-eighths
to nine-tenths was sent to this country. In China the situation was just the opposite. Before 1913 about twice as much
Chinese raw silk was sent to Europe and West Asia as was
sent to the United States. There is a difference between the
European and the American weaving industries. "The
cheap every day silks, turned out in great quantities of one
pattern, are characteristic of the machine industry of America. Limited patterns and sterling quality, catering to the
well-to-do and the rich, are the typical products of the
French industry."[2] "The raw silk of China seems to have
been better adapted to the conditions of the French and the
European industry. Like her tea, China's raw silk is either
excellent or rather poor in quality and it has been so for a
long time. Usually, it is of a better quality and heavier fibre
than the Japanese product. The lack of uniform quality for
a large quantity of material seems to make it very difficult
for the Chinese to make an easy sale of their product in
America. Japanese silk produced with more or less standardized methods, is of a more uniform quality, and therefore fits better the need of the large-scale machine industry
of America. But the best Chinese silk, like her best tea, is
said to be superior to the Japanese product."[3] During the
whole period prior to 1913, therefore, Japan and not China

[1] C. F. Remer: *The Foreign Trade of China*, Ch. IV. For comparative statistical data, cf. *Annual Reports of the Silk Assoc. of
America;* Silk Statistics Section.
[2] F. W. Taussig: *Some Aspects of the Tariff Question*, 1915,
pp. 233-34.
[3] C. F. Remer, *op. cit.*

reaped the benefit of the growing American industry's increased demand.

The European War, however, has brought a considerable
change in this situation. During the war the European
weaving industry was greatly deranged, and the demand for
Chinese silk became uncertain. The Chinese were, therefore,
compelled to send more of their silk to America. Before the
war China sent only one-third of her total export to the
United States, but after the war the United States absorbed
nearly half of her total export. This growth in the importance of the American market for Chinese raw silk has en-
couraged American buyers to exert efforts toward making
Chinese silk more suitable for American use and it has also
made the Chinese more willing to take the suggestions and
specifications of the American weavers.

### The Recent Improvement of Chinese Sericulture to meet the American Demand; and the Future Prospect of China's silk trade with America

"For many years the increasing silk supply from Japan
was able adequately to meet a large part of the growing demand of the American silk manufacturers. But recently,
the popularity of silk in America has so tremendously increased that American manufacturers have begun to feel the
necessity for the extension of the raw material field."[1]
Owing to the scarcity of cultivatable land for mulberry trees,
silk production in Japan has nearly reached its full capacity,
while the silk industry in America is still growing with
rapidity.

Moreover, American silk manufacturers have recently
come to realize the danger of depending upon a single country for the whole supply of such an important raw material.
For two decades Japan has supplied by far the greatest part

[1] The Future of Raw Silk in China, by F. G. Barry, *China Review,*
N. Y., Feb., 1923.

of the raw silk needed in the United States, in some instances
more than four-fifths of the total American import. Under
such a monopolistic condition, the Japanese merchants are
naturally able to control the market, practice cornering, and
raise the price for the material to whatever figure "the traffic
will bear." This was actually the case in 1920, when some
Japanese silk firms held their silk output and raised the
price extremely high with the inevitable result of an immediate slump in the market and the ruin of many American
manufacturers and Japanese merchants. To prevent the re-
currence of such a disastrous practice the best thing is for the
Americans to distribute their silk purchases among different
countries in order to avoid being the victims of Japanese
monopoly. But as has been indicated above, it is of little
avail for the United States to turn to the silk producing
countries in Europe for the solution of this problem. It is
because of these two reasons that to China, once the home
of the entire silk industry, America must look for a solution.

China, on the other hand, has recently come to realize the
great importance of her silk trade with America, and is consequently paying more attention to the production and selling
of this commodity. Silk has for nearly twenty years been
the most important article of export in the foreign trade of
China, and the Chinese have felt the necessity of pushing
the trade abroad. Moreover, the steady rise in price has
recently made the silk trade a very profitable one for China,
and the high profits act as a strong stimulus to further improvement of the material and more aggressive selling in
foreign lands. It is under these conditions that China, once
the best producer and largest supplier of silk, has sought
and accepted the cooperation of the American silk manufacturers in improving the industry and trade.

The first serious attempt to improve Chinese silk was made
in 1909, when the Silk Association of America, at the suggestion of the Silk Throwsters' Association of America,
adopted a resolution to urge the improvement of Canton

filature skeins for the American market.[1] In response to the request, the Cantonese carefully followed the suggestions of the American silk manufacturers as to the method of making standard skeins. The immediate result of this effort was a gain in the American silk trade with China after 1910 over that of previous years, as shown in the following table of distribution :—

PERCENTAGE DISTRIBUTION OF AMERICAN SILK IMPORTS IN QUANTITY

| Average of 5 or 4 year period | China | Japan | France | Italy | Other Countries | Total |
|---|---|---|---|---|---|---|
| 1905-09 | 18.8 | 55.2 | 3.3 | 21.9 | 0.8 | 100.0 |
| 1910-13 | 22.2 | 65.6 | 0.8 | 10.4 | 1.0 | 100.0 |

In order to carry further the improvement thus started, the International Committee for the Improvement of Sericulture of China was formed in Shanghai in 1918 under the auspices of the Foreign Silk Association of Shanghai.[2] Because America is the largest importer of raw silk, the Silk Association of America has concerned itself with the movement, to which it has given active assistance. The Committee has undertaken as its chief work to give instructions to the Chinese farmers of the silk producing regions, and distributing scientifically selected disease-free worm-eggs among them. The movement for the improvement of Chinese raw silk, thus started, has received the hearty support of the American buyers and the Chinese Government and producers. Funds collected from American contributors are being used for the work of the International Committee, the establishment of chairs of sericulture instruction and research work in the colleges in the Nanking and Canton Districts, the building and equipment of sericulture stations in connection with these colleges, and the provision for the

[1] *Annual Report*, Silk Assoc. of America, 1910, p. 24 ff.
[2] *Ibid.*, 1919, p. 30.

services of experts to continue the introduction of the American Standard Silk Skein in Canton and Shanghai by practical demonstration and education.[1] This committee has expanded its activities until it now has seven field stations and a central laboratory in Shanghai and another branch at Chefoo in Northern Shantung.[2]

As an important step toward the scientific improvement of China's raw silk production the Silk Association of America has contributed substantial sums for the erection of two new sericulture buildings, in two of the colleges in China. Events have already proved that assistance to the colleges is a direct means of improving the quality of raw silk.[3]

The campaign to give the American silk trade proper conditioning facilities, which the Silk Association of America started by establishing a conditioning house in New York, was further augmented, when a branch of the United States Testing Company, Inc., was opened at Shanghai in October, 1921. Before the opening of the Shanghai branch, Chinese reelers were, in general, dependent upon visual inspection for control of mill operation.[4] The Shanghai house tests raw silk according to well-known standard methods which are accessible to every one and international in their application. Its certificates will be of material assistance to sellers and buyers in China and will also have great weight in the consuming market in America.[5]

### The American Consumer and the Chinese Producer

Besides the various cooperative efforts between China and the United States to improve the quality and quantity of the Chinese raw silks, there were numerous other activities

[1] *Annual Report* of Silk Assoc. of America, 1922, p. 25.
[2] *To Improve Chinese Silk for American Markets*, *China Review*, N. Y., Dec., 1922.
[3] *The Future of Raw Silk in China*, *Ibid.*, Feb., 1923.
[4] *Annual Report* of Silk Assoc. of America, 1922, p. 25.
[5] *Ibid.*, p. 26.

to promote mutual understanding and good will between the American consumer and the Chinese producer. In 1920 a mission including representatives of the chief branches of American silk manufacture, testing and research and the Silk Association of America, spent more than three months in an active survey of the silk industry in the Orient.[1] The members of this mission gave careful consideration to the possibilities of increased production, improved qualities, the elimination of defects and the determination of grades. Charles Cheney, Chairman of the American Silk Mission, in his official report of the findings of the Mission, called the attention of the American manufacturers to the evident awakening of a new and progressive spirit in China. "The mission," says the report, "found in Canton that no less than eighty-five percent of the filatures in the Canton district have changed their machines and methods and are reeling according to American specifications. A recent estimate by a reliable silk expert is that seventy percent of Canton silk this year will be reeled into American standard skeins. The amount of silk suitable for American consumption has been very largely increased (about doubled), and the so-called new type silk has commanded a much higher price than that reeled in the old way. . . . The ready and general acceptance of the instructions of American buyers denotes an open mind, and the success of the movement should be a valuable lesson which offers a fine argument in favor of further progress. . . . China has within its grasp a golden opportunity to develop and enlarge its old historic industry to an almost unlimited extent."[2]

The Second American Silk Mission, under the leadership of James A. Goldsmith, President of the American Silk Association, left for the Orient in February, 1923, for a further study of the conditions of silk production. Increased

[1] For a fuller account of this mission, cf. The Future of Raw Silk in China, by F. B. Barry, *China Review*, N. Y., Feb., 1923.
[2] *Ibid.*

understanding and cooperation was sure to follow such an undertaking.

The Chinese silk merchants, contrary to their former indifferent attitude toward the American trade, are now taking a lively interest in it. When the First International Silk Exposition was held in this country in 1921 the Chinese silk interests in various sections of the country sent a host of representatives with many samples of their best silks. These delegates also visited many of the American silk factories, with a view to a better understanding of the requirements of their customers. The Second International Silk Exposition of 1923 received the same attention from these Chinese silk magnates. These groups of Chinese delegates carried back to their own country, besides a better understanding of the American market, a more friendly feeling towards this country and a fuller realization of the desirability of cooperation with the American manufacturers for their mutual benefit.

With the recent developments of the Chinese-American silk trade we see a very good prospect for its future expansion. The Chinese silk producer is now giving more and more attention to the American standards and specifications, and making his product more and more fit for American use. Henceforward, there is good reason to expect that America will be a better customer than Europe in China's raw silk market.

### Waste Silk

While raw silk forms the principal material used in silk manufacturing, waste silk is also an important factor in the industry. Waste silk is unreelable material, and must be made into spun silk yarn by a process similar to that used in the spining of cotton and flax. It has mixed with it, to a greater or less extent, a considerable amount of foreign matter. It is said that "Chinese silk waste is particularly poor in this respect, owing to the fact that so large a part of the reeling is done at home on the dirty floor."[1]  As the use of the poor grades of waste, as well as of raw silk, involves a greater amount of time and labor than is needed when better material is used, American manufacturers ordinarily find it necessary to employ the better grades of European waste.  Since the end of the last century, the American importation of Chinese silk waste, though steadily on the increase, has been quite insignificant as compared with that of raw silk.

Brief statistics of this import are shown in Table 36.

TABLE 36

AMERICAN IMPORTS OF WASTE SILK FROM CHINA

| Year | Qty. in 1,000 lbs. | Value in $1,000 | Year | Qty. in 1,000 lbs. | Value in $1,000 |
|------|------|------|------|------|------|
| 1895 | 213 | 95 | 1915 | 2,359 | 1,068 |
| 1900 | 697 | 189 | 1917 | 3,593 | 2,131 |
| 1905 | 114 | 76 | 1918 | 7,831 | 5,677 |
| 1910 | 546 | 253 | 1919 | 4,379 | 4,363 |
| 1913 | 1,905 | 1,012 | 1920 | 5,582 | 8,844 |
| | | | 1921 | 3,636 | 2,337 |
| | | | 1922 | 3,316 | 2,446 |

One of the most striking developments in the American silk business during the war was the expansion of the spun silk industry.[2]  This was caused largely by the war demand for coarse silk cloth with which to make powder bags for the big guns.  The bags are made of silk, as it is essential to use a textile that will burn up quickly and completely, leaving no smouldering remnant.  Spun silk cloth was chosen rather than cloth made of raw silk because of the comparative cheapness of the former.  This special demand raised the quantity and value of American silk waste import from

[1] F. M. Miller, *Some Great Commodities*, p. 170, N. Y., 1923.
[2] *Ibid.*

China during the few years from 1917 to 1920 to abnormally high figures.  In 1920 alone, the value of the imports of this article amounted to nearly nine million dollars.  But as the special demand ceased with the war, and as such manufactures are not likely to be resumed, the American market for Chinese silk waste rapidly declined.

## CHAPTER VIII

### VEGETABLE OILS

#### The United States as a Market for Vegetable Oils

The wide utilization of vegetable oils in American industries and the remarkable growth of Chinese trade with America in these commodities were among the most interesting commercial phenomena of the past decade, and the new development brought about by the World War in connection with their use was for some years very important.  As a result of the war American dependence on vegetable oils was temporarily increased in many ways—new uses of them having been discovered, and minor uses suddenly having taken on greatly added importance.  Oils formerly little known in this country, such as Chinese soya bean oil, were introduced into America for general use, because the supply of some kinds needed in American industries became insufficient to meet the great demand for war production, while that of others, such as palm oil from Africa, was partly cut off during the war.

Probably the most important effect of the war so far on the use of vegetable oils in the half decade, 1916-1920, was the great increase in their consumption as foodstuffs.[1]  The substitution of these oils in liquid or solid form, for animal fats, resulting in a greatly increased consumption of vegetable butters, lards, and flavoring oils, was in part due to the war shortage of animal products.[2]  But even before the war the utilization of these oils in industry had reached very large dimensions, and a number of very interesting and novel uses were being developed, such as the making of artificial leather for book binding, the production of artificial rubber, and of substances similar to celluloid.  The main industrial uses, however, are in making paints and

[1] Vegetable Oils, *The Economic World*, N. Y., Feb. 23, 1918, p. 259.
[2] *Ibid.*

164

varnishes, soaps, candles, linoleum and oil cloths as well as lubricants.[1]

Aside from the cotton belt of the United States, the greatest source of seeds and fruits, from which the vegetable oils are pressed, is the Far East.  And here China is the largest producer, followed by India, Japan, Malaysia and Oceania.  From these primary producing areas some of the seeds have been transported to America to be pressed.

The United States is itself a great producer of vegetable oils.  Her huge production, however, is, with the exception of cottonseed and corn oils, still insufficient for her enormous consumption.[2]  To meet the discrepancy between her production and consumption, the United States has to import a considerable quantity of vegetable oils every year, and her importation is especially large during years of industrial activity.  Table 37 shows her annual imports of some of these oils before, during and after the European War.

TABLE 37

AMERICAN IMPORTS OF VEGETABLE OILS, 1913-22
Unit: One million pounds[3]

| | 1913 | 1918 | 1919 | 1920 | 1921 | 1922 |
|------|------|------|------|------|------|------|
| Cotton seed oil...... | 3 | 18 | 28 | 10 | 1 | ... |
| Peanut oil ........... | ... | 69 | 154* | 95 | 3 | 3 |
| Cocoanut oil ........ | 51 | 356 | 281 | 216 | 190 | 227 |
| Soya bean oil ...... | 12 | 336 | 196 | 112 | 16 | 17 |
| Linseed oil ......... | 1 | ... | 16 | 35 | 61 | 144 |
| Chinese wood oil... | 45 | 43 | 54 | 68 | 27 | 79 |
| Olive oil ........... | 39 | 1 | 70 | 31 | 54 | 88 |
| Palm oil ........... | 50 | 21 | 42 | 41 | 23 | 58 |

[1] *Ibid.*, p. 261.
[2] For complete statistics of production and consumption of vegetable oils in the United States in recent years, cf. U. S. Bureau of Census, *Animal and Vegetable Fats and Oils*, 1922.
[3] Data compiled from the *Commerce and Navigation of the U. S.*

These different oils, of course, come from different countries in the world: for instance; Chinese wood oil, from China; peanut and soya bean oils, from China and Japan; while cocoanut oil, from the Philippines; Palm oil, from Africa; Linseed and olive oils, from Europe.

### China's Oil Trade with the United States

China's oil trade with America is not a new one, though oils have come only recently to assume an important position in the Chinese-American trade. During the latter half of the nineteenth century Chinese wood oil frequently appeared in the list of American imports from China, and before 1900, it was practically the only kind thus imported. When Japan succeeded Russia in the lease of South Manchuria, other kinds, such as soya bean oil and peanut oil, began to be sold in America through Japanese merchants. It was not until 1911 that a substantial volume of oil trade came into existence between China and the United States. Once started, and later under the stimulation of war demands, this line of trade expanded at remarkable strides until the slump in 1921. Table 38 shows the annual value of the American imports directly from China during the last three decades.

TABLE 38

AMERICAN IMPORTS OF VEGETABLE OILS FROM CHINA

| | Year | Value in $1,000[1] |
|---|---|---|
| | 1896-1900 | 110 |
| | 1901-1905 | 262 |
| Annual Average | 1906-1910 | 783 |
| | 1911-1913 | 2,748 |
| | 1914-1916 | 3,398 |
| | 1917 | 12,021 |
| | 1918 | 39,361 |
| | 1919 | 30,955 |
| | 1920 | 18,460 |
| | 1921 | 2,806 |
| | 1922 | 8,364 |

[1] Owing to the different units (the gallon and the pounds) used by the United States customs houses to measure the quantities of different kinds of oils, it is difficult to calculate their aggregate quantity.

It is certainly a remarkable fact that American oil imports from China increased with such rapidity. In 1906-10 the total value of the trade did not exceed three-fourths of a million dollars a year, but only a decade later it amounted to from twenty to forty million dollars a year. Yet these figures, representing only the value of direct imports, do not show the total trade. A great part of the imports from Japan and nearly all from Hongkong come ultimately from China.

Table 39 shows the distribution of American oil imports to the various importing countries in 1918-22. It is seen that during the few years of active warfare in Europe, when European and African oil supplies were temporarily cut off from America, China held the indisputable sway in the American market. Together with Japan and Hongkong, she supplied two-thirds of the total American imports in 1918, and nearly half in 1919.

TABLE 39

DISTRIBUTION OF AMERICAN VEGETABLE OIL IMPORTS

| Year | Value of total American Imports in $1,000 | Value Distribution in Percentages | | | | | | | |
|---|---|---|---|---|---|---|---|---|---|
| | | China including Hongkong | Japan | Philippine Islands | Dutch East Indies | Italy | Spain | England | Other Countries |
| 1918 | 110,909 | 36.8 | 26.0 | 27.7 | 3.9 | 0.7 | 0.3 | .1 | 4.5 |
| 1919 | 130,000 | 25.6 | 22.8 | 19.6 | 2.6 | 1.4 | 13.2 | 2.7 | 12.1 |
| 1920 | 113,490 | 20.2 | 20.7 | 21.2 | 7.0 | 5.0 | 6.5 | 9.8 | 9.6 |
| 1921 | 41,523 | 8.0 | 1.0 | 31.8 | 5.0 | 17.6 | 4.8 | 12.4 | 9.4 |
| 1922 | 59,042 | 14.8 | 1.2 | 27.4 | ... | 14.4 | 4.8 | 17.1 | 20.3 |

In 1921, however, China lost her important position in the trade. She exported to the United States in that year only three million dollars' worth of oils, and her share dropped to

less than one-tenth. The decline in the absolute amount of the trade can be explained, of course, upon grounds which are well known to every business man. They are (1) the business depression which compelled many of the oil consuming factories in this country to close down in 1921 and (2) the imposition of heavy import duties on vegetable oils by the new American tariff act. The first cause resulted first in a maladjustment between demand and supply and then a heavy drop in oil price until it was below the cost of production. But as business depression is only a temporary phenomenon, it can not act as a permanent check upon the oil trade. The second cause, viz., the levying of heavy duties, is, however, a much more serious obstacle to the recovery of the trade, so long as the American Tariff Act of 1922 remains unaltered. As may be noticed in the following comparative list, the American Tariff Act of 1909 admitted all sorts of China's oils free of duty. By the subsequent act of 1913 only peanut oil was taxed six cents per gallon, while the others remained on the free list. These acts, therefore, greatly facilitated their importation during the decade from 1911 to 1920. But in 1921, when business depression set in, the American oil producer felt the need of protection from foreign competition. A heavy rate of duty was then levied by the American Emergency Tariff Act of that year on all sorts of oils coming from China except Chinese nut oil which is not produced in this country. The Tariff Act of 1922 has raised the rate still further and thus practically excluded all Chinese dutiable oils from the American market. This explains why in 1922 there was recovery only in the import of Chinese nut oil but not in those of the other three kinds.

The decline in the relative importance that was held by the Chinese oils in the American oil market a few years ago presents a still more serious consideration as to the possible recovery of China's oil trade with this country. As we have already noticed above, Chinese oils—such as soya bean, peanut, and cottonseed—were imported in some previous years largely as a substitute for some other oils, of which

the supply was either temporarily cut off by the war or became insufficient to meet the extraordinary demand. These other oils thus displaced in the United States have gradually come back to the American market since 1919, and are now displacing their Chinese competitors. It is largely for this reason that American imports of all Chinese oils except wood oil dropped so heavily in 1921-22 as almost to touch their pre-war level.

COMPARISON OF RATES OF AMERICAN IMPORT DUTIES ON SOME VEGETABLE OILS IMPORTED FROM CHINA IN THE TARIFF ACTS OF 1909, 1913, 1921, AND 1922.

| | 1909 | 1913 | 1921 | 1922 |
|---|---|---|---|---|
| Chinese nut oil | Free | Free | Free | Free |
| Cotton seed oil | Free | Free | 20c @ gal.[1] | 3c @ lb. |
| Peanut oil | Free | 6c @ gal. | 26c @ gal. | 4c @ lb. |
| Soya bean oil | Free | Free | 20c @ gal. | 2½c @ lb. |

(a) Soya bean oil. Of all the vegetable oils the United States imported from China during and immediately after the World War, only four kinds were important, viz., soya bean oil, Chinese nut oil (or wood oil), peanut oil, and cottonseed oil. But among these four kinds by far the most important was soya bean oil. It has been regarded as one of the most remarkable developments of American trade with the Orient in recent years. The shortage and the high prices of other oils at that time induced the importation of this oil in quantity, and its similarity or even superiority to cottonseed oil made a ready market for it.[2] During these years soya bean oil was an important constituent of some of the lard substitutes and edible fats being sold in the United States, besides finding a use in industry similar to that of cottonseed oil. The United States was then by far the largest buyer of this oil, importing nearly ninety percent of the total amount sold in the international market.[3]

[1] 1 gallon is roughly equal to 7 pounds.
[2] Vegetable Oils, Economic World, N. Y., op. cit., p. 260.
[3] The Bean Oil Trade, The Trans-Pacific, Oct., 1920, p. 57.

The oil comes from the soya bean, which is grown almost solely in North China, especially Manchuria, where the bean has been known for centuries. In the Far East, few vegetables have attained such importance as this bean. To the Chinese, it ranks very high as an essential food, because of its unusually high nutritive value. Besides bean curd, which is an ordinary food as well as a delicacy, the food products from this bean are bean flour, from which a kind of sphaghetti is manufactured; bean cheese; soy sauce; bean oil; and bean milk. Most of these uses are still unknown to the Americans although some experiments have been conducted in the U. S. Department of Agriculture. When its high value as food is realized the trade in soya beans would undoubtedly be greater than at present. Table 40 shows the American soya bean imports from China and Japan in recent years.

TABLE 40

AMERICAN IMPORTS OF SOYA BEAN OIL.

|  | From China | | From Japan | | Total | |
|---|---|---|---|---|---|---|
|  | Qty. in 1,000 lbs. | Value $1,000 | Qty. in 1,000 lbs. | Value $1,000 | Qty. in 1,000 lbs. | Value $1,000 |
| 1913 | 1,172 | 61 | 7,979 | 379 | 12,340 | 636 |
| 1916 | 27,473 | 1,360 | 70,384 | 3,750 | 98,120 | 5,128 |
| 1918 | 249,968 | 24,571 | 86,831 | 8,255 | 336,825 | 32,827 |
| 1919 | 100,273 | 13,310 | 84,218 | 10,517 | 195,808 | 24,019 |
| 1920 | 59,911 | 7,244 | 52,301 | 6,497 | 112,214 | 13,721 |
| 1921 | 15,239 | 607 | 1,004 | 50 | 16,286 | 660 |
| 1922 | 12,521 | 724 | 3,745 | 222 | 17,294 | 1,013 |

Before the outbreak of the World War, Great Britain was an important exporter of the oil to this country, a large part of the commodity being re-exports of German oil.[1] But since

[1] Beginning in 1910 Germany began to produce the oil, removing the tariff on beans and encouraging the crushers. At the beginning of the war she had developed a considerable oil industry. Vegetable Oils, The Economic World, op. cit.

the war China and Japan have become the sole suppliers, although the ultimate source of the product is from China alone.

Before the war the American market for this oil was unimportant to China; most of her product went to Europe. But during the war America was practically the sole customer for this oil, assuming that a large part of China's exports to Japan was re-shipped to America. Since the recovery of peace in Europe, however, a large quantity of Chinese oils is again on the way to Europe, and trade with America has greatly contracted.

(b) Chinese Wood Oil (Chinese nut oil). Next in importance comes Chinese wood oil which has been imported from China for decades. After the outbreak of the war trade in this commodity received a new impetus. It is extracted from the nuts of two varieties of a tree, native to China, Indo-China, Tonkin and Annam. The Provinces of Szechwan, Kweichow, Hunan and Hupeh in China are most important sources in the order named.[1] The oil is used extensively in China for water-proofing fabrics, paper, for varnish, putty, lacquer and ink.[2] It is largely used in America as a substitute for linseed oil in varnish, water-proofing for cement, linoleum and paint, because of its rapid drying properties. It dries more quickly than linseed oil, but it does not give as elastic a film as the latter. When heated to 500 F. for a short time it solidifies to a jelly-like mass. This property forms the basis of a heat test of the oil which is very useful in determining its purity.[3]

Practically all the wood oil consumed in the United States is provided by China, as is clearly shown in Table 41. From

[1] Laucks, J. F., Commercial Oils, Vegetable and Animal, N. Y., 1919, p. 37.
[2] Ibid., p. 39.
[3] Ibid., p. 37.

Hongkong comes a small part, which, however, is simply the reshipment from South China and Indo-China and Annam.

TABLE 41

AMERICAN IMPORTS OF CHINESE WOOD OIL

| Year | China | | Hongkong | | Total | |
|---|---|---|---|---|---|---|
|  | Qty. 1000 gals. | Value $1000 | Qty. 1000 gals. | Value $1000 | Qty. 1000 gals. | Value $1000 |
| 1913 | 5,858 | 2,659 | 45 | 26 | 5,997 | 2,734 |
| 1916 | 4,901 | 1,947 | 46 | 20 | 4,968 | 1,978 |
| 1918 | 4,649 | 3,896 | 111 | 103 | 4,816 | 4,038 |
| 1919 | 6,048 | 6,808 | 342 | 439 | 7,180 | 8,120 |
| 1920 | 7,436 | 8,690 | 897 | 1,356 | 9,061 | 11,077 |
| 1921 | 3,128 | 2,041 | 301 | 242 | 3,633 | 2,470 |
| 1922 | 10,162 | 7,591 | 255 | 186 | 10,545 | 7,891 |

Even before the war America was the best market for this oil, importing from China about one million dollars' worth of it every year. During and immediately after the war, however, the expansion of the trade was rapid, and until 1920, the value of its annual imports amounted to eleven million dollars, of which about nine million dollars worth came directly from China. This expansion was, however, largely due to price inflation, the actual quantity of the imported oil increasing much less rapidly. In 1922 the quantity of imports set up a new record at ten and a half million gallons.

Among all Chinese vegetable oils, only wood oil is now admitted free of American import duty. Judging from the decidedly rising trend of the quantity of imports during the last decade it is expected that with the recovery of American industrial activities, imports of this oil will increase still further.

For many years the United States absorbed about one-half to two-thirds of the wood oil exports from China, and

in 1922 its share increased to more than four-fifths. This indicates the importance of the American market for this Chinese oil.

(c) Peanut Oil. Another oil of some importance in China's trade with America during and immediately after the War is peanut oil, usually called groundnut oil. This is an oil for the production of which the United States possesses abundant raw material. Quantities of this oil are now being produced in some of the southern states, as it has been found to be suited to almost all the purposes for which other important vegetable oils are used.[1] But in the prosperous years following the European War American production fell short of its consumption by one-half to two-thirds;[2] it became necessary to import a great deal of it for some years.[3]

The countries growing peanuts, besides the United States, are: China, French West Africa, Nigeria, and India. Before the war these countries all shipped the nuts, shelled or unshelled, to Marseilles, which was the sole source of almost all the peanut oil of international commerce. The actual output was over thirty million gallons a year.[4] The United States then imported over a million gallons, chiefly from France, and some from Holland and Germany.

The war more or less cut off the shipments of peanuts to Marseilles, and as a result the trade fell off. On the other hand, pressing in Japan and China received a great stimulus. But for the same reasons as stated above, (viz. business depression, substitution of domestic oil, and heavy import duties) direct imports from China has practically ceased since 1921; and because of the last two reasons, the future of the trade is not promising. For some years these two countries took the lead as world exporters of this oil, and the United States made heavy imports of it therefrom.

[1] Vegetable Oils, The Economic World, op. cit., p. 262.
[2] See U. S. Bureau of Census: Animal and Vegetable Fats and Oils, 1922.
[3] See Table 37.
[4] Vegetable Oils, op. cit., p. 262.

Table 42 shows the American imports of this oil since 1913.

TABLE 42

AMERICAN IMPORTS OF PEANUT OIL FROM

| Year | China | | Hongkong | | Japan | | Total | |
|---|---|---|---|---|---|---|---|---|
| | Qty.<br>1000<br>gal. | Value<br>$1000 | Qty.<br>1000<br>gal. | Value<br>$1000 | Qty.<br>1000<br>gal. | Value<br>$1000 | Qty.<br>1000<br>gal. | Value<br>$1000 |
| 1913 | 11 | 7 | 68 | 42 | ..... | ..... | 1,196 | 821 |
| 1916 | 277 | 119 | 108 | 54 | 708 | 312 | 1,475 | 818 |
| 1918 | 3,509 | 2,998 | 91 | 111 | 4,631 | 4,157 | 8,289 | 7,312 |
| 1919 | 7,030 | 7,339 | 1,062 | 1,461 | 12,354 | 13,058 | 20,540 | 22,010 |
| 1920 | 2,304 | 3,008 | 899 | 1,284 | 9,251 | 12,353 | 12,683 | 16,990 |
| 1921 | 4 | 3 | 212 | 145 | 1 | 1 | 402 | 314 |
| 1922 | 21 | 3 | 1,601 | 170 | 62 | 3 | 2,470 | 281 |

From this table we notice that even after the outbreak of the war and the stoppage of the Marseilles oil trade, China supplied the United States with only one-fourth to one-half of what the latter imported, but this is very misleading. Practically all imports from Hongkong came from China, and this is true of at least one-half of the imports from Japan. This is evidenced by the fact that China exported annually a large quantity of this oil to Hongkong to be distributed to America as well as to Europe. She also exported even more oil to Japan to be re-shipped to the United States than what the United States directly imports from China.

*(d) Cottonseed Oil.* Cottonseed oil is of only temporary importance in China's oil trade with the United States. The latter country has always been by far the largest producer of this commodity because it has been the world's chief

cotton growing country. It is therefore self-sufficient in regard to this oil.

During the few boom years of the World War, however, the demand for this oil was so increased in the United States that a fairly large quantity, averaging more than ten million pounds, valued at one or two million dollars, was imported from China to supplement the native oil. Nearly one-half to four-fifths of the total Chinese imports were absorbed by this country. But after 1920 the American market for Chinese cottonseed oil suddenly dropped because, on the one hand, the demand of American industry could easily be supplied by the domestic product, while, on the other, the heavy import duty raised on this oil by the Tariff Act of 1921 and 1922 has put an end to its competition with the domestic product. Since 1921 no imports in this oil were made into the United States and there is little prospect that Chinese cottonseed oil will sell in any great quantity in this country unless an extraordinary demand should arise and high prices prevail here.

COTTON MANUFACTURES: LACES

Before the European War very little Chinese cotton manufactures were imported into this country. In stating this, however, we must not, of course, forget that in the old days of Chinese-American trade, Nankeens (a kind of cotton cloth) had been for several decades one of the principal imports from China. But with the gradual development of the last century, the importation of Chinese cotton cloths ceased. And until very recently the value of Chinese cotton manufactures imported amounted only to a few thousand dollars a year. They were composed of some cloths and apparel for the use of some Chinese residents in this country.

Immediately following the outbreak of the World War, however, there was introduced in China a new cotton industry which has played quite an important part in the Amer-

ican import trade. Its product has recently taken a growing share in the trade, and in a period of six years it has grown up from nothing to a value of two and a half million dollars a year. This is the trade in handmade laces.

The rise of the Chinese lace industry is an indirect result of the recent Great War. Foreign missionary ladies in Chefoo, Shanghai, Foochow, Amoy and Swatow introduced lacemaking several years before among the Chinese women.[1] When the war broke out in 1914, the American people, who had been using a tremendous amount of lace, were entirely cut off from the sources in European countries. The Chinese lace industry was then only in its infancy. But the Chinese rose to the opportunity offered by the large demands in America. The speed with which they developed their lace industry as if in a twinkling, producing lace of every kind to fill the needs of the American people, shows the ability of the Chinese to take advantage of a good trade opportunity.[2]

In an article on the Chinese lace trade appearing in the *China Review*, Mr. T. E. Pun, a prominent Chinese merchant in New York, wrote as follows:[3]

"Chinese lace compares favorably with the best European lace today. For some purposes American women have even found Chinese lace preferable. It is made more cheaply in China than is possible elsewhere because of the low wages paid in China.

"The Chinese lace industry is scattered throughout the country today. Chefoo, Canton, Shanghai, Foochow, Ningpo, Amoy and Swatow are the centers. The idea generally conveyed to large consumers in this country that the American importers of Chinese lace maintain their own factories or depots in China and have direct control over the workers is without foundation.

[1] Arnold, J., Commercial Handbook of China, Washington, 1919, p. 300.
[2] *Ibid.*
[3] *China Review*, N. Y., March, 1923.

"Chinese laces are being used in the manufacturing of not only women's wearing apparel of every description but also extensively in the making of household articles. A condition that is growing in this country is that American women are again turning to home sewing, and it is natural that they should show a great deal of partiality to handmade lace."

Before the war China was a lace-importing country. Only in the last few years has lace figured as a Chinese export, of which about 80 per cent. was imported by America.

TABLE 43

AMERICAN IMPORTS OF COTTON MANUFACTURES FROM CHINA

| Year | Laces, and Articles Made Thereof | | | All Other Cotton Manufactures, Such as Cloths, Wearing Apparel | Total |
|---|---|---|---|---|---|
| | Laces | | All Other | | |
| | 1000<br>Yards | $1000 | $1000 | $1000 | $1000 |
| 1914 | ..... | ..... | ..... | 46 | 46 |
| 1915 | ..... | ..... | ..... | 27 | 27 |
| 1916 | ..... | 9 | 9 | 43 | 61 |
| 1917 | ..... | 150 | 11 | 163 | 324 |
| 1918 | ..... | 395 | 41 | 30 | 465 |
| 1919 | 7,304 | 1,160 | 192 | 33 | 1,385 |
| 1920 | 7,155 | 1,477 | 542 | 99 | 2,118 |
| 1921 | 17,170 | 2,632 | 340 | 67 | 3,039 |
| 1922 | ..... | 2,438 | 303 | 105 | 2,846 |

Table 43 shows the American import of Chinese laces and other cotton manufactures since 1914. After 1918, the trade in laces and articles made of them expanded with very great rapidity. In 1920 the total value of American lace imports amounted to two million dollars, while in the next two years, in spite of the business depression and price drop, it increased with another large stride to nearly three million dollars a year. It seems quite obvious that so long as the lace using style remains unabated in this country, the future of the trade must be bright, because of the cheap labor in China, and therefore, the cheaper price for hand-made laces.

## CHAPTER IX

### OTHER IMPORTANT COMMODITIES

#### WOOL

In the years immediately preceding 1914, the wool industry of the United States consumed annually about 500,000,000 pounds of wool.[1] Of this total American domestic wool production constituted about three-fifths.[2] While it is as yet too early to determine what part of the expansion in wool consumption which took place during the war years will prove permanent, it is estimated that normal consumption of wool by American mills is now somewhat in excess of 600,000,000 pounds a year.[3] The domestic clip of the United States has not varied far from 300,000,000 pounds in thirty-five years,[4] so that increased consumption must be taken care of by increased imports. Since 1914, the imports of all kinds of wools have been around 350,000,-000 to 400,000,000 pounds a year.[5]

Since the later decades of the nineteenth century wool has held an important place in the American import trade with China. During the fifteen years, 1891-1905, the United States imported from China about 20,000,000 pounds a year, at a value of something more than one and one-half million dollars. It constituted from 5 to 7 per cent of all the American imports from China, and about 10 per cent. of the total American wool imports. From 1906 to 1913, the annual imports from China increased 50 per cent., being around thirty million pounds a year at an average value around three and a half million dollars. Their share in the total

[1] E. M. Miller, *Some Great Commodities*, New York, 1923, p. 276.
[2] *Ibid.*
[3] *Ibid.*
[4] *Ibid.*
[5] Total Imports of Wood into the United States, 1909-13, five-year average, 211,000,000 lbs.; 1914-18, five-year average, 363,000,000 lbs.; 1918, 454,000,000 lbs.; 1919, 446,000,000 lbs.; 1920, 260,000,000 lbs.; 1921, 321,000,000 lbs.

American imports from China increased to 12 per cent; and in the American total wool imports, to 16 per cent.

Before the war, the United Kingdom used to be the biggest wool supplier of this country.[1] China came second, Argentina third, Australia fourth, then New Zealand, Uruguay and Canada took the remaining share.[2] But in spite of her high rank according to the quantity of wool supplied, China's wool was at that time composed exclusively of carpet materials, which commanded a much lower price than those for clothing and combing wools of the other exporting countries.

### TABLE 44

#### AMERICAN WOOL IMPORTS FROM CHINA

| Year | Unmanufactured Wool | |
|---|---|---|
| Average | 1,000 lbs. | $1,000 |
| 1891-1895 | 16,311 | 1,339 |
| 1896-1900 | 22,371 | 1,606 |
| 1901-1905 | 20,518 | 1,914 |
| 1906-1908 | 28,012 | 3,362 |
| 1909-1913 | 33,284 | 3,807 |
| 1914-1918 | 38,545 | 9,089 |
| Calendar Year | | |
| 1918 | 42,910 | 14,235 |
| 1919 | 38,985 | 12,987 |
| 1920 | 15,334 | 5,397 |
| 1921 | 46,804 | 5,483 |
| 1922 | 63,214 | 9,712 |

After the outbreak of the European War, the American de-

[1] Much of the wool import credited to the United Kingdom is merely trans-shipments originated from Australia.
[2] American total wool imports, five-year average, 1909-13: From United Kingdom, 73,486,000 lbs.; from China, 33,284,000 lbs.; from Argentina, 29,856,000 lbs.; from Australia, 18,589,000 lbs.; from New Zealand, 4,533,000 lbs.; from Uruguay, 3,737,000 lbs.; from Canada, 1,163,000 lbs.

TABLE 45

AMERICAN WOOL IMPORTS FROM CHINA, CLASSIFIED

| Year | Clothing Wools 1,000 lbs. | A % of U. S. Total Imports of Clothing Wool | Combing Wools 1,000 lbs. | B % of U. S. Total Imports of Combing Wool | Carpet Wools 1,000 lbs. | C % of U. S. Total Imports of Carpet Wool | Total 1,000 lbs. | D Total % of U. S. Imports of All Kinds of Wool |
|---|---|---|---|---|---|---|---|---|
| Fiscal Year June 30 5-Year Average | | | | | | | | |
| 1909-13 | 1 | .... | 1 | .... | 33,282 | 31.60 | 33,284 | 15.80 |
| 1914-18 | .... | 2.34 | 419 | 2.68 | 31,885 | 39.50 | 38,545 | 10.60 |
| Calendar Year | | | | | | | | |
| 1918 | 6,241 | 2.82 | 1,206 | 12.08 | 311,198 | 44.90 | 42,910 | 9.45 |
| 1919 | 10,506 | 2.56 | 643 | 4.33 | 29,814 | 30.50 | 38,986 | 8.75 |
| 1920 | 8,329 | 0.25 | 2,864 | 25.22 | 11,763 | 32.80 | 15,152 | 5.85 |
| 1921 | 525 | 4.07 | 914 | 6.13 | 37,183 | 38.00 | 46,552 | 14.20 |
| 1922 | 8,455 | 0.49 | 1,495 | 0.96 | 61,533 | 35.50 | 63,214 | 17.20 |
| | 186 | | | | | | | |

mand for all kinds of wool suddenly expanded, while the huge supplies of clothing and combing wools which used to come to America from the United Kingdom practically stopped for some years. Though imports from Argentina, Australia, New Zealand, Uruguay, British South Africa, and Canada, were growing by leaps and bounds, they were still insufficient to fully meet the growing American demand. It was under these abnormal conditions that the United States began to import clothing and combing wools from China. During the five-year war period, the import of clothing wools averaged 6,241,000 pounds a year, constituting 2.34 per cent of the total American imports of clothing wool. From 1918 to 1921 (with the exception of a single year, 1920, which was a year of depression in the woolen and worsted industry in America) the average import from China grew to 8,500,000 pounds, constituting a little more than 3 per cent of the total American clothing wool imports. (See Table 45, column A.)

With regard to combing wool, importation from China since 1914 has fluctuated year by year. During the five-year war period, its quantity averaged 419,000 pounds annually, constituting 2.68 per cent of the total American imports of this kind of wool. It increased in 1918 to 1,206,000 pounds, which was one-eighth of the total, and in 1920 to 2,864,000 pounds, one-fourth of the total. (See Table 45, column B.) The huge increase of the latter year was rather abnormal, due largely to the shortage of this wool in Argentina. When in 1921-22 importation from that country resumed its usual size, China's share again dropped to a little more than one million pounds a year.

As regards carpet wool, China has been for some decades the biggest source of supply for the United States. The annual quantity of imports has remained quite steady since 1909, usually being around 30,000,000 to 35,000,000 pounds a year, constituting one-third to two-fifths of the total American carpet wool imports. (Table 45, column C.)

Taking the aggregate quantity of all these wools, Amer-

ican imports from China remained fairly steady in 1909-20. Throughout the whole period; it fluctuated closely around the figure of 40,000,000 pounds a year. Owing to the enormous inflation of price in some years following the war, however, its aggregate value increased in disproportion to its quantity. During the quinquennium, 1909-1913, it averaged only $3,807,000, but in the next period, 1914-1918, it amounted to $9,089,000 a year with only a small increase in quantity. In 1918 and 1919 the value gained another huge increase, without any increase in the volume. In 1921-22 when the market slumped, the total import value dropped heavily, while the quantity expanded to a record of forty-seven million and sixty-three million pounds respectively. (See Table 44.)

The amount of sheep's wool annually produced in China is roughly estimated at 40,000,000 pounds,[1] although there are no available statistics showing the actual production. In spite of the alleged fact that its quality does not come up to that of American and Australian wool, Chinese wool has begun to be regarded as one of the world's promising products, inasmuch as the demand for wool materials is constantly on the increase.

In China sheep wool comes from Mongolia and Western Asia. Most of it is taken to Tientsin for cleaning, steaming, grading and press-packing in preparation for export. Formerly Japan was its heaviest buyer. But now American importers are competing with the Japanese for this wool. About 46,000,000 pounds a year are shipped abroad, 65 to 75 per cent going to the United States.[2]

According to an American wool importer in the Orient, the reason that the Chinese sheep wool is inferior to American or Australian wools is largely because the sheep of

[1] C. O. Levine, *China in the World Wool Market. The Trans-Pacific*, August, 1922, p. 77 ff.
[2] U. S. Bureau of Foreign and Domestic Commerce, Miscellaneous Series No. 84, *Commercial Handbook of China*, Vol. II, p. 280.

China are not especially wool sheep, being raised chiefly for meat or for their skins. However, much of the inferiority in quality is due to the fact that the wool is sometimes mixed up with dirt and other foreign materials. It is therefore employed chiefly for the manufacturing of carpets, blankets and knitted goods. Although Chinese wool cannot be used for cloth of high quality, it is, because of its low price, coming to be recognized as an important raw material for coarse articles.

Another kind of Chinese wool is camel's hair, which comes from the Mongolian steppes and is also collected at the port of Tientsin for export. It serves for varied uses, among which is the making of camel's hair blankets and rugs. The best of that which goes abroad is said to be used in the finer grades of woolen underwear, by reason of its softness.[1] The exports from China amount to 4,800,000 pounds a year, one-fourth to one-third of which goes to the United States.

In addition to the camel's and sheep's wools, China also exports about 2,200,000 pounds of goat's hair, about one-third of which comes to this country.

The number of the wool-producing sheep and cattle raised in China is small compared with other wool-raising countries of similar size. China, including Mongolia and Tibet, is larger in area than the United States and all her territorial possessions. With the stretches of good grazing lands in Mongolia, Tibet and many inner provinces, it appears that with increasing wool prices, better transportation facilities, a good police system for her mountain regions, and the introduction of improved breeds of sheep, great developments may be expected in the wool industry both in quality and quantity. China may therefore expect to become a more important wool-producing country in the near future, and be in a better position to compete with South America and Australia in the sale of her product to the United States.

[1] *Commercial Handbook of China, op. cit.*, p. 280.

With regard to the trade in wool manufactures, nearly all exports from China are in the form of carpets and rugs. In the course of the past ten years, trade in Chinese carpets and rugs has shown a remarkable development.[1] The chief center of their production is the northern provinces of China, bordering Mongolia and the chief port of export is Tientsin.

It was only nineteen years ago (in 1905) that the United States began to import carpets and rugs from China. Although the volume of this import trade before the European War was quite insignificant, Oriental rugs have earned for themselves a high reputation in this country which is quite disproportionate to their volume of trade. From 1905 to 1913, the annual value of imports did not exceed a few thousand dollars a year.

Since 1914, however, the growth of the trade has been very rapid, and in each of the two years, 1920-1921, this country imported from China a full quarter of a million square yards of these Oriental fabrics, at an average value of one and one-half million dollars. In 1922 the trade doubled its size of the preceding years both in quantity and value. Table 46 shows these imports from China, 1905-1922.

[1] Following data are extracted from the annual Trade Returns of the Chinese Customs, showing the annual value and the destination of China's rug exports, 1913-22:

| Year | Total Exports of Carpets and Rugs from China in 1,000 HK Tls. | Exports to U. S. in 1,000 HK Tls. | % of the Total Exports | Exports to Japan in 1,000 HK Tls. | % of the Total Exports |
|------|------|------|------|------|------|
| 1913 | 100 | 55 | 55% | 6 | 6% |
| 1915 | 165 | 102 | 62 | 50 | 30 |
| 1917 | 796 | 431 | 55 | 329 | 42 |
| 1919 | 461 | 295 | 64 | 70 | 15 |
| 1920 | 1,424 | 1,033 | 73 | 173 | 12 |
| 1921 | 975 | 648 | 66 | 87 | 9 |
| 1922 | 3,300 | 2,697 | 81 | 332 | 10 |

TABLE 46

AMERICAN IMPORTS OF CARPETS AND RUGS FROM CHINA, 1905-1922

|  | Year | 1,000 Sq. Yds. | $1,000 |
|---|---|---|---|
| Average | 1905-1908........ | (a) | 7 |
| Year Ending | 1909-1913....... | (a) | 18 |
| June 30 | 1914-1918....... | 63 | 338 |
| Calendar | 1918............. | 85 | 407 |
| Year | 1919............. | 90 | 442 |
|  | 1920............. | 251 | 2,012 |
|  | 1921............. | 250 | 1,393 |
|  | 1922............. | 469 | 2,595 |

(a) Quantities not reported in these years.

Since the beginning of this carpet and rug trade, the United States has ever been China's best customer.[1] Before the war, the United States took from China more than half of the latter's total export, while after 1914, she took about two-thirds.[2]

### HUMAN HAIR AND HAIR NETS

The increasing importance of the rôle played by so trifling an article as human hair and hair nets in China's foreign trade, especially that with America, deserves to receive our separate attention. It was only fifteen years ago that the United States began to import human hair from China. No hair nets were imported until 1914. But during 1920-22 their aggregate value nearly averaged seven million dollars a year.

With the revolution in 1911, the cutting of queues among the Chinese became very general throughout the south and

[1] See footnote on the previous page.
[2] The reader interested in Chinese carpets and rugs is advised to consult American Vice-Consul J. C. Huston's report on "The Rug Industry of North China," which appeared in *U. S. Commerce Reports* for July 8, 1918; and Rodney Gilbert's report in the same reports for April 25, 1917.

extended gradually throughout the north. So the supply of human hair was greatly augmented, and the trade in it received a new stimulus. This supply has been supplemented by the combings of the women and by barber shop cuttings. Before the war a large part of this supply was directly sent to Europe; only a small part, not more than 4 to 5 per cent, was sold in America. But since 1916 the American market has expanded, and in 1919, 1920 and 1921 it absorbed nearly 50 per cent of China's total exports. Table 47, Column A, shows the quantity and value of the human hair imported into this country from China.

The development of the hair trade is incomparable to the phenomenal growth of the hair net trade. Perhaps none of the infant industries in China has had a more spectacular expansion than that of making hair nets. This industry, though insignificant as it might seem to be, now gives employment to thousands who are providing these articles for millions of American ladies. Although the industry was introduced into China by the Germans only fifteen years ago, in 1920 more than 140,000,000 hair nets were shipped to America from a single Chinese city, and the total annual exports of this product are valued at more than $10,000,000.[1] These nets are used by American ladies to keep their hair in place. A few years ago they were used rather as an adornment or luxury, but now are regarded as a comfort or even a necessity.[2]

The Chinese hair net industry was another product of the war, which promises to be one of permanence. Before the World War, Italy and Galicia shared with China the responsibility for producing most of the hair used in hair nets, while their manufacture centered in Alsace-Lorraine, Galicia and Bohemia.[3] During the period of hostility, however, the industry gradually drifted to China and hair nets are now

[1] The Hair Net Industry in North China, by H. W. Robinson, *The National Geographic Magazine*, September, 1923, p. 327-336.
[2] Hair Nets: *The China Review*, N. Y., January, 1922, p. 56.
[3] The Hair Net Industry in North China, *op. cit.*

practically an exclusive product of that country. The provinces of Shantung and Chihli are the largest producers. A pound of prepaired hair, which costs as much as several dollars, depending upon length and quality, will make over two thousand nets, and a whole gross of hair nets weighs only about one ounce.[1] The nets are made by hand and the girl workers receive about one cent each for their labor. The average person can hardly make ten a day.[2]

As the jet black color of the Chinese hair is not suitable to the use of the American whose hair is usually light in color, the hair before being used in knitting into nets is bleached and re-dyed through the use of chemicals. Formerly the raw hair was shipped from China to Europe or America where the chemical operations were performed, and then sent back to China for manufacture. But as the industry developed, the preparation of the hair has also been transferred in great part to China. Probably nine-tenths of the hair nets exported from China at present are made from hair that has been prepared in that country. The bleaching and dyeing operations performed by the Chinese chemical plants give perfectly satisfactory results.[3] There is also one American firm which has already completed arrangments to prepare its own hair in China under the supervision of expert American chemists.[4]

It seems that American ladies are well satisfied with these nets; they also appear inclined to use more and more of them in the near future. Table 47, Column B, shows the annual value of hair nets imported into this country from China. It is really wonderful that in less than ten years it increased from less than one thousand dollars to more than eight millions. It is worth noticing that in 1921, which was notably a slump year in nearly every line of business, the value of the net trade made a substantial increase in spite of

[1] *Ibid.*
[2] *Ibid.*
[3] J. Arnold, *Commercial Hand Book of China*, Vol. II.
[4] The Hair Net Industry in China, *op. cit.*, p. 333.

the heavy drop of the general price level. Once it establishes itself in the American market, China may rely on it to give employment to thousands of her girl workers so long as the style of net-wearing persists in this country. This trade is also one in which China does not fear the competition of any other country, because China has a vast supply of cheap labor, which is not existent in any other place. A single net requires the tying by hand of one thousand knots or more, for which labor the price paid during the last few years has not varied much from two to two and a half coppers, or about one cent in American currency.

TABLE 47

QUANTITY AND VALUE OF HUMAN HAIR AND ITS PRODUCT IMPORTED FROM CHINA TO THE UNITED STATES

| Year | Human Hair Unmanufactured | | Human Hair Manufactured |
|---|---|---|---|
|  | A | | B |
|  | 1000 lbs. | $1,000 | $1,000 |
| 1913.......... | .324 | 172 | .... |
| 1914.......... | 167 | 60 | 1 |
| 1915.......... | 262 | 70 | 5 |
| 1916.......... | 434 | 74 | 182 |
| 1917.......... | 319 | 85 | 487 |
| 1918.......... | 870 | 340 | 709 |
| 1919.......... | 1,100 | 463 | 2,031 |
| 1920.......... | 1,353 | 604 | 6,257 |
| 1921.......... | 623 | 193 | 8,354 |
| 1922.......... | 629 | 190 | 5,804 |
| 1923.......... | 199 | 79 | .... |

### BRISTLES

Bristles obtained from the hog are the principal material used in brush manufacture.[1] The best grades of

[1] For an exhaustive account of bristles taking part in the American brush industry, see United States Tariff Commission: Tariff Information Series No. 8: *The Brush Industry*, p. 24 ff.

bristles, determined by length, color, stiffness, shape, texture and resiliency, are obtained from hogs living in cold climates; hence Russian and Siberian bristles are known for their superior quality. Russia and China supply most of the bristles used in the American brush industry. Russia ranks first in production, followed in the order named by China, Germany and India. Other countries of Central Europe produce and export considerable quantity of bristles. Those produced in the United States are a by-product of the slaughter houses. They are short and inferior in quality on account of the breeding of the hog and its immaturity when slaughtered. American bristles are used principally in the manufacture of the cheaper grades of brushes, such as shoe and dust brushes.

The introduction of Chinese bristles into the American market was an important event in the brush industry. The objections of the trade to the substitution of Chinese for Russian bristles were largely overcome by the discovery of the proper treatment of the Chinese bristle. The chief obstacle to the use of the Chinese product was the fact that its peculiar characteristics necessitated a method of treatment different from that used in preparing the Russian bristle. Chinese bristles are generally black and range in length from two and one-half to seven inches. They are as resilient as the Russian, but are said to be not so tough or so durable. Yet the United States has been importing bristles from China since the later decades of the last century. Both the quantity and value of this import grew quite rapidly in the past. Thirty years ago in 1894, this country imported only 74,000 pounds of this article at $27,000. Ten years later, in 1904, it increased to 921,000 pounds at $475,000. In another ten years, both the quantity and value nearly doubled the figures for 1904. For the last ten years, China

exported 8,000,000 pounds of bristles a year,[1] of which about two-fifths was sent to America, ranging from less than one and a half million pounds at less than one million dollars before the war, to nearly three and a half million pounds in 1920. (See Table 48, Column A). At present, sorted, bunched and prepared bristles are taking quite an important share in the trade between China and the United States, more than 3 per cent of the total.

TABLE 48

QUANTITY AND VALUE OF BRISTLES AND OTHER ANIMAL HAIRS IMPORTED FROM CHINA TO THE UNITED STATES

| Year | Bristles Sorted, Bunched and Prepared | | Horse Hair Unmanufactured | | Hair of All Other Animals | |
|---|---|---|---|---|---|---|
| | A | | B | | C | |
| | 1000 lbs. | $1,000 | 1000 lbs. | $1,000 | 1000 lbs. | $1,000 |
| 1894 | 74 | 27 | .... | .... | .... | .... |
| 1899 | 389 | 170 | .... | .... | .... | .... |
| 1904 | 921 | 475 | .... | .... | .... | .... |
| 1908 | 1,363 | 800 | .... | .... | .... | .... |
| 1912 | 1,488 | 869 | (b) | (b) | (a) 321 | (a) 80 |
| 1913 | 1,439 | 922 | .... | .... | 418 | 168 |
| 1914 | 1,410 | 934 | 143 | 120 | 10 | 1 |
| 1915 | 2,359 | 1,623 | 194 | 95 | 170 | 17 |
| 1916 | 2,359 | 1,612 | 471 | 178 | 768 | 90 |
| 1917 | 2,385 | 1,728 | 995 | 509 | 656 | 96 |
| 1918 | 3,173 | 3,381 | 678 | 321 | 87 | 51 |
| 1919 | 2,159 | 2,750 | 636 | 351 | 64 | 34 |
| 1920 | 3,357 | 6,168 | 643 | 489 | 93 | 58 |
| 1921 | 2,540 | 3,831 | 782 | 500 | 81 | 38 |
| 1922 | 2,721 | 2,969 | 735 | 490 | 274 | 94 |

(a) Including horse hair.
(b) Included in "Hair of Other Animals."
[1] The total annual export of bristles from China averaged for the last ten years about 60,000 piculs (133⅓ pounds = 1 picul). See data in the Trade Reports and Returns of Chinese Customs.

Before the war England had shared with China the bristle trade of America. During the war period England's share dwindled to very small figures, while China almost got the whole trade. Even after the Armistice, this condition has not changed. China now supplies about 80 per cent of the United States bristle imports, (see Table 49) and, owing to the fact that the price of English bristles is much higher than the Chinese, she will be able to hold the market in the future.[1]

TABLE 49

UNITED STATES IMPORTS OF BRISTLES FROM

| Year | China | | Hongkong | | England | | Total | |
|---|---|---|---|---|---|---|---|---|
| | 1000 lbs. | $1,000 | 1000 lbs. | $1,000 | 1000 lbs. | $1,000 | 1000 lbs. | $1,000 |
| 1913 | 1,439 | 922 | 42 | 30 | 1,050 | 1,169 | 3,559 | 3,492 |
| 1918 | 3,115 | 3,369 | 357 | 558 | 182 | 747 | 4,119 | 5,640 |
| 1919 | 2,126 | 2,727 | 51 | 118 | 558 | 1,468 | 3,081 | 5,932 |
| 1920 | 3,322 | 6,020 | 39 | 58 | 882 | 2,299 | 4,821 | 10,102 |
| 1921 | 2,529 | 3,778 | 102 | 120 | 528 | 761 | 3,414 | 5,341 |
| 1922 | 2,721 | 2,969 | 15 | 15 | 827 | 1,286 | 4,085 | 5,346 |

Data from the United States Navigation and Commerce.

For the making of soft brushes, horse and other animal hair has also been imported from China in increasing quantities. (See Table 48, Columns B and C). But it has not as yet attained a place of importance in the trade.

HIDES AND SKINS

The United States is one of the foremost leather manufacturing countries in the world. It produces an immense

[1] By comparing the small quantity of English imports with its rather big value, we know the price of English bristles is usually two or more times higher than that of Chinese bristles.

quantity of hides and skins from its vast herds of live stock.[1] Yet the quantity of raw material needed by its numerous leather factories is so tremendous that under normal business conditions it has to import each year more than one hundred million dollars worth of hides and skins of various sorts nearly from every nook and corner of the globe. Several years during and immediately after the war, its imports amounted to an annual value of more than two hundred million dollars.

Hides and skins have long assumed an important place in the Chinese-American trade since the closing years of the preceding century. During the two decades, 1891-1913, the trade expanded nearly ten times, as shown in the last column of Table 50. In 1891-95, the quantity of hides and skins imported from China was not reported while the value was less than four hundred thousand dollars a year. In 1911-13 the quantity increased to fifteen and a half million pounds a year, and its value to three and a half million dollars. This growth was partly due to the effect of the American Tariff Act of 1909, which put all hides and skins on the free list.[2] Stimulated by the war and post-war demand during 1914-1920, the quantity and especially its value showed another huge increase. Thus in the single year of 1917, the United States imported from China fifty-nine million pounds of hides and skins at a value of twenty-seven and a half million dollars, whereas in 1920, twenty-nine million pounds at thirty-one million dollars. In 1921-22 these imports declined to nearly their pre-war size, but with the gradual recovery of industrial activities in America, they are now rising again.

[1] For a fuller description of the hide and skin markets in the United States, cf. U. S. Tariff Commission, Information Series, No. 28, Hides and Skins, 1922.
[2] Before 1909, cattle hides were taxed at 15 per cent ad valorem, while other kinds free.

Although Chinese hides and skins have been extensively imported into this country, their share in the total American imports of these materials has never become very big. Before the war, the American tanners and leather manufacturers got their supply of raw materials mainly from Germany, Russia in Europe, the United Kingdom, France, and other Central European countries, British India, Canada, Mexico, Argentina, Brazil, Columbia, Chile, Uruguay, British Africa, New Zealand and Australia, and although their import from China was then already quite large China's average share in 1911-13, was less than four per cent. But during the war and post-war period, the European source of supply was almost completely cut off, and the increasing demand in the United States had to be met by China as well as by other Asiatic and American countries. In 1916-1920, therefore, China's share increased to around ten per cent.; in 1921-22, it stood at 6.5 per cent., showing a substantial increase over that of the pre-war period. (See Table 51.)

China's tremendous production of domestic animals has long served, and will still better serve, the leather industry of this country as a ready source of raw materials.[1] Hides are from cattle, buffalo, horses, and donkeys, whereas skins are from goats, sheep, calves, colts, etc. Heavy hides are used for the production of sole leather, machinery belting, suit cases, trunks, etc., and light hides for light shoes and for uppers. Sheep and goat skins are used for the lightest footwear, gloves, fancy goods, purses, upholstery, etc. Among all the different kinds, imported from China, goat skins are by far the most important kind, usually constituting more than four-fifths of the total value of the imports from that country. Second to goat skins in importance is cattle hides, while all the other kinds have not as yet reached large

[1]Regarding the production of hides and skins in China, see U. S. Bur. of For. & Dom. Com., Special Agent Series No. 173. *Shoe and Leather Trade of China and Japan*, by Bosworth, 1918, pp. 14 ff.

#### TABLE 50

AMERICAN IMPORTS OF HIDES AND SKINS FROM CHINA

| Year | Cattle and Buffalo Hides Qty. 1,000 lbs. | Cattle and Buffalo Hides Value $1,000 | Goat Skins Qty. 1,000 lbs. | Goat Skins Value $1,000 | Sheep, calf, horse, colt and all other Qty. 1,000 lbs. | Sheep, calf, horse, colt and all other Value $1,000 | Total Qty. 1,000 lbs. | Total Value $1,000 |
|---|---|---|---|---|---|---|---|---|
| 1891-95 | | | | | | | * | 379 |
| 1896-1900 | | | | | | | 7,691 | 1,198 |
| 1901-05 | | | | | | | 10,978 | 2,413 |
| 1906-10 | | | | | | | 13,447 | 3,472 |
| 1911-13 | 4,426b | 953b | 9,382 | 2,328 | 1,498 | 246 | 15,308 | 3,727 |
| 1914-15 | 10,893 | 2,316 | 7,601 | 2,006 | 1,762 | 349 | 20,256 | 4,820 |
| 1916-17 | 22,858 | 6,382 | 18,281 | 9,876 | 7,351 | 2,088 | 48,490 | 18,546 |
| 1918 | 5,876 | 1,923 | 13,812 | 8,753 | 3,526 | 1,299 | 23,214 | 11,975 |
| 1919 | 11,050 | 3,720 | 15,217 | 10,942 | 7,129 | 2,487 | 33,396 | 17,149 |
| 1920 | 7,666 | 2,854 | 19,052 | 26,634 | 2,100 | 1,318 | 28,828 | 30,806 |
| 1921 | 1,499 | 263 | 10,586 | 3,508 | 888 | 325 | 12,973 | 4,195 |
| 1922 | 4,655 | 824 | 13,408 | 5,708 | 1,288 | 434 | 19,351 | 6,965 |

* Quantity not reported before 1895.
b Not including Buffalo Hides.

sizes. But as all kinds are imported free of duty, there is no reason why China can not increase her share by sending America more of the other kinds on a competitive basis with other countries.

#### TABLE 51

CHINA'S SHARE IN AMERICAN IMPORTS OF HIDES AND SKINS, 1911-12

| Year | Value of American imports of hides and skins from all countries in $1,000 | Value of American imports of hides and skins from China in $1,000 | % of the total |
|---|---|---|---|
| 1911-13 | 96,789 | 3,727 | 3.9 |
| 1914-15 | 111,211 | 4,870 | 4.4 |
| 1916-17 | 185,334 | 18,546 | 10.0 |
| 1918 | 108,044 | 11,975 | 11.1 |
| 1919 | 306,510 | 17,149 | 5.6 |
| 1920 | 243,878 | 30,806 | 12.6 |
| 1921 | 67,561 | 4,195 | 6.2 |
| 1922 | 107,036 | 6,966 | 6.5 |

#### FURS

Closely related to the importation of hides and skins is that of Chinese furs. Between 1875 and 1890, American furriers, being hard pressed by intense demand for more furs in this country, sought a new source of fur supply and found it in China.[1] From the Orient they imported large quantities of goat and dog skin plates and robes, which were easily worked up into warm and serviceable coats and sleigh robes. "At first the Chinese furs were very low in price, and excellent profit producers for the importers, but in a comparatively short time competition moved prices up in China and profits down in America. The consumption of goat and dog skins was still large, but both animals con-

[1]For early fur trade between China and the United States, see Belden, A. L., *The Fur Trade of America*, N. Y., 1917.

tinue to flourish in China in ample numbers to meet the demand."[1-2]

But between 1891 to 1913 the trade remained practically stationary, amounting annually to about three hundred thousand dollars a year. In fact, the relative importance of Chinese furs in the American market steadily declined as the total Chinese-American trade was growing year after year. During that period the large exporters of furs to the United States were England, Germany, Canada, Australia and Argentina; and the share of China in the trade was only one or two per cent.

#### TABLE 52

AMERICAN IMPORTS OF FURS FROM CHINA, 1891-1922 AND PERCENTAGE OF THE TRADE IN THE TOTAL AMERICAN FUR IMPORTS.

| Year | $1,000 Undressed | Dressed, $1,000 | Manufactures, $1,000 | Total import from China, $1,000 | % of import from China to total American fur imports |
|---|---|---|---|---|---|
| 1891-95 | | | | 389 | |
| 1896-1900 | | | | 281 | |
| 1901-05 | | | | 261 | |
| 1906-10 | | | | 302 | |
| 1911-13 | 124 | 254 | | 377 | 1.5 |
| 1914-15 | 48 | 409 | 136 | 593 | 4.7 |
| 1916-17 | 376 | 764 | 96 | 1,236 | 5.3 |
| 1918 | 2,373 | 467 | 262 | 3,102 | 9.01 |
| 1919 | 5,258 | 223 | 1,845 | 7,326 | 10.2 |
| 1920 | 10,731 | 231 | 1,532 | 12,494 | 13.4 |
| 1921 | 4,047 | 93 | 679 | 4,819 | 11.9 |
| 1922 | 12,125 | 273 | 1,447 | 13,847 | 20.0 |

But a great change in the fur trade has been effected by the war since 1914. During the disturbance of the war, American fur imports from Europe declined rapidly. With Canadian, South American, and Australian furs insufficient to meet the increasing demand in this coun-

[1]*Ibid*, p. 293.

[2]For a fuller description of fur trade in China, see *Ibid*, pp. 427-32.

try, the United States looked once more to China, as she did a half century before, for an additional supply. Under these conditions, Chinese furs were extensively bought by American firms in the East, and the value of the trade rose from half a million dollars in 1914 to three millions in 1918, to seven millions in 1919, and again to twelve millions in 1920. In 1921, the trade suffered a set-back, due to the business stagnation in America. In 1922, it recovered more than its loss in the preceding year, and the value amounted to a record figure of fourteen million dollars. The relative increase of the trade was likewise phenomenal; in 1914 the value of Chinese furs imported by the Americans was only 4.7 per cent. of total American fur imports. In 1918-1921, it averaged more than ten per cent. In 1922, it reached 20%, and China for the first time became the largest exporter of furs to the United States. (See Table 52.)

Chinese furs are imported either undressed, or dressed, or in the form of manufactures. Before 1917, the quantity of dressed furs and manufactures was much greater than that of undressed furs. But since 1918 the import of un-dressed fur has increased a hundred times the value of ten years ago, while that of fur manufactures increased only ten times, and dressed furs has really decreased. This dif-ference in the rates of increase is mainly due to the heavy import duty levied on the dressed furs and fur manufac-tures, while all undressed furs are imported free. Chinese fur trade with the United States has a really brilliant future. As the American people are now becoming more wealthy, their demand for such a luxury as fur goes up correspond-ingly. With her tremendous production of fur-bearing ani-mals, China is able to supply the American tanneries and furriers with many kinds of raw furs.

### Eggs and Egg Products

Although from time immemorial poultry eggs have been an important article in the everyday diet of the Chinese and were thus extensively produced in China, they did not enter into the foreign trade of China until twelve years ago. But within the last ten years the egg trade has rapidly come to assume a position of importance, and Chinese exports of eggs and egg products now amount to ten or twenty million dollars a year. The great part of China's export goes to the United States, while nearly nine-tenths of American imports of these articles come from China. The accompany-ing table shows the recent phenomenal growth of this line of trade between the two countries. In 1912, the value of the trade hardly exceeded ten thousand dollars, but it in-creased to nearly thirteen million dollars in 1919, and eleven million dollars in 1920. In 1921-22, the trade suffered a strong setback as effected by the business depression in America; yet the annual value still stood at four to five million dollars a year.

Eggs are exported from China usually in their preserved condition. They are preserved by the Chinese by a coating of clay and salt, or of lime and will keep for several years without any deterioration of taste or substance.[1] They are exported also in a prepared form of yolk and albumen. Yolk is used for making biscuits and other cakes, whereas albumen is an ingredient for candy manufacture.[2] Since Chinese eggs and their products can be bought at a sub-stantially lower price, they are extensively used by the Amer-ican bakeries and candy factories.

Before 1919, when American imports of Chinese egg products had not as yet assumed very large dimensions,

[1] For a fuller account on Chinese egg industry, see U. S. Bur. of For. & Dom. Com., Misc. Series, No. 84, Commercial Hand of China, by Julian Arnold; Vol. II, pp. 270-271.
[2] A Chinese Egg Plant, China Review, New York, Jan. 1923, p. 14.

their importation was not restricted by the United States. But since that year, American egg producers have become well aware of the competition of China's frozen and powdered egg industry; and on the Pacific coast laws are constantly sought to shut out these products.[1] Formerly, the Chinese producer of dried egg powder usually used zinc as container. It is, therefore, regarded by the United States Health Department that Chinese egg products are poisonous, because they contain zinc substance. This Department, in demanding that the percentage of zinc to be found in those products should not exceed one-tenth of one per cent., has applied a very strict regulation to the Chinese imports,[2] a barrier which caused the Chinese exports to this country to fall off since 1920, and for which Chinese merchants have suffered severe losses.[3] Owing to the method of manufacture, it is impossible to guarantee so low a per-centage of zinc, the yolk being poured on zinc trays during the process of preparation. Other methods have been tried, porcelain has been used, but for some reason the product is not of the same quality as under the old system.[4] According to an American investigator in China, there is little to fear regarding the sanitary effect of Chinese egg products.[5]

Not only have such severe restrictive regulations worked to check the expansion of Chinese egg exports to the United States, but the recently revised American import tariff has also put a second barrier upon the trade. "The American market for frozen and dried eggs from China," thus com-mented the Trade Report of the Chinese Maritime Customs, "has suffered much from the increased duty levied by the raised import tariff which came into force in the United

[1] Ibid.
[2] The Far Eastern Review, Feb. 1919, p. 91.
[3] A Chinese Egg Plant, Ibid.
[4] Ibid.
[5] A description of an American-owned Egg Factory in Shanghai, by F. H. K. Reis of the U. S. Consular Service, China Review, Jan. 1923, p. 14.

States on the 22nd September, 1922.[1] Heavy shipments of these products were made from China during the early part of the year, but practically all exports ceased in August of that year."[2] The future prospect of the egg trade, there-fore, cannot be very bright until these restrictive measures are repealed by the American government.

TABLE 53

AMERICAN IMPORTS OF EGGS AND EGG PRODUCTS FROM CHINA

| Year | Eggs of Poultry | | Egg Yolk, dried, frozen, etc. | | Egg Albumen[*] | | Total Value, $1,000 |
|---|---|---|---|---|---|---|---|
| | Qty. in 1,000 lbs. | Value in $1,000 | Qty. in 1,000 doz. | Value in $1,000 | Qty. in 1,000 lbs. | Value in $1,000 | |
| 1911-13 .. | 111 | 11 | 250 | 16 | | | 27 |
| 1914-15 .. | 1,966 | 229 | 3,718 | 290 | | | 519 |
| 1916-17 .. | 393 | 61 | 6,482 | 1,119 | * | * | 1,180 |
| 1918 ..... | 490 | 105 | 6,736 | 2,455 | 1,353 | 469 | 3,029 |
| 1919 ..... | 475 | 117 | 22,168 | 6,944 | 7,557 | 5,603 | 12,664 |
| 1920 ..... | 847 | 228 | 25,647 | 6,093 | 8,526 | 4,453 | 10,774 |
| 1921 ..... | 1,132 | 246 | 15,326 | 2,300 | 4,498 | 1,119 | 3,665 |
| 1922 ..... | 383 | 61 | 17,566 | 3,099 | 6,441 | 1,995 | 5,055 |

[1] The following table, extracted from the United States Acts of 1909, 1913, and 1922, shows the great increase of import duties on eggs and egg products in 1922 as compared with those in 1909 and 1913.

| Item | Year | 1909 | 1913 | 1922 |
|---|---|---|---|---|
| Albumen, dried ............... | | 3c @ lb. | 3c @ lb. | 18c @ lb. |
| Albumen, frozen or otherwise prepared ............... | | 3c @ lb. | 1c @ lb. | 6c @ lb. |
| Yolk, dried ............... | | 25% | 10% | 18c @ lb. |
| Yolk, frozen or otherwise prepared ............... | | 25% | 10% | 6c @ lb. |
| Eggs of poultry in the shell.. | | 5c @ doz. | Free | 8c @ doz. |

The change from an ad valorem, to a specific, duty usually sig-nifies a great increase in the actual rate in the tradition of American tariff history.

[2] The Chinese Maritime Customs: Foreign Trade of China, 1922, Pt. I, p. 24.

[*] Not separately reported before 1917.

PART III

Some Important American
Exports to China

CHAPTER X.

COTTON GOODS

*China as a Market for Cotton Goods*

Since the middle of the nineteenth century, cotton manufactures have constituted by far the largest single item in
the import trade of China and she is considered the second
largest market for the world's cotton piece goods, ranking
next to India.[1]  For the past half century these goods constituted about one-third of her total imports.  They have
increased in value at a pace nearly as rapid as that of the
rapidly expanding total imports.  Their total import value
for the year 1880 was only 32 million dollars.  In 1900 it
was 51 millions, and in 1920, 306 millions.  For the decade
before the war it averaged more than one hundred million
dollars a year, and since that time the sum has nearly
doubled.  From these figures, one may draw the obvious
conclusion that the Chinese market for cotton goods offers
at the present time a broad field latent with great possibilities.

The development of China's enormous natural resources,
the building of railways which will provide better transportation facilities in the interior, and the economc and
social progress of the people, will unquestionably lead to a
further steady growth in consumption and will no doubt
greatly stimulate the importation of many kinds of foreign
cotton manufactures which are not adequately supplied by
China's own mills.

*Early Prosperity of American Cotton Piece Goods Trade
With China—British Competition*

In China's excellent cotton goods market the United
States shared a very considerable part as soon as her cotton

[1]United States Bureau of Foreign and Domestic Commerce, Special Agents Series No. 107. *Cotton Goods in China*, Letter of
Submittal, p. 5.

205

industry was established. As early as the thirties of the nineteenth century, American piece goods constituted a substantial part of American domestic exports to China;[1] and in the fifties, they became by far the most important item. During the four years 1850 to 1853, piece goods alone made up almost nine-tenths of the total American domestic exports to China,[2] while China became by far the best customer for American piece goods, taking more than one-third of America's total piece goods exports.[3] From these percentages one can easily realize how prosperous was the early trade in cotton manufactures between these countries, and how important was the rôle played by this single article.

But partly due to the destruction during the Civil War of the American merchant marine, which was necessary for carrying the bulky cloths, and partly to the keen competition of Great Britain and India, America lost a very large part of her cotton goods trade with the Orient after 1860. Even though the United States was able to recover some of her lost share during the seventies, American cotton goods have never regained their old high position either in the export list of the United States or in the import list of China. Their absolute value and quantity had sometimes been bigger than those in the fifties, but never their comparative shares.

[1] See tables in Pitkin's *Statistical View of the Commerce of the United States;* also cf. Chapter I, p. 18, *supra.*

| Year | Total U.S. Dom. Exports to China | Total U.S. Piece Goods Exports | U.S. Piece Goods Export to China | % in Total Am. Exp. to China | % in Total Am. Cotton Goods Exp. |
|---|---|---|---|---|---|
| 1850 ..... | $1,486,000 | $3,774,000 | $1,203,000 | 81 | 32 |
| 1851 ..... | 2,156,000 | 5,572,000 | 1,894,000 | 88 | 34 |
| 1852 ..... | 2,480,066 | 6,139,000 | 2,202,000 | 89 | 36 |
| 1853 ..... | 3,213,000 | 6,926,000 | 2,801,000 | 87 | 40 |

Of course, the shrinkage of their comparative shares was also due to the increase or addition of other American exports to China and the huge expansion in the total American cotton goods exports to South America and Europe. But the main reason of this relative decline seems to be that since the very beginning of international competition in the Chinese cotton goods market, the United States has suffered the handicap of a higher manufacturing cost and a resulting higher selling price of her cloth. Price appeal has long been extremely important in China because the income of the majority of Chinese people is usually low. In order to meet this situation England has to a very great extent adopted the practice of adulteration by adding clay and other foreign matter to the cloth.[1] As American manufacturers resisted such temptation and "made honest cloth entirely of cotton," their price must needs be higher, and sometimes, considerably higher, than that of British make,[2] "Although the Chinese have never refused to acknowledge the superiority of the American cottons, as is shown by the higher prices they have always paid for the standard drills and sheetings than for any other goods, the cheap adulterated English goods supply a want in point of low cost which the Chinese cannot overlook and which the Americans will have to combat."[3] Of the Chinese imports of cotton goods in the eighties, therefore, six-sevenths came from Great Britain, and less than one-twelfth from the United States.

One may get an idea of the severe handicap under which this country was and still is placed by reading another typical report from an American consul in China:

[1] *United States Commercial Relations*, 1878, p. 212, Report of the American Consul at Shanghai.
[2] *Ibid.*
[3] *Ibid.*, p. 213.

"There are several large American houses engaged in trade here, but, strange to say, most of the goods sold are purchased from London instead of from American cities. Various explanations are given for this, but the most convincing is that goods can be laid down here at less cost from London than from cities in the United States. Trade is rarely governed by patriotic principles; profit is its guiding star."[1]

Among the minor reasons which accounted for victory of the British over the Americans in their early competition for China's cotton goods trade, the consul enumerated: (1) American merchants did not exercise that care and judgment in packing goods shipped to foreign countries that the English did, and (2) America had not sufficient banking facilities in China to finance the import and practically no merchant marine at her own service, while the banking houses and steamship companies in China were largely under English control.[2]

In spite of such handicaps, American cotton piece goods during the closing years of the last, and the opening years of the present, century still occupied a very respectable position in the American trade with China. As shown in Table 53 both the quantity and value of American cotton cloths exported to China increased about one hundred per cent every five years during the fifteen years 1891-1905, and throughout this period the total value of these cloths constituted nearly sixty per cent. of the total American exports to China. (Table 54, last column.) Of the total cotton piece goods imports of China those from America took a share of twenty-seven per cent. in 1902 and as high as thirty-six per cent. in 1905. (Table 55.)

Most of the cotton fabrics sent to China from this country were plain fabrics, such as sheeting, shirting, jean, duck,

[1] United States House Miscellaneous Documents, No. 268, 51st Congress, 1st Session. *Special Consular Reports*, Vol I, 1890, p. 131, Report of Consul J. T. Campbell of Foochow.
[2] *Ibid.*

together with a very few dyed cottons. Practically all the dyed cottons came to China from England, and in this line the United States has never been able to challenge British supremacy in the Chinese market.

The reason that American cotton piece goods trade with China became very prosperous during the years before 1905 is not difficult to see. Other than England there was at that time practically no one country that could offer any strong competition to the American cotton manufacturer. Although Japan had been exporting plain cotton fabrics to China for some years, her share as compared with that of the United States was still negligible, because her cotton industry was not as yet well developed. In China itself cotton manufacture was then only a "novelty industry." The first cotton mill in China was established in 1891, and in the next twelve years the number had increased to only twelve. As an infant industry these few mills were utterly unable to provide the Chinese consumer with an adequate supply of cotton cloths. On the other hand, the demand of the Chinese people for these cloths became more and more intense year after year as evidenced by the rapid increase of their total imports. This being the situation in the market, the American cotton manufacturer was therefore much benefited.

The American cotton piece goods trade with China reached its zenith in 1905 and 1906, when the quantity attained five hundred million yards and its value nearly thirty million dollars, being almost as great as the share of Great Britain. But these are two rather exceptional years resulting from the war demand in Manchuria.

TABLE 54

QUANTITY AND VALUE OF AMERICAN COTTON CLOTH EXPORTS
TO CHINA,[1] 1891-1922

|  | Year | Quantity, 1,000 Yds. | Value, $1,000 | Value of Total Am. Exports to China, $1,000 | % of Cotton Goods Value to Total |
|---|---|---|---|---|---|
| Five-Year Average | 1891-95 .... | 52,182 | 3,082 | 5,546 | 56.0 |
| | 1896-1900 .. | 146,389 | 7,019 | 11,718 | 60.0 |
| | 1901-05 .... | 249,731 | 13,295 | 24,069 | 55.0 |
| | 1906-10 .... | 123,976 | 10,358 | 25,513 | 41.0 |
| | 1911-15 .... | 75,164 | 5,126 | 20,938 | 25.0 |
| Three-Year Average | 1916-18 .... | 7,308 | 728 | 45,548 | 1.6 |
| | 1919 ........ | 39,216 | 6,410 | 118,275 | 5.4 |
| | 1920 ........ | 28,624 | 7,701 | 152,876 | 5.1 |
| | 1921 ........ | 24,560 | 2,282 | 113,605 | 2.0 |
| | 1922 ........ | 15,884 | 1,940 | 106,074 | 1.8 |

Data compiled from *United States Commerce and Navigation.*

TABLE 55

DISTRIBUTION OF THE VALUE OF CHINA'S
IMPORTS OF COTTON PIECE GOODS BEFORE THE WAR[2]

| Year | Great Britain | Hongkong | Japan | Russia | United States |
|---|---|---|---|---|---|
| 1902 ........ | 55.3% | 8.1% | 2.7% | .... | 26.8% |
| 1905 ........ | 49.2 | 7.3 | 2.5 | .... | 35.5 |
| 1907 ........ | 72.2 | 11.7 | 4.7 | .... | 5.7 |
| 1909 ........ | 54.7 | 12.8 | 8.3 | 1.7% | 18.1 |
| 1911 ........ | 61.3 | 10.5 | 13.8 | 1.4 | 9.5 |
| 1913 ........ | 53.3 | 10.1 | 20.2 | 3.3 | 7.9 |

[1]Including Chinese leased territories.

[2]Data re-copied from United States Bureau of Foreign and Domestic Commerce, Special Agent, No. 107, *Cotton Goods in China*, p. 33.

TABLE 56

IMPORTATION OF COTTON PIECE GOODS INTO CHINA
UNIT 1,000 PIECES, INCLUDING SHIRTINGS, SHEETINGS, DRILLS, JEANS AND T-CLOTH.

| Year | U.S.A. Pieces 1,000 | % | Great Britain 1,000 Pieces | % | Japan 1,000 Pieces | % | Other 1,000 Pieces | % | Total, 1,000 Pieces |
|---|---|---|---|---|---|---|---|---|---|
| *1911 | 1,968 | 12.3 | 11,318 | 70.0 | 2,833 | 17.5 | 22 | 0.2 | 16,160 |
| *1913 | 2,281 | 11.5 | 11,705 | 58.0 | 5,917 | 30.0 | 92 | 0.5 | 19,795 |
| 1914 | 1,040 | 5.4 | 10,473 | 54.0 | 7,728 | 40.0 | 118 | 0.6 | 19,359 |
| 1915 | 638 | 4.5 | 7,591 | 53.6 | 5,717 | 40.5 | 202 | 1.4 | 14,148 |
| 1916 | 413 | 3.5 | 5,455 | 46.2 | 5,589 | 47.3 | 347 | 3.0 | 11,803 |
| 1917 | 72 | 0.5 | 4,397 | 31.4 | 8,046 | 61.0 | 650 | 5.0 | 13,164 |
| 1918 | 101 | 1.0 | 2,634 | 25.3 | 7,007 | 67.2 | 679 | 6.5 | 10,421 |
| 1919 | 622 | 4.5 | 4,592 | 32.5 | 8,899 | 63.0 | ... | ... | 14,116 |
| 1920 | 564 | 4.3 | 5,784 | 43.0 | 7,035 | 52.3 | 55 | 0.4 | 13,438 |
| 1921 | 626 | 6.0 | 3,489 | 33.6 | 5,816 | 56.0 | 449 | 4.4 | 10,380 |
| 1923 | 381 | 3.0 | 4,961 | 40.0 | 6,497 | 52.3 | 586 | 4.7 | 12,425 |

*The difference in the percentages of these two years as shown in this table from those shown in Table 55 is due to the following reasons: (1) The figures in this table were compiled by the Chinese Customs according to the kinds of cloth, while those in the preceding table, according to the port of origin. Thus American cloths, for instance, may be shipped through Canada or Japan. In the former table, they are not credited to the United States, while in this one they are still regarded as American. (2) Table 55 is a distribution of value, while this table is one of quantity. (3) Hongkong, as a trans-shipping port, is eliminated in this table. Therefore in showing the distribution of China's importation of certain kinds of cotton cloths, this table is much more accurate than the other.

### Recent Decline of the Trade

Since 1906 American cotton manufacturers have been losing their ground in China rapidly and American piece goods shipments to China have steadily declined. As clearly indicated in Table 54, the quantity of the trade dwindled from an annual average of 250 million yards of cloths in the five-year period, 1901-05, to 124 million yards in 1906-10, then again to 75 million yards in 1911-15, and finally to 7 million yards in the three-year war period of 1916-18. The value of the trade showed an equally striking downward movement, dropping from an annual average of more than 13 million dollars in the period of 1901-05, to 10 million dollars during 1906-10, and again to 5 million dollars during 1911-15, and finally to less than three-quarters of a million dollars during 1916-18. The share taken by these goods in the American-Chinese trade presented the same waning trend. During the first five years of the present century they constituted fifty-five per cent of the total American exports to China, but during the second five years they dropped to forty-one per cent and then to only twenty-five per cent during the third, and to only three per cent during the three years 1916-18. Since 1919 the trade has recovered a little both in quantity and in value, yet is still far below that of a few years ago. In 1921 the value of American cloth constituted only a little more than two per cent of the total value of American exports to China, although it amounted to something more than two million dollars. On the other hand, we notice that American cotton piece goods were also losing their share in the total piece goods imports of China. As indicated in Tables 55 and 56, the share of America before 1905, if allowance is made for transshipment through Hongkong, was between two-fifths and one-third of the total Chinese imports. But after that time it suddenly dropped to around ten per cent and since the outbreak of the European War, it has constituted barely five per cent. (Table 56.)

This serious loss of American trade has been primarily due to the new competition of Japanese, and more recently, that of Chinese cotton mills, which had the advantage of the use of the cheaper raw material of China and India and in the lower cost of production.[1]

(a) *Japanese Competition.* Let us first take up the Japanese competition and its effects upon American cotton goods exports to China. In the prosperous years of American trade, cotton piece goods of American manufacture exported to China were sold largely in Manchuria. After the Russo-Japanese War Japan had secured a permanent interest and special privileges in that area. Various industries, including cotton spinning and weaving, were soon developed both in Japan and in her leased Manchurian territory. Because raw material, which comes either from British India or from southern and central China, was easily obtainable, and also because labor is cheap in Manchuria, Japan was soon able to manufacture cotton cloths at a much lower price than that of either American or European origin. Taking advantage of the effectiveness of price appeal in the Chinese market the Japanese merchants pushed their sales very strenuously and were soon able to develop a huge market for their cottons, first in Manchuria and later throughout China. Not only did the United States suffer a great deal from this onslaught of Japan, but also Great Britain and some other European countries which had some dealings with China in this article.

The United States now suffered from Japanese competition in the same way that she did from British rivalry in the later decades of the last century, because the price for American goods was usually considerably higher than that for Japanese products. A comparison of these high and low prices, as shown in the accompanying table, should

[1]The subject of Japanese competition in China and especially in Manchuria is dealt with in "Cotton Goods in Japan and their Competition in the Manchurian Market", United States Bureau of Foreign and Domestic Commerce, Special Agents Series No. 86.

TABLE 57

COMPARATIVE PRICE PER PIECE OF COTTON CLOTH.[1]
FEBRUARY, 1914.

| | Japanese | American |
|---|---|---|
| Grey Sheeting ...................... | $2.71 | $3.29 |
| Grey Drill ...................... | 2.89 | 3.34 |
| Grey Shirting ...................... | 3.09 | 3.59 |
| Grey Jeans ...................... | 2.19 | 2.39 |
| White Shirting ...................... | 3.49 | 3.98 |

furnish a sufficient reason for the steady decline of American trade and the rapid expansion of that of Japan. American prices were as a rule twelve per cent higher than the Japanese. For a staple like cotton cloth such a difference is much more than the profit the cloth dealer could expect to earn. According to an American special agent investigating this matter in 1914, the manager of a certain firm in China made the statement that he handled some American goods only occasionally for the purpose of obliging his customers who wanted some of the better-made American goods, together with the much larger quantities of Japanese goods handled as regular lines.[2] Many formerly well known brands of American sheetings and drills were displaced by Japanese goods. The Japanese imitated foreign goods that had a good sale and attempted to bring in a cheaper substitute that resembles as closely as practicable the original article.[3]

The competitive condition described as prevailing before the war still holds good today. The competition has affected the trade of the United States more than that of any other country because American cotton goods trade has been largely confined to coarse sheetings and drills, lines to which

[1] Cotton Goods in China, op. cit., p. 255. These prices are prices for goods landed in Dairen before duty was paid.
[2] Ibid.
[3] Ibid, p. 259.

the Japanese mills have given particular attention and in which they have been most successful because the cost of the raw material is an important factor in the total cost of the goods.

The result of this competition is plainly shown by the figures in Tables 54 and 55. The steady decline of both the quantity and value of American exports to China after 1906 (Table 54) would certainly cause the American cotton manufacturers and exporters serious concern. As regards the distributive shares of China's imports during the decade before the war, Great Britain was not affected by Japanese competition, because her exports to China consisted mainly of the finer kinds of fabrics which Japan had not been able to imitate successfully. The share of the United States, on the other hand, had declined from 26.3 per cent. in 1902 (see Table 55) to 7.9 in 1913, a loss of about 19 per cent., which was almost entirely gained by Japan, whose share increased from 2.7 per cent. in 1902 to 20.2 per cent. in 1913.

After the outbreak of the European War, ocean freight rates were suddenly raised to a prohibitive scale. This added another drawback to the American cloth trade with China because, being a cheap staple, the article could not pay the high transportation rates for such a long distance. Nearly all American cloth trade stopped during the three years 1916-18, and it was Japan that again took full advantage of this opportunity. During the years of active warfare, Japan had supplied more than two-thirds of the piece goods imports of China, while the United States furnished only one per cent. Since the recovery of peace Japan has supplied China with more than half of the latter's total cloth imports, while the United States, though having recovered some of her share lost during the war, has held a humble share of less than five per cent.

(b) *Chinese Competition.* It must not, however, be understood that Japanese competition is the sole cause of the decline of the American trade. This was generally true ten years ago, but now the market situation has greatly changed.

In fact, Japan herself has for some years suffered from a new competition which has sprung up in China itself.

Cotton manufacturing with the use of hand looms is of very ancient origin in China and the industry is today still flourishing. According to the estimate of an American special investigator, the production of the hand looms exceeds in value and quantity the imported piece goods.[1] The cloth woven on these looms is extremely popular among the Chinese. Although that sold in the market is sometimes as expensive as similar foreign goods, it must be remembered that a large proportion of it is made in the homes of the people during their unemployed seasons for their own use. An additional factor in the continuance of hand loom weaving is a spirit akin to patriotism, through which the natives are urged to buy cloth that is made in their own country.

With the recent development of the hand loom industry, China has been rendered to a considerable degree independent of foreign piece goods. Whenever the price of the latter rises, as during the war, there was an increase of hand loom weaving throughout the country to supply the demands of the people. Under such conditions it is utterly impossible for the high priced American cloth to compete with the Chinese home-made cloth.

The hand-loom industry in China is not the only one to offer serious competition to foreign cloth. The machine cotton industry in China, though of comparatively recent development, is now progressing with phenomenal rapidity. The introduction of the modern method of cotton spinning into China is said to date back only to 1890.[2] But during the following thirty years there has been a rapid expansion in this branch of industry. The following table shows the

[1] R. M. Odell: *Cotton Goods in China*; United States Bureau of Foreign and Domestic Commerce, Special Agents Series No. 107, p. 185.
[2] *Bulletin of the Canadian Department of Trade and Commerce*, October 3, 1921. Report of J. W. Ross.

gradual increase in the number of cotton mills in China within the past three decades.[1] In addition to the above, there are twenty-eight mills with 918,000 spindles in the process of erection.[1]

TABLE 58

NUMBER OF COTTON MILLS IN CHINA.

| Year | Number of Mills | Number of Spindles |
|---|---|---|
| 1891 ............................... | 2 | 65,000 |
| 1896 ............................... | 12 | 417,000 |
| 1902 ............................... | 17 | 565,000 |
| 1911 ............................... | 32 | 831,000 |
| 1916 ............................... | 41 | 1,145,000 |
| 1918 ............................... | 49 | 1,200,000 |
| 1921 ............................... | 63 | 1,747,000 |

At first the mills confined themselves mainly to the manufacture of yarn, and the installation of looms was not undertaken very extensively until 1907 and 1908 following the large trade in piece goods during and immediately following the Russo-Japanese War in 1905 and 1906.[2] At present many mills have added power looms to their equipment and have undertaken the manufacture of sheetings and drills.

The principal factors that have contributed to the establishment and growth of the Chinese cotton goods industry are: (1) a supply of native grown cottons of sufficiently good quality for spinning and weaving coarser cloths; (2) an enormous domestic demand for the production of the mills; and (3) abundance of very cheap labor, which makes the cost of production lower than in any other part of the world. With these marked advantages, the Chinese domestic cloth can easily outrival the American and even the

[1] *The Eastern Commerce*, Tokio, November, 1921, Vol. VII, No. 1, p. 32.
[2] R. M. Odell, *op. cit.*, p. 157.

Japanese products. It is the consensus of opinion among those who are engaged in the industry that the time will come in the near future when China will manufacture within her own borders the greater part of the coarser cloth consumed by her vast population.[1] American manufacturers, therefore, can never hope to meet this competition successfully and regain the trade which they once held.

### Future Prospects of American Piece Goods Trade with China

Although it is our conclusion that American trade with China in such coarse goods as sheetings and drills is destined to fall off, it does not follow that the United States will forever keep her hands off the Chinese cotton goods market. There are numerous other lines which are not made either by Japanese or Chinese mills but which are consumed in large quantities by the vast population of China. They are, for example, muslins, cambrics, chintzes, sateens, venetians, velveteens, and other fancy and dyed cottons. Before the war these goods were supplied almost exclusively by England, and since 1915 Japan has shared some part of the trade. At present by far the greater part of the trade in these finer cottons is still in the hands of British merchants. The field in China is a wide one, latent with possibilities, and it is believed that the mills in the United States can furnish many of these cottons on a competitive basis. In a large-scale machine industry in which America's advantage lies, coupled with the advantage of a vast supply of domestic cotton, there is no reason why the American cotton manufacturer should be unable to produce these finer piece goods at as low, or even lower, cost than can his English competitor. Persistent efforts on their part to produce the kinds of goods in demand, backed by a serious determination to cultivate the market on permanent lines, will unquestionably result in a considerable expansion in American

[1] R. M. Odell, op. cit., p. 184.

cotton goods exports to China and enable the Americans, to some extent at least, to regain the important place that they once held in Chinese trade.

### Raw Cotton

Although the United States has suffered a great deal through losing her cloth trade with China, she has, on the other hand, gained a great deal in selling China her raw cotton. In 1921, the value of American cotton sent directly to China amounted to ten million dollars. As the rapid growth of the Chinese cotton industry will greatly expand China's capacity for cotton consumption, it is worth our while to investigate the Chinese market for American raw cotton.

With her boundless area of fertile lands and unlimited amount of cheap labor, China is herself one of the greatest cotton growers in the world, second only to the United States and British India. Though it is impossible to arrive at any accurate estimate of her total cotton production, rough estimates put the yield at 1,000,000 to 5,000,000 bales of 500 pounds,[1] although 2,000,000 to 2,500,000 bales seem to be the more reasonable figures.[2] The annual consumption of all kinds of cotton in Chinese mills, which have today approximately 2,000,000 spindles,[3] is estimated to be about 1,000,000 bales,[4] and that of hand-looms about 1,400,000 bales.[5] These estimates show that China is, on the whole, a self-sufficing country so far as raw cotton is concerned.

In fact, Chinese cotton mills do depend very largely, if

[1] Cotton Goods in China, op. cit., p. 199.
[2] Ibid.
[3] Cotton Mill Statistics of China, the Eastern Commerce, Tokio, Vol. VIII, No. 6, April, 1923, p. 16.
[4] In 1915, Mr. R. M. Odell, author of the Cotton Goods in China, stated that the annual consumption of cotton in Chinese mills having approximately 1,000,000 spindles was about 533,000 bales. Ibid, p. 199.
[5] Ibid.

not entirely, on domestic cotton for their supply of raw material. Nevertheless, the use of foreign cotton in proportion to native cotton is increasing. Moreover, poor local crops, low prices abroad, or favorable rates of exchange, have also resulted in large importation of foreign cotton at certain periods. Sometimes a demand for better grades for spinning fine numbers of yarn also necessitates the purchasing of foreign cotton, especially American, because Chinese cotton is of much shorter staple and unfit for finer manufacture. Of late, especially since 1920, owing to the sudden and enormous expansion of the cotton spinning and weaving industry in China, the import of raw cotton has increased steadily, as shown in Table 59 which is compiled by the Chinese Cotton Mill Owners' Association.[1]

TABLE 59

COTTON CONSUMED BY CHINESE COTTON MILLS

| Kinds of Cotton | Bales of 500 Pounds | | |
|---|---|---|---|
| | Fiscal Year Ending June 30 1921 | 1922 | Half Year Ending January 31, 1923 |
| Chinese | 728,292 | 744,076 | 492,162 |
| American | 29,122 | 154,926 | 58,115 |
| East Indian | 119,029 | 298,365 | 135,330 |
| Egyptian and Sundries | 649 | 1,213 | 4,019 |
| Total | 877,092 | 1,199,115 | 689,626 |

In 1920, 90 million pounds of cotton (or 180,000 bales of 500 pounds) were imported into China; in 1921, 224 million pounds; and in 1922, 237 million pounds (or 475,000 bales). The imports of the last two years practically supplied half of the total estimated consumption of all the Chinese cotton mills.

Table 60 shows the quantity and sources of the imports

[1] Re-quoted by the Eastern Commerce, Tokio, Vol. VIII, No. 6, April, 1923, p. 16.

TABLE 60

CHINA'S IMPORTS OF RAW COTTON FROM THE FOLLOWING COUNTRIES

| Year | U. S. A. Quan. 1,000 Lbs. | U. S. A. % of the Total | Japan Quan. 1,000 Lbs. | Japan % of the Total | Great Britain Quan. 1,000 Lbs. | Great Britain % of the Total | Hongkong Quan. 1,000 Lbs. | Hongkong % of the Total | British India Quan. 1,000 Lbs. | British India % of the Total | Total Import of raw Cotton into China |
|---|---|---|---|---|---|---|---|---|---|---|---|
| 4-Year Average...1902-05 | 1,201 | 7.3 | 135 | 0.8 | 1,090 | 6.5 | 4,549 | 27.5 | 8,304 | 50.2 | 16,538 |
| 5-Year Average...1906-10 | 3 | ... | 697 | 4.2 | 55 | 0.3 | 2,591 | 15.5 | 12,560 | 75.0 | 16,737 |
| 1911-13 | 7,731 | 36.7 | 1,590 | 7.6 | 248 | 1.1 | 2,142 | 10.2 | 8,545 | 40.5 | 21,054 |
| 1914-16 | 6,009 | 14.8 | 4,121 | 10.1 | ... | ... | 2,659 | 6.5 | 27,411 | 67.4 | 40,718 |
| 3-Year Average...1917-19 | 3,714 | 11.1 | 16,975 | 50.8 | ... | ... | 2,266 | 6.8 | 8,859 | 26.6 | 33,997 |
| 1920 | 4,539 | 4.9 | 21,592 | 23.4 | ... | ... | 3,003 | 3.3 | 55,848 | 60.8 | 91,777 |
| 1921 | 68,865 | 30.5 | 18,896 | 8.4 | ... | ... | 4,060 | 1.8 | 130,785 | 58.0 | 225,295 |
| 1922 | 20,704 | 8.1 | 40,376 | 16.3 | ... | ... | 2,328 | 1.0 | 182,864 | 74.0 | 247,657 |

of raw cotton into China in the last twenty years according to Chinese statistics.

Although, according to Tables 59 and 60, there are several countries from which China imports her cotton, the real sources of supply for the Chinese market are only British India and the United States and, to a much smaller extent, Japan. The imports credited to Hongkong refer mainly to American and Indian cotton while the imports from Great Britain were largely, and those from Japan, partly, American.[1] The amount credited to the United States in the above table is, therefore, more or less below the actual quantity imported therefrom. The direct export of raw cotton from the United States to China in the years 1901-1922, are shown in Table 61.

TABLE 61

AMERICAN DIRECT EXPORTS OF RAW COTTON TO CHINA

| Year | Quantity in 1,000 Lbs. | Value in $1,000 | Year | Quantity in 1,000 Lbs. | Value in $1,000 |
|------|------|------|------|------|------|
| 1901 ........ | .... | .... | 1911 ........ | 53 | 8 |
| 1902 ........ | 3,055 | 291 | 1912 ........ | 25,298 | 2,591 |
| 1903 ........ | 1,307 | 123 | 1913 ........ | 3,635 | 464 |
| 1904 ........ | .... | .... | 1914 ........ | 4,490 | 588 |
| 1905 ........ | 2,120 | 176 | 1915 ........ | 7,617 | 734 |
| 1906 ........ | 350 | 40 | 1916 ........ | 6,179 | 729 |
| 1907 ........ | 145 | 16 | 1917 ........ | 2,403 | 403 |
| 1908 ........ | .... | .... | 1918 ........ | 1,958 | 558 |
| 1909 ........ | 221 | 22 | 1919 ........ | 5,814 | 1,786 |
| 1910 ........ | .... | .... | 1920 ........ | 5,690 | 2,092 |
|  |  |  | 1921 ........ | 77,285 | 10,051 |
|  |  |  | 1922 ........ | 18,601 | 3,595 |

Besides these direct exports, there remains a certain portion of American exports to Japan and a very large part of those to Hongkong, which go indirectly to China, but are not included here.

[1] *Cotton Goods in China, op. cit.,* p. 194.

the Chinese cotton industry may reach a stage of improvement where it would be able to produce much fine yarn, and therefore require much cotton of better grade, better methods of cultivation and the efforts of the Chinese cotton growers of the various agricultural colleges and experimental cotton plantations will doubtless result in an improvement in the quality of domestic production to meet the greater part of the home demand.

We notice in Table 60 that whereas in certain periods the United States supplied a considerable part of China's cotton imports, the greater part of the trade still remains in the hands of British India. Indian cotton is usually cheaper in price and suitable for the manufacture of coarser yarn in Chinese cotton mills. American raw cotton, though of a better quality, sells at a high price in the Orient because it has to bear the freight and rail charge for a much longer distance than the Indian cotton.

From Table 61 we can see clearly the relation that exists between the price of American cotton and American cotton exports to China. When the American cotton supply is normal and its price is higher than that of Indian cotton, exports to China are usually small, or decline to nothing. But when American cotton becomes plentiful and its price falls, huge exports are at once on their way to China. Thus in 1912 China made fairly large purchases of American cotton, because of its low price,[1] and in 1921 when the price of cotton was at its trough in the United States, more than 77 million pounds of this fibre were sent to China. China, therefore, cannot be a regular customer for American cotton growers, but serves as a vent for their surplus cotton in a bumper year or at a time of industrial depression.

The annual exports of American cotton to China have amounted to several million dollars in the last few years. Yet, it is unlikely that China will be a good market for American cotton in the future. The present production of fine yarns is comparatively insignificant in that country and is not increasing very rapidly. Although, in the near future,

[1] R. M. Odell: *Cotton Goods in China,* p. 194. Mr. Odell computed that in 1912, American cotton was 12.48 cents per pound in the Orient and Indian cotton 11.77 cents per pound. As the cost of cotton from America was only slightly above that from India, the Chinese mills found it profitable to import more of the former.

## CHAPTER XI.

### MINERAL OILS

#### *China as a Market for Mineral Oils*

It has long been reported by not a few expert geologists that China is in possession of many rich mineral oil deposits. The exploitation of these resources, however, has not as yet been successful. Several experiments have been made in recent years, first by the Standard Oil Company of New York and later by a Japanese firm to produce oil from wells located in some northern provinces in China, but the attempts turned out unsatisfactory.[1] Today, as in former times, China still has to depend solely upon some foreign oil producing countries, especially the United States and The Dutch East Indies, for oils to light up the millions of her city and country homes.

Some fifty or more years ago, mineral oil was not an article of general commerce in China, the import in 1867 amounting to only some thirty thousand gallons of kerosene oil for the foreign community in that country.[2] Beginning with 1870, however, kerosene was rapidly accepted for general use among the Chinese, but not until the end of the last century was it carried far into the interior of the country by the great distributing organizations of some foreign corporations.[3]

The Standard Oil Company of New York, the Texas Oil Company, both of American ownership, and the Asiatic Petroleum Company, of Dutch ownership, now operate their business in China on a large scale, particularly the first and the third, which have many installations in various parts

[1] See Chapter 16, *infra.*
[2] H. B. Morse: *The Trade and Administration of China,* p. 317.
[3] C. F. Remer: *The Foreign Trade of China* (an unpublished dissertation in Harvard University, 1922), Chapter 4, on Kerosene Oil.

225

of the country. No imported article, with a possible exception of cotton cloth, has gained such ground among the masses in China as kerosene. It has found its way into every hamlet far removed from treaty ports and is used by people who may have perhaps never used any other foreign goods. The following figures clearly indicate how during the past half century the Chinese have grown accustomed to the use of kerosene by habit. In 1870 the total importation was just over 280,000 gallons. It increased to 84 million gallons in 1900, and by 1914 it was 225,464,000 gallons, an increase of 80,500 per cent. during a period of thirty-five years.

Since 1914, the import of kerosene oil has suffered a setback in quantity, although its value has increased enormously. Two reasons account for this. In the first place, electrical lighting as a successful competitor of oil lighting has gradually come into general use in China during the last ten years. Secondly, the rising price of illuminating oil during and after the European War has done more than anything else to check the normal expansion of China's oil consumption. It is due to this excessively high price that the Chinese have felt it more economical to install electrical lighting plants not only in cities, but even in many small towns. This substitution of electricty for kerosene will ultimately act as a check on the further expansion of the oil trade, but such a time still lies in the remote future. With such a vast area and so big a population as that of China, the oil trade as it amounts today may be said to have touched China only upon her fringe. There are still numerous places in the internal provinces in which only animal fat and vegetable oils are, as centuries before, used for lighting purposes. No imported mineral oil has as yet reached them because of the poor transportation facilities and the prohibitive rate of freight for long distance. As soon as China's internal transportation facilities are improved, new markets will be found for oil, and another headlong increase in its import will be the result.

Another important change in China's oil import trade must be noted, viz. the rapid increase during the last decade of mineral oils other than kerosene. About a decade ago, the latter was practically the sole kind of mineral oil imported into and consumed by China. Although China began to import some twenty years ago some other kinds such as fuel and gas oil, lubricating oil, gasoline and other naphthas, their quantity and value, even combined together, were at first so small as to be quite negligible. Throughout the first decade of the new century, they constituted less than 2 per cent. of the total oil import with more than 98 per cent. of kerosene. Being stimulated by the war, China has been transforming herself from an agricultural into an industrial stage. With the gradual development of her industry, the use of lubricating oil, naphthas and fuel and gas oil is naturally on the rapid increase. While these oils still constituted less than 2 per cent. of the total oil import of China in 1914, they have grown so enormously in a short period of eight years as to constitute 25 per cent. in 1922 with still greater increase in their absolute quantities and values.

A new era has therefore just dawned upon the oil trade in China. Formerly, only oils for immediate consumptive purposes, viz.: for lighting and illumination, were bought by China. But now she is purchasing more and more oils for further productive use, viz., for the use of machine shops. From the condition of the present growth of China's machinery import trade, one can derive an easy conclusion as to what will be the future of the trade of these machine oils.

### American Oils in the Chinese Markets

The reader might feel that the above general description of China as a market for mineral oils is out of place in a work like this which is to be devoted solely to the discussion of that part of Chinese trade as has connection with America. The writer will certainly be relieved from this criticism if he informs the reader that before 1890, every gallon of

oil imported into China came from America, and at present approximately four-fifths of her oil imports are still American. The United States possesses one of the richest petroleum resources of the world and developed the oil industry at a much earlier date than all the other countries possessing oil deposits. So, until the end of the last century, this country actually monopolized the oil trade not only of China but practically of the whole world.

But American oil supremacy in China did not remain long unchallenged. In the later years of the last century, Russia successfully exploited her oil resources in Siberia, and soon became an important oil exporting country. A few years later, the Russian example was followed by the Dutch East Indies, which, with its rich oil fields in the islands of Sumatra and Borneo, has once acquired such a high rank in oil production as second to no country except the United States. Recently Japan has also produced some oil, though comparatively much smaller in quantity. All these countries are China's immediate neighbors. They have the advantage of propinquity to the market over America, and thus succeeded in introducing their oils into China despite the strenuous effort of the American merchants to oust them by competition.

Russian oil was first introduced into China in 1889,[1] Sumatran in 1894,[1] Bornean in 1901,[1] and Japanese only a few years before the European War. Beginning from 1890, China's oil trade was not solely in the hands of Americans, and we must therefore give American trade a separate description in conjunction with other competing oils. Table 62 shows the general condition of American mineral oil trade with China during the last thirty years.

The outstanding feature of the trade as shown here is that despite the keen competition of Russian and Dutch Indian oils, the export of the American product to China has increased steadily in quantity. Of course, the annual figures

[1] H. B. Morse, op. cit., p. 317.

during the same thirty years show many irregular ups and downs; for instance, the extraordinary expansion during and following the years of the Russo-Japanese War from 1905 to 1908, and the unusual contraction during the years of the active European War from 1917 to 1919; but when the temporary annual fluctuations are eliminated by taking averages of five-year periods, the secular trend is regularly upward.

TABLE 62

AMERICAN MINERAL OILS EXPORTED TO CHINA
(INCLUDING LEASED TERRITORIES)
1891-1922

|  | Year | Quantity in 1,000 Gallons | Value in $1,000 |
|---|---|---|---|
|  | 1891-1895  .......... | 26,173 | 1,854 |
|  | 1896-1900  .......... | 33,804 | 2,711 |
| 5-Year | 1901-1905  .......... | 47,731 | 4,490 |
| Average | 1906-1910  .......... | 81,827 | 6,598 |
|  | 1911-1915  .......... | 94,795 | 6,427 |
|  | 1916-1918  .......... | 80,854 | 5,772 |
| 2-Year | 1919-1920  .......... | 165,781 | 19,934 |
| Average | 1921  ............... | 136,357 | 19,256 |
|  | 1922  ............... | 186,986 | 21,712 |

Data compiled from the U. S. Foreign Commerce and Navigation.

But this does not mean that Russian and Dutch Indian competition is negligible. In fact, from the end of the last century down to the outbreak of the European War, competition in the Chinese oil market had become so keen as to have constituted the whole history of the Chinese oil trade during that period. When Russian oil was once introduced into the Chinese market, it at once got a large share of the trade. Thus in 1890 24.5 per cent. was Russian, and 76.5 per cent. American, (see Table 63) while only two years before, Russian was nil and American one hundred per cent.

TABLE 63

| Year | Total Imports of Kerosene Oil into China — Quantity in 1,000 Gallons | Value in $1,000 | U. S. A. — Quantity | U. S. A. — Value | Borneo — Quantity | Borneo — Value | Sumatra — Quantity | Sumatra — Value | Russia — Quantity | Russia — Value | All Other Countries — Quantity | All Other Countries — Value |
|---|---|---|---|---|---|---|---|---|---|---|---|---|
| 1870 | 281 | | 100 | 100 | | | | | | | | |
| 1880 | 3,439 | 5,189 | 100 | 100 | | | | | | | | |
| 1890 | 80,829 | 10,362 | 76.5 | 80 | | | | | 24.5 | 20 | | |
| 1900 | 83,580 | 14,810 | 41.5 | 45 | | | 19.4 | 18 | 39.1 | 37 | | |
| 1905 | 153,472 | 14,360 | 52.2 | 56 | 7.2 | 5.4 | 31.6 | 29.3 | 8.3 | 8.4 | | |
| 1910 | 161,390 | 18,344 | 59.6 | 53 | 11.8 | 13.0 | 26.5 | 30.5 | 1.4 | 2.9 | .7 | .9 |
| 1913 | 183,984 | 23,069 | 61.0 | 56.5 | 12.8 | 13.6 | 22.8 | 25.3 | 2.3 | 4.6 | .7 | .8 |
| 1914 | 225,464 | 35,582 | 71.2 | 69.4 | 10.6 | 10.1 | 16.3 | 17.0 | .5 | 3.2 | .2 | .3 |
| 1918 | 110,202 | 67,355 | 43.7 | 45.3 | 5.1 | 9.7 | 44.0 | 43.2 | | .6 | 1.8 | 2.0 |
| 1920 | 189,589 | 44,168 | 74.7 | 74.7 | 4.7 | 4.6 | 18.4 | 19.3 | | | | .6 |
| 1921 | 175,220 | 52,657 | 76.8 | 77.0 | 2.1 | 2.1 | 9.0 | 18.4 | | | 4.9 | 4.7 |
| 1922 | 209,191 | | 84.0 | 83.5 | | | | | | | | |

Data compiled from the Chinese Customs Returns.

The distribution is computed according to the kinds of oils, not according to the origins of the imports.

This is enabled by the classification by the Chinese Customs of the oils according to whether it is American or Russian, etc. The distribution as here shown is, therefore, much more accurate than that computed according to the importing country, because much oil imported into China is trans-shipped through Singapore, Hongkong, etc.

During the last decade of the past century, not only Russia's share had greatly expanded, but Sumatra had also made a formidable start to compete with the American oil. As a result, American supremacy was once seriously threatened when in 1900 the share for the United States was only 41.5 per cent, while that for Russia was 39.1 per cent and for Sumatra, 19.4 per cent.

But with her defeat by Japan in 1904-5, Russia lost once for all her commercial, as well as political, stronghold in China, and her newly established petroleum industry at once became impotent to compete on even terms with the strong American and Dutch corporations. Her share dropped from 39.1 per cent. in 1900 to 8.3 per cent. in 1905, and to 1.4 per cent in 1910, and to practically nothing since the outbreak of the European War. (See Table 63.)

Though coming into the market some years later, the Dutch Indian oil, first from Sumatra and then from Borneo, has endured the severe American competition much longer than the Russian. As soon as Dutch oil was introduced into China in 1869, the Royal Dutch Petroleum Company, aided by German agents, was vigorously pushing it in Hongkong and other Chinese coast ports.[1] Since the early years of the new century, therefore, the distribution of kerosene in China has fallen exclusively into the hands of two competing corporations: one being the Standard Oil Company of the United States, the other the Asiatic Petroleum Company of the Dutch East Indies. Formerly, the latter concern also handled some Russian oil. Competition became keener as time went on, and cut-price was the practice usually resorted to by both parties. Around the year 1910, the relations between these competing concerns became so strained that the rivalry practically amounted to war.[2] In one instance we are told that during the first six months of

[1] U. S. Consular Reports, Vol. 58, 1898, p. 23.

[2] See comment by Chinese Customs Commissioner-General, Customs Report, 1910, Part I, p. 49.

1910 American kerosene conquered Sumatra oil in South Manchuria. American oil made a hard fight, showing an advance in quantity of sales in that territory over the preceding year of twenty-nine per cent; and a decline in price of twelve per cent., a phenomenon due to the rate war then in progress between American oil interests and the Dutch exporters.[1] After 1912, this competition is said to have been affected by agreements and understandings of a familiar sort and the market has quieted down as compared with that before that year.[2]

That American oil interests in China suffered a great deal from this severe competition during those years is clearly shown in Table 63. Normally, the United States has a distributive share of from two-thirds to four-fifths of China's total kerosene imports. During the first ten years from 1900 to 1910, when the competition was attaining its zenith, her share dropped to a little over one-half.

From the differences in the percentages between the quantity distribution and value distribution in the different years, as shown in Table 63, it may be noted that during the whole period of competition the trade went, or tended to go, to whichever competitor who offered a lower price for his oil than his rivals. With both the total quantity and its total value as 100 per cent., if, then, a country gets a higher percentage for her quantity and a smaller one for value, the price of her product must be below those of other competitors. If her value percentage is higher than her quantity percentage, the case is just vice versa. Applying this rule of estimating the comparative prices, we see at once from the above distribution table that at the beginning of the Russo-American competition, the price for American oil was much higher than that of Russian, as the former commanded 80 per cent of the total value with 76.5 per cent. of the total quantity, while in the case of the latter,

[1] F. McCormick: American Defeat in the Pacific; The Outlook. Vol. 97, p. 68, January, 1911.

[2] C. F. Remer: op. cit.

24.5 per cent. of oil was sold only for 20 per cent of the total price. The cheap price of Russian oil must have been a very strong selling point among the poorer class of Chinese people, and had tended greatly to expand the Russian trade during the following decade. In 1900, American prices were still much higher than either the Russan or Sumatran, and this largely accounts for the severe drop of American sales and the enormous growth of the other two. This price test holds good throughout the whole period as, for instance, when in 1905 Russian value percentages became higher than her corresponding quantity percentages, that is to say, her price comparatively rose up to be higher than the others, her trade at once fell down. From that time on, Russian price is constantly above those of other competing countries, and this is perhaps the reason that Russia has never been able to recover her lost share of two decades ago.

From 1900 to 1905 the oil prices of Sumatra and Borneo were both below those of the United States. As a result the oil trade of the two former countries in China was flourishing during those years. But a turning point was reached in 1910 when both of the prices of Bornean and Sumatran oils came above that of their strong competitor, who immediately got a greater share in the trade at their expense. It seems quite sure that the gradual recovery of American trade during the interval from 1905 to 1913 was gained solely by cut-price competition. According to normal conditions, American oil cannot be sold cheaper than either Russian or Dutch, because the former has to bear a much larger item of overhead in the trans-Pacific freight. The lower price of American oil during the years around 1910 was, therefore, mainly due to the unusual cut-price policy of the strong Standard Oil Company. Since 1914, both the American and the Dutch prices have remained nearly at an equal level as their value percentages usually equal their quantity percentages. This is, perhaps, the result of the agreement and understanding effected among the competing firms in 1912.

Due to the prohibitive rate of freight, American kerosene trade declined during the three active war years, 1916-1918, to less than half of the total imports of China, and was even exceeded by the Sumatran share in 1918. This drop is, of course, temporary in nature. Soon after shipping conditions came to relief after the Armistice, the United States obtained more than her old share, and now more than four-fifths of the oil is supplied to China from the American wells.

### Trade in Other Mineral Oils

Besides kerosene, America is now sending to China large and increasing quantities of other mineral oils, mainly for the use of the growing industries in that country. Before 1913 kerosene was practically the only oil of commercial importance; the export of other kinds of oils to China being so small that the statisticians of the United States Bureau of Foreign and Domestic Commerce did not even deem it worth while to record them separately. Their total quantity, shown under the name of "Other Oils," was only a little over one million gallons.

But the phenomenal progress of the industrial China following the outbreak of the European War has created a new market for several kinds of American mineral oils other than kerosene. They are, as separately reported by the Bureau, fuel and gas oil, lubricating oil, and naphthas, gasoline, etc. The quantity and value of their export to China during the last ten years are shown in the following table.

First, a few words regarding fuel and gas oil. Before 1918, nearly all imports of this oil into China came from the Dutch East Indies. Handicapped by the high freight rate and long distance, American oil could not compete with the Dutch. But since 1919, when the handicaps were removed, American oil has taken an increasing share; in

1920-21 one-half, and in 1922 two-thirds of China's fuel oil imports were credited to the United States as the place of origin.[1]

TABLE 64

*American Exports of Other Refined Mineral Oils to China*

| Year | Fuel and Gas Oil | | Lubricating Oil | | Naphthas, Gasoline, etc. | |
|---|---|---|---|---|---|---|
| | 1,000 Gal. | $1,000 | 1,000 Gal. | $1,000 | 1,000 Gal. | $1,000 |
| 1913 .... | 1,328* | 210* | | | | |
| 1914 .... | 229 | 6 | 1,472 | 281 | 284 | 54 |
| 1915 .... | 1,777 | 96 | 2,921 | 419 | 472 | 79 |
| 1916 .... | 55 | 3 | 3,326 | 544 | 180 | 37 |
| 1917 .... | 2,846 | 117 | 2,139 | 415 | 245 | 58 |
| 1918 .... | 3,163 | 154 | 4,096 | 1,048 | 245 | 93 |
| 1919 .... | 3,960 | 157 | 5,630 | 1,483 | 1,148 | 386 |
| 1920 .... | 17,131 | 856 | 3,520 | 1,340 | 840 | 352 |
| 1921 .... | 20,001 | 770 | 4,192 | 1,236 | 1,498 | 529 |
| 1922 .... | 19,434 | 695 | 5,098 | 1,308 | 1,447 | 470 |

*Including all other oils, except illuminating oil. Data compiled from *U. S. Commerce and Navigation.*

Somewhat different from the above case is that of naphtha and lubricating oil. In 1914-18, China imported 4,612,-000 gallons of naphthas of which the United States sent 1,426,000 or about 30 per cent. She also imported 21,962,-000 gallons of lubricating oil, of which the United States sent 13,954,000 or 64 per cent. In 1919-21 China's total import was 9,936,000 gallons, of which 3,486,000 or 35 per cent. was American. Her total import of lubricating oil in the same three years was 18,360,000 gallons, of which 13,332,000 or 72 per cent. was American. Although the relative share increased slowly in the face of Dutch competition, yet the absolute quantity in both oils has experienced enormous expansion.

[1] See Chinese Customs Returns.

## CHAPTER XII

### Tobacco

### China as a Market for Foreign Tobacco

The introduction into China of the habit of using foreign tobacco dates back only a few decades. Up to as late as 1867 only home-grown tobacco was used in China and cigarettes were unknown.[1] Even up to the present day native tobacco, together with its necessary adjunct, the old Chinese pipe, is still in wide use everywhere in the country, especially in the interior. But when the cigarette once entered the Chinese market, the Chinese smoker found it more convenient to handle, and the habit of using it has been gradually increasing. However, trade in this article was at first rather small, so small that before 1901 the imports of cigarettes and unmanufactured tobacco into China were not separately recorded by the Chinese Customs, being included under the item "Sundries, unclassified." In 1902, when the item "Cigarettes" was separated from the unclassified item, the value of China's total imports was $1,259,000. The next year, when "Tobacco" was first given a separate figure, its value was only $325,000.

But during the last two decades, the spread of the cigarette habit throughout the whole country has been astonishingly rapid. In 1912, four and four-tenths billion cigarettes were imported into China at a value of $6,493,000; and in 1922 the quantity reached ten billions and its value $23,614,000.

Before the war, the importation of raw tobacco did not keep pace with the growing cigarette trade. In 1904 twelve million pounds of raw tobacco at a value of $1,065,000 were

[1] The *Chinese Customs Returns* gave the first indication of some imports of foreign tobacco in 1867, though the *United States Foreign Commerce and Navigation* shows that after 1850, there was some tobacco exported to China every year.

imported, while ten years later, these figures were sixteen million pounds at $1,834,000. This slow growth is due to the fact that the cigarette industry in China was then still undeveloped, and raw tobacco was therefore not much needed. In the last ten years, however, the trade has made remarkable strides, and in 1922 the imported quantity expanded to more than thirty-five million pounds with a value of $11,461,000.[1]

The growing importation and consumption of tobacco in various forms led some Chinese to believe that this was a second opium curse come to sap the energy of their country and people. Opposing the omni-present reformers, however, were the no less patriotic citizens who were convinced that tobacco was not only a harmless stimulating pleasure for the individual but also a beneficial stimulant to national business prosperity. Among these was the late Kan Chiunam, foremost of China's modern industrialists, who was founder of the Nanyang Brothers Tobacco Company. Many more native concerns for the manufacture of tobacco in various forms were opened following the success of the pioneer venture which together with the establishment of native factories in China by foreign interests resulted in stronger entrenchment of the Chinese tobacco trade and industry.[2]

### American Tobacco in the Chinese Market

Along with China's growing importation of foreign tobacco and cigarettes, American tobacco trade with China has made remarkable progress during the last two or three decades. As shown in Table 65 the total annual American exports of both raw and manufactured tobacco, while worth

[1] For further details on China as a Tobacco Market, cf. U. S. Bur. of For. and Dom. Com., Special Consular Reports, No. 68, *Tobacco Trade of the World*, 1915, pp. 31-34.
[2] *Modern Development in the Chinese Cigarette Trade and Industry*, by Tsze E. Pun, Tobacco, N. Y., April 24, 1924.

only a few thousand dollars thirty years ago, reached thirty millions in 1920. The increase has been especially rapid since 1914 because, on the one hand, the financial ability of the Chinese community to purchase comforts and luxuries has grown and, on the other, British competition, the most formidable competition against American tobacco manufactures before the war, was to a large extent eliminated.

Before 1914 the American share in China's tobacco trade, although important, did not hold the leading position. Cigarettes manufactured in Great Britain constituted by far the greatest part of the total imports into China; and the share of the United States was a poor second. According to the Chinese Customs returns Great Britain supplied China in 1913-14 with seven out of every ten cigarettes imported from foreign lands, while the average of the United States was only one in ten, the other two being shared by Japan, Korea and Russia. England succeeded in maintaining her supremacy up to 1915-16, after which the first place was succeeded to by the United States. With the natural advantage of superior raw material and with European competition withdrawn incident to the Great World War, the American cigarette makers soon became supreme in the trade of the Orient, and, as indicated in Table 65, they are now supplying nine out of every ten cigarettes the Chinese purchase of foreigners.

In the case of raw material, Great Britain, of course, has never been in competition with the United States for she is also obliged to rely upon the United States for a supply of raw tobacco to feed her factories. Although Japan, Korea, Russia and the Philippines have at one time or another shared more or less in the Chinese trade, yet their exports to China have never reached such a quantity as to divest the United States of its largest part. Before 1914, the United States enjoyed one-third of the trade, in 1914-16, about one-half, in 1917-21, two-thirds, and in 1922, more than nine-tenths.

TABLE 65

AMERICAN EXPORT OF TOBACCO, BOTH MANUFACTURED AND UNMANUFACTURED, TO CHINA, 1891-1922

| Year | Tobacco—Unmanufactured | | | Cigarettes | | |
|---|---|---|---|---|---|---|
| | Quantity in 1,000 lbs. | Value in $1,000 | Percentage of China's Total Import | Quantity per 1,000,000 | Value in $1,000 | Percentage of China's Total Import |
| 1891-95 | 146 | 1a | .... | .... | 80 | 16% |
| 1895-1900 | 279 | 21 | .... | .... | 330 | 11% |
| 1901-05 | 825 | 115 | .... | .... | 832 | 18% |
| 1906-10 | 4,140 | 522 | 31% | 594b | 1,085 | 70% |
| 1914-16 | 6,272 | 923 | 35% | 523 | 822 | 90% |
| 1917-19 | 7,944 | 1,283 | 52% | 1,088 | 1,833 | 90% |
| 1911-13 | 13,009 | 4,635 | 56% | 5,854 | 10,289 | 90% |
| 1920 | 18,525 | 13,316 | 63% | 8,509 | 16,096 | 90% |
| 1921 | 19,389 | 8,406 | 63% | 6,444 | 11,659 | 90% |
| 1922 | 32,418 | 10,721 | 92% | 8,580 | 17,035 | 88% |
| 5-year Average | | | | | | |
| 3-year Average | | | | | | |

a Two-year average, 1894-95.
b Three-year average, 1908-10.
Data compiled and computed from the Statistics of the Foreign Commerce and Navigation of the United States.

The mass of the Chinese people, whose purchasing power is still very low, cannot afford to use high grade tobacco. All American products sent to China are naturally of low price, usually as small as one-fourth of a cent (United States currency) for each cigarette.[1] But the very low price has made for the universal use of cigarettes among the Chinese. In order to utilize the cheap labor in China to turn out products for the Chinese markets, foreign tobacco interests have established a number of factories in several of the open ports. The British-American Tobacco Company has been in a dominant position for nearly twenty years.[2]

American tobacco has been used to a large extent by Chinese factories for the manufacture of some of the grades designed to compete with the products of the foreign interests, and there are grades of cigarettes on the Chinese market made of particularly pure American stock. Some American leaf is also used in blending the Chinese fine-cut tobacco used in Chinese pipes.[3]

Although China is even today not a great buyer of American raw tobacco (she took about four per cent of the total American raw tobacco export in 1920-21), she has occupied for some years a foremost place in the American cigarette exporting business. Table 66 shows the American cigarette exports to China along with her total exports. In 1915-1920 China took about two-thirds of the total American export, and in 1921-22, three-fourths.

### The Recent Development of the Chinese Tobacco Industry in Relation to Future American Trade

Despite the recent enormous increase in Chinese imports of American tobacco, both raw and manufactured, the writer is of the opinion that the trade will undergo a great change in the not distant future. The new menace to the further

[1] *Tobacco Trade of the World, op. cit.*
[2] *Ibid.,* p. 32.
[3] *Ibid.,* p. 33.

growth of the American trade is not British or Japanese competition, but the much more formidable rapidly growing native industry. Even many years before the War were cigarettes similar in grade and style to the foreign product made in numerous small Chinese establishments both in the open ports and points in the interior. The sale of this native product has been increasing in considerable quantities.

"The competition," thus reported an American Consul in China in 1915, "offered by Chinese domestic tobacco has always been a hard problem for the American and British tobacco interests. Many Chinese people prefer the local product not only because they are accustomed to the flavor and the price is much cheaper, but also because every one deems preference of domestic products to foreign goods in case of a luxury like tobacco as having a patriotic origin. . . . It is in this trade that the growing preference of the Chinese for domestic goods is particularly felt."

TABLE 66

| Year | Total American Export of Cigarettes per 1,000,000 | American Exports to China per 1,000,000 | % of the Total |
|---|---|---|---|
| 1915 | 2,076 | 1,085 | 52% |
| 1916 | 4,259 | 2,552 | 60 |
| 1917 | 7,020 | 4,949 | 70 |
| 1918 | 12,146 | 6,792 | 56 |
| 1919 | 16,212 | 6,192 | 38 |
| 1920 | 15,834 | 8,507 | 54 |
| 1921 | 8,544 | 6,444 | 75 |
| 1922 | 11,470 | 8,580 | 75 |

What was true of conditions before the war is more true at present because the rapid development of the Chinese tobacco industry, as a result of the high-price stimulation received during the war, has enabled the Chinese concerns to provide more adequately for the expanding home market. The inauguration of the Nanyang Brothers Tobacco Company in 1906 and its wonderful growth since 1914, followed by the organization of many other native companies has resulted in the gradual return to Chinese control of the industry and trade, hitherto dominated by British and then by American interests. Today over ninety-five per cent of the tobacco industry is in Chinese hands and more than seventy per cent of all cigarettes consumed by the Chinese people are home-manufactured.[2] Under such favorable conditions, coupled with an increasing patriotic spirit in favor of domestic products, American exports of cigarettes to China will cease to increase as soon as the Chinese factories can produce an adequate supply to meet the demand of the Chinese community.

The probable future of American trade in raw tobacco seems to be brighter than that in cigarettes, because, on the one hand, the growing industry in China necessitates the use of more material, and, on the other, American tobacco is especially needed in the manufacture of some grades of cigarettes to compete with American manufacturers. Yet the production of Chinese tobacco is of growing importance to the tobacco world. Efforts to improve the quality of the native-grown tobacco, such as the importation of American seeds and cultivating implements and instruction by American trained experts have proved fairly successful. Encouragement of the small producers by the large native companies has resulted in an increase of tobacco production as well as an improvement of its quality, and "Chinese tobacco now equals the American product in color and body although somewhat milder in flavor."[3]

[1] For a more detailed account of the recent growth of the Chinese tobacco industry, see The Growth of China Tobacco Trade, by A. Syhung Lee, *China Review*, New York, November, 1922, pp. 160 ff.
[2] *Ibid.*
[3] *Modern Development in the Chinese Cigarette Trade and Industry*, by Tsze E. Pun, *Tobacco*, April 24, 1924.

This progress in China's tobacco cultivation naturally creates a keen competition for American tobacco in the Chinese market. Some years ago nearly all the raw material used by the native cigarette factories was imported, mainly from the United States. Now the making of Chinese cigarettes usually takes sixty per cent of native, and only forty per cent of imported, tobacco.[1] Not only is the domestic market thus provided for, but export of Chinese tobacco is on the increase for the use of foreign manufactures. In 1918-20 Chinese tobacco exports to the United States alone amounted to five million pounds a year.

Even the British-American Tobacco Company, which formerly used American tobacco exclusively, is now compelled to purchase large and increasing quantities of Chinese domestic tobacco and use it in the manufacture of cigarettes in its factories in China, owing to the inclination on the part of the Chinese to favor native goods. "Buying the native tobacco even in the form of cigarettes," says the same American reporter, "especially appeals to the Chinese at this time when they are anxious to patronize home industry."[2]

On the other hand, the rapid industrialization of China bringing with it higher standards of living for the masses, will undoubtedly result in a greater consumption of articles such as cigarettes. The demand created may be such that even the increased native production will be unable to supply, and together with the demand for imported articles which will always exist in every land, may make it not improbable for the trade in foreign cigarettes to continue unabated.[3]

[1] *Ibid.*
[2] Tobacco Trade of the World, *op. cit.*, p. 34.
[3] *Ibid.*

---

CHAPTER XIII

WOOD, AND WOOD MANUFACTURES

The story of American lumber in China begins with the settlement of foreigners in Shanghai. Commission merchants brought Oregon pine to the port and sold it to the Chinese timber hongs.[1] In 1860 Russell and Company of Shanghai, the great American firm in the early China trade, imported not only lumber but ready-made houses.[2] The failure of the company in 1890 ended this business and until the beginning of the twentieth century, American timber was entirely handled by commission merchants and Chinese hongs. Most of the wood in this period consisted of pine lumber from the States of Oregon and Washington, though considerable redwood from California also found an appreciative market, as did timber from British Columbia.[3]

In 1900 the Pacific Export Lumber Company of Portland was organized with the main purpose of selling lumber across the Pacific. The company chartered steamers and carried timber with some success.[4]

The Robert Dollar Company, which was a very large mill owner and operator on the American Pacific coast, also opened an office in Shanghai at the beginning of the century. It now owns its office buildings and yards at Shanghai, Tientsin, Hankow and Nanking, and has agencies and representatives at other ports in China.[5]

Table 67 shows the gradual increase in the quantity and value of American wood and the value of wood manufactures exported to China since 1891. It is noticed that in the

[1] *China's Growth Stimulates Lumber Trade*, The *Trans-Pacific*, Tokio, Aug., 1922, p. 70.
[2] *Ibid.*
[3] U. S. Dept. of State, Bur. of For. Com. Special Consular Reports, 1897; *American Lumber in Foreign Markets*, p. 219.
[4] *China's Growth Stimulates Lumber Trade*, *op. cit.*
[5] *Ibid.*

closing decade of the last century the average American lumber exported to China was only around ten million square feet a year, valued at less than $100,000. Ten years later, the volume of the trade grew up more than five times, and now, in 1920-22, the quantity of export has increased to an annual average of 114 million square feet, and its value to $2,217,000.

TABLE 67

AMERICAN EXPORTS OF WOOD AND WOOD MANUFACTURES TO CHINA, 1891-1922

| | Year | Wood boards, planks and scantlings | | Wood Manufactures |
|---|---|---|---|---|
| | | Qty. M feet | Value $1,000 | $1,000 |
| 5-year average | 1891-1895 | 5,001 | 48 | 26 |
| | 1896-1900 | 14,792 | 124 | 72 |
| | 1901-1905 | 24,326 | 285 | 256 |
| | 1906-1910 | 53,983 | 684 | 266 |
| 3-year average | 1911-1913 | 71,343 | 776 | 264 |
| | 1914-1916 | 65,901 | 685 | 285 |
| | 1917-1919 | 29,708 | 766 | 992 |
| | 1920 | 117,065 | 4,205 | 1,789 |
| | 1921 | 98,773 | 1,947 | 438 |
| | 1922 | 117,255 | 2,217 | 3,170 |

Data worked out from the statistics in the *Commerce and Navigation of the United States.*

Besides lumber, American wood manufactures have also been exported to China for more than thirty years. Trade in this line has also shown a definite increase from an annual value of about fifty thousand dollars a year in 1891-1900, to more than two million dollars a year in 1920-22.

Table 68 shows the share taken by American lumber in the Chinese lumber market. Before the European War about half of China's soft wood import came from the United States, the other half originated from Japan and

Korea. At the same time Russia and Siberia supplied China with some of their forest product, whose quantity, however, had never been very large. During the World War, the American share dropped from a half to a quarter. This temporary decline was solely due to the prohibitive rates of ocean freight during the years of active warfare and to the impossibility of such a bulky cargo as lumber to bear them. For once, American lumber in China was substituted by Japanese and Korean lumber. But since 1920 American trade has recovered more than its lost share because of the heavy drop of the Pacific freight rates, and now more than two-thirds of China's soft wood import again comes from the States of Oregon and Washington.

As regards the hardwood import of China, the United States has practically no share. All the trade is in the hands of Japan and the British Straits Settlements.[1]

The future of the American lumber business in China is said to be very favorable, although at present lumber has not yet reached the position of being one of the principal imports into China.[2] The eastern part of China is almost denuded of large forests, causing the native supply of lumber to be very limited. As the industrial construction work of various kinds is now advancing rapidly in China, a large and increasing supply of timber must be imported by her for that purpose. Although afforestation is a measure which may ultimately make China self-sufficing in lumber, yet it will be at least some generations before that country can produce a supply sufficiently large to meet the native demand and thus affect foreign importation.

[1] See Chinese Customs Returns.
[2] Lumber Trade, *The Chinese Students' Monthly*, Vol. XVIII No. 1, Nov., 1922, p. 49.

TABLE 68

SOFT WOOD IMPORT OF CHINA, 1911-22, QUANTITY DISTRIBUTION

| From | U.S.A. | | Canada | | Japan and Korea | | Russia and Siberia | | Total |
|---|---|---|---|---|---|---|---|---|---|
| Year | 1,000 sq. ft. | % | 1,000 sq. ft. | % | 1,000 sq. ft. | % | 1,000 sq. ft. | % | 1,000 sq. ft. |
| 1911-13 | 53,769 | 46.5 | 8 | | 57,462 | 49.5 | 2,921 | 2.5 | 115,750 |
| 1914-16 | 46,867 | 27.8 | 1,592 | 0.9 | 109,669 | 64.9 | 5,756 | 2.4 | 169,093 |
| 1917-19 | 23,373 | 23.0 | 10,272 | 10.1 | 60,763 | 59.8 | 6,991 | 7.0 | 101,750 |
| 1920 | 120,504 | 57.5 | 15,011 | 7.2 | 69,234 | 33.1 | 1,314 | 0.6 | 209,402 |
| 1921 | 83,348 | 70.0 | 10,077 | 8.0 | 24,767 | 19.5 | 2,662 | 2.1 | 125,380 |
| 1922 | 142,013 | 61.0 | 27,178 | 11.6 | 42,546 | 18.3 | 20,979 | 9.0 | 233,685 |

(1911-13, 1914-16, 1917-19 are 3-year averages.)

Data computed from Chinese Customs Returns.

---

CHAPTER XIV

INDUSTRIAL MACHINERY AND EQUIPMENT

*China as a Market for American Iron and Steel Machinery*

The rate of progress at which the recent transformation of China from an agricultural to an industrial state is taking place may well be gauged from the expansion recorded year by year in the figures of the various kinds of machinery imported. About thirty years ago, the Chinese Maritime Customs reported the imports under the item of machinery at a total value of about a half million dollars.[1] This trifling sum was only doubled in the course of ten years.[2] Even on the eve of the World War, Chinese imports of all sorts of machinery did not return very large figures, being usually around three or four million dollars a year.[3] But during the last decade, these imports have increased ten times, a growth so phenomenal that it points clearly to the pyrotechnical progress of young industrial China.

"There is," says an American trade commissioner in China, "something in the situation that appeals most strongly to the imagination of a foreign trader. The vast area of the country, the abundant population, the splendid natural resources, both mineral and agricultural, the potential water-power, all in the hands of a people who are intelligent, clever, hard-working, dependable, and likable, will doubtless make China one of the foremost industrial empires of the world."[4]

[1] In 1890, the value of machinery imports into China was 410,000 HK. Taels; exchange rate 1 tl. = $1.27; converted into American currency it is $521,000.
[2] In 1900, the value of machinery imports was 1,450,000 HK Taels; exchange rate, $0.75; converted into American currency, it was $1,088,000.
[3] See Table 69, 1912-13.
[4] U. S. Bur. of For. and Dom. Com., Special Agent Series, No. 215. *Asiatic Markets for Industrial Machinery*, by W. H. Rastall, 1922, p. 247.

248

But before China attains a high stage of industrial development, it is absolutely necessary for her to get from other highly developed countries machinery and equipment for the fitting out of her workshops and plants. At present China is able to produce only such articles as can be manufactured by the simpler forms of industry. There will still be some time before she can reach such a stage of industrial development as that of Europe and North America, and make her own machinery and equipment. So far as the near future is concerned the import of foreign machinery is sure to increase with the industrial progress of the country.[1]

Among the more important enterprises of China are cotton spinning and weaving mills, bean oil mills, iron and steel works, and smelting plants for antimony, tin, zinc, and other ores, silk filatures, match, soap, candle and cigarette factories, distilleries, breweries, canneries and albumen factories, shipbuilding and engineering works, cement works and paper mills. There has been also a great increase during the last two years in the volume of business transacted by flour and rice mills, glass and carpet factories.[1]

Many new enterprises have recently been opened, among which may be mentioned machine-driven hosiery factories, beet and cane sugar refineries, rubber and paint factories, electro-plating works, woolen spinning and weaving mills, biscuit and jam factories, button, umbrella and toy factories.[2] In almost every large city throughout the country modern mills and factories are springing up, which, while turning out in ever-increasing quantities articles which China was in the past obliged to import from foreign countries, have, on the other hand, greatly intensified the demand for foreign machinery, tools, and other equipment.

The corresponding growth of the machinery market in China during the last decade is shown by the import statistics

[1] See *China Year Book*, 1923, ch. on Manufactures.
[2] *Ibid.*

250   TRADE OF UNITED STATES WITH CHINA

in Table 69. The rate of increase has been especially marked since 1918, when Chinese industry was stimulated by the price inflation and business prosperity all over the world. The value of imports increased from ten million dollars in 1918 to 22 millions in 1919, to 31 millions in 1921; then again to 44 millions in 1922 in spite of the general business depression then prevailing in China. Even though this development of industries has been recently much disturbed and retarded by chaotic political conditions in the country, yet the importation of machinery in 1922 was able to hold its own, an evidence which shows that the development is still going on. As soon as the political condition improves, new roads and railways will be built, additional plants and shops installed, and the importation of foreign machinery will make another headlong dash in the expansion of its volume. "The Chinese are now great buyers. But what they are buying today is but a bagatelle of what they will buy tomorrow."[1]

In this highly promising market of the Orient the United States has taken a considerable and increasing share during the past ten years. While before the war China absorbed, according to the United States statistics, annually only less than half a million dollars' worth of American machinery, she took 17 millions worth in 1919, 18 millions in 1920, and 20 millions in 1921 (Table 70). Whereas in 1913 China ranked twenty-eighth among the world markets for American machinery, her rank advanced in 1919 a long way ahead to seventh and again to fifth in 1921. In 1913 the United States supplied less than one-tenth of the total machinery imports of China, the bulk of the business being then in the hands of Great Britain and central Europe. But in 1919-21, more than half of the Chinese demand was met with American machinery. It is most gratifying for the American manufacturer to note that the machinery market of China today is nearly forty times as valuable to him as it was a

[1] C. A. Middleton Smith: The British in China, p. 47.

---

INDUSTRIAL MACHINERY AND EQUIPMENT   251

TABLE 69

CHINA'S IMPORT OF IRON AND STEEL MACHINERY, 1912-22[1]

| Year | Value of Total Import in 1,000 HK Taels | Rate of Exchange of One Tael | Total Value Converted into U.S. Currency in $1,000 | U.S.A. and Canada[2] | Great Britain[2] | Hongkong | Japan | All Other Countries |
|---|---|---|---|---|---|---|---|---|
| 1912 | 4,624 | 0.70 | 3,231 | 11.4 | 34.5 | 15.6 | 10.8 | 22.7 |
| 1913 | 5,778 | 0.73 | 4,218 | 9.8 | 37.2 | 10.3 | 10.2 | 32.5 |
| 1914 | 8,756 | 0.67 | 5,868 | 8.2 | 40.0 | 10.5 | 10.3 | 31.0 |
| 1915 | 4,954 | 0.62 | 3,071 | 15.4 | 41.3 | 11.1 | 17.8 | 14.4 |
| 1916 | 6,655 | 0.79 | 5,257 | 18.7 | 37.2 | 3.9 | 30.8 | 9.4 |
| 1917 | 6,540 | 1.03 | 6,736 | 22.3 | 25.6 | 4.5 | 39.3 | 8.3 |
| 1918 | 8,339 | 1.26 | 10,507 | 31.8 | 15.8 | 4.9 | 44.3 | 3.2 |
| 1919 | 15,482 | 1.39 | 21,520 | 47.0 | 13.4 | 5.0 | 24.1 | 10.4 |
| 1920 | 24,608 | 1.24 | 30,514 | 55.0 | 21.4 | 2.8 | 16.8 | 6.0 |
| 1921 | 57,805 | 0.76 | 43,932 | 43.7 | 36.8 | 2.1 | 13.4 | 4.0 |
| 1922 | 51,541 | 0.83 | 42,779 | 24.0 | 43.2 | 2.5 | 18.0 | 12.3 |

[1] Data from the Chinese Maritime Customs Returns.
[2] Under this heading are included "Agricultural Machinery," "Propelling Machinery, i.e. boilers, turbines, etc.," "Textile Machinery," "Machinery for Brewing, Distilling, Sugar Refining, etc.," "Embroidering, Knitting and Sewing Machines," and "Machinery, every other kind." The percentages as shown here are somewhat different from those compared by W. H. Rastall in his book, Facts and Figures about China, p. 233. The following comment by W. H. Rastall on the amount of machinery from Canada to China comes originally from the United States. To show the value of the Chinese market to American manufacturers by indicating the amount credited to the United States by the authority, the value of machinery from Canada is always credited to the country represented by the last port of shipment, so that the shipments are entered in the Chinese Customs credited to China from the last place, even though it originated in the United States. For example, 1919 returns of the $1,000,000 worth of machinery credited to Hongkong, probably 30 to 40 percent of this was made in New England and shipped via Vancouver. Inasmuch as the United States has supplied to Hongkong, it is clear that the United States has supplied China a good deal more machinery in addition to that strictly credited to it is in the above statement.

---

252   TRADE OF UNITED STATES WITH CHINA

decade ago, and it would be difficult for him to find another place in which his sales could achieve a better record of expansion in volume, rank, and share.

TABLE 70

AMERICAN EXPORTS OF STEEL AND IRON MACHINERY TO CHINA, INCLUDING LEASED TERRITORIES, 1908-22[1]

| | Fiscal year ending June 30 | Value in $1,000 | Calendar year | Value in $1,000 |
|---|---|---|---|---|
| Annual average | 1908-10 | 442 | 1918 | 3,220 |
| | 1911-13 | 425 | 1919 | 16,864 |
| | 1914-15 | 821 | 1920 | 18,217 |
| | 1916-17 | 1,403 | 1921 | 19,652 |
| | | | 1922 | 11,136 |

Among all kinds of American machinery textile machinery has been for several years by far the most important. As we have noted above,[2] the cotton weaving and spinning industry has achieved remarkable progress during the past decade. This has resulted in a huge increase in the import of textile machinery, chiefly from the United States in the three years, 1919-1921.

Although the United States held the lead in the Chinese market during the post-war period, the market is reverting from the transitional period to the pre-war conditions. Taking the total machinery imports of China in the years preceding 1916, Great Britain got the largest share. In the next five years, she dropped to second and third place among the three strong competitors, the United States, Japan, and Great Britain. But in 1921, Great Britain achieved a remarkable recovery and in 1922 again took the lead (See Table 69). As to the other competing countries in Central Europe, Germany and Belgium got a large share before the war. Their trade disappeared entirely during the war and

[1] Data worked up from The Trade of the United States with the World, U. S. Bur. of For. and Dom. Com., Misc. Series.
[2] Chapter on Cotton Goods, supra.

---

INDUSTRIAL MACHINERY AND EQUIPMENT   253

post-war years, but their present effort to regain their shares has been marked with success. Assisted by the depreciating currency and low manufacturing cost (as compared with that in the United States in terms of gold), they are now able to send China many sorts of machinery at a price lower than that offered by the American manufacturer.

Thus outcompeted by Great Britain and the Central European countries, the United States now seems to be losing ground in the Chinese machinery market. In 1920, it supplied China 55 percent of the latter's total purchases. But in 1921, its share dropped to 44 percent, and in 1922 to only 24 percent. This is a serious drop and although the value of the trade in 1922 is still far above that of pre-war years by more than twenty times, yet relatively its share has shrunk to no more than two or three times.

Facing this serious situation the American machinery exporters should do whatever they can to preserve their ground in this highly promising market of China, especially since, as shown in Chapter V, industrial machinery is the chief, if not the sole, line along which China's future imports will certainly expand. Should the United States lose her ground, it would be still harder to regain it again.

Since due to the present gold and exchange situation the price of American machinery is higher than that offered by some Central European countries, or even that offered by Great Britain, the only expedient method by which the Americans can outcompete other bidders in the Chinese market is to finance the new Chinese industries and extend them long-term credits. Formerly China's orders for industrial equipment frequently followed the direction of foreign loans, because it has become the usual practice for the country making loans to insert a clause in their agreement with China to the effect that the materials and equipment to be bought by the funds should be purchased in that country.¹ "It seems clear to me," says one American investigator in the Orient, "that in the East at least, finance and trade go hand in hand, and that neither the profits of trade can be fully reaped nor the trade interest be adequately upheld without incurring the responsibilities incident to financial activity."² Although such a restrictive clause in the loan agreement is very objectionable to the Chinese, yet the Chinese industries need foreign capital to make this further advancement possible. As perceived by everyone, most of the European countries and Japan are at present unable to extend to China the required credit, and here there seems to be a good chance for American traders to get business in China. If other countries could outbid the Americans by a lower price, Americans could outbid them by offering the Chinese industrialists the required credits on liberal terms. Once the trade is gotten hold of, its effect on further expansion is rather cumulative, and the Americans will be able not only to retain their former share, but also to increase it.

### Other Iron and Steel Products

Long before China became a market for iron and steel machinery, she was an extensive purchaser of other iron and steel products, such as tools, bars, sheets, structures, pipes, wires, nails and all other sorts of hardware. For the ten years before the war, the total import of those products into China amounted to ten million dollars a year, of which the Americans got a share of about twelve to fifteen per cent.³ The larger part of China's imports, around eighty percent, came from Europe, mainly from Great Britain, Germany, Belgium, France, and Austria. The rather small American share of the Chinese trade, considering the high development

¹ For detailed discussion on this point, see W. W. Willoughby: Foreign Rights and Interests in China, pp. 344 ff.; also see Rastall: Asiatic Markets for Industrial Machinery, op. cit., pp. 243-5.
² The Far Eastern Review, Shanghai, Vol. II, p. 229.
³ Allowing the United States a certain portion of the trade credited to Hongkong by the Chinese Maritime Customs Returns.

TABLE 71

CHINA'S IMPORTS OF IRON AND STEEL PRODUCTS¹ AND DISTRIBUTION OF THE TRADE²

| Year | Value of Total China's Imports in 1,000 H.K. Tls. | Exchange Rate of One HK Tael | Total Value Converted into U.S. $1,000 | \| Distributive share of exporting countries in % U. S. A. | Canada | Hong kong | Great Britain | Japan | Other Countries |
|------|------|------|------|------|------|------|------|------|------|
| 1913 | 17,374 | $0.73 | 12,683 | 11.2 | ... | 14.7 | 32.9 | 6.0 | 35.1 |
| 1914 | 15,835 | 0.64 | 10,134 | 12.1 | ... | 14.0 | 33.0 | 6.2 | 34.7 |
| 1918 | 29,075 | 1.26 | 36,635 | 40.0 | 7.5 | 11.4 | 8.8 | 29.0 | 3.3 |
| 1919 | 36,237 | 1.39 | 50,369 | 43.8 | 7.6 | 10.1 | 12.1 | 20.8 | 5.6 |
| 1920 | 41,663 | 1.24 | 51,662 | 39.4 | 4.3 | 9.1 | 26.4 | 17.5 | 3.2 |
| 1921 | 38,376 | 0.76 | 29,166 | 39.1 | 0.9 | 11.8 | 25.2 | 10.4 | 12.6 |
| 1922 | 29,687 | 0.83 | 24,640 | 24.6 | | 15.2 | 25.0 | 11.6 | 23.6 |

¹ Including tools, bars, wires, plates, sheets, pipes, tubes, hoops, joists, angles, rails, structures, nails, screws, ties, castings, and other manufactured iron and unmanufactured iron and steel; but excluding machinery, machine tools, iron and steel apparatus and furniture.
² Data worked up from the Chinese Maritime Customs Returns.
³ Footnote on the distribution of China's machinery imports is equally applicable here. A large part of the trade shared by Canada, and a certain portion of that shared by Hongkong are actually American. Among the "Other Countries," Belgium, Germany and France took about 90 per cent of the trade.

and huge production of American iron and steel, was mainly due to the higher American prices.¹

With the outbreak of the European War two great changes came to affect the hardware trade in China, similar to those affecting the machinery trade as indicated above. The first change was the phenomenal expansion of China's imports in these wares due to the rapid progress of her industry. The second was the remarkable increase of the American share in the trade, due to the withdrawal of European competition. Table 71 evidences these changes by showing the total value of China's imports and the distributive shares of some important countries in some pre-war and post-war years. It is seen that China's imports increased from a little more than 10 million dollars a year before the war, to 40 or 50 million dollars a year in 1918-1921. Whereas, the share of the United States increased from 12 percent to more than 40 percent.²

TABLE 72

AMERICAN EXPORTS OF IRON AND STEEL PRODUCTS³ TO CHINA, INCLUDING LEASED TERRITORIES, 1891-1922⁴

| Year | Value in $1,000 | Year | Value in $1,000 |
|------|------|------|------|
| 1891-95 | 109 | 1917 | 7,431 |
| 1896-1900 | 355 | 1918 | 13,148 |
| 1901-05 | 631 | 1919 | 20,528 |
| 1906-10 | 1,451 | 1920 | 24,980 |
| 1911-13 | 1,759 | 1921 | 10,752 |
| 1914-16 | 3,162 | 1922 | 6,074 |

Table 72 shows the gradual growth of the American ex-

¹ See U. S. Bur. of For. and Dom. Com., Misc. Series, No. 50, For Eastern Markets for American Hardware, pp. 24 and 73.
² For an exhaustive description of the Chinese markets for American hardware, see For Eastern Markets for American Hardware, op. cit.
³ Excluding iron and steel machinery.
⁴ Data from the Foreign Commerce and Navigation of the U. S.

ports of these wares to China since 1891. The upward trend of the trade in these lines has never sagged except in 1921 which was, of course, an exceptional year. The value of the trade has increased from $100,000 a year in 1891-95 to $12,000,000 in 1919-20.

But since the gradual coming back of European products to the Chinese markets, the American goods have been once more put under their old handicap of a higher price in competition with those of other countries, and the declining share is the result of this competition. What has just been said about what the American manufacturer should do to preserve their machinery market in the Orient is equally applicable here, because a large part of China's imports of iron and steel products is used for construction and industry.

But, nevertheless, there is a fundamental difference between the future prospect of the Chinese machinery market and the market for other iron and steel products. Regarding machinery, China is depending and will depend for some years or even decades to come upon foreign imports so that the United States as well as other exporting countries, can hope to build a fundamental line of trade in it. But the case is, or at least soon will be, different with other simpler forms of iron and steel manufactures.

Up to the present time most of China's iron and steel products have been imported from the United States and Europe. But, as in the case of cotton goods, manufactured tobacco, and, some fifteen years ago, wheat flour, this is another department in which the new Republic's latent potentialities promise to make it ultimately independent of imports. Little has been done that would enable an accurate estimate of that country's mineral resources to be made, but enough is known to make it certain that it has more iron, and probably more coal, than any other nation of the world. Enough iron and coal to serve the industrial needs of the country for centuries has already been opened up within reach of either railways or navigable rivers. The Hanyang Iron and Steel Works, situated on the middle Yangtse, offer a good illustration of what China may be expected to do toward attaining self-sufficiency in the matter of rails, structures and similar iron and steel manufactures. With skilled labor of a character that would command from $6 to $10 a day in the United States—and say, two-thirds to one-half of those amounts in Europe—available at from fifty cents to one dollar, and with unlimited unskilled labor at hand for twenty to thirty cents a day, the works themselves should be able to make iron and steel at a fraction of the cost in American or European plants. As soon as China is in a position to start more of such iron works,—with the help of foreign capitalists, such an occurrence seems probable at any time—that country will be able to make most of the simpler forms of iron and steel manufactures necessary. My conclusion concerning this line of trade is, therefore, that in the near future China may still largely depend upon America and Europe for these wares, but in ten or twenty years, the demand for imported goods may materially decrease relatively, if not absolutely.

### Electrical Machinery, Appliances, and other Materials[1]

Electrical machinery, appliances, and other materials belong to another field in China in which American trade is going to grow greatly in the near future. The trade now is already quite large, amounting to more than four million dollars' worth in 1920-21, and somewhat less in 1922. Here the quotation in the preceding section that what China is buying today is but a bagatelle of what she will buy tomorrow can be applied with equal accuracy.

[1] Excluding Motor Vehicles, which will be dealt with in the following section.
[2] A detailed survey on China as a market for American electrical goods is found in U. S. Bur. of For. and Dom. Com., Special Agents Series No. 172, Electrical Goods in China, Japan and Vladivostok, by R. A. Lundquist, 1918.

The demand in the old Chinese cities for electrical materials and machinery has grown with amazing rapidity during the last twenty years. It was in 1903 that the Chinese Maritime Customs first reported the imports of electrical goods under a separate item, amounting in that year to only $368,000.[1] Before the war, the total imports of China increased to a little less than two and a half million dollars worth. But in the past decade, the increase has been consistent, and in 1919-22, the total was around ten million dollars (See Table 73). This huge increase has been due to a keen demand for electrical equipment for lighting and operating other plants, for the extension and expansion of existing plants and the installation of others. The employment of electrical current for lighting purposes and for small power plants is rapidly increasing in China.[2] These small power plants are mostly supplied by the United States.[3] The numerous small industries which are operating in China are particularly well adapted to the employment of electricity as a medium of power, the current being easily controlled and shut off when not required.[4]

There is, however, a tendency in the more important establishments in China to install large units, and while a few years ago 200 and 400 kilowatts were considered large, it is now quite common to install units of 1,000 kilowatts and upwards, and a large number of orders were placed in the past few years for privately-owned power-stations for the purpose of supplying power to cotton and flour mills.[5] This increase in the amount of machinery installed has, of course, stimulated the demand for electrical accessories, fittings and all other sorts of electrical materials.

[1] 574,600 HK Taels. Value of tael in that year, $0.64.
[2] See China; Maritime Customs Report, 1920, Part I, p. 10.
[3] The Eastern Commerce, Tokio, Vol. VII, No. 2, Dec., 1921. Market for Machinery and Implements in China, p. 39.
[4] Ibid.
[5] Chinese Maritime Customs Report, op. cit.

In 1922, there seemed to be a setback in the trade. No doubt the surfeited condition of the market in these articles, resulting from overbuying during the two preceding years, coupled with the general depression in trade and a falling exchange explain the contraction in the value of electrical goods in 1922.[1] Despite this setback, it need hardly be said here that the continual growth in the use of electrical plants for power and lighting purposes in China is assured, and that there is a bright future for all sorts of electrical goods.[2]

The share taken by the United States in this line of trade is shown in Table 73 together with those taken by her competitors. Prior to the war American goods did not sell well in China, while British, German, Belgian and Japanese goods were imported in much larger quantities. With Germany and Belgium temporarily eliminated from the field and British commercial activities greatly curtailed following 1915, the electrical manufacturers of the United States began to realize the opportunities in the Orient. The growth of their exports of electrical machinery, appliances and materials to China, as shown by the United States statistics, was as phenomenal as that of iron and steel machinery. In 1913, the value of American exports to China amounted only to $120,000; in 1920 it totalled $4,377,000. Despite the price deflation and the falling of silver exchange in 1921, it increased further to $4,464,000 (See Table 74). In 1913, the United States shared only 6.3 percent of China's total electrical goods imports; in 1920 it was 27.6%, and in 1921 35.2% (See Table 73).

This remarkable advance, however, did not continue in 1922, when the American share dropped to 18.5% with a total value of $1,655,000. This severe drop is explained partly by the general business depression in China with a sudden contraction in her total imports of electrical goods. But the recovery of the business lost to European countries

[1] Chinese Maritime Customs Report, 1920, Part I, pp. 16-17.
[2] Ibid.

TABLE 73

VALUE OF TOTAL IMPORTS OF ELECTRICAL MATERIALS AND FITTINGS[1] INTO CHINA, 1913-22

| Year | China Total Imports of | | Exchange Rate of Tael | Percentage supplied by | | | | | |
|---|---|---|---|---|---|---|---|---|---|
| | HK Tael 1,000 | Converted into $1,000 | | Canada[2] U.S.A. | Great Britain | Hong-kong[4] | Japan | Other Countries[3] | |
| 1913 | 3,159 | 2,306 | $0.73 | 6.3 | 27.2 | 6.8 | 15.2 | 44.5 | |
| 1914 | 3,363 | 2,253 | 0.67 | 4.4 | 23.6 | 10.1 | 22.8 | 39.1 | |
| 1915 | 2,550 | 1,581 | 0.62 | 9.4 | 22.6 | 13.4 | 35.6 | 19.0 | |
| 1916 | 4,197 | 3,316 | 0.79 | 18.0 | 18.9 | 8.4 | 49.6 | 5.2 | |
| 1917 | 5,045 | 5,196 | 1.03 | 21.4 | 8.2 | 9.8 | 58.8 | 1.8 | |
| 1918 | 4,808 | 6,058 | 1.26 | 25.3 | 4.6 | 7.9 | 56.1 | 6.2 | |
| 1919 | 6,110 | 8,493 | 1.39 | 34.4 | 5.8 | 7.5 | 34.2 | 8.1 | |
| 1920 | 9,404 | 11,661 | 1.24 | 27.6 | 13.9 | 3.6 | 40.1 | 14.8 | |
| 1921 | 15,129 | 11,498 | 0.76 | 35.2 | 25.0 | 3.6 | 2.28 | 13.4 | |
| 1922 | 11,261 | 9,338 | 0.83 | 18.5 | 29.6 | 5.7 | 28.1 | 18.1 | |

[1] Under this item are included all the materials and fittings credited by the Chinese Maritime Customs Returns. Data worked from the Chinese Maritime Customs Reports.
"Electrical Material and Fittings" is a special column in the Chinese Maritime Customs credited to the rare items. This item excludes motor vehicles and, possibly, the greater part of electrical machinery. It is unfortunate that the Chinese Maritime Customs do not more clearly report the figures for electrical machinery by itself. "Electrical Materials and Fittings", a special column; "Electrical Machinery, Machinery, Propelling," "Machinery, other kinds," and "Electrical Material and Fittings." The figures here shown are therefore not complete.
[2] A large part of China's imports credited to Canada comes originally from the United States. See note to the preceding section.
[3] Before the war, Germany and, to a less extent, Belgium, practically took nine-tenths of the share under this column. After 1920, many central European countries shared in the trade the majority of American importers have their headquarters in Shanghai and do not take into consideration the fact that the majority of American importers have their headquarters in Shanghai and do not here as important volume. By reason of this, it is probable that to a few Americans electrical manufactures are strongly represented in Hongkong, with South China, and the further fact that a certain volume of imports from Hongkong is and following 1913 area of American origin. U. S. Bur. of For. and Dom. Commerce, Special Agents Series, No. 172, Electrical Goods in China, Japan and Vladivostok, 1918, p. 10. This condition has changed since the war.

during the war, and the formidable efforts of the British to the war, and the formidable efforts of the British to push their goods in the Chinese market are the chief causes of the declining share of the Americans. American electrical goods like other kinds of machinery and equipment are higher in price than those of European make, and are thus handicapped in the post-bellum competition. But the measure of credit extension already suggested before can also be taken by the American manufacturers in this line of trade to offset the disadvantage of higher prices.

TABLE 74

VALUE OF AMERICAN EXPORTS OF ELECTRICAL MACHINERY, APPLIANCES, AND MATERIALS TO CHINA

| Year | Value $1,000 | Year | Value $1,000 |
|---|---|---|---|
| 1913 | 120 | 1918 | 1,493 |
| 1914 | 239 | 1919 | 1,904 |
| 1915 | 242 | 1920 | 4,377 |
| 1916 | 417 | 1921 | 4,463 |
| 1917 | 1,143 | 1922 | 1,655 |

### Motor Vehicles

That China offers the United States one of the greatest fields for the expansion of their motor-vehicle trade is being emphasized by the widespread movement of road construction in China and the rapid increase in her imports of American vehicles during the past few years. A review of the present market discloses an unusual activity in all sections of the vast country in opening up new communications for commercial purposes, and every year thousands of motor cars and trucks are being sent to China to meet the growing demand.

The development of the Chinese market for motor vehicles has come rather suddenly. Only ten years ago, an American consul in China reported to his government that there was no market whatever in most parts of China for auto-

mobiles.' "The country roads there," said the reporter, "are in many places mere cart tracks and are not improved at all, while in cities the streets are entirely too narrow for the use of any wheeled vehicle." [2] At that time a very few machines were owned as a novelty by wealthy Chinese, but the rest of the people could not use them and did not care for them.

But during the past decade conditions in China have been changing very rapidly. The Chinese have now come to recognize the vital necessity of good highways as a means of assisting the development of the vast resources of the country. Many private roads and auto-transportation companies have been formed, or are in process of promotion; and up to the present time hundreds of miles of good roads have been built for motor traffic.[3] Regarded at first as a luxury, the motor car is now recognized in China as a necessity for rapid transit in cities, for suburban and interurban communications, for connecting railways with waterways, and for feeder lines to railways and water-routes. If funds can be obtained for continuous construction and maintenance of these roads, the future looks bright for the development of a huge market for motor vehicles of all kinds. This phase of China's development can be traced largely to the fact that for some ten years, railway construction had been practically at a standstill, with very little hope that funds on a large scale would be forthcoming from abroad for the resumption of work. Cities and towns in the interior of China, which cannot hope to be connected by rail, are

[1] U. S. Dept. of Com. and Labor, Bur. of Mfrs. Special Consular Report, No. 53, Foreign Markets for Motor Vehicles, 1912, pp. 107 ff.
[2] *Ibid.*
[3] For some details on the Chinese good-road movement some years ago, see U. S. Bur. of For. and Dom. Com., Special Agent Series No. 170, *Motor Vehicles in Japan, China, and Hawaii*, 1918, pp. 51 ff. For more recent movement, see *The Market for Motor Vehicles in China*, The Far Eastern Review, Jan., 1922, Vol. 18, No. 1.

turning their attention to the cheaper method of road communication. It is suggested if ways could be found for foreign capital to assist in this development, a great impetus would be given to the automobile trade with China.[1]

The importance of the Far Eastern market has been brought home to the American manufacturers of automobiles and the United States Department of Commerce sent out to China in the spring of 1922 a special automobile expert to study the conditions there and aid American manufacturers to increase their exports.[2]

The increasing value of the Chinese market for American motor vehicles can be realized by referring to Table 75. Before the war, imports into China were so small as to be nearly negligible. In 1912, the total value of imported motor cars was only 282,000 Haikwan Taels, which, according to the current rate of exchange (one tael=$0.70) was only $197,000. The European manufacturers were then selling the Chinese about twice as many cars as the American firms were. During the war, the trade expanded to more than one million dollars' worth a year, with the American merchants supplying two-thirds of it. Now about half of the motor vehicles used in China come from the United States. The success of the Americans is said to be due to the fact that Americans have in general Chinese goodwill, and they have the additional advantage that the American cars recently sold in China have made good.[3]

That China should import only about two million dollars' worth of motor vehicles from the United States in years when her total imports from the latter averaged more than

[1] Finance China's Highway Construction in Order to Increase the Automobile Trade; Far Eastern Review, July, 1922, Shanghai.
[2] *The Market for Motor Vehicles for China, op. cit.*
[3] Motor-Car Market in China, *The Literary Digest*, May 20, 1922, p. 76.

one hundred million dollars is perhaps not startling, but to those who know the conditions in China it is a portent of the most striking development in motor vehicle distribution. For it must be remembered that China has not been a big buyer of motor cars until the last few years. If one can imagine an interprovincial network of macadamized highroads in China, the mind staggers at the probable number of cars that might be sold in that country every year.

TABLE 75

| | China's Import of Motor Cars and Cycles | | | American Exports of Motor Cars and Cycles to China | | |
|---|---|---|---|---|---|---|
| Year | Value in 1,000 HKT | Value of Import from U.S.A. in 1,000 HKT | % of U.S.A. in the Total | No. of Cars | Value in $1,000 | Parts of Cars in $1,000 | Total $1,000 |
| 1912 | 282 | 88 | 31 | .... | .... | .... | .... |
| 1913 | 536 | 119 | 22 | .... | .... | .... | .... |
| 1914 | 608 | 151 | 25 | 144 | 144 | .... | .... |
| 1915 | 431 | 249 | 58 | 123 | 122 | .... | 122 |
| 1916 | 754 | 493 | 65 | 314 | 284 | 22 | 306 |
| 1917 | 957 | 588 | 62 | 645 | 432 | 56 | 488 |
| 1918 | 1,374 | 656 | 48 | 1,058 | 986 | 72 | 1,061 |
| 1919 | 2,450 | 1,461 | 60 | 1,722 | 2,097 | 239 | 2,336 |
| 1920 | 3,877 | 2,231 | 58 | 2,245 | 2,876 | 314 | 3,190 |
| 1921 | 3,868 | 1,844 | 48 | 646 | 703 | 160 | 863 |
| 1922 | 2,495 | 949 | 38 | .... | .... | .... | .... |
| | Data from Chinese Maritime Customs | | | Data from the Commerce and Navigation of the United States | | |

PART IV

American Commercial Policies
and Interests in China

## CHAPTER XV

AMERICAN COMMERCIAL POLICIES IN, AND COMMERCIAL
TREATIES WITH, CHINA

Foreign trade policies are the motive force of trade.
They are, in turn, the result of existing trade conditions.
We are always aided in the interpretation of the history of
international trade by the interaction of the commercial
policies of the respective trading nations, and conversely we
can also understand why these nations follow such and such
a policy toward each other by tracing the various stages of
their trade development. In order, therefore, to understand
what has made American trade with China what it has been,
and to forecast its future prospects it is best to study the
commercial policies of the two nations toward each other.
These policies are, for the most part, embodied in their commercial treaties and agreements as contracted from time to
time. Therefore, in conjunction with their commercial policies, we have also to examine their commercial treaties.

Since the beginning of American trade with China in
1784, we have noticed at different stages that there has been
a great variety of commercial policies adopted by the United
States toward her sister nation on the other side of the
ocean. There was, at first, the policy of non-interference
during the whole period of non-treaty intercourse. There
was the most favored-nation-policy of Cushing when he
concluded with China the first Commercial Treaty in 1844.
There was Parker's land-grabbing policy, when he recom-
mended in 1858 that the United States should create a pro-
tectorate over Formosa. There was Anson Burlingame's perfect sovereignty policy, when he headed the Chinese Mission
to Europe and America in 1868. There was, finally, Hay's
"Open Door" policy, which he enunciated afresh in 1899
and which has been consistently followed by the United
States since that time. But whatsoever these different policies may have been there is clearly a thread of uniformity

269

in all of them. In other words, from the inception of Chinese-American diplomatic intercourse, the United States has, in fact, adopted only a single policy concerning her trade in and with China,—the policy of most-favored-nation treatment. Having realized that China is the biggest potential market in the whole world, the United States desires a fair chance to get an equitable share in her commerce in fair competition. This is the fundamental principle of the most-favored-nation treatment.

But to attain this aim the sovereignty and territorial integrity of China must be preserved, while her door must be kept open to all who desire to enter. So, after the explicit statement of the most-favored-nation treatment in the Cushing Treaty, there followed Burlingame's perfect-sovereignty policy, and Hay's Open Door policy. Even Parker's land-grabbing policy in the early years and the "dollar policy" as advanced by President Taft in 1908 did not deviate at all from this fundamental rule. During the latter-half of the nineteenth century many European powers had one after another stretched their hands to grab some land or other concessions from China, and it is only natural that some American statesmen did not want their own country to lag behind other nations in this respect. Mr. T. Dennett, in the preface of his admirable book *Americans in the Far East During the Nineteenth Century*, says:—

"The tap-root of American Policy has been not philanthropy but the demand for most-favored-nation treatment. One frequently meets the assumption that the Open Door Policy was invented by John Hay and first applied in 1899. The Open Door Policy, in fact, is as old as our relations with Asia. It was pronounced in China as early as 1844, when Caleb Cushing incorporated a most-favored-nation clause into the treaty of Wanghia. It had its full development when Burlingame's Mission concluded for China with the United States the treaty of 1868 and secured from England the Clarendon Declaration. No new principle has ever been introduced since that time. Neither Mr. Hay nor Mr. Hughes appears to have considered that they were creating anything new."

All the commercial treaties and conventions, and other

agreements between China and the United States or between the United States and other countries concerning China, have, therefore, been drawn upon this basis.

### Cushing's Most-favored-Nation Policy

Before 1840 the American Government assumed toward its citizens resident in China an attitude which was not dissimilar to that taken by the Chinese Government toward its own merchants trading with foreigners. This early policy may be designated, not inappropriately, by the much used term of "laissez faire,"—"Let them shift for themselves." The American merchants in Canton, thus left to themselves, adopted a course of conciliation, with the result that as a whole they prospered in their trade. But when the news of the signing of the Treaty of Nanking between China and Great Britain reached America in 1842, it soon became evident to the American Government that a similar treaty was necessary between China and the United States, if Americans were to remain on an equal standing with their competitors in the Oriental market. A special Act was passed by the American Congress in 1843 providing for the creation of the first American Mission to China to deal with commercial treaties.

The mission to China was finally organized toward the end of the year 1843, with Caleb Cushing, as Commissioner. The mission arrived at Macao, February 24, 1844. A formal letter was addressed to the acting Governor at Canton, stating the reason for their coming.[2] After the Governor had memorialized the matter to the Imperial Court, the latter appointed Kiying as the Imperial Commissioner to negotiate with the American Envoy. The actual negotiation of the treaty was simple, and on July 3, 1844, the first commercial

[1] Congress, Globe, 3 Sess., 27 Cong., P. P. 323-325.
[2] For correspondence, see Sen. Doc. 67, 28 Cong., 2 Sess., pp. 2-20; Sen. Doc. 87, 28 Cong., 2 Sess., pp. 5-12.

treaty between the United States and China was signed at Whanghai, near Macao.[1]

The most significant provision in this document was of course the most-favored-nation clause, which was stated in the following words:[2]—

". . . . The citizens of the United States shall, in no case, be subject to other or higher duties than are and shall be required of the people of any other nation whatever. . . . . And if additional advantages or privileges, of whatever description, be conceded hereafter by China to any other nation, the United States and citizens thereof shall be entitled thereupon to a complete, equal, and impartial participation in the same."

Another article of great importance, which established American Extra-territoriality within Chinese territory, also deserves special mention.[3] It runs thus:—

"Subjects of China, who may be guilty of any criminal act towards citizens of the United States shall be arrested and punished by the Chinese authorities, and the citizens of the United States who may commit any crime in China, shall be subject to be tried and punished only by the consul or other public functionary of the United States thereto authorized, according to the laws of their own country. . . . ."

It was further provided that all controversies occurring in China between the citizens of the United States and the subjects or citizens of any other Governments should be regulated by the treaties existing between the United States and such Governments respectively, without any interference on the part of China.[4]

Besides the above provisions, this treaty opened five ports to American commerce[5]—Kwangchow,[6] Amoy, Foochow, Ningpo, and Shanghai—which were previously opened by the treaty of 1842 to British commerce. American citizens

[1] For a full text of the treaty of 1844, see Hertslet's China Treaties, Vol. II (see footnote on p. 539).
[2] Article II.
[3] Article XXI.
[4] Article XXV.
[5] Article III.
[6] Canton.

and families were permitted to reside and trade there, and their vessels and cargoes to enter and clear at will.[1] Fees and charges at these ports were formally abolished and import and export duties were prescribed in a tariff which was made a part of the Treaty.[2] Tonnage dues were also prescribed in the treaty.[3] The exclusive trade with Hong merchants and other monopolies or injurious restrictions were abolished.[4] It also gave the United States a recognized right to appoint consuls in China.[5]

As a basis for the conduct of trade, the American treaty of 1844 was regarded by foreigners as greatly superior to the British Treaty signed with China two years before. It was, in fact, so superior that it became immediately the model for the French treaty negotiated a few weeks later, and also for the treaty with Norway and Sweden, signed in 1847. Indeed, the Cushing treaty became the basis of China's international relations until it was superseded in 1858 by the Treaties of Tientsin. It is true that the United States had never imitated European powers in the use of physical force. It is equally true that she had always enjoyed the fruits of the use of arms by European Powers, inasmuch as the most-favored-nation clause had automatically assured to the United States any trade privileges obtained by others through force.

### American Attempts at Treaty Revision

Following the establishment of formal treaty relationship between China and the United States, there was, as described in Chapter II, an immediate expansion of trade between them. But, nevertheless, the relations between foreign powers and the Chinese Government were rapidly reaching

[1] Article V.
[2] Article XIII.
[3] Article VI.
[4] Article XV.
[5] Article IV.

a critical stage and came to a head in 1853 when the Taiping Rebellion was in the flood tide of its first success in China.

The favorable opportunity offered by the Rebellion for the foreign Powers to advance their interests was utilized to its full extent by the United States as well as by Great Britain, France, and Russia. In 1854 the American Government sent Robert M. McLane to China to secure from the Imperial Government "some important modifications of the Cushing Treaty." Observing that the French and the English would certainly want new concessions, if any were made to the Americans, the Chinese Government energetically refused to accept his proposal.[1]

But in 1856 the time for the revision of the Cushing Treaty fell due, as Article 34 of this treaty prescribed that negotiations for its revision might come up at the end of twelve years. So impressed was the American Government by the steady opposition of the Chinese Government to all proposals for treaty revision that Commissioner Peter Parker was authorized to proceed to his post by way of London and Paris and to confer with the British and French Governments with a view to the adoption of a common policy in China. In the history of the evolution of American policies in China this marks the only step of American cooperation with Europe for the compulsory exploitation of that country.

At Canton, the American, British and French Commissioners were refused an interview by the obdurate Viceroy Yeh. They now tried to get it by force. In the latter part of October, 1856, the British navy fired upon Canton, breaching the city wall, and on the fifteenth of November, the American naval forces destroyed one of the Chinese forts, which was alleged to have fired upon an American ship. Peter Parker, then American Trade Commissioner in China, went even so far as to suggest to the United States Government that if the representatives of the three nations

[1] Parker *Correspondence* S. Ex. Docs. 22: 35-2, pp. 610 ff.

were still not welcome, "the French flag will be hoisted in Korea, the English at Chusan off the coast of Ningpo, and the American in Formosa."[1]

### Parker's Land Grabbing Policy

It has been stated in Chapter II that the United States Government had been considering the starting of the Pacific mail and freight service. But to such a plan an adequate coal supply in the Orient for the fleet was indispensable. With a view to attaining this end, Formosa, then a Chinese Province, had attracted the attention of some aggressive American officials in China. In 1847 officers of both the British and the American navy made surveys of the coal resources of the island. In 1849 the United States brig *Dolphin* made a second expedition for further explorations. The visit of Commodore Perry of the United States Navy to the island in 1854 had stimulated anew the interest of the Americans in it and an American commercial company had been formed to exploit its trade. Here was the opportunity for the ambitious Parker, who, in February, 1857, sent to the American State Department the following message:

"It is much to be hoped that the Government of the United States may not shrink from the action which the interests of humanity, civilization and commerce impose upon it in relation to Tai-Wan (Formosa), at present inhabited by savages, to whose depraved cruelties we have every reason to believe many Europeans, and among them our own friends and countrymen, have fallen victims."

In March he again wrote:

"In event of the establishment of a line of steamers between California, Japan, and China, this source of coal supply will be the most advantageous. That the Island may not long remain a portion of the Empire is possible; and in event of its being severed from the Empire politically, as it is geographically, that the United States should possess it is obvious, particularly as respects the great principle of the balance of Power."[2]

[1] Dennett, Americans in the Far East, p.
[2] Parker *Correspondence*, p. 1208.

To these impetuous proposals that he be given authority to complete the acquisition of Formosa, Parker never received any answer from the Secretary of State. But to his original proposal that the three powers join in taking temporary possession of Korea, Chusan, and Formosa, Secretary Marcy replied that the President did not believe that "Our relations with China warrant the 'last resort' you speak of; and if they did, the military and naval forces of the United States could be used only by the authority of Congress."[1]

### The Tientsin Treaty

William B. Reed, the first American Minister Plenipotentiary to China, arrived in China in 1857 in company with the Russian, French, and English envoys to demand the long awaited revision of the Nanking and Wanghia Treaties. They had been accompanied to China by formidable fleets of war-ships and transports and were fully prepared for hostilities. This time the allied envoys would accept nothing except a concession to the totality of their claims, which the Chinese Government still tried to refuse. On May 20 the British and French fleets attacked the Taku forts and occupied them. The Chinese Government was thus compelled to concede under duress. Negotiations were carried forward with rapidity dictated under the military pressure of the powers. The American Treaty was signed on June 18,[2] and those with Russia, Great Britain, and France were also concluded in due time.

The most important provision in this treaty was a general guarantee of most-favored-nation treatment in all matters of commerce, navigation, and political or other intercourse.[3] The additional concessions gained by the United States were the establishment of diplomatic intercourse with

[1] *Ibid.*
[2] For a full text of the treaty see Herstlet's *China Treaties*, Vol. II, pp. 540-553.
[3] Articles XXX, VI, and XV.

the Chinese Government, with the promise of permanent official residence of diplomatic agents at Peking whenever such privilege should be granted to any other foreign power;[1] the immediate increase of the number of treaty ports from five to eight, and the permission to trade at any other port or place thereafter opened to other foreign countries;[2] a promise to suppress and punish piracy, robbery, and rioting;[3] a revision of tonnage dues, and a promise of religious liberty and toleration.[4] The import and export duties of China were the same as they had been in 1844, except in so far as some of them had been changed by treaty with other nations. Since numerous tariff changes of this kind had been made, a supplementary treaty was concluded, in November, 1858, in which the duties and regulations applicable to the trade of the United States were definitely stated.[5]

The results of these Tientsin Treaties between China, on the one hand, and the United States, Great Britain, France, and Russia, on the other, as affecting American commercial interests in China were numerous. Among the American merchants the pre-treaty traditions of old Canton had entirely disappeared. A new kind of international trade competition had arisen in which the merchants of other nations could bring to their help political and military support. Within the following ten years six other nations,—Germany, Portugal, Denmark, Spain, Holland, and Italy,—were to conclude treaties with China. The result was an intense international rivalry and trade conflict which the American merchants had to face.

[1] Articles IV-VIII.
[2] Article XIV.
[3] Article IX.
[4] Article XXIX.
[5] Supplementary Convention to the treaty of 1858, see Herstlet's *China Treaties*, pp. 552-553.

### Burlingame's Complete-Sovereignty Policy and the Treaty of 1868

Anson Burlingame,[1] the first American Minister to reside in Peking, came to China in 1862. Capable, far-sighted, as well as noble minded, this statesman had a profound sympathy with the Chinese. In 1867 he resigned his post as American minister to serve as envoy of the Chinese Empire to all the Western powers then having treaties with China.

Burlingame's reason for accepting this novel post was not difficult to see. For the benefit not only of China, but also of America and the whole world, it was necessary that the Far East problem should be solved justly and peacefully. The partition of China seemed quite probable if the present "land grabbing" policy of the Westerners was allowed to continue. But in case of such an unfortunate event a wild conflagration in world politics was inevitable. To contribute anything toward the avoidance of such a world calamity was a motive to inspire the best efforts of any man, and Burlingame was fully conscious of the vast issues which might hang on the success of his mission.

The main purpose of Burlingame's Mission was to persuade the Western powers to recognize the sovereign rights of the Chinese Empire, and to treat the Chinese upon a strict principle of equality. That this policy was ultimately the policy of the United States in China is evidenced by the fact that the arrival of Burlingame in America as the head of a Chinese Mission was enthusiastically welcomed by the American people and that soon after his arrival a Sino-American supplementary treaty, usually known as the Burlingame Treaty,[2] was arranged by him with his own government, all eight articles of which were drawn upon

[1] The primary source for Burlingame is: F. W. Williams: *Anson Burlingame and the First Chinese Mission.*
[2] For a full text of this treaty, see Herstlet: *China Treaties*, Vol. II, pp. 554-7.

the principle of the perfect sovereignty of China and treatment of the Chinese upon terms of equality.

Having accomplished its purpose in the United States, the Mission went to London and there secured from the British Government a declaration,[1] which stated that "the Chinese Government is fully entitled to count upon the forbearance of the foreign nations, and the British Government has neither a desire nor intention to apply unfriendly pressure to China."

Thus strengthened by his successful negotiations with the United States and Great Britain, Burlingame moved on to the continent, visiting Paris, Berlin, and arriving at Petrograd in 1870. There he died an untimely death, leaving his work uncompleted.

The Burlingame Mission was the first effort of the United States to establish the Open Door Policy with regard to the territorial integrity of China. Though its immediate results were not great yet the American policies of later times may well have been due in some measure to the effort of this mission.

### Subsequent Revisions of Commercial Treaties in 1880, 1903, and 1920

In general, commercial relations between the United States and China had been fairly well settled by the treaties of 1858 and the additional Articles negotiated in 1868. The treaties which have been concluded since that time are only to supplement but not to supersede them. In conjunction with the "Treaty for the Regulation or Exclusion of Chinese Immigration into the United States," signed at Peking, November 17, 1880, a supplementary commercial treaty between the

[1] The declaration was made by the Minister of Foreign Affairs, Clarendon, so it is commonly known as the Clarendon declaration.
[2] For text, see Herstlet's *China Treaties*, Vol. I, pp. 558-560. This treaty is not a commercial treaty and affects Chino-American trade only indirectly. See *supra*, Chapters III and IV in connection with Chinese Immigration.

two nations was concluded respecting commercial intercourse and judicial procedure,[1] "because of certain points of incompleteness in the existing treaties."[2] This treaty provides a more specific reciprocal pledge in the most-favored-nation treatment concerning tonnage dues, or duties for imports or exports, or coastwise trade,[3] and the absolute prohibition of opium trade between the two countries, the benefits of the favored-nation clause being made not claimable by nationals of either country as against this provision.[4] It also gives Americans a more definite extra-territorial right by providing that controversies arising in China between Americans and Chinese shall be tried by officials of the defendant's nationality in accordance with the law of the defendant's country; but authorized officials of the plaintiff's nationality may take part in the proceedings.[5]

Another occasion for the foreign powers having commercial and other interests in China to revise their existing treaties for the purpose of extending their commercial rights and privileges in China came just at the beginning of the present century, when the Boxer trouble arose in North China. In joint notes regarding conditions for the reestablishment of normal relations between China and the eleven powers involved in this case,[6] December 22, 1900, and January 16, 1901,[7] one provision stated "the Chinese Government will undertake to negotiate the amendments to the treaties of commerce and navigation considered useful by the powers, and upon other subjects connected with com-

[1] For text, see *Ibid*.
[2] Preamble of the Treaty.
[3] Article III.
[4] Article II.
[5] Article IV.
[6] The eleven powers were: Austria-Hungary, Belgium, France, Germany, Great Britain, Italy, Japan, Netherlands, Russia, Spain, the United States.
[7] For a full text of the note see MacMurray, *Treaties and Agreements With and Concerning China*, No. 1901/3, p. 309.

mercial relations, with the object of facilitating them."[1] In view of this provision, the American Government concluded the treaty of 1903 with China.[2] It is to be understood that this treaty is, like that concluded in 1880, to supplement but not to supersede the treaties previously concluded. All the provisions in the previous treaties remain in full effect, except those expressly modified by the present treaty or by other treaties to which the United States is a party.[3] The following is a summary of the document:

(1) Most-favored-nation treatment is pledged in regard to:

(a) All prerogatives, privileges, and immunities to be accorded in either country to diplomatic representatives of the other. (Art. I.)

(b) Attributes, privileges, immunities, and jurisdiction of consular officers of either country in the other. (Art. II.)

(c) Rights and privileges, and immunities of American citizens residing in Chinese ports or places open to foreign residence and trade, as regards their persons and property. (Art. III.)

(d) Duties payable in either country by citizens of the other, with special reference to tariff duties on goods imported. (Art. V.)

(e) Right of citizens, firms, and corporations of the United States to engage in conveyance of passengers and lawful merchandise on navigable inland waters of China. (Art. XII.)

(2) National and most-favored-nation treatment is pledged by China as regards regulations and conditions to be imposed on citizens of the United States desiring to en-

[1] Provision No. 11, *Ibid*, p. 310.
[2] MacMurray, *Ibid.*, 1903/3, pp. 423-452. See also Herstlet, I, 566-78.
[3] Article XVII.

gage in mining operations and other necessary business relating thereto, with special reference to renting of mineral land, payment of royalty, etc.  (Art. VII.)

(3) In connection with tariff duties, the Chinese Government agrees to abolish *Likin* and other transit dues in China, and in compensation, will impose a surtax on imports not to exceed one and one-half times the import duties, and export duties (including surtax) not to exceed 7½ per cent *ad valorem*.  (Procedure detailed.) (Art IV.)  Tariff duties payable by citizens of the United States on goods imported into China are set forth in a schedule which forms a part of the treaty.  But they should be in no case other or higher than those paid by subjects of most-favored nations.  (Art. V.)

(4) Other extensions of American commercial rights and privileges are definitely settled in the following articles :

(a) Americans are permitted to reside, trade, or pursue any lawful avocation in ports or places of China open to foreign residence and trade, and, within localities set apart for foreigners, may rent or purchase buildings, and rent or lease land in perpetuity and build thereon.  (Art. III.)

(b) Right of United States citizens to establish bonded warehouses at open ports for purposes named and subject to conditions stated.  (Art. VI.)

(c) Opening of Mukden and Antung to foreign residence and trade.  (Art. XII.)

All these provisions together with several others are now in full effect except a revision of import tariff as annexed to the supplementary treaty of October 20, 1920,[1] which contains extensive schedules of tariff duties payable on goods imported into China.[2]  Rules concerning customs valuation of merchandise thus imported have also been revised in the

[1] U. S. Treaty Series No. 657.
[2] Annex 1, *Ibid.*

treaty of 1920 to conform to the changed price level at the present time.[1]

### Hay's Open Door Policy—A re-affirmation of the Policy of "Most-favored-Nation" Treatment

The declaration in 1899 of the Open Door Policy by the United States came after the period of a "scramble for concessions" in China.  It was a policy to open the "spheres of interest" that the Powers had hitherto held in China and to put all nations on the same basis commercially as well as politically with a view to maintaining a stable balance of power in the Far East.  In fact it was not to open China's door, because after the wars of 1839, 1858 and 1860 China had already thrown her door wide open.  Up to 1898 there were in China more than thirty ports open to foreign trade, and the different nations were each treated by the Chinese as the most-favored-nation.  So in the real sense of the term it was not China's door that needed to be opened, but rather those of the different powers holding special privileges and creating "spheres of interest" in China.

The balance of power in the Far East at the close of the nineteenth century was unstable to the utmost.  All the European powers wanted to get a foothold in China, and, at the same time, feared their rivals would get ahead of them.  Checks and counter checks were made to protect their own interests on the one hand and to secure "preferential rights" so as to beat their rivals on the other.  In order to establish a firm basis for themselves, all the powers excluded every other and exercised a veto power on the industrial enterprises within their own "spheres."  In addition to the fact that the powers asked the Chinese Government repeatedly to make the so-called "non-alienation declarations," they made arrangements among themselves to define their "spheres of interests."  Such measures, however, could not stop the conflict of interests among the

[1] Annex II, *Ibid.*

powers, but rather intensified it.  Realizing the grave danger of such unlimited competition and emulation, the United States, therefore, stepped at this juncture upon the Far Eastern stage of politics to play a remarkable rôle in eliminating international conflicts and preserving world peace.

Yet the declaration of the Open-Door Policy by the United States was not due solely to the fact that she felt a moral obligation to the civilized world to avert an impending world war.  Aside from all other considerations, the motive underlying this declaration was her own self-interest.  The United States, though having no interest in interfering with political affairs in the Far East, had an intense interest in Chinese trade.  The prospect of American commerce in the East became more bright after the United States purchased the territory of Alaska, acquired the Philippines and proposed the excavation of the Panama Canal.  Should the Western nations be permitted to colonize China, the United States would be the first to suffer from the loss of her immense trade in the future.  John Barrett stated in 1899 the reason why the United States should without further delay proclaim the Open Door Policy[1] as the sole means for protecting American commercial interests in China as follows :

". . . . The tendency of the hour is toward the division of China into spheres of influence of foreign nations, which is only another term for areas of actual supremacy and which will mean the abrogation of the old Tientsin Treaties, which guarantee us absolute freedom of trade throughout China in competition with other nations.  Where spheres of influence are admitted and become general, there may be no portion of this great Empire where we will have equal opportunities with others.  In each sphere we may find preferential duties or rates in favor of the products of the particular land and against us, which, applied to all spheres, will practically exclude us from a fair participation in the immeasurable growing demands of a country that holds 300,000,000 people and reaches over an area of 4,000,000 square miles.

[1] Speech delivered by John Barrett, U. S. Minister to Siam, at the Meeting of the International Commercial Congress in Philadelphia, 1899.  U. S. Bureau of Statistics; *Commercial China*, 1901.

"We have everything to lose and nothing to gain by dividing China into spheres.  Now the development of the markets depends upon our own efforts in fair competition with all the world.  With China divided we must face individual and collective obstacles of all kinds that arise under the new conditions and treaties.

"Were we for a moment to indicate our acquiescence in such spoliation of this great kingdom, there would follow a scramble and rush for China's rich areas that would astonish the world with its wantonness. . . . There would be little doubt that the great opportunity that awaits us in China will be seized, appropriated, and improved by other nations, which will in the end make us a second-rate power in the Pacific."

In this speech the intention of the American Government to make use of the Open Door Policy as a means to preserve her most-favored-nation treatment in China was frankly expressed.  And it was largely due to this underlying motive that the United States was compelled to act.  The policy took effect after John Hay became Secretary of State in September, 1898, though the essence of it can be traced back to 1844.

Further assured by "the formal and often repeated declarations of the British and Japanese Governments in favor of the maintenance throughout China of freedom of trade for the whole world," Secretary Hay, accordingly, sent, on September 6, 1899, to the American Ambassadors at London Berlin, Paris, and St. Petersburg, copies of instructions in relation to the desire of the United States to ask for formal declaration by Great Britain, Germany, France and Russia of the Open Door Policy in the Territory of China.[1]  A few months later he sent the same note to Italy and Japan.  The three propositions as set forth in these notes are reproduced as follows :—

(1) That it will in no wise interfere with any treaty port or any vested interest within any so-called sphere of interest or leased territory it may have in China.

[1] Hay's Correspondence.  Moore, J. B., *Digest of International Law*, Vol V, p. 535 ff.

(2) That the Chinese treaty tariff of the time being shall apply to all merchandise landed or shipped to all such ports as are within such "spheres of interest" (unless they be free ports), no matter to what nationality they may belong, and that duties so leviable shall be collected by the Chinese Government.

(3) That it will levy no higher harbor dues on vessels of another nationality frequenting any port in such sphere than shall be levied on vessels of its own nationality, and no higher railroad charges over lines built, controlled, or operated within its sphere on merchandise belonging to citizens or subjects of other nationalities transported through such "sphere" than shall be levied on similar merchandise belonging to its own nationals transported over equal distances.

Great Britain was the first to accept the proposals of the United States. France followed, then Japan, Italy and later Russia.[1] The response of Germany came last. Nominally, at least, Hay's policy was thus complied with by all the powers concerned.

In the principles of Hay's declaration, we may note three outstanding features. First, it recognized the "spheres of interest" that the powers had hitherto established in China, but in no way were the powers to interfere with the interests vested within their "spheres." Second, it confirmed the sovereignty of China in the collection of the Treaty tariffs within these "Spheres." Third, it did away with economic discriminations which the powers might put on other nations in levying higher harbor dues and railroad fares. It thus put all nations on an equal basis, and was decidedly in accord with the commercial interests of the United States in China.

In order, however, to put the policy on a firm and workable basis, a fundamental prerequisite was required, viz., the independence and territorial integrity of China must be guaranteed. But, meanwhile, Boxer uprisings broke out in

[1] U. S. Foreign Relations, 1899, p. 141.

the Northern Provinces of China; foreign troops rushed to Peking, and Chinese independence reached a critical period. With a view to upholding the policy, the United States first made clear to the other nations the understanding with regard to the territorial integrity and political independence of China before she entered into the settlement of the peace treaty.

After the Boxer trouble all the European nations except Russia seemed for a time to be abiding by the principles of the Open Door. Though Russia had given her pledge to the United States as well as to the world, that the Imperial Government had demonstrated "its firm intention to follow the policy," she did not stand by her words. During and after the Boxer Uprising she attempted through every means to acquire special privileges in Manchuria and to close that territory to all other Nations. Against this Russian aggression Hay made sharp representations by sending notes to the governments of nearly all the European countries and Japan in February, 1902. Without paying any regard to this protest, Russia prosecuted her imperial policy more vigorously than ever. Meanwhile the position of Japan was said to be endangered. For the sake of her own interests Japan declared war upon Russia in 1904. The defeat of Russia at one time eliminated her aggression in North China. But unfortunately Japan came into Manchuria as Russia's successor as a challenger of the Open Door of China.

### The Root-Takahira Declaration

The next chapters in the formal declaration of American policy with reference to the Far East were simply the continuation and re-affirmation of Hay's policy. Whenever the Open Door of China was at stake, the United States seems never to have missed occasion to re-affirm her policy, viz., the Open Door of China or the most-favored-nation treatment of the United States. Thus when Japan after her War with Russia got all the special privileges in Manchuria which Russia previously held, a re-statement of the policy seemed

to the United States to be necessary. This first re-statement came nine years after Hay's exchange of notes. It was in the form of another exchange of notes in November, 1908 between Elihu Root, Secretary of State, and Baron Takahira, Japanese Ambassador at Washington.[1] The notes recognized the growing influence of Japan in the Far East and also the interest of the United States in the Pacific. Their substance was to encourage the free and peaceful development of commerce on the Pacific Ocean, to maintain the *status quo* in that region, to defend the principle of equal opportunity for commerce and industry in China, and to preserve the common interest of all powers—by supporting by all pacific means at their disposal the independence and integrity of China and the principle of equal opportunity for all nations in that empire.

### The Lansing-Ishii Agreement

Nine years passed between the Root-Takahira declaration and a third declaration in 1917 by the Department of State of the United States.[2] The circumstances were different from those in which previous declarations had been made. Japan had entered the World War as an ally of Great Britain. She had wrested Shantung from Germany, and dominated the situation in the Far East. She wanted specific recognition by the United States of her dominant position in Asia. She got it in what was known as the Lansing-Ishii Agreement, an exchange of notes between the American Secretary of State and the Japanese envoy at Washington. This was promulgated in November, 1917. It stated unequivocally that territorial propinquity creates special relations between countries and that, consequently, Japan has special interests in China.

China, of course, was unwilling to be so utterly ignored in

[1] For a full text of the note, see MacMurray, *Treaties and Agreements with and Concerning China*, No. 1908/19, p, 769 ff.
[2] Cf. MacMurray, *op. cit.*, No. 1917/12, p. 1394.

matters affecting her own sovereignty and independence. The Peking Government made public a note in which, following the language of the Lansing-Ishii Agreement "in order to avoid misunderstandings," it declared "the Chinese Government will not allow herself to be bound by any agreement entered into by other nations."

### The Far Eastern Problem after the War and the Reaffirmation of the Open Door Policy in the Washington Conference

The Great War had created in the Far East a very unstable situation. Yet the fundamental issues of the Far Eastern problem in 1920 were virtually the same as those in 1898. They were, first, that China's weakness gave the powers an opportunity to establish various rights in her territory; and second, that a certain power, more imperialistic than the rest, had taken advantage of greater opportunity and established thereby in China a position to the disadvantage of the others—in 1898, that power was Russia, but in 1920 it was Japan. In 1898 the situation was redeemed by the United States by Hay's declaration of the Open Door Policy. In 1920, therefore, it was obvious what the United States should do in conjunction with the interested European nations.

Moreover, the solution of the Far Eastern problem was in fact a prerequisite to the limitation of armaments by the powers. Armaments had been increasing rather than decreasing after the Versailles Peace Conference; their limitation was therefore essential to the effective prevention of a second World War. Realizing the importance of this point, President Harding sent out formal invitations on August 11, 1921, to the Governments of the principal allied and associated powers to participate in the Conference on the Limitation of Armaments and the Discussion of the Pacific and Far Eastern Questions. The Conference was convened on November 11, 1921: nine powers—the United States, Great

Britain, France, Italy, Japan, The Netherlands, Belgium, Portugal, and China participated. The work of this conference is still fresh in our minds and needs no detailed mention here. Suffice it to say that its most important result is the Treaty signed by the nine powers participating in the Conference, with respect to the principles and policies concerning China. In this treaty, the Open Door Policy was for the first time stipulated in an instrument [1] to which China was a party.

Article I of the treaty contains the four fundamental principles according to which the contracting powers should deal with the matters relating to China. It states:

"The contracting powers, other than China, agree:

(1) To respect the sovereignty, the independence, and the territorial and adminstrative integtity of China.

(2) To provide the fullest and most unembarrassed opportunity to China to develop and maintain for herself an effective and stable government.

(3) To use their influence for the purpose of effectually establishing and maintaining the principle of equal opportunity for the commerce and industry of all nations throughout the territory of China.

(4) To refrain from taking advantage of conditions in China in order to seek such special rights or privileges as would abridge the rights of subjects or citizens of friendly states, and from countenancing action inimical to the security of such states."

Article II reinforces the above principles in the following statement:—

"The contracting parties agree not to enter into any treaty, agreement, or understanding, either with one another, or individually or collectively, with any power or powers which should infringe the principles stated in Article I."

Article III makes a careful definition of the Open Door Policy, as follows:—

"With a view to applying more effectively the principles of the

[1] Text of Treaty, see *Washington Conference Minutes*, p. 1621 ff.

Open Door or equality of opportunity in China for the trade and industry of all nations, the contracting powers, other than China, agree that they will not seek, nor support their respective nationals in seeking: (a) any arrangement which might purport to establish in favor of their interests any general superiority of rights with respect to commercial or economic development in any designated region of China; (b) any such monopoly or preference as would deprive the nationals of any other power of right of undertaking any legitimate trade or industry in China, or of participating with the Chinese Government or with any local authority, in any category of public enterprise, or which by reason of its scope, duration or geographical extent is calculated to frustrate the practical application of the principle of equal opportunity."

Article IV dealing with the spheres of influence states:—

"The contracting powers agree not to support any agreements by their respective nationals with each other designed to create spheres of influence or to provide for the enjoyment of mutually exclusive opportunities in designated parts of Chinese territory."

Article V relating to the railways provides:

"China agrees that, throughout the whole of the railways in China, she will not exercise or permit unfair discrimination of any kind. . . . . The contracting powers, other than China, assume a corresponding obligation in respect of any of the aforesaid railways over which they or their nationals are in a position to exercise any control in virtue of any concession, special agreement, or otherwise."

By these articles the Open Door of China is assured and the most-favored-nation treatment of the United States is secured.

### The China Trade Act

The Open Door Policy, so far as it goes, is only a negative measure toward strengthening the hands of American merchants in China. A positive measure taken recently by the American Government toward equalizing the competing power of Americans conducting business in China and toward the further development of American trade with that country is the passage in 1922 by the United States Congress

of a federal trade act, commonly known as the China Trade Act.[1]

"The purpose of this legislation," said Dr. Julius Klein,[2] Director of the Bureau of Foreign and Domestic Commerce, "is to give urgent relief to American merchants engaged in the development of American foreign trade with the Republic of China. Before the European War there were only three or four important American firms located in China. . . . But now the number of those firms, as indicated in the membership of the American Chamber of Commerce of China at Shanghai, has increased from 48 in 1915 to 313 in 1920. . . . In order to make it possible for the United States to enter this expanding field of trade, certain legislative changes are required. It is to meet such needs that the China Trade Act is enacted."

The difficulties which this China Trade Act is intended to overcome were outlined in the report of Mr. Dyer from the Committee on the Judiciary in the House of Representatives and are summarized as follows:

"China is an extraterritorial country, which means that all foreign countries doing business in China must, by treaty, do so under their own laws and regulations. . . . Practically every country interested in the China trade, and this applies especially to our strong competitors, has adopted special laws for the control and promotion of its business in China. America has never done this and as a result American companies doing business in China are subject to the conflicting corporate regulations of the various forty-eight states and our territories. This fact handicaps us specifically as follows:

"First, there is no uniformity, none of the state laws being adapted to foreign trade purposes, and several of the state incorporation laws, being lax, permit the promotion of com-

[1] For a complete text of this Act, see *China Year Book*, 1923, Chapter on China Trade Act.
[2] *The China Trade Act, China Review*, N. Y., October, 1922, p. 116.

panies that are very damaging to our prestige with the Chinese business men.

"Second, our chief competitors in China, the British, Japanese and French, have enacted special regulations governing their companies in China, exempting them from the operation of home income and profits taxation. This places the American firm at a distinct disadvantage, since it cannot build up the necessary reserve to carry over the years of depression and uncertainty. In prosperous years the American firm can meet the competitor, but in slack times it goes bankrupt, while our competitors are going along and getting the business.

"Third, the operation of the home income and excess profits taxation under the various state regulations upon our companies in China, prevents the Chinese business men from forming joint enterprises with American business men. The Chinese are now striving to develop their country industrially and are anxious to cooperate with American merchants who are experienced in the management of industries on a modern basis. Since this Chinese capital coming into an American company is taxed the same as the American capital, the Chinese are thus prevented from co-operating with us.[1]

With a view to remedying these difficulties and promoting cooperation between Americans and Chinese, the Act in its present form makes the following provisions:

(1) It provides federal incorporation of American firms doing business in China under a single set of regulations. This eliminates the confusion resulting from the attempt to apply in China under extra-territorial jurisdiction the conflicting corporate regulations of the forty-eight different states, territories and dependencies.

(2) It provides the machinery for the cooperation of

[1] Re-quoted from C. S. Cooper: *Foreign Trade Markets and Methods*, pp. 273-275.

Chinese and American capital in business and development enterprises by permitting Chinese to own the capital stock of such companies up to 49% of its total and encourages such cooperation by exempting the income of the invested capital of the Chinese from all income and excess profit taxes.

(3) It attempts to provide equality of taxation for the American firm in China in its competition with firms of other nationalities which have been granted similar exemptions by their home governments. The tax exemption is only upon the part of each company's business conducted in China, including Manchuria, Tibet, Mongolia and the British Crown Colony of Hongkong and the Portuguese Province of Macao. The exemption is in proportion to the amount of stock in a China Trade Act Company which is owned by Americans resident in China.

(4) It carries strict provisions covering every kind of activity of a company operating under the act, and also provides penalties for violations. All these strict regulations serve to regulate the conduct of American firms in China and to insure the conduct of a legitimate business in accordance with the laws of the United States and treaties of the United States with China. "By guaranteeing that in the commercial activities of these corporations in China a standard will be maintained, these provisions reflect credit upon the companies themselves as on America as a whole." [1]

In spite of these benefits which are said to be derived from this piece of legislation, the China Trade Act in its present form is not free from criticism even from the point of view of Americans themselves. Some of them attack this act constructively, because they do not feel satisfied with the limited exemption from taxation. They maintain that although the act provides much needed administrative ma-

[1] *A Hail of the China Trade Act*, by C. H. Huston, *Weekly Review of the Far East*, Shanghai, September 20, 1922, p. 148.

chinery for the incorporation of American business in China under an American charter, it falls far short of giving that governmental impetus which American foreign trade in China should have. The act may be considered only as a beginning, a stepping stone. [1] The following paragraph cited from an American Review in China, serves to explain this critical view. [2]

"The China Trade Act was intended to give relief to American business in China in regard to its handicap under the federal income tax requirements. Unfortunately, however, Section 21 of that act, which relates to federal taxation of companies incorporated under it, is so limited as to render that piece of legislation impotent in so far as the promised relief is concerned. Only that portion of the capital invested by American residents in China, but not that invested by those resident outside of that country, is exempt from American taxation. Thus, only purely local enterprises can take advantage of this provision. But, as a matter of fact, American capital in substantial amounts must come from the financial centers of the United States. Branch offices and subsidiary corporations, financed by American enterprises and industries at home will not receive any relief from the act, and as a consequence such act will not be an inducement to the placing of large amounts of capital in China."

There is other opposition to the China Trade Act which is negative in character. It condemns this legislation *in toto* because of the fear of American manufacturers that Chinese capital, incorporated under the law, would use American citizens to procure American protection and exemption from both Chinese and American taxation, so that American industries might suffer from this competition of Chinese capital. [3]

[1] See *A Criticism of the China Trade Act*, by Max Shoop, *Ibid.*, November 18, 1922.
[2] *Ibid.*
[3] *The China Trade Act*. *Far Eastern Review*, Shanghai, May, 1922.

To the Chinese this act is really much more objectionable than it is to Americans. Of course, China is willing to cooperate with American capital in developing her own industry and commerce. Yet if this act confers upon Americans the benefits promised by its originator it does so entirely at the expense of the Chinese. Armed with extra-territorial rights, the act leads Chinese capital into the control of Americans by exempting them both from Chinese and American taxation. No greater injustice could have been done to China both from a political and a financial standpoint, when one understands that by this act China will be deprived of her power to tax her own capital within her own territory. The more such "cooperation" between Chinese and American capital develops, the more the public finance of China is deranged.

Moreover, if some of the American manufacturers should fear that those tax-exempt industrial and commercial concerns incorporated under this law will have too much advantage over similar industries and exporting firms at home, the Chinese conducting business under their own laws and subject to the Chinese system of taxation have ten times more reason to fear that by a wholesale exemption of taxation, the China Trade Act corporation will be able to compete most unfairly in China. Diverting a part of Chinese capital to the hands of Americans and thus enabling them to compete in an unfair manner with businesses still remaining in the hands of Chinese is suicidal to the Chinese. The more of such "cooperation" there is, the less chance for the Chinese to develop their own industry and commerce.

Of course, the Americans can justly argue that they have done no more in this piece of legislation than many of the other countries have done. Yet as a good friend of China, the United States is always expected to do what the other powers are unwilling to do—to aid China and not to aggravate her commercial difficulties. In order to promote their trade, Great Britain, Japan, France and some other powers had, at one time or other, demanded leases and con-

cessions from China, created spheres of influence, and adopted other kinds of colonizing policies. In the face of these unjust aggressions, the United States, instead of following others, has ever clung to her traditional policy of the "Open Door" as a measure to give all nations as well as herself an equal chance in the trade of China. In the present case, America is supposed to secure for her own merchants the same privileges of tax exemption as enjoyed by her competitors. But the same end may be attained by advocating the general repeal of the existing extra-territoriality in China, so that trade of all nationalities would come under the same provisions of Chinese law, either taxed or exempt on the same basis. By so doing, the United States would have not only preserved her traditional magnanimous policy but would also have had another chance of securing the good will of the Chinese as she had before when the "Open Door" policy was declared a quarter of a century ago. The Chinese business men and capitalists as well as the government would be much more willing to cooperate with American capital invested in China when they see not harm but benefit is to follow from such cooperation. As any "cooperation" under the working of the China Trade Act, however, would work to the detriment of the existing financial, juristic, industrial, as well as commercial interests of China, patriotic Chinese citizens will undoubtedly do little to aid such "cooperation."

## CHAPTER XVI
### AMERICAN INVESTMENTS IN CHINA

It goes without saying that China with its immense resources awaiting development is a remarkably good field for investment. Being short of funds of her own, she naturally welcomes the inflow of foreign capital. Half a century ago the development of America was achieved largely through the aid of European funds. Now the United States, besides having paid her foreign debts thus incurred, has become the richest country in the whole world. Foreign investments are also responsible for the recent development of South America. Without the importation of European and American capital the South American states could never have provided themselves so quickly and adequately with the means of railway construction and land improvement, and the volume of their foreign trade could not have attained its present size. The case with China at present is just the same as with the two Americas a few decades ago. The writer has already given the reader some idea of the opportunities for foreign investment in that country, and stated how the expansion of China's foreign trade depends upon the development of her agricultural, mineral and industrial resources. These incredibly rich resources can hardly be developed in the near future if China can not get financial help from outside.

Everyone would like to see an increase in the volume of China's foreign trade, because it would be profitable both to the foreign countries trading with China and to China herself. But it is obvious that China's foreign trade can not expand to any appreciable extent, unless her internal development is achieved first. As a matter of fact, the former is a mere function of the latter. Therefore, any nation desirous of carrying on more trade with China can accomplish this end only by extending her the required financial help.

298

Now the United States has at her disposal the amplest means for investment in foreign lands that any nation has 'ever had. American industry has already attained its adult stage. Further investment of capital will be handicapped by the working of the law of diminishing returns. American capitalists are, therefore, compelled to seek better opportunities in foreign countries. For the last few decades, South America has furnished such a field of good opportunities. But, that continent is becoming less promising for American investors and traders, as its industry, agriculture and commerce are becoming more fully developed.

As the European War has devastated many parts of Central Europe, it would seem that the United States could find plenty of opportunity for her surplus capital in the reconstruction work of many European countries. But the fact that the extreme social and political unrest in Germany, Russia and many of the Balkan States is not likely to end in the immediate future is a discouraging factor in the estimation of American financiers. Moreover, Europe has already become heavily indebted to this country, and any further extension of credit by the latter is extremely unsafe so far as future repayment is concerned. It is only natural, therefore, that American investors should turn their attention to the Far East in seeking the most promising field for their future commitments.

China, on the other hand, naturally looks to America for financial help in the development of her industry and commerce, in preference to any other country. Formerly, most of the European powers were constantly in a state of keen competition with each other for a share in the financing of China, but since the war, this condition has completely changed. With the tremendous task of reconstruction now in their hands, all of the European powers, with the single exception, perhaps, of Great Britain, have neither surplus funds nor surplus energy to be diverted to the improvement of industrial China. Japan has just suffered an unprecedented catastrophe from the severest earthquake ever

known. Her loss in this calamity was so great that she is now in no better position than France or Belgium after they emerged from the war. Certainly, her own reconstruction work will engage for many years to come the whole energy and resources of her people. China, therefore, can hardly expect any help from Japan, even if she were willing to accept it.

Is it not natural, therefore, that China, with no other country in a situation to give her financial help, should in the near future at least, look to America for means of exploiting her undeveloped wealth?

Since the early stage of American and Chinese commercial intercourse, Americans have been fully aware of the good opportunities offered in China. At different times many attempts have been made to take advantage of these opportunities, but so far, little, if any, success has been achieved. The financing of China's future development has long been an extremely confusing topic of international politics rather than a straightforward matter of business interest; and the writer regards it as very regrettable that the United States should have become involved in the financial complications with the result that, in spite of its past and present advantageous situation in China, it has made no more headway in the matter of financing industrial China than a country in a less favorable position. It is hoped that the United States will cast off the fetters and chains of international politics which it has put on itself as well as on other countries and China in the method of financing. Should these chains and fetters remain, there will, in the writer's opinion, be no hope of successful financing such as would result in any appreciable expansion of American trade with China.

In the following pages the writer will attempt to give a brief historical sketch of the various American attempts at making investments in China. This chapter might more appropriately be called the history of the failure of the United States in financing China. It is not difficult to see from these pages why America has so far failed in her en-

deavor to the regret of China as well, perhaps, as of herself. With the experience of the past, it is earnestly to be hoped that the United States will make certain changes in her financial policy in China in order to facilitate future investments over there to the mutual advantage of both countries.

### 1. Early Financing of Railways in China

(a) Canton-Hankow Railway Concession. Among the various opportunities in China as a field for foreign investment, railway construction first attracted the attention of foreign investors. From the close of the Sino-Japanese war until the Boxer Uprising in 1900 the contest to secure railway concessions in China was one of the chief features of the "Battle of Concessions" waged among many European nations.[1] Concessions of railway construction in certain selected parts of China were considered by the powers as an effective means of creating and insuring their respective "spheres of influence." It was not long before the Americans perceived that without taking a share in railway construction they would have an uneven chance for Chinese trade.[2] They, therefore, arranged with the Chinese Government to secure a concession of the Canton-Hankow Railway. This concession was granted to American capitalists in April, 1898, under an agreement executed after due Imperial sanction by the Chinese Minister at Washington.[3] The road was to connect Canton, the great commercial center of South China, with Hankow, the great interior commercial center in Central China. It is about six hundred miles in length and passes through a rich and important agricultural section,

[1] For a historical account of Chinese Railways, see P. H. Kent, *Railway Enterprise in China.*
[2] U. S. Bureau of Statistics (Treasury Department), *Commercial China*, 1901, under the Section of Railway.
[3] *Ibid.* For the texts of the contracts of April 14, 1898, and July 13, 1900, granting the concession for this road, see Rockhill: *China Treaties*, p. 252.

having a population equal to that of the United States at that time, and at its center taps an important iron and coal area.[1] This project at one time constituted what today may be considered the only actual railway concession ever held by American interests in China.[2]

In fact the Canton-Hankow Railway project can hardly be regarded as a concession, but rather as a loan and construction agreement for the building of railways for the Chinese Government.[3] But owing to the fact that the American contractors were not energetic in pushing the work, the project was taken over by the Chinese Government.[4] The failure to complete this project was no doubt very regrettable from the American point of view.

*(b) The Manchurian Railway Schemes of Harriman and Knox.* A second attempt to finance railroad construction in China was made in 1905 by the late Edward H. Harriman, the American railroad magnate.[5] After the close of the Russo-Japanese war Japan was extending its influence in Manchuria at the expense of China and the other non-aggressive powers. The United States, wishing to maintain China's sovereignty in Manchuria and to preserve the open door, suggested to the powers the "commercial neutralization" of the Manchuria railways under an international administration.[6] This proposal was made plainly for the reason that the United States sought to extend its industrial and financial interests in China, more particularly in Manchuria, where she already had an important trade. A few

[1] *Ibid.*
[2] U. S. Bureau of Foreign and Domestic Com., Special Agent Series No. 180. *Far Eastern Markets for Railroad Materials,* p. 109.
[3] *Ibid.* For the text of the agreement between the Chinese Government and American-Chinese Development Company to sell the Hankow-Canton Railway, see MacMurray, Treaties and Agreements with and Concerning China, No. 1905/7, Vol. I, p. 519 ff.
[4] United States Foreign Relations, 1910, pp. 231-269.
[5] See, c. s. "Foreign Trade of China," p. 231.

days after the signing of the Treaty of Portsmouth between Japan and Russia in September, 1905, Mr. Harriman concluded a memorandum agreement with the Japanese Representative, Marquis Ito, providing for the American lease of the South-Manchurian Railway which was ceded by Russia to Japan.[1] This line was to be a part of Mr. Harriman's projected belt line of the world. But owing to popular opposition in Japan, the negotiations did not bear fruit and nothing was heard of Mr. Harriman's scheme until 1908.

In December, 1908, negotiations were opened at New York in regard to the Chinese Eastern Railway, which the Russian Government was willing to sell to American financiers, provided Japan would agree to sell the South Manchurian line.[2] But in 1909 Mr. Harriman died and the purchase of the railway was not effected.

In the next year, 1909, however, Mr. Knox, United States Secretary of State, submitted simultaneously to the British, German, Russian, Japanese and Chinese Governments a scheme for the neutralization of the Manchurian railways, but without having previously received Russia's and Japan's acquiescence.[3] The purport of this scheme was a proposal that the powers addressed should authorize the organization of an international syndicate to buy out the Russian and Japanese railway interests in Manchuria. He suggested further that if the powers were unwilling to join in this general neutralization scheme, they should at least unite in the financing and construction of the Chinchow-Aigun Railway.[4] This scheme had a flavor more political than industrial and commercial, and thus aroused the suspicion of Russia and Japan, and was finally rejected by them.[5] Had either Harriman's or Knox's scheme been put into operation,

[1] United States Foreign Trade Relations, 1910, *op. cit.* A detailed account of these negotiations is given in J. O. P. Bland: "Recent Events and Present Policies in China."
[2] *Ibid.*, p. 318.
[3] J. O. P. Bland, *op. cit.*
[4] *Ibid.*, pp. 317 ff.

American capital would have played a significant rôle in Manchuria, North China and Korea. It is possible that American-Japanese cooperation in the Pacific region would have resulted and the situation of the Far East might have been very different from what it is now.

*(c) Chinchow-Aigun Railway Project.* In 1907 the Chinese Government negotiated with the United States, through the American Consul General at Mukden, for the creation of a Manchurian Bank. This institution, financed by American capital, was to be the financial agent of the Manchurian Government, and was to undertake, together with British financiers, the construction of a line from Chinchow to Aigun as well as other important enterprises for the development of the commerce and industry of Manchuria.[1] Subsequently, in 1909, a preliminary agreement to provide for the financing, construction and operation of this road was signed between the Viceroy of Manchuria on behalf of the Chinese Government, an American banking group, composed of J. P. Morgan and Company, Kuhn, Loeb and Company, The First National Bank and the National City Bank, all of New York, and a British contractor, Pauling and Company.[2] But protests made in behalf of other nationalities, especially Japan, at once followed.[3] As a consequence, no final agreement was ever concluded.

### 2. Financing of Canal Improvement and River Conservation

Since 1910, following a disastrous flood in the Huai district in the northern part of Kiangsu Province, the Chinese Government, at the suggestion of the American National Red Cross, made an attempt to introduce modern scientific

[1] Overlach, T. W., *Foreign Financial Control in China,* New York, 1919, p. 206.
[2] For text see MacMurray, 1909/2, p. 800 ff.
[3] For these protests, see *The Forum,* N. Y., July, 1910, pp. 74-83.

methods of improving waterways, especially that of the Huai River and the connecting Grand Canal, so as to give them a more efficient outlet and thus to prevent further calamities by floods.[1] Through the effort of this American institution, a loan of three million dollars was arranged in the early part of 1916 between the Chinese National Conservancy Bureau and the American International Corporation for the improvement of that portion of the Grand Canal which is included in the Huai River Conservancy.[2] The agreement was signed on May 13, 1916.[3] At the same time the Provincial Government of Shantung also drew up a scheme for improving the northern part of the Grand Canal by contracting with the same corporation for another loan of three million dollars.[4] But since that time neither of these agreements has been heard from.

On November 20, 1917, after a long series of most complicated and difficult negotiations, another loan agreement was signed between the same parties.[5] This agreement provided for the issue of six million dollars worth of bonds for the improvement of the Grand Canal south of Tientsin in the Provinces of Chihli and Shantung. A party of American engineers arrived in China in September, 1918, and at once began to make the survey and collect the necessary engineering data.[6] It is more than three years since the return of these engineers but there is little indication that the work will be started in the near future. The failure of China to get American help is said to have been due largely to the unstable and chaotic conditions of Chinese political affairs, which discouraged foreign investment.

[1] For text of the agreement, see MacMurray, No. 1910/6; p. 1310 ff.
[2] *China Year Book,* Tientsin, 1923, p. 547.
[3] For text, see MacMurray, No. 1916/6, p. 1304.
[4] *Ibid.*, No. 1916/5, p. 1287.
[5] *China Year Book,* Tientsin, p. 547. For text see MacMurray, No. 1916/5, p. 1296 ff.
[6] *Ibid.*

### 3. Financing Other Industrials in China

*(a) The Proposition for the Exploration and Operation of Petroleum Oil Fields.* Since an early period it has been known that petroleum exists in Chihli and Shensi provinces. With a view to exploiting this source of wealth, a contract was signed in February, 1914, between the Chinese Government and the Standard Oil Company of New York for the exploration and operation of these oil fields.[1] According to the agreement, the company was to send experts to make a detailed investigation of the oil fields, and if it should be demonstrated to be profitable, a Sino-American Joint Stock Company was to be organized for its operation.

Subsequently, in 1914, investigations were conducted at many places but according to the Standard Oil experts the deposit was a shallow one. Seven wells were sunk in succession and although oil was seen no oil spring was discovered.[2] In the spring of 1916, boring operations were therefore stopped.[3] Accordingly, the agreement previously entered into was cancelled.

*(b) Contract for Erection of Wireless Stations.* On January 8, 1921, an agreement was made between the Chinese Ministry of Communications and the Federal Telegraph Company, an American corporation, for the erection and operation, as a joint enterprise of the Chinese Government and the American company, of stations for wireless communication.[4] The agreement provided for the erection of a very high-power wireless station at Shanghai, and less powerful stations at Peking, Hankow, Canton and Harbin. It so happened that the Chinese Government had in previous years concluded contracts with the Mitsui Company of Japan

[1] For full text, see MacMurray, No. 1914/3, pp. 1109 ff.
[2] Note of Ministry for Foreign Affairs of China to the American Legation at Peking, April 7, 1917. See MacMurray, p. 1111.
[3] *Ibid.*
[4] *China Year Book*, Tientsin, 1923, Chapter XVII, p. 440.

and the Marconi Wireless Telephone and Telegraph Corporation of Great Britain for the erection of some other wireless stations in China, and had agreed to give them certain time privileges.[1] Both of these companies, through their respective governments, sent protests to the Chinese government against this agreement with the American company, claiming that by granting to the American company the right of participation, their rights under prior contracts were violated. The American Government, however, declined to recognize the validity of such claims by reason of their contravening the treaty rights of American citizens in China and the principle of the "Open Door," and assured the Federal Wireless Corporation of its support.[2] The dispute has been going on for more than two years, and is still pending (1924). The Radio Corporation of America is now behind this activity and it therefore is indicative of the development of an intense American interest in trans-Pacific communications backed by the American State Department.

### 4. American Share in the International Financing of China

In connection with the financing of Chinese enterprises by individual foreign countries, both China and foreign financiers have been very frequently confronted with the difficulties which result from international financial competition, with its struggle for "spheres of interest" and national "control." Due to mutual jealousy and therefore frequent conflict between the capital interests of the different powers, most of the financing propositions have proved unsuccessful. Realizing such a difficulty, those powers that have commercial relations with China in the early years of the present century came to a mutual understanding that international cooperation, instead of competition, should be the guiding

[1] *Op. cit.,* p. 441.
[2] See correspondence between the Chinese Minister at Washington and the United States Secretary of State, *Ibid.,* p. 441.

principle in the financing of China. Mr. Knox's plan to internationalize the railways in Manchuria[1] is an early evidence of American willingness to enter into such cooperation.

*(a) Hukuang Railway Loan.* The first international railway agreement was made in 1908 between the Chinese Government and the Anglo-German banking concerns, for the construction of the Tientsin-Pukow Railway.[2] Negotiations were conducted in the winter of 1908-1909 between the British, German and French banking groups and their respective governments with a view to reaching an understanding as to the degree of "control" to be demanded from China as a condition precedent to future loans.[3] These negotiations were for a loan to construct both the Canton-Hankow and Hankow-Szechuan lines, or, as they are called collectively, the Hukuang Railways.[4] At this point the United States government interfered on the ground that American financiers had secured, in 1904, a promise from the Chinese Government that in the event of the floating of foreign loans for the Hupeh section of the Szechuan road China would consult first the United States and Great Britain.[5] Inasmuch as the United States had not officially relinquished her right to participation, the American Government now demanded the admission of an American banking group. Mr. Knox, then Secretary of State, supported his demand by pointing to the "menace to foreign trade likely to ensue from the lack of proper sympathy between the powers most vitally interested in the preservation of the principle of equality of commercial opportunity," adding that "the Government of the United States regards full and frank cooperation as best

[1] *Supra.*
[2] For text see MacMurray, No. 1908/1, p. 684 ff. For a detailed description of this agreement, see T. W. Overlach, *Foreign Financial Control in China*, N. Y., 1919, pp. 221 ff.
[3] W. Straight, *China's Loan Negotiations*, p. 113.
[4] MacMurray, No. 1911/5, p. 880.
[5] See United States Foreign Relations, 1909 (Vol. 5704), pp. 144 ff.

calculated to maintain the open door and the integrity of China and . . . the formation of a powerful American, British, French and German financial group would further that end."[1]

Due to the personal interference of President Taft,[2] the "Tripartite Banks" invited the American group, in May, 1910, to join them in the combination which they had effected the year before. This invitation was accepted and an inter-group agreement was signed in November, 1910.[3] The final agreement for the Hukuang loan was signed with China by representatives of the four-nation syndicate on May 20, 1911. It provided for a loan of £6,000,000,[4] which was to be obtained by selling the Imperial Chinese Government Five Per Cent Hukuang Railway's Sinking Fund Gold Loan. The construction of the Hukuang railways, however, made but little progress owing to the political and financial state of China during the following revolution.

*(b) The Currency Reform Loan.* The notoriously bad and confusing silver currency system in China has long worked to the extreme hardship of Chinese as well as foreign merchants in their trade dealings. To facilitate their transactions, therefore, some American business men expressed their willingness to extend China financial help to effect an early monetary reform. A preliminary agreement was therefore arranged, in 1910, between the Chinese Government and an American group composed of the four big banking houses to issue and sell America Chinese Government Sinking Fund Gold Bonds to the amount of fifty million dollars.[5] But a little later, at the instance of the American group and

[1] *United States Foreign Relations*, 1909 (Vol. 5704), p. 152.
[2] See Overlach, *op. cit.,* Ch. VII.
[3] For text, see MacMurray, 1910/5, p. 828 ff; also see the *Far Eastern Review*, Vol. XIII, p. 83.
[4] MacMurray, 1911/5, p. 866; also see *Far Eastern Review*, Vol. XIII, Suppl. August, 1911.
[5] MacMurray, No. 1911/2, p. 851.

upon the solicitation of the American Government, the Chinese Government consented to the participation of the British, French and German banks, and the so-called "Four-Power Consortium" was thus formed.[1] On April 15, 1911, a formal agreement was reached between the Chinese Government and the Consortium, authorizing the issue by the four groups of bankers of a Five Per Cent Sinking Fund Gold Loan for an aggregate amount of £10,000,000.[2] However, the outbreak of the Chinese Revolution in August, 1911, against the Manchu Dynasty intervened before satisfactory arrangements had been completed for the flotation of the loan under the terms of the agreement. Under the altered conditions resulting, the "Four-Power Consortium" postponed further action on this project, in order to undertake a reorganization loan required by the newly established republican government.

*(c) The Reorganization Loan.* After the outbreak of the Revolution in 1911, the Chinese Republican Government faced a serious financial stringency and was compelled to ask help from outsiders. On February 27, 1912, Mr. Tang Shao-yi, then Premier of China, discussed with the Quadruple Syndicate the question of a general Reorganization Loan.[3] To enforce the broadest possible internationalization of Chinese financing, the syndicate decided at this time to strengthen its position by inviting the cooperation of Russian and Japanese financiers.[4] But the terms as proposed by the Six-Power Syndicate to the Chinese Government as a basis for making the loan were highly objectionable to China. Some of them were briefly: (1) that China should

[1] See MacMurray, footnote on p. 851.
[2] For full text, see MacMurray, No. 1911/2, pp. 841 ff.
[3] For further details of the negotiations, see Overlach, *op. cit.*, pp. 236-260.
[4] An agreement between the banking groups of the Six Powers was signed, in regard to this loan, June 18, 1912. See MacMurray, 1913/5, p. 1021 ff.

herself create a system of audit in which foreigners should be employed with powers not merely advisory, but also executive so as "to ensure the effective expenditure of loan funds" borrowed for such purposes as might be specified in the loan agreement; (2) that the administration of the Chinese salt tax, which was to be the security of the loan, should be put under foreign supervision, and (3) that for a period of five years China should appoint the group's financial agents to assist in the administration of its work of reorganization.[1]

It was during this time, when very strong opposition to such unendurable terms of foreign supervision was coming from nearly all parts of China, that the sextuple group dwindled into the quintuple group, as a result of the withdrawal of American banking interests from participation.[2] This was brought about by the same sort of opposition from the Wilson Administration to the so-called "dollar policy" which had been initiated under the Taft regime. In a very clear statement, permeated by an admirable spirit of sympathy for the Chinese people, President Wilson announced that the Government of the United States would not accept any responsibility for or exercise any authority in connection with the Six Power Loan to the Chinese Republic.[3] President Wilson felt that the American Government was not justified in taking an official or even a semi-official part in such a loan. He criticized some of the conditions of the six power loan, but his main objection is found in the following words:

"The responsibility on its (American Government's) part which would be implied in requesting the bankers to undertake the loan might conceivably go the length, in some un-

[1] W. Straight: *China's Loan Negotiation*, p. 142 ff.
[2] See *China Year Book*, 1914, p. 379 ff.
[3] For text of the statement, see MacMurray, No. 1913/5, p. 1025; also see *Commercial and Financial Chronicle*, Vol. 96, pp. 824-826, 1913.

happy contingency, of forcible interference in the financial and even the political affairs of that great Oriental state just now awakening to a consciousness of its power and its obligations to its people. . . . The responsibility on the part of our government implied in the encouragement of a loan thus secured and administered is plain enough, and is obnoxious to the principles upon which the government of our people rests."[1]

The American group thereupon formally withdrew in March, 1913, from further participation in the currency loan and the Reorganization loan. But in spite of this withdrawal, the American Government has maintained its interest in the project of China's currency reform.[2]

*(d) Japan's Proposal for Cooperation with America.* The outbreak of the World War in 1914 enabled Japan to increase her influence in China very rapidly by taking over the German holdings and by forcing the infamous Twenty-One Demands upon the Chinese Government. She hoped to control the future industrial development of China and to monopolize the profits therefrom, but in doing so, a huge sum of capital was required which Japan was not in an easy position to supply. The Japanese, therefore, advanced a plan of cooperation with American capital. In the fall of 1915 Baron Yei-ichi Shibusawa, the leading financier of Japan, was delegated to the United States as a national spokesman.[3] While in America the Japanese financier repeatedly told the Americans that they should cooperate with Japan in the "peaceful exploitation" of China. He also pointed out to the American capitalists

[1] C. S. See: *The Foreign Trade of China*, p. 246 (N. Y., 1919).
[2] See MacMurray, *op. cit.*, also see W. W. Willoughby, *Foreign Rights and Interests in China*, p. 99 ff.
[3] See MacMurray, footnote on p. 851. The Reorganization Loan was finally signed at Peking on April 26, 1913, between the Chinese Government and the banking groups of the five nations. For text see MacMurray, 1913/5, p. 1007 ff. For further details, see Overlach, *op. cit.*, p. 257 ff.

the great importance and absolute necessity of cooperation between American capital and Japanese management. For if the United States should fail to adopt this plan, he candidly told the Americans "Our activities in the Chinese market might lead to hostile competition, mutual distrust and bitter animosity which might be mutually disastrous."[1] This means that today, if America wants to invest money in China she will have to do it through Japan. If she should attempt to enter China independently, trouble might ensue.

But both the Americans and the Chinese looked upon this proposal with much disfavor. It was said Japan was not aiming at cooperation, but rather at exclusion.[2] Japan knew that for the development of China foreign capital was absolutely necessary, but if money was permitted to enter there freely from America or Europe, it would lessen her increasing control over China. Japan, however, could not provide the required capital and she fully realized that her position was not yet such as would enable her to slam the door hard and fast against entrepreneurs from the West. Therefore, she proposed to America, and also to Europe, that if they wished to participate in the great economic transformation of China, they should place their investment there under Japanese control.

*(e) The New International Banking Consortium Under American Leadership.* Although the United States had refused to accept Japan's proposal, she realized that it was equally unwise to give a free hand to Japan in loaning money to China. The Six Nation Consortium became a quintuple group after the withdrawal of the United States; but with the outbreak of the war and the downfall of the Czar's government German and Russian interests ceased to exist in the consortium. This left only Great Britain, France and Japan.[3]

[1] *Far Eastern Review*, Shanghai, May, 1915, pp. 487-491.
[2] *Ibid.*, p. 248.
[3] W. W. Willoughby: *Foreign Rights and Interests in China*, p. 499 ff.

But during and immediately after the war, Great Britain and France had become so exhausted financially that they were unable to extend any loan to China. As a matter of fact Japan had been monopolizing the privilege as a lender and had made many loans to finance the warring Chinese factions both to the harm of China herself and to the disadvantage of other investors.

The United States, therefore, wanted to correct the monopolistic situation of Japan, when China needed outside financial help to declare war against the Central Powers. In July, 1918, the Washington government approved a loan to China to be made by a syndicate of American bankers, in association with the bankers of Great Britain, France and Japan in order that China might be enabled "so to equip herself as to be of more specific assistance in the war." [1] An agreement was entered into between the American bankers and their Department of State. The most salient feature of this agreement was that the Department gave assurances to these financiers that if the terms of the loan were accepted by the United States and China, the government would be willing to aid in every way possible, to make prompt and vigorous representations, and to take every possible step to insure the execution of equitable contracts made in good faith by its citizens in foreign lands, in order to encourage and facilitate the free intercourse between American citizens and foreign states which was mutually advantageous. [2] This was the most positive assurance of governmental backing to private investment business, and was then regarded as containing great promise for the extension of American trade and investment in China and for the securing of a place in the Chinese market in the severe post-bellum competition for trade.

With a view to maintaining the Open Door policy perma-

[1] Cf. *The Commercial and Financial Chronicle*, N. Y., Vol. 107, 1918, p. 445.
[2] *Ibid.* Also cf. *The Annalist*, N. Y., Vol. XII, p. 123.

nently, and assuring the "big powers" an equal chance in China, the United States Government went a step further in the proposal to organize the so-called New International Banking Consortium. In 1913 President Wilson announced the withdrawal of the United States from the Six-Power Consortium for reasons already stated. But after only five years the Wilson Administration itself adopted a scheme essentially the same as that so justly criticized by the President.

The New International Banking Consortium was proposed by the United States in 1919. The governments that the United States approached and finally agreed to the scheme were Great Britain, France and Japan. [1] The purpose of this new institution was to finance all future loans to China, industrial as well as political, with, as the American bankers stated it, a view "to help China in the establishment of her great utilities such as the building of her railways, canals, etc., thereby assisting in stabilizing China economically and financially, and making that field a safer one for the initiative of our citizens in private enterprises in commerce, industry, et cetera." [2] One of the conditions was held by the American bankers to be that "there should be a relinquishment by the members of the group either to China or to the group of any options to make loans which they now hold, and all loans to China by way of them should be considered as Four-Power group business." [3]

With regard to government support, the American proposal to pledge "each government to the support of its respective national group rather than to the consortium collectively," was approved by all participating nations. [4]

[1] For full documents and correspondence between the United States and other countries, *China Year Book*, 1921.
[2] Secretary Hughes's letter to the American Group of the Chinese Consortium, March 23, 1921.
[3] American Bankers' Letter to Secretary Lansing, July 8, 1918.
[4] For the full correspondence and negotiations between the powers, cf. *Documents Relating to the International Banking Consortium*, published by Peking Bankers' Assoc., China, 1921.

However plausible this scheme for the international financing of China might seem to be, the new consortium has remained practically moribund since its formation in 1920. [1] It has not yet concluded a single successful negotiation for any large scale enterprise in China. The five-year duration of the consortium as originally stipulated in the agreement will soon expire, and we may perhaps with some certainty prophesy that the scheme will, like most of the other international propositions, end in complete failure.

The failure of this international scheme may be largely accounted for by the opposition of China to the method of financing, and her refraining from asking any loan of the Consortium. It is not to be understood that in her refusal to have any dealing with the Consortium, China is ungrateful to America for the latter's desire to help her. While it is honestly believed by the Chinese people that the new financial machinery set up under the leadership of the United States might ultimately work for the benefit of China, it is not surprising that the Chinese people fear the possible grave consequences of such a method of financing that has the backing of the four controlling political bodies of the world. Much of their opposition is, in the last analysis, not so much to the Consortium as to the fact that it may tend to infringe upon China's sovereign rights by taking China's public finances under foreign supervision, and by granting the land tax of the nation as security for the loan. So long as foreign investment has more of a political than a business flavor, the Chinese will be unwilling to accept the loaning terms, feeling as they do that it is better to remain in national poverty than to suffer from a foreign financial yoke.

Secondly, the Chinese people object strongly to the monopolistic character of the Consortium. Had the Consortium laid down new rules for the game of international finance in China on a basis of free, fair and friendly competition untainted with diplomatic pressure or political co-

ercion, it could not have failed to be "a potential instrument for good," to use the expression of Sir Charles Addis, representative of the British banking group in the consortium. [1] The different banking groups went ahead to combine all their so-called "vested interests" in a consortium of four powers, only at the expense of an open door for other nations. Although such a common pool would insure for the four national banking groups the privilege of equal opportunity, it could be attained only at the expense of China's right of free bargaining. Furthermore, in designating "loans of a public character" emanating from the Chinese Government as its exclusive option, the Consortium has in effect substituted for the regional spheres of interest a fiscal sphere of interest. It is an absolute banking combination, a credit monopoly, so complete and overwhelming that little freedom would be left to China as a money borrower.

The practical business situation, therefore, is that the whole large-scale development of new hopeful, helpful business for the world has been stopped in China. Many enterprises in China are impatiently waiting for outside investments to start business. Yet no one in China is willing to see his government financed by the said Consortium. Commenting upon this situation, the New York Globe made the following laconic yet pertinent statement:

"The four great governments—American, British, Japanese and French—have put the Consortium at the door of China. The consortium holds the door. It cannot open it, because the Chinese do not like its method of opening it. What we have is the consortium as door-keeper and the door fast shut." [2]

[1] In his speech at the Annual Dinner of the China Association, *Chinese Students' Monthly*, N. Y., *op. cit.*
[2] Urging Americans to leave Consortium to Develop Trade with the Chinese. New York *Globe*, reprinted by *China Review*, New York, December, 1921, p. 395.

Having this difficult situation in view, the New York Globe also raises the following questions:

"Might it not pay the United States, and might it not pay China, and might it not pay the world if the United States would get out of this theoretically beautiful but apparently practically useless financial internationalism and go into China with its own American financial resources and there play its own American financial hand without unfairness to other nations but with a vigorous and prompt development of its own interests and of China's interests?" [1]

### 5. Recent Prospects of American Investment in Private Enterprises in China: The Opportunity of an Edge Law Bank in the Far East

Up to the present nearly all the large-scale attempts to finance China have been of a public nature. They consist of dealings either between the American and Chinese Governments or between the Chinese Government and the American banking group. Little has been done by American individual businessmen to finance or establish private industrial enterprises in China. The reason for their inactivity is twofold. First, it is contrary to the traditional policy of the United States to have her nationals establish industrial enterprises in foreign countries. Although by the treaty of 1880 China gave to Great Britain the privilege of establishing manufacturing concerns in her territory, the United States declined to claim the same right by the most-favored-nation clause. The reason for this procedure was given by President Arthur in his annual message of December 4, 1883:

"While it is the duty of the Government to see that our citizens have the full enjoyment of every benefit secured by treaty, I doubt the expediency of leading in a movement to constrain China to admit an interpretation which we have only an indirect treaty right to exact. The transferance to China of American capital for the employment there of

[1] Op. cit.

Chinese labor would in effect inaugurate a competition for the conduct of markets now supplied by our home industries." [1]

Secondly, the United States has lacked the mechanism to facilitate and encourage private investment in foreign lands. Until recently in 1914, American national banks were not allowed to establish branches in foreign lands, and those engaging in foreign banking operations were not allowed to sell their bonds in the home country nor to discount their commercial paper at the Federal Reserve Bank. As a result the American individual investors found much difficulty in putting their money into foreign private enterprises, especially when the latter were of small size and not well known in the world stock market. [2]

Recently, however, the necessity of making investments in private business in China has become obvious. As the nationals of Great Britain and Japan and, before the World War, of Germany, have invested a great deal in private industries in China, the United States is compelled to follow their track, or she will lose her share in the international competition for China's trade. On the other hand, private investment in China is largely non-competitive with American home industry.

In order to facilitate private investment and financing in foreign countries, the United States Congress passed in 1919 a special act known as the Edge Law, providing for the incorporation of banks to engage in foreign banking and financial operations. This act provides for the creation of a system of banks as a part of the American Federal banking machinery, authorized to deal in foreign securities, in addition to their equally important function as financiers of

[1] Moore: A Digest of International Law, V, p. 450. Also cf. United States Foreign Relations, 1883, p. XIII, 1887, pp. 87-92.
[2] For a fuller discussion on this point, cf. Reed: The Development of the Federal Reserve Policy, 1922.

foreign trade. [1] The need and the opportunity for such an American bank in China has long been apparent because it is required to fulfill in China the functions of what are known [2] in America as investment banks or bond houses.

"There are two methods by which the investment operation may be handled. The bank may either buy Chinese bonds, for example, and sell them direct to investors in America, or it may take such securities and pledge them as collateral, issuing its own debentures." [3]

"The Law authorizes the ownership of Edge Law Bank stock by foreign individuals or corporations up to 49% of the total. This makes it possible for such a bank, while holding an American Federal Charter, to be an international cooperative enterprise. It would allow Chinese banks, manufacturers, exporters, and importers to become stockholders along with similar American interests in financing the industrial and commercial enterprises in China, and would also allow Chinese capital to share in the profits arising from the industrial development of their own country." [3]

Such a method of private financing is the very kind that the Chinese most welcome. Yet the extent of the success of such an investment mechanism has still to be demonstrated. Of course Chinese capitalists have always been desirous of cooperating with Americans in developing the resources of their own country. But as long as extra-territoriality in China remains, thoughtful and careful Chinese will never be willing to admit foreign partners freely into their business. According to the regulations of most Chinese industrial companies, the sale of even one share of stock to any one except a Chinese citizen is strictly prohibited because the Chinese always fear, not without good reason, that interference from foreign governments and officials may be aroused on any trifling pretext, and the effect of Chinese civil and com-

[1] Cf. Chapter 17, infra.
[2] China Review, New York, January, 1923, Edge Law Bank in the Far East, by C. M. Bishop.
[3] Ibid.

mercial laws be thus nullified and their own interest endangered.

In concluding this chapter, the writer wishes to state his personal opinion regarding the scheme of American investment in China, both public and private. With regard to public financing, the procedure should be plain and simple, without any political flavor or any monopolistic character. If the financing of railroad construction in China is conducted by foreign governments rather than by foreign capitalists and entrepreneurs, the Chinese will never conclude a loan without great scruples and much hesitation as to the grave consequences which might result therefrom through impairing Chinese sovereignty and independence. For this sole reason public opinion in China has always been strongly opposed to any kind of foreign loan, even though the Chinese realize the tremendous necessity of foreign help. They weigh both the advantages and the disadvantages of an undertaking and decide to take the less disadvantageous step. If the delay of the development of China is a real disadvantage to the Chinese, the international control of their public finance would be ten times more disadvantageous than the other alternative; they therefore have no hesitation in choosing the negative procedure.

Toward the procedure of private investment the Chinese have a more favorable attitude, yet so long as Americans in China are governed by a set of laws different from their own and are under the jurisdiction of American government representatives, they are literally nothing short of "outlaws" from the Chinese point of view. The Chinese will never accept them freely into their business for the fear of foreign interference. How were American enterprises financed by European capital in the latter half of the nineteenth century? How have the South American States been developed by American and European capital? The Chinese dislike being treated differently from the way in which Americans have been treated and have treated others. If all discriminations against China were removed, and the United States would treat China just as she treats South America in the matter of private investment, there is no doubt that a considerable amount of American capital would at once be absorbed by China, and in return, China would be able to pay a handsome profit on American capital. Furthermore, should American capital be successfully used in improving industrial China, American trade with China would expand beyond any assignable limit, owing to the increased purchasing power of the Chinese people, the increasing demand for American machinery and equipment, and the increasing output of such materials as are in great demand in America.

## CHAPTER XVII*

### AMERICAN BANKING INTERESTS IN CHINA

Although Americans have been actively engaging in trade with China for a hundred and fifty years, the development of American banking interests in that country has lagged far behind. Even today American banking facilities over there are still "so small as to be out of all proportion to the American share in the internal and foreign commerce of China, or in proportion to American interests in that part of the world."[1] "Of recent years the part played by American banks has been increasing in importance, but, with the exception of exchange banking, American banks in China are still in such a position as to be able to handle only a very small portion of the possible American business there. American commercial interests have not had the banking facilities provided for them that competitors of other nationalities have. Broadly speaking, American banks in China are foreign exchange institutions. They do a general business, but with few exceptions they major in exchange business."[2]

It is owing to the lack of an adequate banking and financing mechanism that America has many times lost out in competition with other nations in China. Such American banks as had been established there were unable to handle the finances, and, as has been stated above, it was mainly in the control of industrial development in China by European capital that America had been defeated in the Chinese market before and after the Russo-Japanese War.[3] This is particularly true as regards contracts for railway construction. "Out of an estimated total of 7,500 miles of railway con-

---

[1] *China Review*, N. Y., July, 1923, p. 354.
[2] *Weekly Review of the Far East*, Shanghai, June, 1923, suppl. p. 10.
[3] Chapter III, Third Period, *supra*.

cessions granted before December 1, 1898, the Americans had actually accepted or secured only three hundred miles. They had lost several times as much through inability to provide capital on acceptable terms."[1]

Realizing the importance of banking facilities in connection with their trade and investment in the Far East, the Americans had made several attempts in the latter decades of the nineteenth century to organize American banks, but without success. The first attempt was made as early as 1887, which was a year of great activity among foreign investors in China. The Chinese-American bank as projected by the Philadelphia Syndicate was a big financial proposition, but unfortunately, it failed to materialize.[2]

It was not until the dawn of the twentieth century that the first American bank was installed. In 1901 the International Banking Corporation of New York opened its office in Shanghai as the pioneer of the American banks in China.[3] The Guaranty Trust Company of New York followed suit at almost the same time, but its branch was taken over by the International Banking Corporation after a brief period of operation.[4]

In the same year the latter corporation opened another branch in Hongkong,[5] and a year later, another in Canton. For the next five years, there was no further development. But in 1907 two more branches—one in Pekin, the other in Hankow—were installed by the same corporation.[6] One can readily see how inadequate were American banking

---

[1] Dennett, Tyler, *Americans in Eastern Asia*. Mr. Dennett mentions several cases in which this actually occurred.
[2] Cf. Chapter on Investment, *supra*.
[3] *American Banks in China*, *Weekly Review of the Far East*, Shanghai, June 30, 1923. Suppl. p. 11.
[4] *Ibid*.
[5] Since the British Colony of Hongkong is usually considered in the commercial field of China, it is referred to as a part of China in this chapter.
[6] *American Banks in China*, Ibid.

facilities in China, when he learns that it was these five branch banks that were to take the responsibility of financing the growing import and export trade between China, Hongkong and America, which during this period amounted annually to an average of no less than one hundred million dollars.

Owing first to the rapid expansion of Chinese-American trade after the outbreak of the European War, and second, to the increased difficulty of financing trade by the banks of other nations in China, the Americans have greatly extended their banking facilities since 1917. In that year the American-Oriental Banking Corporation was established in Shanghai. In 1918 the American Express Company of New York entered the banking field in the Far East by opening two branches in Shanghai and Hongkong. The next year the Asia Banking Corporation opened seven others, and the Chinese-American Bank of Commerce, a Sino-American institution, was incorporated under a special charter of the Chinese Government. In the following two years more banks were installed, and at the present time there are twenty-eight American banks in China, including the Sino-American institutions. These twenty-eight banks belong to six organizations, only one of which, viz., the International Banking Corporation, was in the field five years ago. A summarized history of these banks is presented in the following table:[1]

---

[1] The following is a little sketch for each of these banking organizations quoted from the same sources:

The International Banking Corporation (capital and surplus $10,000,000; undivided profits $3,200,000)* and the Asia Banking Corporation (capital $4,000,000; surplus and undivided profits $1,489,362) are strong factors in the foreign exchange business of China. These two organizations, especially the former, have been largely responsible for the internationalization of the competition in

(Continued on page 327)

* These and following figures are 1921 figures based upon a list of American banks in the Far East published in the Far Eastern Fortnightly, N. Y., May 23, 1921, p. 5.

| Name of Organization | Home Office | How Organized | Nature of Business | Branches in China | |
|---|---|---|---|---|---|
| | | | | Location | Date established |
| 1. International Banking Corporation | New York | Under the law of Conn. | Foreign exchange banking a specialty | Shanghai | 1901[*] |
| | | | | Hongkong | 1901 |
| | | | | Canton | 1902 |
| | | | | Hankow | 1907 |
| | | | | Peking | 1907 |
| | | | | Tientsin | 1918 |
| | | | | Harbin | 1919 |
| | | | | Dairen | 1923 |
| 2. American Express Company | New York | Under the law of Conn. | Banking, shipping and travel | Shanghai | 1918 |
| | | | | Hongkong | 1918 |
| | | | | Peking | 1921 |
| | | | | Tientsin | 1921 |
| 3. Asia Banking Corporation[1] | New York | Under law of New York | Foreign exchange banking a specialty | Shanghai | 1919 |
| | | | | Hongkong | 1919 |
| | | | | Hankow | 1919 |
| | | | | Tientsin | 1919 |
| | | | | Peking | 1919 |
| | | | | Canton | 1919 |
| 4. American-Oriental Banking Corporation | Shanghai | Under law of Conn. | General banking | Shanghai[a] | 1917 |
| | | | | Chungking | 1922 |
| | | | | Foochow | 1922 |
| 5. Equitable Eastern Banking Corporation | New York | Under law of New York | International banking a specialty | Shanghai | 1921 |
| 6. Chinese-American Bank of Commerce | Peking | Under a special charter of Chinese Government dated April 12, 1919 | Commercial banking | Peking[*] | 1919 |
| | | | | Shanghai | 1920 |
| | | | | Hankow | 1920 |
| | | | | Tientsin | 1920 |
| | | | | Tsinau | 1920 |
| | | | | Harbin | 1921 |
| | | | | Shikaichwang | 1921 |

[1] In December, 1923, the Asia Banking Corporation was absorbed by the International Banking Corporation.

[*] These two are head offices.

Data compiled from the following sources: *American Banks Taking Their Place in China*, by R. C. Bennett, Weekly Review of the Far East, Shanghai, June 30, 1923, supplement, p. 10 ff. *American Banks in the Far East*, Far Eastern Fortnightly, N. Y., May 23, 1921, p. 5.

---

It is predicted that further progress in the development of American banking in China may be expected in the near future, if political and commercial conditions there improve to a degree sufficient to encourage healthy development. Banking institutions already represented there have plans for the opening of new branches and general broadening of their fields of activity and influence, and new organizations contemplate entering this field.

With the passage of the Edge Law by the American Congress, a new era has dawned upon American banking

*Note continued from page 325:*
the foreign exchange business. Their business is not confined exclusively to foreign exchange, but that is their chief interest.

The American Express Company as a banking organization in China is a part of the American Express Company as a shipping, travel, and banking organization throughout the world. Largely as a result of the business developed through its travel department, the American Express Company does a substantial banking business, particularly exchange business.

The American-Oriental Banking Corporation, which belongs to a chain of affiliated American enterprises in China, interests itself more in the field of domestic banking and interior exchange in China. (Paid up capital, $409,950; undivided profits, $37,454). This chain of banks is distinctive among the American organizations in China. The American-Oriental Bank of Szechwan, which is in Chungking, the city at the head of the Yangtze River navigation, may be considered as occupying the frontier position, as it is the farthest inland of all the American banks in China.

The branch of the Equitable Eastern Banking Corporation (capital $4,000,000; surplus and undivided profit $754,000) is especially prominent in the silver business. Enormous shipments of silver are handled through this bank.

The Chinese Bank of Commerce (capital authorized, $10,000,000; paid up, $5,000,000) is relatively young. It entered this field for the purpose of supporting and furthering American and Sino-American enterprises in China and facilitating the sale of Chinese securities in the United States. According to the announcement of the management the extension of this business with branches throughout the whole world is contemplated.

---

interests in China. The so-called Edge Law banks, to be incorporated under this act, are intended to constitute a system as a part of the American Federal banking machinery. They are designed to assist in the development of American foreign trade, as the Federal Reserve banks have done in the development of American domestic trade. Their acceptances are eligible for purchase by the Federal Reserve Banks and their stock eligible for purchase by American national banks.[1]

As importers and manufacturers in the Far East are generally short of funds, the extension of longer term credits is a prerequisite condition to their buying goods from abroad. Those countries able to offer them longer terms of credit will get their trade, while those unable to do so will lose it. Japanese, British, and before the war, German banks have in this respect outrivalled American branches, because the former offer the Chinese importer credits sometimes as long as a year, while the latter cannot extend the period beyond three months. American banks in China employing their capital largely in exchange operations and being limited by law or by the nature of their business to short term loans, had not been in a position to take part in the financing of transactions requiring the longer term of credits such as industrial enterprises in China always require. It was to meet this need that the Edge Law was enacted. Banks incorporated under this act are not permitted to receive deposits, but enjoy the privilege of issuing acceptances up to one year. They have, therefore, a wider margin on which to operate in financing export and import trade.

[1] For further description of the Edge Law and the financing of foreign trade, cf. Moulton, *Financial Organization*, pp. 422-23. Reed: *The Development of Federal Reserve Policy*, pp. 177-180.

---

### SUMMARY AND CONCLUSION

#### *Historical Background of the Trade: Recapitulation*

Indirect commercial relations between the ancient Empire of Cathay and the New World had been existent long before the establishment of the United States as an independent nation. Chinese tea had been regularly imported through England during the colonial days. But it was not until the memorable year of 1784, when the *Empress of China* reached Canton, that Chinese-American trade finally began. Direct commerce between the two great nations bordering on the Pacific has thus run its course for a century and a half, and its growth has practically kept pace with the development of American national life.

With regard to the different directions that the course of Chinese-American trade has taken at different stages, its whole history may be conveniently divided into four periods. The first period is one of informal or non-treaty intercourse, extending from 1784 to 1844. During this period America's enterprising seamen played a very active part in China's foreign trade, a part second in importance to that of no other country. Numerous American ships, no longer handicapped by the restrictive British colonial system, busily plied between the coasts of Asia and America, buying from China tea and silk, for which they paid first with ginseng and specie and later with furs, sandal wood and other products which the American traders got from the South seas.

After 1820 when the early fur trade came to an end and the sandal wood trade had also reached its zenith, new conditions arose to cause a steady growth of this

329

trade. Chinese teas and silks now commanded a better market in the United States because of the gradual growth of the population and wealth in the new Western Republic and the resulting increasing demand for those Oriental luxuries. The Americans, on the other hand, were better able to pay for them with bills of exchange on London, as a result of the English opium traffic in the East. Also gradually increasing in quantity were American domestic exports, among which cotton goods assumed new importance. At the end of this period the American Government, taking advantage of the Opium War between Great Britain and China, followed the British example and sent Caleb Cushing to China and concluded with her the first Sino-American commercial treaty.

The second period of our history is one of temporary trade expansion and then steady decline. It begins with the year 1845 when formal intercourse between the United States and China under the provisions of the treaty of Whanghia began, and ends with the Sino-Japanese War in 1895. This period again falls into two sub-periods with the American Civil War as their dividing line. In the first sub-period the business activity of these energetic merchants attained its high tide. Having a shipping equipment which was second to none in the whole world, the United States was taking a very big share in China's foreign trade during the forties and fifties of the nineteenth century. But the life of this phenomenal expansion was soon cut short by the political confusion and the civil wars in both countries. During the American Civil War, her magnificent shipping, the vital element of her foreign trade, fell into decay. The active American pioneer traders in China gradually disappeared from the market because they were lured homeward by the enticing opportunity afforded by their own country's internal development. While the depreciation

of the value of silver in terms of gold discouraged China from buying more from the United States, the new and strong competition of Japan in tea and silk greatly checked the further expansion of American imports from China. In addition to all these causes there prevailed an ill-feeling between the American and Chinese people as a result of the problem of Chinese immigration. This ill-feeling perhaps contributed more than anything else to the tardy growth of the Chinese-American trade during the latter decades of the last century. During the sub-period of thirty-four years, from 1860 to 1894, the total value of American imports from China increased from thirteen and a half million dollars to only seventeen million dollars, whereas exports thereto dropped from nine millions to six millions.

The third period is one of severe international competition. It began in 1895 and ended in 1913. The easy victory of Japan over China in 1895 radically altered the commercial as well as the political situation in the Far East. The most powerful colonizing empires of the Occident, such as Great Britain, Germany, Russia and France, were quick enough to take advantage of this opportunity to expand their commercial and political influence in China. Japan, also, had made herself an industrial nation and exerted her entire energy toward making China the market of her products. Occupations and leaseholds within Chinese territory became very common, and spheres of influence were viciously established. It was in this period that international competition for Chinese trade was the keenest, and although the United States now gave renewed attention to the development of her trade with China, the expansion of this trade lagged rather behind the normal growth of both the total American foreign trade and the total Chinese foreign trade. Of course, the absolute volume of trade increased nearly two-fold during this period of nearly twenty years, although

the increase was quite irregular. In 1895 American imports from China, including Hongkong, were valued at twenty-three million dollars and exports thereto at twelve million dollars. The corresponding figures in 1905 were thirty-four million and sixty-four millions and in 1913 forty-four millions and thirty-eight millions.

That the expansion of American exports to China during this period was especially slow can be explained by two other reasons. First, the narrow-minded way in which the American Government officials dealt with the problem of Chinese immigration greatly injured the Chinese people's national pride and compelled them to retaliate by a violent boycott movement in 1905 against America. Second, the industrial development in China before the European War was controlled mainly by European capital, and American trade was checked by the "monopolizing" of China's trade by European nations through their loans to China. As to American imports from China, the increase was much more steady and noticeable. Yet, first because of the strong Japanese competition in the American silk market, and East Indian competition in the tea market, and secondly because of the delayed development of the vast mineral and agricultural resources of China and therefore the lack of suitable commodities for the American market, American imports from China were also undermined to a great extent.

The fourth period of our trade history—a period of rapid expansion—was naturally set off by the outbreak of the European War. Because of the inability of the European nations to carry on trade with China during the war, most of their trade was diverted to America. Not only have American demands for Chinese goods greatly expanded, but also Chinese demands for American goods. Thus one finds, on the one hand, a great increase of American imports from China in such goods as antimony, albumen, aniline dyes, indigo, wool, cotton, egg

products, vegetable oils and oil seeds, hides, skins, furs, straw braids and raw silk; and on the other, a corresponding increase of American exports to China in iron and steel machinery and other products, all sorts of vehicles, chemicals and dyes, electrical machinery and materials, rubber manufactures, leather goods, paper products, mineral oils, tobacco, and wood and wood manufactures. In the former periods trade in a great many of the articles mentioned was either non-existent or quite small in volume, but now each item amounted to millions of dollars in annual value.

Throughout this period, the derangement of the gold-silver exchange situation, the shortage of ocean shipping tonnage and the resulting rise of freight rates, worked great havoc in the trade between China and the United States. But later on the mutual demand for more goods from both sides overcame these causes of friction, and the trade increased three to five times, both absolutely and relatively, during a period of ten years. In 1914 American imports from China were valued at thirty-eight million dollars, while in 1923 they were one hundred seventy-six million dollars. In the former year American exports to China were valued at twenty-seven million dollars, and in 1923 they amounted to one hundred seventeen millions. Even after due allowance has been made for the price inflation during and after the war, the real volume of the trade has actually increased two to three times.

### The General Trend of the Trade

In the foregoing section the writer has briefly summarized the various stages of the inception, expansion, decline, and recovery of the trade between the United States and China together with some of the most important economic forces underlying these upward and downward movements. If, however, we combine all these different stages and investigate their general trend as a whole, we find the trade consistently prospering and expanding year after year. As shown in the accompanying chart its secular trend presents a definite upward movement, rising not merely in arithmetical progression, but in geometrical progression.[1]

During the past century American imports from China, with only a few exceptional years, have been consistently greater in value than exports thereto. Yet the general tendency is for their difference to become smaller and smaller in proportion to the total trade, because American exports to China have increased on the whole more rapidly than imports therefrom.

### Future Prospects

In the light of the past we may have some idea about the future. First of all, American trade with China is certain to grow as time goes on, though irregular forces may at any time disturb its smooth course as so many of them did in the past. But whether it will expand at the same rate as during the past century or at a new rate accelerated by the recent cataclismic changes caused by the World War, we have still too short a period in view to be able to forecast correctly. One thing, however, seems rather certain, viz., the trade will from now on fluctuate on a level higher than that which formerly prevailed and will remain on that higher level, perhaps permanently.

[1] The three curves in the accompanying chart represent respectively the annual value of American exports to China, imports therefrom, and the total of the two (in the order from the bottom to the top). They are drawn in the logarithmic scale, thus showing their percentage changes from one year to another. The fitting lines for all these curves, though drawn according to the method of least squares, are not intended to measure their trend with mathematical accuracy, because there can be no single definite trend for so long a period as one century. They are simply intended to show the gradual increase of the trade, and to indicate roughly, but clearly, the four stages of origination, expansion, decline, and revival, as described in the text of this book.

As one may note in the chart, both imports and exports are now far above their normal size indicated by the lines showing their respective trend. Should there have been no World War, the former trend might still represent the normal course. But now world trade relations have been re-adjusted according to a new equation of international demand, and the price levels in both the United States and China have been raised, perhaps permanently; and it seems to be quite improbable that the value of American trade with China will return to its pre-war level.

### American Imports from China

Having thus indicated the general drift of the trade, we will review some important articles which composed or now compose a large part of the imports and exports.

Among the various articles imported from the Old Empire to the New World, tea is one of classical importance. As soon as direct trade with China was made possible by American independence, a large quantity of tea, usually constituting half and sometimes even eighty per cent of the American total imports therefrom, was annually brought from the Orient. But since the middle of last century China's monopoly in tea has been shattered, first by Japanese, and later by British and Dutch East Indian competition. The inefficiency of Chinese methods of cultivation and manufacturing as compared with those followed by the Japanese and East Indian planters and manufacturers, the vicious practice of tea adulteration in China in former years, the heavy tea export duties formerly imposed by the Chinese Government and the poor methods of selling on the part of Chinese tea merchants, have all contributed their share, at one time or another, to the decline of the trade. But according to tea connoisseurs China still produces the best tea in the whole world, though the Chinese tea may not be entirely uniform in quality and therefore somewhat unfit for

the American large-scale method of marketing. Having realized the importance of the American tea market, however, Chinese tea traders and the Chinese Government have made various attempts to improve their method of tea culture in the hope of being able to recover some of their lost shares in the trade of the United States.

Next to tea in point of time of entrance into the American market, but now by far the most important single article among the various American imports from China, is silk. During the early part of the nineteenth century nearly all American silk imports were in the form of manufactured silks, of which a large part came directly from China. But since that time the volume of trade in silk manufactures has dwindled both absolutely and relatively. There are three reasons for the decline and present insignificance of this line of trade: First, Chinese silk goods, being manufactured for the home market only, do not suit the taste and fancy of westerners; secondly, the United States itself has been for half a century one of the largest silk manufacturing countries and can well supply her own needs; and thirdly, the American protective tariff, as applied to silk goods, has been almost prohibitive.

Contrasted with the early decline of trade in silk manufactures was the steady growth of the raw silk trade. Before 1865 the United States bought little raw silk, but since then, due to the rapid development of the silk weaving industry in this country, the importation of foreign raw silk has naturally increased by leaps and bounds. The increase in the silk trade with China, though fairly steady in absolute quantity throughout the last half century, has, however, failed to keep pace with the total American silk import. The reason for this relative decline is twofold; it is due, on the one hand, to the lack of improvement in the method of sericulture and the failure to secure new markets on the part of the Chinese, and, on the other, to the severe competition and the rapid growth of the Japanese raw silk industry. Recently, however, the popularity of silk in America has so tremendously increased that the United States has begun to feel the necessity for extension of its raw material field, and once more it looks to China for a more adequate supply of this article. The Chinese silk raisers have also begun to realize the importance of the American market and have made various attempts to improve the bulk of their silk to suit the large-scale manufacture of the United States. Success in this direction has been quite marked during the last few years and no doubt Chinese silk is going to regain its lost position.

Hides, skins and furs come next in importance as commodities which have for more than thirty years held a prominent place in American import trade with China. At the end of the nineteenth century Chinese cattle and buffalo hides, goat, sheep and calf and horse skins, were imported into America at an average of several million pounds a year. The volume of trade was more than doubled before the European War and since that time it has been quadrupled. Trade in furs, both dressed, undressed and in fur manufactures, has increased in value from an annual average of three hundred thousand dollars a year before the war to several million dollars a year thereafter. China, as we know, has a vast area of pasture land, and is well able to supply the United States with all these things; trade, therefore, in this line of commodities, is certain to expand as the stock-raising industry develops in China.

Closely connected with the hide and fur trade is the trade in wool, both manufactured in the form of carpets and unmanufactured; bristles, and other kinds of animal hairs; because all of them are products of the same animal and for the same reason, therefore, these lines of trade will expand in the future.

There are also several kinds of Chinese hand-labor manufactures, such as hair nets, laces and embroideries, which have recently played an important role in the trade between the two countries.

Besides these Chinese articles just enumerated, there are still several others, each of which, for several years during and immediately after the war, took a great share in American import trade. Among them we must first mention vegetable oils. The wide utilization of these oils in American industries and the spectacular growth of Chinese-American trade in them was one of the most interesting commercial phenomena of the past decade. But America is itself the largest producer of certain kinds of vegetable oils in the world (especially cotton-seed oil), and can supply its own needs under normal conditions. Consequently since 1921 the trade in Chinese oils has declined greatly, and, though we can expect them to retain a place in the trade, they are not likely to amount to anything like the quantity and value of the transactions of a few years ago.

Somewhat like vegetable oils in the rôle played in the trade during and immediately after the European War are antimony, albumen, indigo, raw cotton, raw tobacco, egg products and straw braids. All these articles were imported from China in large quantities at millions of dollars a year as long as American business, during 1915 to 1920, sustained its prosperity. In 1921 to 1922 trade in them dropped heavily both in quantity and value. As all these articles are raw materials used by American industries for further production, it is predicted that American imports in these lines will more or less recover as soon as American business conditions become normal.

Generally speaking, American imports from China, like her imports from all other Oriental countries, and from South America, are composed mainly of raw and semi-raw materials. The most important and promising are

raw silk, hides and skins, furs, straw braids, wool, bristles, vegetable oils, etc. The tendency in the future will be toward a gradual increase in these lines. This is because, on the one hand, the increasing activity of American industries will result in more intense demand for these materials, and, on the other, China will be able to supply the United States with a larger quantity of such articles as her agriculture, together with her simpler forms of industry, is gradually developing. The importation of finished or consumers' goods, on the contrary, shows a tendency toward decreasing importance. These goods consist of tea, silk textiles, etc. Nevertheless, China has been able to export to the United States some kinds of hand-work manufactures whose relative importance is on the increase, because China, having an immense supply of cheap labor, is able to outrival any nation in the world in such hand-made articles as laces, embroideries, hair-nets, etc.

### American Exports to China

In passing to the consideration of American exports to China, we find that only two decades ago the most important article was cotton cloth. During the fifties of the nineteenth century, cotton goods constituted in some years nine-tenths of the total American domestic exports to China, amounting to more than two million dollars a year. But after 1860 further expansion was checked, partly because of the destruction, during the Civil War, of the American merchant marine, which was necessary for carrying the bulk cloth, and partly because of the keen competition of Great Britain. In spite of these handicaps, American cotton cloth still occupied a very respectable position in the export list during the closing decades of the last, and the opening years of the present, century. These cloths, during that period, still constituted nearly sixty per cent of the total American exports

to China, at a value of several million dollars a year. But since 1906 they have been losing ground rather rapidly, first because of Japanese and, later, Chinese competition, until now they constitute scarcely five per cent of the total American exports to the Oriental Republic. It is unlikely that in the future the United States will be able to regain its lost position in this line of trade.

But it must not be understood that the United States will forever keep its hands off the Chinese cotton goods market. There are numerous other lines of finer cottons, which are not made by either Japanese or Chinese mills, but which are consumed in large quantities by the Chinese. At present trade in these cottons is almost exclusively in the hands of Great Britain, but there is no reason why American cotton manufacturers should be unable to produce these finer goods and send them to China on a competitive basis.

Next to cotton goods are kerosene oil and tobacco. In the recent remarkable growth of tobacco imports of China American tobacco has taken a share which increased from less than one-fifth, at the beginning of the present century, to more than four-fifths during the last few years. China has been for many years the largest purchaser of American cigarettes, and now buys a fairly large quantity of American raw tobacco. But despite all these recent developments in the American tobacco trade with China, it can hardly be expected that, in the future, trade along this line will undergo further expansion at such a remarkable rate as that of recent years. The tobacco industry, in China, like her cotton industry, is rapidly advancing and, if it were not for the present huge demand for foreign tobacco in that country, her home-manufactured tobacco could well supply the market. Recent efforts in China to improve the quality and increase the quantity of domestic tobacco has resulted in marked success, and during the last few years China has become to a small extent a tobacco exporting country. While a substantial increase in Chinese purchases of American tobacco leaf will undoubtedly result in the immediate future, the future development of this trade will ultimately depend on the course of native leaf production in China itself.

As regards mineral oils, the old empire had been an excellent market for the American output, although Russian and Dutch East Indian competition has caused the American trade to fluctuate widely. Before 1890 every gallon of oil imported into China came from America, and the trade expanded from almost nothing in the sixties to an average of thirty million gallons in 1891 to 1900, increasing to nearly a hundred million gallons before the war, and finally to one hundred and sixty million gallons in the last few years. In the closing years of the last, and the opening years of the present, century, the American Standard Oil Company had a hard fight in the East, first with the Russian oil interests and later with the Dutch, but, owing to its huge strength, has succeeded in defeating them, and now holds the key to the Eastern oil trade.

It has been reported by geologic experts that rich mineral oil fields are in existence in China itself. But the exploitation of these resources has not been successful. Today, as in former times, China still has to depend upon foreign oils for lighting purposes, and so long as this demand persists, American oil trade with China is certain to grow.

Moreover, as industrial China is taking shape, she needs more and more of fuel and gas oil, lubricating oil, naphthas, etc., in addition to illuminating oil, which was the only important kind imported in former times. The United States, with her very rich oil resources and a well developed refining industry, is naturally in a greatly ad-

vantageous position to reap the benefit of this expanding market.

Lumber is another important American product which was introduced into the Orient in the closing decade of the last century. As China has no great forests of her own, her increasing demand for lumber for construction and manufacturing purposes must be met by increasing imports. In fact, her imports have actually grown tenfold since 1900, amounting now to more than ten million dollars a year, of which more than fifty per cent comes from the United States. While lumber has not yet reached the position of being one of the principal imports in China, those in the trade see a splendid future for it. America, being in possession of rich forest resources in its Pacific States, is certain to reap the profit of the growing Chinese trade.

American leather goods, rubber manufactures and paper products are the other lines of trade, each of which has recently amounted to millions of dollars annually.

We now come to several other lines, which, quite insignificant only a decade ago, are now playing such an important part in the trade that they practically constitute the larger part of American exports to China. These are iron and steel machinery and other manufactures, electrical appliances and materials, motor vehicles and other carriages, chemicals and drugs, and all other sorts of finer products of the highly developed American industries. The reason for such a rapid expansion along these lines can be readily found in the two-fold fact that while China's demand for these industrial equipments and provisions has greatly increased, due to her recent industrial development, the United States is now better able to supply China with these articles due to the increased output of her various industries and diminished competition in the Orient since the war.

From what has been said above, we can realize the

general trend of the American export trade with China. First of all, manufactures of the simpler forms, which formed the largest part of American exports to China in the past decades, are now decreasing in importance, both in absolute quantities and in relative shares, and this tendency will continue in the future. To repeat again, industrial China has recently made remarkable progress, and she is adding every year a number of flour mills, cotton factories, tobacco plants, iron and steel workshops, paper mills, leather factories, etc., to the host of those already in existence. At one time before 1906 American flour commanded a good market in China, but owing to China's achievement in the milling of flour, this line of trade has already declined to an insignificant volume. This is also true of American cotton cloths, of manufactured tobacco and will be true of all other simpler forms of manufacture such as leather goods, paper products, etc.

Up to the present time, most of China's iron and steel products, such as rails, structures, bars, wires, sheets, plates, pipes, etc., have been imported from America and Europe, and the volume of trade along these lines has grown rapidly. But this is another department in which the new republic's latent potentialities promise to make it ultimately independent of import. China possesses many fabulously rich deposits of coal and iron, and, if enough capital can be obtained, can manufacture the simpler forms of iron and steel products in her own country.

The writer will not multiply instances calculated to show the unlikelihood that the United States or any other foreign nation will be able to build up a permanent trade with China in the simpler articles of manufacture, for which that country has the raw materials. The Chinese people can successfully elaborate, and are successfully elaborating all sorts of raw materials of which nature has given them so great a store, and it will not, therefore,

profit foreign nations, especially the United States, to endeavor to build up trade with them along these lines. The American manufacturers may sell China flour, cotton goods, cigarettes, metals, leather goods and paper products for a while, but it will not be long before they will face a decreasing demand as has happened in not a few instances before.

Now let us consider what line of American exports to China may hold a promise of better and longer success.

In the past the products of American factories, designed for the American market and for a class of people living on a relatively high wage-scale, were of better quality and consequently more expensive than those goods should be if they are successfully to compete for the trade of the Orient, where the individual earning capacity, and therefore the purchasing power, is relatively small. Other countries having a greater demand at home for cheaper goods are in a better position to supply the Oriental market than is the United States. So far as America is concerned, this condition is clearly shown in its decreasing share of China's import trade in 1921 to 1923. This condition will continue until an improvement in their economic condition increases the earning and purchasing power of the Chinese masses. When the buying capacity of the Chinese shall have increased to the point where it will be able to furnish a market for the sale of more expensive American goods, American trade will doubtless expand still a great deal more.

Now let us take note of the fact that the recent development of industrial China will benefit American trade more than that of any other country. As pointed out above, China is annually increasing her own output of all the simpler forms of manufactures under very favorable natural conditions and under a low wage-scale. These products are manufactured, under the impulse of the new movement, to supply the demand for cheaper goods, and thus offer more serious competition to those countries now underselling the Americans in the Chinese market than to the higher class American products. Within the next decade or two China will develop into a great manufacturing nation, while at the same time her demand for a better and different class of goods than she herself can produce will materially increase. Goods which involve high mechanical skill and nicely standardized processes, should be supplied more and more by the United States, which has not, and will not have, any serious rival in those lines.

A good opportunity is already evident and will surely continue to improve, for the Americans to export to China such lines as industrial machinery, locomotives and the higher class of rolling stock, motor vehicles and electrical railway equipment; many classes of agricultural machinery and a long list of other things, such as typewriters, cash registers, sewing machines, and the like, in which are to be found the fullest expression of American ingenuity. This marks the easiest and practically the only chief line of future advance which may lead to permanent American success in the Chinese market.

### Some Features of the Trade Relations

As to the general trade relations between the United States and China, there have been several significant features worthy of notice. One of them is the *purity of motive* which has characterized their commercial intercourse since its very beginning. There is no ulterior aim on the one side and no suspicion on the other, as contrasted with so much of these which have marked the history of China's trade with other powers. Here commerce is carried on with no other consideration than that of a legitimate profit of business. The Chinese are strictly a peaceful business people with a keen business sense. They perceive and appreciate and therefore

do not hesitate to iterate and re-iterate their desire for closer commercial relations with the Americans.

*Identity of interest* is another significant feature of the Chino-American trade. The interests of China and those of the United States run along parallel lines with a peculiar consistency, and there is no fundamental conflict or clash to mar the development of their commercial intercourse. In fact no two countries could be better qualified than the United States and China to cooperate with each other in bringing about the realization of the immense possibilities of trade in the Pacific and in effecting the economic development of East Asia to their mutual benefit.

The third feature is their *interdependence*. Every one realizes that further development of the foreign trade of the United States in the future will to no small extent depend upon the extension of her market in China, because, being a vast country of fabulously rich resources together with an immense population, China is the greatest potential market in the whole world. China, in turn, if she desires to have her vast resources developed and population enriched, must look mainly to the United States for the initial capital, for a large part of machinery and equipment, and also for a reciprocal market, almost as unlimited as China herself, to dispose of her raw or semi-raw materials which the developed Chinese industries will turn out in the near future and of which American manufacturers will feel in great need.

### American Dependence on Chinese Market for Further Extension of Trade

The total imports of China during the last fifty years have expanded with remarkable rapidity. Yet, in spite of the phenomenal increase, the value per capita is now still less than two dollars, in which the United States shares to the extent of nearly forty cents. Insignificant as this figure might seem to be, yet, during the year immediately following the World War, the United States sent goods to China an-

nually amounting to an average of more than 150 million dollars. If China imports in future as much as Japan, which now buys about eighteen dollars' worth of American goods per capita, it will mean that the market in China will become ten times more valuable than it is now.

The wide use in America of water and electric power and the application of labor-saving machinery and scientific management to the manufacture of articles of all kinds have greatly increased and are still increasing the output of American mines, farms and factories. To dispose of these products the United States has turned her attention more to Europe and South America than to the Far East. It is true that before the World War Europe usually took more than 60 per cent of the total exports of the United States. During and immediately after the War, there was an almost unlimited market for American output. But now the whole situation has become, or is becoming, quite different. Europe is now greatly indebted to the United States, and according to the plain theory of international trade, it will sooner or later have to send more goods to the United States than it can buy from, in order that international payments between Europe and America, whether on their capital account or on interest account, may be balanced. In the future, therefore, the United States can not expect as good a market in Europe as she had before or during the War, and she must seek some outlet, other than Europe, for her increasing output.

It is the general opinion of American exporters that, besides Europe, the leading market for American manufactures is South America, Eastern Asia being the next. Prior to the War the continent territorially contiguous to the United States was naturally highest in favor among American manufacturers and merchants, whereas in Eastern Asia there prevailed international political conditions which were not conducive to any considerable trade expansion. Now, however, with China's "Open Door" re-affirmed in the Washington Conference, conditions have become more favorable for foreign commerce and investment. In order to

show that China will in the near future be a market, for American goods, as good as, or even better than, South America, let us take a comprehensive view of the possibilities of China as compared with those of South America.

The imports of South America in 1914 amounted to $671,000,000 or $11.92 per capita, while exports amounted to $882,000,000 or $15.7 per capita. In 1923 [1] imports increased to $1,274,000,000 [1] and exports to $1,410,000,000, or $20.45 and $24.24 per capita respectively. [2] Comparing with these figures those of the principal market in the East, that is, China, we find her total imports were $381,391,000 in 1914, and her exports, $238,672,000 or 95 cents and 60 cents per capita respectively. In 1922 her total imports increased to a value of $784,392,000, and her exports to $544,560,000 or $1.96 and $1.37 per capita respectively. In the case of South America the increase in the per capita figures during the past one decade was, for imports, from $11.92 to $20.45, an increase of 71 per cent and, for exports, from $15.70 to $24.24, an increase of 54 per cent. But in the case of China the increase in per capita imports during the same period was from 95 cents to $1.96, an increase of 106 per cent; and in per capita exports it was from 60 cents to $1.37, an increase of 128 per cent. The rapidity with which China's import trade increases is, relatively speaking, one and a half times greater than that of South America, and that of her export trade nearly two and a half times greater.

Again, let us make the point more clear by comparing the trade between these countries and the United States with that between China and the United States. During 1914 [3] United States exports to South American countries were valued at $116,329,000 or 17.3 per cent of their total imports,

[1] Fiscal year ending June 30.
[2] Figures compiled and percentages computed from statistical data given in the *World Almanac*, N. Y., 1914.
[3] Fiscal year ending June 30.

and imports therefrom, $221,770,000 or 25.2 per cent of their total exports.[1] During the fiscal year 1922-23 the corresponding figures were $259,000,000 or 20.4 per cent for exports; and $470,000,000 or 33.4 per cent for imports.[2] Her exports to China in 1914 were $24,699,000 in value, or 6.4 per cent of China's total imports, and her imports therefrom, $26,943,000, or 11.3 per cent of China's total exports. During 1922, the corresponding figures were $140,274,000 or 18 per cent for exports, and $80,991,000 or 16.5 per cent for imports. It is again evident that the growth of American trade with China has been relatively more rapid than the growth of her trade with South America.

From this concrete analysis of trade statistics we come to the conclusion that if the United States desires to further extend her foreign commerce, she can not do much either in Europe or in South America. To the Orient she must look, and especially China—"the one great potential market in the world."[3]

The United States not only wants a market where the needs are commensurate with her present capacity to produce and manufacture, but she requires a demand that will increase with her increasing output. China is such a market for the products of American industry.

### China's Dependence on the United States for Further Development and Trade

Let us now consider the question of China's dependence on the development of her American trade as an index of her industrial development and commercial success. This also needs some explanation. In the first place China's American trade has for the past century been very necessary to her in the sense that she has depended to no small

[1] Figures quoted from U. S. Bur. of For. and Dom. Com., The For. Com. and Navigation, 1914.
[2] Figures compiled from the *World Almanac*, 1924.
[3] *China Review*, N. Y., November, 1922.

extent upon the favorable balance of this trade to pay off the unfavorable balances in her trade with other nations. At first her unfavorable balance was due solely to the large and expensive importation of opium. But afterward it was due largely to the lack of development of her industry. As a result, the annual balance of her foreign trade has, for nearly a hundred years, been invariably against her. This one-sided balance has been a long and heavy drain on China's resources, the rapid accumulation of foreign debts and a gradual impoverishment of her people. But fortunately in this unhappy state of things China has had a consistently stable balance in her favor in her trade with the United States, since direct trade was established between them in 1784, except for a very few years. According to the official trade statistics of the United States, the balance averaged about $15,000,000 throughout the last four decades of the nineteenth century. During the first fourteen years of the present century, the average balance in China's favor dropped to $7,200,000. But in the following period of nine years, 1914-1922, it again increased to $42,000,000. These favorable balances greatly helped China in counterbalancing her other unfavorable balances and thus mitigated the severity of foreign exploitation, from which she has long suffered. A balance in favor of China is, however, not a discouraging factor for the United States. Her trade with China consists largely of raw materials or semi-finished products which feed her numerous factories and mills, and double or treble their original values when they are resold in their finished state.

Secondly, it is to the huge American market with its unlimited purchasing power that China will look in the near future for the disposal of a part of her immense mineral and agricultural output which her rapidly developing industry is going to produce. China has pasture land in Mongolia, Tibet, Eastern Turkestan and some inner

provinces to an area of several million acres, on which she will be able to raise tens of millions of sheep, goats, cows, horses, hogs, etc. From these animals there will be an immense output of hides, and skins, furs, bristles and wool, for which there is a great demand in the United States for the manufacture of leather, clothing and other articles. She has more than twelve million acres of farm land in Manchuria which under proper methods of cultivation will yield more than one hundred million bushels of soya and other beans, the oil of which has recently played a very important part in American industry. She has also an unlimited supply of cheap labor, which will produce a very great quantity of raw silk with the newly improved method of sericulture, of high grade teas, of handmade laces, hair nets, etc., all of which the United States is anxious to buy. In a word, China must in turn look to the United States for the disposal of the increasing products of her rapidly developing industry and agriculture.

In short, China wants just what the United States is well able to offer; viz., all sorts of machinery, iron and steel manufactures, and electrical appliances, chemicals, drugs, etc. They are normally the products of large scale production and highly developed industry, and no one nation on the glode can excel the United States in this respect. On the other hand, the United States wants just what China is well able to offer, viz., raw silks, hides and skins, furs, vegetable oils, wool and other products of manual work, such as carpets, hair nets, laces, etc. They are mostly the products of simpler forms of industry. As these simpler forms of industry are springing up at a remarkably rapid pace, with a huge supply of cheap labor at her disposal, China will be able to supply the growing demand of the United States for such material and products to whatever extent the United States cares to go. The steady advance of industrial China, therefore, is a

good thing for America. It will be some time before China attains to the height of the complex industrial activity which prevails in the United States, but in the meantime the more China develops her simpler forms of industrial activities, the greater will be her demand for American goods. At the same time, the development of these simpler forms of industry in China will give the United States a more adequate and perhaps a cheaper supply of materials. *Here lies the identity of commercial interests between these two countries; and here also lies their interdependence.*

In addition to the factors we have mentioned, there is also the strong and sincere friendship which has existed ever since the beginning of trade between the United States and China. This is of course a valuable asset to both parties—an asset which money cannot buy as well as a strong guarantee for successful trade.

### Improving the Chinese-American Trade Relations

How, then, can the trade relations between the two great republics of the Pacific be best improved to their mutual advantage? In the writer's opinion, the most effective measure to aid the development of Chinese-American trade is American investments in China in the spirit of true American justice. The truth of the old adage that "trade follows capital" is especially brought out in the Orient today because until China is in a fairly advanced stage in a modern industrial sense, the reservoirs of Chinese trade can but be barely tapped. But what are the most crying needs for the advancement of industrial China? None is more indispensable to the development of China than disinterested foreign capital and expert scientific aid. In Chapter XVI the writer has endeavored to point out why he believes China is the best field for American investments today and why China looks mainly to America for capital. To this American capitalists have been partly alive and have expended some efforts in the past to cooperate with the Chinese in the building of railways, conservation of canals, exploitation of mineral resources and the promotion of new industries in China. But unfortunately for both, most, if not all, of these attempts have so far failed to bear fruit, as we have witnessed in reviewing the history of American investments in China. Although this utter failure may be attributed to a great many reasons, yet two principal causes are quite evident, viz., first, the misguided policy of American capitalists in mixing up their investments with national and international politics; and, second, the unsettled state of affairs in China at the present time.

Regarding the first of these two causes, the writer believes that unless foreign business men, whether Americans or others, who are interested in China, are willing to make their investments purely on a business basis without resorting to the wires and strings of foreign chancelleries, the Chinese people can not but look upon their capital without fear as to the grave consequences which might result from accepting their aid, such as have actually happened in the past to the impairment of Chinese political sovereignty and economic independence.

As to the second cause, the present unsettled state of Chinese affairs is a problem inevitable to such a period of transition as is now under way in China, and there is no ground for despair. Already are there encouraging signs pointing to a speedy settlement of China's internal troubles. One has only to recall the discouraging state of affairs in the United States immediately after independence was won from England and for the many decades following as well as the troublous periods following the establishment of the French Republic, not to speak of the rise of democracies in other parts of the world, to realize that the budding Chinese Republic has made remarkable progress in traversing the thorny path of democracy.

China is fundamentally sound, socially and economically. Her present unhappy plight is not entirely through her own fault; for it the Powers are partly responsible. The problem of China today has become an integral part of the greater problem of world peace and it is the part of wisdom for the Powers, especially the United States, to extend to China sympathetic cooperation in its solution. The proper development of industrial China will require not alone the cooperation of foreign capital but what is as indispensable, the hearty cooperation of foreign scientific and technical experts in the working out of her industrialization. America has been generous in proffering China aid in the educational field in the past and to America China must look for expert technical assistance hand in hand with financial cooperation in her development. With the ushering in of modern industrialization, bringing with it financial reorganization and an efficient marshalling of her tremendous resources, the prevailing chaotic condition in the present transitional period which is to a large part an economic problem, viz., the masses struggling for a living under the seething conditions caused by congested population and undeveloped resources, will likewise disappear as the morning fog under the rising sun.

The American Government and American financial interests have not been insensible to China's dire need of foreign capital in recent years. As a result, various means to foster Chinese-American cooperation were devised. Thus, the International Banking Consortium was formed under American leadership, the China Trade Act and the Edge Banking Law have been passed by the American Congress, and some joint Chinese-American commercial and industrial enterprises have been projected. Unfortunately, the Consortium has failed to accomplish its desired end and is now in a lethargic state, while the China Trade Act and the Edge Banking Law do not tend

to become instruments of Chinese-American cooperation for reasons already discussed in previous chapters.

The urgent need of China today, to restate it again, is that of disinterested foreign financial and technical cooperation with the Chinese for the industrial development of the great Asiatic country, to the benefit of both. While foreign financial interests have been willing to invest in China under their own special conditions, often, however, to the detriment of China, there is the urgent problem of working out this cooperation so that it will not be to the impairment of Chinese sovereignty and independence to be acceptable to the Chinese people as well as to afford foreign investors the necessary guarantees for the safety of their capital. In the present situation, the Government and people of the United States have a great opportunity. It is indeed a worthy responsibility because of the traditional friendly relations between the two peoples, for upon the proper working out of the problem of Chinese-American financial, industrial and commercial cooperation hinges the problem of China and the future peace of the world.

## INDEX.

# 译 者 后 记

　　本书原作者是我国现代会计事业的先驱、著名会计学家潘序伦先生(1893—1985)。潘序伦先生从事会计事业达 60 年之久,作为中国现代会计事业的奠基人、"中国现代会计之父",他为我国会计事业的发展做出了卓越的贡献,他的功绩不仅为业界也为世人所敬仰;作为上海立信会计学院、立信会计师事务所、立信会计出版社的创始人,他为立信事业的发展殚精竭虑、呕心沥血、奋斗终生,他的务实作风和高贵品格影响着一代又一代立信人,使得"三位一体"立信事业永葆青春、蓬勃发展、蒸蒸日上。

　　作为一名立信人,译者也时常被先生刻苦求学、积极创业、热心教育、潜心研究、终身为会计事业奋斗的精神所感动、所激励,同时也希望能为发扬光大先生的事迹、纪念传承先生的思想作出自己的努力。后来在收集、整理潘序伦先生所编撰(译)图书、学术论文目录的过程中,产生了翻译、出版潘序伦先生博士学位论文的想法。

　　潘序伦先生在美国哥伦比亚大学的博士学位研究方向是政治经济学,最后提交了以中美贸易关系为研究内容的学位论文 *The Trade of the United States with China*,这虽然有异于成为其终身职业的会计学,但两者并非毫无关系,这一学习、研究经历不仅扩展、完善了知识结构,训练了学术研究素养,论文中多处体现的中美(含其他西方列强)之间的不平等关系也使潘序伦先生认识到学习外国先进技术、引进西方会计学术思想的必要性,事实上这也奠定了其成为学贯中西的会计学泰斗的基础。因此这篇学位论文也是先生重要的学术成果之一。

　　另外,该学位论文虽在先生的自传及后人的纪念文章中多有提及,但由于该论文只有英文版,且仅在美国国会图书馆、上海立信会计学院图书馆等机构有收藏,因此,见其全貌者并不多,了解其详细内容者更少。在上海立信会计学院图书馆江淇馆长、郑鑫尧老师的鼓励下,本人决定翻译该论文,一为揖录先生之学术成果方便学界同仁之参考之用,更为感念先生开创立信事业之功德。

　　上海立信会计学院校长唐海燕教授对本书的翻译、出版给予了多方面的指导与关心,并提出了宝贵的建议。本文译稿经由上海立信会计学院程新章教授全文审阅,出版工作得到了立信会计出版社的大力支持。

　　在本书即将正式出版之际,译者对上述及其他所有对潘序伦先生博士学位论文翻译、出版工作给予关心、帮助的立信同仁一并致以最真诚的感谢。

　　本文翻译,历时三年,反复斟酌,数易其稿,但由于本人水平有限,译稿之中谬误之处在所难免,敬请批评、指正。

李湖生

2013 年 8 月